Society for Arabian Studies Monographs No. 5

Series editors D. Kennet & St J. Simpson

Natural Resources and Cultural Connections of the Red Sea

Proceedings of Red Sea Project III

Held in the British Museum

October 2006

Edited by

Janet Starkey

Paul Starkey

Tony Wilkinson

BAR International Series 1661

2007

This title published by

Archaeopress
Publishers of British Archaeological Reports
Gordon House
276 Banbury Road
Oxford OX2 7ED
England
bar@archaeopress.com
www.archaeopress.com

Archaeopress
10 years

BAR S1661
Society for Arabian Studies Monographs No. 5

Natural Resources and Cultural Connections of the Red Sea: Proceedings of Red Sea Project III. Held in the British Museum October 2006

ISBN 978 1 4073 0097 9

Printed in England by Chalvington Digital

All BAR titles are available from:

Hadrian Books Ltd
122 Banbury Road
Oxford
OX2 7BP
England
bar@hadrianbooks.co.uk

The current BAR catalogue with details of all titles in print, prices and means of payment is available free from Hadrian Books or may be downloaded from www.archaeopress.com

Society for Arabian Studies Monograph Series

Series editors D. Kennet and St J. Simpson

The *Society for Arabian Studies Monograph Series* was launched in 2004 with the intention of encouraging the publication of peer-reviewed monographs on the archaeology, early history, ethnography, epigraphy and numismatics of the Arabian Peninsula and related matters. Creating a specific monograph series within the *British Archaeological Reports International Series* is intended to allow libraries, institutions and individuals to keep abreast of work that is specifically related to their areas of research. Prospective authors are encouraged to contact either of the series editors for more details.

Dr Derek Kennet
Department of Archaeology
Durham University
South Road
Durham DH1 3LE
England
Derek.Kennet@durham.ac.uk

Dr St John Simpson
Department of the Middle East
The British Museum
London WC1B 3DG
ssimpson@thebritishmuseum.ac.uk

Already published:

D. Kennet with a contribution by Regina Krahl (2004), *Sasanian and Islamic pottery from Ras al-Khaimah: classification, chronology and analysis of trade in the Western Indian Ocean*, Archaeopress BAR S1248, Society for Arabian Studies Monographs No. 1, £32.00, ISBN 1841716081

P. Lunde and A. Porter, eds (2004), *Red Sea Trade and Travel in the Red Sea Region: Proceedings of the Red Sea Project I held in the British Museum October 2002*, Archaeopress BAR S1269, Society for Arabian Studies Monographs No. 2, £33.00, ISBN 1841716227

Janet C.M. Starkey, ed. (2005), *People of the Red Sea: Proceedings of Red Sea Project II held in the British Museum October 2004*, Archaeopress BAR S1395, Society for Arabian Studies Monographs No. 3, £30.00, ISBN 1841718335

N. Durrani (2005), *The Tihamah coastal plain of South-west Arabia in its regional context c. 6000 BC – AD 600*. Archaeopress BAR S1456, Society for Arabian Studies Monographs No. 4, £32.00, ISBN 1841718947

Contents

List of Figures, Maps and Tables

Figures and Illustrations

Maps and Plans

Tables and graphs

Acknowledgements

Red Sea III followed two successful conferences held at the British Museum in association with the Society for Arabian Studies. This phase of the project was generously supported by the British Academy, the Leigh Douglas Memorial Trust, The Seven Pillars Trust, and the Triplow Foundation, for which many thanks are due.

We are indebted to the British Museum, London, for hosting the Phase I, II and II of the Red Sea Project. We were extremely honoured to be able to host the event in this prestigious venue. Particular thanks are due to St John Simpson for his unflappable calmness and all the support provided by the British Museum; to our new Treasurer, Douglas Stobie for his effective financial management; to Rob Carter, Sarah Searight and St John Simpson for all their efforts to find financial support for the Project; to Durham and Edinburgh Universities for logistical support, and to Corina David for her patience and keen attention to detail; to Francine Stone for her support in the final session; to Ionis Thompson for her continuing support in setting up all the relevant committee meetings as secretary to the Society; and atp ll the members of the committee including Professor Dionisius Agius, Dr St John Simpson, Sarah Searight and Dr Shelagh Weir for their academic expertise and advice.

We are indented to Dave Martin for producing an excellent mini-exhibition whilst he was in the throes of a major exhibition of his own, in Edinburgh, as well as Ruth Wood for helping at the event. Special thanks are due to Christine Lindner for all the hard logistical work and continuing enthusiasm, when I was organising the event for much of 2006 via internet cafés in Cairo, down the Red Sea, Sinai and around Lebanon. All the chairs (Professor Dionisius Agius, Dr Lucy Blue, William Facey, Dr Jacke Phillips, Dr St John Simpson, Professor Paul Starkey, Dr Shelagh Weir, and Professor Tony Wilkinson) provided effective leadership for their individual sessions and had wonderful time management skills. Further thanks are also due to Sarah Arenson for her kindness and generosity.

We would also like to thank all the contributors to this volume and to the conferences and associated workshops in all phases of the Project for all their hard work and amazing ability to meet our deadlines. There is now an effective network of over a hundred academics interested in the Red Sea region and a website based in Durham that is being developed to co-ordinate this interest. Thanks are also due for financial and academic support on an impressive range of contributors' research projects which are acknowledged at the end of each relevant paper. Many contributors had to face serious logistical challenges to meet our requests for proofs, images and bibliographic references. The selection and preparation of the Proceedings of Red Sea Phase III were made in consultation with several academic readers. Papers have been revised, rethought and resubmitted within a relatively short time scale and from an amazing variety of locations. In early May, for example, over 40 percent of contributors were scattered around the Middle East on field trips or archaeological excavations — but still managed to find internet cafés and postal facilities so send us updated material. All our appreciation goes to the contributors who worked without complaint on the task to produce some excellent results on a wide range of topics. Finally, we should like to thank colleagues at Archaeopress for all their support in the production and distribution of this and previous volumes on the Red Sea.

Introduction

Janet Starkey, Paul Starkey and Tony Wilkinson

The Red Sea lies between Africa and Asia, a salty sea noted for its wonderful corals and desert hinterlands. Although in many ways an inhospitable region, it was an arena for many civilizations and commercial activities on both sides of or across the Sea. In 2001 members of the Society for Arabian Studies, aware that the Red Sea as a focus for study had long been neglected, gathered to explore the possibilities of setting up a series of events that focused on the Red Sea. The aim was to provide a multi-disciplinary forum for a wide range of first-class scholars who were pioneering research on the region.

In a recently published article, M.P.M. Vink uses the term 'thalassology',[1] from the ancient Greek *thalassa* meaning 'sea', which he gleaned from P. Horden and N. Purcell.[2] By taking a similarly 'aquacentric' perspective the aim has been not only to advance our knowledge about the Red Sea but also to explore artificial distinctions of supposedly distinct regions and myths of continents (Africa, Asia, Arabia, etc.) traditionally associated with the region by illuminating interactions across the Red Sea, however intrinsically unstable this maritime region might be over time.[3]

The first conference was in 2002 with the theme 'Trade and Travel in the Red Sea Region',[4] and the second in 2004 on 'People of the Red Sea'.[5] The first two conferences were timed to coincide with relevant exhibitions held at the British Museum. The third, 'Red Sea III: Natural Resources and Cultural Connections of the Red Sea' was also organized by the Society for Arabian Studies at the British Museum and held on Friday 27 and Saturday 28 October 2006.

Named sessions in Red Sea III included 'The Ecological Environment of the Red Sea', 'Corridors of Cultural Contact', 'Early Red Sea Harbours and their Hinterlands', 'Ships and Boats of the Red Sea', 'Rise and Fall of Red Sea Ports from Preclassical to Late Antiquity', 'The Red Sea and its Cultural Connections', 'War and Commerce in the Red Sea', and 'Navigation and Naval Expeditions'. Topics included maritime networks; commercial connections, traditions and industries — in particular, the location and significance of harbours, boats, boat-building and navigation; caravan routes across the Eastern Desert, and trade in coffee and spices.

There was also an associated exhibition by David Martin, entitled 'Sketches from the north Red Sea'. David Martin's encounter with the Red Sea, in June 2006, came as part of a longer journey, travelling across land, from Cairo to Central Europe. This project was the result of his success in the prestigious Alastair Salvesen Travel Scholarship competition run by the Royal Scottish Academy, and involved working in sketchbooks as he travelled looking at themes of cultural and personal change and transformation. The sketches, essentially works in progress which will be developed into paintings, formed an exhibition in the Royal Scottish Academy in Edinburgh in March 2007.

Figure 0:1 'Nuwaiba', © David Martin, 2006

Over a hundred people participated in Phase III. They came from Europe and the UK, the Middle East and the United States. Particularly encouraging were the many first-class presentations by a range of younger scholars from the UK and Europe and we look forward to hearing more from them in the future. Many of the papers given at Red Sea III presented cutting-edge research and the latest new discoveries from the earliest times to the present day. They were provocative, thoughtful and well presented, opening light on a wide range of potential research projects and hitherto unexplored interconnections and themes.

The dynamics of the interdisciplinarity of the Red Sea Projects is part of the key to their success. Scholars were able to exchange ideas and broaden approaches to their own subject

1 Vink 2007: 41–62.
2 Horden and Purcell 2006: 723.
3 Vink 2007: 58.
4 Lunde and Porter (eds) 2004.
5 Starkey (ed.) 2005.

interests. Many of us are familiar with Braudel's concept of 'deep structure' and his *longue durée* approach to the Mediterranean that focuses on the sea and ocean basins as frameworks of interdisciplinary historical analysis. For Braudel, the Mediterranean Sea 'had its own unity, a distinct sphere of influence' — which he explores through his 'evocative metaphor of multiple "skeins of history".'[6] How far this sense of unity can be applied to the region of the Red Sea has been debated at each stage of the Red Sea Projects, for the Sea, paradoxically, could also be an obstacle as well as a channel of communication.

The Text

The book is divided into four major sections that explore the major themes of the book: I. Natural Resources of the Red Sea; II. The Sea: Boats and Navigation; III. Harbours: Ways of Life and Cultural Connections; and IV. The Cultural Connections of the Red Sea.

Natural Resources of the Red Sea

The first section focuses on the landscapes and seascapes of the Red Sea with papers on the natural resources and ecological connections of the Red Sea — fish, corals, minerals and plants. The papers reflect its landscapes, the material manifestations of relations between human cultures and their biophysical environments; and its seascapes, that is, the combination of adjacent land, coastline and sea of the Red Sea. It includes papers on Environmental Archaeology which present some of the latest research in the field, beginning with a paper by R. Neil Munro and Tony J. Wilkinson who sketch the changing environment of the Yemeni Tihāmah plain and the adjacent highlands over the last 20,000 years or so. Between 20,000 and 15,000 years ago both the Tihāmah and the Yemen highlands were significantly drier than today: sand dunes were well developed and *wādī* flow was probably more intermittent. With the post-glacial rise of sea level, offshore sources of sand were covered up and dune development on the Tihāmah was suppressed. During the early to mid-Holocene period (*ca.* 9,000 to 3000 BC), soil development reflected a more verdant environment, with extensive lakes set in the highlands and a more humid climate. More recently there was significant degradation of the environment; whilst growing populations had significant impact on the natural environment.

Lamya Khalidi's paper, based on fieldwork in the Tihāmah coastal plain, takes up many of these themes of archaeological landscape by exploring settlement strategies and material culture in the third to first millennium BC in the region which had became a corridor for culture contact by the third millennium BC. She supports her analysis with technical data on predominant tool types to show Red Sea maritime traditions that culturally linked the African and Asian coasts of the Red Sea. Tools included geometric microliths of obsidian. This material probably originated in the Horn of Africa rather than from highland Yemen and may well reflect local trade links between Africa and Arabia.

The significance of fish from the Red Sea in the diet of Crusaders in Petra is explored in a paper by Stephan G. Schmid and Jacqueline Studer. Recent excavations in the Wādī Farasah East at Petra revealed fortifications, Crusader tombstones and evidence of long-distance trade with the Red Sea, with impressive quantities of Red Sea parrotfish being discovered in a Nabataean cistern that had been re-used as a rubbish pit in medieval times. Indeed, evidence suggests that parrotfish from the Red Sea were a main component of the diet for Crusader soldiers controlling the Wādī Farasah in medieval Petra.

A reanalysis of botanical and zoological specimens collected by the ill-fated Danish Expedition to Arabia between 1761 and 1763 is presented by Nigel Hepper. The Danish Expedition included not only the geographer Carsten Niebuhr (who is mentioned in many papers in this volume) but also the naturalist Pehr Forsskål who made a huge collection of dried wild and cultivated plants and pickled fish and other animals. These samples were sent back to Europe by Niebuhr after Forsskål's death. Forsskål also provided detailed notes and lists of Arabic names, which are still being studied 230 years later in Denmark and Britain by zoologists, botanists and philologists. In 1775 Forsskål's notes were published posthumously in three volumes: one about animals, one about plants, and one which included drawings of both plants and animals by the Expedition's artist, G.W. Baurenfeind, who also died on the expedition.

Following papers that focus on archaeological landscapes, flora and fauna, and on maritime resources, Steve McMellor and David Smith provide useful if sobering data on the sea itself, focusing on current research on the coral reefs of the Red Sea by using a case study of the Ras Mohamed National Park with the incredible natural beauty of its marine environment. The reefs of the Red Sea are of major biological interest, for about 15 per cent of the fish species are endemic. The authors identify major threats to the reefs including pollution, changes in sea-surface temperatures, coral disease and damage by divers. They aim to develop a long-term monitoring programme to ensure the sustainable use of this very important natural resource.

The Sea: Boats and Navigation

The region's cultural landscape includes ships, seafarers and naval presences. The second section continues to focus on the Sea itself with a fascinating group of papers about its boats and navigational difficulties.

---

6 Vink 2007: 59.

The perceived navigational difficulties of the Red Sea have long played a central role in the construction and discussion of models of trade, cultural connections and maritime networks in that region. As Julian Whitewright discusses in his paper, sailing and navigation on the Red Sea must be addressed in terms of the capabilities of vessels at specific points in time rather than just focusing on the environmental conditions of the Red Sea. He also rationalizes the capabilities of ancient ships within their economic contexts, by studying ships in the Roman period. Whitewright re-assesses previously published data and recent archaeological finds from Roman Red Sea ports. The role of these vessels and the ports which they serviced in the maritime networks of the region are reconsidered on the basis of both their contemporary technology and economic conditions.

Although vessels were built on the shores of the Red Sea, others were imported overland from Mediterranean shipyards from Pharaonic times up to the Ottoman era. Thus, whenever a naval action was planned in the Red Sea, warships were imported to the Red Sea to carry out the battle. The absence of the specialized warship from the Red Sea arena had far-reaching implications for the development of ship construction, for piracy, for the nature of international trade in the area, and for global balance of power. Sarah Arenson explores this strange phenomenon by focusing on medieval Arabic sources.

Not only were ships imported from Mediterranean shipyards, but for over 1400 years the Red Sea has been part of the nautical culture on the Indian Ocean. Indeed, the construction of ships in the Red Sea has been similar to those in other areas of the Indian Ocean during this period. Norbert Weismann describes the features of ships and boats in the Indian Ocean such as construction principles, stem-posts, types of rudder and sails over this period. For example, the evidence for the exclusive use of settee or Latin sails in the Red Sea before the fifteenth century is poor. Square sails seem to have been used widely up to the sixteenth century and remains of the transitions from square to settee sails could be found up to the nineteenth century.

James Edgar Taylor's paper on the Red Sea *jalbah* opens with a tentative attempt to identify some of the factors influencing the movement of technical terms between local and regional cultures. It then employs these to challenge the accepted origin of the word *jalbah* and argue the case for a hitherto unrecognized one. It then considers the possible influence of the *jalbah* on ship design and the word *jalbah* on the names of ship types elsewhere. It draws from a number of European and Arabic texts, both classical and modern.

It is important to emphasize the importance of indigenous knowledge for any clear understanding of maritime cultural traditions and ways of life. For example, boat ornamentation is a widespread custom among mariners and fishermen. Its evidence is not confined to the Red Sea; it is customary, for example, among the coastal communities of the East African coast, the Southern Arabian coast and the Arabian / Persian Gulf and Oman. Dionisius A. Agius's paper focuses on the ornamentation of boats in the Red Sea and surrounding waters. Based on fieldwork in the Arab Gulf States and in the Red Sea he describes a variety of decorative motifs. His focus is on the symbolism behind boat decoration, and their cultural messages and influences.

Sarah Searight's paper returns to the hazards of navigating the Red Sea and focuses on the improvement of navigational aids as communications between India and Europe increased from the eighteenth century. Cultural, political and commercial connections expanded after the Bombay Marine / Indian Navy recognized the potential of steam navigation. This led to the crucial charting of the waterway, just in time to meet the demands of the larger steamboats commissioned by P&O for their Calcutta-Suez run. The opening of the Suez Canal in 1869 and increased navigation in the waterway demanded improved charts and navigation aids, and in the 1870s cable-laying for the Indo-European Telegraph improved communications. All this was against a background of commerce, war, anti-slavery manoeuvres, vastly increasing pilgrimage traffic, quarantine measures and so on. Admiralty Pilots and charts, lighthouses, 'lights' and buoys have also followed the internationalization of this crucial route between east and west. Her paper provides up-to-date information on the twenty-first century charting of the Red Sea — which is still crucial to safe navigation.

Harbours: Ways of Life and Cultural Connections

The cultural landscape includes harbour-towns, with long-distance trade in 'luxury' or, rather, lucrative goods (including textiles and especially silks, ceramics, tea, coffee, and spices), and basic commodities providing an underlying 'historical unity' to the region.[7] The third group of papers explores the ways of life and cultural connections of the harbours of the Red Sea and their hinterlands from pre-Classical Antiquity to the nineteenth century.

As Kenneth A. Kitchen describes, careful study of the geographical features of the western and eastern coastlines of the Red Sea and their hinterlands reveals striking contrasts between the two margins of the Red Sea, not least in the far greater number of anciently navigable inlets for use as natural harbours on the west side as opposed to the eastern one. There are also considerable contrasts between their respective hinterlands, in extent of climatic sub-regions (and related fauna and flora), mineral resources, linked land-routes,[8]

---

7 Chaudhuri 1990, cited in Vink 2007.

8 It is well established that the ancient road and route system in the Eastern Desert in Graeco/Roman times consisted of a complicated route system linking seaports as well as mines

their human users and their purposes. Involved with all this are modes and practical conditions of early navigation, identities of such navigators and their reasons for such travel in pre-Classical Antiquity.

The second paper in this group describes the latest discoveries of the cedar boat timbers and coils of ship ropes from the Egyptian coastal site of Marsā Gawāsīs, which confirmed that this was the sea port for Punt in the Middle Kingdom (*ca.* 2055–1650 BC) and early New Kingdom (*ca.* 1550–1069 BC). Kathryn A. Bard, Rodolfo Fattovich and Cheryl Ward describe how five parallel rock-cut rooms in the fossil coral terrace were used as a kind of ship arsenal: they found coils of rope, ship timbers and decking, just as the sailors left them almost 4000 years ago. Large cedar, pine, oak and ebony wood and charcoal as well as copper fastenings were found, as well as fragments of exotic ceramics from the Yemeni Tihāmah, the region of Aden and possibly Eritrea, suggesting that in the early to mid-second millennium BC the Egyptians had maritime contacts with both Arabian and African regions of the southern Red Sea.

So who lived in the Egyptian ports, such as Myos Hormos? The term 'Ichthyophagi' (fish-eaters), was used by Greek and Roman writers to describe a number of discrete communities that shared a common coastal fishing economy along the Erythræan Sea coast (which included what is now the Red Sea, Indian Ocean and Persian Gulf). Distinctions between different *Ichthyophagi* groups were recognised in antiquity. One such group, Ptolemy's *Arabaegypti Ichthyophagi*, inhabited the coastal region of the northern Red Sea and are the focus of Ross Thomas's paper. Tantalizing survey data along the Egyptian Red Sea coast has revealed the presence of shell middens, historically attested features of an *Ichthyophagi* maritime landscape. At the port sites of Myos Hormos and Berenike, newly discovered artefact and epigraphic evidence means that *Ichthyophagi* identity is now archaeologically attested. Ross Thomas then debates to what extent the 'Arabaegypti Ichthyophagi' can be classified as an 'ethnic identity'.

There has been considerable debate as to why certain ports in the Red Sea developed in particular locations. Walter Ward challenges the relevance of Facey's paper about the significance of winds on travel, presented at Red Sea I[9] — for trade in late antiquity seems to run counter to his conclusions. Ward focuses on the rise of Clysma and Aila at the extreme north of the Red Sea and the abandonment of Myos Hormos, Leuce Kome, and by the mid-fifth century, Berenike. This paper argues that the 'perceived' threat to merchants' security by nomadic groups along the eastern frontier (Saracens) and in the Eastern Desert (Blemmyes / Eastern Desert Dwellers) led to the shift of Roman trade routes to more easily defended ports such as Aila and Clysma. Walter Ward believes that the accounts of raids created a 'perceived' threat, which convinced merchants to move their operations to ports in the north which they believed to be safer.

Suez is a provincial capital at the head of the Gulf of Suez (Baḥr Qulzum) and to the north west of the mouth of the modern Suez Canal. It is the site of the Ptolemaic fortress of Clysma and was identified by Abū'l-Fidā as the medieval Qulzum; by 1927 it was a town of 40,523 inhabitants. The town was a busy crossroads for travellers from Palestine, Cairo and India; for pilgrims to and from Makkah;[10] and the embarkation point for travellers on the overland route via Alexandria and Cairo, to and from India. From the mid-nineteenth century it was a harbour that flourished (or declined) on the economic fortunes of the Suez Canal. Janet Starkey continues the focus on northern ports and describes the town and its maritime trade in the eighteenth and nineteenth centuries. Using travellers' literary landscapes of Suez as her starting point, she describes its economic and cultural connections including those associated with coffee as a commodity.

Extending the Cultural Connections of the Red Sea

The Red Sea region was affected by the periodic migration of nomads within and into the region; by the rise and spread of Christianity from the Mediterranean from Roman times, followed by Islam from the Ḥijāz from the seventh century AD; by the impact of a succession of empires, including the Ottoman empire, with epicentres beyond the Red Sea; and by European maritime expansion and even infiltration by Chinese traders. As K.N. Chaudhuri comments in relation to the Indian Ocean, a sea provides the 'means of travel, movements of peoples, economic exchange, climate, and historical forces that created elements of cohesion. Religion,

and quarries in the desert. Jonatan Krzywinski described (in a paper presented at the conference but not published in this volume) a new route in Wadi Halous across the Eastern Desert of Egypt which he argues was used by local people. He showed that a remarkable aspect of this local route to Berenike is the many petroglyphs showing both hunting (ibex and gazelles) and camel caravan motifs. As well as these motifs he found evidence of Blemmy graves but no Graeco/Roman installations.

9 Facey 2004: 7–18.

10 Note should also be made of an additional paper presented at the conference not included in this volume, but nevertheless of significance in the understanding of cultural connections of the Red Sea. As Dr 'Adil Salahi, the Executive Director of Al-Furqan Islamic Heritage Foundation, London, described in his paper 'Red Sea Voyages in the Red Sea by the Prophet Muhammad's Companions', the Arabs of Makkah travelled regularly for trade, and had two annual trips which took them to Syria and Yemen. These trading expeditions were central in the flourishing Makkan economy prior to Islam and indicate that a regular route of travel existed between Makkah and Abyssinia, across the Red Sea.

social systems, and cultural traditions, on the other hand, provided the contrasts.'[11] The final section of the book therefore focuses on a series of overlapping cultural zones from many historical periods in order to try to understand cultural exchange and connections between the Red Sea and surrounding regions.

External trading contacts were not simply around the Red Sea and its immediate hinterlands in the Middle East but also further afield, even in the first millennium BC, as Paul Sinclair describes in his paper. Archaeological investigations along the coast of East Africa and the islands of the Zanzibar archipelago have focused on the extensive open sites containing architectural remains of the Swahili civilization and documentary evidence for trade from the early first millennium AD onwards. Recent research by Felix Chami and newly explored archaeological sequences from Kuumbi Cave in south-east Zanzibar indicate the presence of possible South Asian Early Historic and Historic ceramics and imported glass beads possibly from the Mediterranean Basin.

The section continues by exploring the Arabian presence from Late Antiquity. It also includes evidence of contact further afield, outside the Arabian Peninsula and the Middle East, with data on external trading contacts on the east coast of Africa in the first millennium BC. As Tim Power describes, Late Antique sources attest to an Arabian presence in pre-Islamic Egypt which is apparently absent from the archaeological record. However, explorers and archaeologists working in the Eastern Desert of Egypt have repeatedly noted 'enigmatic settlements'. These do not readily conform to familiar Graeco-Roman models, and instead find parallels in the Umayyad Levant and North Africa.

While states on the Red Sea and Indian Ocean rim in the ancient period were primarily inland states, maritime long-distance exchange facilitated by the monsoon winds brought these societies, separated by huge stretches of water, into close commercial contact over a period of centuries. Eivind Heldaas Seland uses an historical source for this trade, the *Periplus of the Erythræan Sea*,[12] to reveal a picture of inland states which took an active interest in maritime trade. These states interacted in a system where political centres on high ground inland mobilized key resources from extensive hinterlands in order to coordinate and facilitate long-distance maritime exchange from coastal settlements established and maintained specifically for that purpose. In his paper he argues that maritime trade as an agent of change in Red Sea and Indian Ocean societies is reflected in the consistent use of terminology describing hierarchies of settlements in the *Periplus*. This, in turn, broadens our understanding of the relationship between ocean, coast, inland and inland-periphery in the regions participating in the monsoon exchange, and enables us to develop a descriptive model of the first-century Indian Ocean state.

Underlying themes of the book are the spiritual and religious connections of the Red Sea region and beyond. Roberta Tomber turns our attention to India, by asking what role Indian Ocean trade played in the diffusion of Christianity, and what role Christians and Christianity played in Indian Ocean trade. The origins of Christianity in India are intermingled with legend, and it is commonly held that St Thomas arrived in southern India in the mid-first century AD on a trading ship originating in Alexandria. His landing spot is thought to have been the important Malabar port of Muziris, only recently located on the ground in the modern state of Kerala. It is in this region that St Thomas is said to have established seven churches. In the fourth century AD the Christian population converted by St Thomas was boosted by refugees from East Syria or the area of modern-day Iraq. Today Christians account for only 3 per cent of the overall population in India, but *ca.* 20 per cent of that in Kerala. She provides archaeological evidence for Christianity on the Red Sea, from 'Aqabah, Abū Sha'ar, Myos Hormos, Berenike, Adulis and Aksum. While there is limited evidence for Christianity during the first century AD, by the fourth century these sites were united by a strong Christian element known not only from documents but also from structures and artefacts.

Between 1405 and 1431, the Ming dispatched seven major naval expeditions to the Indian Ocean under the overall command of the eunuch Cheng Ho / Zheng He. The fourth expedition, which set out in 1413, was the first to sail beyond South Asia. It crossed the Indian Ocean and put in at Hormoz, already the major emporium of the Gulf. This expedition was accompanied by Ma Huan, a convert to Islam, who acted as translator and chronicler to this expedition and two more, those of 1421 and 1431; for unknown reasons he did not take part in the fifth expedition of 1417. His *Ying-yai sheng-lan*, 'The Overall Survey of the Ocean's Shore', begun on his return from the expedition of 1413 and expanded and revised after succeeding expeditions, was published *ca.* 1451. As Paul Lunde describes in his paper, the chapters devoted to the Arabian ports are full of interest, but have attracted surprisingly little attention from scholars working on the history of the Arabian Peninsula. Ships from the Chinese armada put in at La'sa, Dhofar, Aden and Jiddah, and on the last voyage, Ma Huan made the pilgrimage to Makkah and may have visited al-Madīnah. Rasūlid and Mamlūk chronicles mention the arrival of the Chinese junks in Aden. His paper examines these Arabic sources to see how far they coincide with Ma Huan's account and what the chroniclers made of Chinese imperial pretensions in the Indian Ocean and Red Sea.

The final paper in this section focuses on a specific individual, the career of the Turkish traveller and cartographer Piri

[11] Chaudhuri 1990: 104, and 383–7, cited in Vink 2007.
[12] Casson 1989.

Reis b. Hajjī Meḥmed (*ca.* 1470–1553/4), who was active during the period when the Ottomans were extending their empire over much of the central Arab world. Piri Reis is perhaps best known today for his 'world map' dated 1513, preserved in the Istanbul Topkapı Saray Library; but he was also the author of a major navigational work, the *Kitab-ı Bahriyye*, designed as a complete manual for Turkish navigators in the Aegean and Mediterranean seas. With the Ottoman advance into Syria and Egypt in 1516–1517, however, the focus of his career appears to have switched from the Mediterranean to the Red Sea and he is said to have seen active service in the Ottoman Red Sea fleet based in Suez, recapturing Aden from the Portuguese in 1549 and besieging Hormoz in 1552. Paul Starkey's paper examines some of the controversies that have attended accounts of his later career, including the allegation made by Ottoman historians that he was executed in Cairo for dereliction of duty, and considers the significance of his career in the context of European-Ottoman relations in the Red Sea area of the time.

Overall, although many papers continue to focus on the Red Sea region as seen from the perspective of outsider communities, it is evident that local cultures and indigenous knowledge were of considerable significance. For example, in terms of local communities the ancestors of the *Icthyophagi* were arguably the prehistoric occupants of the coastal shell middens, and as early as the sixth millennium BC these groups had links across the waters from Arabia to north-east Africa. Similarly the settlement systems of the Himyarites as well as other trading communities around the Red Sea had a long history extending back to the second and third millennium BC. The practices of these long-established communities would have contributed, to some degree, to the development of later maritime developments. Therefore, if we are to understand the long-term development of the Red Sea, it may be the tension between outsider views and an understanding of indigenous knowledge through local communities that will provide the most productive way forward.

Conclusions

The final session of Red Sea Project III, coordinated by Francine Stone who initiated the Red Sea Project in the early 2000s, and Janet Starkey who organised Red Sea Projects II and III, was dedicated to the discussion of the first three stages of the project and was followed by an open forum on what to do next with the Red Sea Project. Possible subjects for discussion, either at small workshops or future major conferences, included fishermen's cultures, particularly their songs and music; architecture and the conservation of sites such as Sawākin, al-Mukhā' and Massawa; the use and distribution of conch shells; the various manifestations of the *ḥajj*, as well as more on boats, navigation, routes and cultural links. The need for future emphasis on the importance of indigenous knowledge on these topics for any clear understanding of maritime cultural traditions and interpretation of archaeological data was stressed. The Peninsula is a crossroads of complex cultural and natural connections with the Red Sea, the Gulf, Arabian Sea, the East African coast, the Indian Ocean and beyond. Whatever else is planned, it is important not to lose sight of Arabia as a focal point with its fascinating archaeological and cultural heritage waiting to be further explored.

References

Casson, L. 1989. *The Periplus Maris Erythræi*. Princeton: Princeton University Press.

Chaudhuri, K.N. 1990. *Asia before Europe: economy and civilization of the Indian Ocean from the rise of Islam to 1750*. Cambridge and New York: Cambridge University Press.

Facey, W. 2004. The Red Sea: the wind regime and location of ports. 7–18 in P. Lunde and A. Porter (eds). 2004. *Trade and Travel in the Red Sea Region. Proceedings of Red Sea Project I held in the British Museum October 2002*. BAR International Series 1269. Oxford: Archaeopress.

Horden, P. and Purcell, N. 2006. The Mediterranean and 'the new thalassology'. *American Historical Review* 111(3): 723.

Lunde, P. and Porter, A. (eds). 2004. *Trade and Travel in the Red Sea Region*. Society for Arabian Studies Monographs 2. BAR International Series 1269. Oxford: Archaeopress.

Starkey, J.C.M. (ed.). 2005. *People of the Red Sea*. Society for Arabian Studies Monographs 3. BAR International Series 1395. Oxford: Archaeopress.

Vink, M.P.M. 2007. Indian Ocean Studies and the 'new thalassology'. *Journal of Global History* 2: 41–62.

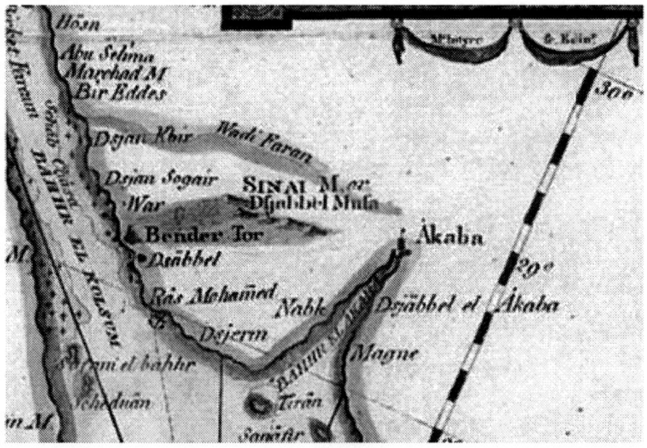

Map 0:1 The Red Sea, from Carsten Niebuhr's map, 1762

The Contributors

Dionisius A. Agius is a linguist and maritime ethnographer, currently Professor at the University of Leeds. Author of several books on maritime material culture, he is currently working on traditional boat-building, boat-types, maritime trade and ethnography of the Red Sea region. He is general editor of *Al-Masāq: Islam and the Medieval Mediterranean*, an international journal covering all aspects of the Mediterranean cultures (8th-15th century). His recent publications include *In the Wake of the Dhow: The Arabian Gulf and Oman* (Reading: Ithaca, 2002) and *Seafaring in the Arabian Gulf and Oman: The People of the Dhow* (London: Kegan Paul, 2005). The latter was awarded a major prize by the Abdullah Al-Mubarak Al-Sabah Foundation and the British-Kuwait Friendship Society for the best scholarly work on the Middle East published in the UK in 2005. In September 2007, he will take up the Chair in Arabic and Islamic Material Culture at the University of Exeter.

Sarah Arenson. A medieval maritime historian, Born 1940 in Jerusalem, she now lives in Caesarea. Co-founder of the Department for the History of Maritime Civilizations at Haifa University and currently Associate Researcher at the Recanati Institute of Maritime Studies, Haifa University, Israel.

Kathryn A. Bard is Associate Professor of Archaeology at Boston University, Boston (USA). She has directed or co-directed archaeological projects in Egypt and Ethiopia. Since 2001 she has been directing with Rodolfo Fattovich the Joint UNO/IsIAO and BU Expedition at Marsā Gawāsīs (Egypt).

Rodolfo Fattovich is Professor of Ethiopian Archaeology and lecturer in Egyptian Archaeology at the University of Naples "l'Orientale," Naples (Italy). He has directed or co-directed archaeological projects in Egypt, Sudan and Ethiopia. Since 2001 he has been directing with Kathryn A. Bard the Joint UNO/IsIAO and BU Expedition at Marsā Gawāsīs (Egypt).

F. Nigel Hepper is retired from Kew Herbarium where he worked as a plant taxonomist and editor of the revised Flora of West Tropical Africa. He has also been interested in historic expeditions to Africa and the Middle East, as well as the botany of ancient Egypt and the Bible, which resulted in several publications.

Lamya Khalidi received her PhD from the Department of Archaeology at the University of Cambridge in 2006. Her dissertation focused on late prehistoric (3rd – 1st millennia BC) culture-contact and interaction along the Tihamah Red Sea coastal plain, Yemen. She received a B.F.A. with a minor in archaeology from the University of Michigan and an M.Phil in archaeology from the University of Cambridge. Since 1994 she has assisted in excavations in Beirut, Lebanon and Petra, Jordan and spent two years excavating and surveying in the northern Jezira, Syria on the sites of Tel Chagar Bazar and Tel Hamoukar. In 2001, she joined the University of Chicago Dhamar Survey Project in the Yemeni highlands where she assisted in excavations and survey. She has since directed four survey projects in Hazm al Udayn (the western escarpment) and the Tihāmah coastal plain, Yemen, as well as a reconnaissance mission in Eritrea. She is currently a research associate at the Centre Français d'Archéologie et de Sciences Sociales in Sanaa, Yemen.

Kenneth A. Kitchen is Professor emeritus (Brunner and personal chairs) at the School of Archaeology, Classics and Egyptology, University of Liverpool. Active expertise in both Egyptology and Semitics; pursuing these and other fields world-wide: e.g. Egypt (extensive epigraphic fieldwork); Anatolia, Syria / Lebanon and both Palestines west and east of the Jordan; Gulf states and Yemen; Brazil (museum collections) etc. extensive publication in several disciplines: Egyptian text-editions, history, foreign relations (Near East, Africa, Aegean); early West Semitic, and systematic backgrounds to Old Testament; Pre-Islamic Arabia; Egypt and Aegean area.

Paul Lunde was raised in Saudi Arabia and is a graduate of the University of California (Berkeley) and SOAS. He has lived and studied in the Middle East and for many years conducted research in the Vatican Library, the archives of the Propaganda Fide, and the Archivo de Indias in Seville. Specializing in Arabic geographical literature, he has written extensively on related topics. His most recent book is *Islam: Culture, Faith and History* (Dorling Kindersly, 2002).

Steve McMellor is a PhD student with the Coral Reef Research Unit, Department of Biological Sciences, University of Essex. His research is based on the development of a classification scheme for coral reef health and he is also developing an urgently needed Index of Biotic Integrity to act as a diagnostic monitoring and management tool. In 2006 he produced a number of monitoring reports with David J. Smith on Ras Mohammed National Park for the Egyptian Environmental Affairs Agency. He is also involved in the monitoring of Indonesian reefs in the Wakatobi Marine National Park, Sulawesi.

R. Neil Munro, an independent consultant since 1996, started his career with Hunting Technical Services in 1972 and now runs RN Munro & Associates, Dirleton, Scotland. He has made soil, geomorphological, and land use surveys in all the countries that border the Red Sea. He is currently completing a study of stabilized dunes in Arabia, including the Yemen Tihāmah.

Tim Power is an Islamicist and archaeologist, currently a doctoral candidate at the Khalili Research Centre, University of Oxford. His thesis is on the economic development of the medieval Red Sea. His archaeological experience in the Red Sea region includes seasons with Steve Sidebotham in the Eastern Desert of Egypt and Ed Keall in the Yemeni Tihāmah.

Sarah Searight has specialized for many years in the Middle East. She is the author of *The British in the Middle East* (1969), *Steaming East* (1991), and *Yemen: Land and People* which was published to coincide with the opening of the British Museum's 'Queen of Sheba' exhibition in 2002. She lectures on Islamic art and architecture, is a founder member of the Association for the Study of Travel in the Near East and is Chair of the Society for Arabian Studies.

Stephan G. Schmid has been Professor of Archaeology at the University Paul Valéry (Montpellier III, France) since 2002. From 1996 to 2002 he was deputy director of the Swiss School of Archaeology in Greece. He obtained a PhD from Basel University with a doctoral thesis dealing with Nabataean fine ware pottery in 1996 and a habilitation from Sorbonne University (Paris I, France) in 2002. Research activities: Nabataean studies, Greece in Hellenistic and Roman times, Hellenistic sculpture. Direction of excavations at Eretria (Greece) from 1996 to 2000 and from 2000 to present at Petra (Jordan).

Eivind Heldaas Seland is Lecturer in Ancient History and World History at the Department of History, University of Bergen, Norway. His research interests are the relationship between trade and state power and between the Mediterranean world and the Red Sea and Indian Ocean regions in the ancient period.

Paul J.J. Sinclair is Professor of African and Comparative Archaeology, Department of Archaeology and Ancient History, Uppsala University, Sweden http://www.arkeologi.uu.se. Professor Sinclair has worked for over thirty years in Africa as an archaeologist, excavating at Great Zimbabwe and Manyikeni in Mozambique, and has carried out fieldwork in Comores islands, Jenne Jenno, Mali and the Nile Delta. His interests include GIS applications and spatial archaeology, urbanism and socio-environmental interactions and landscape dynamics. In 1993, with T. Shaw, B. Andah and A. Okpoko he produced *The Archaeology of Africa* (London: Routledge). Current interests include urbanism and landscape dynamics in riverine contexts throughout the tropics.

David J. Smith, Senior Lecturer in Marine Biology and Director of the Coral Reef Research Unit, University of Essex. He is also Associate Editor of *Global Change Biology*, Lead Scientist for the Mitsubishi Global Coral Reef Task Force: Indian Ocean, and Director of Operations, Wallacea. His main research interests are Coral Reef Systems, Water Pollution Biology and Natural Resource Management. He has carried out many projects including those Ras Mohamed National Park, Sinai and Wakatobi Marine National Park, S.E. Sulawesi, Indonesia.

Janet Starkey is a Research Associate at the Department of Anthropology, Durham University and publishes on the anthropology of the Middle East. She has undertaken fieldwork among the Beja of the Red Sea Hills. Recent publications include *Travellers in Egypt* (1999), *Desert Travellers from Herodotus to T.E. Lawrence* (2000), *Unfolding the Orient* (2000) and *Interpreting the Orient* (2000) and she has recently edited *Red Sea II: People of the Red Sea*. She is currently researching the eighteenth-century 'natural historians' of Aleppo, Alexander Russell, MD and Patrick Russell, MD.

Paul Starkey is Professor of Arabic at Durham University, where he lectures on Arabic language and literature and on Middle Eastern culture, and is a Co-Director of the Centre for the Advanced Study of the Arab World (CASAW). He has written extensively on Arabic literature and translated a number of Arabic novels. He was a founder member and past President of the Association for the Study of Travel in Egypt and the Near East (ASTENE), and a former editor of the *British Journal of Middle Eastern Studies*.

Jacqueline Studer is conservator at the Muséum d'histoire naturelle at Geneva since 2002. From 1988 to 2002 she was a researcher at the Department of Archaeozoology of the same museum. She obtained a PhD from Geneva University (Switzerland) in 1991 with a doctoral thesis dealing with the fauna of the final Bronze Age in Switzerland. Research activities: studies on the exploitation of animals by protohistoric farmers (Bronze and Iron Age) in Switzerland and France. Studies on the fauna of the Near East (Jordan and Syria), since 1989 in collaboration with the Swiss-Liechtenstein excavations led by Basel University at Petra (Jordan).

James Edgar Taylor of the Society for Nautical Research was born in 1926 to an East Anglian family of shipwrights and seafarers. Qualifications: BSc (Civil Engineering), BA (Arabic with Linguistics), MA (Arabic Literature & Literary Criticism). Occasional writer and lecturer on aspects of Arab culture, especially dhows and pearl diving. Ex-Indian Army, Colonial Engineering Service and Industry. Sojourned in India, East Africa and the Middle East, where he studied the construction and sailing of dhows as a hobby.

Ross Iain Thomas is currently studying for a PhD on the maritime cultures of the Erythræan Sea trade at the Department of Archaeology, University of Southampton. His interests include archaeological evidence for earthquakes, maritime cultures and ethnicity. He has worked on archaeological sites in 'Aqabah, al-Quṣayr al-Qadīm /Myos Hormos on the Red Sea and in the Eastern Desert of Egypt and Sudan.

Roberta Tomber has worked extensively on archaeological sites throughout the Roman Empire, specializing in pottery. Since 1996 she has been involved particularly in the ports of the Red Sea (Berenike, Myos Hormos and Aila/Aylah) and their role in Indian Ocean commerce. Between 2002 and 2004 she held an AHRB funded grant (with David Peacock) at the University of Southampton to continue this work on Indo-Roman trade, which included extensive fieldwork in India. She is currently an Honorary Research Fellow in the Department of Archaeology, Southampton and a Visiting Fellow in the Department of Conservation, Documentation and Science at the British Museum.

Cheryl A. Ward is Associate Professor at the Department of Anthropology, Florida State University, Tallassee, USA. She is a specialist in nautical archaeology with particular reference to ancient Egyptian boats and long experience as principal or co-principal investigator in the Mediterranean Sea, Black Sea and Red Sea.

Walter Ward. Walter Ward's first archaeological experience occurred while attending North Carolina State University, at 'Aqabah, Jordan, site of ancient Aila. He is currently attending the University of California at Los Angeles and working on his dissertation on the later Roman province of Third Palestine.

Norbert Weismann of Ruhr-Universität Bochum. General practitioner and assistant lecturer. He has studied Arab shipbuilding since 1992 and undertaken fieldwork in Oman, Kuwait, Qatar and UAE.

Julian Whitewright is a PhD candidate at the Centre for Maritime Archaeology, University of Southampton. His research interests centre upon maritime technological change in the Mediterranean, Red Sea and Indian Ocean during the first millennium AD. This subject is approached from an ethnographic, historical and practical perspective as well as an archaeological one.

Tony J. Wilkinson, Professor of Archaeology, Durham University, and previously Professor in Near Eastern Archaeology at the University of Edinburgh. With interests in Landscape Archaeology, Geoarchaeology and the Archaeology of the Middle East, he has worked in Yemen, Oman and Saudi Arabia, and was Assistant Director, British Archaeological Expedition to Iraq, Baghdad. He has published extensively on Mesopotamia, Syria and other sites in the Middle East: in 2005 he was awarded the James R. Wiseman Book Award of the Archaeological Institute of America for *Archaeological Landscapes of the Near East* (Arizona 2003).

Part I: Natural Resources of the Red Sea

Environment, Landscapes and Archaeology of the Yemeni Tihāmah

R. Neil Munro and Tony J. Wilkinson

Introduction

The dominant feature of the Red Sea coast of south-west Arabia is the Tihāmah Piedmont coastal plain, with its dramatic backdrop of mountains that rise inland to heights in excess of 3,000 m. This paper examines landscapes of the Tihāmah Piedmont and human occupation during the late Quaternary. We review the physical landscape and environment with emphasis on the aeolian landforms that cover significant parts of the Tihāmah, and describe the characteristics of these and other landform features, together with aspects of the climate and how it has controlled sand transport in the past and present. The implications of environmental change for long-term human settlement and migration are also examined. These include the formation of linear dunes during periods of Pleistocene low sea levels, as well as the later stabilization of dunes by soils in the early Holocene, and the modern period of active sand dune movement. Finally, now that more is known about the archaeology of the Tihāmah it is appropriate to review how emerging patterns of human occupation might have been configured in terms of the physical and human geography of the region as well as long-term environmental change.

Previous Studies

Landforms of the Tihāmah

In 1763 the Danish explorer Carsten Niebuhr[1] gave a convincing description of the Tihāmah, noting it to be a 'sandy, unhealthy, though friendly place'. The same could be written today. To those that visited and reported on the Tihāmah, its sandy nature was well known: 'an arid coastal plain....consisting of alluvial and wind-blown deposits thirty to sixty miles wide',[2] whilst Huzayyin[3] noted the occurrence of sand storms on the Tihāmah. After Niebuhr's visit in 1763 over two hundred years were to pass before nationwide soil surveys by Cornell University[4] described alluvium and both modern and ancient dunes on the Tihāmah.[5]

Yet, despite these early reports of a sandy environment, many influential studies of global and / or regional distribution of aeolian landforms[6] have not indicated that the Tihāmah has active or relict aeolian dunes. Palaeogeographic maps for the 8,000 BP timeline[7] suggest that the entire Tihāmah comprizes fluvial sediments, whilst Edgell[8] indicates that most of the Tihāmah is an alluvial plain, with only a few sand dunes in the Wādī Zabīd area.[9]

On the other hand, geological maps of Yemen[10] show the presence of modern dunes, but they do not indicate ancient aeolian landforms. Geological and hydro-geological maps of Yemen at a scale of 1:250,000[11] referred to most of the Tihāmah as 'undifferentiated superficial deposits' and missed the major areas of ancient dunes. They did, however, map loess / ancient dunes in northern parts of the Tihāmah close to the escarpment, and indicated the existence of raised coral reefs up to 10 km inland to the north-east from al-Ghulayfiqah (south of Wādī Sihām).

To the modern visitor, the Tihāmah is a complex mosaic of sand dunes and sand sheets, juxtaposed with active and inactive alluvial fans, and along the coast small areas of mangrove forests and tidal to supra-tidal *sabkha* flats.

Halcrow and Partners (1978) in development planning for the Wādī Surdud; and in the Wādī Rima' by Anderson (1979). Later, FAO–IC (1990 and 1991) described ancient dunes as part of a project preparation plan for the TEPP. Though their interpretations differed, these authors recognized that there were various semi-stabilized linear dunes and rolling sand plains overlain by more active dunes. Hunting Technical Services (HTS) (1999) provided sedimentological data for aeolian and alluvial landforms throughout the Tihāmah.

---

[1]   Niebuhr 1792.
[2]   Naval Intelligence 1946.
[3]   Huzayyin 1945.
[4]   King, *et al.* 1983, 1985, Forbes 1985, van Waveren 1990.
[5]   Dune ridges were also noted by Tipton and Kalmbach (1974) and MMP–Hunting Technical Services (HTS) (1982, 1983) during the Wādī Mawr feasibility studies; by

[6]   Meigs 1966, McGinnies, *et al.* 1968, Glennie 1970, Snead 1972, Sarnthein 1972 and 1978, Cooke and Warren 1973, Petrov 1975, Sarnthein and Diester-Haas 1977, Breed, *et al.* 1979, Leeder 1981, Wells, 1989, Pye and Tsoar 1990, Summerfield 1991, Thomas and Shaw 1991, Cooke, *et al.* 1993, Lancaster 1995, Thomas 1997, Allison 1997, Goudie, *et al.* 1999, Williams, *et al.* 2003.
[7]   Pachur and Altman 1997.
[8]   Edgell 2006.
[9]   Data from TEPP report by El-Hassan 1999.
[10] Geukens 1966, Grolier and Overstreet 1975, 1976, Kruck 1983, 1984, 1991, Kruck, *et al.* 1996.
[11] Robertson Research 1991a, 1991b, 1991c, 1993a.

These features have been variably documented in a number of published and official studies.[12]

The above summary indicates the degree to which the Tihāmah remains an unknown land, and one that has been misinterpreted by many reviewers; errors which, in turn, have been compounded by reviews of reviews. Whilst reviewers cannot expect to visit every spot on earth, they generally fail to refer to the locally distributed 'grey' literature prepared by governments or international development agencies. For the Tihāmah at least, this paper hopes to put the record straight.

Previous archaeological research

The Tihāmah, although visited frequently, has not been the focus of many major archaeological projects. Nevertheless, this account has benefited from and builds upon earlier synthetic studies and reports by Durrani, Stone, Tosi, Keal and Hehmeyer, Phillips, and Khalidi.[13] Among the various published reports, those on the Saudi Arabian Tihāmah south of Jizan also provide useful insights into environmental change. For example, Zarins and Zahrani[14] showed that Neolithic settlements and middens were placed on stabilized red sand dunes that were assumed to be a product of late Pleistocene aridity, and are overlain by active dunes. Middens in the Wādī Rima', dated to 8,084 to 8,480 years BP by Tosi,[15] occur 10 km inland of the present coastline and were cited by Edgell[16] somewhat misleadingly as evidence of the rapid aggradation of the Tihāmah Plain during the Holocene.

Geology and Present-Day Environments

Methods

For this study the landforms of the Tihāmah have been mapped according to the Australian 'Land System' approach.[17] A 'Land System' is defined as a group of landforms with a recurrent pattern over a large area and with distinctive features of geology, geomorphology, water resources, climate, soils, ecology and land use that distinguish it from other 'Land Systems'. The Red Sea coastal plain, namely the Tihāmah Piedmont, is a 'Land Region', a broader unit in which there are several 'Land Systems'. This undulating and gently sloping plain contains complex patterns of active and stabilized aeolian sands, extensive older and recent alluvial fans, as well as coastal *sabkha* and mangrove plains that hug the coast. Geomorphological mapping (by Munro) of the Tihāmah Piedmont identified eight land systems covering some 17,550 km^2 of the Tihāmah (Table 1:1). The disposition of these is shown in Map 1:1.

Climate and Sediment Movement

Although the climate of the Tihāmah is arid, the eastern areas along the Piedmont receive a mean annual rainfall of 300–400 mm, which is sufficient for rain-fed cultivation. To the west, however, rainfall declines rapidly attaining *ca.* 100 mm at the coast itself.[18] Facey has shown how the annual movement of the Inter-Tropical Convergence Zone (ITCZ) set seasonal limits to maritime trade and warfare over several millennia prior to the steamship era.[19] The ITCZ is and has been responsible too for shaping the evolution of the Tihāmah's distinctive landscapes of aeolian, alluvial and coastal landforms.

The ITCZ follows the position of the sun's zenith with a time lag of some five weeks[20] and separates the trade winds of both hemispheres. Over Arabia, during the northern hemisphere summer, it brings rainfall to the 'Asir and mountainous areas of Yemen and Oman, though not beyond, into interior Arabia.[21]

In winter (January) Yemen lies on the southern edge of the high-level polar westerly winds, but at the surface strong subsidence associated with high pressure results in cool easterly winds blowing towards areas of low pressure over Egypt and Arabia. The canalizing effect of the Red Sea trough causes these winds to become south-westerly. These drive the currents northwards and bring sands onshore on parts of the Tihāmah coast.

By spring (April) the subtropical anticyclone of the ITCZ is moving rapidly northwards with high-level westerly and north-westerly winds, but at the surface south-easterly and south-westerly winds blow along the Red Sea trough. The northerly surface flow is also responsible for the northerly longshore drift of sediments along the coastline. In addition, winds blow from the south-west and south, and move sandy and shelly carbonate sediments onshore. These winds, which are generally stated to be the strongest, affect fishing operations, by creating high sea conditions, and also affect agriculture by blowing sand.

12 Al-Hubaishi and Müller-Hohenstein 1984, Barratt 1987a, 1987b, Hunting Technical Services (HTS) 1992, 1993, 1999, 2002, Scholte, *et al.* 1991, 1992.

13 Durrani 2005, Stone 1982, Tosi 1985 and 1986, Hehmeyer and Keall 1993, Phillips 1998 and Khalidi 2006.

14 Zarins and Zahrani 1985.

15 Tosi 1986.

16 Edgell 2006.

17 Christian and Stewart 1952, Christian 1958, Mitchell 1973.

18 Naval Intelligence 1946, Rathjens, *et al.* 1956, Williams 1979, Taha, *et al.* 1981, Siraj 1984, Gun and Abdul Aziz 1995, Fisher and Membery 1998, UK Hydrographic Office 2004, DHV 1990: 11.

19 Facey 2004.

20 Brown and Cochemé 1973.

21 Huzayyin, 1945.

Table 1:1 Land Systems on the Tihāmah, Yemen

Land System	Geomorphic Units	Soil Features	Vegetation / Land Use
Zabīd: Active coalesced alluvial fans with channels: 5974 km^2	Channel bed; low terrace; bunded flood irrigation silt plains; outwash silt 'deltas' at distal end; sand sheets, hummocks and dunes; truncate ancient dunes in east.	Deep silty and loamy soils	Bunded fields fed by spate irrigation channels: cereals, bananas, cotton, vegetables, flowers. Dom Palm *(Hyhaene thebaica)* in low lying areas.
Sihām: Older coalesced alluvial fans that are either stable or are being eroded by rilling and deflation: 2210 km^2.	Slightly undulating plain with anthropogenic terraces; deflation plains. Probably several generations of fans.	Deep loams to clay loams; subsurface gravels.	Bunded fields with runoff irrigation for cereals etc; patches of dense *Commiphora spp* and *Acacia spp.* bushland.
Rasiyan: Active and older braided streams & terraces in arid zones: 1372 km^2.	Bouldery to sandy ephemeral braided stream beds; low terraces; dark patinas on boulders of oldest terraces.	Bouldery to silty soils.	Pump irrigated on silty soils.
Mansuriyah: Soil-stabilized aeolian sand plains: 3432 km^2	Slight undulating sand plains; ancient coastal foredunes to 20m height; active dunes/sand sheet cover.	Hard blocky relict paleosol (*Torrispamments, Ustipsamments)*, with moderate silt+clay, sand-filled polygonal crack network. Cambic Arenosols (FAO-UNESCO, 1977)	Tussock grassland of *Panicum turgidum, Odyssea mucronata*; occasional *Acacia tortilis, Acacia ehrenbergiana* and *Cadaba rotundifolia trees;* rainfed millet close to Escarpment.
Bayt al-Faqīh: Soil-stabilized aeolian sand formations comprizing linear dune ridges and interdune corridors; some gullied areas: 2377 km^2	Rolling, linear, sand ridges, with soil cap over stratified sands; gullying of soil with sandy with outwash fans. Interdune areas now covered by sand sheets, but some areas of loamy alluvial silts remain.	Polygonal features with hard blocky paleosol topsoil (as above), over stratified to massive structured sands. Some additional buried paleosol layers.	*Acacia ehrenbergiana* woodland groves, and tussock grasses (*Panicum turgidum, Odyssea mucronata).* Also, *Leptadenia pyrotechnica* on sand hummocks and rainfed millet on rain stabilized dunes; *Ziziphus spina-christi* and *Balanites aegyptiaca* trees with cereals on loamy interdune plains.
Rima': Active aeolian sand sheets and dunes of Interior Plains overlies old dunes and alluvium: 1196 km^2	Barchans, transverse dunes and sand sheets. Limited parabolic development on borders of W Rima'; limited seif dunes.	Negligible soil formation inn loose stratified sands. *Typic Torrispamments*	Sparse grasses and herbs on sand hummocks: *Lasiurus scindicus, Leptadenia pyrotechnica. Scattered Acacia ehrenbergiana, Salvadora persica, Cadaba rotundifolia, Tamerix aphylla;* rainfed millet.
Mujaylis: Coastal dunes and sand sheets, overlies old dunes: 294 km^2	Parabolics up to 800 m long and 400m wide pass inland to barchan and transverse dunes; hummock dunes and sand sheets widespread; locally foredunes up to 20 m high often at mouths of wadis, and seif dunes; older eroded aeolianites with yardangs; coastal sand spits, bars and partly infilled lagoons. Recent aeolianite formation, with embedded garbage, cemented by $CaCO^3$ from salt sprays (Pye & Tsoar, 1990).	Negligible soil formation in loose stratified sands. *Typic Torrispamments*. Sands can be dominated by mineral or shell fragments.	Tussock grasses *Odyssea mucronata on parabolics; Halopyrum mucronatum and Tamerix aphylla close to coast. Cadaba rotundifolia; Dipterygium glaucum, Panicum turgidum* on barchans
Luhayyah: Coastal sabkha, beaches and mangrove flats: 615 km^2	Mangrove woodland; tidal and supratidal sabkha plains; sand sheets.	Deep saline and gypsic sands, silt loams and clays. Typic and Gypsic Salorthids.	*Suaeda fruticosa, Suaeda spp., Salsola spinescens;* Mangrove: *Avicennia marina* and *Rhizophora mucronata*
Bajil: Ridges and hills on limestone and volcanics: 80 km^2	Steep sided bedrock ridges some with kartsic features, salt hills; associated scree slopes.	Very shallow Lithosols with residual loams in karst pockets.	*A. ehrenbergiana* scrub. Limestone quarried at Bajil.

Source: Field Surveys by R.N. Munro, 1998-2000. Identification of vegetation was aided by Barratt, *et al* (1987a, b); HTS (1992, 1993); Stone (1985); Wood (1985a, 1985b, 1997); al-Hubaishi and Müller-Hohenstein (1984); Scholte, *et al* (1991, 1992). Information on soils gained from TESCO-Viziterv-Vituki (1971); Anderson, 1979; MMP-HTS, 1982; King, *et al.*, 1983; FAO-UNESCO, 1977.

During summer (July) northerly to north-westerly (*shamāl*) surface winds blow towards the low-pressure area of the ITCZ. In July the ITCZ lies a short distance north of Yemen, and in August as it moves south again the period of highest rainfall is encountered: at the latitude of al-Ḥudaydah rains may moisten sands within 15 km of the coast, stabilizing dunes that are then planted for rain-fed millet.

Currents in the Red Sea are reversed, and north to north-westerly winds induce a southerly surface flow that moves out of the Bāb al-Mandab into the Indian Ocean. During this period sand movement is southerly, and also sands are driven onto north-facing beaches but with less intensity than was the case with the south-westerlies of spring.

In autumn (October and November) the ITCZ shifts to the south of Yemen. Strong high pressure re-develops over Arabia, with the north-easterly trades being re-established at the surface over much of Yemen, but in the Tihāmah these veer round to the south-west.

Geomorphological Framework of the Escarpment and Yemen Highlands

The landscape of the Great Escarpment and Tihāmah is the direct product of events initiated some 30.5 million years ago which resulted in the uplift of the Afro-Arabian dome and associated volcanism along the margins of the future Red Sea / Gulf of Aden Rift. The extensive volcanism buried earlier Tertiary and Mesozoic sedimentary groups and the underlying Precambrian metamorphic basement.[22] Large-scale volcanism ended 26.5 million years ago when the thickness of the volcanic pile had reached about 5 km, and pre-volcanic formations had been elevated some 2.5 km, an average rate of surface uplift of 0.08 mm per year.[23] Since then erosion has removed up to 3 km of crust, mostly towards the Red Sea, but at least 2 km remain.[24] A new phase in the region commenced around 26 million years ago as the Red Sea trough opened in response to tectonic plate movements which resulted in rifting and the separation of Asia from Africa. Volcanism and granite intrusion continued on the flanks of the rift in Yemen whilst the older sedimentary and Basement Complex rocks were subjected to folding and extensional faulting.[25] At the same time there was erosion on the flanks of the volcanic ranges and sedimentation into the subsiding basins of the Red Sea rift valley and the lowlands of the Rub' al-Khālī. In the Red Sea, during this phase of rift opening, thick accumulations of evaporites and clastic sediments were deposited by Tihāmah streams in a semi-arid climate.[26] Rifting ceased in the onshore area of the Red Sea rift and Tihāmah during the late Miocene (*ca.* 12 million years ago), but remained active in the centre of the Red Sea 60 km offshore, where oceanic crust is extending.[27]

In contrast to the Tihāmah, the Highland Plateau Land Region of Yemen consists of volcanics, rugged mountain massifs and dissected plateaux on sandstone and limestone, ranging in elevation from 1000 m to 3660 m. These include accumulation plains in down-faulted depressions (*graben*) often with internal drainage. Between the Saudi Arabian border and the Bāb al-Mandab, the Escarpment is drained by twenty-five river basin catchments, ranging in size from 61 to 7,867 km^2, which drain a total area of 33,100 sq km of the Great Escarpment.[28]

Geographical Sub-divisions

The following geomorphological sub-divisions provide the context for everyday life and frame the economic activities of the Tihāmah communities (Map 1:1):

Alluvial Plains on the Tihāmah

Main Tihāmah wādīs. The main *wādī* basin streams debouch from the mountains via incized channels. These are often braided, carry sandy to gravelly alluvium and some flow year round. The *wādīs* become ephemeral westwards as waters become subsurface and channel features may disappear completely.

Low Terrace and flood plain. Being just above the level of the river channel, these areas are often seasonally inundated and can be irrigated from the river.

Middle Terrace (Holocene). Coalesced alluvial fans of silt formed, in part, from the accumulation of spate irrigation deposits guided by canals and terraced boundaries. These form where the principal *wādīs* (for example, Wādī Sihām, Rima', Mawr, Surdud, Kuway') discharge their sediments to the Tihāmah Piedmont (and occasionally to the ocean), during extreme flood events.[29] The infiltration of water from seasonal floods and base flow helps recharge the groundwater of shallow aquifers and sustain irrigated agriculture and dune stabilization programmes.

Middle Terrace: sub-recent. Largely inactive alluvial fans that have displaced the ancient dunes to form extensive plains that partly infill the inter-dune corridors of the ancient linear dunes. They are progressively being buried by the eastward creep of aeolian sand sheets and dunes, as well as deposition of sands transported by gully erosion of the dune ridges.

22 Davison, *et al.* 1994.
23 Davison, *et al.* 1998.
24 Davison, *et al.* 1994, 1998.
25 Davison, *et al.* 1994.
26 Nichols and Watchorn 1998.
27 Ibid.
28 Hunting Technical Services (HTS) 2002.
29 Van der Gun and Abdul Aziz 1995.

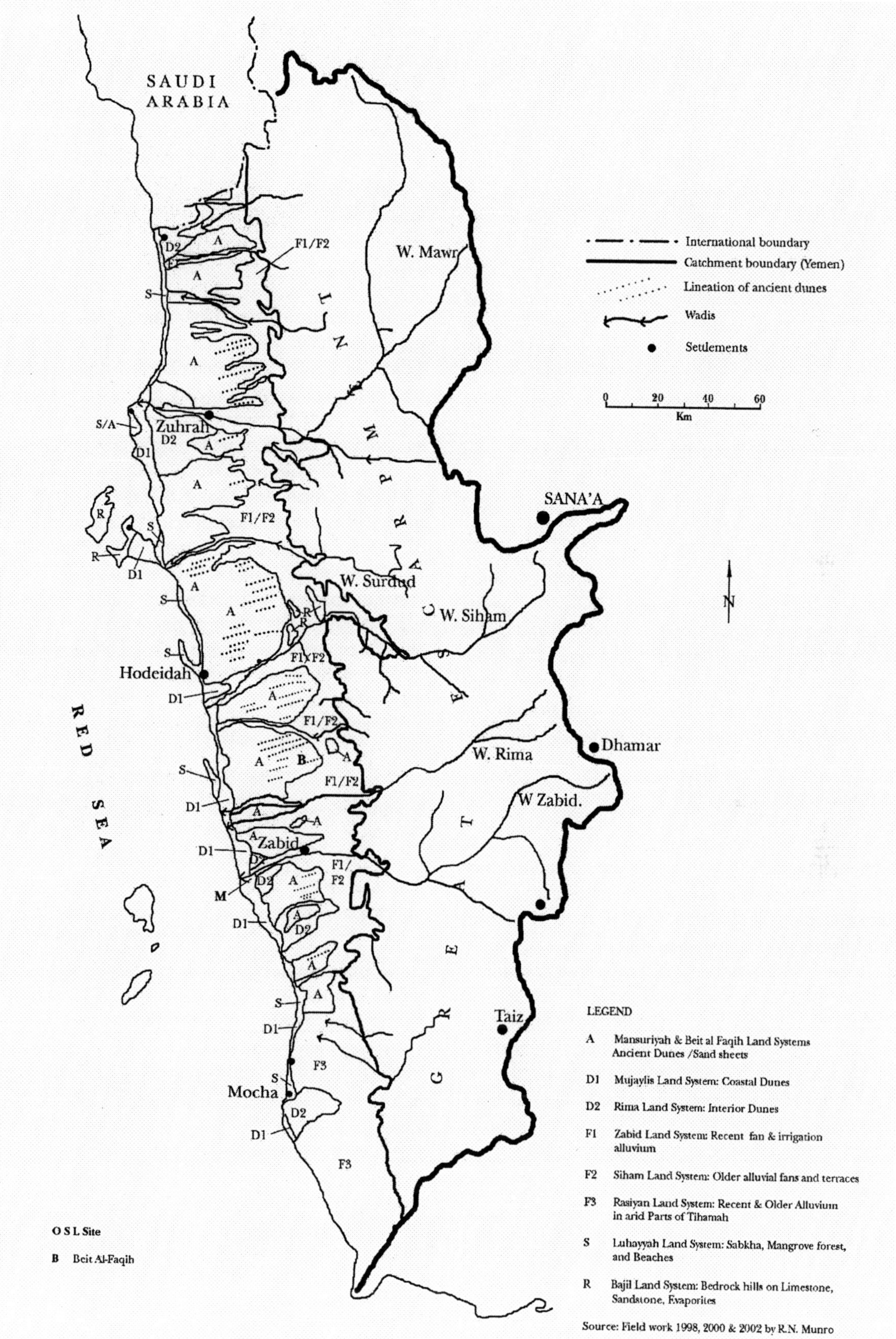
SAUDI ARABIA
International boundary
Catchment boundary (Yemen)
Lineation of ancient dunes
Wadis
Settlements
0 20 40 60
Km
W. Mawr
W. Surdud
W. Siham
W. Rima
W Zabid.
SANA'A
Dhamar
Taiz
Zuhrah
Hodeidah
Zabid
Mocha
RED SEA
GREAT ESCARPMENT
N
O S L Site
B Beit Al-Faqih
LEGEND
A Mansuriyah & Beit al Faqih Land Systems Ancient Dunes /Sand sheets
D1 Mujaylis Land System: Coastal Dunes
D2 Rima Land System: Interior Dunes
F1 Zabid Land System: Recent fan & irrigation alluvium
F2 Siham Land System: Older alluvial fans and terraces
F3 Rasiyan Land System: Recent & Older Alluvium in arid Parts of Tihamah
S Luhayyah Land System: Sabkha, Mangrove forest, and Beaches
R Bajil Land System: Bedrock hills on Limestone, Sandstone, Evaporites
Source: Field work 1998, 2000 & 2002 by R.N. Munro

Map 1:1 Tihāmah Land Systems (RNM)

High Terrace Complex: In the central and northern areas these consist of up to 20 m of coarse gravels, the soils of which thicken down-slope where they can be irrigated by run-off irrigation. In the central Tihāmah the loamy coalesced alluvial fans appear to underlie ancient dunes and also include beds of lacustrine deposits. In the southern areas the characteristic braided drainage patterns are coated with dark 'desert varnish' except where there is a shallow weakly developed soil.

Coastal Deposits

The coastal belt of the Red Sea includes fringing coral reefs which occupy considerable lengths of coastline and extend several kilometres offshore. Landward of these, strips of fringing mangrove forests, which occur almost as far as al-Mukhā', may have been more extensive during the early to mid-Holocene. Offshore sand bars and spits also occur at intervals along the coast and a shell sand cuspate foreland lies at the coastal end of the Wādī Zabīd. Time-sequence aerial photography and satellite imagery demonstrate that these features are in a state of continuous change.[30] In places raised areas of shoreline marked by supra-tidal *sabkha* and lagoons abut against truncated sandy alluvial fans and older aeolian dunes. Estuaries (*khūr*) occur where several *wādīs* reach the sea, and deltas occasionally form along the coast in response to periodic floods which result in large volumes of sand being swept out to sea. In places, older aeolian-alluvial formations reach the coast where they are directly eroded by the sea.

Aeolian Formations

Aeolian features of the coastal region differ from those inland. Though the boundary between coastal and interior is not precise, there does appear to be a hiatus between the vegetated and irregular coastal shell-rich sand coastal dunes, and the interior, quartz-sand rich, and poorly vegetated dune-fields and sand sheets. These changes appear related to interplay between various factors: seasonal and diurnal changes in winds; a decline inland of wind-blown salts and moisture; a decline inland of shell fragments in sands; a very arid interior zone; and a steady increase in rainfall towards the mountain front. In both environments, dune sands have a uni-modal particle size distribution, in contrast to the bimodality of most alluvial sediments.

Coastal Dunes

Along the southern Red Sea coast a complex of shoals, sand bars, spits and cuspate forelands are replaced in some offshore localities by coral reefs.[31] Ocean currents deliver a steady supply of sediments to the coast; long-shore drift is northerly in spring but southerly in autumn and follows the ITCZ.[32] On-shore winds feed fore-dune ridges that lie parallel to the coast at locations where conditions are suitable for sands to come onshore, and these spawn parabolic dunes colonized by *Odyssea mucronata* grass. Large sand hummocks with the deep-rooted salt-tolerant tussock grass *Halopyrum mucronatum* are common in many coastal areas. Coastal *seif* dunes formed of dark sands, rich in ferromagnesian and heavy minerals, are migrating across the main road to Salif, and having disrupted traffic on the road, drift on northwards to the sea!

Interior Dunes

In the interior of the Tihāmah, mobile barchan dunes, parabolic dunes and transverse ridges are dominant and generally poorly vegetated. Barchan dunes, one to four metres high and five to twenty metres across, usually form down-wind of transverse dunes and in turn may supply sand to new chains of transverse dunes further downwind. In the Wādī Zabīd transverse dunes with wavelengths of 50 to 70 m form dunes some 50 m across, with gaps of 25 to 70 m between dunes. Interior linear dunes, in the form of *seif*-like ridges, occur in parts of the Tihāmah, but generally are localized and small. *Seif* dunes also occur on the eastward edge of some transverse dunes that are advancing into farmlands south of the Wādī Zabīd. Whilst dune slip faces show northwards or southwards movement, depending on seasonal winds, the resultant vector for sand drift is eastwards.

Movement of Modern Dunes

Recent assessments of sand dune movement[33] have shown that the range of movement is very variable, from –300 m (where the sand has drifted backwards, uncovering land due to seasonal wind changes) to +400 m. Mean annual movements range from 18–41 m *per annum.*

Rates of movement of parabolic dunes advancing northwards into the Wādī Rima' have been estimated by comparing multi-temporal aerial photography for 1973 and 1987 together with SPOT satellite imagery for 1997–1998. Farmers were also questioned on rate of burial of houses at a village near al-Madaniyah. Their answers confirmed the aerial photographic measurements, that since 1987 there has been an average north-easterly movement of some 7.2 m per year, and in total the dunes have advanced some 80 m across the channel of the Wādī Rima' onto the edge of the farmlands.

30 Hunting Technical Services (HTS) 1999.

31 Barratt, *et al.* 1987a.

32 Barratt, *et al.* 1987a, 1987b, Hunting Technical Services (HTS), 1999.

33 The following results derive from a study by Munro which formed part of his assessment of Tihāmah sand dunes made for the TEPP (Hunting Technical Services (HTS) 1999) and which included field measurements between 1998 and 2002, and a synthesis of earlier studies (reported in FAO-IC 1991).

At al-Qaza, south of Wādī Rummān, large 15 m high transverse dunes lie on the edge of an extensive transverse-dune sand sea. These dunes, which are largely static and immobile for parts of the year when winds are blowing southwards and out of the plantations, were said to have moved 100 m in twenty years and buried houses and date palms.

Near Maghras in the Wādī Zabīd, dunes were measured to be advancing into farmland at 10 m over an 11-year period but elsewhere the rate is even faster. At Mujaylis (Wādī Zabīd), where parabolic dunes are burying valuable date plantations, average annual movements between 1973 to 1987 were from 15.4 to 16 m per year, whilst from 1987 to 1998 they were from 9.1 to 10.9 m per year.

In the central Tihāmah (Wādīs Sihām, Rummān and Zabīd in particular), the encroachment of modern dunes onto ancient dunes, inter-dune corridors and alluvial plains poses a very serious problem for agriculture. In addition, the steady flow of sand sheets between dunes can filter through a farm, and estimates from other regions with similar dunes suggest that this will be at least 15 m^3 per m per year. Data collected by Munro indicate that winds exceeding 5.5 m per second (20 km per hour) occur in every month of the year but are strongest in July and August when interior sands are moved eastwards by sea breezes. Such winds also deflate silts from the alluvial lands.

Much of the build-up of the sand seas between the main *wādīs* has occurred during the Holocene. At rates of 10 m per year dunes will advance the forty kilometres from the present coastline to the towns of Zabīd or Bayt al-Faqīh in 4,000 years. Significantly, Niebuhr did not describe active dunes at Bayt al-Faqīh in 1763,[34] whereas they are dominant now.

Wind Direction and Dune Movement

Overall, the dominant winds on the Tihāmah are from the north-west or from the north-north-west to north in summer[35] and from south-south-east to south in winter.[36] This appears to be due to the strong funnelling effect on winds, either as north-west or south-east flows, in the centre of the Red Sea rift valley, what Pedgley termed 'rift flow'.[37] Winds coming through the Bāb al-Mandab are constricted by the Tihāmah escarpment to the north-east (rising to almost 3000 m) and the Tadjoura Mountains (1200 m) on the south.

Pedgley noted that because most climatic stations are land-based, they record diurnal effects of land and sea breezes, but fail to show the regional movement of air masses.[38] The overall movement is for winds to blow along the middle of the Red Sea either from the north-west or from the south-east, but only ships in the centre of the Red Sea can record this. On the ground, however, the actual movement of winds, and of course sand, will be the vector of the prevailing sea or land breeze and the rift flow at the time. Thus, a southerly air stream will produce a south-easterly vector when it meets the westerly sea breeze. These changes will also affect currents and the supply of sand to the beaches.[39]

The movement of sands along coastlines by long-shore drift is due to the circulation of ocean currents and wave action, and it is well known that these currents vary with the seasons and the passage of the monsoon.[40] The supply of sediments to the coastline of Yemen is a principal factor in dune development along the Red Sea Tihāmah coast of Yemen,[41] and ultimately results in sand drifting as far inland as the Great Escarpment.

A key feature of the climate of the Tihāmah is that south-westerly to westerly winds develop due to diurnal effects or the land-sea-breeze system.[42] During the day the Tihāmah heats up faster than the Red Sea resulting in an easterly flow of wind, as the trade winds are inverted. This flow reaches its maximum in the early afternoon, with rising warm humid air forming convection cells and storms over the escarpment. This is also the period of maximum sand movement. During the night differential cooling is reduced and cool air from the highlands flows down to the Tihāmah and the Red Sea, so that for much of the year in the early hours there is a light easterly surface flow. This abruptly changes at around 06:00 hours, becoming by 10:00 hours either a south-westerly flow in winter and spring, or a west to north-westerly flow in summer. At 18:00 hours it turns around again to the east.[43]

Ancient Aeolian Landforms

In the Bayt al-Faqīh Sand Ridges Land System, the 1:50,000 scale topographic maps of the Tihāmah show that the linear core of the sand ridges is from 250 to 500 m across and their heights range up to 20 m above the inter-dune floor. At Bayt al-Faqīh, exposed sections for samples and associated OSL dating has reached 11 m into the dune sequence, which is estimated to attain a total thickness of 40 m.

34 Niebuhr 1792.
35 Guilcher 1952, Brown, *et al.* 1989.
36 Red Sea Pilot: UK Hydrographic Office 2004.
37 Pedgley 1966a, 1966b.
38 Ibid.
39 Barratt 1987a.
40 Naval Intelligence 1946, UK Hydrographic Office 2004.
41 Hunting Technical Services (HTS) 1999.
42 Williams 1979.
43 Data from al-Madaniyiah station in Wādī Rimah, given in Williams, 1979, confirmed by RNM in IFAD 2003.

Inter-dune corridors are typically 1 to 2 km across and often 15 km long (Figure 1:1). The corridors are enhanced to the east where the terrain, although rolling, continues to be aligned east to west. The ridges show a number of Y-shaped junctions, characteristic of linear dunes[44] that tend to open out to downwind to the east. The present slope on the ridges, in the Mansūrīyah area, varies from 4 to 9 per cent, which is thought to approximate to the slope of the ancient dune when it was stabilized. Gullying of ancient dunes and deposition of eroded sediments down-slope as alluvial fans is a common feature of the ancient dunes as a result of runoff generated by intense rainfall.[45]

Figure 1:1 Landsat image of Tihāmah with ancient dunes (RNM)

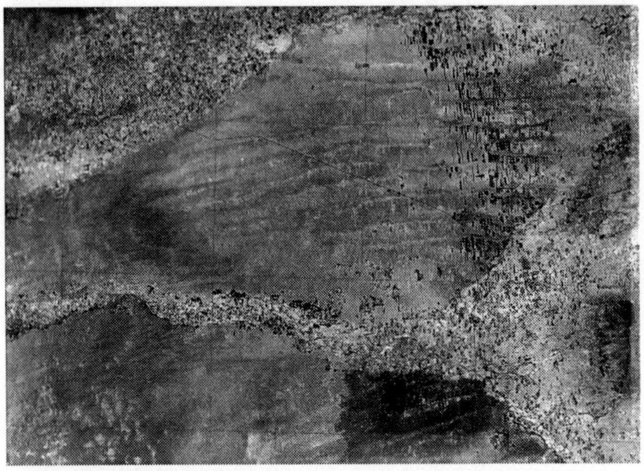

The ancient sand ridges were distinguished as older aeolian formations on the basis of several diagnostic features that are repeated throughout the Tihāmah: they retain features typical of linear dunes, with rounded ridges, Y-shaped junctions and inter-dune corridors up to 1 to 2 km wide; south-facing slopes appear steeper. The loamy textured dunes lack alluvial gravel greater than 2 mm, have a dark coloured, strongly structured surface soil, with moderate organic matter, and often exhibit polygonal sand-filled cracks up to 1 m diameter.[46] The layers immediately below the paleosol have root concretions of calcium carbonate,[47] and there has been some disturbance to the stratification. At greater depths aeolian strata are original and fresh and lack evidence of bioturbation. In places, additional buried soil layers or layers of secondary carbonate are apparent. Where the paleosol is exposed within moister parts of the Tihāmah the surface of the ancient dunes can be cut by gullies. In coastal areas, the original stratification of older dunes has been preserved by carbonate cementation of the sand to produce aeolianites. The sand ridges are aligned approximately east-north-east / west-south-west and east-west lineation (60 to 90 degrees), whereas modern dunes are drifting more to the north, at 45 to 60 degrees.

A key section (Site M1005) in a sand quarry close to Bayt al-Faqīh showed recent sands overlying a paleosol layer on stratified aeolian sands. The stratigraphy is given in Table 1:2.

Optical Dating of Aeolian Sands

Optically stimulated luminescence (OSL) has provided Quaternary scientists with a valuable tool to date quartz and feldspar minerals potentially back to 1 million years ago.[48] OSL dating was attempted on six samples from the Bayt al-Faqīh-1 section.[49] Due to apparent contamination with poorly bleached InfraRed sensitive minerals (possibly feldspars), Single Aliquot Regeneration (SAR) analysis on quartz grains provided age determinations on only three out of the six layers (Table 1:3). Future OSL dating on the Tihāmah is recommended to use a range of minerals, such as feldspars used by Preusser and colleagues in the Wahiba Sands, Oman.[50]

The upper layers of the section provide a very young date for sand accumulation at just over a hundred years. But this is not surprising, as sand accumulation has been observed to be very substantial in a short period. The Bayt al-Faqīh OSL dates do provide the first direct indication of a Pleistocene age for aeolian sand deposition in the Tihāmah. The deposition of the essentially unmodified pre-paleosol sands ranges from 10.1 to 12.5 thousand years BP, and as these lie at the top of a thick aeolian fill it is likely that the record can be extended further back into the Pleistocene. The age of the paleosol and associated carbonate rhizo-concretion formation must postdate 10.1 thousand BP and this fits in well with early Holocene records elsewhere in Arabia.

44 Mabbut 1977, Cooke and Warren 1973.

45 Talbot and Williams 1978 and 1979.

46 In the laboratory: sub-rounded grains of quartz show thick clay mineral and iron oxide coatings, indicated by high Fe, Al, K, Mg, Ti; silt + clay content ranges up to 7.5% (by dry sieving) up to 8.3% (by laser granulometry); laser granulometry shows that sands are unimodal, of very coarse silt to coarse sand with mean grain size from 2.52 to 3.68 Phi; the mineralogy of the sands includes quartz, feldspars, ferromagnesian minerals, and rock fragments; shell fragments are usually absent suggesting they have been leached out.

47 Known as rhizoliths, or *dikaka* according to Glennie and Evamy 1968.

48 Aitken, 1991, 1994, 1998, Bøtter-Jensen, *et al.* 2003.

49 Collected in sealed tubes in 1998, and analysed at SUERC by Munro during 2005; Sommerville, *et al.* 2005.

50 Preusser, *et al.* 2002.

Table 1:2 Bayt al-Faqīh – 1 (Site M1005)

OSL Layer / OSL Lab/ Sample Number	Depth m	Sampled Depth m	Description of Layers
Not OSL tested / -/ R38	0 - 1.00	0-.30	Active sand hummock on crest of sand ridge. 3.1 % Silt + Clay
1-A / SUTL 1721/ R39	1.00 – 3.00	1.80	Upper Sand of older hummock. Layered sands. Living roots. 6.0% Silt + Clay
1-B / SUTL 1722/ R40	3.00 –6.20	3.40	Massive homogeneous sub-recent aeolian sand with stratification. Living roots. 9.2% Silt + Clay
1-1 / SUTL 1723 / R41	6.20–6.45	6.20–6.45	Blocky, sandy palaeosol. Slightly hard, moderate medium to coarse subangular blocky structure. Polygonal cracking pattern, <1 m diameter, cracks infilled with stratified aeolian sands & extend down to 1 m. Living roots common. 7.8% Silt + Clay
1-2 / SUTL 1724/ R111	6.45–7.00	6.95	Sand. Dry and soft, breaking to loose sand. Weak, fine to medium subangular blocky. Sandy subsoil with $CacO^3$ concretions. Remains of dead roots. Living roots. Weak traces of stratification. 4.8 % Silt + Clay
1-3 / SUTL 1725/ R42	7.00–8.00	7.40	Soft sand with few $CaCO^3$ concretions. Dry and loose. Weak fine subangular blocky structure. Weak traces of stratification. Living roots 3.3% Silt + Clay
1-4 / SUTL 1726/ R112	8.00–11.4	8.00	Sand with $CaCO^3$ concretions *in situ*. Dry and loose. Original stratification preserved in patches. 1.9% Silt + Clay

Source: Fieldwork by RN Munro. Silt+Clay % data determined by laser granulometry at PRIS, Reading.

GPS Location: UTM 38P. 0318450. N 1606860; Elevation 130 m. SUTL: Scottish Universities Thermoluminescence Lab, East Kilbride.

Table 1:3 Results of OSL Dating at Bayt al-Faqīh, Yemen

Sample	Assumed Water content (%)	ED (Gy)	Background Dose Rate ($mGya^{-1}$)	Age (ka before AD 2000)
1721	2 ± 2	No Determination	3.12 ± 0.11	No age determination
1722	2 ± 2	0.34 ± 0.04	3.27 ± 0.11	0.105 ± 0.01
1723	4 ± 4	No Determination	3.23 ± 0.15	No age determination
1724	2 ± 2	No Determination	3.14 ± 0.11	No age determination
1725	2 ± 2	32.21 ± 6.6	3.18 ± 0.12	10.1 ± 2.1
1726	2 ± 2	41.86 ± 3.57	3.36 ± 0.12	12.5 ± 1.1

Source: Sommerville, Burbidge, Sanderson and Munro, 2005

Cycles of Erosion and Sedimentation on the Tihāmah Escarpment and Piedmont

The principal origin of Tihāmah dunes was sands blowing inland from coastal beaches:[51] The complex climate-driven cycle of sediment movement includes:

- Deposition of aeolian dust (silt plus clay) on land surfaces of the Highlands, Great Escarpment and Tihāmah from deflation sources in the interior plains of Arabia and the Tihāmah, and its incorporation into soils, dunes and other surfaces;
- Erosion of contemporary or earlier dust deposits, and coarser detritus, by rainfall, runoff and gravity processes in the Highlands and Great Escarpment (trapping of products on terraces in the Escarpment);
- The transportation of these coarse- to fine-grained materials by stream flow onto the Tihāmah;
- Erosion of ancient dunes by gullying of soil layer, with deflation of finer sized sediments.
- Deposition of silty to loamy sediments in the spate irrigation and runoff agriculture systems of the Tihāmah. Terraces and coalesced fans of similar content show that these processes occurred during earlier alluvial phases;
- Deposition of coarser sediments in *wādī* channels. Floods can reach the coast during extreme events to form deltas;
- Deflation of silty alluvium from exposed soils in the spate irrigation systems and other alluvial formations;
- Limited deflation of sandy sediments from *wādī* channel floors onto adjacent aeolian landforms;

[51] Hunting Technical Services (HTS) 1999.

- Seasonal long-shore drift (northwards or southwards) of sandy and / or shelly sediments in coastal waters, with formation of bars, cusps, spits;
- Fragmentation of near-shore and off-shore coral reefs during (normally spring) storms;
- On-shore emergence of sands according to coastal alignment and prevailing current direction and formation of wide range of coastal fore-dunes and parabolic, hummock, barchan and *seif* dunes; northerly movement in spring, southerly movement in summer;
- Eastwards sand drift resultant towards the Great Escarpment, with limited dust entrapment.

Palaeoenvironments

Environmental change in the Tihāmah encompasses both rise and fall of sea level as well as global climate change. Although the Red Sea was not dry during the last glacial period, during the Late Glacial Maximum, around 18,000 BP, opposite the mouth of the Wādī Zabīd the Red Sea coastal plain was up to 75 km wide, that is, approximately double the width of the present Tihāmah. This would have resulted in the *wādī*s, already depleted of flow thanks to the drier atmospheric conditions, having to traverse a broader belt of plain. Consequently there must have been greater loss of water into the arid sediments of the plain with the result that *wādī*s rarely would have discharged into the sea. In addition, as has been suggested for the coasts of Oman and the United Arab Emirates,[52] the broad expanses of plain that extended between the lowest Pleistocene shoreline and that of today would have supplied a vast reservoir of sands that could be whipped up by winds and transported inland to form dunes.

Thus, during the Late Glacial period not only were climatic conditions drier because of the weaker monsoon, but also the local geography probably resulted in less surface water and more sand movement than is the case today within the relatively narrow Tihāmah.

Overall, south-west Arabia has experienced three broad environmental phases over the last 20,000 years (Figure 1:2).

Late Glacial Period and Formation of Ancient Linear Dunes

A broad phase of arid climate during the late glacial period between about 20,000 and 12,000 years ago. At this time the highlands were cool and dry, with more intermittent *wādī*s, local dune formation, and even some periglacial conditions on the highest mountains.[53] At this time the Tihāmah was also dry with the extended coastal plain providing a source for aeolian sand.

The remarkable lineation of the ancient dunes is oriented at right angles to the coastline at the coast, but veers slightly clockwise from west-south-west to east-north-east to east-west with distance inland. It is therefore valid to ask why, when modern dunes of the Tihāmah interior are dominantly of the transverse type, did the ancient dunes form a regularly spaced linear pattern at right angles to this?

Linear dunes are widespread and their origins much debated: 'roll-vortices' have been invoked as the cause, but these have not been satisfactorily observed in the field. Such alignments are now generally explained to be more the result of the steady play of one or more dominant wind directions, with the crests being modified by seasonal or diurnal local winds.[54]

In central and southern Arabia linear dunes veer round from an easterly flow in the Nafud, to southerly in the al-Dahna and northern Rub' al-Khālī, until they become south-westerly where they reach the Yemen massif, due to rotation of the earth.[55] On the west side of the Yemen mountains the Tihāmah linear dunes appear to continue this trend, but these are confined to the Yemen coast because there are no equivalent sets of linear, or other dunes, in eastern Eritrea or Ethiopia. That the dune lineations almost join up would appear to be a coincidence.

We suggest that the linearity of the Tihāmah dunes was the result of the same combination of north-west and south-west winds as today, but with modifications due to reduced impacts of the ITCZ and lowered sea levels during the glacial periods. A model for the Tihāmah may have seen one or more winds (north-west and south-west) blowing obliquely and steadily towards a roughly east-west linear and un-vegetated ridge, with a slight modification by diurnal sea breezes originating far to the west.

During the Late Glacial Maximum easterly sea breezes would have been enhanced by the rapid diurnal heating of the exposed coastal plain at low elevations, in contrast to cooler, more elevated parts of the Tihāmah. The exposed coastal plain would have provided an extensive area for dunes to develop and evolve, and it is probable that barchans and transverse dunes were initiated far to the west of the present coastline. Evolution into linear dunes must have occurred only relatively close to the Escarpment, an analogous situation being the transition from transverse, barchanoid or sand sheet fields in the Jafura Desert of north-east Saudi Arabia through sand drifts into the archetypal linear dunes of the Rub' al-Khālī.

52 Glennie 1998.
53 el-Nakhal 1993, Wilkinson 1997.
54 Thomas 1997.
55 Glennie 2005.

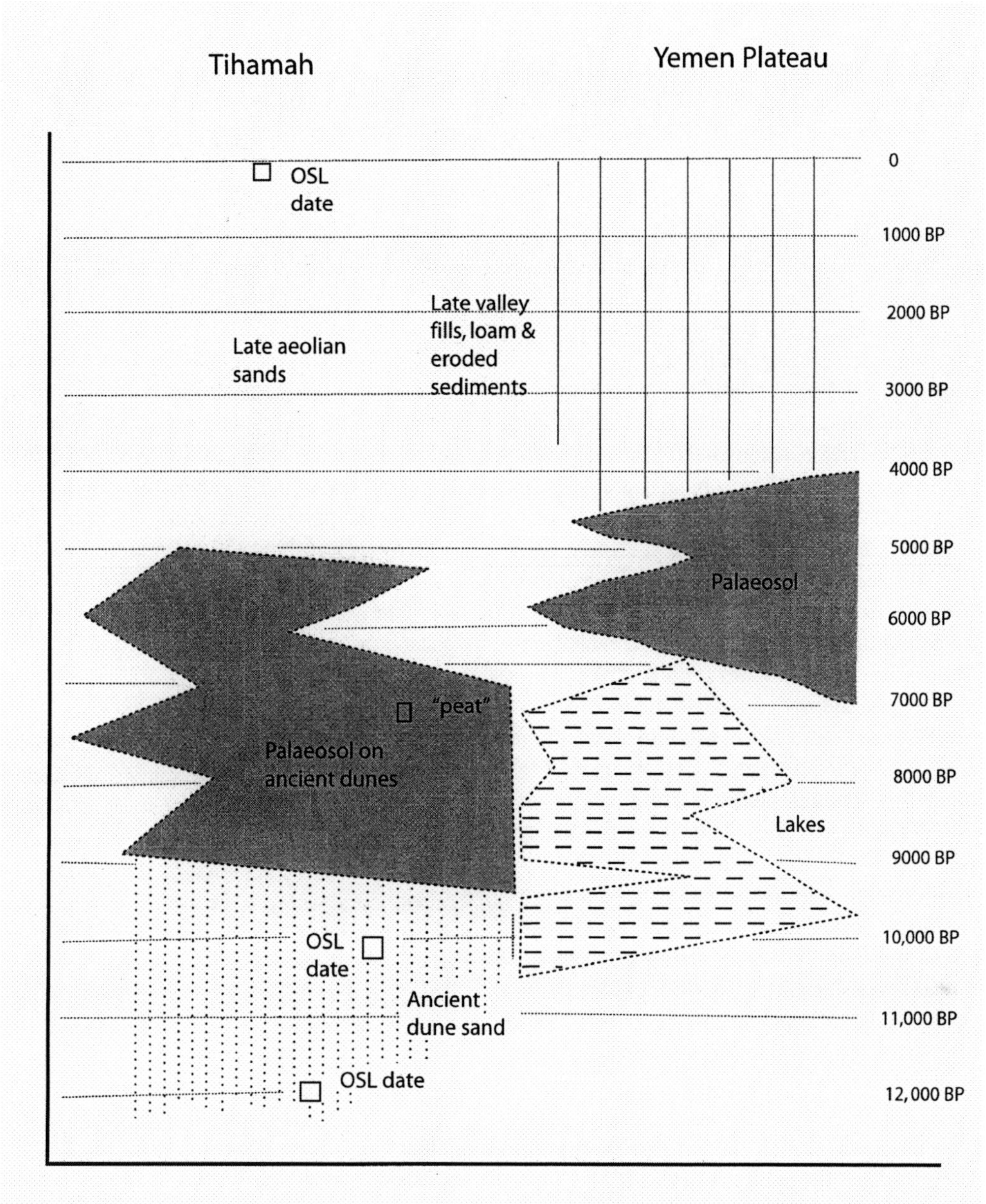

Figure 1:2 Comparative chart showing sequence of environmental change on plateau and Tihāmah. (TJW)

The late glacial maximum at around 17,000 to 18,000 BP was hyper-arid, cool in winter and hot in summer, depending upon the position of the sun, at which time arboreal and shrubby vegetation may have been extremely limited on the interior parts of the Tihamah sands. The lower parts of the exposed areas of ancient dunes on the Tihāmah show fresh-looking fine stratified sands, with evidence of fine depositional layering on a flat topped and convex flanked dune surface. The lower layers of the dunes, with the exception of some deeper paleosol and / or carbonate enrichment layers, lack calcified root casts or any evidence of bioturbation that would suggest biological activity. All of this points to rapid accumulation of sands in a hyper-arid environment. The diurnal range in temperature, which is such an important feature today, was probably greater than at present. The extensive and exposed sediment-rich coastal shelf enabled westerly winds, once generated and moving towards the Escarpment zone, to fine-tune the movement and sorting of sands to create the linear dunes characteristic of the Tihāmah. In this context, the shell sand that is so common at the coast appears to have been progressively reduced in content by the impact of other grains. The climate was less modified by the monsoonal rains, which today lead to seasonal stabilization of the dunes in eastern parts of the Tihāmah, and the lack of bioturbation in the depositional layers of the linear dunes suggests they were probably largely devoid of vegetation.

Early Holocene Wetter Phase

Following a transitional period during which sea levels were rising rapidly and the monsoon was gaining strength, by around 10,000 BP the environment of south-west Arabia, from the interior to the Tihāmah, became significantly wetter. It must be appreciated, however, that sea levels continued to be lower during the early Holocene, being *ca.* –40 m below present sea level at 10,000 BP. It then rose to 1–2 m above present-day sea level by 7,000 BP to 6,000 BP, at which time we have considerable evidence for human occupation of the coastal fringe.[56]

From around 10,000 BP, many of the high plains around Dhamar accommodated lakes. This approximates to the time when the isotopic record from Qunf cave in southern Oman had started to register increasing moisture.[57] The OSL dates from the lower palaeodune sands of the Tihāmah suggest that conditions were still relatively arid before 10,100 BP, but shortly thereafter the formation of the deep moderately humic paleosol on the megadunes indicates that the dunes had become more stable and that conditions were somewhat moister. Although we have no evidence for lakes in the Tihāmah during the early Holocene, the palaeosol record for increased moisture can be appreciated within the context of local archaeological evidence as well as within a broader environmental framework. First, hints that conditions were more verdant along the east–west valleys that crossed the Tihāmah come from the seventh millennium BC site of al-Shuma, which included evidence for freshwater crab.[58] The presence of this in association with abundant shells of *Terebralia palustris*, usually associated with coastal mangroves, suggests that the lower valleys were fringed with mangroves, in close proximity to freshwater or estuarine conditions. Finally, the evidence of a log of wood from a 'peat' buried below some 5 m of alluvial silts exposed in a marine cliff at the mouth of the Wādī Zabīd,[59] provides evidence for a more verdant coastal environment in the period 5070–4820 BC. This places it firmly within the moist period of the plateau.

Climate proxy records from ocean cores and cave sites such as Qunf Cave indicate that the monsoon was demonstrably stronger and more rain would have fallen over southern Arabia during the early and mid-Holocene.[60] In addition, the significantly wetter highlands would have been discharging greater quantities of water to the Tihāmah. Finally, the narrow coastal plain would have been more readily traversed by water from the *wādīs*, which may have included increased year-round flow, with the result that there was a greater chance of flow reaching the sea. This moister Tihāmah with more stable dunes would have witnessed increased opportunities for human settlement, although it must be emphasized that lack of archaeological fieldwork still leaves us with a relatively sparse archaeological record, except for along the coastal fringes and selected *wādīs*.[61] In addition to the more verdant environment and the slightly raised sea level, the coastal belt was fringed, at least locally, by coastal mangrove woodlands, which themselves provide a rich habitat for shellfish gathering and fishing activities.

Although the duration of the early-mid Holocene moist period in interior Arabia and the highlands is becoming better understood,[62] the chronology of the wet phase on the Tihāmah is much less clear. On the plateau, immediately to the west of the Tihāmah many lakes were drying around 6000 BC, but that conditions remained relatively verdant can be suggested from the presence of the humus-rich 'Jahran Soil', many exposures of which continued until as late as 4,000 BP (that is, 2000 BC). Although we have no radiometric dates for this transition in the Tihāmah, the presence of overlying dune sands enables us to tentatively estimate the termination of the mid-Holocene moist phase to around 4,500–5,000 years ago. This transition may also correspond to a postulated recession of coastal mangrove woodlands that occurred around the same time.[63]

Evidence for high sea level comes from the elevated coastal deposits, such as mangrove, lagoons, sand bars, coral reefs, beach ridges or supra-tidal *sabkha*. In the Yemeni Tihāmah, the latter do occur and abut against the older alluvium and ancient dunes, and as noted above, raised coral reefs have been reported at a considerable distance and at a relatively high elevation inland.[64] For much of the coastline the evidence for a higher shore is at the most four kilometres inland, and is usually less. Only in the mouths of some Wādīs (Mawr, Sihām, Kuway', Rima', and Zabīd) is there doubt, as recent alluvium may have in-filled coastal inlets that probably extended some distance inland at the end the Late Glacial Maximum when the *wādīs* had cut deep channels (*khūr*) through older formations and coral reefs in response to the very low sea levels. In quite a few areas in fact the coast is being eroded where older alluvium and sand dunes reach the coast.

Late-Holocene Drying

On the Yemen plateau, Late-Holocene drying is evident from the disappearance of lakes, the cessation of soil formation, specifically the humic soils of the plateau and *Sayhad*,[65] and in places, renewed dune formation. On the Tihāmah, as described above, sand dunes were reactivated, and cracks in the paleosols accumulated aeolian

56 Tosi 1986, Zarins and Zahrani 1985, Zarins and Badr 1986, Khalidi 2006.

57 Fleitmann, *et al.* 2003.

58 Cattani and Bokonyi 2002.

59 Keal 2004: 43.

60 Parker, *et al.* 2006.

61 Khalidi 2005a.

62 McClure 1976, Lezine, *et al.* 1998, Parker, *et al.* 2004, Parker, *et al.* 2006, Fleitmann, *et al.* 2003.

63 Khalidi 2006: 195, 279.

64 Robertson Research 1991a.

65 Wilkinson 1997, Brinkmann 1996.

sand, although it appears that dune formation varied from place to place over the last 5,000 years. On the high plateau around Dhamar, there is no evidence for renewed dune activity, but sediments derived from soil erosion are common, together with evidence for the building up of anthropogenic soils behind field terraces, and for the accumulation of a thin layer of aeolian dust (*loess*) over prehistoric sites.[66] The evidence for increased soil erosion provides a compelling case for increased run-off from destabilized hill-slopes which might have resulted in increased flood peaks along *wādīs*. Consequently during the preceding moist period, higher rainfall on the plateau, combined with less run-off from the vegetated surfaces and deeper soils, would probably have contributed to greater groundwater re-charge and a more even year-round flow of water in the Tihāmah *wādīs*. In contrast, during the last 5,000 years water flow in the *wādīs* would have been more episodic, with higher flood peaks and less 'base flow' as well as increased sediment in the rivers. Probably the only evidence for this from the Tihāmah is the wood within peat deposit (mid-Holocene year-round moisture?) and the overlying flood silts (late-Holocene increased flood peaks) recorded by Keal near Midamman.[67] Unfortunately, there is insufficient archaeological information for Neolithic settlement in the Piedmont fringe of the Tihāmah and the tributary valleys to suggest how the human communities might have responded to such conditions.

Archaeological Sites in their Environmental Context

Although the Tihāmah continues to be under-explored archaeologically, some general points can be made about long-term patterns of archaeological settlement (Map 1:2). These provide a model to be tested by future research.

a) Today the mountains immediately east of the Tihāmah are patchily populated,[68] but these same areas have received little attention from archaeologists. On the other hand the plateaus to the east around Dhamar are now quite well known archaeologically, and were rather densely occupied from at least 3000 BC.[69]

Map 1:2 Long-term settlement zones identified in text. (TJW)

b) The major east-west *wādīs* within relatively broad mountain valleys appear to have been less densely occupied than both the Tihāmah plain to the west and much of the moist highlands to the east.[70] In the middle and upper reaches of many *wādīs*, there are fewer opportunities for large-scale irrigation works, mainly because the *wādīs* are incized well into the flanking Pleistocene river terraces. That there may also have been a dearth of settlement in the past is suggested by archaeological surveys in the Wādī Zabīd by Lamya Khalidi and Krista Lewis that demonstrated that, in contrast with the highlands to the

66 Wilkinson 2005.
67 Keal 2004.
68 Geiser 1977.
69 Wilkinson, *et al.* 1997.
70 Geiser 1977.

east, settlements of the third, second and first millennium BC were relatively sparse.[71] Interestingly, this negative evidence for long-term settlement was echoed by Wood who pointed out that:

> The botanical interest of these valleys lies partly in the fact that they are one of the few examples of a natural vegetation climax found in Yemen ... The survival of the valley forest communities till the present time is largely due to their isolation and to the very small populations that live in the area.[72]

c) The Tihāmah plain immediately west of the Piedmont, including the zone of coalescing alluvial fans located where the major east-west *wādīs* debouch into the coastal plain (Holocene Middle Terrace, above), is an important locus for recent settlement. This transition zone forms a broad north-south corridor which occupies the land between the central dune belt and the Piedmont itself. Whereas the main topographic alignments (that is, the valleys themselves) are oriented east to west, their resultant alluvial fans together with associated zones of Piedmont run-off agriculture combine to form an attenuated north-south zone that has been exploited for runoff and *sayl* (flood) cultivation.[73] These traditional modes of farming dwindle upstream into the middle reaches of the valleys and as a result, today the associated settlement is significantly denser where the valley widens out into the sub-Piedmont corridor. Where the broad alluvial fans have been in use for centuries for *sayl,* run-off and rain-fed farming,[74] population densities are significantly higher today than on the dune fields to the west or the mountains immediately to the east.[75]

Sayl and run-off cultivation appear to be a long-term practice in this region. This is evident from the massive depth of up to 6 m of silts accumulated in the Wādī Zabīd alluvial fan, which, at least in part, are the result of the long-term flood-water farming. Unfortunately, there is little direct evidence for the ancient practice of run-off agriculture in this zone apart from occasional instances of buried field banks, 'berms' and diversion structures,[76] as well as hints of former irrigation channels within the sediments. Whereas the above features appear to have been associated with flood (*sayl*) agriculture, a number of water conduits and piped-water supplies designed to conduct low discharge flows from perennial sources were also recovered.[77] By applying copious quantities of silt-rich water to the fields on the Wādī Zabīd alluvial fan the practice of *sayl* agriculture resulted in the ground surface rising significantly over the centuries, so that earlier agricultural landscapes were buried together with perhaps an unknown number of associated settlements. Therefore, although a number of Iron Age to Islamic sites are known from the sub-Piedmont corridor (see below), it remains likely that many prehistoric and early historic settlements have been buried below the aggrading alluvial and irrigation sediments.

That the sub-Piedmont corridor might have formed a long-term axis of settlement and movement can be inferred from both the presence of the modern north-south road from Hays, Zabīd, Bayt al-Faqīh, and after a deviation behind al-Ḥudaydah, from al-Zaydiyah to Sūq 'Abs in the northern Yemeni Tihāmah. Significantly, the medieval pilgrim route towards Makkah also followed this alignment, but without the deviation to al-Ḥudaydah.[78] The presence of a north–south axis of settlement is especially evident for the area between Zabīd and Abs in the northern Tihāmah where numerous small communities occupy the cultivable *sayl*-irrigated and rain-fed lands between the escarpment and the dune belt.[79] Rather than forming a single line, this forms a broad passageway some 20–30 km in width, along which some of the more significant ancient sites of the Tihāmah are found:

- *Prehistoric megalithic sites*: al-Muhandid; al-Saba'a / al-Uqsh; al-Jerahi; Manāsīb al-Rukba al-Mahbūb.[80]
- *Early Historic (Iron Age)*: Kashawba';[81] al-Hamid and Waqir.[82]
- *Islamic*: Dayr al-Khadāmah;[83] al-Kadrā';[84] Zabīd,[85] Hays, Old Mansūrīyah, as well as the earlier phases of Bayt al-Faqīh itself.[86]

Overall, this broad alignment of settlement, which can be seen to extend north–south through much of the Yemeni Tihāmah, provides a long-term path of movement and occupation that parallels the coast, but is rather distinct from the alignment of coastal settlement. Although some ancient settlements were presumably sedentary, others may have been associated with mobile pastoralists, in which case the sub-Piedmont corridor can be seen as forming a long-term path of movement, both between sedentary communities, as well as a landscape through which mobile groups moved.

---

71 Khalidi 2005b: figure 1.
72 Wood 1985b: 15.
73 DHV 1990.
74 Makin 1977.
75 Geiser 1977.
76 Hehmeyer and Keall 1993: 26; Hehmeyer 1995.
77 Hehmeyer and Keall 1993: 27; Hehmeyer 1995: 48.
78 Keall 1983: figure 1.
79 Geiser 1977.
80 Khalidi 2005b.
81 Also known as STN: Ciuk and Keall 1996, Durrani 2005: 85–6, Khalidi 2006: 202–3.
82 Phillips 2005, Durrani 2005: 75–84.
83 Al-Radi 1985: 51.
84 Ibid.: 53.
85 Keall 1983.
86 Al-Radi 1985: 54–5.

d) The coastal settlement belt consisting of Neolithic shell middens, Bronze and Iron Age site complexes, occasional Red Sea ports and specialist sites such as salt-processing installations. This settlement zone can also be recognized to the north of the frontier in Saudi Arabia, where it is continued by the sites of Sihi and the abundant shell middens of the Farasān Islands.[87] The settlements of this zone can be seen as functionally related to the coastal zone with copious evidence for fishing and shell-fish collection, as well as some animal husbandry.[88] Nevertheless, as recent surveys demonstrate, these settlements are not limited to the coast but extend some 5 km or more inland, usually along the main *wādī* beds that flow from the main inland valleys.[89] Any coastal sites occupied prior to around 6000 BC to 7000 BC (that is, when sea level attained its present elevation or nearly so) will have been submerged below sea level as a result of the rapid rise of sea level during the earlier Holocene.

e) Today the Bayt al-Faqīh Sand Ridges Land System, which extends some 20–30 km inland from the coast, can be divided into settled and less settled zones. The eastern part of this zone falls (just) within the zone of rainfall that permits rain-fed farming, and as a result the ridges and intervening valleys are frequently under field crops.[90] However the western parts receive insufficient rainfall, and are too high above water sources, to be used for agriculture, and this area, which is less populated today, may in later prehistory have served as a pastoral reserve for communities either rooted on the coast or inland corridor, or moving along the riverine corridors.[91] Although towns such as Bayt al-Faqīh, which is entirely sited on relict dunes, can be traced back to at least the Rasūlid period (thirteenth to fifteenth centuries BC), the long-term exploitation of this belt must await more archaeological studies.

Settlements on Ancient Dunes

In the dune ridge and inter-dune valley country, between the Wādī Sihām and Wādī Rima' (Figure 1:1), and also north of the Wādī atowards Wādī Surdud, field surveys and analyses from topographical maps (1:100,000 and 1:50,0000 scales) show that dozens of traditional Tihāmah settlements lie on the dune ridge tops and are in danger of being over-run by mobile sand sheets and dunes. Very few settlements occur in the more loamy soils of the inter-dune areas. Whilst elevation offers security for a site it would seem strange for it to be placed on an active dune. The ridges are in fact the ancient linear dunes with surface ridge-line and flanks stabilized by the early Holocene paleosol. We suggest that settlements were established on the dune ridges prior to the present cycle of mobile dunes, when the inter-dune areas would have been subject to occasional flooding.

Land use on the sand ridges has until recently been confined to rain-fed agriculture for millet and cowpeas. The establishment of some 70 km of irrigated forestry windbreaks on the sand has indicated how rapidly a variable plant cover can be established on dune sands.[92]

Conclusions and Future Research

The Tihāmah, like other parts of southern Arabia, provides some evidence for climate cycles of aridity and moisture comparable (although less distinct) to those of the interior and highlands. During prehistoric and early historic times the area was probably much better vegetated and more verdant than today with dense mangrove woodlands (*Avicennia*) along the coast and extensive stands of woodland (such as *Acacia –Commiphora* woodland) in the inland parts of the Tihāmah. Therefore the combined effects of climatic drying, and particularly long term collection of wood for fuel and construction have resulted in the present day degraded desertic environment.

The five-fold classification of the terrain into coast, Tihāmah dune fields, sub-piedmont corridor, interior valleys and mountains may provide a useful analytical framework for future surveys. Particularly, the broad north-south sub-Piedmont corridor deserves further consideration as a focus for long term agricultural communities based around rain-fed, run-off or *sayl* agriculture. In addition, this corridor must have served as the locus for the movement of populations between sedentary settlements within this zone, as well as for the movement of mobile pastoralists from north to south. This north-south axis of movement must, in places, have coincided with the east-west movement of people through the major valleys, and such intersections must have been the places where human groups of diverse origins met and interacted.

In terms of its relationships across the Red Sea, Khalidi (this volume) provides evidence for links between the prehistoric shell middens of the Tihāmah and obsidian sources in the Horn of Africa.[93] The perception that such cross-Red Sea linkages were significant is perhaps compounded by the separation that is apparent between the emerging pattern of archaeological settlement in the Tihāmah, the relatively high density of settlement on the high plateaus of the Yarim–Dhamar–Sana'a plateau with a relative dearth of settlement between.[94] This pattern of sites is, in part, an artefact of a lack of archaeological surveys in the major east–west *wādīs* and the mountains that

87 Bailey 2006.
88 Tosi 1986, Cattani and Bokonyi 2002, Khalidi 2005b.
89 Khalidi 2005a.
90 DHV 1990.
91 Khalidi 2006: 195.
92 IFAD 2003.
93 See also Fattovich, *et al.* this volume for similar interactions in the second millennium BC.
94 Lewis 2005: figure 1, Khalidi 2005b figure 1.

separate them. It is therefore a task for archaeologists in future to test this distribution of archaeological sites.

Significantly, the Tihāmah contrasts with the apparently similar coastal plain of the Bāṭinah, in Oman. Not only does the Bāṭinah lack the vast and long-term occurrence of sand dunes, but also the distribution of rainfall and hydrology is entirely different, with the Tihāmah benefiting from both higher rainfall in the Piedmont fringe, and also significant recharge of waters from rainfall on the highlands to the east. Significantly both plains, despite their local areas of soil fertility, exhibit relatively few archaeological sites. In the case of the Bāṭinah, this is because any early coastal settlements may have been destroyed or obscured by long term cultivation and building in the palm gardens that dominate these areas,[95] whereas in the Tihāmah, it is likely that the high discharges of silt directed onto the agricultural areas of the alluvial fans and associated *wādīs* have resulted in the submergence of settlements and their associated landscapes below metres of sediment, except where 'taphonomic windows' (for example, at Kashawba' and al-Hamid) are favourable to site preservation. Significantly, on the Bāṭinah, such agro-alluvial deposition, although present, was less significant because the sources of water — wells and perennial (that is, clear water) *falaj*es — did not result in such deep sedimentary accumulations.

The present study has been a broad reconnaissance on the Tihāmah that has attempted to open a small window on a significant period of human history. A more ambitious programme is needed to enhance the picture. This would see cores drilled through the ancient dunes at various parts of the Tihāmah, in order to provide a more comprehensive programme of OSL dating of aeolian sediments. Such a study would ascertain the stratigraphic relationships between the aeolian and alluvial succession, make a wide range of sedimentological studies of Quaternary formations and relate these to ecological change on land and with the marine and coral reef records. It would also investigate the pattern of early settlement on stabilized dune ridges and later population movements.

References

Aitken, M.J. 1991. Optical Dating. *Quaternary Science Reviews* 11: 127–31.

——. 1994. Optical Dating: a non-specialist review. *Quaternary Science Reviews* 13: 503–8.

——. 1998. *An Introduction to Optical Dating.* Oxford: Oxford Science Publications.

Allison, R.J. 1997. Middle East and Arabia, 507–21 in D.S.G Thomas (ed.), *Arid Zone Geomorphology: process, form and change in drylands.* London: Wiley.

Anderson, I.P. 1979. Soil Survey and Irrigation Suitability Classification of Wadi Rima. *Montane Plains and Wadi Rima' Project. Project Record,* 30 (YAR–01–43 / REC–30 / 79). Tolworth, UK: Land Resources Division.

Bailey, G. 2006. Early prehistory in the Farasan Islands and the Southern Red Sea. Paper delivered at the Seminar for Arabian Studies, London, 27 July 2006. On-line at http://www.arabianseminar.org.uk/abstracts2006-.html#bailey

Barratt, L., Dawson-Shepherd, A., Ormond, R. and McDowell, R. 1987a. *Marine Conservation Survey.* I: *Preliminary Coastal Habitats Species along the Yemen Arab Republic Coastline.* YAR Marine Conservation Survey. Report to IUCN (International Union for Conservation of Nature), Geneva, by The Tropical Marine Research Unit Ltd, York University. Gland: IUCN.

Barratt, L., Dawson-Shepherd, A. and Ormond, R. 1987b. *Marine Conservation Survey.* II: *Preliminary Coastal Zone Management Recommendations for the Yemen Arab Republic.* YAR Marine Conservation Survey. Report to IUCN (International Union for Conservation of Nature), Geneva, by The Tropical Marine Research Unit Ltd, York University. Gland: IUCN.

Bøtter-Jensen, L., McKeever, S.W.S. and Wintle, A.G. 2003. *Optically Stimulated Luminescence Dosimetry.* Amsterdam: Elsevier.

Breed, C.S., Fryberger, S.G., Andrews, S., McCauley, C., Lennartz, F., Gebel, D. and Horstman, K. 1979. Regional Studies of sand seas using Landsat (ERTS) imagery, 305–97 in E.D. McKee (ed.), *A Study of Global Sand Seas.* US Geological Survey Professional Paper, 1052. Washington D.C.: US Government Printing Office.

Brinkman, R. 1996. Pedological characteristics of anthrosols in the al-Jadidah basin of Wadi al-Jubah, and native sediments in Wadi al-Ajwirah Yemen Arab Republic, 45–211 in M.J. Grolier, R. Brinkman and J.A. Blakely (eds), *Environmental Research in Support of Archaeological Investigations in the Yemen Arab Republic, 1982–1987.* Washington, D.C.: American Foundation for the Study of Man.

Brown, G.F., Schmidt, D.L. and Huffman A.C. 1989. *Geology of the Arabian Peninsula: Shield Area of Western Saudi Arabia.* US Geological Survey Professional Paper, 560A. Reston, Virginia: US Government Printing Office.

Brown, L.H. and Cochemé, J. 1973. A study of the Agroclimatology of the Highlands of Eastern Africa. *WMO Tech.* Note 125. Geneva: World Meteorological Organization.

Cattani, M. and Bokonyi, S. 2002. Ash-Shumah: an early Holocene settlement of desert hunters and mangrove foragers in the Yemeni Tihamah. Volume 92: 3–52 in S. Cleuziou, M. Tosi and J. Zarins (eds), *Essays on the*

[95] Costa and Wilkinson 1986: 234.

Later Prehistory of the Arabian Peninsula. Serie Orientale, Roma. Rome: ISIAO.

Christian, C.S. and Stewart, G.A. 1952. *General Report of Survey of Katherine-Darwin Region (1946)*. CSIRO Australia. Land Research Series. 1. Canberra: CSIRO.

Christian, C.S. 1958. The concept of land units and land systems. *Proceedings of the 9th Pacific Science Congress, 1957*, 20: 74–81.

Ciuk, C. and Keall E. 1996. *Zabid Pottery Manual 1995*. BAR International Series 655. Oxford: Tempus Reparatum.

Cooke, R.U. and Warren, A. 1973. *Geomorphology in Deserts*. London: B.T. Batsford.

Cooke, R.U., Warren, A. and Goudie, A.S. 1993. *Desert Geomorphology*. London: University College London Press.

Costa, P.M. and Wilkinson, T.J. 1987. The Hinterland of Sohar. Archaeological Surveys and Excavations within the Region of an Omani Seafaring City. *Journal of Oman Studies* 9: 1–238.

Davison, I., al-Kadasi, M., al-Khirbashi, S., al-Subbary, A.-K., Baker, J., Blakey, S., Bosence, D., Dart, C., Heaton, R., McClay, R., Menzies, M., Nichols, G., Owen, L.A. and Yelland, A. 1994. Geological evolution of the southeastern Red Sea Rift margin, Republic of Yemen. *Bulletin of the Geological Society of America*, 106: 1474–93.

Davison, I., Tatnell, M.R., Owen, L.A., Jenkins, G. and Baker, J. 1998. Tectonic geomorphology and rates of crustal processes along the Red Sea margin, north-west Yemen. 595–614 in B.H. Purser and D.W.J. Bosence (eds), *Sedimentation and Tectonics of Rift Basin: Red Sea–Gulf of Aden*. London: Chapman and Hall.

DHV. 1990. Environmental Profile Tihama. DHV Consultants, Netherlands.

Durrani, N. 2005. *The Tihamah coastal plain of South-West Arabia in its regional context: c.6000 BC–AD 600*. Society for Arabian Studies Monograph 4. BAR International Series 1456. Oxford: Archaeopress.

Edgell, H.S. 2006. *Arabian Deserts. Nature Origin and Evolution*. Place: Springer.

Facey, W. 2004. The Red Sea: the wind regime and location of ports. 6–17 in P. Lunde and A. Porter (eds), *Trade and Travel in the Red Sea Region. Proceedings of the Red Sea Project I.* Society for Arabian Studies Monographs 2. BAR International Series 1269. Oxford: Archaeopress.

FAO–IC. 1990. *Tihama Environmental Protection Project. First Phase Preparation Mission. Environmental Protection*. FAO–IC Report No. 61 / 90; IF–YEM 32. Rome: FAO–Investment Centre.

——. 1991. Annex 1. Land Protection, Annex 6. Assessment of Desertification through the use of aerial photography 1976–1987. *Tihama Environmental Protection Project. First Phase Preparation Report.* FAO / IFAD Co-operative Programme. FAO–IC Report No. 148 / 91. IF–YEM 39. Rome: FAO–Investment Centre.

FAO–UNESCO. 1977. *Soil Map of the World*, 1:500,000. Volume VII, South Asia. Rome: FAO.

Fisher, M. and Membrey, D.A. 1998. Climate. 5–38 in S.A. Ghazanfar and M. Fisher (eds), *Vegetation of the Arabian Peninsula. Geobotany*, 25. Dordrecht: Kluwer.

Fleitmann, D., Burns, S.J., Mudelsee, M., Neff, U., Kramers, J., Mangini, A. and Matter, A. 2003. Holocene Forcing of the Indian Monsoon Recorded in a Stalagmite from Southern Oman. *Science* 300: 1737–9.

Forbes, T.R. 1985. Landforms, soils, and climate of Wadi Zabid in the Tihama. 10–13 in F. Stone (ed.), *Studies on the Tihamah: the report of the Tihamah Expedition 1982 and related papers*. Harlow: Longman Group Limited.

Geiser, U. and Steffen, H. 1977. Map of Population distribution, administrative division and land use in the Yemen Arab Republic. Berne: Swiss Technical Cooperation Services. Sana'a: Central Planning Organization.

Geukens, F. 1966. *Geology of the Arabian Peninsula, Yemen.* US Geological Survey Professional Paper 560–B. Reston, Virginia: US Geological Survey.

Glennie, K.W., 1970. Desert Sedimentary Environments. *Developments in Sedimentology* 14. Amsterdam: Elsevier.

——. 1998. The desert of SE Arabia: A product of Quaternary climatic change. 279–92 in A.S. Alsharhan, W. K.W. Glennie, G.L. Whittle and C.G.S. Kendall (eds), *Quaternary Deserts and Climatic Change.* Rotterdam: Balkema / Brookfield.

——. 2005. *The Desert of Southeast Arabia*. Manama, Bahrain: GeoArabia–Gulf Petro Link.

Glennie, K.W. and Evamy, B.D. 1968. Dikaka: plant and plant-root structures associated with aeolian sand. *Palaeogeography, Palaeoclimatology, Palaeoecology* 4: 77–87.

Goudie, A.S., Livingstone, I. and Stokes, S. (eds). 1999. *Aeolian Environments, Sediments and Landforms*. Chichester: John Wiley.

Grolier, M.J. and Overstreet, W.C. 1975. Preliminary geologic map of Tihama between Zabid and Hudaydah, Yemen Arab Republic (Scale 1:500,000). *United States Geological Survey Miscellaneous Investigation Series: Open File Report* 76–739. Reston, Virginia: US Geological Survey.

——. 1976. Geologic Map of the Yemen Arab Republic (Scale 1:500,000). *United States Geological Survey Miscellaneous Investigation Series.* Map I–1143–B. Reston, Virginia: US Geological Survey.

Guilcher, A. 1952. Formes et processus d'érosion sur les récifs coralliens du nord du banc Farasan (Mer Rouge). *Revue de Geomorphologie Dynamique* 3 (6): 261–74.

Gun, J.A.M. van der and Abdul Aziz, A. 1995. The Water Resources of Yemen. A summary and digest of available information. *Water Resources, Arab Republic of Yemen Project (WRAY)* Report WRAY–35. Sana'a: Ministry of Oil and Mineral Resources, and Delft: TNO Institute of Applied Geosciences.

Halcrow, Sir William. 1978. Soils and Land Capability. *Wadi Surdud. Development on the Tihama* 4. Sana'a: Ministry of Agriculture and Fisheries.

El-Hassan, B.A. 1999. *Environmental protection studies and activities in the Tihama Plains of Yemen*. Sana'a: UNCCD National Workshop to Review the National Action Plan to Combat Desertification and Resource Degradation.

Hehmeyer, I. 1995. Physical evidence of engineered water systems in Medieval Zabid. *Proceedings of the Seminar for Arabian Studies* 25: 45–54.

Hehmeyer, I. and Keall, E. 1993. Water and Land Management in the Zabid Hinterland. *Al-'Uṣūr al-Wusṭā (The Bulletin of Middle East Medievalists)* 5(2): 25–7.

Hunting Technical Services (HTS). 1992. *National Land and Water Conservation Project— Woodland Resources Mapping Project: Technical Manual*. Sana'a: Ministry of Agriculture and Water Resources, General Directorate of Forestry and Rangelands. Hemel Hempstead: Hunting Technical Services.

——. 1993. *Tihama Land Cover Change Study*. Ministry of Agriculture and Water Resources. Hodeidah: Tihama Development Authority. Hemel Hempstead: Hunting Technical Services.

——. 1999. Aeolian Sand Formations of the Tihama: Geomorphology and Assessment of Sand Stabilisation Programmes. Unpublished Technical Report by R.N. Munro, Hunting Technical Services (HTS) Ltd. for the Tihama Development Authority, Hodeidah. (Report and maps: http://www.wossac.com). Hemel Hempstead: Hunting Technical Services.

——. 2002. Study of the Integrated Drainage Systems of the Tihama Plains and Wadi Basins. Unpublished Technical Report by R.N. Munro, Hunting Technical Services (HTS) Ltd. for the Tihama Development Authority, Hodeidah. (Report and maps: http://www.wossac.co). Hemel Hempstead: Hunting Technical Services.

al-Hubaishi, A. and Müller-Hohenstein, K. 1984. *An Introduction to the Vegetation of Yemen. Ecological basis, floristic composition, human influence*. Eschborn: Deutsche Gesellschaft für Technische Zusammenarbeit (GTZ).

Huzayyin, S.A. 1945. Notes on climatic conditions in S.W. Arabia. *Royal Meteorological Society, Quarterly Journal* 71: 129–40.

IFAD. 2003. Land Conservation. Annex 1 (author: R.N. Munro), in *Interim Evaluation Report of the Tihama Environment Protection Report.* Rome: International Fund for Agricultural Development.

Keall, E.J. 1983. The dynamics of Zabid and its hinterland: the survey of a town on the Tihamah plain of North Yemen. *World Archaeology* 14 (3): 378–92.

——. 2004. Possible connections in antiquity between the Red Sea coast of Yemen and the Horn of Africa. 43–55 in P. Lunde and A. Porter (eds), *Trade and Travel in the Red Sea Region. Proceedings of the Red Sea Project vol. 1.* Society for Arabian Studies Monograph 2. BAR International Series 1269. Oxford Archaeopress.

Khalidi, L. 2005a. The prehistoric and early historic settlement patterns of the Tihamah coastal plain (Yemen): preliminary findings of the Tihamah Coastal Survey 2003. *Proceedings of the Seminar for Arabian Studies* 35: 115–27.

——. 2005b. Megalithic Landscapes: the development of the late prehistoric cultural landscape along the Tihamah coastal plain (Republic of Yemen). 359–75 in A.M. Sholan, S. Antonini, M. Arbach (eds). *Sabaean Studies: Archaeological, Epigraphical and Historical Studies in Honour of Yusuf M. Abdullah, Alessandro de Maigret and Christian J. Robin.* Università degli Studi di Napoli: Naples–Sana'a.

——. 2006. Settlement, Culture-Contact and Interaction along the Red Sea Coastal Plain, Yemen: The Tihamah cultural landscape in the late prehistoric period, 3000–900 BC, unpublished PhD thesis, University of Cambridge.

King, J.W., Forbes, T.R. and Ghanem, A.E.A. (eds). 1983. *Soil Survey of the Yemen Arab Republic.* Final Report by Cornell University to the United States Agency for International Development (USAID). Ithaca, New York: Cornell University.

King, J.W., Forbes, T.R. and Ghanem, A.E.A. 1985. Benchmark Soils of the Yemen Arab Republic. *World Benchmark Soils Report* 1. Washington DC: SMSS.

Kruck, W. 1983. Sana'a Sheet. *Draft Geological Map of the Yemen Arab Republic, 1:250,000.* Hanover: Federal Institute for Geosciences and Natural Resources, and Sana'a: YOMINCO.

——. 1984. al-Hudaydah Sheet. *Draft Geological Map of the Yemen Arab Republic, 1:250,000.* Hanover: Federal Institute for Geosciences and Natural Resources, and Sana'a: YOMINCO.

——. 1991. *Geological Map of the Yemen Arab Republic, 1:250,000* (8 Sheets). Hanover: Federal Institute for Geosciences and Natural Resources, and Sana'a: YOMINCO.

Kruck, W., Schaffer, U. and Thiele, J. 1996. Explanatory Notes on the Geological Map of Yemen Arab Republic. *Geologisches Jahrbuch, Reihe B: Regionale Geologie Ausland*, 87: 1–105.

Lancaster, N. 1995. *Geomorphology of Desert Dunes*. London: Routledge.

Leeder, M.R. 1981. *Sedimentology. Process and Product.* London: George Allen and Unwin.

Lewis, K. 2005. The Himyarite site of al-Adhla and its implications for the economy and chronology of Early Historic highland Yemen. *Proceedings of the Seminar for Arabian Studies* 35: 129–41.

Lézine, A.-M., Saliège, J.-F., Robert, C., Wertz, F. and Inizan, M.L. 1998. Holocene Lakes from Ramlat as-Sab'atyn (Yemen) Illustrate the Impact of Monsoon Activity in Southern Arabia. *Quaternary Research*, 50: 290–9.

Mabbutt, J.A. 1977. *Desert Landforms*. Cambridge: MIT Press.

Makin, M.J. 1977. Yemen Arab Republic Montane Plains and Wadi Rima' Project: a land and water resources survey. Irrigation and agricultural development in Wadi Rima', volume 1. Report YAR–01–29 / REP–16 / 77. Tolworth, Surrey: Land Resources Division.

McClure, H.A. 1976. Radiocarbon Chronology of Late Quaternary Lakes in the Arabian Desert. *Nature* 263: 755–6.

Sir M. MacDonald & Partners (MMP)–Hunting Technical Services (HTS). 1982. Wadi Mawr Project. Inception Study. Unpublished technical report by Sir M. MacDonald & Partners and Hunting Technical Services Ltd. to the Ministry of Agriculture and Fisheries, Yemen. Cambridge: MacDonald & Partners.

——. 1983. Wadi Mawr Project. Notes and General Information. Unpublished technical report by Sir M. MacDonald & Partners and Hunting Technical Services Ltd. to the Ministry of Agriculture and Fisheries, Yemen. Cambridge: MacDonald & Partners.

McGinnies, W.G., Goldman, B.J. and Paylore, P. (eds). 1968. *Deserts of the World: an appraisal of research into their physical and biological environments*. Tucson: University of Arizona Press.

Meigs, P. 1966. *Geography of Coastal Deserts. Arid Zone Research* XXVIII. Paris: UNESCO.

Mitchell, C.W., 1973. *Terrain Evaluation*. London: Longman.

el-Nakhal, H.A. 1993. The Pleistocene cold episode in the Republic of Yemen. *Palaeogeography, Palaeoclimatology and Palaeoecology* 100: 303–7.

Naval Intelligence Division. 1946. Western Arabia and the Red Sea. *Geographical Handbook Series* BR 527. London: Naval Intelligence Division.

Nichols, G. and Watchorn, F. 1998. Climatic and geomorphic controls on rift sedimentation: Oligo-Miocene synrift facies in the Gulf of Aden, Yemen. *Marine and Petroleum Geology*, 15: 505–18.

Niebuhr, M. 1792 [repr. 1969]. *Travels through Arabia and Other Countries to the East*. Tr. R. Heron. Edinburgh: publisher.

Pachur, H.J. and Altman, N. 1997. The Quaternary (Holocene, *ca.* 8000 a BP). 111–125, in H. Schandelmeier, P.O. Reynolds and A.K. Semtner (eds), *Palaeogeographic-Palaeotectonic Atlas of North-Eastern Africa, Arabia and Adjacent Areas*. Rotterdam: Balkema.

Parker, A.G., Eckersley, L., Smith, M.M., Goudie, A.S., Stokes, S., Ward, S., White, K. and Hodson, M.J. 2004. Holocene vegetation dynamics in the northeastern Rub' al-Khali desert, Arabian Peninsula: a phytolith, pollen and carbon isotope study. *Journal of Quaternary Science* 19(7): 665–76.

Parker, A.G., Davies, C. and Wilkinson, T.J. 2006. The early to mid-Holocene moist period in Arabia: some recent evidence from lacustrine sequences in eastern and south-western Arabia. *Proceedings of the Seminar for Arabian Studies* 36: 243–55.

Pedgley, D.E. 1966a. The Red Sea Convergence Zone. I: the horizontal pattern of winds. *Weather* 31(10): 350–8.

——. 1966b. The Red Sea Convergence Zone. II: Vertical Structure. *Weather* 31(11): 394–406.

Petrov, M.P. 1975. *Deserts of the World*. New York: Wiley.

Phillips, C.S. 1998. The Tihamah *c.* 5000 to 500 BC, *Proceedings of the Seminar for Arabian Studies* 28: 233–7.

——. 2005. A preliminary description of the pottery from al-Hāmid and its significance in relation to other pre-Islamic sites on the Tihāmah. *Proceedings of the Seminar for Arabian Studies* 35: 177–93.

Pleijsier, L.K. 1978. Aspects of Soil and Soil Salinity in the Tihama Region. Yemen Arab Republic. *UNDP / FAO Agricultural Services Project, Yemen*. Technical Paper YEM 73 / 011. Rome: FAO.

Preusser, F., Radies, D. and Matter, A. 2002. A 160,000-Year Record of Dune Development and Atmospheric Circulation in Southern Arabia. *Science* 296: 2018–20.

Pye, K. and Tsoar, H. 1990. *Aeolian Sand and Sand Dunes*. London: Unwin Hyman.

al-Radi, S. 1985. Archaeology Survey Report. 53–55 in F. Stone (ed.), *Studies on the Tihamah: the report of the Tihamah Expedition 1982 and related papers*. Harlow: Longman Group.

Rathjens, C.S., Rathjens, C.J., Samlenski, E. and Kerner, G. 1956. Contributions to a study of the climatology of Southwest Arabia. The Climates of Sana and the Yemen. *German Weather Service: Marine Weather Office*, Publ. 11. Hamburg.

Robertson Research Int. 1991a. Geological Map of Yemen (2 sheets at 1:1 million; 35 sheets at 1:250,000). *The Natural Resources Project*. AFESD and UNDP. Wales: Robertson Research International.

——. 1991b. Hydrogeological Map of Yemen (2 sheets at 1:1 million; 35 sheets at 1:250,000). *The Natural Resources Project*. AFESD and UNDP. Wales: Robertson Research International, Wales.

——. 1991c. Topographical Map of Yemen (2 sheets at 1:1,000,000 and 35 sheets at 1:250,000). *The Natural*

Resources Project. AFESD and UNDP. Wales: Robertson Research International.

——. 1993. *Geology of Yemen*. Report to the Government of Yemen. Wales: Robertson Research International.

Sarnthein, M. 1972. Sediments and history of the Post-glacial Transgression in the Persian Gulf and North-West Gulf of Oman. *Marine Geology* 12: 245–66.

——. 1978. Sand deserts during glacial maximum and climatic optimum. *Nature* 272: 43–6.

Sarnthein, M. and Diester-Haas, L. 1977. Eolian sand turbidites. *Journal of Sedimentary Petrolology* 47: 868–90.

Scholte, P., al-Khuleidi, A.-W. and Kessler, J.J. 1991. *The Vegetation of the Republic of Yemen (Western Part)*. Environment Protection Council. Agricultural Research Authority. Netherlands: DHV Consultants BV.

Scholte, P., Kessler, J.J. and al-Khuleidi, A-W. 1992. *The Vegetation Map of the Western Part of the Yemen Arab Republic. A summary of the Vegetation Types*. Environment Protection Council. Agricultural Research Authority. Netherlands: DHV Consultants BV.

Siraj, A. 1984. Climate of Saudi Arabia. 6: 32–52 in W. Buttiker and F. Krupp (eds), *Fauna of Saudi Arabia*. Basle: Pro-Entomologia.

Snead, R.E. 1972. *World Atlas of Physical Features*. New York: Wiley.

Sommerville, A.A., Burbidge, C., Sanderson, D.C.W. and Munro, R.N. 2005. Report on Luminescence Dating of Sediments from Yemen and Saudi Arabia. *SUERC Unpublished Report Series*. East Kilbride: Scottish Universities Environmental Research Centre.

Stone, F.L. (ed.). 1985. *Studies on the Tihamah: the report of the Tihamah Expedition 1982 and related papers*. Harlow: Longman Group.

Summerfield, M.A. 1991. *Global Geomorphology*. Harlow: Longman Scientific and Technical.

Taha, M.F., Harb, S.A., Nagib, M.K. and Tantawy, A.H. 1981. The Climates of the Near East. 183–255 in K. Takahashi and H. Arakawa (eds), *Climates of Southern and Western Asia, World Survey of Climatology* 9. Amsterdam: Elsevier.

Talbot, M.R. and Williams, M.A.J. 1978. Erosion of fixed dunes in the Sahel, Central Niger. *Earth Surface Processes* 3: 107–13.

——. 1979. Cyclic alluvial fan sedimentation on the flanks of fixed dunes, Janjari, Central Niger. *Catena* 6: 43–62.

TESCO–Viziterv–Vituki. 1971. Final Report, *Survey of the Agricultural Potential of the Wadi Zabid*. 12 Technical Reports. SF / FAO. Budapest: Tesco–Viziterv–Vituki.

Thomas, D.S.G. 1997. Sand seas and aeolian bedforms. 373–412 in D.S.G. Thomas (ed.), *Arid Zone Geomorphology, Form and Change in Drylands*. London: John Wiley.

Thomas, D.S.G. and Shaw, P.A. 1991. Relict desert dune systems: interpretation and problems. *Journal of Arid Environments* 20: 1–14.

Tipton and Kalmbach Inc. 1974. *Development of Wadi Mawr for Tihama Development*. Hodeidah: TDA, Denver, Colorado: Tipton and Kalmbach Inc.

Tosi, M. 1985. Archaeological activities in the Yemen Arab Republic, 1985: Tihamah coastal archaeological survey. *East and West* 35: 363–9.

——. 1986. Archaeological activities in the Yemen Arab Republic, 1986: Neolithic and protohistoric cultures. Survey and Excavation on the Coastal Plain (Tihamah). *East and West* 36: 400–14.

UK Hydrographic Office 2004 (14th edn). *Red Sea and Gulf of Aden Pilot*. Exeter: UK Hydrographic Department.

Waveren, E. van 1990. The Soils of Wadi Mawr. *FAO Soil Survey and Land Classification Project,* AG: YEM / 87 / 002, Field Document 11. Sana'a: Ministry of Agriculture and Water Resources.

Wells, G.L. 1989. Observing earth's environment from space. 148–92 in L. Friday and R. Laskey, *The Fragile Environment. The Darwin College Lectures*. Cambridge: Cambridge University Press.

Wilkinson, T.J. 1997. Holocene Environments of the High Plateau, Yemen. Recent Geoarchaeological Investigations. *Geoarchaeology* 12 (8): 833–64.

——. 2005. Soil Erosion and Valley Fills in the Yemen Highlands and Southern Turkey: integrating settlement, geoarchaeology and climate change. *Geoarchaeology* 20(2): 169–92.

Wilkinson, T.J., Gibson M. and Edens, C. 1997. The archaeology of the Yemen high plains: a preliminary chronology. *Arabian Archaeology and Epigraphy* 8: 99–142.

Williams, J.B. 1979. Climate of the Montane Plains and Wadi Rima'. *Montane Plains and Wadi Rima Project*. Project Record 42 (YAR–01–48 / REC–42 / 79). Tolworth: Land Resources Development Centre.

Williams, M.A.J., Dunkerly, D.L., De Decker, P., Kershaw, A.P. and Chappell, J. 2003. *Quaternary Environments*. London: Arnold.

Wood, J.R.I. 1985a. An Outline of the Vegetation of the Yemen Arab Republic. 29–43 in J.W. King, T.R. Forbes. and A.E.A. Ghanem (eds), *Soil Survey of the Yemen Arab Republic*. Ithaca, New York: Department of Agronomy, Cornell University.

——. 1985b. The Vegetation of the Tihāma. 14–17 in F. Stone (ed.), *Studies on the Tihāma: the report of the Tihāma Expedition 1982 and related papers*. Harlow: Longman.

——. 1997. *A Handbook of the Yemen Flora*. Kew: Royal Botanic Gardens.

Zarins, J. and Zahrani, A. 1985. Recent Archaeological Investigations in the Southern Tihama Plain. The Sites of Athar and Sihi, 1404 / 1984. *Atlal* 9: 65–107.

Zarins, J. and Badr, H. 1986. Archaeological investigations in the Tihama Plain II 1405 / 1985. *Atlal* 10: 36–57.

Acknowledgements

The geomorphological and sand dune stabilization fieldwork that supports this study was made by R.N. Munro (RNM), during 1998–2000 for the Tihāmah Development Authority (TDA) on the International Fund for Agricultural Development (IFAD) funded Tihāmah Environment Protection Programme (TEEP), in support of the establishment of 70 km of irrigated forestry shelterbelts designed to halt sand dune incursion onto irrigable lands in the Wādīs Siham and Zabid. RNM made sedimentological studies (dry sieving). In acknowledgement, RNM wishes to give extended thanks to former TDA Chairman, Ibrahim al Doumi, for permission to use data for his doctoral research; to TDA HQ and regional staff, in particular Adnan Saleh, Khalid Sheikh, Mohamed Abdulrahman, Dr Babiker el-Hassan, Zein al Haig and Abdulazeez Al Jalleel for field support; to Andrew Warren at University College London for general support and advice; and to John Allen of Yemen Hunt, Hodeidah for logistical support.

Professor Ken Pye facilitated laboratory work by RNM at the Department of Geology, Reading (particle size analyses by laser granulometry; x-ray diffraction; geochemical analyses; scanning electron microscope); optically stimulated luminescence (OSL) dating, the first achieved on the Tihāmah, was made at the Scottish Universities Environmental Research Centre (SUERC) (Sommerville, *et al.*, 2005), East Kilbride under the instruction of Drs David Sanderson, Chris Burbidge and Anne Sommerville; Dr Osman el Tom facilitated soil analyses at the Land and Water Research Centre, Wad Medani, Sudan; and five wind measurement stations, made by ELE International Ltd., were established on the Tihāmah in 1999 (IFAD, 2003).

333The Formation of a Southern Red Seascape in the Late Prehistoric Period: Tracing Cross–Red Sea Culture-Contact, Interaction, and Maritime Communities along the Tihāmah Coastal Plain, Yemen, in the Third to First Millennium BC

Lamya Khalidi

Yemen holds a geographic position that naturally lends itself to trade and interaction on a number of different levels. With the Red Sea to the west and the Arabian Sea and Indian Ocean to the south, Yemen, as it is defined geo-politically today, has for millennia had direct access to the seaways of the Indian Ocean and Red Sea worlds (Map 2:1). While its interior is a mosaic of topographies and landscapes, including the high-altitude mountains that loom at 3800 m above sea level over its desert interior to the east, the Tihāmah coastal plain to the west and the south-western coast near Aden to the south, these extreme geographical contrasts have not acted as an impediment to overland and maritime trade and interaction from the early historical periods onward.

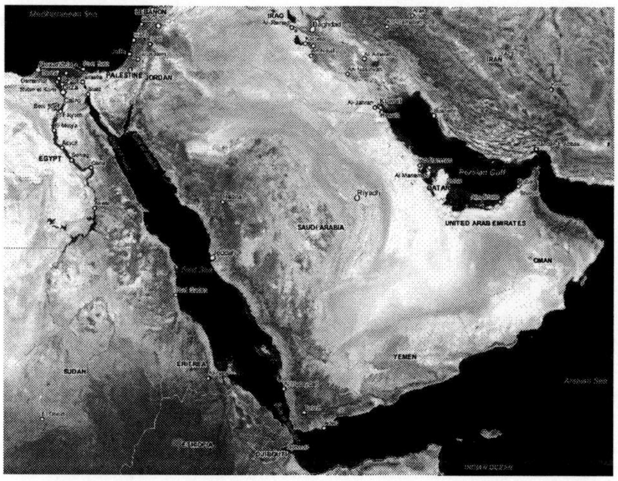

Map 2:1 Satellite map situating the Arabian Peninsula and more specifically Yemen within its larger geographic context, with the African Horn to the west and south and India to the east.

Early historical sources vouch for the existence of extensive overland trade routes during the period of the rise and fall of the South Arabian desert-kingdoms and later the highland kingdom of Ḥimyar, in the mid- to late-first millennium BC. However, prehistoric interaction remains elusive due to a dearth of comprehensive and systematic prehistoric research in certain regions[1] and at major geographical interfaces where evidence for culture-contact and interaction would be more noticeable. This paper presents data that demonstrate that by the third millennium BC, there was regular maritime interaction between the Yemen and Horn of Africa coasts.

Fieldwork carried out between 2003 and 2005 by the Tihamah Coastal Survey[2] along the Yemeni Tihāmah coastal plain began to define prehistoric settlement in relation to its contemporary landscapes and to trace inter- and intra- regional interaction, which proved to be multi-directional. Using systematic survey strategies to show densities and distributions of materials across settlements, micro-zones and macro-zones, as well as tracing the introduction of certain materials and tool types, the data collected clearly point to the corridors of the Red Sea as the means by which most of the obsidian found along the Tihāmah arrived and by which the two opposing coasts were culturally intertwined.[3]

Most of the data recovered were compared with material culture typologies from regions of Yemen with a longer history of prehistoric research. These included typologies formulated by the Italian Archaeological Mission in the Khawlān area[4] and those of the Dhamar Survey Project in the central highland area.[5] In addition, results were compared to those of a survey mounted in the western escarpment area along the Wādī Zabīd,[6] an area chosen

---

1 For a more detailed discussion see Crassard and Khalidi 2005.

2 Survey project directed by L. Khalidi, carried out in cooperation with the Yemeni General Organization for Antiquities, Museums and Manuscripts (GOAM). The team members included Dr Krista Lewis, Ahmed al-Mosabi and Essam Hamana. In 2003 the fieldwork was funded by a Fulbright IIE grant.

3 Khalidi 2006.

4 Costantini 1986, Costantini 1990, De Maigret 1981, 1988, 1997, De Maigret, *et al.* 1990, Fedele 1984, 1985, 1990, Francaviglia 1989.

5 Barbanes 2000, Edens 1999, Edens and Wilkinson 1998, Edens, *et al.* 2000, Ekstrom and Edens 2003, Gibson and Wilkinson 1995, Wilkinson, *et al.* 1997, Wilkinson 1997, 2003, Wilkinson and Edens 1999.

6 The Hazm al-'Udayn Survey was directed by L. Khalidi and carried out in cooperation with GOAM. The team members included Dr Krista Lewis and Muhammad al-Qadhi. Fieldwork was funded by a grant from the American Institute for Yemeni Studies (AIYS). See

precisely because it lies midway between the highland and lowland study areas. Finally, a landscape and site reconnaissance in Eritrea[7] added a comparative African perspective to the study of the Yemeni Red Sea coast.

Sites surveyed in the Tihāmah were relatively dated based on three carbon-dated late prehistoric sites in the coastal plains area, namely the site of al-Midamman in the central Tihāmah, excavated by Keall and the Royal Ontario Museum,[8] and the site of Sabir near Aden.[9] Finally, the work of the Italian Archaeological Mission to the Tihāmah that concentrated on early Holocene settlements[10] near the foothills was useful in relatively dating earlier and later period sites.

Fieldwork concentrated on systematic survey with a focus on archaeological landscape methodology. The main study area falls in the central Tihāmah, between the Wādīs Zabīd, Rima' and Kuway'. The eastern boundary of the survey area is situated near the site of Kashawba', approximately halfway across the 30–60 km wide coastal plain, while the western boundary consists of the littoral itself where the majority of transects walked began or ended.

The Tihāmah is a hyper-arid flat coastal plain with a subtropical climate. This plain is wrought with sand dunes in differing stages of erosion and formation and is green with agriculture and wild vegetation near the *wādī*s and their deltas. Given the sparse vegetation cover along most of the plain, there is little protection from sand and wind erosion and the deflation of ground surfaces is widespread, making it a difficult terrain to cover. Sites are often partially buried by shifting sands or have been heavily deflated. Given these difficulties, the survey began by sampling a range of terrains. Certain landscape features such as the coast and the river deltas were proven to be more intensively inhabited in the prehistoric period. These river deltas acted as natural conduits for contact and movement and were more favourable due to their proximity to crucial resources.

The central Tihāmah survey recovered 133 sites in total, sixty of which were relatively dated to the early Holocene period and 49 of which were late prehistoric.[11] Aceramic mono-specific shell middens dominate the early Holocene sites, which date between the seventh and fifth millennium BC. These were mainly located along the littoral and along the banks of the rivers and deltas where stable mangrove tidal creeks once flourished and provided the source of sustenance for the hunter-forager populations inhabiting the area.[12] The inter-fluvial steppe included light scatters interspersed with light concentrations of molluscan shell, occasional lithic tools and equid remains. These signatures can be interpreted as debris left over from temporary hunting camps in areas that were lightly forested and were ideal roaming grounds for wild equid and ostrich in the early Holocene. The tool kit of these periods consisted of bifacial parallel pressure-flaked projectiles made mainly from jaspers, rhyolites and cherts that were acquired in the *wādī* beds. What appear to be the earliest projectiles are large in size and standardized in their shape and workmanship. By comparison with the site of al-Shumah, these can be dated to sometime in the seventh millennium BC.[13] None of these bifaces are made from obsidian, a material that does not seem to appear on sites in the area before the sixth millennium BC[14] when the same bifacial tradition was carried out but with gradual changes in the form, size and workmanship. A technologically parallel bifacial industry, but one entirely restricted to obsidian, appears on sites comparable to one excavated by the Italian Archaeological Mission and dated to the fifth millennium BC.[15] These tools are also standardized and are all smaller in size and thinner than their predecessors. During these periods, settlement distribution is relatively similar, with sites continuously distributed along the *wādī* and the edges of the tidal creeks. In addition, there is evidence for seasonal or temporary presence in areas of the inter-fluvial steppe and a drop-off of early Holocene sites towards the interior.

The appearance of ceramic sites is confirmed by the early third millennium BC onward at sites such as Ma'alaybah near Aden,[16] as well as during the early occupational phases at the sites of al-Midamman and Sabir.[17] These sites are characterized by an altogether new material culture repertoire, one that includes a sand-tempered and high-fired ceramic tradition with intricate decorative elements and forms. Ceramics found on the surface of sites are dominated by decorated oval-cross sectioned handles and fenestrated vessel fragments as well as hole-mouth pots and burnishing. The appearance of these ceramics is accompanied by a new settlement strategy which includes multiple period shell middens with later ceramic elements evenly clustered along the *wādī* banks and areas of the littoral, and large sites located where the

Khalidi 2006: 48–122.

7 An archaeological reconnaissance survey was carried out by L. Khalidi in Eritrea with the cooperation of the National Museum in Eritrea. Fieldwork was funded by CAORC.

8 Keall 1998, 1999, 2000, 2004.

9 Buffa 2002, 2003, Buffa and Vogt 2001, Vogt 1997, Vogt and Sedov 1997, 1998, excavated by Vogt and Sedov, and the site of Sihi in the Saudi Tihāmah, excavated by Zarins (Zarins and Al-Badr 1986, Zarins and Zahrani 1985).

10 Cattani and Bokonyi 2002, Tosi 1985, 1986 as well as the work of Phillips (Phillips 1997, 1998, Phillips 2005).

11 Khalidi 2006: 179.

12 Cattani, *et al.* 2002: 33.

13 Ibid.: 34.

14 Ibid.: 44.

15 Tosi 1986: 407.

16 Buffa 2002, 2003.

17 Buffa, *et al.* 2001: 446, Keall 1998: 146.

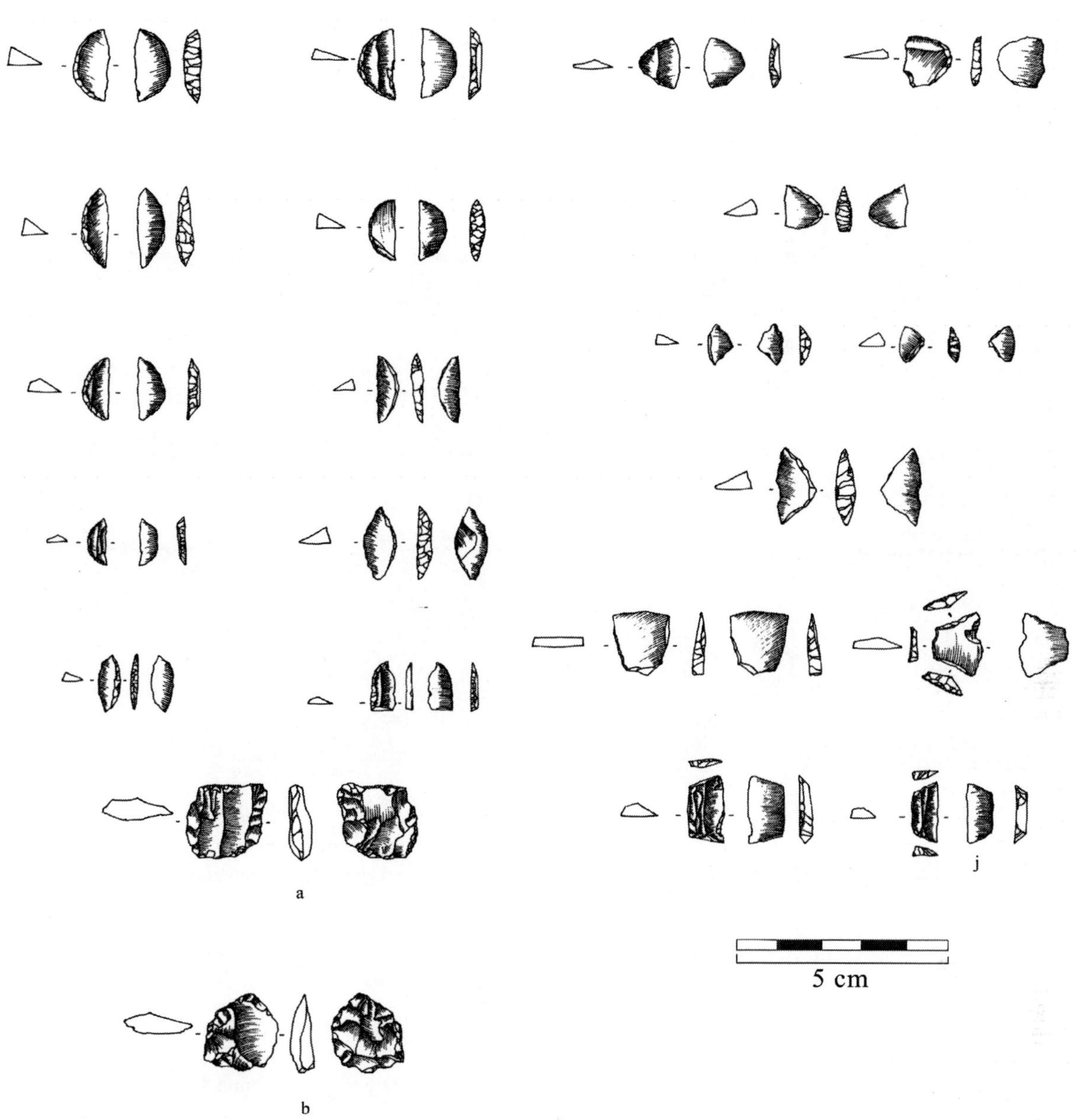

Figure 2:1 Obsidian geometric microliths: circle segments (left). All of these circle segments are retouched on the circular edge and are either made from bladelets or from flakes; arches, triangles and trapezoids (right).

(a, b) Tool or waste?: obsidian pièces esquillées. *The* pièce esquillée *is characterized by removals from opposing ends (bipolar flaking). This effect is often acquired when the stone acts as a wedge or chisel during indirect percussion on anvil. The force of the hammer on one end and the anvil on the other produces removals from both ends as well as the scaled edges typical of these pieces. Drawn by J. Espagne*

main *wādī* course reaches the sea and at the formation of the deltas.

The larger sites such as al-Midamman and Kashawba' are characterized by dense pottery middens, low mounding and, in most cases, earlier third to second millennium BC megalithic elements often re-used in the foundations of early first millennium BC partitioned buildings.[18]

Survey work in the Tihāmah coastal plain has yielded a surprisingly diverse and rich lithic assemblage. In many ways these tools have provided the most accurate chronological indicators for sites in the area. Furthermore, the types and densities of the primary materials available have been useful not only in determining the period, but also in tracing contact and interaction in the case of non-available stone resources. Both the smaller and larger late prehistoric sites are characterized by a remarkable increase in the density of obsidian, present in the form of

[18] Keall 1998: 140, 145.

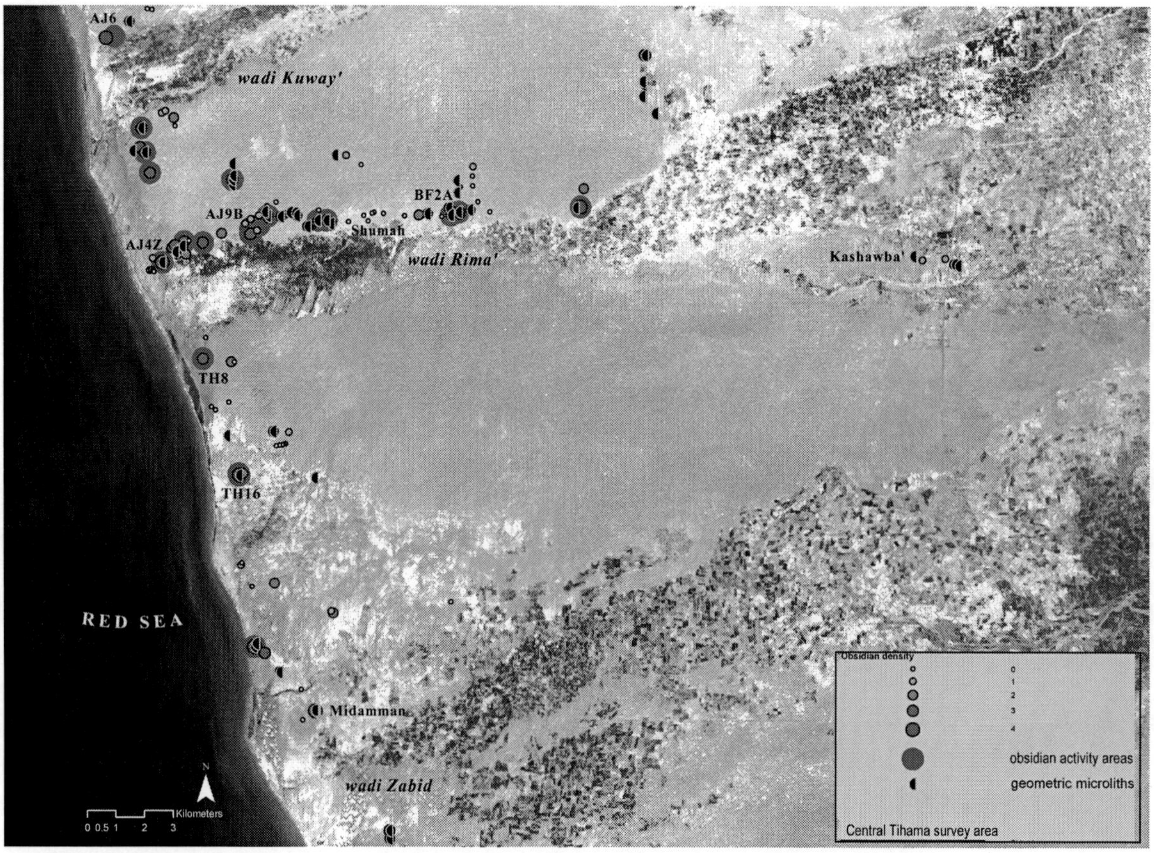

Map 2:2 Satellite map of the Central Tihāmah Survey Area located between the wādī Zabīd to the south and the wādī Kuway' to the north. The circles represent the density of obsidian present in the area (the smallest circles = no obsidian, while the largest circles constitute activity areas with the highest densities of obsidian debitage).

Map by L. Khalidi.

relatively large amounts of small debitage and waste, small globular flake cores and a tool kit consisting of geometric microliths and *pièces esquillées* made from obsidian (Figure 2:1).

Site interaction can be interpreted on a micro-regional level on the basis of the form (tool, debitage, waste) of the obsidian, its context and its distribution. Obsidian geometric microliths and small *pièces esquillées* are found side by side, the latter synonymous with a bipolar flaking technique and an economic use of small amounts of material.[19] The two technologies are found on smaller dispersed sites along the littoral and the riverbanks as well as on significantly larger sites located at the junctures of the rivers, that is to say, along the shoreline and towards the interior where the delta begins to form. Besides the obsidian tools, waste and debitage characterize the lithic assemblages on these sites. Activity areas have been identified where the densities of obsidian are relatively high and the lithic waste suggests knapping (Map 2:2). As at the sites of al-Midamman[20] and Sihi,[21] the presence of small obsidian cores, *batonnêts*, and a high frequency of small flakes and blades present a signature for a bipolar flaking technique on anvil and the preparation of backed geometric microliths by percussion and perhaps on anvil.

The highest density of obsidian is found on sites near the mouths of the deltas and along the littoral, which suggests that the obsidian was arriving by sea (see Map 2:2). The lithic assemblage further suggests that obsidian was being worked in the Tihāmah itself and appears to have arrived in the area in small pre-prepared nodules. Activity areas can be identified interspersed along the riverbanks towards the larger interior sites. Systematic survey was not conducted east of these large interior sites. However, the western escarpment survey located along the interior Wādī Zabīd demonstrated a massive drop-off of obsidian density in the mid-altitude region. Furthermore, the obsidian in this region was of a poorer quality and did not resemble the obsidian of the Tihāmah, nor of the site of al-Midamman, which lies along the Wādī Zabīd and the Red Sea coast.

19 Crassard in press.

20 Crassard in press, Rahimi 2001.

21 Zarins, *et al.* 1986: 43, 48.

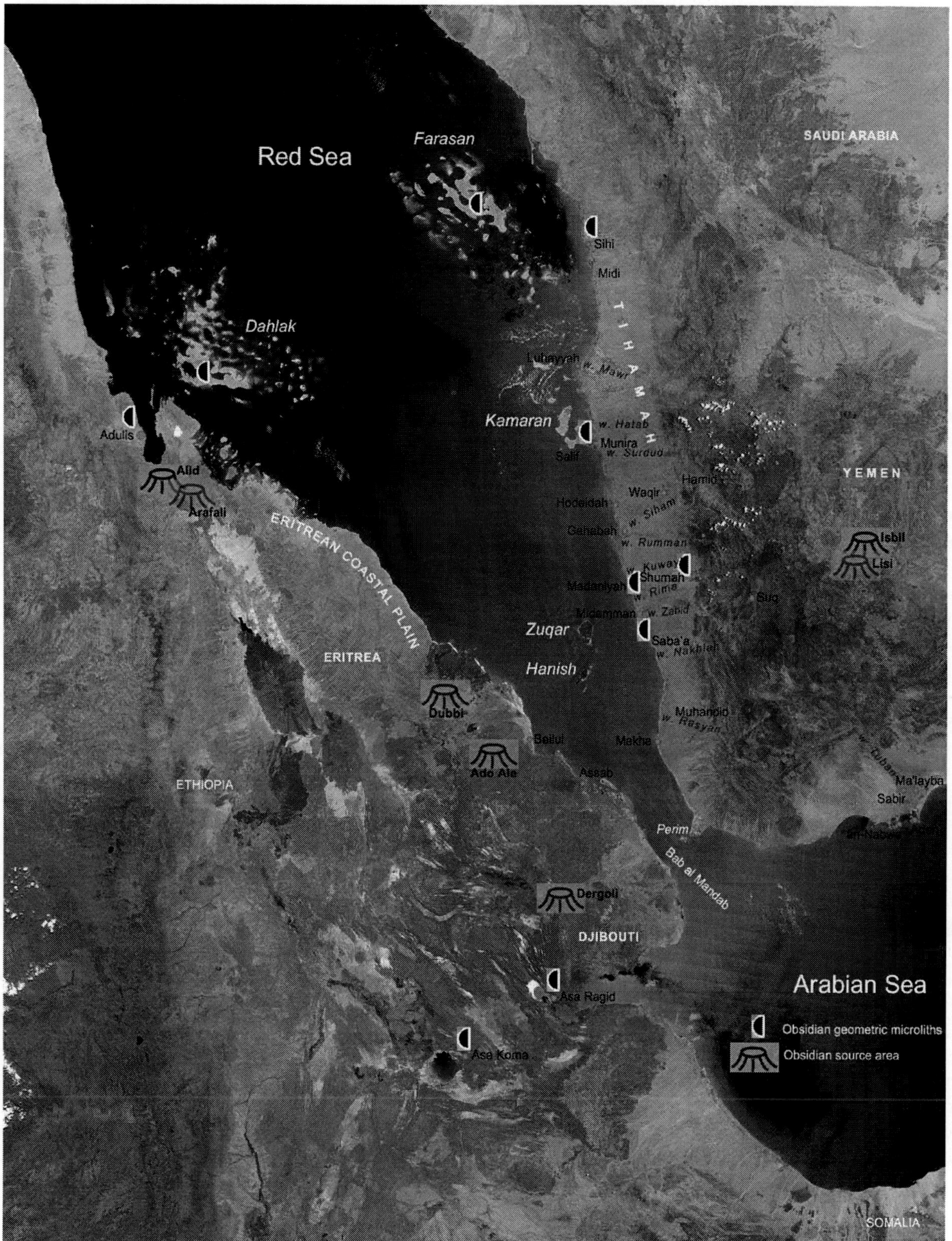

Map 2:3 Satellite image illustrating the location of obsidian source areas and recovered late prehistoric (third to end of first millennium BC*) obsidian geometric microliths in the southern Red Sea regions of Southwest Arabia and the African Horn. Geometric microliths have also been found on sites along the coast of northern Eritrea and Sudan (not on map). These tools are evenly distributed along the length of the Tihāmah coastal plain, while their absence along most of the Eritrean coastline could be explained by the lack of archaeological fieldwork in the area. Map by L. Khalidi.*

In addition to the obsidian densities and distribution signalling its sea-borne transportation, thirty-two samples of this stone collected from fourteen sites were sent to Vincenzo Francaviglia[22] for sourcing analysis. The results also point to a non-Yemen highland origin and most likely to Horn of Africa sources (Map 2:3). Different analytic approaches were used for sourcing the obsidian including traditional XRF, radioactive XRF and tube-XRF in order to retrieve major, minor and significant trace elements. The raw data was studied using discriminant analysis and conventional bi-elemental plots. According to Francaviglia, the results of the plots show that of the samples chosen from these sites, the majority definitely do not originate from known sources in Yemen, that is, Jabal Lisi and Jabal Isbil.[23] In the case of Renfrew's Nb / Zr plot, some ten samples fall in the range of archaeological obsidians from the Wādī Surdud also in the Tihāmah, while some fourteen samples are very similar to obsidian samples from other sites in the Tihāmah and in Eritrea. In bi-elemental plots borrowed from magmatology, some of these thirty samples can be interpreted as having a clearer correlation to certain Ethiopian and Eritrean samples.

The fact that a significant number of the archaeological samples are similar to samples from Eritrea and Ethiopia is important since a large obsidian source area exists directly across the Red Sea.[24] Isolated samples in some of the plots also demonstrate that some of the samples are not related to any analysed archaeological or source samples from either continent. In view of the fact that more archaeological samples from the Arabian side have been analysed and compared to the central Tihāmah survey material, it is likely that these isolated obsidians pertain to un-characterized source areas in the southern Red Sea region, and most likely in the Beilul area in Eritrea. Although an African origin is not certain for all of the obsidian specimens analysed, a discussion of microlithic technologies that are directly related to an African tradition establishes an undeniable contact between the two coasts of the Red Sea.

In most parts of the world, geometric microliths are synonymous with a Palaeolithic and Mesolithic lithic tool technology.[25] The occurrence of these tools in such late contexts in Yemen is extremely perplexing when viewed out of geographic context. This lithic technology occurred in tandem with a bipolar flaking technique throughout the Tihāmah coastal plain and on contemporaneous sites of the third–first millennium BC. Furthermore, both technologies were made on obsidian only. The late occurrence of obsidian geometric microliths and *pièces esquillées* is contemporaneous with a similar phenomenon across the Red Sea.[26]

At the site of Asa Koma in Djibouti (see Map 2:3), for example, 23 per cent of the tool assemblage (consisting of *ca.* 16,000 obsidian tools)[27] were obsidian geometric microliths. In addition, a large number of *pièces esquillées* are represented in association with *bâtonnets*, a waste produced from the bipolar flaking technique. Based on C-14 samples, the dates obtained for this site fall in the second millennium BC.[28] All of the characteristics of the lithic tradition of this site match those of the Tihāmah. Although the site differs in many ways (stone access-ibility, different ceramic tradition) the contemporaneity suggests a parallel mode of existence that is bridged by the Red Sea.

The contemporaneous presence of obsidian geometric microliths on sites along the Horn of Africa coast is common. However, there is a clear temporal distinction between the occurrence of a geometric microlith toolkit in the Tihāmah and its occurrence in the desert fringe and Haḍramawt interior of Yemen where isolated geometric microliths made mainly on chert appear in mid-first millennium BC early historical contexts.[29] The late occurrence of geometric microliths in eastern Yemen, in relation to the contemporaneous late prehistoric occurrence along the opposing shores of the southern Red Sea coast, strongly suggests that the Red Sea was an extension of both coasts and constituted an arena for a seaborne lifestyle. Although some of the obsidian found does not match any archaeological or source samples from either side, the clear link that existed across the Red Sea, demonstrated by the occurrence of contemporaneous lithic tool kits and technologies on both coasts, articulates what is also clear from the results of the obsidian analysis: that the majority of the obsidian originates on the Horn of Africa coast. In addition, the comparison with the Horn of Africa coast demonstrates that the tradition of geometric microliths is more ancient in the Tihāmah than elsewhere in Yemen.[30]

The systematic study of site context, the material, the technology, the waste, and the tools, viewed in relation to their density and distribution, constitute the evidence for the interpretation of material procurement strategies in this area of the Tihāmah coastal plain, as well as for site interaction within the micro-region. Viewed in relation to

22 Institute of Applied Technology at CNR – Istituto per le Tecnologie Applicate ai Beni Culturali, Rome.

23 This data was analysed and interpreted by Dr Francaviglia, personal communication 19 July 2004.

24 see Dubbi and Ado Ale.

25 Andrefsky Jr. 1998: 194.

26 Arkell 1954, Blanc 1952: 355–7, Callow and Wahida 1981: 36, Fattovich 1997: 276, Joussaume 1995: 33–6, 52–3, Paribeni 1907, Zarins 1989: 359.

27 Joussaume 1995: 33–6.

28 Ibid.: 32.

29 Caton Thompson 1938, 1944, 1953, Caton Thompson and Gardner 1939, De Maigret and Antonini 2005: 20, Pl.34a, Inizan and Francaviglia 2002, Sedov 1991.

30 Rahimi 2001.

the landscape evidence and the obsidian source analysis for the prehistoric period, it can be surmised that the majority of the obsidian was procured from the shores of the Horn of Africa, possibly from the Dubbi and / or Ado Ale sources, and arrived in modest quantities as small pre-prepared nodules on the shores of the Tihāmah. Until systematic survey is conducted in this area of the Eritrean coastal plain, it is unclear which sources were being quarried and by whom. It is most likely that fishing and sailing communities had direct access to the source. However, bartering or gift exchange with those who had access is also possible. It is also unclear whether the obsidian was arriving at the large sites that lie at the interface of the rivers and the sea, or else at all of the sites along the coastline. It can further be surmised that the obsidian was then dispersed upriver and knapped at the various smaller riverbank sites. Relatively high obsidian densities and activity areas are visible both along smaller littoral sites as well as at larger coastal sites such as TH8 and al-Midamman (see Map 2:2). Moreover, activity areas are also common along smaller riverbank sites. What is apparent is that the communities of the Tihāmah were clearly linked to those of the opposing coast and were familiar with the seaways of the Red Sea. Regular interaction between these communities may have paved the way for later large-scale maritime trade routes.

It has been demonstrated that the notion of boundaries erodes, and the cultural continuities that permeate imaginary territories are illuminated when the Red Sea is viewed as a point of contact and integration and when transitional communities are studied on a micro-level.

References

Andrefsky Jr., W. 1998. *Lithics: macroscopic approaches to analysis*. Cambridge Manuals in Archaeology. Cambridge: Cambridge University Press.

Arkell, A.J. 1954. Four Occupation Sites at Agordat. *Kush* 2: 51.

Barbanes, E. 2000. Domestic and defensive architecture on the Yemen plateau: eighth century BCE–sixth century CE. *Arabian Archaeology and Epigraphy* 11: 207–22.

Blanc, A.-C. 1952. L'Industrie sur obsidienne des îles Dahlac (Mer Rouge). 355–7 in *Actes du II Congres Panafricain de Préhistoire*. Paris : A.M.G.

Buffa, V. 2002. The Sabir cultural sequence in the frame of the archaeology of coastal Yemen and northeast Africa Bronze Age: A provisional view. *Вестник древней истории* (Наука) 2 : 175–84.

———. 2003. De l'âge du Bronze à la formation des royaumes sud-arabiques. Une synthèse de la periode de transition de la préhistoire récente à la periode sud-arabique. PhD thesis, Université Aix- Marseille I.

Buffa, V. and Vogt, B. 2001. Sabir — Cultural Identity between Saba and Africa. *Migration und Kulturtransfer, Berlin, 2001. Akten des Internationalen Kolloquiums* 2(1): 437–50.

Callow, P. and Wahida, G. 1981. Fieldwork in Northern and Eastern Sudan. *Nyame Akuma: Bulletin of the Society of Africanist Archaeologists* 18: 36.

Cattani, M. and Bokonyi, S. 2002. Ash-Shumah: An Early Holocene Settlement of Desert Hunters and Mangrove Foragers in the Yemeni Tihamah. 3–52 in S. Cleuziou, M. Tosi, and J. Zarins (eds), *Essays on the Late Prehistory of the Arabian Peninsula*, XCII, *Serie Orientale Roma*. Rome: ISIAO.

Costantini, L. 1986. Plant impressions in Bronze Age pottery from Yemen Arab Republic. *East and West* 34: 107–15.

———. 1990. Ecology and farming of the protohistoric communities in the Central Yemeni Highlands. 187–204 in A. De Maigret (ed.), *The Bronze Age Culture of Hawlan at-Tiyal and al-Hada (Republic of Yemen)*. Rome: ISMEO.

Crassard, R. in press. Obsidian lithic industries from al-Midamman (Tihama coast, Yemen). In E.J. Keall (ed.), *Pots, Rocks and Megaliths*. BAR International Series. Oxford: Archaeopress.

Crassard, R. and Khalidi, L. 2005. De la pré-histoire à la préhistoire au Yémen: des données anciennes aux nouvelles expériences méthodologiques. *Chroniques Yéménites* 12: 1–18.

Edens, C. 1999. The Bronze Age of Highland Yemen: chronological and spatial variability of pottery and settlement. *Paléorient* 25: 103–26.

Edens, C. and Wilkinson, T. 1998. Southwest Arabia during the Holocene: recent archaeological developments. *Journal of World Prehistory* 12: 55–119.

Edens, C., Wilkinson, T. and Barratt, G. 2000. Hammat al-Qa and the roots of urbanism in southwest Arabia. *Antiquity* 74: 854–62.

Ekstrom, H. and Edens, C. 2003. Prehistoric Agriculture in Highland Yemen: new results from Dhamar. *Bulletin of the American Institute for Yemeni Studies* 45: 23–35.

Fattovich, R. 1997. The Contacts between Southern Arabia and the Horn of Africa in Late Prehistoric and Early Historical Times: a view from Africa. 273–86 in A. Avanzini (ed.), *Profumi D'Arabia*, II, *Saggi di Storia Antica*. Roma: 'L'ERMA' di Bretschneider.

Fedele, F.G. 1984. Fauna of Wadi Yana'im (WYi), Yemen Arab Republic. *East and West* 34: 117–21.

———. 1985. Research on Neolithic and Holocene paleo-ecology in the Yemeni highlands. *East and West* 35: 369–73.

———. 1990. Man, land and climate: emerging interactions from the Holocene of the Yemen Highlands. 31–42 in S. Bottema, G. Entjes-Nieborg, and W. Van Zeist (eds), *Man's Role in the Shaping of the Eastern Mediterranean Landscape, Proceedings of the Inqua / Bai Symposium on the Impact of Ancient Man on the Landscape of the Eastern Mediterranean Region and the Near East.* Rotterdam / Brookfield: A.A. Balkema.

Francaviglia, V.M. 1989. Obsidian sources in ancient Yemen. 129–34 in A. De Maigret (ed.), *The Bronze Age Culture of Khawlan at-Tiyal and al-Hada (Yemen Arab Republic).* Roma: IsMEO.

Gibson, M. and Wilkinson, T. 1995. The Dhamar Plain, Yemen: a preliminary study of the archaeological landscape. *Proceedings of the Seminar for Arabian Studies* 25: 159–83.

Inizan, M.-L. and Francaviglia, V.M. 2002. Les périples de l'obsidienne à travers la mer Rouge. *Journal des Africanistes* 72: 11–9.

Joussaume, R. 1995. Les premières sociétés de production. 15–63 in R. Joussaume (ed.), *Tiya-l'Éthiopie des Mégalithes: Du biface à l'art rupestre dans la Corne de l'Afrique.* Poitiers: P. Oudin.

Keall, E.J. 1998. Encountering megaliths on the Tihamah coastal plain of Yemen. *Proceedings of the Seminar for Arabian Studies* 28: 139–47.

———. 1999. Archäologie in der Tihamah: Die Forschungen der Kanadischen Archäologischen Mission des Royal Ontario Museum, Toronto. Zabid und Umgebung. *Jemen-Report: Mitteilungen der Deutsch-Jemenitischen Gesellschaft e.V.* 30: 27–32.

———. 2000. Changing settlement along the Red Sea coast of Yemen in the Bronze Age. 719–29 in P. Matthiae, A. Enea, L. Peyronel, and F. Pinnock (eds), *Proceedings of the First International Congress on the Archaeology of the Ancient Near East.* Rome.

———. 2004. Possible connections in antiquity between the Red Sea coast of Yemen and the Horn of Africa. 43–55 in P. Lunde and A. Porter (eds), *Trade and Travel in the Red Sea Region.* Society for Arabian Studies Monographs 2 and BAR International Series 1269. Oxford: Archaeopress.

Khalidi, L. 2006. Settlement, Culture-Contact and Interaction along the Red Sea Coastal Plain, Yemen: the Tihamah cultural landscape in the late prehistoric period, 3000–900 BC. PhD thesis, University of Cambridge.

Maigret, A. De 1981. Two prehistoric cultures and a new Sabaean site in the eastern highlands of North Yemen. *Raydan* 4: 1–13.

———. 1988. The Sabaean archaeological complex in the Wadi Yala. Rome: IsMEO.

———. 1997. L'âge du Bronze sur les Hautes-Terres. 34–9 in C. Robin (ed.), *Yémen: au pays de la reine de Saba.* Paris: Flammarion / Institut du Monde Arabe.

Maigret, A. De, and Antonini, S. 2005. South Arabian Necropolises: Italian excavations at al-Makhdarah and Kharibat al-Ahjur (Republic of Yemen). Rome: IsIAO, volume IV.

Maigret, A. De, Bokonyi, S., Castiello, B., Costantini, L., Di Mario, F., Fedele, F.G., Francaviglia, V.M., Gianni, A., Marcolongo, B., Palmieri, A.M. and Zarattini, A. 1990. *The Bronze Age Culture of Hawlan at-Tiyal and al-Hada (Republic of Yemen).* XXIV. *Istituto Italiano per il Medio ed Estremo Oriente: Centro Studi e Scavi Archeologici.* Rome: ISMEO.

Paribeni, R. 1907. Ricerche nel Luogo dell'Antica Adulis (Colonia Eritrea). *Monumenti Antichi* 18: 445–51.

Phillips, C. 1997. Al-Hamid: a route to the Red Sea? 287–95 in A. Avanzini (ed.), *Profumi D'Arabia: Atti Del Convegno, Saggi di Storia Antica 11.* Roma: 'L'ERMA' di Bretschneider.

———. 1998. The Tihamah *ca.* 5000 to 500 BC. *Proceedings of the Seminar for Arabian Studies* 28: 233–7.

Phillips, C.S. 2005. A preliminary description of the pottery from al-Hamid and its significance in relation to other pre-Islamic sites on the Tihamah. *Proceedings of the Seminar for Arabian Studies* 35: 177–93.

Rahimi, D. 2001. Geometric microliths of Yemen: Arabian Precursors, African Connections. Parting the Red Sea: Holocene interactions between Northeastern Africa and Arabia. *Society for American Archaeology.* Unpublished symposium paper.

Sedov, A.V. 1991. On the Origins of the Agricultural Settlements in Hadramawt. 67–86 in *Arabia Antiqua: early origins of South Arabian states.* Roma: Serie Orientale Roma LXX.

Thompson, G. Caton. 1938. Geology and archaeology of the Hadramaut, Southern Arabia. *Nature* 142: 139–42.

———. 1944. The Tombs and Moon Temple of Hureidha (Hadhramaut). XIII. Reports of the Research Committee of the Society of Antiquaries of London. Oxford: Oxford University Press.

———. 1953. Some Palaeoliths from South Arabia. *Proceedings of the Prehistoric Society* 19: 189–218.

Thompson, G. Caton, and Gardner, E.W. 1939. Climate, irrigation and early man in the Hadramaut. *Geographical Journal* 93: 18–38

Tosi, M. 1985. Archaeological activities in the Yemen Arab Republic, 1985: Tihamah Coastal Archaeology Survey. *East and West* 35: 363–9.

———. 1986. Archaeological activities in the Yemen Arab Republic, 1986: survey and excavations on the coastal plain (Tihamah). *East and West* 36: 400–15.

Vogt, B. 1997. Sabr: une ville de la fin du IIe millénaire dans l'arrière-pays d'Aden. 47–8 in C. Robin (ed.), *Yémen: Au pays de la reine de Saba.* Paris: Flammarion / Institut du Monde Arabe.

Vogt, B. and Sedov, A. 1997. La culture de Sabr, sur la côte yéménite. 42–6 in C. Robin (ed.), *Yémen: Au pays de la reine de Saba.* Paris: Flammarion / Institut du Monde Arabe.

———. 1998. The Sabir culture and coastal Yemen during the second millennium BC: the present state of discussion. *Proceedings of the Seminar for Arabian Studies* 28: 261–70.

Wilkinson, T.J., Edens, C. and Gibson, M. 1997. The Aarchaeology of the Yemen High Plains: a preliminary chronology. *Arabian Archaeology and Epigraphy* 8: 99–142.

Wilkinson, T.J. 1997. Holocene environments of the High Plateau, Yemen: recent geoarchaeological investigations. *Geoarchaeology* 12: 1–32.

———. 2003. The organization of settlement in highland Yemen during the Bronze and Iron Ages. *Proceedings of the Seminar for Arabian Studies* 33: 157–68.

Wilkinson, T.J. and Edens, C. 1999. Survey and excavation in the Central Highlands of Yemen: results of the Dhamar Survey Project, 1996 and 1998. *Arabian Archaeology and Epigraphy* 10: 1–33.

Zarins, J. 1989. Ancient Egypt and the Red Sea trade: the case for obsidian in the predynastic and archaic periods. A. Leonard Jr. and B. B. William (eds), *Essays in Ancient Civilization presented to Helene J. Kantor. SAOC* 47: 339–68.

Zarins, J., and al-Badr, H. 1986. Archaeological investigation in the Southern Tihama Plain II (including Sihi, 217–107 and Sharja, 217–172) 1405/1985. *Atlal* 10: 36–57.

Zarins, J., and Zahrani, A. 1985. Recent archaeological investigations in the Southern Tihama Plain: the sites of Athar, and Sihi, 1404/1984. *Atlal* 9: 65–107, plates 69–96.

Acknowledgments

The fieldwork was funded by the Fulbright IIE, CAORC and the American Institute for Yemeni Studies. I would like to thank the directors and staff of four institutions, the Yemeni General Organization for Antiquities, Museums and Manuscripts (GOAM), the National Museum in Eritrea, the American Institute for Yemeni Studies (AIYS) and the Centre Français d'Archéologie et de Sciences Sociales de Sana'a (CEFAS) that facilitated my stay and my fieldwork in Yemen and Eritrea. Fieldwork would not have been possible without the very few but valuable team members: Krista Lewis, Ahmed al-Mosabi, Essam Hamana and Muhammad al-Qadhi. Finally, I would like to thank several individuals whose help with the material analysis and whose encouragement was invaluable to this research, namely Vincenzo Francaviglia, Marie-Louise Inizan, Tony Wilkinson, Augusta McMahon, Fiona Marshall, Edward Keall, Vittoria Buffa, Marsha Levine, Rémy Crassard and Julien Espagne.

Products from the Red Sea at Petra in the Medieval Period

Stephan G. Schmid and Jacqueline Studer

Introduction

From 1999 (exploration season) and 2000 (first excavation season) respectively, an international project authorized by the Department of Antiquities of Jordan and organized by the Association for the Understanding of Ancient Cultures (AUAC) has been focusing on the ancient structures within the Wādī Farasah East, on the south-eastern periphery of the ancient city of Petra.[1]

Figure 3:1 Petra, Wādī Farasah East. General view of the lower terrace of the Soldier's Tomb complex (Schmid)

Figure 3:2 Petra, Wādī Farasah East. Tentative restitution of the lower terrace of the Soldier's Tomb complex (Wirth & Wirth Architects, Basel)

The aims of the project are to understand the functioning of one of the most prominent funeral complexes of the Nabataean capital. Since a visit by the 'Deutsch-türkische Denkmalschutzkommando' during the First World War it was suspected that the structures in the Wādī Farasah East belong to a more complex unity.[2] Excavations by The International Wadi Farasa Project (IWFP) revealed indeed that rock-cut structures such as a richly decorated tomb and a splendid banqueting hall, together with a two-storied and freely built entrance complex, were inter-connected through a huge *peristyle* courtyard (Figures 3:1 and 3:2). The overall plan and organization of this complex are clearly dependent on the luxury architecture of the Hellenistic and Roman Mediterranean, as displayed in the palaces and *villae* of the upper classes. On the upper terrace of the Wādī Farasah East, a partially rock-cut installation was installed by the Nabataeans in close connection with a huge water basin, the latter being an integral part of a highly sophisticated water management system (see below).

The excavations revealed a precise chronology for the structures, which were initially built during the third quarter of the first century AD, underwent some changes in the early second century AD and collapsed during the violent earthquake of AD 363. In the medieval period a small Crusader community developed within the ruins of the Nabataean structures, apparently defending the access to the 'High Place' on Jabal Mattbah, where a Crusader fortification may have been installed. As for the Nabataean funeral complex, the excavations indicate that it was once richly decorated by wall paintings, polychrome marble slabs and even heating installations in some rooms. These elements are a clear indication of a regular use of the installations going far beyond occasional visits in order to commemorate the deceased.

Comparative studies indicate that such complex installations are rather the rule than the exception within Nabataean funerary architecture. This means that we have to entirely rethink the conception of the famous Nabataean rock-cut façades. As a matter of fact, the façades were an integral part of bigger complexes and they were looking on an interior courtyard, invisible or only partially visible from the outside.

1 Preliminary reports are regularly published in the *Annual of the Department of Antiquities of Jordan*, starting with volume 44, 2000; see also electronic versions of the reports at www.auac.ch/iwfp as well as Schmid 2001; Schmid 2004; Schmid 2006a.

2 Bachmann, Watzinger and Wiegand 1921: 75–94.

Medieval remains in the Wādī Farasah East

It seems as if the complex of the Soldier's Tomb and related structures, as briefly described above, were destroyed during the violent and well attested earthquake of AD 363.[3] The complex had been by this time probably abandoned and no longer regularly maintained for several years. This can be concluded from the fact that most of the floor slabs that originally formed the walking level inside the buildings and within the central courtyard had already disappeared and that when collapsing due to the earthquake, the column drums were falling onto a layer of up to 10 cm of fine sand. Since the latest coins found within destruction debris can be dated to between AD 350 and 360, the earthquake of AD 363 seems the best candidate for that destruction.[4]

After this event, the complex seems to have been abandoned until the medieval period, when on both the lower and the upper terrace, new activities were recorded.[5] These activities clearly show defensive aspects. Constructed in a hurry and without too much care, most structures clearly indicate the builders' aim to hide and to protect themselves. For instance, on the lower terrace, the massive retaining wall that during the Nabataean period zigzagged across the valley in order to increase its static resistance to the natural pressure, was now reinforced and led in a straight line across the whole valley in order to completely lock it up (Figures 3:3 and 3:4). The entrance to the Soldier's Tomb also shows manifest indications of the fear of the medieval builders. In order to considerably narrow the access to the rock-cut tomb, architectural elements of the collapsed Nabataean structures, including several column drums, were used to build a kind of a bastion in front of the opening (Figure 3:5). Apparently in great hurry, the builders even used fragments of the mutilated statues from the *attica* zone of the tomb, as can be illustrated by several fragments of arms and legs found within the medieval walls. This, as well as other indications, point to a medieval reuse of the area in the shape of a small fortress as indicated by Figure 3:6.

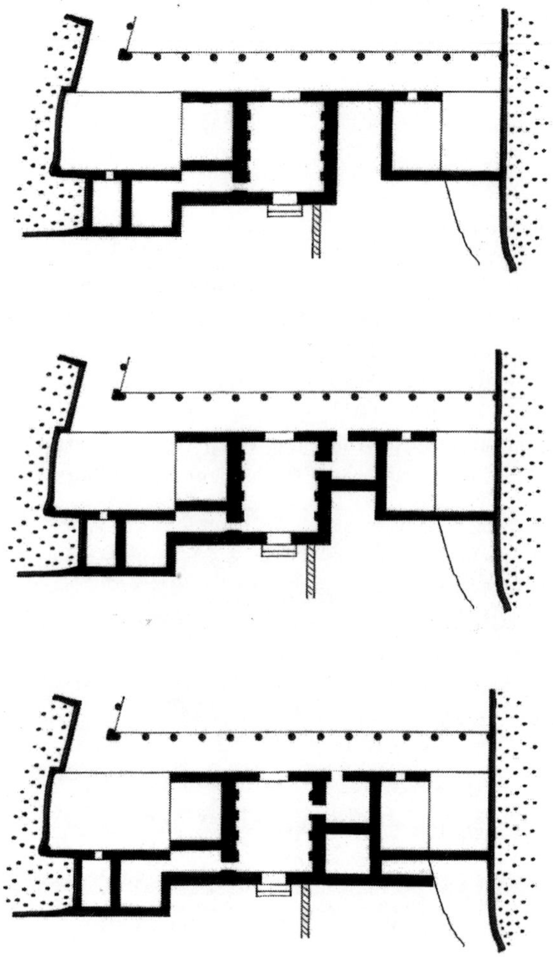

Figure 3:3 Wādī Farasah East, lower terrace. Three phases of main wall; top: Nabataean, centre: Roman, bottom: Medieval (Schmid)

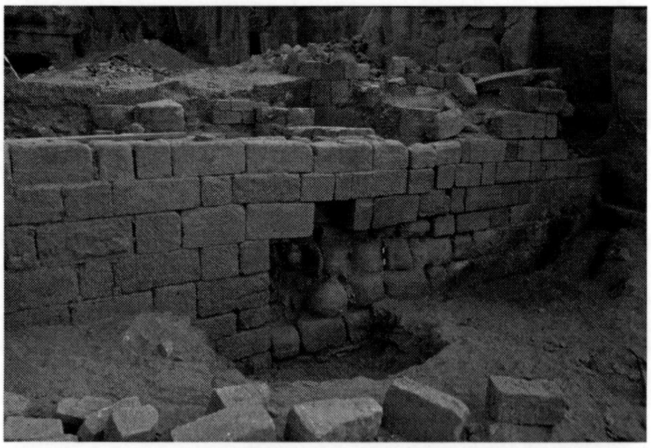

Figure 3:4 Wādī Farasah East, lower terrace. Main wall; in the centre clearly visible the area of the Medieval extension (Schmid)

3 On the earthquake, see Russell 1980.

4 On comparable coins from comparable contexts, see Peter 1996.

5 See Schmid 2006b for an overview of the medieval elements in the Wādī Farasah East.

Figure 3:5 Wādī Farasah East, lower terrace. Entrance to the Soldier's Tomb with Medieval walls using column drums and architectural elements (Schmid)

Figure 3:6 Wādī Farasah East, lower terrace. Tentative restitution of the Soldier's Tomb complex in Medieval times (Schmid)

So far, the clearest evidence for the medieval period was obtained from the upper terrace of the Wādī Farasah East. As briefly mentioned above, the main structure of that terrace is the huge water basin, clearly visible in the form of its massive retaining wall on the right of Figure 3:7. In the Nabataean period a partly rock-cut and partly free-built structure (on the left on Figure 3:7) was closely connected to the basin. As a matter of fact, this structure turned out to be the Nabataean version of a Hellenistic-Roman *peristyle* house.

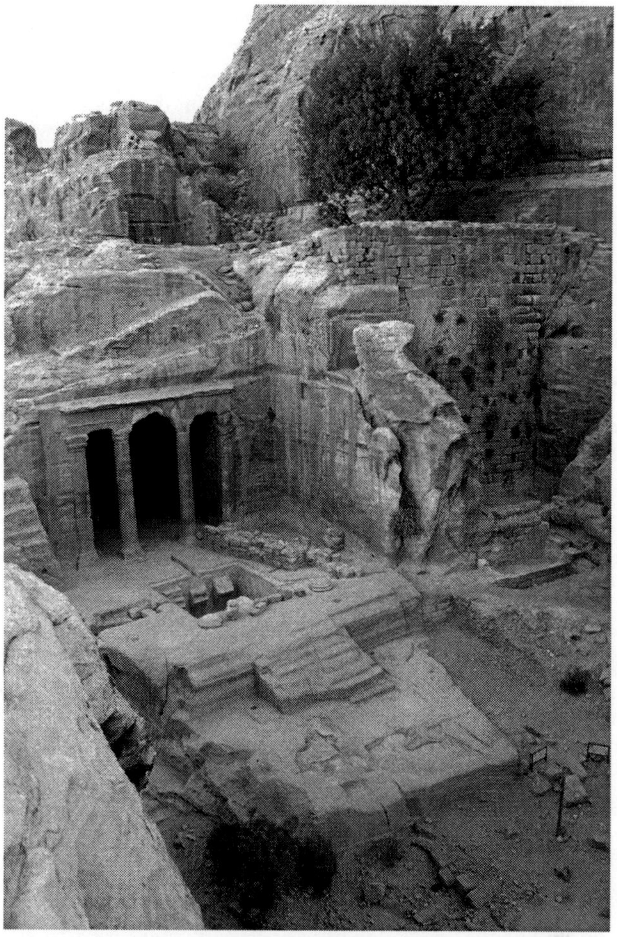

Figure 3:7 Wādī Farasah East, upper terrace. Nabataean peristyle house, partially rock-cut, partially built (left) and Nabataean water basin (right) (Schmid)

A small courtyard was built around a cistern that in turn was cut in the rocky plateau (Figure 3:8) while two comfortable rooms connected to the courtyard were cut into the rock on the southern side of the construction. Further, the *peristyle* had an upper floor that allowed a free circulation between the house and the water basin and related structures. The whole unity shows similarities to rich Hellenistic houses like the ones known from Delos or to Roman villas as seen in Pompeii.[6] The central cistern was fed from water coming from the huge retaining basin and led into it through a built and rock-cut water channel. Related to the large cistern measuring 4 x 4 m is a smaller overflow basin, showing a common depth of 2.40 m with the cistern (Figure 3:8).

6 For the Delian houses, see, for example, Kreeb 1988; Trümper 1998; on Pompeii, see Zanker 1995 and generally on Italian houses Clarke 1991.

Excavation of the area of the former *peristyle* courtyard revealed further information. The material from the cistern's fill contained much of the stone blocks that were originally used in order to build the three massive vaults that covered the cistern. This massive destruction debris probably explains why the large cistern was not reused in the Medieval period, contrary to the small cistern next by (see below). The fill of the bigger cistern contained in its upper part some medieval pottery,[7] in the middle part were late Roman and Byzantine elements, including a fragmentary Greek inscription, and in the lower part exclusively Nabataean pottery. In the lower fill also two column bases of attic type were found, belonging to a type common in first-century AD Petra.[8] Towards the bottom of the large cistern considerable amounts of plaster that originally covered the walls of the cistern were found; these must have fallen into it when it was destroyed. These plaster remains were used in order to get a precise dating for the construction of the cistern: several small pottery fragments found within the plaster belong to phase 3a of Nabataean pottery,[9] indicating, therefore, a *terminus ad quem* of the second and third quarter of the first century AD for the construction of this cistern and the related structures. The covering of the cistern and its considerable depth show that drinking water in large quantities was needed for the *peristyle* house. The clearly indicated use of large quantities of drinkable water strongly points to a profane use of the entire complex and against a cultic or funeral aspect. The profane aspect of our complex is further supported by its opening towards the south. Such an orientation, combined with the courtyard in front of it, guarantees less heat in summer and less cold in winter. Therefore, according to Vitruvius, such was the location of the most important rooms in the Greek house, the *triclinia* or *andrones*.[10] Indeed, similar arrangements were identified within rich houses and palaces of the late Classical and Hellenistic periods in Greece.[11]

Excavation of the small cistern revealed that it was almost exactly the same depth as the large cistern, i.e. roughly 2.40 m, while its length is 1.45 m and its width 1.00 m. Unlike the large cistern next to it, the small one was apparently reused during a long period of time, as it contained large amounts of medieval pottery, some of it lavishly painted (Figures 3:9 and 3:10). This pottery can be dated to the eleventh to thirteenth century AD and is usually called 'Ayyūbid-Mamlūk pottery.[12] More neutrally, such painted pottery can be called *Middle Islamic Hand-Made Geometrically Painted Ware.*[13] So far no wheel-thrown and no glazed pottery has been found. As previously suggested, this could point to a rather local aspect of that medieval occupation. So far, all of the motifs of the handmade painted pottery seem to fit the known, repertoire previously attested for Jordan.[14]

Figure 3:8 Wādī Farasah East, upper terrace. Cistern in front of Nabataean house with small basin (right) and Medieval walls (left) (Schmid)

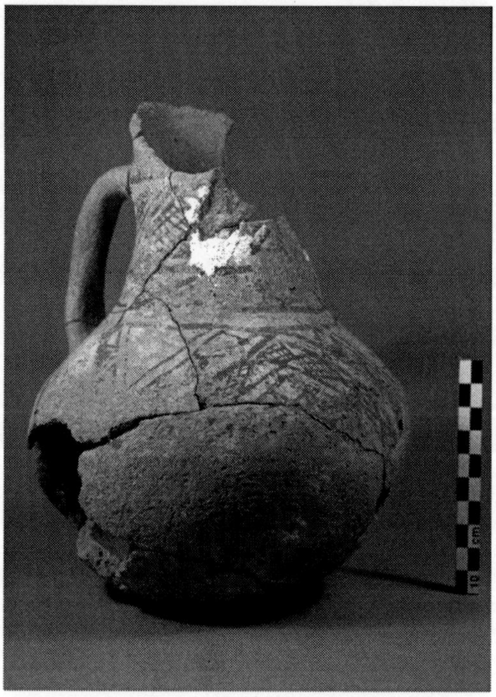

Figure 3:9 Wādī Farasah East, upper terrace. Middle Islamic Hand-Made Geometrically Painted Ware from small basin (Schmid)

7 See also IWFP 2001.

8 McKenzie 1990: pl. 50e, and 50g.

9 On the typology and chronology of Nabataean fine ware pottery, see Schmid 2000.

10 Vitr., *de archit.* VII 149, 3f.

11 Reber 1998: 166–9; Zoppi 1991–1992.

12 For similar pottery, see Walmsley and Grey 2001: 153–9; Tonghini and Vanni Desideri 2001; Pringle 1984, 1985; on local aspects of Late Islamic pottery in central and southern Jordan see Brown 1987, 1988, 1991: 232–41; in general terms on that period in Jordan, see Walmsley 2001.

13 Johns 1998.

14 Homès-Fredericq and Franken 1986: 242f.

Figure 3:10 Wādī Farasah East, upper terrace. Middle Islamic Hand-Made Geometrically Painted Ware from small basin (Schmid)

The intense sieving of the contents of the small cistern revealed large amounts of bones. This is of particular interest as they can be surely connected to the eating habits of the above-mentioned medieval community (see below). In conclusion, the small cistern seems to have served as a kind of rubbish-pit during the medieval period. Further, late modification related to the built and rock-cut structure indicates also that on the upper terrace the same defensive aspects ruled during the medieval period. Once the large cistern was filled in, several walls were built at the spot, showing a rather careless technique and a lot of reused material (Figures 3:11 and 3:12). These walls belong to the medieval period, as is underlined by the considerable amount of pottery from the eleventh to thirteenth century that was found, including some handmade painted shards (Figure 3:13) belonging to the same types as discussed above. Beside the painted pottery large quantities of plain, hand-made pottery were found, including a pottery lamp. Medieval household activities are attested, for example by a stone mortar. Interestingly, within the debris between the medieval walls, five tombstones were found, including one showing a cross and others showing a kind of symbol of the tree of life (Figures 3:14 and 3:15). The tombstones were dumped in that area and it has not been possible so far to localize the spot of their primary use and, therefore, the cemetery of the medieval Wādī Farasah community.

Figure 3:11 Wādī Farasah East, upper terrace. Medieval walls on top of Nabataean cistern from North (Schmid)

Figure 3:12 Wādī Farasah East, upper terrace. Medieval walls on top of Nabataean cistern from East (Schmid)

Figure 3:13 Wādī Farasah East, upper terrace. Middle Islamic Hand-Made Geometrically Painted Ware from Medieval structures (Schmid)

The precise connection and interpretation of these tombstones is also rather difficult. Both the cross and the symbol of the tree clearly belong to Christian funerary iconography.[15] The question remains, however, whether we can connect them to a Crusader occupation or to a substrate of a local Christian community. The type of cross represented on the tombstone (Figure 3:14) does also occur on Crusader coins,[16] but for the rest, unfortunately, the funerary iconography of the Crusaders has been analysed only very summarily so far.[17]

Figure 3:14 Wādī Farasah East, upper terrace. Gravestone with cross from Medieval structures (Schmid)

It becomes, however, all the more evident that an important medieval occupation has to be located in the Wādī Farasah East, possibly connected with a Crusader fortress on top of Jabal al-Madhbah.[18] As the medieval walls on the left of Figure 3:11 contain a threshold and, therefore, most probably formed the main entrance to the complex during that period, and since it runs in the direction of the eastern column of the Nabataean *peristyle* house, it can be supposed that during this later occupation the space between the columns was closed by secondary walls and access was given only via a small corridor (Figure 3:16). This hypothesis is confirmed by a nineteenth-century sketch by Linant de Bellefonds that shows the 'Garden Triclinium' still with some remains of walls between the columns,[19] and even on photographs published by Brünnow and von Domaszewski as well as by Dalman, remains of these walls were still clearly visible.[20]

Figure 3:15 Wādī Farasah East, upper terrace. Gravestone with tree of life from Medieval structures (Schmid)

15 On these symbols, see *Dictionnaire d'archéologie chrétienne et de liturgie* 1, 2. Paris: Letouzey et Ané 1907: 2691–709 s.v. arbres [H. Leclerq] and *Dictionnaire d'archéologie chrétienne et de liturgie* 3, 2. Paris: Letouzey et Ané 1914: 3045–131 s.v. croix et crucifix [H. Leclerq] especially 3054 no. 3362 for a stylized tree as symbol on a tombstone.

16 Boas 1999: 183f.

17 In general, see, for example, Boas 1999: 226–36.

18 Vannini and Vanni Desideri 1995: 512.

19 Laborde and Bellefonds 1828, repr. 1994: pl. 30.

20 Brünnow and Domaszewski 1904: 276 figure 308; Dalman 1908: 195 fig. 116.

Figure 3:16 Wādī Farasah East, upper terrace. Tentative restitution of Medieval remains (Schmid)

A medieval occupation of that part of Petra has been supposed since Brünnow and von Domaszewski found what they believed to be a Crusader tombstone inside the Nabataean *peristyle* house,[21] that is, only a few metres from the spot were we found five more in the last few years. The impressive amount of new data on the medieval period occupation collected so far by the International Wadi Farasa Project needs some explanation. For the time being, it seems very tempting to connect these observations with a supposed Crusader fortress on top of Jabal al-Madhbah.[22] The fact that the medieval Wādī Farasah community apparently put considerable efforts into the restoration and even extension of the main terracing wall of the lower terrace (see above) could indeed point to a military character of this occupation. Although a very logical interpretation, the problem is that so far no medieval reuse or occupation of the Jabal al-Madhbah is attested and the small Crusader post in the Wādī Farasah East remains, therefore, rather isolated and in a not very advantageous strategic situation.[23]

Faunal remains

As pointed out above, an assemblage of animal bones was recovered from the smaller overflow-basin on the upper terrace of the Wādī Farasah East. According to the archaeological context this structure was probably used as a rubbish pit by the soldiers stationed in Wādī Farasah during the eleventh to thirteenth centuries AD. The presence of Crusaders in the *wādī* is attested too by a huge retaining wall and other architectural finds which appear to correspond to a guard post controlling the route to the top of Jabal al-Madhbah where a medieval castle may have stood (see above).

The faunal sample recovered from the cistern represents a homogeneous unit. It comprises 936 bones of which 573 (63 per cent) represent remains of terrestrial mammals and 359 (39 per cent) bones of fish.[24] Bones of birds were not found, while molluscs are represented by a fragment of a Red Sea shell *Pinctada margaritifera*, and three fragments of land-snail. Sheep and goat (caprines) were the most common mammals, with more sheep represented than goats (3:1). Isolated remains of cattle (representing a calf aged less than one year old) and a small wild carnivore (a beech marten or a marbled polecat) were recovered; the latter may represent an intrusive element. A minimum number of eight caprines are represented, including at least six young animals (less than two years old) and two senile adults. Body-part representation shows a bias in favour of forelimb (23 per cent), hindlimb (25 per cent) and cranial elements (30 per cent), with relatively few trunk and lower foot elements.[25] The first two body-part categories are especially rich in meat, while the cranium contains the brain and tongue, which are considered culinary delicacies in many cultures. Fine filleting marks (on two hyoid bones) indicate consumption of the latter organ. The assemblage had been ravaged by dogs or small-sized wild carnivores. A total of twenty-eight bones show typical canid gnawing, and a further three exhibit surface erosion resulting from ingestion by carnivores. The majority of long bones lack ends, while destruction of the soft trunk elements (vertebrae and ribs) may also be attributed to carnivore activity. Consequently, carnivores, possibly dogs, appear to have played a critical role in determining skeletal element representation in the sample. There is a marked under-representation of lower limb elements — metapodials and foot bones. Since these are amongst the most robust bones in the skeleton,[26] it seems unlikely that carnivore action is solely responsible for their rarity. These elements are common discards of primary butchery: indeed, their absence may indicate that the caprines were not slaughtered on-site. Marks relating to carcass processing and food preparation are found on 5 per cent of caprine bones. Of particular interest is the presence of short and superficial cut marks which relate to

21 Brünnow and Domaszewski 1904: 275 fig. 307; Dalman 1908: 196 fig. 117; Brünnow 1909: 249f.; Lindner 1997: 104 with n. 10.

22 Vannini and Vanni Desideri 1995: 512.

23 See the remarks by Bellwald 2006: 72–4.

24 Schmid and Studer 2003 : fig.32.

25 Ibid.: fig. 33.

26 Lyman 1994: Table 7.6.

dismemberment of the hindlimb and upper forelimb from the carcass (acetabulum of pelvis, proximal radius), and others which indicate separation of the skull and mandible (occipital condyles and hyoid). Of the 27 ribs represented, 16 have had at least one end severed. This is a common butchery pattern resulting from division of the carcass into two equal portions, by cutting vertically through the rib cage down the vertebral column.

A third of the assemblage is made up of fish bones. This relatively high proportion of fish bones is undoubtedly due to the fact that all sediment from the basin was sieved using a fine 0.5 cm mesh. Although the frequency of fish reflects their importance in the diet, due to their small size they contributed significantly less protein than sheep and goat. All of the 218 identified fish bones from Wādī Farasah represent Red Sea species. With the exception of a single bone of a wrasse, the clown Coris (*Coris aygula)*, all material belongs to parrotfish, a common Red Sea fish family which inhabit the coastal waters and feed on the coral reefs.[27] The ichthyofaunal assemblage from Wādī Farasah contains a minimum number of eleven individual fishes. The largest individuals are two Bluebarred parrotfish (*Scarus ghobban*) with a standard length of slightly more than 50 cm. This species can attain a length of at least 57 cm and is the largest *Scarus* living in the Red Sea.[28] A second, slightly smaller parrotfish of the genus *Scarus*, with a length of around 40 cm, is represented by a dozen bones. The clown Coris (*Coris aygula)* also falls within this medium-large sized group. It is represented by an isolated lower pharyngeal bone (Figure 3:17) that derives from an individual with a standard length of about 40 cm.

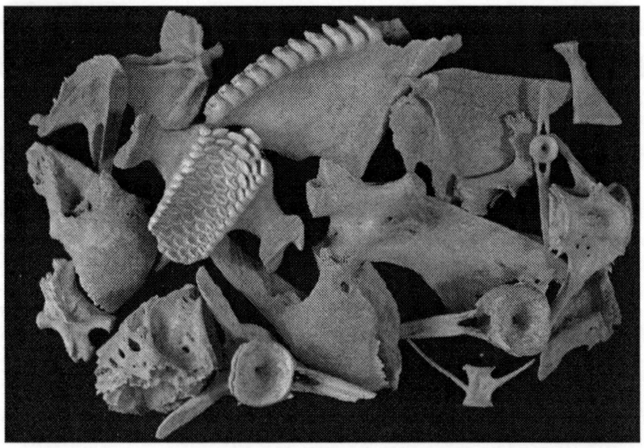

Figure 3:17 Wādī Farasah East, upper terrace. Parrotfish remains from small basin (Museum d'Histoire naturelle, Geneva)

Seven parrotfish represent medium-sized individuals (25–35 cm), while the smallest parrotfish had a standard length of 20 cm. It is important to note that the different size classes of parrotfish are represented at Wādī Farasah by all skeletal elements, demonstrating that complete fish were brought to the site.

As shown above, the Wādī Farasah assemblage exhibits several distinguishing features: a very high proportion of fish compared to mammalian remains; a narrow range of species with sheep and goat the major meat source; a biased body part representation with few foot and trunk elements, which may in part be due to human activity and partly due to carnivore action. The limited diet, of caprine meat and parrotfish, may well reflect the menu of soldiers garrisoned in a guard post and fed rations brought in from elsewhere. The high frequency of fish remains, as well as the preferential selection of meat-rich limb bones for sheep and goat, may be understand as representing food that can be easily stored or prepared. It is therefore interesting to explore whether these features are typical of such sites. Two Crusader assemblages from the southern Levant which may serve for comparison with Wādī Farasah are the village fortress of al-Burj al-Aḥmar (the Red Tower), located on the coastal plain of Israel, and Belmont Castle located on the outskirts of Jerusalem.

The site of al-Burj al-Aḥmar has been identified as a Templar fort, which was occupied from AD 1191 to 1390. Phase B, which represents the Crusader construction phase, yielded only 16 bones of sheep/goat, 6 of cattle and 1 equid bone.[29] A larger sample was retrieved from Phase C, which dates to AD 1191–1248 and contained 49 pig bones, 8 sheep / goat remains, and several bones of goose and chicken which, according to the archaeo-zoologist, may relate to a single meal. No cattle or equid bones were recovered. The assemblage from al-Burj al-Aḥmar therefore differs markedly from that of Wādī Farasah. It contains hunted and/or trapped terrestrial *taxa*: deer, gazelle, hare, while of the domestic animals, birds (chicken and goose) as well as pigs were the most common *taxa* consumed. Surprisingly few remains of sheep, goat and cattle were recovered. No data was given in the report on skeletal element representation or on the age and sex of animals represented and no fish remains are reported from this site.[30] Horwitz has suggested that the al-Burj al-Aḥmar assemblage primarily contained domestic animals that could easily be raised within the enclosed environment of a village-fortress, while those which require access to pasture located outside the confines of the site, were not kept.[31] It may be concluded then, that the al-Burj al-Aḥmar assemblage reflects exploitation of local animals: either those kept within the confines of the fort, or else those hunted in its immediate environs.

27 Randall 1983: 126, Bellwood 1994: 7.
28 Randall 1983.
29 Cartledge 1986.
30 Ibid.
31 Horwitz 1999: 375–6.

The second assemblage is derived from Belmont Castle located on the outskirts of Jerusalem. It has been suggested that it represents a rural manor house which was converted by the Hospitallers (after AD 1140), into a castle.[32] The animal bone assemblage recovered from the Crusader phase at Belmont comprises 860 identified remains.[33] Unlike Wādī Farasah or al-Burj al-Aḥmar, it is characterized by almost equal frequencies of caprines (29 per cent), cattle (21 per cent) and pigs (27 per cent). Birds, primarily chicken, constitute 20 per cent of the remains and fish less than 2 per cent. Isolated bones of camel and equids were also recovered as well as remains of two wild species, fox and fallow deer.

Sheep and goat appear to have been kept in similar numbers by the Crusaders. Croft noted that 42 per cent of caprines died before reaching 2.5 years of age, which is a mortality pattern associated with meat rather than milk production.[34] The small size of the bone sample does, however, necessitate caution in interpreting these remains. Half the cattle were slaughtered as juveniles and 40 per cent lived into adulthood, reflecting a mixed exploitation pattern. Clearly pigs were slaughtered for meat, with 66 per cent culled as infants, 10 per cent as juveniles and 30 per cent as sub-adults with none surviving into adulthood. This demonstrates that the Crusaders did not breed this species. Body-part representation of caprines, cattle and pigs at Belmont Castle was similar and all skeletal elements are represented. Trunk and cranial parts were not studied in the same manner as at Wādī Farasah. Even without these skeletal parts, when the other body-part categories are calculated in the same manner for both sites, even without these skeletal parts, it is clear that lower foot elements (20 per cent) as well as forelimbs_ (20 per cent) and hind limbs (12 per cent) are represented in higher proportions at Belmont than at Wādī Farasah. Unfortunately, no species' identifications are available for the sixteen fish remains from Belmont. Irrespective of their aquatic origin, they would have been imported to the site.

In contrast to Wādī Farasah, primarily locally available species were exploited at the other two Crusader military sites in the region, especially domestic herd animals. Literary sources indicate that the communal kitchen of the Crusader hospital in Jerusalem prepared pork and/or mutton three days of the week, while the private kitchen serving nobility offered lighter foods such as chicken, pullet, pigeon, partridge, lamb, kid, eggs and fish.[35] The presence of mainly young sheep / goat at both Wādī Farasah and Belmont Castle would indicate that prime meat animals were consumed at both sites. However, the high frequency of Red Sea fish recovered from Wādī Farasah is unique, and does not appear to be a signature of Crusader military sites in the southern Levant.

Table 3:1 presents currently available data on the presence of imported fish species in Crusader sites from the region. Although only a few relevant data sets are available, it is evident that even sites located on the Mediterranean Sea coast contained remains of traded fish, with parrotfish recovered from both Jaffa and Ashqelon, sites that are located respectively 250 km and 225 km from the source. Like Wādī Farasah, both these sites are located on trade routes, indicating a direct association between the two.

Given the great distance to the Red Sea from these sites, it is probable that parrotfish were caught in the Red Sea and then preserved by sun-drying, smoking or salting. Drying arrests bacterial decay and prevents infestation by flies but not by insects such as dermestid beetles. Dried fish may however be stored for several months. Salting of fish facilitates even longer storage.[36] Today, Egyptian fisherman preserve parrotfish as dried and salted boneless fish fillets,[37] while Bedouin fisherman prepare complete small parrotfish or emperors.[38] The presence at Wādī Farasah of bones from different parts of the skeleton indicates that whole fish and not only fillets were imported. Once preserved, the fish could easily be transported and stored until required for consumption, making it a perfect dietary element for military rations as at Wādī Farasah.

Van Neer, *et al.* have summarized available data on trading of fish for archaeological sites in the Eastern Mediterranean. They concluded that the wide distribution of Nile fish in the Islamic and Crusader periods (traded dried), followed the same pattern as in Roman and Byzantine times, 'indicating the continuing potential for exchange of needs and benefits between the two neighbouring regions'.[39] The same conclusion may be reached for parrotfish which, as illustrated in their gazetteer,[40] occur in Roman-Byzantine sites throughout the southern Levant. Some examples are: Tell Hesban (250 km from source), the Armenian Monastery, Jerusalem (240 km from source), Tel Ashqelon (225 km from source), Ein Gedi (220 km from source), Horvat Karkur (200 km from source) and En Boqeq, Tel Malhata and Upper Zohar (190 km from source).

32 Pringle 2000: 213.
33 Croft 2000.
34 Ibid.: 179.
35 Pringle 2000: 218–9.

36 Van Neer, *et al.* 2004.
37 Hamilton-Dyer 1994.
38 Studer, personal observations on the Sinai coast of the Gulf of 'Aqabah, 2004.
39 Van Neer, *et al.* 2004: 129.
40 Ibid.

Site	Site Location	Fish Species	Source	Source to Site distance in km
Caesarea	Mediterranean coast	Nile perch	Nile River	400
		Catfish	Coastal river/ Sea of Galilee	0 70
		Tilapia	Coastal river/ Sea of Galilee	0 70
Jaffa	Mediterranean coast	Parrotfish	Red Sea	250
Tel Ashqelon	Mediterranean coast	Catfish Parrotfish	Coastal river Red Sea	50 225
Belmont Castle	Jerusalem		Red Sea Mediterranean Sea Nile River Jordan River Coastal rivers	240 50 410 32 45
Wādī Farasa	Petra	Parrotfish	Red Sea	250

Table 3:1 Traded fish found in Crusader sites (after Van Neer, et al. *2004: Table 3, completed by J. Studer)*

NISP	EZ	EZ	JH	WF
	Nab	LR	Byz	Cr
MAMMAL	83%	64%	9%	61%
BIRD	8%	14%	1%	1%
FISH	2%	38%	90%	38%
parrot fish	4%	20%	73%	99.6%
other species	96%	80%	27%	0.4%

Table 3:2: Synoptic table of faunal remains in the Petra area (J. Studer)

Examination of faunal data for earlier sites in the Petra region indicates that parrotfish were exploited in all periods (Table 3:2). They constitute only 4 per cent of the identified fish remains from Nabataean levels and 20 per cent in Late Roman deposits from the city of Petra.[41] Parrotfish increase to 73 per cent in the Byzantine period when they are the most common fish species in the region.[42] This pattern is maintained in the Crusader period.

Red Sea Scaridae also made their way to Egypt and are found in Roman sites along the desert trade routes such as al-Zarkeh (*ca.* 65 km inland on the Qifṭ–al-Quṣayr al-Qadīm road), Mons Porphyrites and Mons Claudianus (each *ca.* 50 km inland on the Abū Sha'ar–Nile road), and at the site of Shenhur in the vicinity of Coptos in the Nile Valley, where 'the Romans controlled and taxed the Red Sea transit traffic *en route* to Alexandria, where goods could be put on sale, processed into artisanal products or transhipped into the Mediterranean.'[43] As illustrated in Table 3:2, there is continuity in exploitation of this fish family as a food source, probably because they are

41 Desse-Berset and Studer 1991.

42 Studer 2001.

43 Van Neer, *et al.* 2004: 137.

extremely suitable for drying/salting, and are still commercially exploited in this manner.

Conclusions

It may be concluded that parrotfish were an easily available food source and became an increasingly common trade item from the Early Roman period onwards. Thus, despite their relatively isolated location inland, the Crusaders in Petra appear to have participated in regional trade systems or perhaps even controlled the caravan route between Petra and 'Aqabah. Although the Crusaders had placed several garrisons between Shobak and 'Aqabah (that had two small fortresses), they never had the means to control the territory in Transjordan on a wider scale.[44] It is, therefore, more likely that the different concentrations of Crusader populations, like the one in the Wādī Farasah East, were provided with food and other goods by trading with the local population. Especially in our case, this can be shown when comparing the situation inside Petra and more specifically in the Wādī Farasah East with results from the village of Wādī Mūsa.[45] In the area of Khirbat al-Nawafla, near the spring of 'Ayn Mūsa, nowadays an integral part of Wādī Mūsa, important quantities of remains from Red Sea parrotfish were found.[46] In contrast to Wādī Farasah East, at Khirbat al-Nawafla important traces of agricultural production and various handicrafts were attested for that period. This is a clear indication that in Transjordan the Crusaders were essentially dependent on the local and regional economy being under the control of the local population.

References

'Amr, K. 2006. Die Kreuzritter und die Oliven von les Vaux Moïses, 6–26 in Ritterhausgesellschaft Bubikon (ed.), *Die Kreuzzüge. Petra — Eine Spurensuche.* Tann: Ritterhausgesellschaft Bubikon.

Bachmann, W., Watzinger, C. and Wiegand, Th. 1921. *Petra. Wissenschaftliche Veröffentlichungen des deutsch-türkischen Denkmalschutz-Kommandos, Heft 3.* Berlin/Leipzig: Walter de Gruyter.

Bellwald, U. 2006. Die Kreuzritter in Petra. Warum waren sie dort? 60–80 in Ritterhausgesellschaft Bubikon (ed.), *Die Kreuzzüge. Petra — Eine Spurensuche.* Tann: Ritterhausgesellschaft Bubikon.

Bellwood, D.R. 1994. A Phylogenetic Study of the Parrotfishes Family Scaridae (Pisces: Labroidei), with a Revision of Genera. *Records of the Australian Museum*, supplement 20. Sydney: Australian Museum.

Boas, A.J. 1999. *Crusader Archaeology. The Material Culture of the Latin East.* London & New York: Routledge.

Brown, R.M. 1987. A 12th-Century AD Sequence from Southern Transjordan. Crusader and Ayyubid Occupation at el-Wu`eira. *Annual of the Department of Antiquities of Jordan* 31: 267–88.

——. 1988. Summary Report of the 1986 Excavations: Late Islamic Shobak. *Annual of the Department of Antiquities of Jordan* 32: 225–45.

——. 1991. Ceramics from the Kerak Plateau. 168–279 in J.M. Miller (ed.), *Archaeological Survey of the Kerak Plateau.* Atlanta, GA: Scholars Press.

Brünnow, R.E. 1909. Review of G. Dalman, Petra und seine Felsheiligtümer. *Zeitschrift des Deutschen Palästina-Vereins* 32: 247–51.

Brünnow, R.E. and Domaszewski, A. v. 1904. *Die Provincia Arabia. Auf Grund zweier in den Jahren 1897 und 1908 unternommener Reisen und der Berichte früherer Reisender.* Strassburg: Trübner.

Cartledge, J. 1986. Faunal remains. 176–86 in D. Pringle, *et al.* (eds), *The Red Tower 'al-Burg al-Ahmar'.* London: British School of Archaeology in Jerusalem.

Clarke, J.R. 1991. *The Houses of Roman Italy, 100 BC–AD 250. Ritual, Space and Decoration.* Berkeley: University of California Press.

Croft, P. 2000. The faunal remains. 173–94 in R.P. Harper and D. Pringle (eds), *Belmont Castle.* Oxford: Oxford University Press.

Dalman, G. 1908. *Petra und seine Felsheiligtümer.* Leipzig: Hinrich.

Desse-Berset, N. and Studer, J. 1996. Fish Remains from Ez Zantur (Petra, Jordan). 381–7 in *Petra, Ez Zantur I. Ergebnisse der Schweizerisch-Liechtensteinischen Ausgrabungen 1988–1992.* Terra Archaeologica II. Monographien der Schweizerisch-Liechtensteinischen Stiftung für Archäologische Forschungen im Ausland. Mayence: von Zabern.

Hamilton-Dyer, S. 1994. Preliminary report on the fish remains from Mons Claudianus, Egypt. *Offa 51, Archaeo-Ichthyological Studies, Neumünster*: 275–8.

Homès-Fredericq, D. and Franken, H.J. (eds). 1986. *Pottery and Potters — Past and Present. 7000 Years of Ceramic Art in Jordan.* Tübingen: Attempto Verlag.

Horwitz, L.K. 1999. The Sumaqa Fauna. 369–78 in S. Dar, *A Roman and Byzantine Jewish Village on Mount Carmel, Israel.* BAR International Series 815. Oxford: Archaeopress.

Johns, J. 1998. The Rise of Middle Islamic Hand-Made Geometrically Painted Ware in Bilad al-Sham (11th-13th Centuries AD). 65–93 in R.-P. Gayraud (ed.), *Colloque international sur l'archéologie islamique. IFAO, Le Caire, 3–7 février 1993.* Cairo: Institut français d'archéologie orientale.

44 See the overview in 'Amr 2006: 18-21; Bellwald 2006: 76–80.

45 'Amr 2006: 21–6.

46 Ibid.: 24–5 with figure 32.

Kreeb, M. 1988. *Untersuchungen zur figürlichen Ausstattung delischer Privathäuser*. Chicago: Ares Publishers Inc.

Laborde, L. and Linant de Bellefonds, L.M.A. 1828; re-éd. 1994. *Pétra retrouvée. Voyage de l'Arabie Pétrée*. Ch. Augé and P. Linant de Bellefonds (eds). Paris: Pygmalion.

Lyman, R.L. 1994. *Vertebrate Taphonomy*. Cambridge: Cambridge University Press.

Lindner, M. 1997, 6th edition. Beschreibung der antiken Stadt. 17–36 in M. Lindner (ed.), *Petra und das Königreich der Nabatäer. Lebensraum, Geschichte und Kultur eines arabischen Volkes der Antike*. München / Bad Windsheim: Delp.

McKenzie, J.S. 1990. *The Architecture of Petra*. Oxford: Oxford University Press.

Peter, M. 1996. Die Fundmünzen. 91–127 in *Petra — Ez Zantur I. Ergebnisse der Schweizerisch-Liechtensteinischen Ausgrabungen 1988–1992* (= Terra archaeologica II). Mainz: von Zabern.

Pringle, D. 1984. Thirteenth-Century Pottery from the Monastery of St. Mary of Carmel. *Levant* 16: 91–111.

——. 1985. Medieval Pottery from Caesarea. The Crusader Period. *Levant* 17: 171–202.

——. 2000. Summary and discussion. 195–219 in R. P. Harper and D. Pringle (eds), *Belmont Castle*. Oxford: Oxford University Press.

Randall J.E. 1983. *Red Sea Reef Fishes*. London: Immel.

Reber, K. 1998. *Die klassischen und hellenistischen Wohnhäuser im Westquartier*. Eretria 10. Lausanne: Payot.

Russell, K.W. 1980. The Earthquake of May 19, AD 363. *Bulletin of the American Schools of Oriental Research* 238: 47–64.

Schmid, S.G. 2000. *Die Feinkeramik der Nabatäer. Typologie, Chronologie und kulturhistorische Hintergründe. Petra — Ez Zantur II 1. Ergebnisse der Schweizerisch-Liechtensteinischen Ausgrabungen* (= Terra archaeologica IV. SLSA/FSLA. Mayence: von Zabern.

——. 2001a. The International Wadi Farasa Project (IWFP). Between Microcosm and Macroplanning: a first synthesis. *Palestine Exploration Quarterly* 133: 159–97.

——. 2001b. The International Wadi Farasa Project (IWFP). 2000 Season. *Annual of the Department of Antiquities of Jordan* 45: 343–57.

——. 2002. The International Wadi Farasa Project (IWFP). 2001 Season. *Annual of the Department of Antiquities of Jordan* 46: 257–77.

——. 2004. The International Wadi Farasa Project (IWFP). Progress on the Work in the Wadi Farasa East, Petra. *Palestine Exploration Quarterly* 136: 163–86.

——. 2006a. Hellenistische und römische Luxusarchitektur im Spiegel nabatäischer Grabkomplexe. *Numismatica e antichità classiche. Quaderni ticinesi* 35: 253–81.

——. 2006b. Kreuzritteralltag in Petra — Das Beispiel des Wadi Farasa. 45–59 in Ritterhausgesellschaft Bubikon (ed.), *Die Kreuzzüge. Petra — Eine Spurensuche*. Tann: Ritterhausgesellschaft Bubikon.

Schmid S.G. and Studer, J. 2003. The International Wadi Farasa Project (IWFP). Preliminary Report on the 2002 Season. *Annual of the Department of Antiquities of Jordan* 47: 473–88.

Studer, J. 1996. La faune romaine tardive d'Ez Zantur, à Petra. 359–75 in *Petra, Ez Zantur I. Ergebnisse der Schweizerisch-Liechtensteinischen Ausgrabungen 1988–1992*, Terra Archaeologica II. Monographien der Schweizerisch-Liechtensteinischen Stiftung für Archäologische Forschungen im Ausland (SLSA / FSLA). Mayence: von Zabern.

——. 2001. Observations on Animal Bones from Jabal Harûn. 384–6 in J. Frösen, *et al.* (eds), The 1998-2000 Finnish Jabal Harûn Project: Specialized Reports. *ADAJ*, 45: 377–92.

——. 2002. Dietary Differences at Ez Zantur Petra, Jordan (1st century BC–AD 5th century). 273–81 in H. Buitenhuis, A.M. Choyke, M. Mashkour and A.H. al-Shiyab (eds), *Archaeozoology of the Near East* V, ARC-Publicaties 62. Groningen: ARC.

Tonghini, C. and Vanni Desideri, A. 2001. The Material Evidence from al-Wu'ayra: A Sample of Pottery. 707–19 in *Studies in the History and Archaeology of Jordan*, 7. Amman: Department of Antiquities.

Trümper, M. 1998. *Wohnen in Delos. Eine baugeschichtliche Untersuchung zum Wandel der Wohnkultur in hellenistischer Zeit*. Rahden: Verlag Marie Leidorf.

Van Neer, W., Lernau, O., Friedman, R., Mumford, G., Poblome, J. and Waelkens, M. 2004. Fish remains from archaeological sites as indicators of former trade connections in the Eastern Mediterranean. *Paléorient* 30: 101–48.

Vannini, G. and Vanni Desideri, A. 1995. Archaeological Research on Medieval Petra. A Preliminary Report. *ADAJ* 39: 509–40.

Walmsley, A. 2001. Fatimid, Ayyubid and Mamluk Jordan and the Crusader Interlude. 515–59 in B. MacDonald, R. Adams and P. Bienkowski (eds), *The Archaeology of Jordan*. Sheffield: Sheffield Academic Press.

Walmsley, A.G. and Grey, A.D. 2001. An Interim Report on the Pottery from Gharandal (Arindela), Jordan. *Levant* 33: 139–64.

Zanker, P. 1995. *Pompeji. Stadtbild und Wohngeschmack*. Mayence: von Zabern.

Zoppi, C. 1991–1992. L'architettura abitativa in età ellenistica. Il modello vitruviano e i documenti superstiti. *Rendiconti della Accademia di archeologia, lettere e belle arti, Napoli* 63: 157–98.

Continuing Studies of Plants and Animals and their Arabic Names from the Royal Danish Expedition to the Red Sea, 1761–1763

F. Nigel Hepper

The Royal Danish Expedition set out from Copenhagen in January 1761 heading for the Red Sea and Arabia Felix, as the north Yemen was called in those days. This expedition is principally known for the remarkable exploits of Carsten Niebuhr who was the sole survivor. However, there were several other members, notably Pehr (Peter) Forsskål who was the industrious naturalist.

Figure 4:1 Pehr Forsskål before the Arabia-Felix expedition

Before he died in Yemen he made a huge collection of dried plants, pickled fish and other animals which were sent back to Europe by Niebuhr, as well as detailed notes.

It may come as a surprise to learn that even after some two hundred and thirty years Forsskål's collections and notes are still subjected to continuing studies which are yielding important new information.[1] The latest studies are centred on the Arabic names of the plants and animals by Professor Philippe Provençal of Aarhus University in Denmark.

Initiation of the expedition

In 1756 the German theologian Professor Johann Michaelis of Göttingen University proposed an expedition to Arabia to study the geography, its inhabitants and the plants and animals found there in order to throw light on those mentioned in the Bible. New translations of the ancient manuscripts of the Bible were taking place and scholars wished to make as correct renderings as possible. The proposal was made to the Danish Foreign Minister J.H.E. Bernstorff, who was a Hanoverian and a scholar in his own right. Bernstorff was greatly taken by the proposition and he soon obtained the support of Frederick V, the king of Denmark, to finance the expedition which was to be of the highest status since it was the first such Danish expedition.

There were many difficulties in finding suitable scholars to take part in such an arduous expedition which would be away for several years. Eventually the following were selected: Friedrich Christian von Haven (Danish), a philologist and ethnologist of Göttingen University to observe customs and habits of the country; Pehr (Peter) Forsskål (Swedish), a naturalist and student of Carl Linnaeus and trained in Oriental languages at Göttingen, to make zoological and botanical collections, in particular those mentioned in the Bible; Carsten Niebuhr (German), a mathematician and astronomer of Göttingen University who was to learn Arabic and survey the lands visited; George Wilhem Baurenfeind (German), an artist who would draw objects found and local scenes, also to assist members of the expedition; Christian Karl Cramer (or Kramer) (Danish), a recently qualified medical doctor to observe local diseases and to assist the sick; Berggren, the servant for the expedition, previously in the service of a Swedish Colonel of the Huzzars in Pomerania. All the members were designated of equal rank, although Niebuhr held the purse; and they were instructed to keep a diary. First, however, there had to be a great deal of preparation over several years before their departure from Copenhagen.

Departure from Copenhagen

Five of the members were to start from Copenhagen in January 1761 and the sixth (von Haven) was to join at Marseille. The Danish warship 'Groenland' under Commander Fisker was designated to carry the expedition to Constantinople. Amazingly, it took Groenland many weeks to reach the Atlantic Ocean as each time they tried to leave the Skagerrak the ship was blown back and they had to await a favourable wind. Once in the Atlantic, storm winds nearly blew them on to the Icelandic coast, but they just survived and headed for Cape St Vincent, Gibraltar and Marseille, where they docked on 14 May.

1 Hepper and Friis 1995.

At last the Swedish botanist, used to semi-arctic flora, could make herbarium specimens of Mediterranean type plants on the Estac hills behind the coast, and even visit the famous botanical gardens at Montpellier while their ship was re-victualled and merchant ships collected. 'Groenland' was detailed to protect a flotilla of three ships heading from Marseille for Constantinople. Forsskål was very busy in France where he listed 265 plant species; at least eighty-five of them he collected as herbarium specimens. They set sail for Malta on 3 June where the members went ashore for a week and Forsskål listed eighty-seven plant species and collected at least twelve of them. On 3 July they reached Smyrna (İzmir) and then on to the island of Tenebos (Bozçaada), where they left 'Groenland'. The ship was no longer going to Constantinople owing to smallpox raging there, but undaunted, the expedition reached the city in a Turkish ship. Stops at the Dardanelles and elsewhere enabled Forsskål to prepare a list of 481 plants and to collect 170 of them. This was the first systematic account of the Turkish flora when it was published posthumously having been edited by Niebuhr.[2]

During the Mediterranean voyage Niebuhr had suffered from severe dysentery and feared for his life: thankfully he survived. Unfortunately at the same time there had been a conflict of interests and personalities, between von Haven and Forsskål in particular. Von Haven thought he should be leader and in control of finances instead of Niebuhr. He questioned the viability of the whole expedition by writing a critical letter to Minister Bernstorff when he sent him a list of thirty-four Arabic manuscripts he had purchased. Von Haven's antagonism to Forsskål was such that he even threatened to do away with him. When Dr Cramer noticed von Haven buying a considerable quantity of arsenic he feared the worst, even though von Haven passed the packets to Cramer for safe-keeping.

However, preparations for departure for Egypt continued, and, dressed in Oriental costumes, they all left Constantinople on 8 September in a Turkish ship carrying female slaves bound for Alexandria. It was only when they reached Rhodes that Cramer showed to Niebuhr, Baurenfeind and Forsskål the packets of arsenic. Worryingly, Cramer thought that perhaps von Haven might have kept some himself and the hand-over was a blind. These three members took the revelation so seriously that they immediately wrote a long letter to the Danish Ambassador, von Gahler, whom they had met in Constantinople, requesting permission for von Haven to be separated from the other members of the expedition. Although von Gahler was an experienced diplomat, this situation was too serious for him to decide alone, so he referred the matter to to Bernstorff. Not only was correspondence between Constantinople and Copenhagen slow and unpredictable, but the bombshell received by Bernstorff took time to consider — so much time that it was not until the following summer that Niebuhr received a decision from Bernstorff via von Gahler. And how unsatisfactory it was: in effect, nothing was to be changed and the expedition must continue.

Twelve months in Egypt

Von Gahler had been told to help the expedition by ordering passports in Constantinople and letters of recommendation for Egypt and beyond. He had even tried to reconcile the members by making them publicly apologize to one another and he hoped all would be well.

Their Turkish ship docked at Alexandria on 26 September 1761 and a new enthusiasm gripped the expedition members. Everything was different and exciting. They spent several weeks in Alexandria learning Arabic, meeting expatriates and carrying out individual researches. On 31 October the time had come for them to continue their journey via Rosetta (Rashīd) and sail up one of the two main branches of the Nile. After five days they arrived at Cairo and dispersed to their lodgings already booked by von Gahler. Little did they realise that their planned month in Egypt would be extended to over twelve while they waited for a response from Denmark.

Figure 4:2 Egyptian Henbane called Hyoscyamus muticus *by Linnaeus and* H. datora *by Forsskål after its Arabica name* Datora*; drawn by Baurenfeind in Egypt*

[2] Forsskål 1775: XV–XXXVI.

During their enforced sojourn several of the members were very busy researching and recording everything that interested them in Egypt. Niebuhr surveyed the Pyramids with great accuracy and noted the place-names along the eastern branch of the Nile to Damietta. Baurenfeind completed numerous splendid drawings of towns and scenery, even local shoes and head-dresses.

It was the industrious Forsskål who interests us here since it was he who catalogued 576 plants (at least 256 of them collected) and dozens of zoological specimens with their local names in Arabic, written in both Arabic and Latin letters.

Forsskål was a compulsive note-taker — not merely rough notes but finished ones with names and descriptions of new species suitable for publication. Did he take this precaution in case he died before he was able to finalize his field notes? If so, he was well advised as it turned out, for Niebuhr was able to publish Forsskål's work posthumously, as well as Baurenfeind's biological drawings.[3] Forsskål's notes made in Egypt also included many ethnographic observations which are only now being reinterpreted by Professor Friis and myself. These are under eight headings: 1, *Foliation (tree phenology)*; 2, *Shade trees*; 3, *Fruit trees*; 4, *Sweet-smelling herbs with petals*; 5, *Cereals*; 6, *Fodder*; 7, *Plants used for food, colouring, medicine*; and 8, *Timber;* as well as 9, *Wild Plants*. This information has never been available in a usable form to horticulturists, pharmacists and historians.

Departure from Egypt

By August 1762 the time had come to leave for Arabia. After a farewell party with dancing girls as entertainers, the members joined a caravan on leaving Cairo for where they soon expected to board a ship for the Red Sea voyage to Yemen. First, however, von Haven had to fulfil his royal instruction to visit Sinai in order to copy some hieroglyphic inscriptions and to report on the manuscripts in St Catherine's Monastery. Although no use had been made so far of the poisonous arsenic, only Niebuhr would agree to accompany von Haven through the rugged terrain to the monastery. Sadly, they were refused entry to it owing to the letter of introduction not having been signed by the right bishop! When Bernstorff was informed of this disaster he was furious and told them to return to Sinai on the way back. However, von Haven was dead by the time Niebuhr received these instructions.

While von Haven and Niebuhr were away, Forsskål, Cramer and Baurenfeind were bored, having little to do but collect sea creatures and spiders and to await the explorers' return.[4] On 10 October they all boarded an Ottoman vessel with three smaller ones in tow loaded with pilgrims, prostitutes and cattle for Jiddah *en route* to Makkah. A tragedy was averted when a woman using a hot smoothing iron caused a small fire aboard the ship. Then it was realized that the pilot was unable to navigate the ship out of sight of land so there was always a possibility of grounding on coastal rocks.

On safe arrival at Jiddah they had a great welcome, but had to wait for some six weeks until a coffee ship arrived to carry the expedition to Mocha (al-Mukhā'). Niebuhr busied himself surveying the town, and since only fourteen species of plants were available in the desert Forsskål went fishing at Jiddah where he collected at least fifty-two species of fish new to science. Baurenfeind managed to make some splendid drawings of local people, such as a fisherman and a bread seller.

Figure 4:3 Chaetodon unicornis, *one of the numerous fishes in the Red Sea caught by Forsskål and drawn by Baurenfeind*

On 18 December they boarded the coffee ship which they found uncongenial and ill-equipped for carrying passengers. Unfortunately, the friendly Arab businessman who agreed to take their chests full of botanical and zoological specimens to the customs at Mocha later turned out to be a charlatan. On 29 December the expedition members disembarked at Loheia. Here they had a good welcome from the emir and populace who offered no threat. They soon headed inland to Bayt al-Faqīh, the main commercial centre on the coastal plain called the Tihāmah. They remained at Bayt al-Faqīh until 7 March

[3] Forsskål 1775a, 1775b.

[4] See J. Starkey, this volume, for more details of their visit to Suez.

when they returned to the coast at al-Ḥudaydah (Hodeida), and then travelled inland to Zabīd, another Tihāmah town. From here they penetrated the mountains by deep valleys with the coffee trees from which Mocha coffee is obtained. In each locality Forsskål amassed splendid collections of plants which were dried as herbarium specimens. His main localities were Bulgose and Hadie where the rocky terrain provided a wide range of habitats that supported a diverse flora from marsh plants to succulents. At the end of March he climbed up to the montane plain around Jiblah with its temperate flora which he collected in early April.

Back on the lowland the temperature was increasing, but instead of returning to the cooler mountains they went to Mocha, which became a cauldron in summer. Here they met up with the entrepreneur who had taken their boxes, but all he wanted was payment and he declined to help them through customs. The officials destroyed the carefully packed up specimens; the snakes horrified them as they feared these foreigners wanted to poison people; then there was uproar when the bottles of fish were found by the Muslim officials to be pickled in alcohol. The members were locked out of the sheds without cooking pots or beds and their house was ransacked. At last they met three English merchants bound for India and gradually the expedition members were accepted and their remaining chests were returned unopened. By this time von Haven was sickening; he died on 25 May and was buried in the Jewish cemetery. Permission to leave Mocha for Ta'izz was repeatedly refused, and as conditions were atrocious they considered abandoning Arabia Felix altogether. However, they managed to obtain a permit for Ta'izz in the foothills from where they hoped to reach the emir who held court at Sana'a.

While at Ta'izz, busy Forsskål used the time to study the extraordinary cactus-like flora (mainly *Euphorbia* species) of the stony outcrops. But even he succumbed to malaria and by the time they left Ta'izz and began the fearsome ascent up the Sumara Pass on 5 July Forsskål had fallen seriously ill. He had no water and his donkey was unable to carry him; he eventually arrived at Jerim on the montane plains strapped to a camel. Forsskål, aged thirty-one, died on 11 July and was buried in the Jewish cemetery which has by now disappeared. According to his will he bequeathed his belongings to Baurenfeind in grateful thanks for his splendid drawings of plants and animals. Sadly, Baurenfeind himself did not have long to enjoy the benefits of this bequest as he also fell ill and perished on the way to India.

Niebuhr continued to Sana'a where he met the Imām of Arabia Felix. But as soon as they could Niebuhr made a direct return via Bayt al-Faqīh to Mocha in order to board a merchantman to India. He continued to Bombay (Mumbai) with Forsskål's precious notes and specimens which he sent off on a Danish ship that went to China before returning to Denmark in 1766. Regrettably, by then interest in the expedition had waned and Professor Ascanius put the specimens in an attic where they stayed for a decade until studied by Professor Martin Vahl. Even the great Linnaeus was not allowed to study them since he was Swedish, not Danish.

Linnaeus did unofficially study a number of plants grown from seeds sent to him by Forsskål by an arranged subterfuge — hence several Mediterranean and Egyptian plants were named and described by Linnaeus as new to science, not knowing that Forsskål had already come to the same conclusion and provided another name. Forsskål was commemorated by Linnaeus in the new genus *Forskohlia tenacissima*, a member of the nettle family which is perhaps appropriate for his prickly personality.

Figure 4:4 Carsten Niebuhr in Arab dress; drawn by Baurenfeind in Sana'a where the costume was presented by the Imam

Figure 4:5 Forskohlea tenacissima, *a plant of the nettle family first collected by Forsskål and named in his honour by Carl Linnaeus*

Niebuhr himself had a formidable return journey ahead of him: by sea to Muscat and by land to Persepolis and Basra, continuing to Baghdad, Jerusalem and Constantinople, before reaching Copenhagen on 20 November 1767. Certainly Niebuhr[5] earned himself the highest place in the annals of exploration, and the other members, especially Forsskål, also gained a redoubtable place in history.

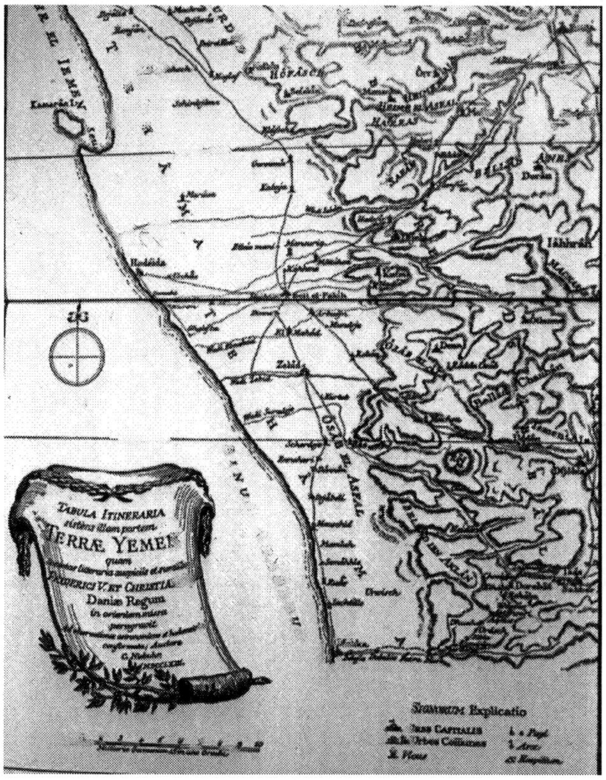

Map 4:1 Part of Carsten Niebuhr's map of 'Terræ Yemen' or Arabia-Felix

5 Niebuhr 1772, 1774–1778.

Continuing Research

The impression of total failure of the Danish Expedition to unravel the scientific and scholarly mysteries of these lands could easily be obtained from this account of the disasters that befell its members. Thankfully, that is far from the case. As indicated above, before Forsskål's demise he had made vast collections of plants and animals, many of which were new to science from lands scarcely visited by naturalists. He had collected some 256 plants from Egypt and over 500 from north Yemen, mostly new to science. During the last two and a half centuries several botanists and zoologists have made intensive studies of these collections — and active research still continues.

Major investigations of the plants were carried out by the Danes Martin Vahl, C. Christensen, Mrs Fox Maule and Ib Friis; by the Frenchman A. Deflers; the German Georg Schweinfurth and the British botanists Dorothy Hilcoat, John Wood and myself, as well as numerous lesser studies. In 1994 Ib Friis and I published a 400-page volume,[6] being the results of our re-identification of all of the existing 1750 plant specimens in Copenhagen and other herbaria, totalling well over 2000 sheets. Many other species were listed in Forsskål's notes. Mrs Fox Maule worked out that he noted 2093 plant species, of which 693 came from the Red Sea area including north Yemen. Over 500 of them are represented by herbarium specimens and many were new to science, given Latin names, described and published — those specimens on which the description was based are called type specimens and they must be carefully preserved as standard reference material. The same applies to the zoological material collected by Forsskål which now is housed in the Zoological Museum of Copenhagen: there are fifty-eight type specimens of fishes alone.[7] Provençal comments[8] that as a result of Forsskål's studies 'the Red Sea seems to form a linguistic entity regarding the Arabic names of marine life'.

Another line of botanical research is Forsskål's lists of street trees, garden ornamentals and crops in Egypt and Yemen. These were published as tables giving his identification in Latin and the vernacular names in Arabic. Provençal comments,

> It was honourable of Forsskål that he was scrupulous enough never trying to render the names of animals and plants more classical in his notations. He thus has provided us with a unique and very precious documentation of zoological and botanical terms from a region which was and in many ways still is isolated and poorly known, but

6 Hepper and Friis 1994.

7 Klausewitz and Nielsen 1965: 9.

8 Provençal 2002: 157–61.

which has a tremendous interest for the philology and linguistic of Semitic languages.[9]

— and he posthumously congratulates Forsskål for having fulfilled to a very wide degree the purposes for which he was sent on the expedition.

References

Forsskål, P. 1775a. *Descriptiones animalium.* Niebuhr, C. (ed.). Copenhagen: Möller.

——. 1775b. *Flora Aegyptiaco-Arabica.* Niebuhr, C. (ed.). Copenhagen: Möller.

Hansen, T. 1964. *Arabia Felix: the Danish Expedition of 1761–1767.* J. and K. McFarlane (English tr.); London: Collins.

Hepper, F.N. and Friis, I. 1994. *The Plants of Pehr Forsskål's* Flora Ægyptiaco-Arabica. Royal Botanic Gardens, Kew.

Klausewitz, W. and Nielsen, J. 1965. On Forsskål's collection of fishes in the Zoological Museum of Copenhagen. *Spolia Zoologica Musei Hauniensis,* Copenhagen. 22: 1–29.

Niebuhr, C. 1772. *Beschreibung von Arabien : Aus eigenen Beobachtungen und im Lande selbst gesammleten Nachrichten.* Copenhagen: Gedruckt in der Hofbuchdrukery bey Nicolaus Møller. In Leipzig zu bekommen bey B.C. Breitkopf und Sohn.

——. 1774–1778 *Reisebereibung nach Arabien und anderen umbiegendenlandern.* Copenhagen: Gloyer & Oldhausen.

Provençal, P. 2002. The cultural significance of the results in natural history made by Arabic Travel 1761–1767 — Peter Forsskål's contribution to Arabic lexicography. Pages 157–61 in J. Wiesehöfer and S. Conermann (ed.), *Carsten Niebuhr (1733–1815) und seine Zeit.* Stuttgart: Franz Steiner Verlag.

Acknowledgements

I am grateful to Professor Ib Friis and Professor Philippe Provençal for their help and for the English translation of Thokild Hansen's book listed above.

[9] Ibid.

Coral Reef Conservation and the Current Status of Reefs of the Ras Mohamed National Park in the Northern Red Sea and Gulf of 'Aqabah

Steve McMellor and David J. Smith

The Importance of Coral Reefs

Coral reefs are by definition three-dimensional, shallow water structures dominated by reef-building hard corals and are the most biologically diverse of shallow water marine ecosystems. It is believed that although coral reefs represent less than 0.2 per cent of total ocean area, they contain more species per unit area than any other ecosystem.[1] Estimates of the total number of people who are reliant on coral reefs for their food resources, range from 500 million[2] to over one billion.[3] Some 30 million of the world's poorest and most vulnerable people in coastal and island communities are totally reliant on reef-based resources as their primary means of food production, sources of income and livelihoods.[4] As well as providing direct food resources, coral reefs provide coastal protection and sustain valuable tourism industries.[5] Due to increasing population size, the reliance on reef resources is set to increase over coming decades, while the reefs themselves are predicted to decline.

Threats to coral reefs

Most coral reefs around the world are over-exploited and damaged by over-extraction, pollution, excess sediment and inappropriate development. Coral reef scientists also predict massive destruction of coral reefs in coming decades due to the effects of global climate change. Their loss will destroy the social fabric of many coastal communities, and ruin the massive tourism industry that supports many of the developing tropical countries.[6] The current 'State of the Reefs' report states that some 20 per cent of the world's coral reefs have already been destroyed and show no prospect of recovery, while a further 24 per cent are under imminent risk of collapse through human induced pressures and a further 26 per cent are under a longer-term threat of collapse.[7] The threat to coral reefs worldwide was assessed according to a number of common factors such as coastal development, over-exploitation and destructive fishing practices, impacts of inland pollution and soil erosion and from marine-based pollution.[8] The study observed that of the world's reefs, 27 per cent were at high risk, 31 per cent at medium risk and just 42 per cent were considered to be at a low-level risk from the combined factors.

Coral reefs around the world continue to decline due to both natural and anthropogenic influences. Threats are becoming more serious because of the high demand for marine-sourced products and weak enforcement of existing laws in many regions.[9] Despite the potential long-term stability of coral reefs in the face of many disturbances, concern is increasing that anthropogenic induced environmental changes may be beginning to exceed the limits of tolerance of reef organisms to factors such as UV radiation, water temperature and human predation.[10] Humans may be affecting the frequency, intensity, distribution and duration of many types of disturbance. By fishing out keystone predators and increasing nutrient concentrations, humans may be inadvertently contributing to outbreaks of coral predators such as the Crown of Thorns starfish (*Acanthaster planci*) also known as COTs. Such fishing activity is now pervasive throughout the tropics and now extends further offshore than in the past. Unsustainable fisheries reduce the abundance of many target species and can also remove whole functional groups such as grazing Parrotfishes (Scaridae), which can lead to phase shifts from coral to algal dominated systems. Even on heavily studied reefs, identifying such shifts has often been unrecognized, because of the increasing instability of coral reef ecosystems before their collapse. These phase shifts of tropical reefs to less desirable states can have devastating economic effects on maritime developing nations.[11] This extensive deterioration highlights the need for efficient monitoring, assessment methods and the implementation of strategic conservation management.[12]

Anthropogenic enhanced climate change caused by increasing greenhouse gas emissions is now becoming accepted as a major threat to coral reef systems. Increasing ocean temperatures are leading to increased incidence of coral bleaching, where the relationship between coral host and their symbiotic algae breaks down.[13] It is, however, worth noting that during the 1998 worldwide bleaching event, when an estimated 16 per cent of the world's reefs were severely impacted, there was little impact upon the reefs of the Red Sea, with bleaching only reported in a few isolated places. If the corals of the

1 Ahmed, *et al.* 2004.
2 Wilkinson 2004.
3 Whittingham, *et al.* 2003.
4 Gomez, *et al.* 1994.
5 Spalding, *et al.* 2001.
6 Wilkinson 2004.
7 Ibid.
8 Bryant, *et al.* 1998.
9 Hidayati 2003.
10 McClanahan, *et al.* 2002.
11 Bellwood, *et al.* 2004.
12 McKenna, *et al.* 2001; Bellwood, *et al.* 2004.
13 Brown 1997; Smith, *et al.* 2005.

Red Sea are more resistant to bleaching or environmental conditions within the Red Sea itself are preventing widespread impacts, then the reefs of the Red Sea take on a global importance.

As well as increased temperatures it is believed that climate change will lead to an increase in the frequency and severity of storm events, possibly not giving reefs time to recover between events.[14] Finally, the volume of carbon dioxide entering the atmosphere is now predicted to lead to an acidification of the world's oceans, leading to a shift in pH and subsequent reduction in calcification rates which would impact many reef organisms, especially the reef-building Scleractinian corals.[15]

The Red Sea

The reefs of the Red Sea are of particular importance to global biodiversity as they are part of the third centre of reef biodiversity, after the Indo-West Pacific and Caribbean regions. This third area encompasses the western Indian Ocean and East Africa.

The Red Sea is a relatively 'new' sea formed in the Eocene some 40 million years ago when a fault developed between what is now the Arabian Peninsula and North Africa. This fault created a narrow sea connected at the northern end to the Mediterranean, formerly known as the Tethys Sea. The Red Sea as it is today was formed some five million years ago when Sinai uplifted, cutting the water body off from the Mediterranean and opened a shallow channel to the Indian Ocean, allowing entry of Indo-Pacific organisms to the water body. Subsequent isolation from the Indian Ocean led to speciation and the current situation, with so many endemic species unique to the Red Sea. The Red Sea was again linked to the Indian Ocean some 15,000 years ago at the end of the last Ice age.[16] Current literature suggests that between 210 and 270 species of Scleractinian coral are found within the Red Sea, and around 1,000 species of fishes, some 15 per cent of which are endemic.

All types of coral reef are represented in the Red Sea: fringing reefs, barrier reefs, patch reefs and atolls are all present. Reefs were historically recorded as 'luxuriant and plentiful in the central Red Sea and rather less so in the north and to the south.'[17] In total there are some twenty marine protected areas (MPA) within the Red Sea region encompassing a range of sizes and designations across seven Red Sea nations covering a total of 17,670 km^2.

The Kingdom of Saudi Arabia is the largest coral reef nation in the region, with an extensive coastline facing the Red Sea. Large parts of Saudi Arabia's Red Sea coastline are undeveloped. Sewage pollution and land reclamation are concerns around many of the larger cities. Oil pollution is a threat to reefs around some of the major ports and refineries. Away from these urban areas coastal development remains limited and the reefs are in relatively good condition[5]. Fishing is not a major industry in the country, and there is little or no artisanal fishing. Saudi Arabia has four Red Sea marine protected areas (MPA) covering 7,298 km^2.

The reefs of Eritrea are extensive and suffered little human impact before the 1990s. Since then there have been small increases in both the coastal population and fisheries.[18] Artisanal fisheries exist but are not extensive. There is also a commercial fishery for the aquarium trade. Eritrea has one MPA covering 2,000 km^2.

Sudanese fisheries and tourism account for less than three per cent GNP, and subsistence fisheries are only locally important. While large parts of the Sudanese Red Sea region are still in a pristine state, environmental threats, notably from habitat destruction, over-exploitation and pollution, are increasing rapidly, requiring immediate action to protect the region's coastal and marine environment.[19] Sudan has one proposed MPA covering 260 km^2.

Djibouti has two MPAs covering almost 13 km^2, as fisheries contribute little to the national economy. Current threats to coral reefs come from the tourism, shipping and coastal development sectors.[20]

Fringing reefs border up to 50 per cent of the Jordanian coast supporting a high diversity of coral and associated fauna. Jordan's coral reefs are in good condition, supporting up to 90 per cent cover of Scleractinian corals.[21] Pollution from industry, primarily in the form of phosphates and fertilisers, constitutes the major threat to coral reefs. Jordan has one MPA covering 2 km^2.

Israel has one MPA covering 0.5 km^2 at Eilat.[22] The Israeli Red Sea coastline is probably the most widely studied section of reef in the Red Sea.

Yemen has a relatively developed Red Sea coastline compared to its neighbours. Oil pollution together with sewage and industrial development may be having localized impacts. Fisheries are important, including an offshore trawl fishery, but also line and net fisheries, with reports of over-fishing in some areas.[23] Yemen has not declared any MPAs along its Red Sea coast.

14 Crabbe and Smith 2006.
15 Kleypass, *et al.* 2006.
16 Lieske and Myers 2004.
17 Admiralty (GB) 1946.
18 Spalding, *et al.* 2001.
19 Pilcher and Nasr 2000.
20 Pilcher and Abdi 2000.
21 Spalding, *et al.* 2001
22 Pilcher and Zaid 2000.
23 Spalding, *et al.* 2001.

Egypt has ten Red Sea MPAs covering 8,096 km^2. Egypt's extensive coastline incorporates a significant proportion and a considerable range of the coral reefs found in the Red Sea. Human activities along this coastline are highly varied. The coastline includes areas of quite intensive use and considerable reef degradation, but also areas which remain relatively remote and inaccessible, and which are largely unaffected by humans.[24] Marine fishing is not a major industry in Egypt: there is a small amount of commercial fishing in the southern reef areas in the Gulf of Suez. In contrast, pollution from shipping and oil spillage are a significant threat, notably along the coastline of the Gulfs of Suez and 'Aqabah. Ship groundings have also been a problem, causing direct physical destruction to some reefs, and raising concerns about the potential economic repercussions arising from any damage to the major tourist beaches and dive sites.[25] Egypt has legally protected over 35,000 km^2 of the major tourist destination areas which encompass extensive and diverse coral reefs and associated fauna, and which are also important sea turtle and seabird nesting or foraging habitats.[26]

Ras Mohamed National Park

History of the Ras Mohamed National Park

Located at the southern tip of the Sinai Peninsula, Ras Mohamed has always had immense strategic importance from the time of the Ancient Egyptians who controlled trade on the Red Sea. The strategic importance of the area was elevated in global terms with the construction of the Suez Canal at the end of the nineteenth century. This meant that whoever held the area of Ras Mohamed *de facto* controlled the trade between Europe, Africa and Asia. The Ras Mohamed area was declared as a military zone by the Egyptian army along with the rest of the Sinai Peninsula following the Suez War in 1956. In 1967, Israel occupied Sinai and held the area until the signing of a peace agreement between Egypt and Israel in 1979; Egypt regained the Sinai in phases ending in 1982.

The first legislation to institutionalize conservation was Ministerial Decree No. 349 of 1979 which established the Egyptian Wildlife Service as the first governmental authority concerned with the protection of wildlife in the country. The Presidential Decree of 5 March 1980 established a mechanism for identifying and protecting threatened areas and species through cooperation between provincial governors, the Academy of Scientific Research and the Ministry of Agriculture. Subsequently, Ministerial Decree No. 472 of 5 May 1982 ensured the prohibition of hunting of all birds and animals in a number of sites in the Sinai as well as banning fishing or harming molluscs. Eventually the introduction of Law No. 102/83, passed on 20 July 1983, provided for the legal framework upon which the government could establish protected areas throughout the whole of Egypt. It is through this law that Ras Mohamed was declared a protected site. This also created the Egyptian Environmental Affairs Agency (EEAA) which now administers Ras Mohamed through its Nature Conservation Sector. From 1988 an entrance charge was levied on all visitors at the main Park gate.

By 1991, the EEAA was restructured and together with the help of some foreign partners such as the European Commission, UNEP and the World Bank (amongst others), it began to effectively manage Ras Moḥamed, which was subsequently declared as a National Park. In August 1997 the EEAA became a department of the newly established State Ministry of Environmental Affairs (SMEA). It should be noted that both Egyptian and international Non-Governmental Organisations (NGO) also participate in the maintenance of Ras Mohamed and are mainly active at the level of research, monitoring and education.

The Ras Mohamed National Park covers an area of roughly 750 km^2. The Park houses a particularly high diversity of flora and fauna, including coral reefs, seaweed and seagrass beds, mudflats, mangroves and other salt-tolerant vegetation. The management plan, developed with financial and technical assistance from the European Commission, includes the development of infrastructure and training for rangers and scientific staff. The Ras Mohamed National Park was established in 1983 as Egypt's first national park, although it is generally agreed to have existed as a 'paper park' until 1988, when the Egyptian government handed the task of management to the EEAA in response to the area's growing popularity as a dive tourism destination.[27]

The Ras Mohamed National Park exists at the southern-most tip of the Sinai Peninsula (Map 5:1), protruding into the Red Sea. It is bordered on one side by the Gulf of Suez and on the other by the Gulf of 'Aqabah.[28] The coastal plain is narrow with granitic mountains descending almost directly into the sea. To the north and the west are large alluvial plains, the northern part of which has undergone rapid and constant development since the mid-1980s and now forms the tourist resort of Sharm el-Sheikh.

The cape of Ras Mohamed consists of a large bay and inlet with cliffs of raised fossilized corals backed by low undulating barren hills.[29] In the east and in the west there are clear water creeks with sandy shores.

24 Ibid.
25 Ibid.
26 Pilcher and Zaid 2000.
27 Shehata 1998.
28 Frouda 1984.
29 Samuel 1973.

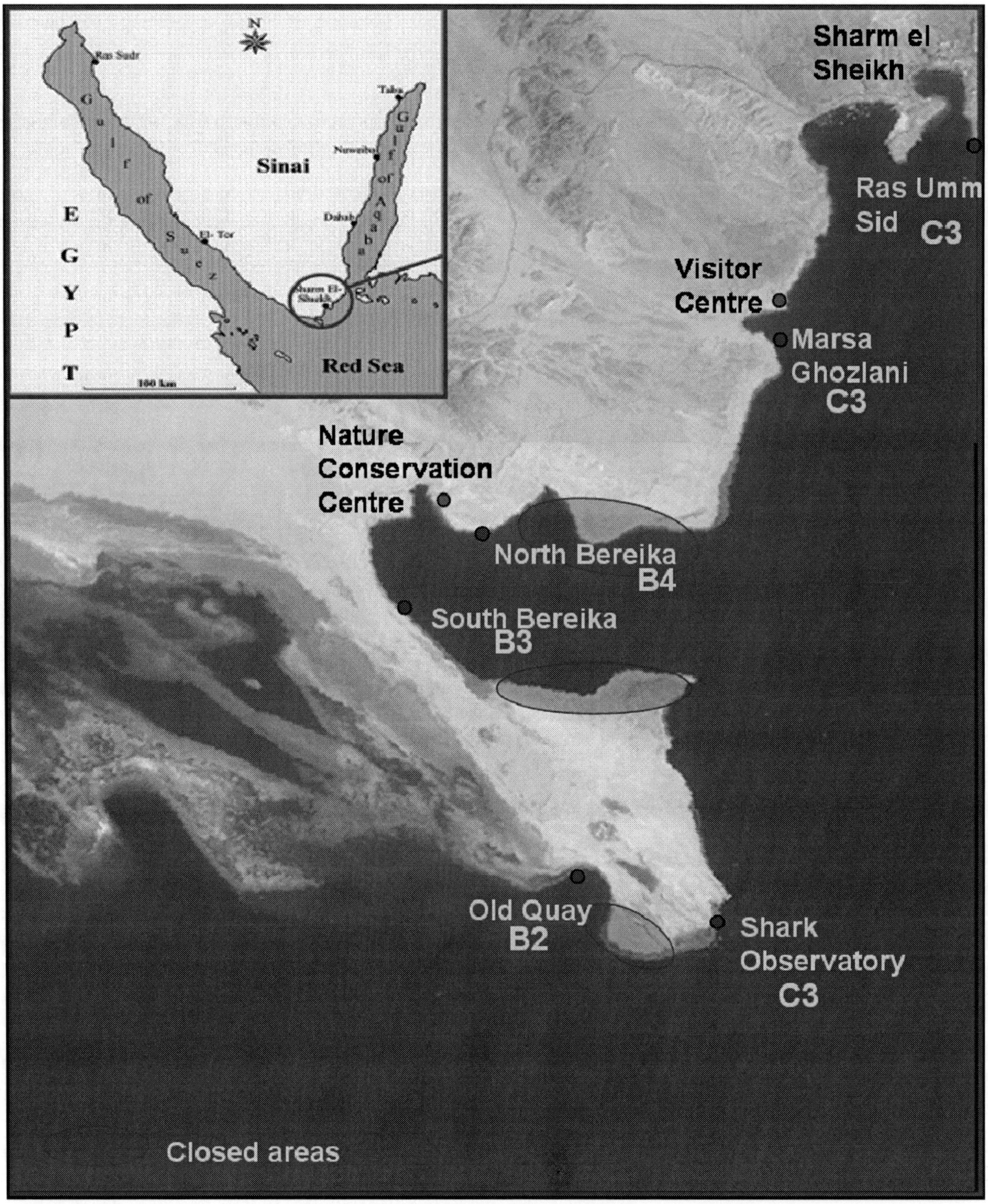

Map 5:1 Ras Mohamed National Park with conservation scores assigned to six of the Park's reefs (Letter ranks reef benthos from A–E; Number ranks fish community from 1–5; A1 being the highest value). Image from Landsat Millennium Coral Reef Archive, courtesy Image Science and Analysis Laboratory, NASA.

The high bluffs of Ras Mohamed itself are connected to the mainland by a narrow land bridge, 3.5 km long and 1 km wide. The southern tip of the headland is an island separated from the mainland by a shallow channel filled with mangroves. Exposed coral reefs are found adjacent to open water areas of over 100 m in depth. The fringing reef encircles the entire headland and ends in cliff-like ledges at 70 m and 100 m water depth. By the headland there is an extensive terrace at approximately 15 m depth.[30] Nearly all areas of shoreline within the Park have well developed

[30] Wells 1987.

fringing reefs, often with steep walls dropping thousands of metres in places.

Water temperatures in the Park range from 21°C in January to almost 30°C in August. Salinity is elevated above 40 parts per thousand due to high levels of evaporation and slow rates of water exchange between the Red Sea and the main Indian Ocean basin, which is due to the shallow water connection between these two bodies. Lack of riverine inputs and associated run-off and sedimentation give rise to the world renowned visibility of the regions' waters.

Monitoring and Management

Monitoring is essential for any type of informed natural resource management to be implemented. Stakeholders need to know what is there, what condition it is in and what threats it is facing. Stakeholders may be traditional or historic users such as Bedouin subsistence fishermen, but now also include tourism interests in many Red Sea nations.

The Regional Organisation for the Conservation of the Environment of the Red Sea and Gulf of Aden (PERSGA) was established in Saudi Arabia in 1996 and is a multinational body responsible for the development and implementation of regional programmes for the protection and conservation of the marine environment of the Red Sea and Gulf of Aden. PERSGA plays an active role in promoting regional cooperation and has recently supported regional environmental assessments, MPAs, navigation risks and marine resources management.

Although there appear to have been a number of studies and monitoring programmes attempted in the Ras Mohamed National Park, the data they produced is unfortunately lacking.[31] Any sort of informed management action requires a solid foundation on which to base decisions, often in the form of an in-depth biological survey. The hermatypic Scleractinian corals are arguably the most important component of the reef as they are the reef builders themselves, and without them reef growth would be very limited. Although important, they are by no means the only organism important to overall reef health.

Degradation of tracts of reef often involves a 'phase shift' from coral dominated to algal dominated states, which in turn has knock-on effects to the fish abundance and diversity.[32] A complex interaction between hard corals, soft corals, algae and levels of fish and urchin grazing can lead to these phase shifts, but it often requires the simultaneous occurrence of several factors, such as increased nutrients and removal of important herbivorous fishes, along with ongoing degradation of hard corals. It is due to the complex nature of competition on a coral reef that many of these other factors need to be recorded and considered, before any management action can be taken. It is of vital importance to stakeholders and managers that early detection of changes in these interacting factors be monitored, alongside measures of coral cover, to allow the early identification of possible phase shifts in community structure.

The link between the health of the benthic and fish communities is already well established in coral reef ecology. It has been shown that substratum biodiversity was positively correlated with overall fish species richness,[33] although total live cover did not show a significant correlation to fish diversity or abundance. It is also known that benthic habitat characteristics affect reef fish assemblages,[34] and hence the availability to humans of natural reef resources. Often these are characteristics which provide habitat for fish and also for fish prey species, such that the benthic and fishery components of a reef system are highly interdependent, with a natural or anthropogenic impact on one community having a knock-on effect on the other.

The Ras Mohamed National Park was originally designated to protect an area of important natural resources which was at risk due to the development of the dive tourism industry. The hermatypic corals provide habitat and resources for a huge variety of different organisms, and the sustainable development of tourist activities should be based around the protection of the reef builders themselves.

Any form of reef assessment must include the fish species present as they perform vital roles in the maintenance of diversity on a healthy reef system. Many fish species are important algal grazers and as such help maintain the competition for substratum between benthic organisms, by keeping the faster growing algae in check.[35]

Removal of predators by over-fishing is known to deplete both biomass and diversity of other non-target fish species.[36] Unlike many reef areas worldwide, the Ras Mohamed National Park is not subject to adverse fishing techniques or over-extraction of resources. However, it is still vital to monitor the fish assemblages for signs of impact or change.

Performance criteria and management

Science and research play a major role in providing the information required to plan and decide on management actions for coral reefs.[37] Accurate environmental valuation is integral to the development of appropriate pricing and charging policies, which are vital to the emerging science

31 Pilcher and Nasr, 2000.
32 McCook 1999; Bryant, *et al.* 1998.
33 Roberts and Ormond 1987.
34 Friedlander and Parrish 1998.
35 Sluka and Miller 2001; Thacker, *et al.* 2001.
36 Jennings and Polunin 1997.
37 Ablan, *et al.* 2004.

of environmental economics.[38] In fact, it is logical to suppose that the successful management of ecosystems depends on the early detection of change and the causes of such change.[39] Management also depends upon the communication of scientific results to the broader public, and this can fail if the evidence of change and causality is not synthesized in a transparent manner. Studies suggest that the most appropriate way to identify ecological change should be focused on the responses of a wide range of ecological groups rather than individual species or factors.

Once a baseline has been established, management goals can be set and the performance of management action can be monitored by comparing attribute values over time. This also allows the setting of benchmarks of performance and monitoring rates of change in the system, providing valuable feedback to stakeholders for management.

Specific threats to Ras Mohamed reefs

Natural threats include predation on the important reef building corals by *Acanthaster planci*, the Crown of Thorns Starfish (COTs), and corallivorous gastropods such as *Drupella* spp. and *Coralliophilla* spp. Both of these organisms are natural components of any reef system and usually occur in small numbers where they feed directly on hard coral tissues. However, outbreaks or population explosions of both of these coral predators are known to occur and have both been recorded over recent years in and around the Ras Mohamed National Park with devastating effects.

Feeding aggregations of *Drupella* spp. have caused considerable coral damage on reefs across the Indo-West Pacific. They usually aggregate in small clusters of less than ten individuals, but have been recorded in densities from around 200 to over several thousand individuals over a relatively small reef area. These gastropods have adapted *radula* for stripping the live coral tissue from the skeleton, leaving behind characteristic white feeding scars that are quickly colonized by turf algae.[40] The populations tend to exhibit stable periods punctuated by rapid population increases, often associated with changes in ecological structure. The outbreaks tend to occur in areas with high coral cover.[41]

The Ras Mohamed National Park has recently (1998–2002) suffered a catastrophic outbreak of COTs, with thousands of individuals being removed from the reefs of the Park.[42] Again, the COTs is a predator of the reef-building *Scleractinia* and such outbreaks can lead to a collapse in reef structure, resulting in very slow recovery of the impacted reefs. Recovery can take at least twelve years even if the structural integrity of the reef remains intact.[43] The current 'State of the Reefs' reported that coral cover was reduced by 65 per cent during the recent outbreak at some sites in the Gulf of 'Aqabah.[44] The loss of the hard coral cover often leads to shifts in community structure to an algal dominated system. This in turn can affect the community structure of fish populations with changes in the abundance of various roving herbivores, such as the Surgeonfishes (Acanthuridae) and Parrotfishes (Scaridae).[45] Loss of coral cover (from COTs outbreak) can lead to a reduction in reef accretion. This can then allow increased erosion of the reef structure due to the loss of the delicate balance between accretion and erosion.

Other natural threats to the region's coral reefs include coral bleaching and coral disease. Coral bleaching is the loss of symbiotic zooxanthellae due to a number of different stresses, the most commonly reported being elevated sea surface temperature (SST). The incidence of coral diseases is believed to be increasing worldwide, yet little data exists for the entire Indo-Pacific region. It has been suggested that the increasing incidence of disease may be linked to declines in marine environmental health generally, due to anthropogenic influences.[46]

Major anthropogenic threats include the continued development of the tourism industry with direct physical impacts on the reefs caused by the visiting divers and snorkellers. Tourism activity in and around the Ras Mohamed National Park is intense with over 75,000 divers per year reported at some sites.[47] The 'State of the Reefs' report also reports major indirect anthropogenic threats from tourism in the form of land-fills, dredging and sedimentation, sewage discharge and effluent from desalination plants all associated with continued coastal development.[48] There needs to be a balance between the need for tourism, which is a major part of the Egyptian economy, and the need to conserve the resources which drive the tourism, that is, the reefs. Anthropogenic impacts on coral reefs can be assumed to be cumulative with natural impacts and as such, both these sources of stress are important in controlling reef community structure.[49]

Status of the reefs of the Ras Mohamed National Park

The goal of this project was to establish a baseline dataset for the reefs of the Ras Mohamed National Park, that is, to identify what is there, what condition it is in and what threats the reefs may be facing. This data was then compiled into a report for the Egyptian Environmental Affairs Agency to support management of the Park, and also submitted to the Australian Institute of Marine

38 Spurgeon, 2004
39 Fabricius and De'ath 2004.
40 Cumming 1999.
41 McClanahan 1994.
42 Saleh 2005.
43 Hart and Klumpp 1996.
44 Wilkinson 2000.
45 Hart, *et al.* 1996.
46 Green and Bruckner 2000.
47 Kotb, *et al.* 2004.
48 Fabricius and De'ath, 2004.
49 Grigg and Dollar 1990.

Science for inclusion in the next 'State of the Reefs' report to be published in 2008. This biennial report provides a global overview of reefs and reef resources worldwide.

i) Benthic community

The percentage cover of hard corals did not vary significantly between any of the study sites. Marsā Ghozlani showed the lowest hard coral cover at 20.8(±1.1) per cent, with the highest cover found at South Marsā Bereika at 33.3(±2.4) per cent. The uniformity of coral cover at all sites is somewhat surprising as the sites were selected for their varied factors, such as sheltered and exposed, heavily dived and minimally dived. This suggests that some other over-riding factor, such as the COTs outbreak in 1998, has had a more important influence on the benthic communities. The levels of hard coral cover are now higher than immediately after the outbreak, but are still significantly lower than before the COTs outbreak (Graph 5:1).

Total live benthic cover (hard corals, soft corals and sponges) showed a very highly significant difference between sites, with the Old Quay site having the highest cover recorded at almost 60 per cent. The Ras Umm Sid and South Marsā Bereika sites also showed total live cover >40 per cent. The generic richness of the hard corals varied significantly between sites, with South Marsā Bereika having significantly more genera than Shark Observatory, with no significant difference between the other sites. There was a significant difference between sites when considering the number of individual colonies, and a relatively small mean colony size of just 0.15(±0.01) m (Graph 5:2).

Both South Marsā Bereika and Marsā Ghozlani had higher numbers of hard coral colonies than did the Old Quay site which had the fewest. Significant differences were also found in the abundance of coral rubble between the sites. Rubble cover was lowest at the Shark Observatory site and highest at the South Marsā Bereika site.

The mean hard coral cover within the Park has increased from 20.3 per cent in 2005 to 25.7 per cent in 2006. Although this increase is statistically significant, the power of the sampling design will only reliably account for changes in excess of around 5 per cent. Hence this change is only very slightly above this threshold and data from future years will be necessary to identify if this is a real trend in increasing coral cover as this study suggests. There were no detectable annual variations in many of the other recorded benthic parameters.

The dominant Scleractinian coral Genera included *Acropora*, *Seriatopora*, *Pocillopora*, *Stylophora*, *Porites* and *Montipora*. There was also significant abundance of the Octocoral *Millepora*. All of these Genera are common to all Indo-Pacific reefs.

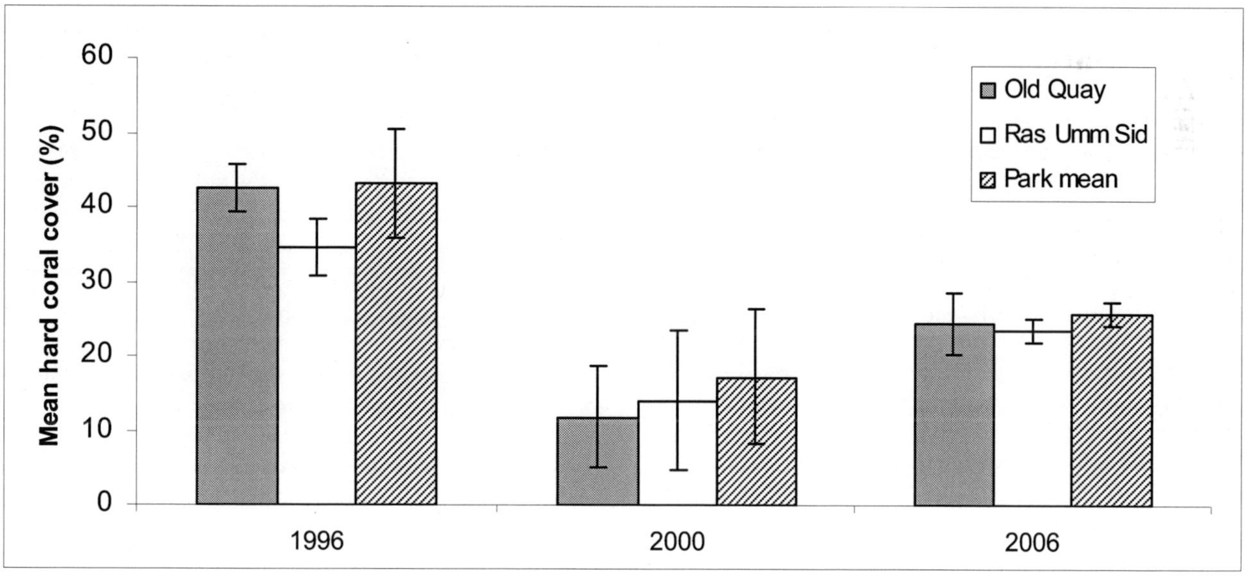

Graph 5:1 Mean (±s.e., n=8) Scleractinian coral cover before and after COTs outbreak compared with current status at two sites within the Park and also for the Park mean value

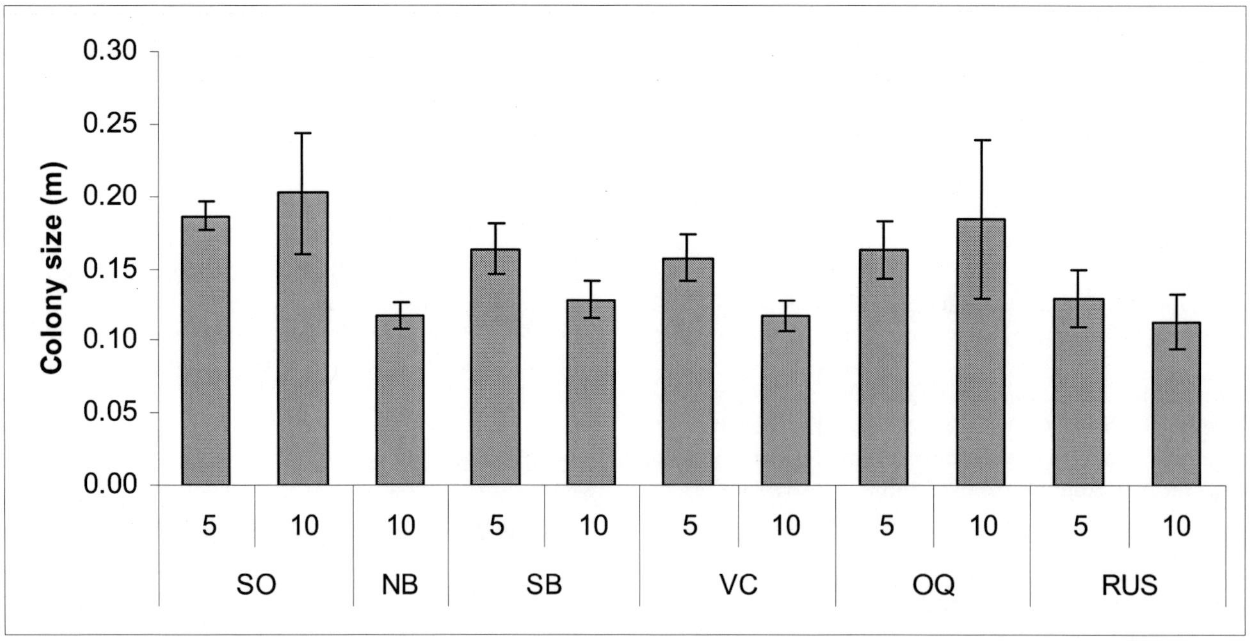

Graph 5:2 Mean (±s.e., n=8) Scleractinian coral colony size at six sites within the Ras Mohamed National Park

The rate of coral recruitment is important in maintaining the balance between reef accretion and reef erosion. The use of randomly placed quadrants identified a mean recruitment rate for Scleractinian corals of 1.21 (±0.13) new recruits per m^2 per year. There was no significant difference in the number of recruits between the different sites. This suggests that recruitment is fairly stable throughout the Park and although the figures are somewhat lower than other reported studies, the uniformity of the recruitment rates suggests that there is plenty of available substratum and there are no site specific impacts preventing recruitment. Grazing by Parrotfish may be keeping recruitment rates lower than would be expected in a region where the fish population was being exploited.

In summary, the benthic communities of the Ras Mohamed National Park appear to be continuing to recover from the devastation caused by the COTs outbreak in 1998. Although there was significant coral bleaching in the Red Sea in 1998, this did not affect the Ras Mohamed region. Although large areas of bare substratum exist, these are generally free of turf algae and available for recruitment of other benthic invertebrates.

ii) Fish community

The abundance of fish varies surprisingly little between the sites. This may be due to the protection offered by the Ras Mohamed National Park. Fishing is prohibited in all areas of the Park and has been for some period of time. Historically, the marine resources were exploited at a subsistence level by the Bedouin, but they now form the core of the tourist dive-boat industry. Providing the Bedouin with alternative incomes has meant that the fishing ban is generally observed and that there are only minor infringements. This lack of fishing pressure means that natural competitive interactions are occurring and hence most of the fish communities are similar in abundance and composition, with local differences attributable to natural variations, possibly linked to localized reef conditions and habitat structure.

The number of reef fish species observed during this study relates to around 10 per cent of the reported total 1,000 species present in the Red Sea. This value compares favourably with earlier studies,[50] with this study identifying species richness as almost double that of the previous study, though the two different survey methods used mean that the data are not statistically comparable.

It is interesting to note the variation in the individual samples, as the fish surveys were carried out at a similar time of day to avoid any diurnal variation. The greatest variation was recorded at the Shark Observatory site, attributable to the varied strength of the currents at this very exposed site. When the current was running at this site it was often moderate to strong, and hence larger numbers of pelagic species were recorded, such as Jacks and Trevally. The lowest variation was found at the North Marsā Bereika site which had the most stable, sheltered conditions, but the lowest overall abundance of fishes. This is important in a wider context as it suggests that changes in weather patterns and currents can affect the availability of natural resources.

.

50 Leujak 2005.

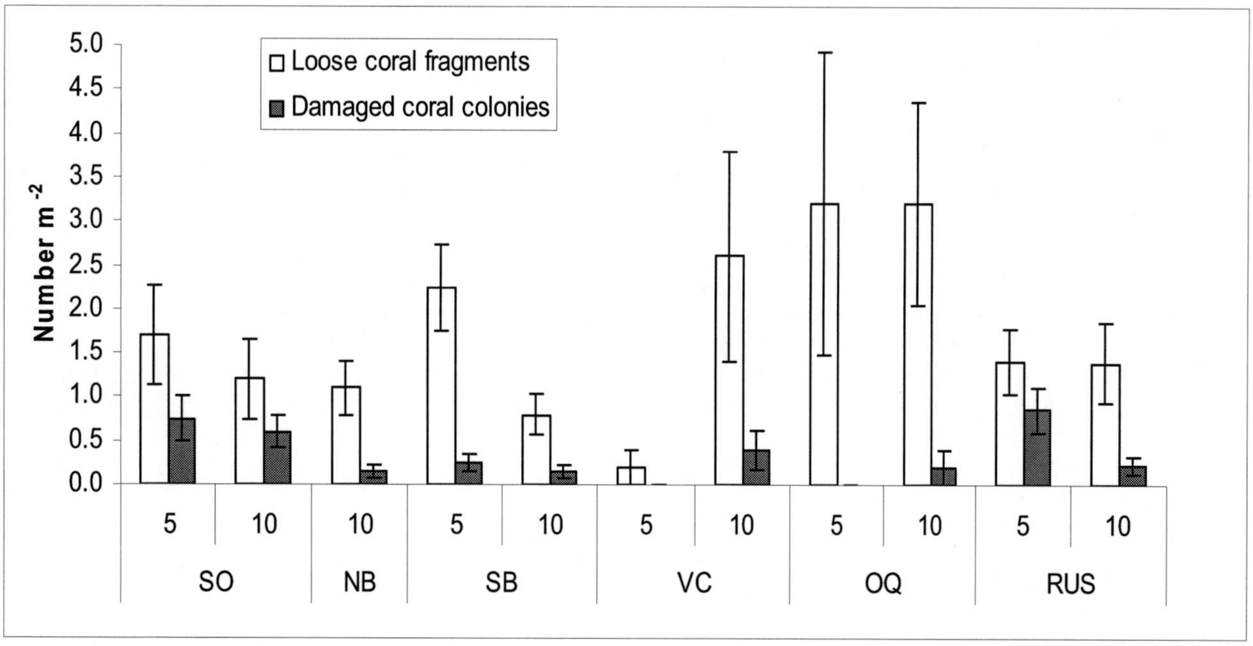

Graph 5:3 Mean (±s.e., n=8) number of loose damaged coral fragments and number of damaged coral colonies at six sites within the Ras Mohamed National Park

Those sites with highest fish abundance tended to have lower diversity as they were dominated by vast numbers of several common planktivorous species, such as the Anthiases (*Pseudoanthias squamipinnis*), which were found in great numbers at some sites. The two low abundance sites did not appear to be dominated by a few species and hence showed greater diversity.

With regard to the functional redundancy of the fish populations at the study sites, there were very limited differences between sites, with similar numbers of species from each family present. The exceptions were the increased Butterflyfish (Chaetodontidae) species richness at the Old Quay and South Marsā Bereika sites and the lower richness of Damselfishes (Pomacentridae) at the Shark Observatory site. Many Damselfish also show close associations with branching coral colonies, which were limited in number at this site, possibly helping to explain their reduced abundance there.

The only available data for temporal comparison is that provided by the ReefCheck database for the Butterflyfish, Grouper (Serranidae) and Parrotfish families. The species richness and hence functional redundancy of the Butterflyfish has shown a steady decline within the Park from the mid-1990s to the present survey, with the current richness less than a third of the recorded levels before the 1998 COTs outbreak, in line with the 'State of the Reefs' report.[51] The removal of coral substrata by the COTs would have impacted the obligate coral eating species, which are known to migrate to seek food elsewhere,[52] leaving the non-corallivores behind, and giving a lower species richness.

In summary, all of the sites in this study have similar fish populations, although the exposed Shark Observatory, Ras Umm Sid and Old Quay sites are characterized by low species diversity but high abundance, while the sheltered Marsā Ghozlani, North and South Marsā Bereika sites show low abundance but high diversity

iii) Threats

The survey results suggest that COTs (*A. planci*) are not currently a significant problem on the reefs of the Ras Mohamed National Park, with no quantitative values for their abundance. The sighting of the odd single individual suggests that the reefs within the Park have now returned to their normal, non-outbreak state.

As with the COTs, the population of the corallivorous Gastropod *Drupella* spp. seems to be in a natural state with just a few individuals aggregating on certain corals especially of the *Acropora* genus. Again, their presence in such small densities is no cause for concern and a natural part of the reef communities. Both these populations need ongoing monitoring as large increases in their abundance could have a considerable effect on the coral communities of the Park, especially in tandem with other impacts. Thankfully, no signs of coral bleaching or disease were recorded in any of the surveys, and only a single incidence of disease was observed while diving within the Park in general. As both bleaching and diseases have previously been identified within the Park, it is again essential to continue to monitor for either impact.

51 Wilkinson 2000.
52 Crosby and Reese 1996.

As the impacts of Scuba divers and snorkellers are one of the greatest threats to the health of the Park's benthic communities, it makes sense to include their effects in any monitoring programme. The number of broken coral fragments throughout the Park seems somewhat higher than would be expected naturally and it seems logical to attribute this to anthropogenic damage caused by divers and snorkellers (Graph 5:3). The high number of broken colonies at Shark Observatory may be due to the high number of visitors this site receives; the fact that more fragments are not also found here can be attributed to the wall-style topography meaning that fragments sink into the depths and are not recorded as they are at some of the sites with sloping topographies. Establishment of monitoring in closed areas will also provide data to monitor the rates of recovery of the reefs from the COTs outbreak. This is needed as there does seem to be a relationship between the rates of increase in coral cover since the outbreak and the number of visitors to each site.

Conservation Strategies

The reefs of the Red Sea are of particular importance to global biodiversity as they are part of the third centre of reef biodiversity. However, unlike the majority of this region, the Red Sea was not overly impacted by recent bleaching events, such as that of 1998 which caused widespread devastation to the region's reefs. It is not known if this is due to some kind of adaptation by the corals in the Red Sea or whether the enclosed nature of the Red Sea will help to protect the area's reefs from elevated sea temperatures more than the surrounding areas. Whatever the reason for the lack of severe impacts, this highlights the global importance of the Red Sea reefs in terms of resilience to climate change, which is seen as probably the greatest threat to coral reefs worldwide. For this reason alone, but also due to the economic importance to the respective economies, there is a requirement to continue to monitor the reefs of the Red Sea to allow informed management decisions to be made.

The use of a multi-attribute index to classify the condition of reef habitats has a number of advantages for both management and for the dissemination of complex biological data to all levels of stakeholder, from the local community to NGOs, park authorities and managers, governments and international funding bodies.

The data collected as part of such monitoring programmes has a clearly defined use in the region's conservation strategies. As well as allowing informed management decisions to be made, it also allows the monitoring of the performance of management actions. If the action is successful the index values should improve with time; if not, then this indicates that either the management action is not effective or that there is a further impact occurring which the management strategy has not taken into account and will therefore allow ongoing re-assessment of management actions.

Key to the management of all coral reef ecosystems is sustainable management of the reef resources for multiple uses, from fisheries to tourism. This monitoring project has been initiated in the Ras Mohamed National Park; however, it is envisaged that if successful in providing managers and stakeholders with the necessary information to allow informed management to be achieved, the methodology could be supplied to Park authorities throughout the Red Sea to allow a standardized conservation strategy to be implemented for this important region. This would allow the monitoring and management of all Red Sea reefs with a truly collaborative and standardized initiative, which could facilitate the conservation and sustainable use of these important natural resources.

References

Ablan, M.C.A., McManus, J.W. and Viswanathan, K. 2004. Indicators for management of coral reefs and their applications to Marine Protected Areas. *NAGA Worldfish Center Quarterly* 27(1 and 2): 31–9.

Admiralty Great Britain. Naval Intelligence Division. 1946. *Western Arabia and the Red Sea.* Geographical Handbook Series. Oxford: Oxford University Press.

Ahmed, M, Chong, C.K. and Balasubramanian, H. 2004. An overview of problems and issues in coral reef management. 70: 2–11 in M. Ahmed, C.K. Chong and H. Cesar (eds), *Economic Evaluation and Policy Priorities for Sustainable Management of Coral Reefs. Conference Proceedings.* Penang: Worldfish Center.

Bellwood, D.R., Hughes, T.P., Folke, C. and Nyström, M. 2004. Confronting the coral reef crisis. *Nature* 429: 827–33.

Brown, B. 1997. Coral bleaching: causes and consequences. 65–74 in H.A. Lessios and I.G. Macintyre (eds), *Proceedings of the 8th International Coral Reef Symposium* Vol. 1. Panama: Smithsonian Tropical Research Institute.

Bryant, D., Burke, L., McManus, J. and Spalding, M. 1998. *Reefs at Risk: a map based indicator of threats to the world's coral reefs.* Washington DC: World Resources Institute.

Crabbe, M.J.C. and Smith, D.J. 2006. Storm and stress: modelling strategies for recruitment and survival of corals in Discovery Bay, Jamaica, and in the Wakatobi Marine National Park, S.E. Sulawesi. 382–9 in Yoshimi Suzuki, et al. (eds), *Proceedings of the 10th International Coral Reef Symposium. Okinawa.* Tokyo: Japanese Coral Reef Society.

Crosby, M.P. and Reese, E.S. 1996. *A manual for monitoring coral reefs with indicator species: Butterflyfish as indicators of change on Indo-Pacific reefs.* Silver Spring MD: Office of Ocean and Coastal Resource Management, NOAA.

Cumming, R.L. 1999. Predation on reef building corals: multiscale variation in the density of three corallivorous gastropods, *Drupella* spp. *Coral Reefs* 18: 147–57.

Fabricius, K.E. and De'ath, G. 2004. Identifying ecological change and its causes: case study on coral reefs. *Ecological Applications* 14(5): 1448–65.

Friedlander, A.M. and Parrish, J.D. 1998. Habitat characteristics affecting fish assemblages on a Hawaiian coral reef. *Journal of Experimental Marine Biology and Ecology* 224: 1–30.

Frouda, M.M. 1984. Ras Mohamed: The first National Park in Egypt. *Courser* 1. Cairo: The Ornithological Society of Egypt.

Green, E.P. and Bruckner, A.W. 2000. The significance of coral disease epizootiology for coral reef conservation. *Biological Conservation* 96: 347–61.

Gomez, E.D., Aliño, P.M., Yap, H.T. and Licuanan, W.Y. 1994. A review of the status of Philippine reefs. *Marine Pollution Bulletin* 29: 62–8.

Grigg, R.W. and Dollar, S.J. 1990. Natural and anthropogenic disturbance on coral reefs. 439–52 in Z. Dubinsky (ed.), *Coral Reefs* 25. *Ecosystems of the World.* Amsterdam: Elsevier.

Hart, A.M. and Klumpp, D.W. 1996. Response of herbivorous fishes to crown-of-thorns-starfish (*Acanthaster planci*) outbreaks. 3. Age, growth, mortality and feeding ecology of *Acanthurus nigrofuscus* and *Scarus frenatus*. *Marine Ecology Progress Series* 132(1–3): 11–19.

Hart A.M, Klumpp, D.W. and Russ, G.R. 1996. Response of herbivorous fishes to crown-of-thorns-starfish (*Acanthaster planci*) outbreaks. 2. Density and biomass of selected species of herbivorous fish and fish habitat correlations. *Marine Ecology Progress Series* 132(1–3): 21–30.

Hidayati, D. 2003. Coral reef rehabilitation and management program in Indonesia. 303–19 in *Proc. 3rd International Surfing Reef Symposium. Regan, New Zealand, 22–25 June 2003.*

Image Science and Analysis Laboratory, NASA–Johnson Space Center. 17 August 2006. Remote Sensing of Coral Reefs at NASA. Retrieved 6 November 2006 from URL <http://eol.jsc.nasa.gov/reefs/Overview-2003/scie.htm>

Jennings, S. and Polunin, N.V.C. 1997. Impacts of predator depletion by fishing on the biomass and diversity of non-target reef fish communities. *Coral Reefs* 16: 71–82.

Kleypas, J.A., Feely, R.A., Fabry, V.J., Langdon, C., Sabine, C.L. and Robbins, L.L. 2006. Impacts of ocean acidification on coral reefs and other marine calcifiers: a guide for future research, Report of a workshop held 18–20 April 2005, St. Petersburg, FL, sponsored by NSF, NOAA and USGS.

Kotb, M., Abdulaziz, M., Al-Agwan, Z., Al-Shaikh, K., Al-Yami, H., Banajah, A., DeVantier, L., Eisinger, M., Eltayeb, M., Hassan, M., Heiss, G., Howe, S., Kemp, J., Klaus, R., Krupp, F., Mohamed, N., Rouphael, T., Turner, J. and Zajonz, U. 2004. Status of the coral reefs in the Red Sea and Gulf of Aden in 2004. In C. Wilkinson (ed.), *Status of the Coral Reefs of the World: 2004.* Townsville: Global Coral Reef Monitoring Network GCRMN/AIMS. Available on-line at http://-www.aims.gov.au/pages/research/coral-bleaching/scr-2004/.

Lieske, E. and Myers, R.F. 2004. *Coral Reef Guide Red Sea*. London: Collins.

Leujak, W. 2005. Monitoring coral communities in South Sinai, Egypt, with reference to visitor impacts. Unpublished PhD Thesis. UCL University Marine Biological Station, Millport, Isle of Cumbrae, Scotland.

McCook, L.J. 1999. Macroalgae, nutrients and phase shifts on coral reefs: scientific issues and management consequences for the Great Barrier Reef. *Coral Reefs* 18: 357–67.

McClanahan, T. 1994. Coral-eating snail *Drupella cornus* population increases in Kenyan coral reef lagoons. *Marine Ecology Progress Series* 115: 131–7.

McClanahan, T., Polunin, N. and Done, T. 2002. Ecological states and the resilience of coral reefs. *Conservation Ecology* 6(2): 18.

McKenna, S.A., Richmond, R.H. and Roos, G. 2001. Assessing the effects of sewage on coral reefs: developing techniques to detect stress before coral mortality. *Bulletin of Marine Science* 69(2): 517–24.

Pilcher, N. and Abdi, N.D. 2000. The Status of Coral Reefs in Djibouti. In C. Wilkinson (ed.), *Status of the Reefs of the World.* Townsville: Global Coral Reef Monitoring Network GCRMN/AIMS.

Pilcher, N. and Nasr, D. 2000. The Status of Coral Reefs in Sudan. In C. Wilkinson (ed.), *Status of the Reefs of the World.* Townsville: Global Coral Reef Monitoring Network GCRMN/AIMS.

Pilcher, N. and Zaid, M.M.A. 2000. The status of coral reefs in Egypt: 2000. In C. Wilkinson (ed.), *Status of the Reefs of the World.* Townsville: Global Coral Reef Monitoring Network GCRMN/AIMS.

Roberts, C.M. and Ormond, R.F.G. 1987. Habitat complexity and coral reef fish diversity and abundance on Red Sea fringing reefs. *Marine Ecology Progress Series* 41: 1–8.

Saleh, B.M. 2005. Impacts of *Acanthaster planci* infestations on reefs of the Ras Mohamed National Park 1998–2003. Unpublished MSc Thesis. Suez Canal University.

Samuel, R. 1973. *The Negev and Sinai.* London: Weidenfeld and Nicolson.

Shehata, A. 1998. Protected areas in the Gulf of Aqaba, Egypt: a mechanism of integrated coastal management. 310–9 in *ITMEMS Proceedings*.

Sluka, R.D. and Miller, M.W. 2001. Herbivorous fish assemblages and herbivory pressure on Laamu Atoll, Republic of Maldives. *Coral Reefs* 20: 255–62.

Smith, D.J., Suggett, D.J., Baker, N.R. 2005. Is photoinhibiton of zooanthellae photosynthesis the primary cause of thermal induced bleaching in corals? *Global Change Biology* 11: 1–11.

Spalding, M.D., Ravilious, C. and Green, E.P. 2001. *World Atlas of Coral Reefs*. UNEP World Conservation Monitoring Center. Berkeley Ca.: University of California Press.

Spurgeon, J. 2004. Valuation of coral reefs: the next 10 years. In M. Ahmed, C.K. Chong, and H. Cesar (eds), *Economic Evaluation and Policy Priorities for Sustainable Management of Coral Reefs. Conference Proceedings*. Penang: Worldfish Center.

Thacker, R.W., Ginsburg, D.W. and Paul, V.J. 2001. Effects of herbivore exclusion and nutrient enrichment on coral reef macroalgae and cyanobacteria. *Coral Reefs* 19: 318–29.

Wells, S. 1987. *Draft Directory of Coral Reefs of International Importance*. Cambridge: IUCN / CMC.

Whittingham, E., Campbell, J. and Townsley, P. 2001. *Poverty and Reefs: a global overview.* London: DFID-IMM-IOC / Paris: UNESCO.

Wilkinson, C. (ed.). 2004. *Status of the Reefs of the World: 2004*. Volume 1. Townsville: Global Coral Reef Monitoring Network GCRMN/AIMS.

Part II: The Sea: Boats and Navigation

How Fast is Fast?
Technology, Trade and Speed under Sail in the Roman Red Sea

Julian Whitewright

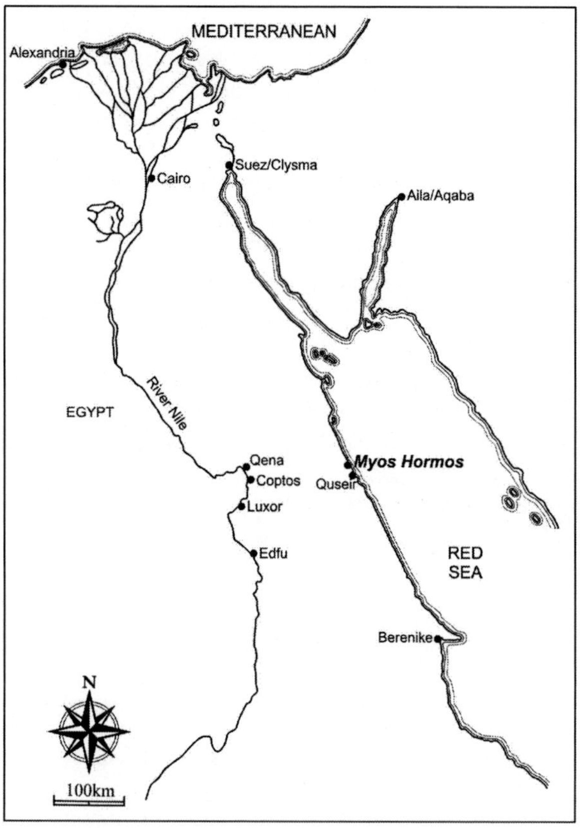

Map 6:1 The northern Red Sea showing the location of Myos Hormos (after Peacock and Blue 2006: figure 1)

The Red Sea represents one of the great maritime highways of the ancient and modern world. It has formed one of the primary geographical connections between the cultures of the Mediterranean world and those of the Indian Ocean, as well as allowing Red Sea cultures to move in either direction. Trade routes have utilized the orientation of the Red Sea from prehistoric times up to the present day; the construction of the Suez Canal has further emphasized the advantageous nature of north / south travel through the Red Sea as a link between East and West. The focus of this paper is on the use of the Red Sea as a trade route and cultural link during the Roman period, specifically the first three centuries of the first millennium AD. Particular emphasis is placed upon an understanding of the relationship between environmental conditions and ancient ship technology as a way of elucidating the maritime routes of the Red Sea and the corresponding overland routes in the Eastern Desert.

Roman Red Sea Trade

Throughout the early first millennium AD Roman commerce with the wider Indian Ocean was funnelled through the ports of Myos Hormos, Berenike and Clysma, located on the Egyptian coast in the northern third of the Red Sea (Map 6:1).

Some indication of the scale of the Roman involvement in the wider trade networks of the Indian Ocean can be found in Strabo's remark that 'now one hundred and twenty ships sail from Myos Hormos to India'.[1] It is worth noting that Strabo is only referring to ships sailing to India. Roman vessels trading with the southern part of the Red Sea and the Gulf of Aden are not included — neither are ships sailing down the coast of East Africa. All of these Roman merchant ships would have had to begin and end their voyage in one of the northern Red Sea ports. As well as Roman ships sailing from Egypt to India, it also seems likely that vessels of Indian Ocean origin were sailing to the northern end of the Red Sea. The author of the *Periplus Maris Erythræi*, a first-century AD merchant guide to the Red Sea and Indian Ocean, says of Eudaemon Arabia (Aden) 'in the early days of the city when the voyage was not yet made from India to Egypt, and when they did not dare to sail from Egypt to the ports across this ocean, but all came together at this place and it received cargoes from both countries.'[2] It is easy to imagine ships of different cultures engaged in trade on the Indian Ocean converging on the Red Sea in order to reach the markets of the Mediterranean.

The two ports of Myos Hormos and Berenike were central to this long-distance trade. They acted as entrepôts into the Roman Empire for the goods, many of them luxury items, arriving from Arabia, East Africa, India and places further to the east.[3] Once unloaded, goods were trans-shipped across the desert to Coptos on the Nile. The journey from Berenike to Coptos took twelve days across the Eastern Desert,[4] while the route from Myos Hormos required six or seven days of desert travel.[5] From Coptos goods were taken by boat to Alexandria from where they could be shipped to the wider Roman world. Goods ex-

1 Strabo *Geography* 2.5.12.
2 Passage 26, tr. Schoff 1912.
3 Peacock and Blue 2006: 3.
4 Pliny *Natural History* 6.102–3.
5 Strabo *Geography* 17.1.45.

ported from the Roman Empire to the Indian Ocean probably followed the reverse route.

The Red Sea wind regime

The geographical advantages of the Red Sea are obvious, the north / south corridor which it provides between the Indian Ocean and Mediterranean being clear from even the briefest glance at a map. However, seafaring and navigation on the Red Sea are far from simple. As with any body of water, the ease with which a sailing ship can be navigated between two locations is dependent to a large extent on the nature of the wind the vessel encounters. A fair wind will allow a relatively faster voyage to be made than if unfavourable winds are encountered. Understanding the wind regime of the Red Sea is therefore important in understanding the sailing vessels and the ports which they used. The data on Red Sea wind patterns presented here (Figures 6:1–6:5) is derived from the work of Davies and Morgan.[6] In the northern third of the Red Sea, where the ports of Myos Hormos and Berenike are located, the prevailing wind blows from the north for most of the year. This is especially the case between June and September when the frequency of northerly winds is between 75 and 94 per cent. The frequency of northerly winds moderates slightly during the winter. However, it is still 67 per cent in the vicinity of Berenike and Myos Hormos from October to December and 74 per cent between January and March. The central third of the Red Sea experiences more mixed conditions. Northerly winds again dominate during the summer, although the wind is more variable and sometimes blows from the west. During the winter the frequency of northerly winds declines and a southerly wind may be active for 39 per cent of the time from October to December and 33 per cent between January and March. The southern third of the Red Sea follows a similar, albeit more polarized, pattern to the central third. Northerly winds dominate during the summer, prevailing for as much as 75 per cent of the time during September. During the winter the pattern is reversed and southerly winds prevail for 70 per cent of the time from October to December and 55 per cent between January and March. The wind in the Gulf of Aden follows a general pattern of prevailing wind blowing into the Gulf (from the Indian Ocean) during the winter and out of the Gulf during the summer.

A vessel attempting to sail from the straits of Bāb al-Mandab to the coast of Egypt is likely to encounter unfavourable northerly winds at some point on its route. Throughout its history of use as a corridor for travel and trade the presence of persistent northerly winds must have been an added complication to northward sailing on the Red Sea, while making southbound travel relatively simple.[7] The problem of northward navigation has drawn the attention of both ancient and modern authors. Strabo comments that the road from the Nile to Berenike was cut because 'the Red Sea was hard to navigate, particularly for those who set sail from its innermost recess'.[8] Recent scholarly investigation into Red Sea voyaging has identified the problems associated with sailing against the northerly wind.[9]

It is no surprise, given the nature of the wind patterns in the Red Sea, that trade routes were utilized when the winds in the Red Sea and the Indian Ocean were at their most favourable.[10] If the voyage from Egypt to India and back is used as an example, this meant leaving Egypt in August in order to have northerly winds on the voyage down the Red Sea. Ships then sailed across the Indian Ocean on the tail end of the south-westerly monsoon, reaching the Indian coast sometime in September. The return voyage could have been made at any stage after this point, as long as the north-easterly monsoon in the Indian Ocean had begun. Pliny records that vessels left India at the beginning of the Roman month of December and no later than early January.[11] Such a departure date would have given ships a fair wind back to the Gulf of Aden. Vessels then had to sail up the Red Sea and hope that the southerly winds in the southern two-thirds were as frequent and long-lasting as possible. Pliny says that the ships sailing from India to Egypt 'after entering the Red Sea, continue the voyage with a south-west or south wind'.[12] It seems likely that the earlier a ship set off from India (assuming the north-east monsoon had begun) the better its chance of quickly working its way up the Red Sea to the Egyptian ports of Myos Hormos and Berenike. Effective use of diurnal winds would also have played a role in successful northward navigation. Although difficult to accurately quantify, Davies and Morgan note that daytime heating of the land relative to the sea slants the wind, and this has the effect of making one tack more favourable than the other.[13] Successful exploitation of this would have aided a vessel in its voyage northward and it seems unlikely that an experienced seafarer would have overlooked this opportunity.[14]

6 Davies and Morgan 1995: 29–30.

7 Cf. Facey 2004: 11.

8 Strabo *Geography* 12.1.45.

9 Casson 1980; Sidebotham 1989: 198–201; Facey 2004.

10 Cf. Casson 1980.

11 Pliny *Natural History* 6.106.

12 Ibid.

13 Davies and Morgan 1995: 28.

14 The advantageous use of diurnal winds is mentioned by Ibn Mājid in his account of navigating the Red Sea; he noted that they occur mainly on the African coast of the Red Sea and rarely on the Arabian coast. For a translation and commentary see Tibbets 1971: 256 and 370.

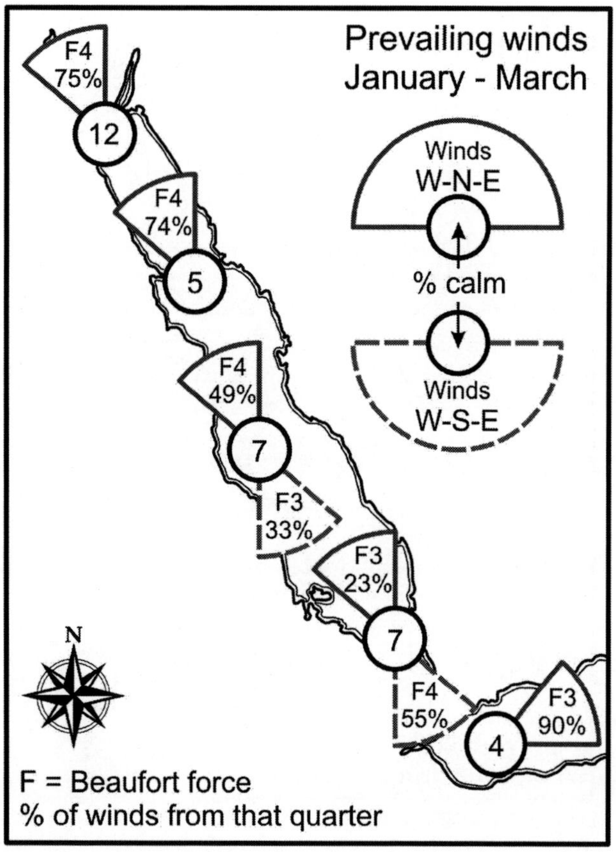

Figure 6:1 Prevailing Red Sea winds, January to March (after Davies and Morgan 1995: 29)

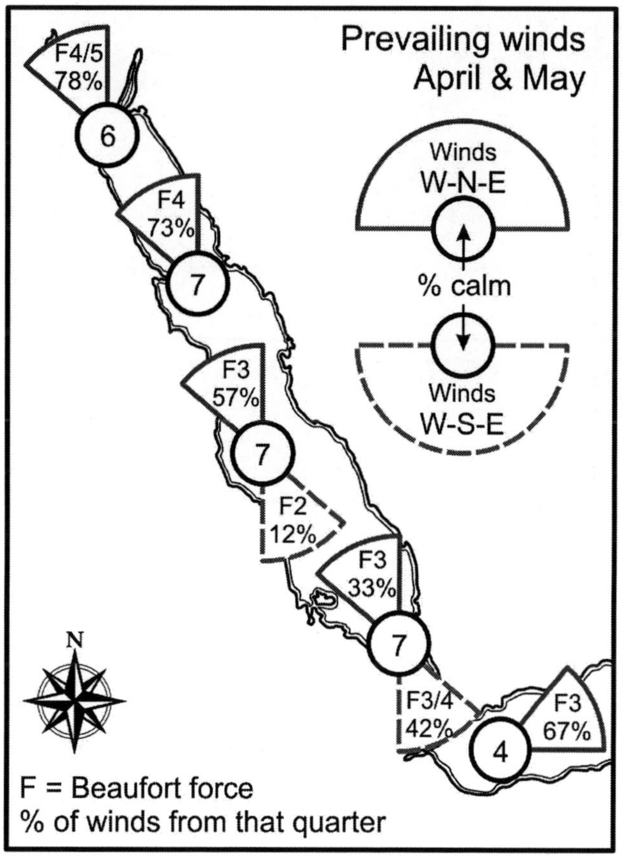

Figure 6:2 Prevailing Red Sea winds, April and May (after Davies and Morgan 1995: 29)

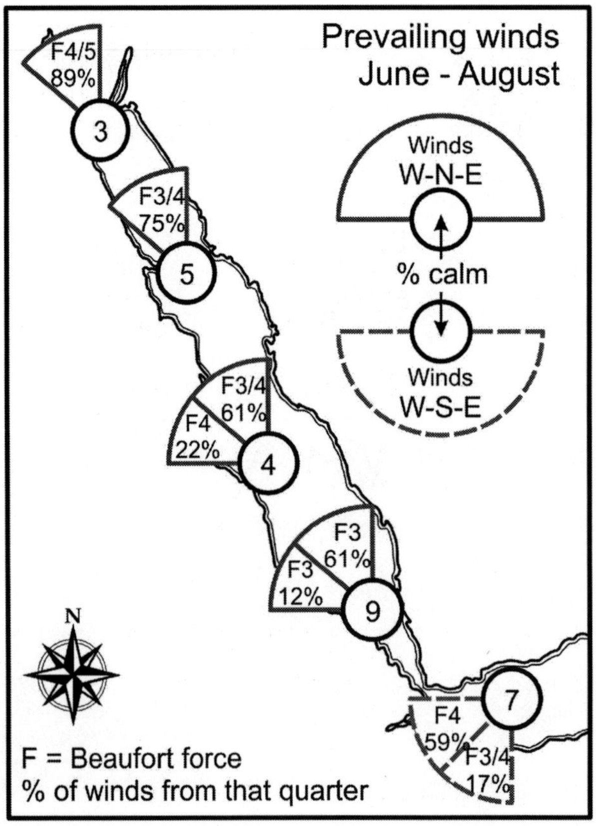

Figure 6:3 Prevailing Red Sea winds, June to August (after Davies and Morgan 1995: 29)

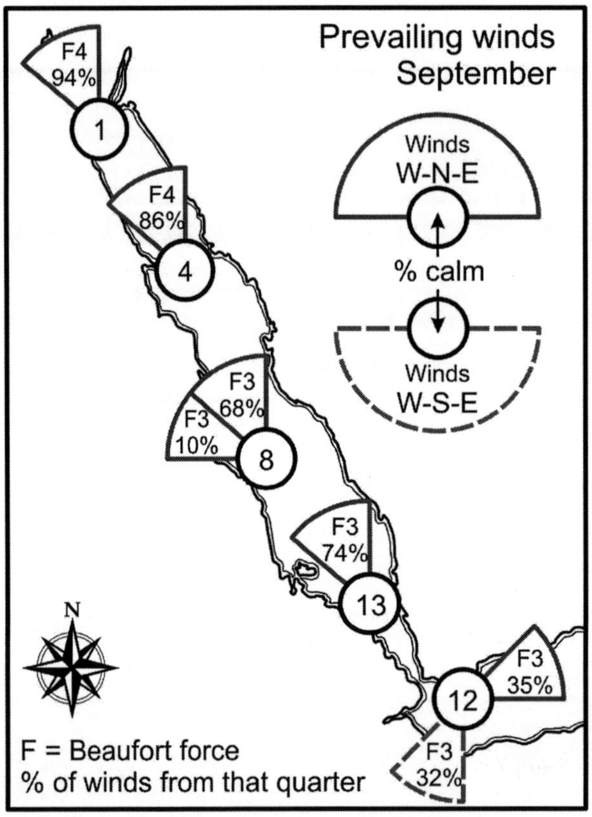

Figure 6:4 Prevailing Red Sea winds, September (after Davies and Morgan 1995: 29)

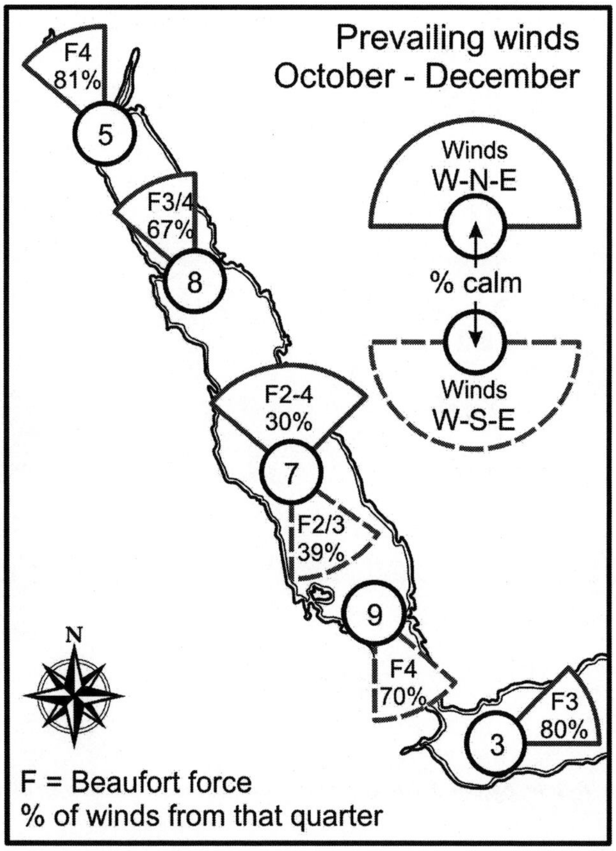

Figure 6:5 Prevailing Red Sea winds, October to December (after Davies and Morgan 1995: 29)

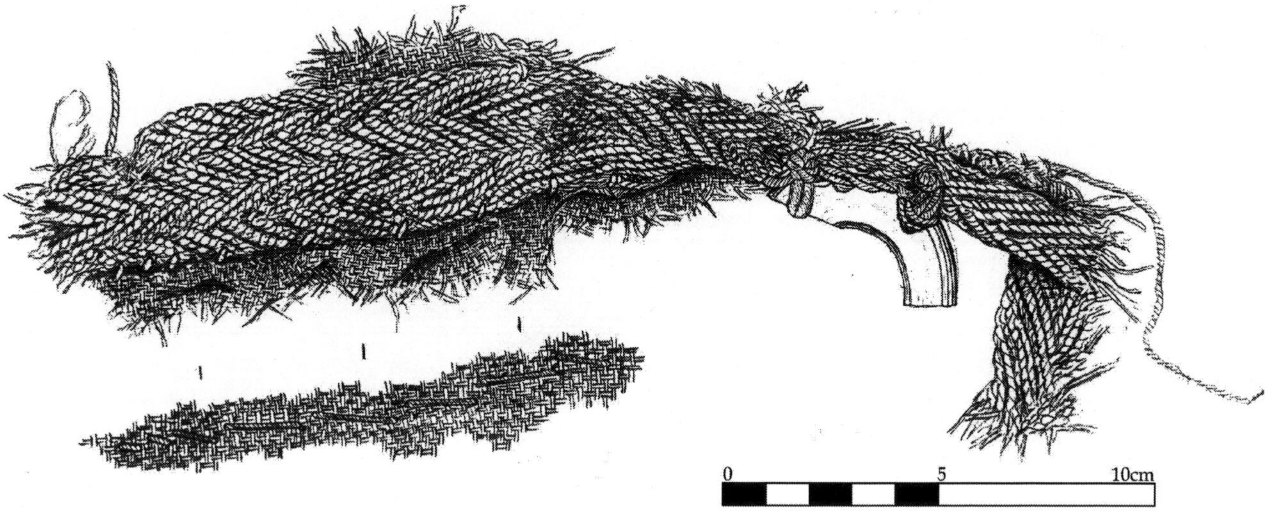

Figure 6:6 Roman sail and brail ring from Myos Hormos, late first / early second century AD (J. Whitewright)

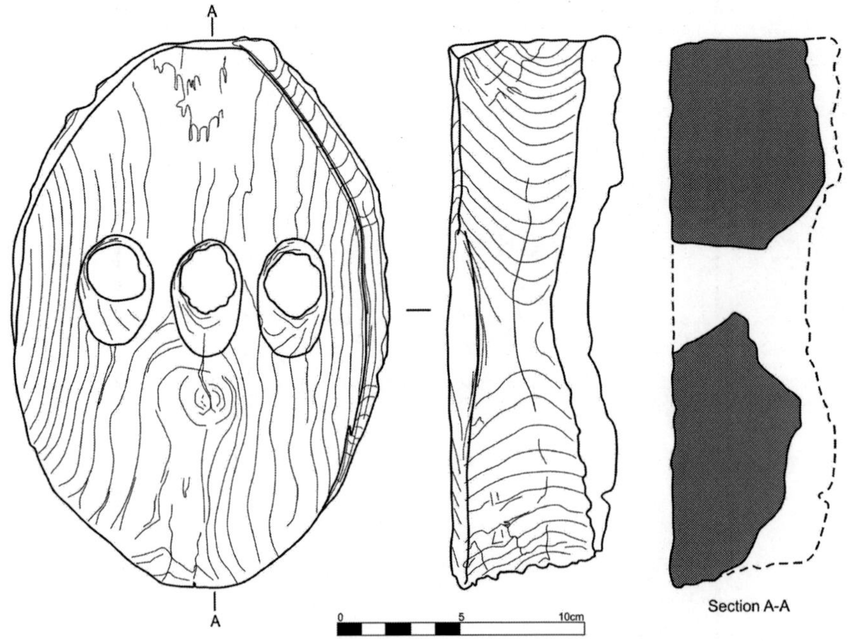

Figure 6:7 Roman deadeye from Myos Hormos, mid / late second century AD *(J. Whitewright)*

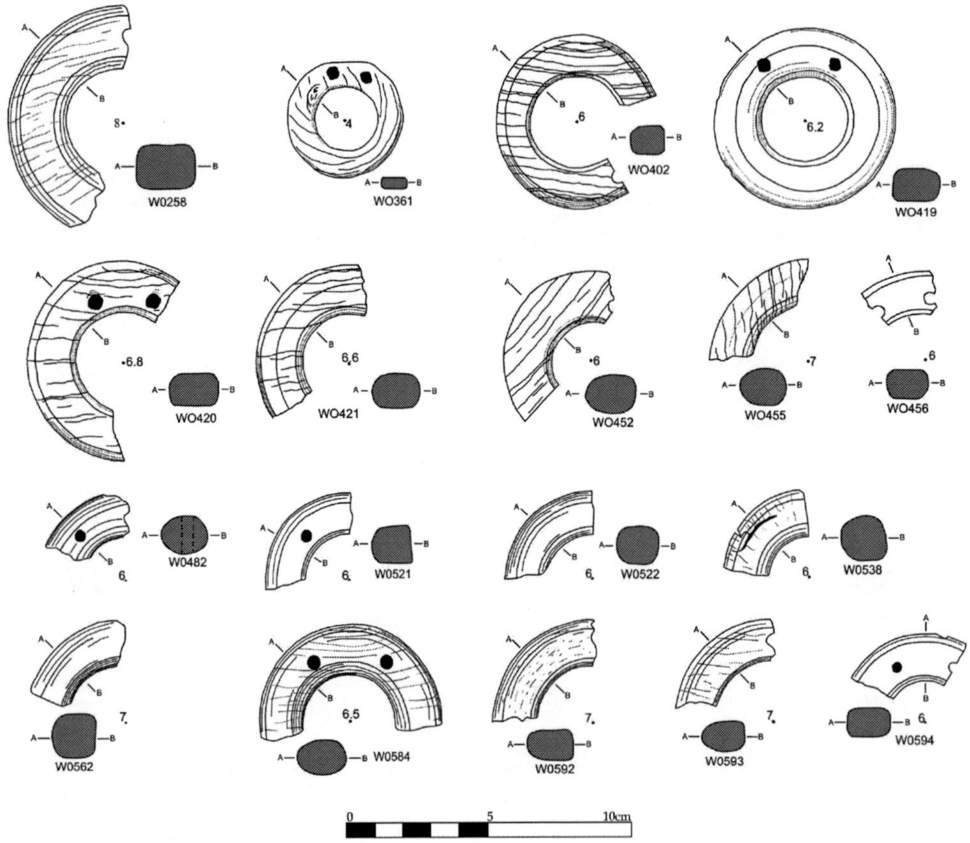

Figure 6:8 Example of wooden brail rings from Myos Hormos, first century BC *– third century* AD *(J. Whitewright)*

With the problem of sailing to windward in mind, it is interesting to observe that the authors of the *Red Sea Pilot* note that 'Anyone used to sailing to windward will not find the Red Sea markedly worse than anywhere else.'[15] Sailors native to the Red Sea or other areas where upwind sailing was a part of life may have taken for granted the techniques required to sail to windward and continued their voyages accordingly, once northerly winds were encountered. Sailors from areas where favourable trade winds generally prevail during the sailing season, such as the Indian Ocean, may have had far more difficulty adapting to the unfamiliar conditions of the northern Red Sea.

The northerly wind and the location of ports

The environmental reality of prevailing northerly winds has led to the location of Red Sea ports being considered in terms of the wind patterns before other contributing factors. In general, this theory concludes that a port situated as far to the South as possible, within the overall context of a specific culture, will be preferable to a more northerly port. The main reason for this has been the assumption that northward sailing is so difficult as to make transport or travel overland a more favourable option. This viewpoint is best summed up in Casson's statement regarding the relative merits of Berenike and Myos Hormos; 'Berenike was well over 200 miles south of Myos Hormos, which meant, for returning vessels, that much less beating against the northerlies which prevail in the Red Sea above latitude 20° north.'[16] Quite simply, there was no reason to waste time sailing against the prevailing northerly winds in order to reach Myos Hormos when Berenike would serve perfectly well and was located over 200 miles to the south.

The assumption that ports needed to be located as far to the south as possible only takes into account the prevailing wind regime which complicates Red Sea navigation, particularly in the northern third. No account of the actual sailing ability of ancient ships or the difference in costs of transporting goods overland rather than by sea has been included. Such a line of argument also overlooks the fact that ports such as Myos Hormos and Clysma were located at the northern end of the Red Sea and were used extensively during antiquity. Archaeological evidence from Myos Hormos indicates that a significant quantity of the rigging material found there originated in the Indian subcontinent. This material included sail cloth (Figure 6:6), a deadeye (Figure 6:7), and brail rings (Figure 6:8). Sailing ships engaged in trade between the Red Sea and the Indian Ocean must have been capable of reaching the port, despite the direction of the prevailing wind. Likewise, in the medieval period it is Myos Hormos, under the new name of al-Quṣayr (later known as al-Quṣayr al-Qadīm) which is reused as a port of trade, rather than the more southerly port of Berenike. Proximity to the river Nile and by inference faster land communication, rather than a southerly location, may have been an underlying cause of the reuse of Myos Hormos in the Islamic period. This is implied by Qalqashandī writing in the fourteenth century, who states that 'Al-Quseir is on the northern side of Aidhab and some of the ships frequent it; it is near to Qus and Aidhab is far from Qus.'[17] The location of ports in the Red Sea during antiquity was obviously dependent on more than just the direction of the prevailing wind.[18]

Roman sailing ships on the Red Sea

An indication of the potential capability of merchant ships engaged in trade on the Red Sea is impossible without first establishing the nature of the rig and sail plan of the vessels concerned. The archaeological remains of the rigging of vessels utilizing the port of Myos Hormos during the Roman period fall within the same rigging tradition as other published finds from the Mediterranean.[19] The general form of the sail fragments (Figure 6:7), deadeye (Figure 6:8) and brail rings (Figure 6:9) is consistent with rigging finds from classical contexts within the Mediterranean basin and observations of rigging depicted in iconographic sources[20]. These finds comprise most of the components required to rig a sailing vessel within the classical Mediterranean tradition.[21] Brails, and brail rings in particular, are components unique to the Mediterranean sailing rig. Their use is inconsistent with any of the other forms of sailing rig known to have been used at this time in the Mediterranean or Indian Ocean.[22] As a result of this, it seems reasonable to assume that Roman sailing vessels engaged in trade in the Indian Ocean and sailing from the Egyptian Red Sea ports were outwardly similar in appearance, operation and capability to their Mediterranean contemporaries, at least in terms of the sailing rig.

The Mediterranean square-sail rig of the Roman Imperial period was a sophisticated and highly developed sailing rig. By the first century AD, the Mediterranean square rig consisted of all the component parts required to sail on all

15 Davies and Morgan 1995: 26.
16 Casson 1980: 22, n. 2.

17 1913: 465.
18 Cf. Ward, this volume.
19 Whitewright 2007.
20 As well as Mediterranean sources which depict Roman square-rigged vessels, a pot sherd from the port of Berenike has a graffito of a square-rigged ship in the Roman style, dating between AD 50 and AD 70, see Sidebotham 1996: 315–7.
21 Whitewright, forthcoming.
22 Ibid.

points of sailing. A strong system of standing rigging, comprising shrouds, forestay and backstay, was in place to support the mast both laterally and longitudinally on all courses a vessel may have sailed. Likewise the running rigging of such ships was designed to act as efficiently as possible. The system used for shortening sail, known as brails, allowed ancient mariners to reduce the size of their sail at a moment's notice. Brails also allowed sailors to change the overall shape of the sail depending on the course being sailed and in doing so to sail a vessel in the most efficient manner for a given course. It seems likely that all of these features would have allowed Mediterranean sailors in the first millennium AD to sail on both upwind and downwind courses, if they so wished. Textual sources from the Mediterranean refer to sailing techniques and practices which are consistent with vessels sailing to windward and which would not be used on any other course.[23] Likewise the invention and use of a small foresail or *artemon* on the Mediterranean rig is indicative of an ability to sail an upwind course — the *artemon* being of only limited use on other sailing courses.

Textual evidence survives from the ancient world which provides a further indication of the ability of Roman sailing ships to make ground to windward. Records from the Roman Mediterranean detail the time taken to sail between different locations in the Roman Empire.[24] Some of these voyages are recorded as having taken place with fair winds and some with foul winds. In the context of the ancient world 'foul' winds generally refer to winds from a contrary direction. Put simply, voyages made with a foul or unfavourable wind would have been voyages made in an upwind direction. Analysis of such voyages can give an indication of the overall speed of a vessel between two places in the form of *Velocity Made Good* (Vmg), in other words, the relative speed of the vessel directly to windward. The importance of Vmg as a way of recording a vessel's sailing capabilities has been observed during the trial voyages of replica vessels from Scandinavia.[25] Reference to eight voyages, listed here (Table 6:1), indicates that the Roman sailing ships of the period, presumably rigged with the standard Mediterranean square-sail rig, could attain an average Vmg of 1.9 knots. The actual figure might be slightly more or less depending on the exact nature of conditions encountered *en route*, the state of repair of the vessel and the ability of its crew. A Vmg of 1.9 knots equates to a distance of about 45 nautical miles sailed over a 24-hour period in upwind conditions. Sailing trials of replica vessels from the Viking era, carrying a square-sail rig broadly similar to that used by the Romans, returned a Vmg to windward of between 1.5 and 2 knots.[26] This compares favourably with the data derived from historical sources for Roman ships. Roman merchant ships on the Red Sea were rigged with the same sailing rig as Mediterranean vessels; they would have been operated in the same way and would have had a similar performance. This would have included being able to sail on an upwind course at an average of 1.9 knots Vmg. For comparative purposes it is worth noting that historical records of Roman merchant ships contain a fastest average speed, over a distance of 670 nautical miles between Corinth and Puteoli, of 6.2 knots.[27]

	Route	*Distance (nm)*	*Time (days)*	*Vmg (kts)*
1	Rhodes — Gaza	410	7	2.4
2	Alexandria — Marseilles	1500	30	2.1
3	Puteoli — Ostia	120	2.5	2
4	Gaza — Byzantium	855	20	1.8
5	Rhodes — Byzantium	445	10	1.8
6	Caesarea — Rhodes	400	10	1.7
7	Alexandria — Cyprus	250	6.5	1.6
8	Sidon — Chelidonian Isles	350	9.5	1.5
			Average	*1.9*

Table 6:1 Sailing times of Roman merchant ships in unfavourable Mediterranean conditions (data derived from Casson 1995: 288–9)

Seasonal currents in the Red Sea

Having considered the wind regime of the Red Sea and assessed the potential capabilities of the Roman vessels which sailed upon it, one further important environmental factor remains: namely, the seasonal currents of the Red Sea, which vary in both direction and intensity during the year. The Red Sea has a very high salinity level due to the lack of permanent rivers, the lack of regular rainfall and the continual solar evaporation.[28] A direct result of this is that in order to replace water lost by evaporation, water must flow in through the straits of Bāb al-Mandab. This water of average salinity is more buoyant than the existing seawater and a counter-current is formed. Incoming water flows northward in the upper area of the water-column, while denser, more saline water flows outward at the bottom.[29] Northwards-running currents reach their peak in the winter when they are pushed in by the easterly winds

23 Augustine refers to the use of the *artemon* to balance the sailing rig and keep the bow of the vessel at the correct angle to the wind while sailing close-hauled, tr. Casson 1995: 240, n. 70; Aristotle *Mech.* 851b observes the practice of brailing up one portion of a vessel's sail when it is necessary to sail to windward, tr. Casson 1995: 276.

24 Casson 1995: 288–9.

25 Englert 2006: 39.

26 Vinner 1986: 224.

27 Casson 1995: 284.

28 Davies and Morgan 1995: 37.

29 Ibid.

prevailing in the Gulf of Aden. During the winter, these currents flow northwards as far as the site of Myos Hormos up to a speed of 0.5 knots.[30] Such a figure may seem insignificant, but when taken as a ratio of the Vmg made good against the wind by a Roman sailing ship it represents an additional 25 per cent or more of the speed of the vessel on a direct course: a far more significant figure. Even when faced with northerly winds a vessel would still have been able to make steady progress towards its destination. The currents decrease between January and April before flowing southward during the summer, when the north wind is at its strongest.[31] This final point lends further emphasis to the need for vessels to return to the Red Sea as quickly as possible in order to avoid fighting both wind and currents during their journey northward.

Discussion

The evidence presented above strongly suggests that Roman sailing vessels engaged in navigation on the Red Sea and Indian Ocean were rigged in the same fashion as contemporary ships in the Mediterranean. This sailing rig comprised all the component parts required for upwind sailing. Textual sources detailing the time taken to sail between specific places in the ancient Mediterranean suggest that Mediterranean sailors had the technical knowledge and ability to sail upwind at an average Vmg of 1.9 knots. It is valuable here to reiterate the statement made by Davies and Morgan regarding upwind sailing in the Red Sea, that 'Anyone used to sailing to windward will not find the Red Sea markedly worse than anywhere else.'[32] Sailors of a Mediterranean tradition, in vessels rigged in the Mediterranean fashion, would seem to have been well-equipped to tackle northward travel in the Red Sea. These conclusions regarding the capability of Roman sailing ships can be applied to possible trade routes in the northern Red Sea. Three potential routes based on known locations of ports and road systems can be identified (Map 6:2):

* Route A: Sail to Berenike, overland transport to Coptos.
* Route B: Sail to Berenike, sail to Myos Hormos, overland transport to Coptos.
* Route C: Sail directly to Myos Hormos, overland transport to Coptos.

To travel from Berenike to Myos Hormos by sea would require a voyage of roughly 200 nautical miles. A vessel sailing north and by-passing Berenike altogether in order to sail directly to Myos Hormos would be required to sail 150 nautical miles further than the same vessel sailing directly to Berenike only.

Using the average Vmg of 1.9 knots would allow the voyage from Berenike to Myos Hormos to be made in 4½ days. If the lowest Vmg of 1.5 knots was applied it would take a vessel 5½ days and the fastest Vmg of 2.4 knots would see the voyage completed in 3½ days. For a vessel sailing past Berenike and straight on to Myos Hormos, the extra time required would be 3½ days at an average speed, and c. 4 days and 2½ days for the slowest and fastest Vmg respectively. A vessel with a strong southerly wind, sailing at the fastest documented long-distance average speed of 6.2 knots, would be able to complete the journey between the two ports in 32 hours and the straight-on route in 24 hours.

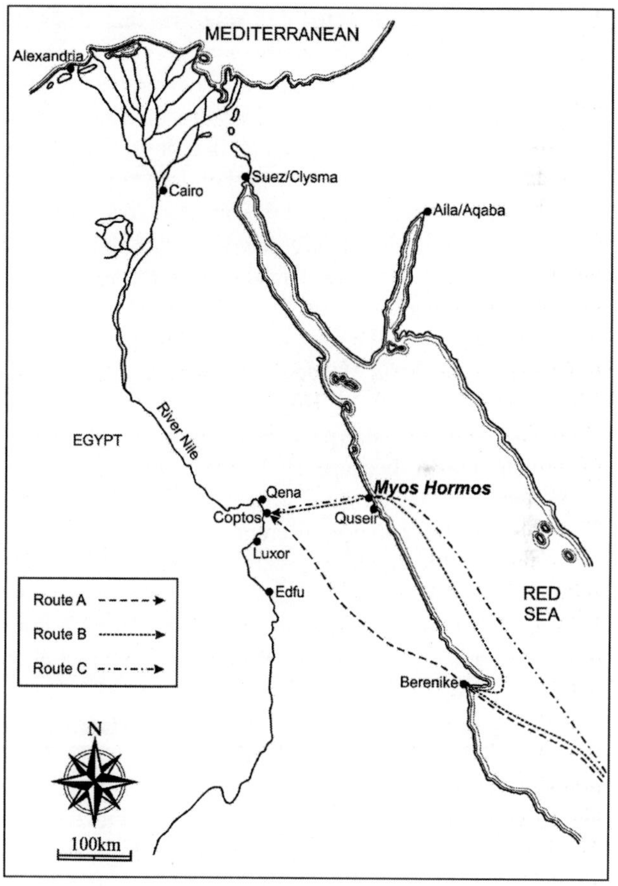

Map 6:2 Northern Red Sea, showing three alternative routes to Coptos

Textual sources referred to above include details of the length of time taken to travel from the Red Sea ports to Coptos, where customs duties were levied. Both desert journeys would have utilized the watering stations located at various points along the route. The journey between Berenike and Coptos across the Eastern Desert is known to have taken twelve days and the journey from Myos Hormos to Coptos required seven days travel through the Eastern Desert. The three routes can therefore be summarized, according to the time taken to complete them (and the elements comprising them):

[30] Davies and Morgan 1995: 40–44.
[31] Ibid.
[32] Ibid.: 26.

* Route A: 12 days (12 days overland).
* Route B: 12 days (4.5 days sailing plus 7 days overland).
* Route C: 11 days (3.5 days sailing plus 7 days overland).

In each case at least seven days of desert transport is required, the difference being made up in extra desert transport on the overland route from Berenike to Coptos and extra time spent sailing if the route via Myos Hormos was selected. From a purely economic standpoint, the difference in cost between the different routes is therefore the difference in cost between four and five days sailing and five days of desert transport. This assumes that factors such as offloading times and costs are the same in each port.

It is widely acknowledged by scholars that seaborne transport in the Roman Empire was generally cheaper than transporting the same goods via overland routes.[33] The principal difference in cost between the routes is the difference in cost between four to five days' sailing and five days of overland transport; therefore route A will only become cheaper if land transport is cheaper than seaborne transport. It would be convenient at this point to be able to calculate the relative cost differences between the different routes. Scholars of the ancient economy have generally calculated the relative cost of different types of transport on the basis of documents such as Diocletian's edict of prices (AD 301).[34] Horden and Purcell have noted the unsuitability of this type of approach to the calculation of transport cost because such costs do not concern economic costs but merely list maximum haulage rates.[35] They also note the many different ways in which goods were moved (pack animal, cart, coastal vessel, large sailing ship, and so on) and also the many different reasons for moving goods in the first place (tribute, military requisition, 'straight' trade, rent, redistribution within a single estate, etc), factors which further complicate direct cost comparison.[36] Duncan-Jones notes that the 'Edict of Diocletian'' has a total disregard for regional variation,[37] a statement seemingly at odds with his attempt to apply a ratio derived from the edict to Empire-wide differences in transport costs. With all of the above in mind it would seem unwise to attempt to calculate the cost of transport in the Red Sea and Eastern Desert based on the costs of moving different goods, for different reasons, through a different environment in the Mediterranean. It may simply be best to highlight the reasons for the difference in cost between seaborne and land-based transport as seen by the economist Adam Smith who observed of coastal shipping 'six or eight men, therefore, by the help of water carriage, can carry and bring back in the same time the same quantity of goods between London and Edinburgh, as fifty broad wheeled wagons, attended by a hundred men, and drawn by four hundred horses.'[38]

Analysis of Roman ship technology and its potential capability under sail has been outlined above. A previous reliance on the Red Sea wind regime as a means of explaining the location of port sites has been challenged by a reassessment of the sailing capabilities of Mediterranean ships; vessels rigged in an identical fashion are archaeologically proven to have been present on the Red Sea in antiquity. This, in combination with a fresh study of wind and current patterns in the Red Sea, has allowed a model of the potential routes and their relative travel times to be calculated. Given the uncertainty of our ability to accurately calculate the relative transport costs of shipping goods by land and sea in the Roman empire, it must suffice to say that the shipping route via Myos Hormos would have been economically cheaper in antiquity because of the reduction in the quantity of overland shipping this route entailed.

Conclusion

Such analysis is based primarily on economic and environmental considerations. If they were the only contributing factors then it seems unlikely that a port other than Myos Hormos, providing as it did a convenient trade-off between navigable winds and minimum overland transport, would have been required. Such a view, at best, accounts for only some of the factors which dictated where ships sailed and people traded during antiquity. Other reasons, rooted in political, social or material origins, may have dictated which Red Sea port merchants chose to utilize at various times. The presence of other contributing factors has been indicated by the myriad of methods and reasons for trade and exchange which so complicate any attempt to directly compare the cost of different forms of transport (above). Likewise, sailors of a Mediterranean background were seemingly suited to Red Sea conditions and in particular upwind sailing. Seafarers and navigators from the Indian Ocean may have been less familiar with the techniques and technology required for upwind sailing, and as a result they may have been limited to using a more southerly port, at least until they learned or adopted the practices required for upwind sailing. This situation may be paralleled in later periods when Indian Ocean merchant ships seem to sail only as far as Jiddah, vessels local to the northern Red Sea performing the function of trans-shipping goods from Jiddah to Egypt.[39] At a more unquantifiable level, certain merchants may have preferred certain ports because they were offered

33 Duncan-Jones 1982: 366–9; Finley 1999: 126–30; Greene 1986: 39–44; Horden and Purcell 2000: 151; Temin 2001: 176, 188–9; Yeo 1946: 230–3, 236.

34 For example, Duncan-Jones 1982: 366–9; Yeo 1946.

35 Horden and Purcell 2000: 377.

36 Ibid.

37 Duncan-Jones 1982: 367.

38 Campbell and Skinner 1976: 32–3.

39 Facey 2004: 9–11.

incentives to go there or simply had family or other social ties with the place. There are many potential reasons why a vessel should sail to one Red Sea port rather than another. This paper has attempted to show that the wind regime of the Red Sea, which had previously been seen as one of the most important factors in the location of Red Sea ports, is simply one of a myriad of contributory factors. This paper has also attempted to demonstrate that the potential of ancient shipping, at least when built in a Mediterranean tradition, has so far been underplayed. The maritime technology in use in the Red Sea would have allowed merchant vessels to navigate to all parts of the Red Sea during the Roman period.

References

Campbell, R.H. and Skinner, A.S. 1976. *Adam Smith: An inquiry into the nature and causes of the wealth of nations*. Oxford: Clarendon Press.

Casson, L. 1980. Rome's trade with the East: the sea voyage to Africa and India. *Transactions of the American Philological Association* (1974–) 110: 21–36.

———. 1995. *Ships and Seamanship in the Ancient World*. London: The Johns Hopkins University Press.

Davies, S. and Morgan, E. 1995. *Red Sea Pilot*. St Ives: Imray, Laurie, Norie & Wilson Ltd.

Duncan-Jones, R. 1982, 2nd edition.. *The Economy of the Roman Empire: quantitative studies*. Cambridge: Cambridge University Press.

Englert, A. 2006. Trial voyages as a method of experimental archaeology: The aspect of speed. 35–42 in L. Blue, F. Hocker and A. Englert (eds), *Connected by the Sea. Proceedings of the Tenth International Symposium on Boat and Ship Archaeology, Roskilde 2003*. Oxford: Oxbow.

Facey, W. 2004. The Red Sea: The wind regime and the location of ports. 7–18 in P. Lunde and A. Porter (eds), *Trade and Travel in the Red Sea Region. Proceedings of the Red Sea Project I*. BAR International Series 1269. Oxford: Archaeopress.

Finley, M.I. 1999. *The Ancient Economy* (updated edition). Berkeley: University of California Press.

Greene, K. 1986. *The Archaeology of the Roman Economy*. London: Batsford.

Horden, P. and Purcell, N. 2000. *The Corrupting Sea*. Oxford: Blackwell.

Peacock, D.P. and Blue, L. (eds). 2006. *Myos Hormos — Quseir al-Qadim. Roman and Islamic Ports on the Red Sea*. Volume 1: *Survey and Excavations 1999–2003*. Oxford: Oxbow Books.

Pliny. 1961. *Natural History*. H. Rackham (tr.). Loeb Classical Library. London: Willian Heinemann.

al-Qalqashandī. 1913. *Ṣubḥ al-A'shā*. III. Cairo.

Schoff, W.H. 1912, repr. 2001. *The Periplus of the Erythraean Sea. Travel and trade in the Indian Ocean by a merchant of the first century*. Delhi: Munshiram Manoharlal.

Sidebotham, S.E. 1989. Ports of the Red Sea and the Arabia–India Trade. 195–223 in T. Fahd (ed.), *L'Arabie préislamique et son Environnment historique et culturel*. Strasbourg: Strasbourg University.

——. 1996. The Ship Graffito. 315–7 in S.E. Sidebotham and W.Z. Wendrich (eds), *Berenike 1995. Preliminary report on the 1995 excavations at Berenike*. Leiden: CNWS.

Strabo. 1969. *Geography*. H.L. Jones (tr.). Loeb Classical Library. London: William Heinemann.

Temin, P. 2001. A Market Economy in the Early Roman Empire. *The Journal of Roman Studies* 91: 169–81.

Tibbets, G.R. 1971. *Arab Navigation in the Indian Ocean before the Coming of the Portuguese*. London: The Royal Asiatic Society of Great Britain and Ireland.

Vinner, M. 1986. Recording the Trial Run. Sailing into the Past. 220–5 in O. Crumlin-Pedersen & M. Vinner (eds), *Proceedings of the International Seminar on Replicas of Ancient and Medieval Vessels, Roskilde 1984*. Roskilde: Viking Ship Museum.

Whitewright, R.J. 2007. Roman rigging material from the Red Sea port of Myos Hormos. *International Journal of Nautical Archaeology*. 1–11. On-line at http://-www.blackwell-synergy.com/doi/pdf/10.1111/j.1095-9270.2007.00150.x

——. Forthcoming. Tracing technology: the material culture of maritime technology in the ancient Mediterranean and contemporary Indian Ocean. In R. Bockius (ed.), *Between the Seas: Transfer and exchange in nautical technology. Proceedings of the Eleventh International Symposium on Boat and Ship Archaeology, Mainz 2006*. Oxford: Oxbow.

Yeo, C.A. 1946. Land and Sea Transportation in Imperial Italy. *Transactions and Proceedings of the American Philological Association* 77: 221–44.

The Red Sea — a Bridge or a Barrier? The Case of Naval Warfare

Sarah Arenson

The Red Sea is a narrow body of water separating Africa from the Arabian Peninsula and Asia. The Isthmus of Suez is an even narrower stretch of land which, until some kind of a navigable channel was in operation, separated the Mediterranean Sea and Atlantic Ocean from the Indian Ocean. These two apparent 'obstacles' cannot be seriously considered as such, for there is evidence from the earliest times in human history of both east-west and north-south cross connections. The three Red Sea conferences of the Society for Arabian Studies have shown clearly the multiple ties between the various regions bordering the Red Sea. These ties are expressed in demographic, economic, cultural and many other aspects of human existence. Yet the division between the different regions bordering the Red Sea is also apparent in many other fields. Outstanding among them is the clear difference in boat-building techniques[1] which continued for several millennia, until the sixteenth century AD when the Indian Ocean was reached by European fleets, mainly Portuguese, Dutch and English.

This paper will focus on the north-south axis, rather than the east-west, by following the case of naval warfare in the region, mainly during the Middle Ages under Muslim rule. The nature of naval warfare in the Red Sea was, to my mind, inseparably connected with the development of ship construction. Lacking archaeological evidence, the source material is basically Arabic written works —chronicles, histories and so on. My starting point is a precious piece of information dating to the beginning of the tenth century AD by Ibn Rustah, a Muslim, Persian author. Dealing with pioneers in various fields, he describes an innovation in ship-building technique: 'The first who sailed the sea in ships which are tarred and nailed, rather than sewn and oiled, and their form is flat rather than having two poles, is al-Ḥajjāj ibn Yūsuf.'[2]

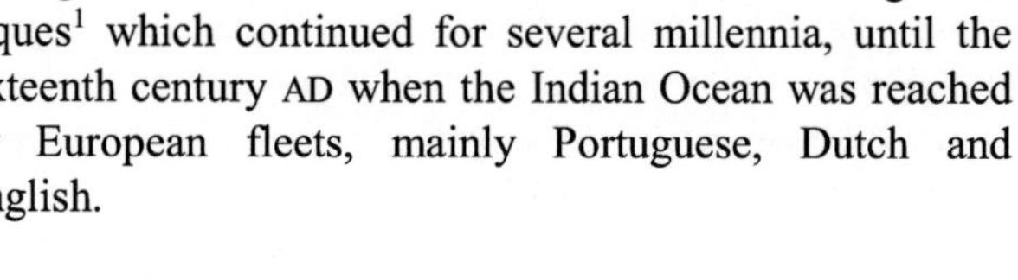
وأول من اجرى في البحر السفن المقيرة المسمرة غير المخروزة
المدهونة والمسطحة غير ذوات الجآجئ الحجاج بن يوسف

Figure 7:1 Ibn Rustah Arabic text

This description sums up the differences in hull construction between the Mediterranean and Indian Ocean boat-building traditions in three ways: (a) Joining the planks: sewing versus nailing; (b) Water proofing: using oil versus tar; (c) General profile: double-ended versus a flat vessel. Setting aside other features in rigging and steering that are connected to the ship profile and will not be dealt with here, points (a) and (b) are indeed the major differences between the two shipbuilding traditions. Ibn Rustah was writing at a time when a revolutionary process was taking place in Mediterranean shipbuilding, that is, the shift from shell-first to skeleton-first construction.[3] The move from mortise-and-tendon plank joints to nailing them onto skeleton frames, entailed a move from tarring to true *calfatage*,[4] which is not yet known to our author.[5] The dichotomy between sewing and nailing is most distinctive.

al-Hajjaj was the governor of Iraq from AD 694 to 714 under the Umayyad caliphs, 'Abd al-Malik and al-Walīd. He needed reliable warships to fight the pirates at the entrance to the Persian Gulf.[6] It is unlikely that he would have pioneered new ship-building methods if he was only building merchant vessels. The issue of government-owned merchant vessels is beyond the scope of this paper; indeed, most merchantmen were owned and built by private individuals, rather than government owned. The effort of importing raw materials and expert shipwrights was justified only in the case of state-initiated programmes, such as those that enforced the new Muslim rulers and secured the safety of vital waterways.

Another piece of revealing information comes to us from the middle of the tenth century AD, with another Persian-Muslim text ascribed to Sulaymān al-Mahrī ('Sulayman the Merchant'), who was active in the eastern trade about one hundred and fifty years after al-Ḥajjāj was writing:[7]

> Now we know something, which our predecessors did not know … namely that the ocean bordering on China and India is connected with the Mediterranean … It has been proven by a part of a sewn Arab ship hull, found in the Mediterranean. The ship must have been wrecked and this

1 Arenson 1982.

2 Ibn Rustah 1967: 195–6. See below for Arabic text.

3 Pomey and Rieth 2005: 29–33.

4 Caulking: i.e. filling all the joints and interstices between the boards that make up the external coating of the hull and the bridge in order to make it water-tight. Editor's note.

5 Basch 1986: 187–96; Arenson 1991: 24.

6 Baladhury 1968: 435–6, 444–6.

7 Reinaud 1845: 87–88. See below for Arabic text.

part of the hull was carried by the waves to the Caspian Sea, from there to the Black Sea, whence it got into the Mediterranean … Now we know that only the ships of Siraf[8] are sewn, while Syrian and Byzantine ships are nailed and not sewn.

مصرنا هذا فانه بلغنا انه وجد فى بحر
الروم خشب مراكب العرب المخروزة
التى قد تكسرت باهلها فقطعها الموج
وساقتها الرياح بامواج البحر فقذفته
الى بحر الخزر ثم جرى فى خليج الروم
ونفذ منه الى بحر الروم والشام فدل
هذا على ان البحر يدور على بلاد
الصين والسيلا وظهر بلاد الترك

Figure 7:2a and 7:2b al-Hajjaj Arabic text

والخزر ثم يصب فى الخليج ويفضى الى
بلاد الشام وذلك ان الخشب المخروز
لا يكون الا لمراكب سيراف خاصة
ومراكب الشام والروم مسمورة غير
مخروزة وبلغنا ايضا انه وجد ببحر الشام

The merchant, as well as his editor, obviously did not know about the sewn boats of the Mediterranean,[9] and their knowledge of the northern waterways was also imperfect, for it is clear from this passage that al-Ḥajjāj's project did not have any prolonged impact on the eastern shipbuilding industry. The basic difference between the two traditions is again focused around the different hull-construction methods: in the Arabian Sea ship hulls are sewn, while in the Mediterranean they are nailed. Al-Ḥajjāj, then, was not a pioneer, for his endeavour itself did not lead a change. Rather, some scholars believe there was 'a constant interchange of naval technology in the construction of vessels between the two areas';[10] however, the sources do not support this assumption. Indeed, the sewing tradition in the area continued to the beginning of the modern era, while the character of naval warfare was also unchanged.

The sewn ships served well as trading vessels. They actually carried the vast medieval international commerce across the Arabian Sea with hardly any interference.[11] This type of ship, called later by the Europeans the *dhow*, was the principle agent of maritime transport on the southern maritime routes leading to the new Muslim capitals and major consumption centres in Iraq, Iran, Egypt and elsewhere. In the later Middle Ages, during and after the Crusades, when European demand for eastern goods increased considerably, the same *dhow*-type vessels continued to ply the southern seas and performed quite successfully. Our knowledge of these ships is derived primarily from travellers' accounts. Ibn Jubayr, writing in the 1180s, described in detail their general nature and construction methods.[12] The iconographic sources, foremost among them the miniature illuminations to al-Ḥarīrī's *Maqāmāt*,[13] also give a good impression as to what they looked like. Other travellers, such as Ibn Baṭṭūṭah[14] and Marco Polo,[15] as well as the aforementioned Ibn Jubayr,[16] complain of the poor quality of the ships and the misery of the seafarers, while praising the expertise of the crew. Nonetheless, these ships were seaworthy and served their purpose: carrying merchandise and men to their destination.

There is little doubt that Mediterranean-type ships plied the southern seas from Pharaonic times, through Phoenician, Hellenistic and Roman times, and maybe even later. The archaeological evidence for this assertion is scarce, but historical sources point in this direction. The famous squadrons of Queen Hatshepsut, the biblical Ophir line of King Hiram of Tyre and King Solomon of Jerusalem, the Phoenician voyages of discovery described by Herodotus, the Hellenistic and Roman commercial network with the East[17] — all these endeavours, which were initiated by Mediterranean naval powers, relied on Mediterranean-type ships, built in Mediterranean shipbuilding centres. These ships reached the Gulf of Suez through the predecessors of the Suez Canal or by camel-caravans in the Eastern Desert of Egypt,[18] or travelled to the Gulf of 'Aqabah through the southern part of what would later become Israel.

8 A major commercial port at the head of the Persian Gulf in the 'Abbāsid period
9 McGrail and Kentley 1985.
10 Christides 1987: 88.

11 Nougarede 1964: 95–122.
12 Ibn Jubayr 1907: 70–74.
13 al-Ḥarīrī 1992.
14 Ibn Baṭṭūṭa 1879–1893: IV, 158–63.
15 Marco Polo 1958: 66.
16 Ibn Jubayr 1907: 70–74.
17 Taylor 1971: 38–40, 56–61.
18 Hallberg 1974: chapter 1.

Undoubtedly, the bulk of the maritime activity in these seas was carried out by local craft, but there was constant presence of the great empires with their vessels. Nonetheless, the great powers did not have any influence on the local shipbuilding industry. It may be concluded with some certainty that the sewn merchantmen were equal to their task, and their ships may even have been better suited to the warmer seas and local coasts, full of reefs and coral shoals. In the Middle Ages, with the Christian-Muslim border stabilized at the Levantine coast, Mediterranean merchantmen disappeared from the scene for several centuries. It is a curious fact that the dramatic change in ship-building in the Indian Ocean did not evolve locally, nor did it spring from long-standing contact with the adjacent maritime civilizations of the Mediterranean and South-East Asia, but occurred after the violent invasion of Atlantic powers, far-removed and completely alien to local traditions.

In the military sphere, the picture described by our sources is very different. There were no reliable warships that could be used for a naval campaign south of Suez. It seems that whenever the need arose for warships in the Red Sea, a curious routine was set in motion: Mediterranean-type warships were constructed in Mediterranean arsenals, dismantled and carried on camel-back to one of the ports of the Red Sea. There they would be reassembled, armed and launched, ready for battle. The famous naval action of Renauld de Châtillon, the Crusader Lord of Transjordan, in the winter of AD 1182–1183 is a well-known example,[19] but it is worthwhile noting that his adversary Saladin also moved Mediterranean fighting vessels to the Red Sea on several occasions, for example when he sent his fleet against that of Renauld; and twelve years earlier, when he captured Jazīrat Fir'awn, in the Gulf of 'Aqabah.[20] As late as the sixteenth century, the Ottomans were fighting the Portuguese in the Red Sea with Mediterranean war fleets.[21]

This phenomenon is not unique to the Middle Ages: the same practice is reported in earlier periods. A few well-known examples will suffice: Ptolemy the Second defeated the Nabateans in the Gulf of 'Aqabah *ca.* 275 BC by using *quadriremes*.[22] In 25–24 BC, the Roman Emperor Ælus Gallus carried out an unfortunate *trireme* campaign to Aden.[23] The excavations in al-Quṣayr al-Qadīm[24] revealed the first archaeological evidence that proved that this was the case also in Pharaonic times, namely that Mediterranean-type ships were carried overland to the Red Sea, although these may have been merchant ships. The same is true for the Persian Gulf, where this discourse had started with al-Ḥajjāj's campaign. The Assyrian King Sancheriv (705–681 BC) transferred Phoenician shipwrights to Nineveh, where they built a war fleet to fight 'the land of the sea';[25] Alexander the Great brought Phoenician fleets to the Persian Gulf during his long march east;[26] centuries later, in 1291 AD, just as the Crusader Kingdom of Jerusalem was coming to its end, the Mongol ruler of Iraq arranged for Genoese galleys to be built on the Euphrates, in order to fight their common enemy, the Mamlūks of Egypt.[27]

In Classical times, warships launched into the southern seas were certainly those that also carried out the naval campaigns in the Mediterranean. Indeed their names are usually mentioned — *biremes, triremes* and other boats using methods of oar-propulsion such as *quadriremes*. In medieval times, they were mostly galleys used by Christian powers and their equivalents in the Muslim navies — *ghurab, shini, shalandi, qita'*.[28] Notwithstanding the differences between these various types of ships, they were all basically different from the ships built in the ports of the Red Sea, Persian Gulf and the Arabian Sea. In the case of the Red Sea, their construction took place in Mediterranean arsenals, using local shipwrights and Mediterranean building materials, especially the timber, that is, pine and not teakwood. It may be assumed that while the ancient canal linking the Nile with the Red Sea was in use, the ships could pass through it, but we have no direct evidence for this practice. In the Persian Gulf and beyond, the ships were probably constructed *in situ*, using imported materials and expertise.

These practices are understandable in the case of Mediterranean sea-powers pushing into foreign waters, but need an explanation when dealing with countries such as Egypt and Iraq, that had shores bordering the Indian Ocean and its gulfs and whose harbours served as important maritime centres, at least at certain periods in their history.

Egypt, with coasts on both the Mediterranean and the Red Sea, is an enigma. Throughout its medieval history, it had close relations with Makkah and al-Madīnah, a flourishing trade with the Far East and a constant need to protect its long eastern border.[29] Nonetheless, it seems that Egypt always used Mediterranean warships to patrol its eastern waters, and that these did not influence the local ship industry, even during periods of intensive maritime activity, as under Umayyad and Fāṭimid rule. al-Quṣayr, 'Aydhāb, al-Ṭūr and other coastal towns served at different periods as important ship-building centres, but

19 Ibn al-Athīr 1966: XI, 490–1; Lebrousse 1977; Facey 2005.
20 Ibn al-Athīr 1966: XI, 365.
21 Hess 1970; Guilmartin 1974: 7–15.
22 Strabo XVII, ch. 1, 44–45.
23 Strabo XVII, ch. 1, 23; Plinius II, 168.
24 Sayed 1983: 30.
25 Possibly the site of modern Kuwait? Luckenbill 1927: II, sections 318–21.
26 Arian VII, chapters 19–20.
27 Adam 1906: II, 551; Richard 1970.
28 Agius 1998, 2001.
29 Labib 1965.

they produced sewn merchantmen, and were unaffected by the Mediterranean tradition. As warships, these boats were definitely inferior to the Mediterranean type, unsuited for carrying heavy equipment such as rams, landing bridges, catapults and mangonels,[30] and could hardly have taken blows and projectiles, which were commonly used in the naval manoeuvres of the time. Technical innovations in the military field, are quickly adopted in the civil sphere. It is but logical to assume that once superior warships were introduced, the techniques used would be adopted for merchant vessels. A comparison that comes to mind is the famous story of the first Punic War, when the Romans captured a Phoenician man-of-war in 262 BC[31] and then joined the club of Mediterranean naval powers, reserved exclusively hitherto for the Phoenicians, Greeks and Etruscans. In the southern seas, it is clear that although Mediterranean-type ships were constantly present, they did not influence local tradition.

On the whole, naval activity in the region was very sporadic. When describing Gallus' campaign, Strabo said: 'Now this was the first mistake of Gallus, to build long boats, since there was no naval war at hand, or even to be expected. For the Arabians are not very good warriors even on land, rather being hucksters and merchants, to say nothing of fighting at sea.' [32] Strabo was using derogatory language, but the same facts may be stated positively: in the Arabian Sea, the style of conduct was not violent, but relied rather on friendly diplomatic agreements and a general *laissez-faire* policy. Even on the private scale, commercial partnerships were not strictly legally defined, but rather based on good-will and personal trust, as is evident in the Geniza documents and the recently discovered fragments from al-Quṣayr al-Qadīm.[33]

Strabo's statement remained valid for the Arabian Sea for hundreds of years to come, although in the Mediterranean the same Arabs rapidly developed into a naval power to be reckoned with. G.F. Hourani, in his pioneering study of this topic,[34] has commented on the lack of naval tradition even with the seafaring tribes of south and east Arabia. Most modern treatments of the subject of Muslim eastern seafaring deal mainly with commercial expansion;[35] they note the technical characteristics in ship construction and types, but fail to notice the absence of warships and naval actions from the eastern sphere. A.R. Lewis, in his study of Indian Ocean shipping in the late Middle Ages,[36] concludes that the eastern system of free trade lasted from pre-Islamic times to the Age of the Great Discoveries and was totally different from the monopolistic, violent maritime commerce prevailing in the West.

Piracy, however, continued to be a major problem throughout the Middle Ages.[37] The South Arabian tribes engaged in piracy from times immemorial, as an extension of the caravan robbery on land. The straits of Tiran, Bāb al-Mandab, Hormoz and the adjacent islands (Socotra, Bahrain, and at the mouth of the Indus), were much-feared pirate nests. State or regionally organized campaigns against them usually failed. This endemic situation is another aspect of the lack of naval power in the area. When the few descriptions of naval action in the area are studied carefully, they are revealed as anti-piracy campaigns, using mostly armed merchantmen to carry fighters to the scene of the battle, as in al-Ḥajjāj's first attempts at controlling the head of the Persian Gulf. The deep-rooted reasons for this state of affairs are beyond the scope of this paper. D. Ayalon has drawn attention to the contempt with which the Mamlūk elite class, raised to rule as mounted warriors, treated the field of naval warfare.[38] A glimpse into this mentality is found in an eloquent passage, quoted in the name of a Persian sage, talking of the difference between land and naval tactics:

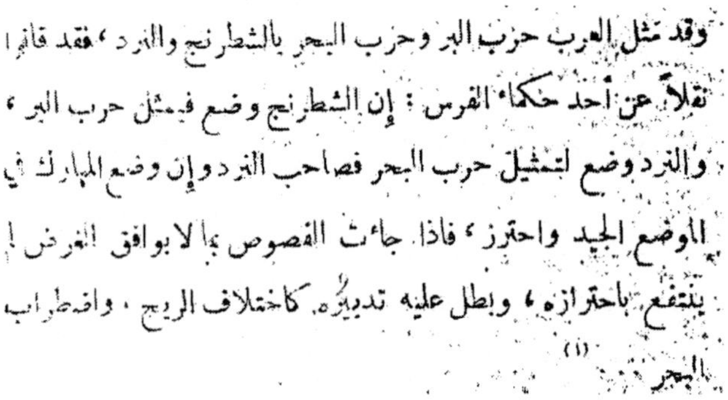
وقد مثّل العرب حرب البر وحرب البحر بالشطرنج والنرد ، فقد قالوا
نقلاً عن أحد حكماء الفرس : إن الشطرنج وضع فيمثل حرب البر ،
والنرد وضع لتمثيل حرب البحر فصاحب النرد وإن وضع المهارك في
الموضع الجيد واحترز ، فاذا جاءت الفصوص بما لا يوافق الغرض لا
ينتفع باحترازه ، وبطل عليه تدبيره ، كاختلاف الريح ، واضطراب
البحر (1)

> Chess is similar to land battle, while backgammon represents a sea battle. The backgammon player places his pieces in choice positions and stays on guard, but the dice come up with what does not agree with his plan, so there is no use for his watchfulness, and his stratagem comes to nothing, as with the shifting winds and the ever-changing sea. [39]

Figure 7:3 Sea battles compared to backgammon

The absence of specialized warships had far-reaching implications on the nature of maritime commerce and the dominion of the seas. In the Arabian Sea, commerce was free and open to all, and the style of international relations up to the Great Discoveries was not violent, but depended on diplomatic missions — like that of the queen of Sheba

30 Mangonel: a military engine for throwing stones etc. [OED]. Editor's note.
31 Polybius II, 20–22; Morrison and Coates 1996: 43.
32 Strabo XVI, ch. 4, 23.
33 Goitein, 1967: 164–86; Guo 1999–2001.
34 Hourani 1951: 55, see also 31.
35 Mahir 1940: 190; al-Ḥimawī 1945: 60; al-'Ibādī and Salīm 1972.
36 Lewis 1976: 468, 475.
37 Toussaint 1977.
38 Ayalon 1985.
39 al-Ḥimawiī1945: 112.

in the tenth century BC or the Ming dynasty voyages at the beginning of the fifteenth century AD. At the end of the Middle Ages, fusion of the seafaring traditions of the Mediterranean and Atlantic Ocean led to the European victory over the oceans and the dominion of the whole of the known world.[40] In the East, no mutual influence occurred between the seafaring traditions of the Mediterranean and the Indian Ocean. The absence of the Oriental warship may be regarded as a major factor in the naval supremacy of the West at this crucial moment in history.

References

Adam, Guillaume. 1906. Recueil des historiens des Croisades. II: 549–55 in C. Kohler (ed.), *Recueil des historiens des Croisades. Documents arméniens.* Paris, Imprimerie Nationale.

Agius, D. 1998. Maqrizi's evidence for the Gurab: the galley of the Mamluks. 185–97 in U. Vermeulen and J.M.F. Van Reeth (eds), *Law, Christianity and Modernism in Islamic Society: proceedings of the eighteenth congress of the Union européenne des arabisants et islamisants held at the Katholieke Universiteit Leuven (3 September–9 September 1996).* Leuven: Peeters.

———. 2001. The Arab Salandi. 49-60 in U. Vermeulen and J.M.F. Van Reeth (eds), *Egypt and Syria in the Fatimid, Ayyubid and Mamluk Eras.* Leuven: Peeters.

Arenson, S. 1982. Ships and Shipbuilding: the Red Sea and Persian Gulf. 11: 245–51 in *Dictionary of the Middle Ages.* New York: Scribners` Sons.

———. 1996. The mystery of the oriental warship. 4: 21–28 in H. Tzalas (ed.), *Proceedings of the International Symposium on Ship Construction in Antiquity (TROPIS), 1991.* Athens: Hellenic Institute for the Preservation of Nautical Traditions.

———. *ca.* 1991. The medieval ship and technological decadence, the case of the East. 213–7 in C. Villain-Gandossi, S. Busuttil, P. Adam (eds), *Medieval Ships and the Birth of Technological Societies*, Volume 2 *The Mediterranean area and European integration.* Valletta: Said.

Arrian. 1966–1967. *Anabasis*, E.I. Robson (tr.). London: Heinemann; Cambridge: Harvard University Press.

Ayalon, D. 1965. The Mamluks and naval power: a phase in the struggle between Islam and Christian Europe. *Proceedings of the Israel Academy of Sciences and Humanities*, 1: 1–12.

Balādhurī, Aḥmad ibn Yaḥyā. 1866; repr. 1968. *Kitab futūḥ al-buldān*, M.J. De Goeje (ed.). Leiden: E.J. Brill.

———. 1916–1924. *The Origins of the Islamic State*, K.P. Hitti and F.C. Murgotten (tr.). New York: Columbia University; London: King.

Basch, L. 1986. Note sur le calfatage: la chose et le mot. *Archaeonautica* 4: 187–98.

Christides, V. 1985–1987. Some remarks on Mediterranean and Red Sea ships in ancient and medieval times: a preliminary report. *TROPIS* 1: 75–82; 2: 87–99.

Facey, W. 2005. Crusaders in the Red Sea: Renaud de Châtillon's Raids of AD 1182–1183. 87–98 in Janet C.M. Starkey (ed.), *People of the Red Sea.* BAR International Series 1395. Oxford: Archaeopress.

Goitein, S.D. (tr. and ed.). 1967. *A Mediterranean Society: the Jewish communities of the Arab world as portrayed in the documents of the Cairo Geniza.* Volume 1, *Economic Foundations.* Berkeley and Los Angeles: University of California Press.

Guilmartin, J.F. Jnr. 1974. *Gunpowder and Galleys, Changing Technologies and Mediterranean Warfare at Sea in the Sixteenth Century.* Cambridge: Cambridge University Press.

Guo, Li. 1999–2001. Arabic documents from the Red Sea Port of Quseir in the seventh/thirteenth century. *JNES* (Chicago), 58: 161–90; 60: 81–116.

Hallberg, C.W. 1931; repr. 1974. *The Suez Canal: its history and diplomatic importance.* New York: Columbia University Press.

al-Ḥarīrī. *Maqāmāt.* Bibliothèque Nationale, Schefer Collection, Ms. Ar. 5847, reproduced in full in R. Ettinghausen. 1977. *Arab Painting.* London: Macmillan.

Hess, A.C. 1970. The evolution of the Ottoman seaborne empire in the age of the oceanic discoveries. *American Historical Review* 75: 1892–919.

al-Ḥimawī, Muḥammad Yasin. 1945. *Tārīkh al-ustul al-'arabi.* Damascus.

Hourani, G.F. 1951. *Arab Seafaring in the Indian Ocean in Ancient and Early Medieval Times.* Princeton: Princeton University Press.

Ibn al-Athīr. 1966. *al-Kāmil fī al-tārīkh.* C.J Tornberg (ed.). Beirut: Dār Ṣādir, XI. Reprint of edition published by Tornberg (Leiden, 1853–1867) under title: *Ibn-el-Athiri Chronicon quod perfectissimum inscribitur.*

Ibn Baṭṭūṭa. 1879–1893; repr. 1914–1927, 1958–. *Voyages d'Ibn Batoutah [Riḥlat ibn Baṭṭūṭa]*, C. Defremery and B.R. Sanguinetti (eds and tr.). Paris: Imprimerie Nationale, IV.

al-'Ibādī, A.M. and Salīm, A.A., 1972. *Tārīkh al-baḥriyya al-islamiyya fī miṣr wa-al-sham.* Beirut.

Ibn Jubayr. 1907. The travels of ibn Jobayr. [*Riḥlat Ibn Jubayr*]. W. Wright (ed. and tr.). Leiden: A.J. Brill.

40 Villain-Gandossi, *et al.* 1989–1992.

Ibn Rustah. 1967. *al-Mujallad al-sābi' min Kitāb al-a'laq al-nafīsah*, M.J. De Goeje (ed.). Reprint of the Leiden 1879 edition, Leiden: Brill.

Labib, S.Y. 1965. *Handelsgeschichte Ägyptens in Spätmittelalter (1171–1517)*. Wiesbaden: F. Steiner.

Lebrousse, H. 1977. La guerre de course en Mer Rouge pendant les croisades. 1: 36–77 in M. Mollat (ed.), *Course et Piraterie: études présentées à la Commission internationale d'histoire maritime à l'occasion de son XVe colloque international pendant le XIVe Congrès international des sciences historiques, San Francisco, août 1975*. Paris: Institut de recherche et d'histoire des textes: Éditions du Centre national de la recherche scientifique.

Levenson, J.R. (ed.). 1957. *European Expansion and the Counter-Example of Asia, 1300–1600*. Englewood Cliffs, N.J.: Prentice-Hall.

Lewis, A.R. 1976. Les marchands dans l'Océan Indien, AD 1100–1500. *Revue d'histoire Économique et Sociale* 54: 468–75.

Luckenbill, S. 1927. *Ancient Records of Assyria and Babylonia*. Chicago: University of Chicago Press.

Māhir, Su'ād. 1940. *al-Baḥriyya fī misr al-islamiyya*. Cairo.

Marco Polo. 1958. *Travels*, P. Latham (ed. and tr.). Harmondsworth: Penguin.

McGrail, S. and Kentley, E. (eds). 1985. *Sewn Plank Boats*. BAR international Series 276. Oxford: Archaeopress.

Morrison, J.S. and Coates, J.F. 1996. *Greek and Roman Oared Warships 399–30 BC*. Oxford: Oxbow.

Nougaredes, M.P. 1964. Qualités nautiques des navires arabes. 95–122 in *Océan Indien et Méditerranée, Travaux du 6e Colloque International d'Histoire Maritime*. Paris: SEVPEN.

Plinius the Elder. 1938–1962. *Natural History* [*Naturalis Historia*], H. Rockham, *et. al* (tr.). London: Heinemann.

Pomey, P. and Rieth, E. 2005. *L'Archéologie navale*. Paris: Errance.

Reinaud. M. 1845. *Relation des voyages faits par les Arabes et les Persans dans l'Inde et la Chine dans le IXe siècle de l'ère Chrétienne*. Paris: Imprimerie royale.

Richard, J. 1970. Les navigations des occidentaux dans l'Océan Indien et la Mer Caspienne. 353–63 in M. Mollat (ed.), *Sociétés et compagnies de commerce en Orient et dans l'Océan Indien*. Paris: Travaux du VIIIe CIHM.

Sayed, Abdel Monem, A.H. 1983. New light on the recently discovered port on the Red Sea shore. *Chronique d'Égypte* 58: 23–37.

Strabo. 1959–1960. *The Geography of Strabo* [*Geographica*], H.L. Jones (tr.). London: W. Heinemann; Cambridge, Mass.: Harvard University Press.

Toussaint, A. 1977. La course et la piraterie dans l'Océan Indien. 2: 703–43 in M. Mollat (ed.), *Course et Piraterie: études présentées à la Commission internationale d'histoire maritime à l'occasion de son XVe colloque international pendant le XIVe Congrès international des sciences historiques, San Francisco, août 1975*. Paris: Institut de recherche et d'histoire des textes: Éditions du Centre national de la recherche scientifique.

Features of Ships and Boats in the Indian Ocean

Norbert Weismann

Introduction

For over 1,400 years the Red Sea has been part of the nautical culture on the Indian Ocean. The construction of the native ships in the Red Sea from this time should therefore be very close to those in other areas of the Indian Ocean. There is no evidence of an isolated or Mediterranean-influenced development in ship and boat construction on the shores of the Red Sea during this time. What is known about the features of ships in the Indian Ocean in this period? These features include construction principles and types of rudder and sails and they will be discussed with an indication of their probable date of appearance. Examples discussed include stem-posts of all known native ships in the Indian Ocean. Since AD 1800 Indian Ocean stern-posts have been constructed only at the front edge of the hull, and have not been intended as an important part of a longitudinal framework. Inner stem-posts connect the hull with the true stem-post, but are not fixed to the keel. Another feature discussed in this paper is the lanceolate and longitudinal bended bottom. Even in the twentieth century the remains of this old construction principle could be found. Such a bottom enabled the building of boats or even small ships without a central keel and with broad planks, and was an important feature of sewn constructions. Thirdly, the evidence for the exclusive use of settee or Latin sails before the fifteenth century is poor. Square sails seem have been used widely up to the sixteenth century and remains of the transitions from square to settee sails could be found even in the nineteenth century.

The *sanbūq*

The wooden ships of the Red Sea are not well known. There is no typology and only few records of constructional details of ships in this part of the Indian Ocean. Therefore the descriptive typology of Indian Ocean ships by Hawkins is used in this article.[1] This typology has its weaknesses,[2] but it is almost complete and easy to use.

The Arabs do not write much about their ships, they simply use them. European travellers from about AD 1500 were also investigating the society and nature of Arab countries rather than the construction of ships. The names they give for the ships in the Red Sea are mostly used in other parts of the Indian Ocean as well.[3] The first detailed record of a *sanbūq* of the Red Sea was made by Le Masson, an engineer working on the Suez Channel and published by E. Pâris in 1882.[4] This drawing shows the same features as ships in other parts of the Indian Ocean. The particular construction of the hatchway carling (Arabic: *taḥt al-ğālī*) on this *sanbūq* (Figure 8:1) is, for example, very similar to the hatchway carling of the cargo *badan* 'al-Khammam' (Figure 8:2) built 1938 on the island of Mashira in Oman.[5]

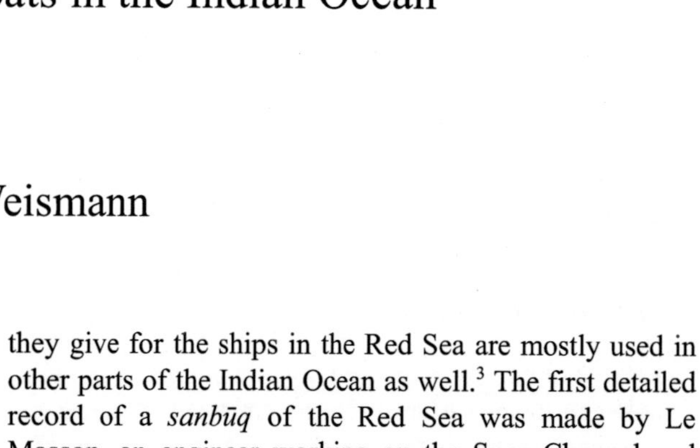

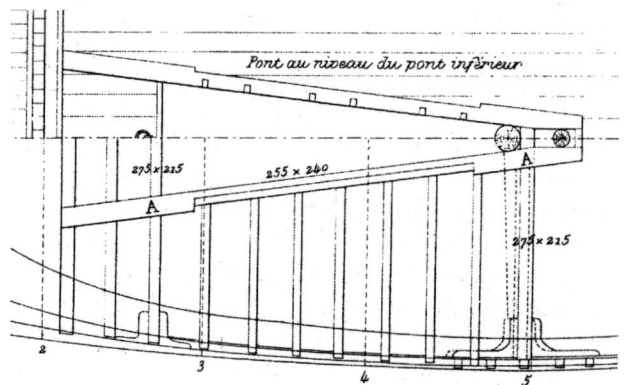

Figure 8:1: Detail of a drawing by Le Masson of a sanbūq *of the Red Sea (Pâris 1882: 157)*

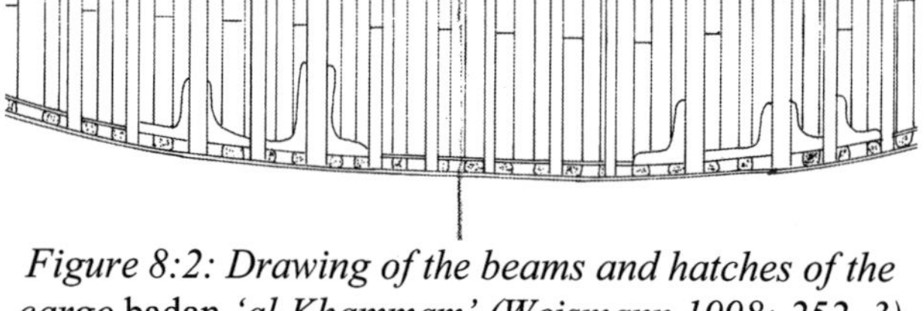

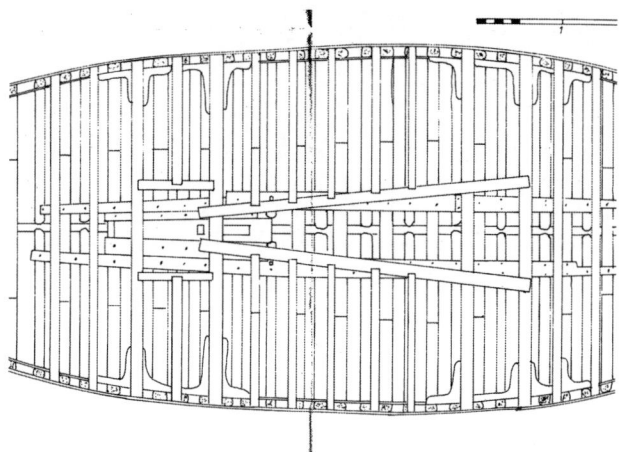

Figure 8:2: Drawing of the beams and hatches of the cargo badan *'al-Khammam' (Weismann 1998: 252–3)*

1 Hawkins 1977: 135–41.
2 See, for example, Prados 1997: 185–98.
3 Niebuhr 1772.
4 Pâris 1882.
5 Weismann 1998: 237–57.

The *sanbūq* seems to be common in the Indian Ocean as well as in the Red Sea. In 1878, Klunzinger[6] described the *sanbūq* as the most numerous type of ship in al-Quṣayr. In some pictures of Jīzān, taken in 1938 by Alan Villiers,[7] many *sanābīq* are depicted and prove the predominance of this type at least in this place and at this time. Other distinctive types of the Red Sea are the *za'īmah* and the *zārūka*.

Characteristic features

Some features are found on all ships in the Muslim-dominated Indian Ocean from the nineteenth century, and probably in earlier times too, though there is no proof of earlier styles. If a wreck in the Red Sea should ever be found, its features could be taken as evidence of the style of vessel built in the Arab ship-building tradition.

Stem and stern posts

The most important features are the function and style of stem and the stern posts. In the European tradition these posts are part of a longitudinal framework. On the Indian Ocean, these posts strengthen only the foremost and aftermost edge of the hull. There are no knees, no connection to the keel able to take any torque. Instead, any nailed ship stem and sternpost are only secured against slip-out by iron pieces. The planks are fitted into a notch in the post and fixed only to the inner stern and stem post. Posts and inner posts are connected by barbed nails or, more recently, by bolts; the inner posts are not joined to the keel (Figures 8:3–8:4).

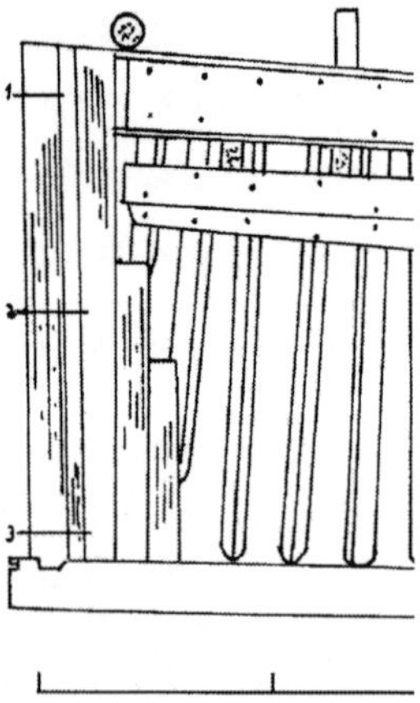

*Figure 8:3. Stem post: inner stem post and keel of the cargo-*badan *'al-Khammam', longitudinal section (Weismann 1998: 252–3)*

Figure 8:4 Stem post and keel of an abandoned badan *in al-Askarah, Oman (Weismann 1998: 244)*

In al-Quṣayr, in the northern part of the Red Sea, the construction of wooden boats that still exist is influenced by the boat-building tradition and styles of construction used in the nearby Mediterranean Sea. Nevertheless, the stem posts of these boats have no joints to the planks, and the inner-stem posts are bent along the stem. From the twentieth century, the double ribs shown in Figure 8:5 have not been common in other parts of Indian Ocean. A model of a *dhow* from Bombay, made in 1850, also shows such double ribs.[8]

Figure 8:5 Keel, stem post, inner stem posts, rips and planks of a small boat in the Mövenpick Hotel, al-Quṣayr, Egypt (photograph by Weismann 2001)

Knees

The knees are also a characteristic feature of boats and ships in the Indian Ocean. There are no hanging knees, only lodging knees (Arabic: *karwah*), see Figure 8:2. That means that the ribs and the beams are not built as a closed framework. There are a few exceptions where the main sheet bitt and the small bulkhead enclose the foredeck abaft. Even on recent constructions, as seen on a big *brig*

6 Klunzinger 1878: 288.
7 Alan Villiers photographic collection, National Maritime Museum, Greenwich, London.

8 Weisman 2001.

built in Spring 2006 in Ras al-Khaimah, UAE, only lodging knees are used.

Main sheet bitt

The main sheet bitt (Arabic: *qā'im*) was also a unique feature on every Indian Ocean sailing ship. It could be found on every depiction of Arab sailing ships. On bigger ships the main sheet bitt is fixed by a hanging knee, but in one exception from the rule only lodging knees are used. It was sometimes covered with planks, which could be easily replaced when worn out. Inside the *ghanjah* 'Fatḥ al-Khayr' from Sur, Oman, the bitt is partly covered too; the reason for this is unknown. On a photograph by Alan Villiers, made 1939, of the *būm* 'Triumph of Righteousness' the use of the main sheet bitt is depicted (Figure 8:6). On ships built to be powered by engines the main sheet bitt is much smaller or has totally disappeared, as is seen on many wooden ships calling at Dubai in the twenty-first century.

Figure 8:6 Main sheet bitt in use, starboard, būm 'Triumph of Righteousness' *(photograph by Alan Villiers 1939, catalogue no. 5461–32)*

Mast partner

There is only one kind of mast partner on traditional ships in the Indian Ocean. The middle part (Arabic: *fils* or *samām*) with the grooves for the mast and the characteristic mast post is only fitted into cuts on the ribs and futtocks, while the side parts (Arabic: *nashshāb*) are nailed onto the rips or futtocks, securing the mast partner against slipping out sideways (Figure 8:7). On small boats the mast partner was not so elaborate: it is just a piece of wood with grooves, fitted in and nailed on the ribs.

Figure 8:7 Mast partner, replica of the būm *'al-Muhalab', Kuwait (photograph by Dziamski 2003)*

Joinings

In Figure 8:8, a drawing of a *badan* used for fishing[9] from Oman, nearly all the methods used by shipbuilders in the Indian Ocean for joining parts since the eighteenth century are shown, including sewing, oblique wooden pegs, nails, clinched nails and skew nails.

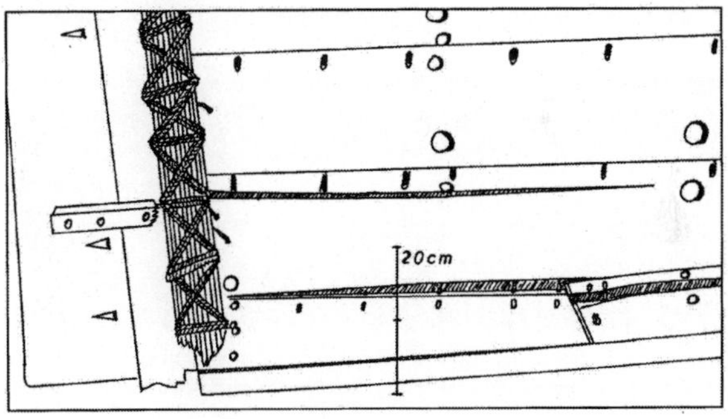

Figure 8:8 Drawing of the bow of a badan *for fishing, Qurm, Oman (photograph by Weismann 1995)*

Arab ship-builders also use iron connecting pieces to join the parts of the stem post. Other iron pieces connect the stem post and the keel (Figure 8:9). Sometimes barded nails were used to connect outer and inner stem posts. On recent constructions, bolts are used instead.

9 Weismann 1995: 175–83.

Figure 8:9 Connecting piece on the ghanjah *'Fatḥ al-Khayr', Sur, Oman (photograph by Dziamski 2004)*

Stern construction

The construction of the square stern is a distinctive feature of traditional Arab ships in the Indian Ocean as well. It is very simple. A stout floor is laid on the after-edge of the bottom; stern timbers run along the edge of the hull; then planks are used to close the stern, and more stern timbers connect the planks and strengthen this construction. Figure 8:10 shows the stern construction on the *sanbūq* 'Dhebe' from Sahd in Oman.

Figure 8:10 Stern construction, sanbūq *'Dhebe', Sadh, Oman (photograph by Dziamski 2005)*

On the much bigger *ghanjah* 'Fatḥ al-Khayr' from Sur in Oman the same construction is used, only strengthened by lodging knees attached to the main floor. Instead of one, three floors are used tightly together.

Lanceolate bottom plank

The typical feature of the lanceolate bottom plank does not appear on all ships in the Indian Ocean but only in some types of boat. On a potsherd from the first century AD, found by Weißhaar in Tissamaharama, Sri Lanka, a ship with a round bottom is depicted.[10] Further depictions exist, for example, that in a manuscript of the *Maqāmāt* of al-Ḥarīrī from Baghdad, painted about 1220. The descendants of these ships with round bottoms still exist as in various boat types including the *badan* and *battīl*. *Badan*-like ships appear in African graffiti as early as the fifteenth century.[11] The *badan* was built in the nineteenth century with a bent lanceolate bottom plank and side keels. Such a construction enables the use of wide planks, which is advantageous in the case of sewn ships (Figure 8:11).

Remains of this kind of bottom and keel could still be found, for example, on the *bānūsh* of the northern Bāṭinah coast in Oman. In the twentieth century the foremost bottom part was straight on the *badan* and *battīl*. Figure 8:12 shows some construction principles of a *baggārah* which is used for fishing in Sohar, Oman, with the keel plank, side keels, stem post and inner stem posts.

Square and settee sails

It is sometimes difficult to decide if in old sources settee or square sails are depicted. Three criteria may be used to solve the riddle. First, the settee rig is normally hoisted on a forward-raking mast, while square sails are normally used with vertical masts. Secondly, rigs with settee sails have a much bigger yard / mast relation than square sail rigs on seagoing ships. For a *būm* in the twentieth century this relation is about 2, whilst on European ships of the sixteenth century it was about 0.6. Thirdly, on square-sail rigs the yard is fixed on its middle, but this is not the case on settee-rigged ships. Up to the thirteenth century, only images with square sails could be found. Figure 8:13 shows a copy of a miniature in a manuscript by Muḥammad ibn Mubārak Ḥākim al-Qazwīnī made in 1526. The masts of this ship are vertical and the yard / mast relation is about 1.

A hero stone from Bhuji, India from the fifteenth century shows a transition to a settee sail: because the mast is raking, the yard / mast relation is about 1.5, and the yard is not fixed in the middle (Figure 8:14). The earliest depiction of a settee sail seems to be on a hero stone in Armada, India from the fourteenth or fifteenth century. Here the mast is raking forward too; the yard / mast relation is about 1,5 and the yard is fixed below its middle (Figure 8:15).

[10] Zick 1996: 178–85.

[11] Garlake 1964.

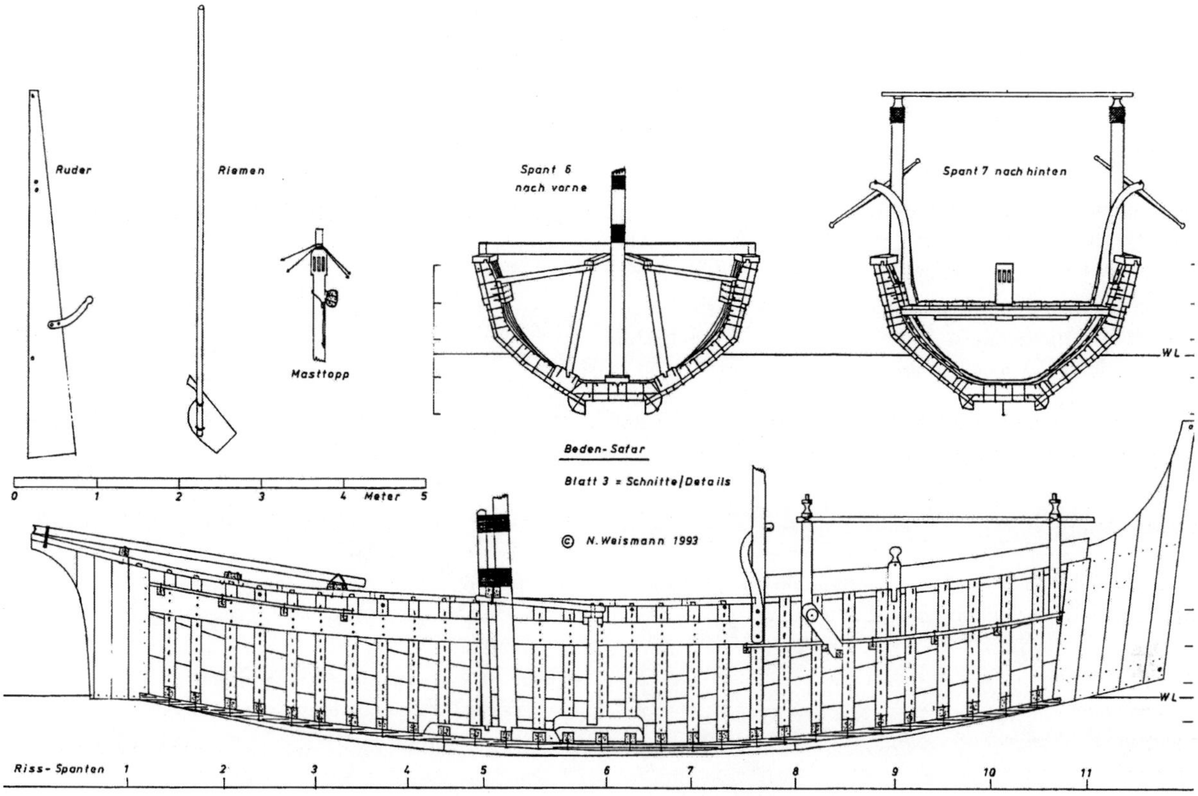

Figure 8:11 Sections of a badan safar *(Weismann 1994: 165)*

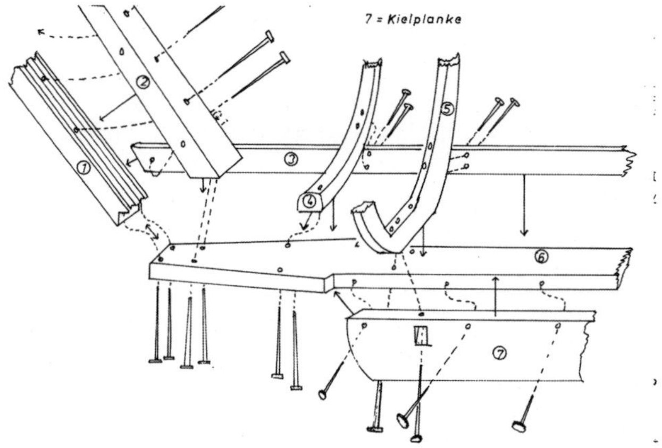

Figure 8:12 Foremost part of the keel plank on a baggāra *for fishing, Sohar, Oman (drawing by Weismann 1994: unpublished)*

Figure 8:13 Miniature from al-Qazwīnī 1526

Conclusion

Ships and boats in the Indian Ocean from AD 1800 onwards have characteristic features that make them identifiable. Such features include the construction of the main hatch, stem and stern, mast partner and main sheet bitt. Other features common in European ships, such as hanging knees, are generally not to be found on Indian Ocean ships. The repertoire of fastenings is limited and known. A lanceolate, rounded bottom plank with side keels occurs in some types in earlier times. The relations in the length of mast and yard, the raking of the mast and the point where the yard is fixed to mast seem to be helpful to identify a seete rig in old sources.

Figure 8:14 Hero stone in Bhuji, India, fifteenth century (Swamy 1997: 127)

Figure 8:15 Hero stone, Armada, India; fourteenth–fifteenth century (Swamy 1997: 126)

References

Garlake, P. and Garlake, M. 1964. Early Ship Engravings of the East African Coast, I. *Tanganyika Notes and Records* 63: 197–206.

al-Ḥārirī. 1220. *Maqāmāt*. Bibilothèque nationale de France, Department of Oriental Manuscripts. Ms Arabe 5647; 2003, facsimile repr. Lebanon?: Touch@rt.

Hawkins, C.W. 1977. *The Dhow: an illustrated history of the dhow and its world*. Lymington: Nautical Publishing Co.

al-Qazwīnī, Muḥammad ibn Mubārak Ḥākim (Shāh). 1526. *Du traite d'histoire naturelle écrit en arabe, sous le titre de...* . Bibliothèque nationale de France, Paris; Department of Oriental Manuscripts, Suppl. Persan 333 fol. 9.

Klunzinger, C.B. 1878, 2nd edn. *Bilder aus Oberägypten, der Wüste und dem Rothen Meere*. Stuttgart: Levy and Müller.

Niebuhr, C. 1772. *Beschreibung von Arabien: aus eigenen Beobachtungen und im Lande selbst gesammelter Nachrichten / abgefasset von Carsten Niebuhr*. Copenhagen and Leipzig: N. Möller; repr. 1969. Graz: Akademische Druck- und Verlagsanstalt.

Pâris, É. 1843. *Essai sur la construction navale des peuples extra-europeéns*, 2 vol. Paris: Arthus Bertrand.

——. 1882; repr. of first edn, 1972. *Souvenirs de Marine*. Hamburg: Butzinger.

Prados, E. 1997. Indian Ocean Littoral Maritime Evolution: the case of the Yemeni *Huri* and *Sanbuq*. *Mariner's Mirror* 83(2) (May): 185–98.

Swamy, L.N. 1997. *Boats and Ships in the Indian Art*. New Delhi: Harman Publishing House.

Weismann, N. 1995. Ein Fischer — Beden in Qurm (Sultanat Oman). *Das Logbuch*, Brilon (31 Jg. 1995) 4: 175–83.

——. 1998. The cargo-beden Al-Khammam. *International Journal of Nautical Archaeology* 27(3) (August): 237–57.

——. 1994. Der Beden Safar, eine Rekonstruktion nach Unterlagen von Admiral Pâris. *Das Logbuch, Brilon* 3 (30 Jg. 1994): 60–167.

Zick, M. 1996. Scherbenzählerei – oder: die Bürokratie des Archäologen. 178–85 in G. Graichen, M. Siebler (eds), *Schliemanns Erben*. Mainz: Phillip von Zabern.

Decorative Motifs on Arabian Boats: Meaning and Identity

Dionisius A. Agius

الزخارف ما زين من السفن

Ornamentation adorns the ship.[1]

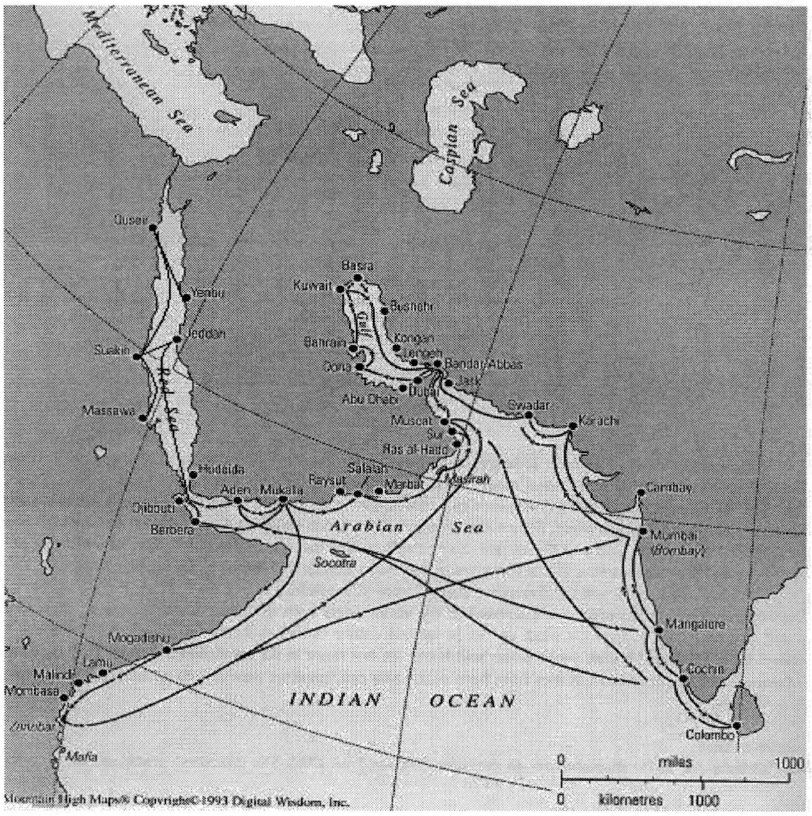

Map 9:1 Main ports and routes of dhow activities based on interviews with mariners, 1985–2004

Ornamentation of boats is a practice found within disparate communities of the Red Sea, the southern Arabian coast and the Arabian Gulf and Oman. Their boats have a variety of decorative motifs: the *oculus* on the stem or sternposts; circular conventionalized forms carved or painted on the stem-heads; tassels, flags, umbrellas and cowrie shells decorating stem- or sternposts; goatskin decoration covering the stem-head, and textual painting or carving on the sides of the aft deck or the transom.

This paper is concerned with the design and evolution of boat decoration and raises a number of questions: What is the symbolism behind boat decoration? Do decorative motifs express a cultural message typical of one region or are they representative of a wider community? How many of these motifs can be said to be Islamic? How much have foreign influences dictated the pattern process? What is the significance of the colours in these motifs? In response to these questions and others a number of possibilities will be considered.

Introduction

During the course of my work on dhows I became intrigued by their ornamentation. I noticed that in the Arabian Gulf and Oman boats were often decorated, albeit sparingly, contrasting with the colourful fishing boats of the Red Sea. I found over the years that this subject of ornamentation on boats is more complicated than I first thought when I started to research into the different types of motif. What appears to be simple turns out to have many layers of meaning. As is to be expected, there are regional differences in the type and use of ornamentation but the question is how different are they and what, if anything, can they tell us about the people who build, own and man the dhows on which they appear?

1 *al-Zakhārifu mā zuyyina min al-sufun*. Ibn Sīda. 1898–1903. I: 26.

Ornamentation on boats is a practice found within disparate Arabian communities. The boats have a variety of decorative motifs consisting of embellishment with objects or the use of carving, embossing and writing and the application of colour; their history goes back to antiquity. With the exception of Hornell 1923 and 1938, LeBaron Bowen 1955 and 1957, Prins 1970 and Shihāb 1983, decorative motifs on Arabian boats remain a much under-studied theme; much of their concern was on the 'eye' (the *oculus*), its meaning in maritime art, and its provenance. I would like to go further and explore if this art is homogenous within the whole region (the Red Sea, southern Arabian coast, Arabian Gulf and Oman) and how far decorative motifs are an outward expression of a unity of culture. Further, how far can we claim that ornamentation on Arabian boats of the Red Sea, the southern Arabian coast and the Arabian Gulf are part of Islamic art? This paper attempts to answer these questions.

The subject of ornamentation on boats is a universal one but my focus in this study is based on field work conducted in the African Red Sea ports and those of the Arabian Gulf and Oman, interviewing over two hundred mariners, shipwrights and merchants. The majority of my interviewees were over sixty years old; one sea captain in Sawakin (Sudan) was 120 years old and a pearl diver in Muharraq (Bahrain Island) was 112 years old (see map above).[2]

Figure 9:1 Dilmun seal with goat headstem (after Al-Khalīfa and Hamar 1982: 31)

2 Muhammad Yaqoob of Bahrain (born 1879) was interviewed on 24 April 1991 and Hussein 'Abd al-Hamid 'Abd 'Allah of Sawakin (born 1884) interviewed on 24 November 2004.

Zoomorphic motifs: their significance

From the Bronze Age, right through the Islamic period, zoomorphic motifs such as the animal headstems are recurring features in boat models and graffiti. Mesopotamian seals show animal or bird heads on both raised prows and sterns;[3] consider the Dilmun seal (1800 BCE) with a headstem of a goat (Figure 9:1).

The theme occurs in the *Maqāmāt* illustration of al-Ḥarīrī (d. AH 516 /AD 1122)[4] and the Persian miniatures, copies of which portray animal-shaped prows as in a British Library manuscript,[5] or bird-shape stem heads in a Chester Beatty Library manuscript.[6] The parrot-shaped stemhead on a Kuwaiti cargo *baghlah* is a good example of this kind (Figure 9:2).

Figure 9:2 The parrot-shaped stemhead of a Kuwaiti baghlah, 1999 (photograph by author)

It has been suggested that these motifs are an echo of human sacrifice when the severed head was fixed to the prow. Sacrificing humans was well known in pre-Islamic Arabia.[7] Human sacrifice was then replaced by animal sacrifice and it is still the custom today in the Red Sea, the southern Arabian

3 LeBaron Bowen 1955: 32.

4 BN Ms Arabe 3929, fol. 155v.

5 BL Add 15531, fol. 012a. I am grateful to Charles Melville who drew my attention to this illustration (communication 18 June 2004).

6 CBL Sa'dī Gulistān Herat 1427. My thanks go to Robert Hillenbrand who alerted me to this manuscript (communication 11 May 1998).

7 It is said that al-Mundhir, King of Hira, sacrificed the poet 'Abīd b. al-Abraṣ (d. *ca.* AD 554) after a vow he made to kill any person that approached him on a certain day. The poet happened to be that person, see Lyall 1981: xxvii–xxviii. It is also known that prisoners were offered as sacrifice and it is these that were stuck to the stempost of the ship.

coast and the Arabian Gulf to sacrifice a sheep or goat at the launching of a boat or ship; a custom also prevalent in the Mediterranean until fairly recent times.[8] The flayed goat skin is dressed on the stemhead — such as the stempost of a *battīl kārib* at Kumzar, Musandam Peninsula (Figure 9:3a) and the *zārūk* at the Mina, Sawakin (Figure 9:3b).

Figure 9:3a A goat-skin on a battīl kārib *stemhead, Kumzar, 1996 (photograph by the author)*

Figure 9:3b The zārūk *stemhead decorated with a goat-skin, Sawakin, 2004 (photograph by the author)*

It is interesting that the two ox-like horns at the stem-head on both dhows could be part of the ritual of the animal sacrifice. It seems that the horns are for the purpose of decoration and not, as I was told, designed originally for holding the rigging or anchor rope.[9]

Ornaments: protection and security

Ornaments are typical of decorative motifs on boats and ships. Bronze Age or Late Neolithic vessels hang tassels from their stern (Figure 9:4); the practice of hanging decoration is seen on graffiti from the Egyptian Eastern Desert and Dilmun seals.

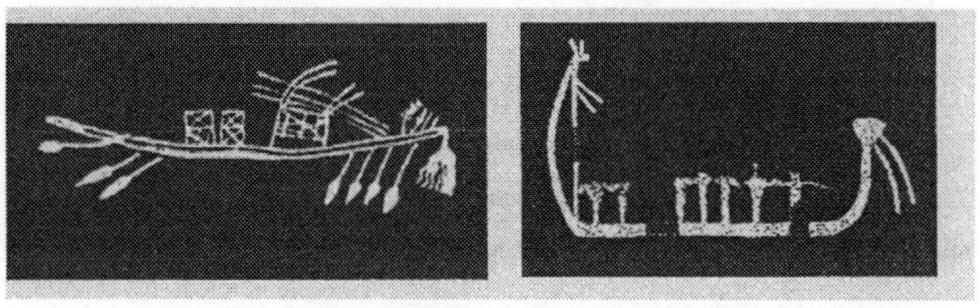

Figure 9:4 Hanging decorations on Dilmun vessels (after Flinders Petrie 1920: pl. XXXII and Winkler 1938: pl. XXXIX)

In modern times tassels (*kasht*) are hung from the *zārūka* stemhead in Kumzar or a *shū'ī*'s stempost at Ras al-Hadd (Figure 9:5):

Figure 9:5 A tassel hanging from the tip of a shū'ī *stemhead, Ras al-Hadd, 1998 (photograph by the author)*

Tassels and palm fronds were suspended from the bow of the East African *mtepe* and in more recent times the *battīl*s and *zārūka*s of the Musandam Peninsula. Bands of cowrie shells (*zanzūl*s) decorate the *fashīn* (false sternpost) of a *battīl* in Kumzar (Figure 9:6).

8 Information from Ġużeppi Maniscalco, Marsaxlokk, Malta (interviewed on 30 January 1996) and Ġrizi Muscat, Malta (10 September 2000).

9 Interview with Salih Zaid Muhammad Jumaa al-Kumzari on 25 November 1996; for further details see Agius 2002: 112.

Figure 9:6 Decorating the fashīn *of a* battīl, *Kumzar, 1996 (photograph by the author)*

I was told by my informants in Kumzar that the decoration of cowrie shells around the tall stern fins of a *battīl bahwī* is to commemorate a wedding in the village.[10] It is difficult to establish the original meaning of these decorative motifs, but it is generally understood that pendulous decorations such as tassels, flags umbrellas, shells, ostrich eggs and feathers[11] serve as amulets to guard the boat against the evil eye. One perhaps might compare this custom with the bridle ornaments of the Arabian camels which are hung around their noses, also to confer protection.

The *oculus*

Painting eyes is well known in different cultures and its cult is widespread from the Mediterranean to China. Red Sea vessels reported by LeBaron Bowen, such as the *hūrīs*, *za'īmahs*, *jalbahs* and the Adeni *sanbūqs* were decorated with *oculi* on the transom;[12] the now extinct East African double-ended *mtepe* had *oculi* carved and painted on each side of the stem and sternposts.[13] Rarely is the eye represented in the Arabian Gulf dhows; an exception is this Kuwaiti deep-sea *baghlah* which is striking with a painted eye on the transom (Figure 9:7).

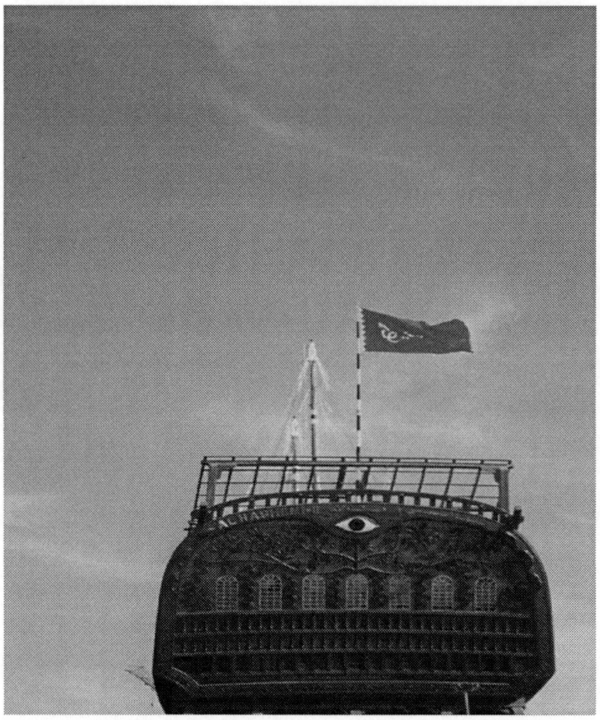

Figure 9:7 A painted eye on the baghlah *transom stern, 1998 (photograph by the author)*

The *oculus* is represented in two forms: the anthropomorphic eye design related to the Egyptian eye often associated with Ra, the Sun god and the eyes of Horus depicted on mummy coffins (Figure 9:8a); the other form, the stylized eye, a persistent recurring motif, having evolved into a patterned circle such as on the fourth century (BCE) Greek *bireme* (Figure 9:8b) and the crude eye on a modern stempiece of a *sanbūq*, at Mirbat (Figure 9:9).

Figure 9:8a The eye of Horus on a mummy coffin (after Lee Davis 1978: 155)

10 Interview with 'Abdallah bin Muhammad al-Kumzari on 24 November 1996.

11 Morton Nance 1914: Figure 7; 1920: 36, Figs. 14, 15; Foster 1949: 19.

12 LeBaron Bowen 1955: 6, 12; see also Prins 1970: 327–9.

13 Burton 1872: 74.

Figure 9:8b Stylized eyes on a Greek bireme *(after Landström 1961: 42–3)*

Figure 9:9 A crude circled eye on a sanbūq *stempiece, Mirbat, 1996 (photograph by the author)*

The *oculus* is perhaps the most ubiquitous motif. Symbolically, it is said to guard 'the soul of the boat'[14] and to drive off any malignant spirits which endanger the vessel. Its shape is particularly appropriate in this context as it harmonizes with the shape of the boat and waves of the sea. That the *oculus* is of an early Egyptian provenance is possible but its presence in the Eastern Indian Ocean makes the search for its origin more difficult. However, it must be said that there is an uncanny resemblance to the way the eye is depicted in Pharaonic Egyptian painting.

The Arabesque motif

Another common motif is the Arabesque design, characterized by its stylized floral forms, which is found on many dhows of the Arabian Peninsula, such as the Kuwaiti *baghlah*, the Omani *ghanjah* and the Indian *kotia.*[15] The Arabesque motif may be found as purely geometric forms such as the 'rosette' made of interlaced lines. One finds arabesque floral and geometric carved decoration carved on fairly recent dhows, such as the stempost of a *jālbūt* in Kuwait (Figure 9:10a) or a modern racing *hūrī* at al-Bateen, Abu Dhabi (Figure 9:10b).

Figure 9:10a A floral design carved on a Kuwaiti jālbūt *stempost, 1998 (photograph by the author)*

Figure 9:10b A floral motif on a racing hūrī*, Abu Dhabi, 1997 (photograph by the author)*

---

14 Hornell 1938: 348.

15 Agius 2002: 49–58; 2005: 13–6.

Hawkins noted three typical ornamental rosettes on the Arabian *būm* sternpost (Figure 9:11):

Figure 9:11 Ornamental rosettes on an Arabian būm *sternpost (after Hawkins 1977: 74)*

Its form is ancient; consider its presence on the hull sides of two thirteenth-century *Maqāmāt* illustrations of al-Ḥarīrī (d. AH 516 / AD 1122); one represents a cargo ship (Figure 9:12a) and the second is a river boat (Figure 9:12b).[16]

Figures 9:12a and 9:12b Rosettes carved or painted on thirteenth-century vessels (after al-Rāmhurmuzī 1883–1886: 91, 167)

Such patterns are well known in architectural art; they decorate the walls of mosques such as the Divrigi mosque, Turkey AH 626–627 / AD 1228–1229 and the Alhambra palace, al-Andalus (thirteenth and fourteenth centuries AD).[17] The tradition of floral design is found on doors like the ones at Dar'iyyah in Saudi Arabia, which are well preserved in spite of the ruined town.[18] Although it is a design found throughout the world and clearly ancient, it is found in abundance in Persian art and can be traced back from there to the ancient civilizations of the Near East: for example, carved rosettes are found on Iron Age shell 'buttons' (or medallions) at Sharm, Fujairah[19] and a 'rosette' of cup marks appears in the Jabal Jusassiyyah petroglyph in Qatar.[20] Also, though not common, one finds the Arabesque expressed by motifs of half a palmette leaf of a palm tree in a scroll of flower patterns along the bulwarks of a Mutrah *sanbūq* (Figure 9:13).[21]

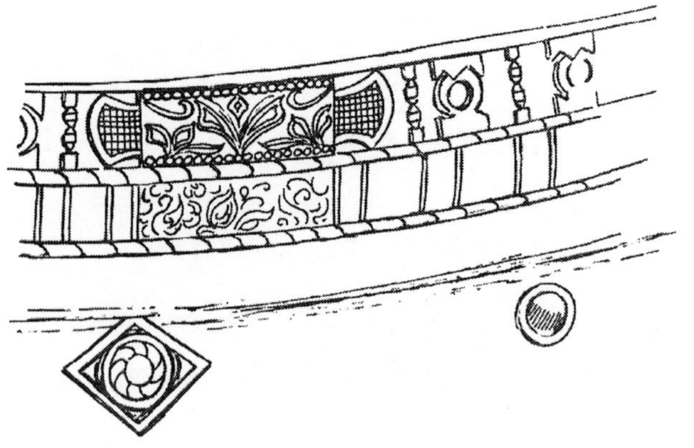

Figure 9:13 Palmette leaf motif with flower patterns on an Omani sanbūq *(after Sassoon 1970: 194, Figure 9)*

Geometrical designs

Geometric designs are usually rectilinear, such as circles, zigzags, triangles, and so on. The star motif is formed by intersecting quadrants of a circle: it can be seen in the Musandam Peninsula on the foredeck of a *battīl* in Qadah (Figure 9:14a), also found on the aft side of a *zārūk* in Sawakin (Figure 9:14b).

Figure 9:14a A star on a Qadah battīl*, Musandam, 1996 (photograph by the author)*

16 BN Ms Arabe 5487 (dated AH 634/ AD 1237).

17 Written communication Sharon Laor-Sirak 24 May 2006.

18 Agius 2005: 206.

19 Hellyer 1998: 22.

20 Kapel 1983: 37 (others are shown, see Figs. 18, 21 Site 72, 307, 401, 525).

21 Sassoon 1970: 194, Figure 9.

Figure 9:14b Star and intersecting quadrants on a Sawakin zārūk *stern fin, 2004 (photograph by the author)*

One recurrent design is the triangle. Smaller triangles are elaborately decorated on the stern fins of the Sawakin *zārūk* illustrated above and on the upper sides of the hull of the Mirbat *sanbūq* (Figure 9:15).

Figure 9:15 Triangles depicted on a sanbūq *stern fin, Mirbat, 1996 (photograph by the author)*

Such triangles are also typically found on Persian carpets. Prins reports seeing an *mtepe* in the 1950s that had geometrical designs carved and painted on the sides of bow, stern and rudder, like the border of a Shirazi carpet.[22] Double-ended *jalbah*s of Aden, Mukalla and Yemen and sewn boats at Shihr are reported to have had green triangles; *sanbūq*s from East African ports, invariably, are said to carry green triangles with eyes painted blue on the stemhead.[23] This triangle-*oculus* complex is common today with Maltese and Sicilian fishing boats. *Hūrī*s in the Aden harbour, LeBaron Bowen noted in the 1950s, had green triangles with *oculi*, fore and aft. He also observed *oculi* in triangular areas on tarred hulls of Adeni dugouts.[24] On small *būṭ*s and *za'īmah*s, he reports that the green triangle had gradually started to disappear.

Abstractness in maritime art

Although geometric designs are, by definition, precise, one finds in maritime art that each motif is individually drawn freehand so that not one motif is exactly the same as another. The process of decorating in its different forms is controlled by the eye and this is also true of the art of building a dhow; no dhow-type is similar to its model. No plans are required but the accuracy of eye provides the stability and seaworthiness of the structure of the vessel. The patterns of boat decorating are not rigidly stylized: they are an informal form of personal expression and one is struck by their simplicity and beauty.

From what has been said there is a mixture of anthropomorphic images and pure geometric designs on boats. This raises an intriguing question: why do anthropomorphic motifs occur in an Islamic culture where figurative art is prohibited? Figurative art only exists on the periphery, such as the Persian miniatures which portray images of persons and objects; and in this art the face of a sacred personage is always blurred and painted white. Islamic art dictates that nature is not allowed to be reproduced: no work of God the Creator should be imitated; thus, no Muslim is allowed to reproduce nature in other words, it is prohibited 'to transform nature into an imagery so as to make it visibly unreal'.[25] It can be transformed into something which is not represented by an object but by a feature which is an abstract.

Abstract designs are the purest forms of Islamic art and calligraphy is the quintessence of the abstract form, being both beautiful yet devoid of any object of creation. The art of writing, Burckhardt explains, 'awakens in the Muslim a sensitivity to the interplay of abstract lines, an interplay which is both geometric and rhythmic.'[26] Examples of textual painting and carving are found among Arabian boats; all examples I found are in the *naskhī* form, a simplified style of writing.

The art of writing on Arabian boats

Textual painting is typical of the Sawakin *zārūk* in Sudan while the Southern Arabian *sanbūq* has an elaborate carved transom embellished with writing in high relief. Textual carving is almost extinct today. I have classified these writings into three categories: (a) names of boats, (b) poetic lines, and (c) invocatory prayers.

(a) Names of fishing boats painted on the sides of the bows and stern of the Sawakin boats express words of hope, luck, livelihood and blessing of Allāh, others are place-names: بشائر *bashā'ir* (good omens), بغداد *Baghdād*, الجاموس *al-jāmūs* (buffalo), حماس *ḥamās* (fervour), رجاء *rajā'* (hope), الرحال *al-raḥḥāl* (the wanderer), ساحلي *sāḥilī*

22 Prins 1959: 213.

23 LeBaron Bowen 1955: 8–10; see Figure 6.

24 LeBaron Bowen 1952: 200.

25 Burckhardt 1976: 32.

26 Ibid.

(coastal), طالب الله *ṭālib Allāh* (seeker of Allāh), مواهب *mawāhib* (talents), العسيري النجد *al-Najd al-'Asīrī* (al-ʿAsīr),[27] المهاجر *al-muhājir* (the emigrant),[28] نوره *nūruhu* (His light).[29]

(b) Poetic verses painted on the aft side of a *zārūk* at the Mina in Sawakin show a very personal message (Figure 9:16):[30]

Figure 9:16 Writing on the zārūk *aft-side, Sawakin, 2004 (photograph by the author)*

على الشواطئ ترسى السفن
وعلى القلوب ترسى الذ كريات

Off the coast the boats anchor in the hearts lie memories

One *zārūk* gave the title of a song by the Saudi ʿAbd al-Majīd 'Abdallāh

رحيب والله رحيب

Amazing! O Allāh, it is wonderful!

(c) Invocatory prayers occur carved on the stern of a *sanbūq* in Sadh, Dhofar; the date and year and the name of the carver are included at the end of the prayers (Figure 9:17):[31]

Figure 9:17 Invocatory prayers on a Sadh sanbūq, *Dhofar, 1996 (photograph by the author)*

right side top

بسم الله الرحمان الرحيم يا الله
يا حافظ الارواح في الالواح

In the Name of Allāh, Most Gracious, Most Merciful
O You who preserve life on board ship.

right side bottom

و يا منجي الالواح في اللجج البحري
تحفظ لناهذا السنبوق المسمى الذيب
يا الله يا رازق يا الله يا حافظ

O You who rescue ships on the deep ocean[32]
Save and guard this *sanbūq* called *The Wolf*
O Allāh, O Provider, O Allāh, O Saviour.

left side top

بسم الله الرحمان الرحيم
نسالك التوفيق والغفور والرضا

In the Name of Allāh, Most Gracious, Most Merciful
We ask for mediation, forgiveness and favour

left side bottom

واتي لنا الارزاق من حيث
لا تدري تاريخ ٨ رجب عام ١٣٧١
ياس كهيعص----

Provide us with livelihood, knowingly or
without your knowledge. Dated 8 Rajab 1371 (1951)
Yā-Sīn; Kāf-Hā'-Yā'-'Ayn-Ṣād[33] (----)[34]

---

27 South-west Saudi Arabia: the Najd mountainous district between al-Hijaz and Yemen.

28 May be a reference to the *muhājirūn* — the Makkans who, in the early years of Islam, emigrated to Medina.

29 Recorded by author 4 December 2004.

30 Recorded by author 28 November 2004.

31 Recorded by author 17 November 1996.

32 The end of the first line in Arabic should read اللجج البحرية, the adjective following the plural noun is feminine singular.

33 These letters known as the 'abbreviated letters' are believed

These writings demonstrate a mental process which, when combined with the visual experience, creates something of unique beauty, but its function is clear: to convey a poetic or spiritual meaning. By writing on its planks, the *nakhoda* (sea captain) and/or the owner invoke God to protect the boat from wreckage or piracy. Not only would Arabic writing represent the values of an artistic creativity but it conforms to an Islamic life and the precepts of the faith. Consider the writing on the door lintel, examples of which I saw in al-Quṣayr, Sawakin and Sadh on the southern Arabian coast. The doorway is the symbol of the family just as the boat is another family (the owner and the crew). In both cases the writing demonstrates a sense of belonging.

Attitudes to decorative motifs

Let me now turn to the attitudes of seafaring communities towards their own decorative motifs. One of the most striking features of the boats in the Red Sea is the bright colours used on the outside. What is the significance of these colours? Table 1 shows that the most common colours in the two harbour towns of al-Quṣayr and Sawakin are red, blue and green. Turquoise blue is, of course, associated with protection against the evil eye, that is, protection against someone who is envious.

Ettinghausen's explanation that colour is a response to environment makes sense up to a point. He argues that the desert and the barren landscape of the Arabian shores and the Red Sea, the scarcity of water, the fierce sun and damp nights are elements that render life monotonous. The psychological relief from this 'unrelieved monotony' led to the use of colour in clothing and in the objects that are used.[35] But then how can one explain that the dhows of the Arabian Gulf and the Oman region are almost devoid of colour? The painting of the sharp-pointed stem-head of a *būm* in black and white, or white and blue on the stem-head of *sanbūq*s in the Gulf is all that we have. In general, most of the Arabian Gulf dhows look brown, though with fish oil rubbed into the planks, they contrast very well with the green-blue sea.

Final remarks

It may be said in general that the themes of decorative motifs can be symbolic or representational; some may be following in a tradition from late classical and Byzantine prototypes. The rosette is a Persian influence and this is visible on the Arabian Gulf boats because of the Shī'ite dominance in the communities there. Of the 150 mariners I interviewed in the Arabian Gulf, seventy percent told me they were Shī'ites; the figure may be higher as some were reluctant to give such information due to political and religious sensitivities. In contrast to the more flowing lines of the rosette are the triangles and star motifs which seem to belong more to the Sunni communities who settled on the coast, influenced as they are by Bedu tribal art. This is not a clear-cut divide but there is evidence to support nomadic influences. Tellingly, no sign of the rosette occurs on the Red Sea fishing boats owned by the Rashāyida, a Saudi (Sunni) tribe who have been settled on the African coast for at least one hundred years.

The desert and the sea have space in common. When it comes to forms, Burckardt comments, nomads simplify them and render them as symbols while sedentary people develop nomadic art with forms reminiscent of nature.[36] Thus, nomadic art enjoys rhythm and space while sedentary art has melody but limits space.[37] Maritime culture lies at a crossroads between two polarities: nomadic and sedentary. Nomads were in contact with the merchants and traders who came with their goods at the harbour front to trade goods and fish when the ship anchored. Others came to the shore for seasonal work in October as mariners and returned to their pasture land in May. Artistic motifs on objects that are traded produce ideas that are borrowed and become part of the maritime art repertoire. Its adaptation is a balance between motifs developed by the town and the desert settlers.

To return to the questions raised at the beginning of this article: maritime art cannot be said to be completely homogenous within the region of the Red Sea, southern Arabian coast and the Arabian Gulf and Oman because one or more motifs can predominate in one area of the region but not another. For example, although the *oculus* is common to the whole Arabian Peninsula, the rosette is typical of the Arabian Gulf states but not of the Red Sea. How far is maritime art an expression of a unity of culture? Some motifs such as pendulous decorations and the *oculus* predate Islam as we have seen, but nevertheless seem to have originated across the whole region. There is no doubt that they do demonstrate a unity and stability over the centuries. It is only when it comes down to individual motifs that one sees the regional differences. The greatest expression of unity is, of course, Islam and it is calligraphy in maritime art that distinguishes this region from the western Indian Ocean boats.

When one considers the ornamental intricacy of buildings such as the Alhambra in Spain and the high degree of detail and colour susceptibility in Persian miniature painting, Islamic maritime art is relatively simple. However, it gives us a unique glimpse into the customs and folklore traditions of a pre-Islamic society as well as reflecting customs and beliefs of modern Arabian and African communities.

to have a mystic meaning; the first group relates to the Prophet Muḥammad, see Sūrat YāSīn 37: 1; the second group of letters is found in the first *āya* (verse) of Sūrat Maryam 19: 1.

34 The owner or carver's name is not readable.

35 Ettinghausen 1976: 68.

36 Burckhardt 1976: 37.

37 Ibid.

Table 9:1 Colours of dhows Sawakin and al-Quṣayr (2001–2004)						
	red / red ochre	black	green	blue/turquoise blue	yellow	white
zārūk	√	√	√	√	√	
shaṭṭiyya	√			√	√	√
ramaṣ	√			√		
falūka	√		√			
gaṭīra	√		√	√		
hūrī	√			√		

Archives

BL British Library, London

BN Bibliothèque Nationale, Paris

CBL Chester Beatty Library, Dublin

References

Agius, D.A. 2002. *In the Wake of the Dhow: the Arabian Gulf and Oman*. Reading: Ithaca.

——. 2005. *Seafaring in the Arabian Gulf and Oman: the people of the dhow*. London: Kegan Paul.

Burckhardt, T. 1976. Introduction to Islamic Art. 31–38 in [Dalu Jones and George Michell (eds)], *The Arts of Islam. Hayward Gallery*. London: The Arts Council of Great Britain.

Burton, R.F. 1872. *Zanzibar, City, Island and Coast*. London: Tinsley.

Ettinghausen, R. 1976. The Man-Made Setting: Islamic Art and Architecture. 57–88 in B. Lewis (ed.), *The World of Islam: faith, people, culture*. London: Thames & Hudson.

Foster, W. (ed.). 1949. *The Red Sea and Adjacent Countries at the Close of the Seventeenth Century*. London: The Hakluyt Society.

Grabar, O. 2006. *Islamic Art and Beyond*. III. *Constructing the Study of Islamic Art*. Aldershot: Ashgate.

Hawkins, C.W. 1977. *The Dhow: an illustrated history of the dhow and its world*. Lymington: Nautical Publishing Co.

Hornell, J. 1923. Survivals of the Use of Oculi in Modern Boats. *Journal of the Royal Anthropological Institute of Great Britain and Ireland* 53(3): 289–321.

——. 1938. Boat Oculi Survivals: Additional Records. *Royal Anthropological Institute of Great Britain and Ireland* 68(2): 339–49.

Ibn Sīda, Abū l-Ḥasan ʻAlī b. Ismāʻīl. 1898–1903. *Kitāb al-mukhaṣṣaṣ*, volume X. Bulaq.

Al-Khalīfa, ʻAbd Allāh bin Khālid and ʻAbd al-Malik Yūsuf al-Ḥamar. 1982. *Al-Baḥrayn ʻabr al-tārīkh*, volume I. Manamah: Wizārat al-Iʻlām.

Landström, B. 1961. *The Ship*. London: George Allen & Unwin.

LeBaron Bowen, R. Jr. 1952. Primitive Watercraft of Arabia. *The American Neptune* 12(3): 186–221.

——. 1955. Maritime Superstitions of the Arabs. *The American Neptune* 15(1): 5–48.

——. 1957. Origin and Diffusion of Oculi. *The American Neptune* 17(4): 262–91.

Davis, V.L. 1978. Pathways to the Gods. 154–201 in Jules B. Billard (ed.), *Ancient Egypt*. Washington DC: National Geographic Society.

Lyall, C.J. 1981 (Ist edn 1930). *Translations of Ancient Arabian Poetry*. Westpoint, Connecticut: Hyperion.

Nance, R.M. 1914. Terradas and Talismans. *The Mariner's Mirror* 4(1): 3–13.

——. 1920. Fresh Light on 'Terradas' and 'Gelves'. *The Mariner's Mirror* 6(2): 34–9.

Petrie, W.M. Flinders 1920. *Prehistoric Egypt*. London: British School of Archaeology in Egypt.

Potts, D. 1998. Maritime Beginnings. 8–43 in Peter Hellyer (ed.), *Waves of Time*. London: Trident Press.

Prins, A.H.J. 1970. Maritime art in an Islamic context: oculus and therion in Lamu ships. *The Mariner's Mirror* 56(3): 327–39.

al-Rāmhurmuzī, Buzurg b. Shahriyār al-Nākhudā. 1883–1886. *Kitāb ʻajāʼib al-Hind* [Livre des merveilles de l'Inde], P.A. Van Der Lith (ed.) and L.M. Devic (tr.). Leiden: E. J. Brill.

Sassoon, C. 1970. The dhows of Dar Es Salaam. *Tanzania Notes and Records* 71, 185–200.

Shihāb, Ḥasan Ṣāliḥ 1983. *al-Marākib al-ʻarabiyya: tārīkhuhā wa anwāʻuhā* [Arabian Ships: their history and types]. Kuwait: Mu'assasat al-Kuwayt lil-Taqaddum al-ʻIlmī.

Winkler, H.A. 1938–1939. *Rock Drawings of Southern Upper Egypt*. London: Egypt Exploration Society, Oxford University Press.

Acknowledgements

This research was partially funded by grants from the British Council (1990–1996), Ministries of Information in Kuwait, Bahrain, Qatar and the Emirates (1990–1996), the Leverhulme Trust (1996–1998) and Arts and Humanities Research Council (2002–2005).

The Red Sea *Jalbah* or *Jalabah*. Local Phenomenon or Regional Prototype?

James E. Taylor

Word transfer and the derivation of names for Arab ship types

Speculation about the derivation of the names given to the different types of Arab dhows has occupied the attention of scholars from a variety of disciplines but the intrusion of wishful thinking, guesswork and, at times, flawed logic has cluttered the field with dubious assertions, nowhere more clearly evident than in the case of the *jalbah* or *jalabah.* Much error might have been avoided by the adoption of a rigorous analytical approach based on an understanding of the factors involved in the word transfer process that lies at the heart of the matter.

In order to establish that a word of one language is derived from a word of another one it is necessary to demonstrate: (1) an agent; (2) a motive: (3) a communication route; (4) the correlation of circumstances; (5) chronological credibility. In other words, if a word is to move from one language to another, it requires someone or something to carry it, a justification for moving it, and a believable route along which it might travel. Moreover, the various events and circumstances associated with the transfer must correlate in a credible manner in a credible time frame.[1]

One of the circumstances essential to a word transfer that we need to bear in mind is the presence of some form of intercourse focused on the object or idea represented by the transferred word. This is exemplified in a later paragraph where the absence of an object on which to focus a discourse reinforces the argument against an Iberian origin for the word *jalabah.* Also, we need to be aware of the possibility that an idea or word originating in a cultural or linguistic community 'A' and transmitted to a community 'C' via a community 'B' is ascribed by the people of 'C' to the intermediary 'B' rather than the originator 'A'. Thus Marx[2] launched the theory that the Chinese word 'zaw' was transmitted to India where he claims that it metamorphosed into the word 'dhow', which was picked up by the first English travellers to India and thought to be of Indian provenance. Although there are strong grounds for believing that Marx was mistaken, his theory does illustrate something that could quite conceivably happen.

There are two fundamental questions that we need to ask ourselves:

1. Why should a culture adopt a loan word instead of coining a word of its own? This usually happens when:

1.1 There is some sort of commercial, technical or cultural transfer in which a name accompanies the idea or thing to which it applies. This is particularly apparent nowadays in the transfer of technical terms from English to a variety of other languages. But this is no more than the current manifestation of an observable tendency for words to flow from the more advanced culture to the less advanced one, a striking example of which is to be found in the large body of Arabic words in the KiSwahili language, where it is evident that the words derived from Arabic are pitched at a more advanced technical and cultural level than those of Bantu origin. Of course, one meets a flow in the opposite direction when an advanced culture encounters something new in a less advanced one and adopts the local name, exemplified by such words as 'tea', 'orange', 'cocoa', etc., absorbed into English usage along with the product to which each of them relates.

1.2 There is an exchange of words and ideas between cultures that are in communication with each other, such as when traders and seamen cohabit with local women and sire families by them. Of such we find reference in *Periplus Maris Erythrœi*: 'They (the merchants of Muza (al-Mukhā')) send out to it (the coast of Africa) merchant craft that they staff mostly with Arab skippers and agents who, through continual intercourse and intermarriage, are familiar with the area and its language.'[3] Then, about fifteen hundred years later, Barbosa wrote, 'And in this land of Malabar there are Moors in great numbers who speak the same tongue as the Heathens of the land ... They marry as many wives as they can support and keep as well many heathen concubines of low caste. If they have sons or daughters by these they make them Moors, and oft-times the mother as well.' [4] A powerful inducement for seamen and traders to maintain a second household in foreign parts was the long period of waiting on shore for the monsoon winds to change direction and waft them back home. Obviously, the language exchanges worked in both directions and so it is probable that the huge Arabic element of the Swahili lexicon is a

1 These criteria, especially the last two, may be usefully applied *mutatis mutandis* to the appraisal of other theories of a historical nature. Thus the late Thor Heyerdahl's theory that the trade between Ur, Magan, Dilmun and the Indus valley city states was conducted in ships made of reeds is not chronologically credible and overlooks the fact that a reed boat on a seal found in the Indus Valley probably had religious rather than historical significance.

2 Marx 1946.

3 Casson 1989, v.16.

4 Barbosa 1918–1921

phenomenon of great antiquity, pre-dating the *Periplus* and the rise of Islam.

1.3 Finally, one must not underestimate the effect of swank: people of all races and all walks of life are prone to flourish the occasional foreign word as a token of their erudition, especially when the word is from a dominant or more prestigious culture. I found the Swahili people particularly susceptible to the lure of the foreign word or phrase, as we also perceive in many of the ship names recorded by Prins[5] and Gilbert.[6]

2. What moves a modern scholar to attribute a word in one language to a source in another?

2.1. The usual reason is similarity of articulation of the word together with similarity in the characteristics of the named object, such as form, function, venue and so on. This inspired the theory that the name of the Arab *jalabūt* was derived from the English jolly boat that it closely resembles. But similarity of articulation as a means of tracing the borrowing of words from one language by another is not a completely trustworthy tool, especially where the two languages are cognate, when that which at first sight appears to be a word transfer may well be two different manifestations of a common, ancient root.

The derivation of *jalbah / jalabah*

In his study of East African vessels, Prins[7] suggests that the word *jalbah* is derived from the Portuguese or Spanish word *gelba*, merely citing the authority of Kindermann,[8] who linked the *jalbah* to the *gelba* about thirty years before him, in what came to be an accepted authority on the names of the different types of Arab ships. However, Kindermann only claims linkage without implying which is the source language and which the receptor but the fact that his source is the Dozy-Engelmann, *Glossaire des mots espagnols et portugais dérivés de l'arabe* [A Glossary of Spanish and Portuguese Words derived from Arabic] suggests that Arabic was the source language and that *jalbah* not *gelba* was the source word. Moreover, the earliest uses of the word *jalbah* in writing were first by Buzurg ibn Shahriyār[9] in about AD 953, when he writes of *jilāb*[10] from ports of the Red Sea travelling in the Indian Ocean, and then by Ibn Jubayr,[11] who crossed the Red Sea in a *jalbah* in 1183. Thus we have firm evidence that the word was used in the Indian Ocean more than five centuries before the arrival there of the Portuguese. In the days of Buzurg and Ibn Jubayr, the Iberian Peninsula was ruled by Arabs, and so I suppose one could argue they might have picked up the word from their Portuguese subjects but although there were viable communication routes between al-Andalus, Baghdad and the Red Sea, it is almost impossible to conceive of a context in which such a word transfer might have occurred prior to AD 953, since there is no record of *jilāb* or anything remotely like them[12] ever plying in the Mediterranean and hence there was no subject on which to focus a discourse, no catalyst to spark a transfer.

So far as I am aware, no one has previously considered the possibility of a purely Arabic origin for the word *jalbah*, possibly because it is not used to define a ship in the English-speaking Arabist's *vade mecum*, E.W. Lane's *Lexicon.*[13] But while Lane does not mention the *jalbah* as such, he does define the Arabic verb *jalaba* thus: 'He drove, or brought, conveyed or transported, a thing, or things, such as camels, sheep, goats, horses, captives, or slaves, or any merchandise, from one place to another, or from one country or town to another, for the purpose of traffic', which is exactly what the *jalbah* did! Indeed, Ibn Jubayr first encountered the word at the Red Sea port of Aydhab, where he makes quite a point of the fact that the town was without resources, that all means of sustenance had to be imported and that the main income of the population was from transporting pilgrims to and from Jiddah *en route* to Makkah. There are precedents in Arabic for Arab ship types to be named in accordance with their functions;[14] and, if, as we believe, the *jalbah* was an indigenous Arab creation it was unlikely to be given a foreign name. Hence it is almost certain that *jalbah* is not a loan word at all but one coined by the Arabs to denote a particular kind of merchant ship; and given the importance of the import/export business to the people of 'Aydhāb it is not inconceivable that the word and even the ship originated there.

Descriptions of the *jalbah*

Descriptions of the *jalbah* improve with age. Writing in 1920, Moore mentions a vessel called a *jalba*; but from his description of its 'curved stem something like a sambuk's but overhanging less, a high raking stern, a very much notched rudder and a single mast'[15] it appears that the word *jalbah* was employed locally for what is more usually known as a *za'īma.*[16]

5 Prins 1965.

6 Gilbert 2004.

7 Prins 1965: 77.

8 Kindermann 1934: 19.

9 Buzurg ibn Shahriyār al-Rāmhurmuzī.

10 The broken plural form of the word *jalbah*.

11 Abū al-Ḥusayn Muḥammad ibn Aḥmad ibn Jubayr al-Kinānī.

12 The medieval European ship known as the 'cog' bears a superficial resemblance to the *jalbah* but it mainly circulated in northern waters and had not made its appearance at the time when the *jalbah* was first mentioned in print.

13 Lane 1863–1893.

14 For example, the warship and hunting canoe, both known as the *ṭarrād* or *ṭarrādah*, from the verb *ṭarrada* meaning 'he attacked, chased, hunted'.

15 Moore 1920.

16 One needs to be aware of a tendency for Arabs to use the

In 1877 the word *jalbah* appears to have acquired a specialized meaning in Aden, for Hunter[17] reports:

> Country crafts are built from 1 to 150 tons, and of course, as already described, there is considerable diversion in construction, but the principal point is how the bottom is made; this varies even in vessels of the same class. Flat bottom, or Markâbi, are used for coasting and harbour purposes; deep, or Gilâbi, for sea-going craft.

In 1625 Lobo,[18] *en route* to the Red Sea, sighted 'a gelve,[19] or kind of boat, made of thin boards, sewed together, with no other sail than a mat.' A comment of Sulaymān al-Mahrī (*ca.* 1511) 'indeed, you return in the land route, (by) the way of the *jilāb* and the anchorages'[20] has been interpreted by Shihāb[21] to mean that 'the jalbah was one of the heavy cargo ships not as suited as lighter ships to combating the waves and winds of the deep sea, but followed a course running abreast of the land, especially in the Red Sea.' Elsewhere, Shihāb dismisses Ibn Jubayr's and Marco Polo's criticism of the *jalbah's* rickety design and weak construction and reaffirms that it was a heavy cargo ship, on the grounds that the *jilāb* that Ibn Baṭṭūṭah saw in the port of Jiddah were large and strong enough to carry camels along with goods and passengers.

The most valuable descriptions of the *jalbah* are those given by Ibn Jubayr (1184), Ibn Baṭṭūṭah (1326) and probably by al-Muqaddasī (AD 986) as well.[22] They generally agree on its principal features, which are:

- A planked hull in which the planks were stitched together with cords made from coconut fibre.
- No decking.
- A sail made from palm matting. (From the impracticability of a fore-and-aft sail made from palm matting we can infer that the sail was a square one.)
- A central rudder turned by means of a yoke and lines (mentioned only by al-Muqaddasī).

Unfortunately, none of them say whether the vessel was flat-bottomed or vee-bottomed. As previously mentioned, Hunter states that in Aden the word *Gilâbi* is used for deep-hulled sea-going vessels. Although it implies that the *jalbah* is vee-bottomed, which suits my next argument, this usage is not reported anywhere else and the definition of the word *markab* is unusual, and so I am cautious about relying on it.

The *jalbah / mtepe* connection

Figure 10:1 Photograph of a model of an mtepe *in the Science Museum, London*

Apart from the manner of steering, the characteristic features of the *jalbah* are the same as those of the *mtepe*[23] (Figure 10:1) that flourished until recently on the East African coast and this raises the possibility that the *mtepe* was in fact the surviving relic of the *jalbah*, or was at least influenced by it. Of course, one might argue that the *mtepe* could have influenced the *jalbah,* but nowhere in substantiated history do we find the products of Africa being exported in African ships until modern times; so how could the *mtepe* have possibly influenced the *jalbah* if it never ventured into the *jalbah's* home waters until recently? Moreover, the word *mtepe* does not appear in print until 1870 when Steere[24] included it in his lexicon of Swahili words about 900 years after Buzurg first mentioned the *jalbah*, which suggests that the *jalbah* long pre-dated the *mtepe*. Its omission from Owen (1833)[25] is particularly significant because his mission, 'to carry out surveys of the East African and Arabian coasts including collecting information of the numbers and characters of the natives, their occupations, modes of subsistence etc., the nature of the soil and also of the productions of the surrounding country',[26] included a study of the local boats by his Lieutenant, who mentions a vessel answering the description of the *mtepe*, but which he calls a 'dow'. Neither Sulivan (1873)[27] nor Colomb (1873),[28] who both

name of a locally popular type of ship generically in casual speech. Thus in some ports of the Yemen almost anything that floats is either called a *za'ima* or, if it is small, a *hūrī.*

17 Hunter 1877: 84.

18 Lobo 1887.

19 One suspects that 'gelve' is a corrupt rendition of *jalbah.*

20 Sulaymān al-Mahrī, *ca.* 1511.

21 Shihāb 1983.

22 Al-Muqaddasī describes at length a vessel in which he travelled in the Red Sea but does not mention its name.

23 The *mtepe* was steered by means of a tiller, whereas the vessel described by al-Muqaddasī was steered by means of a yoke and lines.

24 Steere 1870.

25 Owen 1833.

26 Extract from Owen's instructions from the Lords Commissioners of the Admiralty.

27 Sulivan 1873.

28 Colomb 1873.

were active in the suppression of slave traffic off the East African coast, use the word *mtepe* in their journals.

On the origins of the *mtepe*

Periplus Maris Erythræi (*ca.* AD 50) states that the East African coast, known as Azania, was under the suzerainty of South Arabians and had been so since ancient times, thus providing the most likely means and communication route for technical and cultural transfers to East Africa. It also mentions the existence of sewn vessels at Rhapta,[29] an ancient port in the vicinity of modern Dar-es-Salaam. Chittick[30] rightly questions the tendency of authors to cite the sewn ships of Rhapta as evidence of the existence at the time of ships of the *mtepe* type, pointing out that the use in the Greek text of the diminutive *rhapton ploiarion* instead of *ploion*, the word normally used for ships, suggests something quite small. I would go further and question the tacit assumption that the unknown author of the *Periplus* was necessarily referring to sewn vessels sheathed with sawn planks and not some other material that would suggest an indigenous creation, since there is no evidence that the technique of sawing logs into planks was anything but an imported innovation and there was no specific mention of sawn planks until the first European travellers appeared on the scene, about 1,500 years later.

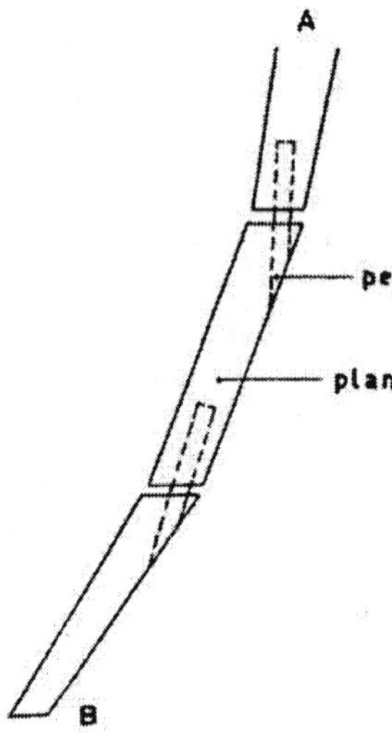

Figure 10:2a Cross-sectional drawing of an mtepe *hull showing treenailing (Prins).*

The method of planking furnishes a useful clue to the origin of the *mtepe*. Prins's cross-section of an *mtepe* hull (Figure 10:2a) shows the treenails driven obliquely upwards; but upward driving is not practicable because (1) it would preclude the possibility of dowelling the garboard strake[31] to the keel; (2) it would be very difficult to achieve a hearty upward stroke of the driving mallet in the cramped conditions in which the first few strakes are fixed; and (3) the transmitted momentum of the mallet blows would tend to separate the strakes already fixed.

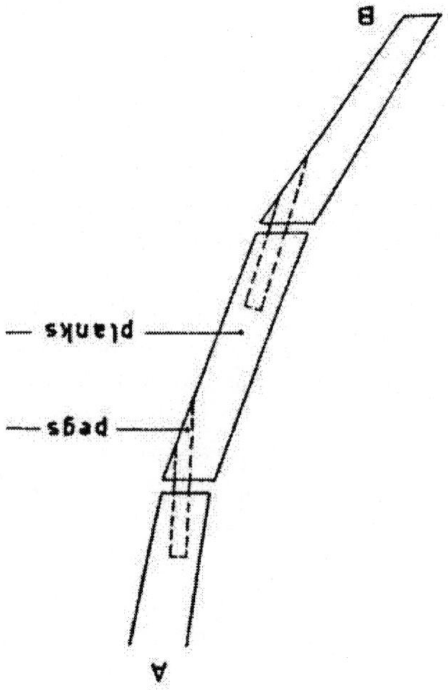

Figure 10:2b The image of Fig 10:2a inverted to show a more credible method of treenailing

The image becomes credible if we invert it (Figure 10:2b) so that the treenails appear to be driven downwards, which agrees with the explanations of Lydekker[32] and Hornell[33] (Figure 10:3),[34] who studied the matter when *mitepe*[35] were still to be seen. It also coincides with the method of treenailing described by Shihāb and Bowen as the norm in southern Arabia (Figure 10:4) and the one recently used to construct a replica of the *mtepe* in Zanzibar.[36] This points to South Arabian rather than Maldivian influence on the *mtepe*, for Millar[37] reports that shipbuilders in the Maldives drive their dowels perpendicularly (Figure 10:5) which implies a radically different planking technique. One might argue that Maldivian shipbuilders had switched from oblique treenails to perpendicular ones since olden times but what motive was there for them to take what I regard as a retrograde step? Other things being equal, the obliquely driven dowel is theoretically stronger in

29 The name of this place is said to be derived from the Greek word for 'sewn', but could equally be derived from the Arabic ربط = to bind.

30 Chittick 1980.

31 The garboard strake is the first strake to be fitted alongside the keel.

32 Lydekker 1919: 89.

33 Hornell 1941: 60, 65.

34 Adams 1985, contradicts the statements of Lyddeker, Hornell and Prins, claiming the treenails of the *mtepe* to be driven perpendicularly as in Figure 10:5. His grounds for doing so are flimsy.

35 The word *mitepe* is the plural of *mtepe.*

36 Abdul Sheriff, Khamis Abdalla and Ame Mshenga 2006.

37 Millar 1993: 9–16.

longitudinal and transverse shear than the perpendicular one; moreover, oblique tree-nailing is the easiest way of ensuring that the two holes for a treenail are in the perfect alignment necessary for a treenail to realise its full potential, since they are drilled as one, with the two adjacent planks set up in their final positions; and it implies a planking technique that requires less skill and less labour than perpendicular treenailing. Further evidence of Arabian influence is to be found in the Swahili shipwright's use of the same Arabic word *'maliki'* for the garboard strakes of the *mtepe*[38] as South Arabian shipwrights use for the garboard strakes of the dhow[39] and, more significantly, the use of the word '*makumbi*' derived from the ancient Arabic word *qanbar*,[40] for the coir rope used to stitch the planks together, rather than the modern Arabic term *līf Hindī*. Moreover, these are just two of a significant nucleus of Arabic technical terms used for various key elements of the *mtepe* and its rigging. Chittick[41] is of the opinion that the characteristic features of the *mtepe* are not found in the Maldives; and dismisses the probability of any influence on the *mtepe* from the sewn boats observed by Speke[42] and Stanley[43] on Lake Victoria. I am inclined to agree with him in this because sewing is the only feature they have in common. Indeed, there is every possibility that it was Arabs from the coast who first introduced the technique of sewing planks together to the Central African lakes, since there is no firm evidence to suggest that the stitching technique predated their appearance on the shores of these lakes.

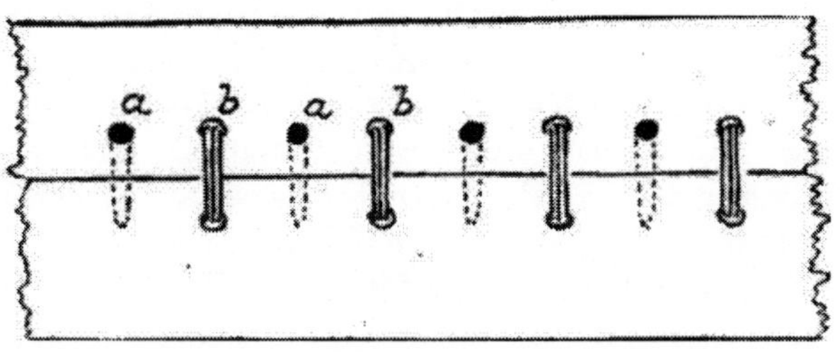

Figure 10:3 An external side view of a joint between adjacent planks of an mtepe showing treenailing and stitching (Lyddeker and Hornell). Key to drawing: a = a treenail; b = the stitching cord

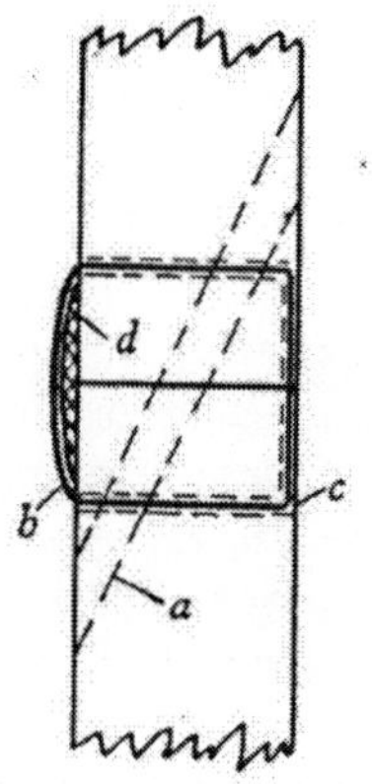

Figure 10:4 Cross-section through a joint between adjacent planks of a stitched hull as used in South Arabia (Baron and Shihab). Key to drawing: a = a treenail; b = the stitching cord; c = external groove to protect cordage: d = internal caulking strip

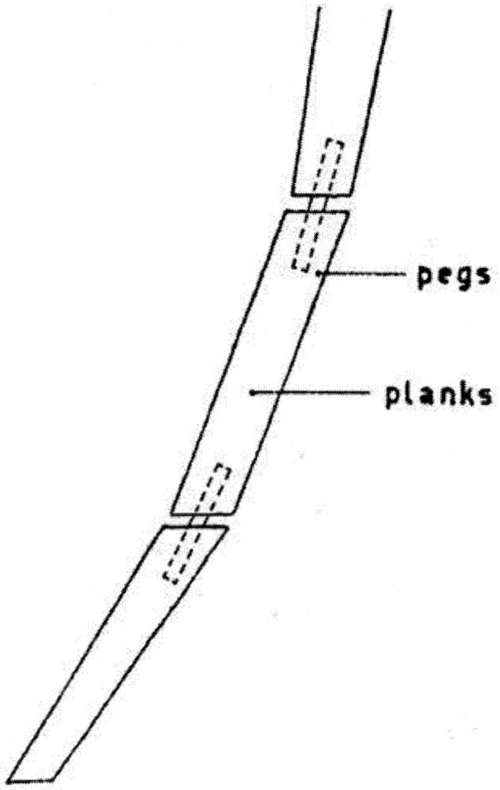

Figure 10:5 Cross section of a hull showing treenailing as practised in the Maldives (Millar).

---

38 Nabahany 2006 where he says (in verse), 'Wa mwando wa kuafiki, Na ubao ni maliki' [The first plank to be joined on is the *maliki*].

39 Shihāb 1983: 103, Figure 102.

40 First used by Ibn Baṭṭūṭah.

41 Chittick 1980: 298.

42 Speke 1863: 391.

43 Stanley 1890: 286.

According to Lydekker, the natives of the Bajun Islands off the Kenya coast claim a crew of shipwrecked Wadiba[44] from the Laccadive or Maldive Islands introduced the *mtepe* there, sometime before the coming of the Portuguese. Were this true one would expect the names of the many fundamental elements of the *mtepe* that are derived from Arabic to have been derived from the Laccadivan language, Malayalam, or the Maldivian, Dhiveli. Jewell[45] is ambivalent. On the one hand he writes, without giving his reasons: 'These craft appear to be of African origin and owe nothing to outside influence', which, of course, conflicts with Lydekker's account. Then, on the other hand, he relates the legendary story of the vessel's distinctive prow: 'The bird-like prow is alleged to represent the head and neck of the she-camel, which, as is narrated in the Koran, was sent from heaven to the Thamud, an ancient Arabian tribe, which refused to accept it as a divine token and hamstrung it', which hints at an Islamic Arab origin. Prins[46] writes:

> Surveying this meagre evidence, we see that the four threads lead in three different directions: one to the Persian Gulf and Shiraz, two to a country where the coconut has some ritual meaning — either the Maldives, the Laccadives or South India, and the last to the shores of Arabia, perhaps the Red Sea. It would be interesting to know whether there is a sequence in the three notions, as obviously they do not belong together.

However, I believe that he places too much emphasis on the Wadiba's use of timber obtained from the coconut palm, since Barbosa mentions that it was the only shipbuilding timber available in the Maldives and Laccadives and, according to the legend, the Wadiba were happy enough to switch to mangrove wood in East Africa.

One important consideration that lends credence to an Arab to African transfer of shipbuilding technology is the Arab visitors' practice of breaming[47] and repairing their ships in African ports whilst awaiting the arrival of the monsoon winds that would return them to their home ports. Both Villiers[48] and Jewell[49] describe the operation as carried out in modern times; however, frequent mention of the damage suffered by dhows and the need to repair them in foreign ports that appear in Buzurg's *'Ajā'ib al-Hind* bears witness to its great antiquity. One suspects that the employment of local boatmen to assist in the work would inevitably lead to their acquisition of Arab shipbuilding techniques in the same way that Indian shipwrights became highly skilled in European methods of ship construction through assisting in the repairing and building of Portuguese and, later, British ships.

A possible metamorphosis of the word *jalabah* / *jalbah*

Dozy[50] states that the word *jalbah* can take the sound plural *jalabāt* as well as the more widely used broken plural *jilāb*. The word *jalabāt* has the same combination of consonants and the same pattern of long and short vowels as the word *jalabūt*, applied to a type of dhow that still survives in the Gulf today. Hence it is not impossible that *jalabūt* is a corrupted form of the plural *jalabāt*, or even of the singular *jalabah*, for the final '*h*' of the singular is pronounced as a '*t*' whenever it is followed by a vowel, even when that vowel is the first phoneme of the succeeding word, which it frequently is. It is not difficult to envisage how the pronunciation of the word might have been corrupted when one bears in mind the heterogeneity of a typical dhow crew and passengers — Omani, Yemeni, Somali, Swahili, Iranian and Indian — and the mixture of languages and pronunciations they used to communicate among themselves and with the traders and officials they dealt with in their various ports of call. The idea of a *jalbah* to *jalabūt* transfer is supported by Sir James Campbell,[51] who claims the word *galbat* to be generally used by the natives in Bombay waters for large foreign vessels and attributes it to *jalba*, which he defines as a word for a small boat used on the shores of the Red Sea. This implies a transfer route from the Red Sea to Bombay to the Persian Gulf, which is perfectly compatible with the trade routes of the Indian Ocean at the time. The first recorded uses of the word *jalabūti* for a type of dhow occur in Roebuck (1811)[52] and in Lorimer (1908–1915)[53] when, as we can deduce from Moore (1920) and Campbell (1896), the word *jalbah* and its plural *jalabāt* were still active in the dhow mariner's vocabulary; hence there is no chronological incompatibility in a *jalbah* to *jalabūt* transfer. The only argument against such a transfer is that the characteristics of the *jalabūt* are more like the English jolly boat than the Arab *jalbah* and that the word *jalabūt* does not appear to have clearly distinguished Arabic singular and plural forms, which suggests an incompletely Arabized loan word.

Moreover, a number of distinguished scholars believe the word *jalabūt* to be derived from the word *gallevat*, either

44 'Wa' is a Swahili plural prefix that precedes a noun denoting race, tribe or nationality and *Dībā Maḥl* is the Arabic name for the Maldives whereas the Laccadives were called *Juzur al-Fāl* so it is possible that the Wadiba were from the Maldives rather than the Laccadives; but one cannot be 100 per cent certain of this because the Arab geographers always referred to the *Dībajāt*, which possibly included the Laccadives (Tibbetts 1971: 460).

45 Jewell 1976.

46 Prins 1965: 84.

47 Breaming: cleaning the ship's bottom of marine growth and applying anti-fouling compositions.

48 Villiers 1940.

49 Jewell 1976: 2.

50 Dozy 1877.

51 Campbell 1896.

52 Roebuck 1811.

53 Lorimer 1908–1915.

directly, from *gallevat* to *jalabūt* or indirectly from *gallevat* to jolly boat to *jalabūt.* The case for an indirect derivation via 'jolly boat' is a strong one. First, the straight, perpendicular stem and transom stern of the *jalabūt* resemble similar features in the British naval jolly boat, whilst its bowsprit and jib-staysail provide a further hint of European influence (Figure 10:6). Secondly, Hunter[54] lists among the native craft that frequented and plied in Aden harbour, '"Jolly boats", built after the model of an English rowing boat with stronger and heavier frames and very rough workmanship.' What could be more natural than to accept the name along with the design? However, Hunter's jolly boats were essentially harbour-going rowing boats whereas the *jalabūt* are deep-water sailing ships that can attain a length of fifty feet and a displacement of 75 tons, so the naming of the Aden 'jolly boat' and the naming of the *jalabūt* are not definitively linked. If they were, one might expect to see *jalabūt* strongly represented in the waters around Aden but one does not.

Figure 10:6 A small jalabūt *of Bahrain*

The strongest objections to a direct derivation *gallevat* to *jalabūt* are firstly appearance: the *gallevat* had a distinctive 'grab' bow[55] and was primarily a rowed boat that sometimes hoisted a sail whereas the *jalabūt* has a bow that is bolt upright and is primarily a sailing boat that is seldom rowed,[56] and secondly timing and topicality: the *gallevat* became obsolete about the second half of the eighteenth century,[57] whereas the *jalabūt* did not appear in records until the end of the nineteenth; a gap of at least a hundred years in which the name is likely to have been forgotten. If new types of Arab ships were named by scholars or lovers of naval tradition, one could imagine them wishing to conserve a time honoured appellation, but can one really envisage an Arab seaman or the shipwright who built the first *jalabūt* searching the history books for a suitable name and picking that of an Indian type, which the former never manned and the latter never built?

Was the *jalbah* the archetypal Arab ship?

The mediaeval Arab navigator and would-be poet Ibn Mājid opens his treatise on the nautical sciences, *Kitāb al-Fawā'id fī uṣūl al-baḥr wa'l-qawā'id* (The Book of Useful Things on the Principles and Rules of the Sea) with the following discourse on the origins of Arab navigation:[58]

> The first man who organised such a thing (seafaring) and built a ship was Noah, on the advice of the Almighty through Gabriel.[59] This ship was put together in the form of the five stars of the Great Bear, and the stern of the ark is the third star of the Great Bear (γ Ursa Major) and the keel is the fourth (δ Ursa Major), fifth (ε Ursa Major) and sixth (ζ Ursa Major) stars, while its bow is the seventh star (η Ursa Major). Even at this time the people of *Zanj* and *Qumr* (Madagascar) and *al-Rīm*[60] and the land of *Sofāla* called the fifth and sixth stars of the Bear *'al-Hīrāb'* (the keel of the ship)...When the Ark had come to rest, men learnt the art of shipbuilding along all the shores of the sea in all the climates (of the earth) which (God) had divided amongst the children (of Noah), *Jāpheth, Sām,* and *Hām* who is the second Adam, and everyone began to build ships in the maritime lands and in the gulfs and on the shores of the Encircling Ocean.

How much can we infer from this tale? Certainly it suggests that the lines of the archetypal Arab sailing ship were firmly established on this stellar model by the end of the fifteenth century, when Ibn Mājid committed the legend to print. However, it is quite probable that the profile was established much earlier because a double ended hull having a straight, sharp stem and stern, as exemplified by the *jalbah*, the *mtepe*, the al-Ḥarīrī ship[61] and the *massoolah* boat of the Coromandel coast, and even the north European 'cog', is one of the simplest and easiest planked hull forms to build; and hence the one that

54 Hunter 1877.

55 The term 'grab bow' means a bow having an inclination of about 30° to the horizontal. It is derived from a supposed resemblance to the bow of a galley, which is known in Arabic as a *gharab*.

56 The only occasions that I have ever seen a *jalabūt* rowed is when it was engaged in pearl fishing and changing position over the pearl banks where the distances involved were too short to warrant hoisting the sail.

57 Yule and Burnell 1886.

58 From Tibbetts 1971: 69.

59 Muslims believe that the Holy Qur'ān is the speech of God revealed through the mouth of the angel Gabriel.

60 The East African coast near Mombasa.

61 That is to say the ship depicted by Yaḥyā bin Maḥmūd al-Wāṣitī in the 39th or Omani *maqāmah* of his edition of *al-Maqamāt* written by Abū al-Qāsim bin al-Ḥarīrī.

early shipwrights are likely to have stumbled upon first. To check the legend I superimposed a photograph of the Great Bear upon a photograph of the model of a *mtepe* displayed in the Science Museum (Figure 10:7),[62] having first adjusted the scale of the pictures to ensure that the length of the *mtepe* keel was the same as the distance between the fourth and sixth stars of the Great Bear. The inclination of the *mtepe* stern was a perfect match and that of the bow was about 1 in 12 (4° 45′) steeper than that given by the seventh star, which is, I suggest, within the variation to be expected between different shipwrights. Is it a coincidence that this profile closely approximates that of the *mtepe* or, bearing in mind that Ibn Mājid links the people of the East African coast (*Zanj* and *al-Rīm*) to the legend, could it be that a vessel similar to the *jalbah* and the *mtepe* was in fact the archetypal Arab sailing ship?

Figure 10:7 A photograph of the constellation Ursa Major *(The plough) superimposed on the* mtepe *of Figure 10:1*

62 'The distinctive shape of the Plough in Ursa Major (as shown in the photograph used to compile this illustration) would have presented itself to a sixteenth-century navigator with hardly any difference visible to the naked eye.' Jennifer Downes, Curator of Astronomy at the Royal Observatory, personal communication.

Appendix

Jilabah, *jalabah* or *jalbah*?

In the unvowelled text of Ibn Jubayr's *Rihlah*, the plural is given as *j-lāb* and of the twenty-nine common broken plurals derived from the trilateral root that were identified by Wright[63] the only one having the long vowel *ā* between the second and third radicals is *fi'āl*, with *kasrah* on the *fā'*, therefore it is probable that the correct plural is *jilāb*. In other words, the missing short vowel is 'i'. The singular is given by Ibn Jubayr as *j-l-bah*; and according to Wright, the plural *fi'āl* can only admit singulars of the forms: *fa'latun*, *fa'alatun*, and very rarely *fi'latun*. Since the form *fi'latun* is so very rare, we can conclude that the singular of *jilāb* is either *jalbah* or *jalabah*.

References

Abdul Sheriff, Khamis Abdalla and Ame Mshenga. 2006. *Shungwaya* the *Mtepe* sails again. Paper presented at the ZIFF Conference: Sails of History: Citizens of the Sea, Zanzibar.

Abū al-Ḥusayn Muhammad bin Ahmad bin Jubayr al-Kinānī, *al-Rihlah*. Beirut: Dār Ṣādir.

Adams, R.M. 1985. Construction and qualitative analysis of a sewn boat of the Western Indian Ocean, unpublished MA thesis, Texas A & M University.

Barbosa, D. 1866. *A Description of the Coasts of East Africa and Malabar in the beginning of the 16th Century*. Hon. H.E.J. Stanley (tr.). London: Hakluyt Society.

——. 1918–1921. The Book of Duarte Barbosa: An account of the countries bordering on the Indian Ocean and their inhabitants. In volume 39 of Hakluyt Society 2nd series. London: Hakluyt Society.

Buzurg ibn Shahrīyār al-Rāmhurmuzī. 1886. *'Ajā'ib al-Hind*. Leiden: Brill.

Campbell, Sir J. 1896. Volume 13 of *Bombay Gazetteer*. Bombay: The Bombay Presidency.

Casson, L. 1989. *The Periplus Maris Erythræi*. Princeton: Princeton University Press.

Colomb, Capt. P.H. 1873. *Slave Catching in the Indian Ocean. A Record of Naval Experiences*. London: repr. Dawsons, 1968.

Chittick N.H. 1980. Sewn boats in the western Indian Ocean, and a survival in Somalia. *International Journal of Nautical Archaeology and Underwater Exploration* 9(4): 297–309.

Dozy, R.P.A. 1881. *Supplément aux dictionnaires arabes*. Leiden: Brill.

63 Wright 1977: I, 199–226.

Gilbert, E. 2004. *Dhows and the Colonial Economy of Zanzibar 1860–1970*. Oxford: James Curry.

Hornell, J. 1941. The sea-going mtepe of the Lamu Archipelago. *The Mariner's Mirror,* 27(1): 60, 65.

Hunter, F.M. 1877. *An Account of the British Settlement at Aden, in Arabia.* London: Trübner & Co.

Jewell, J.J.H. 1976, rev. edn. *Dhows at Mombasa.* Nairobi: East African Publishing House.

Kindermann, H. 1934. *'Schiff' im Arabischen Untersuchung über Vorkommen und Bedeutung der Termini.* Bonn: Zwickau.

Lane, E.W. 1863–1893. *Arabic English Lexicon*. London: Williams & Norgate.

Lobo, J. 1887. *A Voyage to Abyssinia*. Samuel Johnson (tr. from the French translation by Abbé Legrand). London: Cassell.

Lorimer, J.G. (ed.) 1908–1915. *Gazetteer of the Persian Gulf, Oman and Central Arabia*. Calcutta: Government Printer; repr. Slough: Archive Editions, 2003.

Lydekker, C.J.W. 1919. The '*Mtepe*' Dhau of the Bajun Islands. *Man* 19 (June 1919), 89.

Marx, E. 1946. The derivation of the words 'dhow' and 'junk'. *The Mariner's Mirror* 32(3): 185.

Millar, K. 1993. Preliminary report on observations made into the techniques and traditions of Maldivian shipbuilding. *Bulletin of the Australian Institute for Maritime Archaeology* 17(1): 9–16.

Moore, A. 1920. The craft of the Red Sea and the Gulf of Aden. *The Mariner's Mirror* 6: 99.

Nabahany, Sheikh Ahmed, 2006. Swahili Dhow Building Tradition. Paper presented at the ZIFF Conference: Sails of History: Citizens of the Sea, held in Zanzibar, in 2006.

Owen, Capt W.F.W. 1833. *Narrative of Voyages to explore the Shores of Africa, Arabia and Madagascar.* London: Richard Bentley.

Prins, A.H.J. 1965. *Sailing from Lamu: A Study of Maritime Culture in Islamic East Africa*. Assen: Von Gorcum.

Roebuck, T. 1811. *An English and Hindoostanee Naval Dictionary*. Calcutta: Printed by A.H. Hubbard, Hindoostanee Press.

Shihāb, Ḥasan Ṣāliḥ. 1983. *Al-Marākib al-'arabiyya: tārīkhuhā wa anwā'uhā.* [Arab Ships: their history and types]. Kuwait: Mu'assasat al-Kuwayt lil-Taqaddum al-'Ilmī [Department of Geography, Kuwait University].

Speke, Capt J.H. 1863. *Journal of the Discovery of the Source of the Nile.* Edinburgh: William Blackwood & Sons.

Stanley, Sir H.M. 1890. *Through the Dark Continent: or, The sources of the Nile around the great lakes of Equatorial Africa and down the Livingstone River to the Atlantic Ocean,* London: Sampson Low, Marston, Searle & Rivington.

Steere, Bp E. 1870. *A Handbook of the Swahili Language as spoken at Zanzibar.* London: Society for the Promotion of Christian Knowledge.

Sulaymān al-Mahrī. 1971. *'Umdat al-Mahriyya fī ḍabṭ 'ilm al-baḥriyya* verified by Ibrāhīm Khūrī. Damascus.

Sulivan, Capt. G.L. 1873. *Dhow chasing in Zanzibar Waters and on the Eastern Coast of Africa.* London: Sampson Low, Marston, Low & Searle.

Tibbetts, G.R. 1971. *Arab Navigation in the Indian Ocean before the Coming of the Portuguese,* London: Royal Asiatic Society of Great Britain and Ireland.

Villiers, A. 1940. *Sons of Sindbad.* New York: C. Scribner's Sons.

Wright, W. 1977, 3rd edn. *A Grammar of the Arabic Language*. Cambridge: Cambridge University Press.

Yule, H. and Burnell, A.C. 1886. *Hobson-Jobson.* London: John Murray.

Acknowledgments

I gratefully acknowledge the kind help received from the following: Dr Ḥasan Ṣāliḥ Shihāb for a casual remark that first drew my attention to the possibility of a *jalbah/mtepe* link; Ann Davies and David Boyd of the British Astronomical Association for providing me with the photograph of the constellation Ursa Major used to compile Figure 10:7; Jennifer Downes, Curator of Astronomy at the Royal Observatory for the quotation in footnote 62; The Director of the Science Museum, South Kensington for providing a 35mm slide of a model *mtepe* along with permission to publish it; Janet Starkey and Christine Lindner of the RSPIII team for their very considerable help to a first-time contributor.

Navigating a Hazardous Sea

Sarah Searight

Two Red Sea conferences have covered much of the ancient and medieval knowledge of the Red Sea, as well as the early modern experience of Portuguese navigators and such Age of Enlightenment travellers as Carsten Niebuhr, James Bruce, John-Louis Burckhardt and others. William Facey's paper in the *Proceedings* of Red Sea I on the wind regime (particularly severe in the Gulfs of 'Aqabah and Suez) and location of ports provided an extremely valuable description of the hazards of navigation handled by the *nakhodas* in the many types of indigenous vessel introduced to us by Dionisius Agius and others in this volume of *Proceedings*.

The eighteenth-century wreck on the reefs of Sadana Island (off the Egyptian coast) described by Cheryl Ward in the *Proceedings* of Red Sea I[1] is an example of the type of hazards dotted around the 2,350 km between the Bāb al-Mandab and Suez. This paper is an overview of how that sea has been made less hazardous in the light of its increasing use from the early nineteenth century as a highway between Europe and the East. Notably, there was the foresight of the Bombay Marine / Indian Navy in recognizing the potential of steam navigation in speeding up communications between Europe and India; this led to the first crucial charting of the waterway, most notably by Robert Moresby and Thomas Elwon in 1829–1833. The Gulf of Aden was surveyed by Captain Haines in 1835–1838; his charts are still the basis of some modern charts. These measures were just in time to meet the demands of the larger steamboats commissioned by the Peninsular and Orient (P&O) shipping company for their Calcutta-Suez run. The opening of the Suez Canal and increased navigation in the waterway demanded improved charts and navigation aids. In the 1870s cable-laying for the Indo-European Telegraph was another aspect of improved communications; all this against a background of commerce, war (movement of troops in particular), anti-slavery manoeuvres, increasing pilgrimage traffic and quarantine measures. Admiralty *Pilots* and charts, lighthouses, lightships and buoys have also followed the internationalization of this crucial route between East and West. In the twenty-first century charting and surveying the Red Sea is still vital to safe navigation.

In the nineteenth century, the treacherous Red Sea entered a new era of communication between the rapidly expanding economy of an industrializing Britain and the needs and raw materials of British India. In a wide variety of ways this was powered by steam, most notably in the context of this paper, by the marine steam engine. This paper carries on from the remarkable 1829–1833 survey of Robert Moresby and Thomas Elwon,[2] and particularly from the opening of the Suez Canal in 1869. But we should bear in mind the background to the sea described in earlier papers — discussions about ports and winds, Punt, al-Quṣayr, the Portuguese, as well as Cheryl Ward's wreck, all of which have provided in a variety of ways a picture of this tricky waterway which was about to become a major international highway.

From Suez at the northern end to the Bāb al-Mandab at the southern end the Red Sea is 2,350 km long. It is at its widest at Qunfidhah in modern Saudi Arabia — 350 km, with an average width of 200 km. At the Bāb al-Mandab it is a mere 30 km wide. At the northern end it divides into two narrower waterways, the main one, the Gulf of Suez, being 100 km long, the narrow, storm-tossed Gulf of 'Aqabah 180 km long.

In the central Red Sea channel, 'deeps' descend as much as 1,500 fathoms (2,830 m). However, coral reefs line either coast and these, according to the Admiralty's *Red Sea Pilot*, are 'more numerous and more extensive than in any other body of [equal] water.'[3] This explains the popularity of the Red Sea today with the diving fraternity.[4] Divers also relish the rich marine life in and around the ships that have come to grief on the reefs and now rest on the bottom. Long strips of coral reef lie parallel to and about half a kilometre or more from the shore, usually a few metres below the surface, with the more extensive reefs on the eastern, Arabian shore rather than on the west. Inshore channels, reached through gaps in the reef, are therefore sheltered and sometimes quite deep. They were used by local vessels as well as by the small under-powered paddle steamers of the 1830s and 1840s to collect coal and provisions.[5] In daylight a careful watch can distinguish reefs by changes in the colour of the

1 Ward 2004: 165–71.

2 Elwon, T. 1873 (New ed. corr.). *The Red Sea* surveyed by Captain T. Elwon, Commander R. Moresby, Lieutenants H.N. Pinching & T.G. Carless, I.N. 1830–1834, engraved by Davies & Company. []. London: published at the Admiralty. 1 chart on 5 sheets; 81 x 319 cm., on sheets 81 x 66cm or smaller. First ed.: 1873, replacing and partly based on the same surveys as the *Chart of the Red Sea* by T. Elwon, H.N. Pinching and R. Moresby, first published 1836.

3 Admiralty. 1955: 272.

4 J.-J. Cousteau being the most celebrated. See Cousteau 1971.

5 Ingrams 1988 I: 809–14.

water, although this is more difficult in summer when reefs can be confused with a brown scum of seaweed. Inshore navigators are advised against sailing at night. A modern sailing guide to the Red Sea stresses, as indeed did Moresby, the importance of using your eyes in waters of recognized treachery; also, as the Admiralty *Pilot* advises, 'keep the sun astern when in coral waters and beware the midday sun.'[6]

For today's shipping the principal hazards are in the north, in and around the shallow Gulf of Suez, and in the south, beyond the Zubayr Islands, where again the depth in the main shipping channels is sometimes reduced to a minimum of 28 m in shoal patches. There are several archipelagos, including the Hanish Islands, with the Haycock and Marhabbaka Islands south of these, the Zubayr and Farasān Islands (with many wrecks there, to the delight of Jean-Jacques Cousteau),[7] the Dahlaks (126 islands), as well as individual hazards such as Mayyum or Perim Island just north of Bāb al-Mandab, and Avocet Rock. Several are volcanic and there is a long history of seismic activity.[8] Red Sea winds are notorious, as we know from Will Facey. 'Fresh gales and close-reefed topsail breezes' are a constant occurrence according to the Admiralty's *Pilot*, as well as 'head winds, rough seas, poor visibility, sand and dust storms, mirror calms, rapid or unpredictable winds.'[9] As the first century AD *Periplus of the Erythraean Sea* and all subsequent nautical guides make clear, you have to choose sailing months with care.[10]

However, armies cannot wait on winds and generals in different parts of the world need to know what is going on elsewhere, as was highlighted by the Anglo-French wars at the beginning of the nineteenth century. The French invasion of Egypt was ultimately defeated, despite a British expedition despatched from India in 1801 in an attempt to take the French from the rear via the Red Sea. Regular trade and communication with India was conducted via the Cape and was notoriously slow, as the Marquis of Wellesley complained from India in 1800: 'in the present year I was nearly seven months without receiving one line of communication from England ... so that I suffered almost insupportable distress of mind ... Speedy, authentic and regular intelligence from Europe is essential to the trade and government of this country.'[11]

It just so happened that his plea coincided not only with the first few puffs of the marine steam engine but also with increasing attention focusing on the Red Sea in combination with an overland route through Egypt as the best potential for improved communication between Britain and India. A tiny paddle steamer, the 'Enterprize', rounded the Cape of Good Hope in 1826; three years later another experimental vessel, the 'Hugh Lindsay', was despatched from Bombay up the Red Sea to Suez. By that time Bombay Marine (renamed in 1832 to the Indian Navy) was keen enough on the route to despatch Commanders Moresby and Thomas Elwon in two sailing brigs — the 'Benares' and the 'Palinurus' (appropriately named after Aeneas' pilot in the *Aeneid*) — to conduct the first complete survey of the Red Sea.[12]

'Great dangers and privations were inseparable from such a service,' wrote Moresby in his subsequent *Sailing Instructions*.[13] The survey was conducted mainly in coastal waters, using local pilots. The 'Benares' was caught forty-two times on coral reefs; the Gulf of 'Aqabah was a nightmare; the 'Palinurus' was nearly wrecked on Zabarga Island (also known as St John's or Emerald Island because of ancient peridot mines and still a major hazard); everyone suffered from chronic ill health. But the *Sailing Instructions*, published in 1841 together with two sheets of charts of a higher quality than anything that had previously been available, were vital for the increased traffic, including as they did details not only of navigational hazards but also the practicalities of where food and provisions were available, how friendly or otherwise the locals were, and so on. While the focus of this paper is on the post-Moresby scene, nevertheless, as Andrew Cook of the India Office Library has pointed out, those charts and instructions were reprinted in 1874 virtually unchanged. What had changed of course was the volume of traffic. In general all charts were maintained by the East India Company until 1863 when the task was taken over by the Admiralty.

There were two reasons for this increased traffic: first, the vastly increased trade between Britain and its Indian domain, demanding swifter communication; and secondly, the success of the three-legged, Overland Route through Egypt. This used steamers from Europe to Alexandria, then continued overland to Suez where, hopefully, steamers were waiting for the onward journey to India.[14] Steamers heading for Suez were sometimes caught in the Straits of Tiran at the entrance to the Gulf of 'Aqabah, hence the names of the reefs there — Gordon Reef, Thomas Reef, Woodhouse and Jackson Reefs. Cheryl Ward's diving expeditions have also found innumerable wrecks there. P&O's vessel 'Carnatic' was wrecked on Shadwan Island in 1876 with a cargo of wine and London Soda. The Admiralty *Pilot* notes that wrecks on Ras Muḥammad on the southern tip of the Sinai Peninsula 'are conspicuous and helpful'.[15] Certain ports presented part-

6 Morgan and Davies 1995; Admiralty 1955: 11.
7 Cousteau 1971.
8 Ambraseys, *et al.* 1994. Moresby 1841: 25 noted smoke issuing from Jabal Ṭayr.
9 Admiralty 1955: 38.
10 Casson 1989: 11–12.
11 Wellesley 1836: letter of 6 October 1800.

12 Searight 2003: 40–47.
13 Moresby 1841.
14 Searight 1991: 30–50 and 72–88.
15 Admiralty 1955: 101.

icular problems; some, such as Aden, are better surveyed than others. Jiddah, for instance, is particularly tricky ('with strong and variable currents') and several ships have, in recent years, been grounded on the reefs at the entrance. The same applies to the approach to Massawa through the Dahlak archipelago, as tricky today as in the nineteenth century. Massawa completed a new 12-metre deep berth in 2002 and handled 237 ships in 2004.

From the 1830s Anglo-French rivalry over control of the Red Sea and its western littoral led to greater involvement in the adjoining territories. The British acquired Aden in 1839 and gradually revived its ancient role as the major entrepôt between the Indian Ocean and the Mediterranean. Political and economic interest in Abyssinia led almost inexorably to the taking of British hostages by the Emperor Teodor and subsequently to Britain's Abyssinian Expedition of 1868 to release them.[16] The expedition, mounted from Bombay, was a logistical nightmare. The transport of 12,000 men from Bombay, as well as 1,000 Spanish mules from Suez, led to a detailed survey of the route from Aden to Massawa and of Annesley Bay where the expedition disembarked, 'through treacherous Red Sea waters',[17] and to marking the channel with temporary buoys and beacons. Some 20,000 tons of coal had to be moved to Aden having been sent from Wales round the Cape. Ten transport ships shifted the troops to Africa and three hospital steamers stood by for the wounded. There were no groundings and no wrecks: a remarkable achievement.

A year later, in 1869, the Suez Canal was opened with maximum fanfare. It was relatively shallow and narrow and several vessels ran aground on the inaugural passage. It is interesting to compare the dimensions then and now, as a reflection of what the Canal has to cope with today. When opened in 1869 the Canal had a cross-sectional area of 304 m^2; effective width was 44 m and water depth 10 m. By 2001 the cross-sectional area had risen to 4,800 m^2, effective width was 200–210 m and depth 22.5 m. It is currently being deepened to 26 m to cater for larger tankers and bulk carriers, and with the container vessels already at sea or on the drawing board;[18] this will of course put extra pressure on the need to provide the data on which reliable charts elsewhere in the Red Sea can be based. Back in 1869 and immediately thereafter, the success of the Canal was ensured by some revolutionary developments in ship design and propulsion systems: the compound expansion engine, the efficient use of the screw propeller (paddles were totally unsuited to the Canal) and long low iron hulls. Better charts and better marking of hazards became essential to the safety of shipping steaming up and down the Red Sea. Moresby's charts were expanded from two to five sheets in the 1860s because of the increased traffic; they were also republished virtually unchanged in 1874.

Communication was not just by steamship; telegraph was equally crucial, thinking back to the poignant isolation felt by the Marquis of Wellesley fighting the French in India. The Abyssinian expedition highlighted the need for better telegraph communications and in 1870 Brunel's *Great Eastern*, crucially stable in rough seas, was loaded with cable (a thousand miles of it in the second-class saloon), unreeling from Bombay as far as Perim where the task was handed over to a smaller vessel to be taken on up the Red Sea. Kipling later wrote:

> They have wakened the timeless Things; they have killed their father Time;
> Joining hands in the gloom, a league from the last of the sun.
> Hush! Men talk today o'er the waste of the ultimate slime,
> And a new Word runs between: whispering, 'Let us be one!'

At four shillings a word it would have cost Kipling nine pounds and eight shillings sterling to send this to England.[19]

With the increase in traffic came a substantial increase in the number of pilgrims heading for Makkah. With those coming from the east, particularly India, came the danger of cholera. Dire epidemics in Europe, for instance in 1858, traceable to the pilgrimage, led to the establishment of quarantine stations — at al-Ṭūr in the Gulf of Suez, at Jiddah, on Flint Island and other islands in Aden harbour, and at Kamaran Island just off the coast of Yemen.[20] The route to Kamaran was therefore well lit: the lights as well as the quarantine station being the responsibility of the government in India. The entrance to the bay in which the quarantine area lay was tricky and the conditions in the station far from perfect: the quarantine huts could accommodate 6,000 pilgrims at one go, a situation which must have been quite a challenge to health authorities. Some 38,000 were said to have passed through as late as 1955. The responsibility for occasional quarantine regulations is now in Saudi hands; otherwise one dreads imagining what Kamaran would be like today.

The process of laying the telegraph cable highlighted a number of serious problems including inaccuracies in existing charts: 'it will be a somewhat perilous highway for strange vessels until this is done,' wrote the engineer with the project, J.C. Parkinson.[21] From the later nineteenth century, regular charting of the Red Sea was in

16 Marston 1961: 340–56 provides details of and references to relevant correspondence. See also Hozier 1869 who gives the fullest account of the expedition.

17 Marston 1961: 346.

18 R. Facey, personal communication.

19 Parkinson 1870: 193.

20 For more details see Searight 2005: 113–14. Also Admiralty 1955: 149.

21 Parkinson 1870: 237.

general in the hands of those powers controlling territories adjoining the sea — the Ottoman empire, Egypt, Britain (more particularly the government in India), France, and Italy. Inshore waters on the eastern side were theoretically charted by the Ottoman authorities as far as Mayyun / Perim where Britain took over; on the western shore charting was largely in the hands of the Egyptians; then, as the 'scramble for Africa' took hold towards the end of the century, the Italians and the French assumed responsibility in those areas under their control.

Nowadays the surveying and charting of the major routes and coastal waters attempt to be more systematic and on-going, with pressure from the International Maritime Organisation for national authorities to take responsibility for producing the data required in order to prepare new charts. The principal charts today are maintained by the UK's Hydrographic Office, the French Dépôt de la Marine and the US Department of Marine. For coastal waters there is input from the Regional Organisation for the Protection of the Environment of the Red Sea (PERSGA) based in Jiddah and funded by countries bordering the Red Sea and Gulf of Aden. There are also blueback commercial charts,[22] intelligence reports, and diving reports. But they still leave much to be desired; Haines's charts of the Gulf of Aden for instance still provide the basis of modern charts in much of the area. Facey maintains that the shallow Gulf of Suez is relatively well charted despite hazards of oil platforms and terminals, but the deep central section of the Red Sea, entered at the Strait of Gubal, needs much more work given ever-increasing ship sizes (particularly oil tankers); in fact, the middle section of the Red Sea has never been properly surveyed. There have been a number of accidents around the few shoals: Shadwan at the mouth of the Gulf has seven fairly recent wrecks on its reefs; other treacherous reefs (well lit however) are al-Akhawain (the Brothers) and Abū al-Kizan / Zabargad, and harbour entrances (especially Jiddah's). Ra's Muḥammad at the mouth of the Gulf of 'Aqabah has a good cluster of wrecks, including the 'Dunravon' in 1876 and is now noted for the groupers which live inside. Coastal areas need constant updating. A wreck popular with divers is the 'Umbria' wrecked at the entrance to Port Sudan in 1940, on its way to Eritrea with a cargo of 360,000 bombs. Another war casualty (bombed this time, in 1941, rather than wrecked on treacherous reefs) was the complete army surplus store aboard the *'Thistlegorm'* discovered by Cousteau in 1956.[23]

Lights in the Red Sea and Gulf of Suez were initially installed by various interests, including the British at Aden and Perim, and the Ottoman Turks on the island of Abū ʿAlī and on the Zubayr Islands off the Yemeni Coast (these were later taken over by the British in Aden).[24] After the Second World War, the lights were operated from Djibouti. Nowadays the lights are the responsibility of national authorities — Egypt, Jordan, Saudi Arabia, Yemen, Sudan, Eritrea, Djibouti and Somalia — with international coordination and some finance. Maintenance is variable and the lights sometimes weaker than claimed. Shipping companies such as P&O were heavily involved in the early establishment of lights: recently, P&O was recommending better lighting of the Soqotra archipelago because of the hazard of fog at the eastern end of Qalansu.[25]

Captain Roy Facey himself has been focusing on the most hazardous shallow area of the southern Red Sea, in particular round the Hanish archipelago, where huge oil tankers and ever larger container vessels are most at risk. Improvements include a new lighthouse on Hanish al-Kubra (Greater Hanish) but perhaps even more significantly Facey has been involved in updating a north-south routeing of vessels either side of the Hanish islands, known as a 'traffic separation scheme'. One of the earliest of such schemes was introduced in the Gulf of Suez and several now operate in the Red Sea and Gulf of Aden (also part of Captain Facey's 'beat'), in the hopes of preventing collisions between fast-moving monster vessels trying to stick to timetables imposed by owners.

Not only is the north-south traffic a problem; there is also the traffic that joins and leaves the main shipping route to call at ports on either side of the Red Sea.[26]

One hazard, the Avocet Rock, has a particularly poignant history that also highlights the problems of making accurate surveys using the technology available, until 30 years ago, in an area where a hazy horizon could make sun and star sights rather inaccurate. It stands to the north of the main group of Hanish Islands which were extensively surveyed in the 1870s. In 1886 this new rock was reported, having been struck by 'SS Avocet'.

22 Fisher 2001.

23 Cousteau 1871.

24 One former lighthouse keeper, a Maltese named Joe Lapira, spent eight years on Abū 'Alī lighthouse 'and believe me, I loved every moment of those years,' he writes in a personal communication.

25 Personal communication from Mr Joe Lapira who looked after Abū 'Alī and Jabal al-Ṭayr lights, on maintenance, supplies, supervision etc.

26 Capt. Facey mentions a special chart of the Gulf of Suez, Admiralty Chart No. 5501: 'exceptional care is needed when overtaking'! See also the 2005 annual report of the UK's Marine Accident Investigation Branch, which records significant increases in both collisions and groundings from the incidents that it investigated during 2005.

Map 11:1 Kamaran Island 1915 (Ingrams 1993: VI, 835)

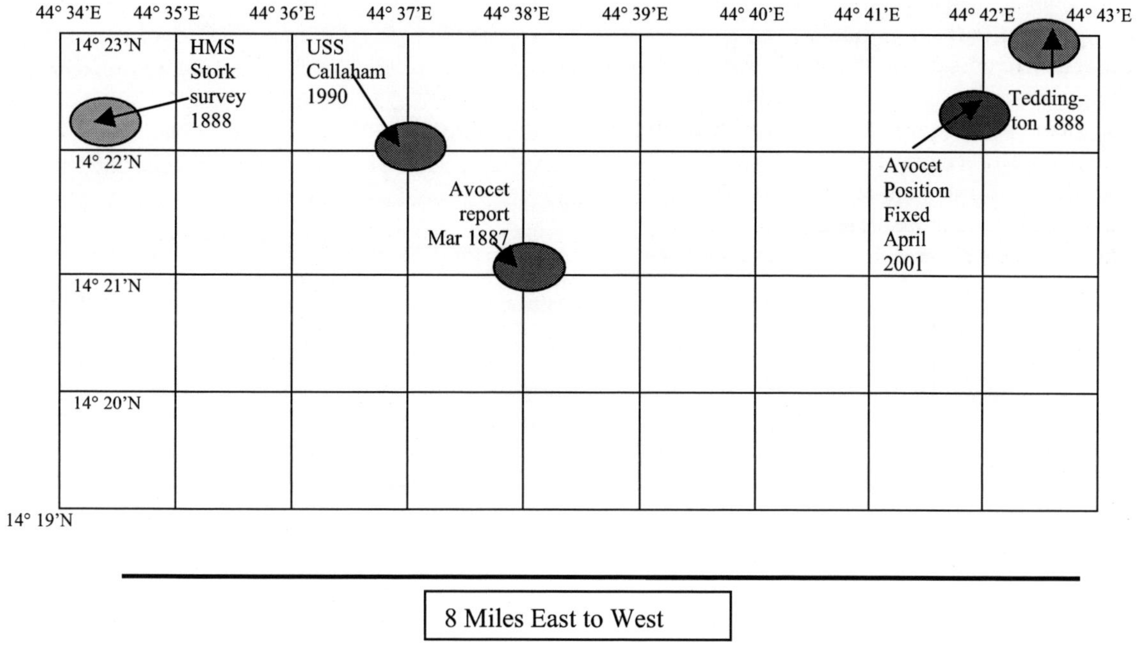

Figure 11:1 Trying to fix the Position of the Avocet Rock – between 1887 and 2001[27]

27 Survey results for the Avocet Rock, southern Red Sea (Courtesy of Cardline Surveys, reproduced with the kind permission of

The captain of the 'Avocet' reported hitting a rock but was disbelieved and dismissed and is said to have died a broken-hearted man. His family, wanting to clear his name, then set about trying to locate the rock with two small rowing boats with a chain suspended between them. Eventually they snagged a rock and reported its position, but several other incidents, and surveys, placed it quite differently, varying by as much as eight miles. Its position and extent, a plateau with a surface 6 m below sea level extending some 400 x 400 m, was only finally established in 2001 during the PERSGA survey. This gives some idea of the problem of making accurate surveys in the Red Sea.[28]

In a recent contribution to PERSGA's annual report on the state of the Red Sea environment, Captain Facey highlights the significance of the Red Sea as a trading route,[29] one of several factors in the ancient and modern history of the waterway and part of the background to the series of conferences established by the Society for Arabian Studies. The object of this paper has been to bring that history up to the present, when the route carries between seven and eight percent of world trade. Important constraints to its further growth are the shallow, narrow Gulf of Suez with all its industrial *impedimentia*. In recent years the increasing size of vessels using the Red Sea, moving at higher speeds, in greater numbers, and using ever expanding Red Sea ports, has led to more groundings and collisions. More detailed charts and routeing measures are crucial, together with the international cooperation essential to their implementation. One of the objectives of the conferences has been to stimulate research into relations between either side of the great waterway — people, religion, ports, environment, linguistics, trade — relationships that have been developed over at least five thousand years. To that melting pot, as in many ways it has proved to be, we now add the international element to reinforce the other element in Red Sea history: a link, with all its hazards, between the worlds of the Mediterranean and the Indian Ocean.

References

Admiralty. *Red Sea and Gulf of Aden Pilot* (many editions, published at varying intervals and now the responsibility of the UK Hydrographic Office, c/o the Ministry of Defence at Taunton; here I have referred to the 1955 edition).

Admiralty Naval Intelligence Division. 1920. *Handbook of Arabia.* London: HMSO.

Ambraseys, N.N., Melville C.P., and Adams R.D. 1994. *The Seismicity of Egypt, Arabia and the Red Sea* Cambridge: Cambridge University Press.

Casson, L. 1989. *The Periplus Maris Erythræi: text with introduction, translation and commentary.* Princeton: Princeton University Press.

Cousteau, J-J. 1971. *Life and Death in a Coral* Sea, tr. J.F. Bernard. London: Cassell.

Dawson, L. 1885. *Memoirs of Hydrography.* Eastbourne: H.W. King.

Day, A. 1967. *The Admiralty Hydrographic Service 1756–1919.* London: HMSO.

Fisher, S. 2001. *The Makers of the Blueback Charts.* St Ives: Imray, Laurie, Norie & Wilson.

Hoskins, H. 1928. *British Routes to India.* London: Longmans.

Hozier, H.M. 1869. *The British Expedition to Abyssinia.* London, Macmillan.

Ingrams, L. and Ingrams, D. (eds). 1993. *Records of Yemen 1798–1960.* [Slough]: Archive Editions.

Low, C.R. 1877. *The History of the Indian Navy 1613–1863.* London: Charles Rathbone.

Marston, T.E. 1961. *Britain's Imperial Role in the Red Sea Area 1800-76.* Hamden, Conn.: Shoe String Press.

Moresby, R. and Elwon, T. 1841. *Sailing Instructions for the Red Sea.* London.

Morgan, E. and Davies, S. *ca.* 1995. *Red Sea Pilot.* St Ives: Imray, Laurie, Norie & Wilson.

PERSGA. 2006. *State of the Marine Environment Report for the Red Sea and Gulf of Aden.* W. Gladstone (ed). Jiddah: Regional Organization for the Conservation of the Environment of the Red Sea and Gulf of Aden.

Parkinson, J.C. 1870. *The Ocean Telegraph to India.* Edinburgh and London: Blackwood.

Ritchie, G.S. 1995. *The Admiralty Chart: British Naval Hydrography in the 19th century.* Cambridge: Cambridge University Press.

Searight, S. 1991. *Steaming East: the forging of steamship and rail links between Europe and Asia.* London: Bodley Head.

———. 2003. The Charting of the Red Sea. *History Today* 53(3), March: 40–7.

———. 2005. Jiddah in the nineteenth century: the role of European Consuls. 109–16 in J.C.M. Starkey (ed.), *Proceedings of the Second Red Sea Conference: People and Places.* BAR International Series 1395. Oxford: Archaeopress.

Ward, C. Luxury Wares in the Red Sea: the Sadana Island shipwreck. 165–171 in P. Lunde and A. Porter (eds), *Trade and Travel in the Red Sea Region. Proceedings of Red Sea Project I.* BAR International Series 1269. Oxford: Archaeopress.

28 UK Hydrographic Office. Further details in report to London's Middle East Association in January 2006.

29 Facey 2006.

Wellesley, R. (Marquis of). 1836. *The Despatches and Correspondence of the Marquis of Wellesley during his administration in India.* M. Martin (ed.). 5 Vols. London: John Murray.

Acknowledgements

In the preparation of this paper I am particularly grateful to Dr Andrew Cook in the India Office Library on the East India Company's role in early charting work, to Miss Leila Ingrams and her *Records of Yemen*, and to the International Maritime Organisation, but my greatest debt is to Captain Roy Facey who is employed by the Yemeni government as the Port Development Adviser at the port of Aden, and was for six years the Navigation Safety Adviser to the World Bank for the Red Sea and Gulf of Aden as part of the team working on the Regional Organization for the Conservation of the Environment of the Red Sea and Gulf of Aden (PERSGA), Jiddah, Strategic Action Programme.[30] Captain Facey most generously supplied me with diagrams, articles, statistics and anecdotes, thereby bringing the whole nautical Red Sea scene up to date.

30 For details about the PERSGA Strategic Action Plan see http://www.persga.org/about/Projects/SAP/Overview.asp.

Part III: Harbours: Ways of Life and Cultural Connections

Red Sea Harbours, Hinterlands and Relationships in Preclassical Antiquity

K.A. Kitchen

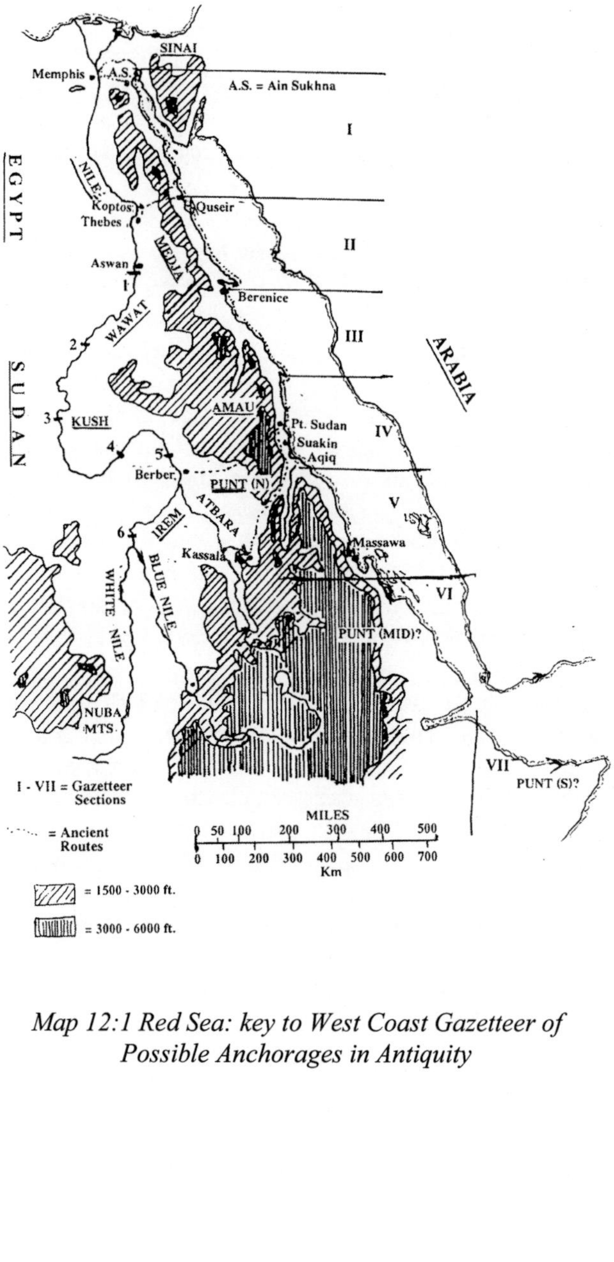

Map 12:1 Red Sea: key to West Coast Gazetteer of Possible Anchorages in Antiquity

Introduction

The interplay between the physical geography of seacoasts and hinterlands and varying human use and exploitation of such regions offers us a changing and often colourful panorama throughout the centuries. This can be seen through the intersection, in turn, of physical geography, archaeology and written sources, down the west and east sides of the Red Sea, extending out into the Gulf of Aden. A partial gazetteer down the west (African) coast, for possible landing-places for ancient shipping, was presented back in 1971.[1] Here, with slight corrections, that listing is completed (nos 81ff.) through to Ras Hafun (no. 132) on Somalia's north-eastern seaboard, plus a parallel gazetteer for the east (Arabian) coast, from the Isle of Tiran similarly out to Bir 'Alī (classical Kane) on Arabia's south-west coastland (nos 1–57).

Striking contrasts emerge when the western and eastern coasts and hinterlands are compared. The most apparent is that the west coastline offers about 130 possible inlets and coves suitable for harbouring the boats and ships of far antiquity (plans being given of a typical eighteen sites, Map 12:5), whereas the eastern coast appears to offer only about fifty to sixty such workable landings (not much more than one-third of the west coast figure), if we eliminate the probably illusory options of a series of coral islets that almost certainly did not exist in (say) *ca.* 2500, 1400 or even 600 BC. We stay with genuinely terrestrial *khors*, *marsās*, *sherms* and suchlike more permanent inlets of rock, earth and sand / gravel beach, not with coral-formations of uncertain and often much more recent dates. We shall review the anchorages and then the hinterlands for the west and east coasts in turn, and then the historical / cultural relationships involved with these remarkable settings on both sides of the Red Sea.

Potential Anchorages, West Coast, Suez to Ras Hafun

These are here divided now into seven successive zones from north to south-east; cf. Map 12:1. Zone I runs from Suez (ancient Clysma) down to al-Quṣayr and the ancient

---

[1] Kitchen 1971: 197–202, for our nos 1–81. These gazetteers derive from intense scrutiny of multiple sources which are not always internally or mutually wholly consistent, hence, minor errors may be present in some cases; but they serve to show that conditions permitted of day-to-day ancient navigation.

harbours just to its north (Map 12:2). Facing across to the west-Sinai seaboard for the north half of its length, this area had prevailingly north winds (fine for sailing south) all year round (and so, down to about 20° latitude), which meant that ancient expeditions from far south returned north no further than the al-Quṣayr-area harbours (no. 16, Marsā Gawāsīs, ancient Sawaw; later, no. 18b, al-Quṣayr al-Qadīm / Myos Hormos), and not against contrary winds all the way back to Suez. In fact, the Pharaonic expeditions to Punt used Marsā Gawāsīs as their main sea-base both ways, as it was within good reach of the Nile port of Coptos, and the latter's shipbuilding and other major facilities. However, from recent work at 'Ayn Sukhna (no. 3bis),[2] which enjoyed a direct short route west to the Nile at Memphis, ancient Egypt's administrative capital, it seems clear that 'Ayn Sukhna in part operated as a staging-post for products from Sinai, notably copper and turquoise, particularly in the Middle Kingdom (early second millennium BC), while copper was also obtainable locally and was worked there. So, this zone included an important east-west link: Sinai mines — 'Ayn Sukhna (with smelting, and more mining) — Memphis. It is noteworthy that some officials responsible for Middle-Kingdom inscriptions found at ᶜAyn Soukhna recur in texts of the same reigns in the east Sinai mining-sites (Serabit el-Khadim; Serabit); they clearly travelled back and forth along this link-route.

Zone II (Map 12:2) runs from the al-Quṣayr ports (nos 18–19) south to Berenike (no. 33). From al-Quṣayr to Berenike, we have (in about 192 miles) some fourteen possible stopping-places beyond al-Quṣayr, nos 22–23 being mutually adjacent; so, the average distance between stops is fourteen or fifteen miles, and never more than seventeen to twenty miles except in two cases (thirty and thirty-three miles between nos 29–30 and 32–33 respectively), in both cases close to a thirty-mile average day's sailing.[3]

In turn, Zone III (Map 12:3) runs from Berenike (no. 33) to Ras Abu Shagara and the twin inlets of Dungunab Bay / Muḥammad Qol (nos 57–58). Counting these twins as one (and likwise the adjoining nos 49–50, Marsās Wasi', Abū Fanadir), we have a distance of about 278 miles, with twenty-three potential stopping-places (some, very close together) beyond Berenike, averaging distances apart of twelve miles, with figures rarely reaching more than seventeen to twenty-four miles in distance, except two cases of thirty-mile intervals (nos 43 to 44; nos 56 to 57 / 58), a distance matched by a day's average sail (cf. above).

With Zone IV (Map 12:3), we reach coastal Punt, from Ras Abu Shagara (by nos 57–58) down to Ras Kasar / Brassy Bay (no. 80), a maximum run of some 224 miles with many short-distance spans; of all these (with nos 76–77 and 78–79 being 'twin-units'), only one distance extends beyond twenty-two to twenty-four miles and often much less, namely the forty miles or so between Trinkitat (no. 77) and 'Aqīq Gulf shore (no. 78), only ten extra miles (two or three hours) above an average day's sail, just once. This represents (Zones II–IV) the main scope for such Egyptian trips during the Old, Middle and New Kingdoms (*ca.* 2500–1170 BC), and probably for corresponding Puntite ventures in reverse up to al-Quṣayr / Marsā Gawāsīs in the New Kingdom, *ca.* 1450–1380 BC. For sketch-plans of two dozen assorted possible anchorages, see Map 12:6. From Punt, the Egyptians obtained gold / electrum, aromatics (incense, myrrh), special timbers ('ebony', *dalbergia melanoxylon*), ivory, panther-skins and other exotica.

In later periods, from the Saïte 26th Dynasty (664–525 BC) onwards, new Egyptian enterprises may have moved further south, if the original (north) Punt was less accessible (for example, because of internal Nubian politics, or opposition by Napatan kings in that region). One Saïte text shows clear interest in Punt.[4] So, our new Zone V (nos 81–88, latter, 88, being Adulis) and Zone VI (nos 89–106, latter, 106, being Djibouti) in Map 12:4, would take us first to the Massawa-Adulis region ('Middle Punt'?), with additional sources of gold.[5] By this period, too, Egyptian exploration may finally have reached our new Zone VII (Map 12:4; nos 107–132, latter at Ras Hafun, classical Opone), namely northern Somalia with its wealth of aromatics (South Punt?). This would be indicated by recent finds from dramatically further south — of south-Egyptian marl pottery of ca. 10th–7th centuries BC (and perhaps a little later?), from deposits in the caves of Mafia Island off the Tanzania coast.[6] To reach so far, the Egyptians would have to have passed by Somalia. In terms of practical ancient trade-travel, they would not conceivably have gone through the region of the rising kingdom of Napata, then push somehow all the way via the Sudd swamps (or adjacent uncharted mountains), then on via Kenya and Tanzania, to end up on a small island with no resources to offer them! Coming by sea, they might well have used an island base from which to conduct business with mainland folk for trade in their products, before the Greeks did so with historic Azania hereabouts still later. However, this proto-Azania (as at Rhapta) could offer them neither gold nor aromatics, only ivory and tortoiseshell, to judge by the later data (first century AD) from the *Periplus*.[7]

2 Full monograph, ᶜAbd el-Raziq, Castel, Tallet and Ghica 2002; useful summary, ᶜAbd el-Raziq, Castel and Tallet 2006.

3 A figure already discussed in Kitchen 1971: 195–96.

4 Translated, Kitchen 1993: 602.

5 See Fattovich 1991: 264, Abb. 1, map of products.

6 See Chami 2004: 98–99 and Figure 38.

7 Casson 1989: 60 / 61, §16.

Potential Anchorages, East Coast, Tiran Island to Bir 'Alī (Kane)

Here, by contrast, our roughly corresponding seven zones have much less to offer at first sight. Zone I (nos 1–10) takes us from Tiran I. across to the strategic Aynuna Bay (no. 2) and hinterland valley, quite possibly the Greek Leuce Kome. South therefrom in some 157 miles, we have in principle about ten possible anchorages (taking nos 6b, c as equivalent to one), giving an average run of fifteen to sixteen miles, with some close-neighbouring places, and no spans of more than twenty to twenty-five miles apart, except for thirty-five miles between nos 3 and 4, and the initial thirty miles from Tiran to Aynuna. But the coastlands are forbidding, and in antiquity nobody flourished there except impoverished fisher-folk and hostile bandits and pirates, all to be given a wide berth.[8] By contrast with the mineral potential in Egyptian and Nubian Red Sea deserts, of gold and semi-precious stones, nothing but harsh desert and the dreaded post-volcanic *harra* lay east of the main east coastline and steeps of the Red Sea from Aynuna southwards for far enough, other than scattered and remote oases (al-'Ulā, Taymā', etc.)

Zone II (nos 11–16) down to Yanbū' (no. 16) is more of the same, for yet another 180 miles, and likewise our Zone III (nos 17–21) as far as Jiddah (no. 21), close on another 170 miles (*ca.* 274 km) south. From Tiran until Yanbū', nothing here along the Red Sea's east coast or within western Arabia's interior behind its western hilly curtain backing that coast held anything for questing traders or explorers. Little wonder the captain of the *Periplus* recommended his readers to speed down the middle of the Red Sea as fast as possible!

However, from Yanbū' to Jiddah (hinge of Zones III and IV), there was potential opportunity inland (south-east from al-Madīnah to north-east of Makkah), at the gold-bearing district of the well-named Maḥd al-Dhahab ('Cradle of Gold'),[9] now almost 540 miles (*ca.* 870 km) from Tiran, to Jiddah, and averaging about 130 miles (*ca.* 200 km) inland from the coast. Further gold-deposits extend southwards to around Wādī Baysh and northern Hawlan, giving a 370–mile (*ca.* 590 km) north-south 'golden zone'. There is the intriguing possibility that here, on the south of ancient Havilah (certainly in the north-west quadrant of Arabia), was the land of Ophir, known to have produced gold in the early first millennium BC: 'gold of Ophir: 30 shekels' is a prosaic notation from an Iron II ostracon (eighth century BC) found at Tell Qasile in central west Palestine long since.[10] Only two centuries before this, the Phoenician Hiram I of Tyre (in league with Solomon) had organized shipping expeditions to Ophir, specifically for gold and timber, *'almug*, probably tree-aloe, also known in western Arabia, around the 'Asīr region — whose upland woodlands herald better conditions further southwards still. So, from the early first millennium onwards, early (if fleeting) attempts would seem to have been made to exploit gold and timber from north of the Red Sea, down behind its eastern flank.[11]

With Zones IV (nos 22–29, to al-Qunfidha) and V (nos 30–39, 40, to Jizan and Khor Wahlan), we begin to approach the south Tihāmah and the famous South Arabia of irrigable uplands and eventually of inland oases again (Marib's 'gardens'). Their *ca.* 139 miles for eighteen possible stops (several being close together) averaged eight miles per stretch, in which few exceed twenty-seven to thirty miles (notably nos 25–26 at *ca.* 44 miles; and nos 37–38, Widan to Khor Abu as-Saba'a, *ca.* 40 miles).

Zone VI (nos 41–56) takes us from Luhiya (no. 42b) to al-Mukhā' (no. 50), and round at last to Aden (no. 53), before finally Zone VII brings us to Bir 'Alī / Kane (no. 57) in south-westernmost Ḥaḍramaut, hence to the traditional lands of myrrh and incense. On this final part, Luhiya to Aden (nos 42b — 53) is some 330 miles (*ca.* 530 km), with eleven stages (taking nos 43 and 44 together), averaging thirty miles each, and the only 'long' ones being Kamaran to Hodeida (al-Ḥudaydah) (*ca.* 40 miles), and then all stops, Perim Island to Aden (80 miles), and those beyond, out to Kane. However, this run is known better from later sources; and in any case, once landed at Bir 'Alī / Kane, the aromatics travelled rather by the overland route to the Levant, not by Arabia's inhospitable western sea-coast, which needs no detailed treatment here. Zones IV–VII, see Map 12:7.

Hinterlands and Relationships

In economic terms, the hinterlands have (on both west and east sides of the Red Sea) been drawn in already: gold, aromatics and the rest. Superficially, in terms of climate, ecology and types of topography, there is an outward semblance of correspondence between the regions immediately west and east of the Red Sea. Southwards from Suez and 'Aqabah respectively, both shores are backed by rocky, mountainous deserts down to approximately 20° latitude, before (on both sides) rising massifs (Ethiopian highlands; Arabian 'Asīr and south-west highlands) show varied vegetation, both woodlands and grasslands (Ethiopia) and monsoon-fed terrain and streams and dependent irrigation (south-west Arabia). And thereafter, further south, the Horn of Africa reverts to semi-desert at

8 Cf. the *Periplus*, Casson 1989: 63, §20.

9 See for this area, Roberts 2002: 133–54, with map at 119; cf. H. von Wissmann's map, at rear of Grohmann 1963, at coordinates approx. 23⁰ N and 41⁰ E. Also, Dawson 1979, minerals map on p. 25 (missing from recent editions of that book).

10 Recent edition, Renz / Röllig I 1995: 229–31, no. 2.

11 Detailed references will be found in Kitchen 1997: 143–47; Hiram / Solomon ref., 1 Kings 9:26–28 and 10:11.

best, as does the southern strip of Arabia (backed up northward by the totally desertic Rub' al-Khalī). But there remains finally the matter of the human organizational profiles — what societies in early times flanked this sea, and how did their changing relationships affect what happened in and around it?

However, there are striking contrasts. On the west side, for some 1,400 miles (*ca.* 2,200 km), south to north, the massif and deserts are bounded by the Nile from the Sudd to the Mediterranean sea — which supported the greatest African civilization(s) of antiquity. By contrast, no such river relieves the west-Arabian deserts from Sana'a to the same northern sea. Instead, Arabia's most powerful west-side societies were the kingdoms of Saba, Main, Qataban and Ḥaḍramaut (all eventually fused in Ḥimyar), based strictly within the SW quadrant of the Peninsula. Most of 850 miles (*ca.* 1200 km) separated them from the oasis-based minor kingdoms of the Qurraya group ('Midian'), then in turn Qedar / Dedan and Lihyan, before the Nabateans took over. Between the south-west and north-west were hundreds of miles of weary desert travel marked only by occasional wells (the 'incense route'). Adding in the contrast in sailing / anchorage conditions between the east and west coasts, the resultant human histories (both political and cultural) of both regions adjacent to these coasts were markedly different.

First: in Africa. Here, at the height of her political power, three times repeated, Egypt took control over Lower Nubia ('Wawat'), in the third millennium (Old Kingdom), then in the early second millennium (Middle Kingdom), and in the later second millennium (New Kingdom, 'Empire' period). In the oldest period, various chiefs actively ruled their own segments of Nubian Nile valley, in Wawat, and (above or below the Second Cataract) in Irjet and Satju. Beyond them, Egyptian traders visited Iam (between the second and third if not Fourth Cataracts), a possible precursor to both the later Kush and Irem. Egypt traded with these people-groups cum chieftaincies, by either of two routes: the central one, up the Nile from Aswan, and the western desert one, via the oases (via Kharga possibly as far as the Selima Oasis, close to the Third Cataract).[12] And at all periods, the products of inner (that is, more southerly) Africa came into Egypt via intermediaries, with appropriate price mark-ups. This situation led to Egyptian state use of ships upon the Red Sea to reach the aromatics of Punt and its gold-bearing region ('mines' of Punt), to bypass expensive intermediaries (Hatshepsut's explicit aim), in all three main periods of power.

But Nubia also had its centres of power. Even the most powerful Middle-Kingdom rulers had to be content with a southern boundary no further than the Second Cataract. The early second millennium saw the rise of Kush, a formidable kingdom between the Second and Fourth Nile Cataracts, based in the Dongola Reach, with its spectacular capital at (modern name) Kerma.[13] So much so, in the Second Intermediate Period of Egypt (*ca.* 1780–1540 BC, 13th to 17th Dynasties), that (i) Egypt's kings proper eventually ruled only in southern Upper Egypt (Aswan to Coptos, sometimes Abydos), between the Semitic Hyksos fifteenth Dynasty in the north, and the kingdom of Kush south from Aswan. And (ii) in the seventeenth Dynasty, *ca.* 1600 BC, we now know that Kush even gathered its subordinates and allies (Wawat; east-desert Medjayu; Khent-hen-nufer in S. Kush; and Punt!) and invaded Upper Egypt successfully![14] The New Kingdom soon reversed all that, by conquering Kush; but Irem beyond it was not controllable, and Punt remained reachable only by the Red Sea. After the Libyan period (945–715), the kings of Napata in full Pharaonic style took over the rule of both lands to the Mediterranean, albeit briefly (715–664). Thereafter, south of Egypt proper, the successive kingdoms of Napata and Meroe ruled supreme in north-east Africa to the Red Sea, until Hellenistic and late Roman times respectively. To avoid these powerful kingdoms, Egypt renewed her Red Sea maritime line of communication (from the seventh century) to territories well south of 'old' (North) Punt, via the Massawa area ('Middle Punt'? for gold) and the N. Somali coast-region ('South Punt'? for aromatics), ultimately to Tanzania (Mafia Isle finds, cf. above). This may have been an attempt to bypass the Arabian aromatics trade — to cut costs?

Second: Arabia as a contrast. Here, it was the dominant group of kingdoms (Saba through to Ḥaḍramaut, later eventuating into a unified Ḥimyar) that controlled both the production and distribution of the precious aromatics and other exotica within their territories. From this group, in the early first millennium, we see a main 'incense-route' bifurcating into two branches: (i) north then east (via Teima), to reach the Middle Euphrates at Hindanu in the eighth and probably ninth centuries already,[15] and (ii) much more famously up the west side of Arabia via southern Transjordan, going north-west to Gaza, or north on towards Damascus. In Arabia, the successive north-west transmitters of such caravans were the al-'Ulā oasis powers Qedar / Dedan, then Lihyan prior to the Nabataeans. But not without occasional (but always ephemeral!) foreign interventions: such were the possible short-lived Phoenician / Hebrew maritime visits to Ophir, for gold (Mahd al-Dhahab? Wādī Baysh zone?) and timber (north 'Asīr?) in the tenth century; the Neo-Babylonian intervention in the sixth century (Teima), and the longer Minean presence in the second century (al-'Ulā); then Rome in Western Arabia in the late first

12 See map, Kitchen 1982: 262.

13 See Kemp 1982: 749–56; the Egyptianizing titles of two rulers may indicate Kerma kings imitating Egyptian style under the influence of their Egyptian officials.

14 See Davies 2003: 18–19.

15 Liverani 1992.

(Ælius Gallus; Caesar's naval raid on Aden). No single power or pair of powers (local or foreign) was able to rule the entire route in pre-classical or even classical antiquity, by contrast with the African hinterland to the Red Sea (Egypt; Kush / Napata / Meroe) thanks to the parallel highway and water / food resource there provided by the immense length of the Nile.

But also third: Arabia with Africa. Long ago there began (e.g.) a debate as to whether the Egyptian-attested term 'Punt' (so closely tied in with Africa) had also extended east across Bāb al-Mandab in south-west Arabia at least. For this, there is no real evidence: but from Arabia into Africa, definitely. Most recently, probable indicators have been reported at the new excavations at Marsā Gawāsīs, of Middle-Kingdom date (*ca.* twentieth–nineteenth centuries BC): fragments of pottery of Malayba type comparable with wares found also around the Aden area in south-west Arabia, and also of a type found in Wādī (O)urq, along the Yemeni Red Sea coast; with these may be contrasted also the finding of a Kassala-type fragment, from what would be the heart of south-east (Sudani) Punt.[16] In the latter case, a Nubian / Puntite pot probably became part of the effects of an Egyptian ship returning from Punt. In the former cases, South-Arabian Bronze-Age pottery probably came across Bāb al-Mandab with early Arabians eager to participate in the wider aromatics trade that reached northwards; and so, some of their vessels (like the Kassala pot) found their way up through Punt, and into Egyptian ships as utility items, but most likely they have no direct bearing on the location or extent of Punt — only on the extent of its trade-connections. Perhaps those who first brought them west over Bāb al-Mandab were, who knows, distant precursors of the Genebtyw of the Late Bronze Age, half a millennium later, who shared briefly (and probably from south-west Arabia) in the Red Sea trade with Egypt.

References

'Abd el-Raziq, M, Castel, G., Tallet, P., and Ghica, V. 2002. *Les inscriptions d'Ayn Soukhna* (MIFAO 122). Cairo: IFAO.

'Abd el-Raziq, M., Castel, G., and Tallet, P. 2006. Ayn Soukhna et la mer Rouge. *Égypte Afrique et Orient* 41: 3–6.

Casson, L. 1989. *The Periplus Maris Erythraei.* Princeton: University Press.

Chami, F. 2004. The Egypto-Graeco-Romans and Panchaea / Azania. 93–103 in Lunde, P. and Porter, A. (eds), *Trade and Travel in the Red Sea Region, Proceedings of Red Sea Project I.* BAR International Series 1269. Oxford: Archaeopress.

Davies, W.V. 2003. (a) Sobeknakht's Hidden Treasure. *British Museum Magazine* 46: 18–19. (b) Sobeknakht of Elkab and the coming of Kush. *Egyptian Archaeology* 23: 3–6.

Dawson A., *et al.* (eds). 1979. *The Kingdom of Saudi Arabia.* 4th ed. (Minerals map is omitted in later editions.) London: Stacey International.

Fattovich, R. 1991. The Problem of Punt in the light of recent field work in the Eastern Sudan. 257–72 in vol. 4 of Sylvia Schoske (ed.), *Akten des vierten Internationalen Ägyptologen-Kongresses München 1985.* Hamburg: Helmut Buske Verlag.

Fattovich, R. and Bard, K. 2006. À la recherche de Pount, Mersa Gaouasis et la navigation égyptienne dans la mer Rouge. *Égypte, Afrique et Orient* 41: 7–30, 53–56.

Grohmann, A. 1963. *Arabien* (Kulturgeschichte des Alten Orients: Handbuch der Altertumswissenschaft, III.1: 3.3.4). Munich: Verlag C.H. Beck.

Kemp, B.J. 1982. 749–56 in Clark, J.D. (ed.), *Cambridge History of Africa*, I, Cambridge: University Press.

Kitchen, K.A. 1971. Punt and How to Get There. *Orientalia* 40: 184–207.

——. 1982. *Pharaoh Triumphant, the Life and Times of Ramesses II.* Warminster: Aris & Phillips [now Oxford: Oxbow].

——. 1993. The land of Punt. Chapter 35, pages 587–608 in Shaw, T., Sinclair, P., Andah, B. and Okpoko, A. (eds), *The Archaeology of Africa, Food, Metals and Towns.* London / New York: Routledge.

——. 1997. Sheba and Arabia. 126–153 in Handy, L. (ed.), *The Age of Solomon, Scholarship at the Turn of the Millennium.* Leiden: Brill.

Liverani, M. 1992. Early Caravan Trade between South-Arabia and Mesopotamia. *Yemen* 1: 111–115, with map. 113.

Renz, J. and Röllig, W. 1995. *Handbuch der althebräischen Epigraphik*, I. Darmstadt: Wissenschaftliche Buchgesellschaft. Cited as Renz and Röllig I.

Roberts, R.J. 2002. *A Passion for Gold.* Reno / Las Vegas: University of Nevada Press.

16 See briefly Fattovich and Bard 2006: 26.

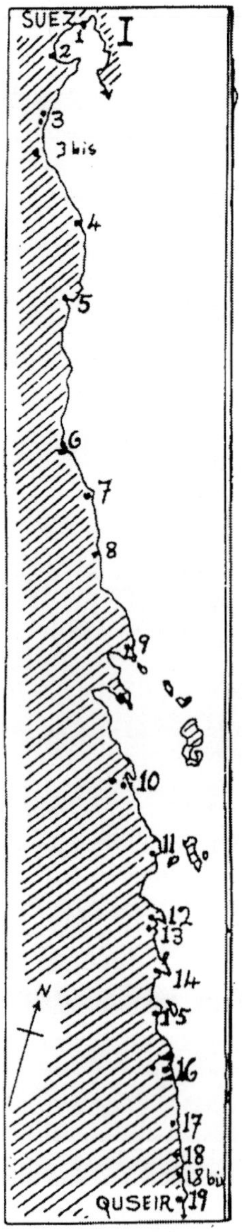

MILES

0 100

Approx. Scale Only

I. From Suez to Quseir

1. Suez, ancient Clysma,
c. 8 miles to
2. Adabiya Bay, SW anchorage
c. 18 mls (round cape) to
3a. Birs Odeib, Themada; shore
c. 22 mls to Ras Abu Diraj
3b Ain Sukhna, near 3a.
4. Ras Abu Diraj, shore,
c. 23 mls to
5. Mersa Thelemet, inlet,
c. 30 mls to
6. Ras Abu Bakr, N. bay,
c. 25 mls to
7. Ras Gharib, anchorage,
c. 17 mls to
8. Ras Shukheir, N. bay,
c. 30 mls to
9. Mersa Zeitiya, inlet,
c. 34 mls to
10. Abu Shaʿr inlet,
c. 16 mls to
11. Hurghada, shores,
c. 15 mls to
12. Mersa Abu Mokhadig, inlet,
c. 3 mls to
13. Sherm el-ʿArab, inlet,
c. 15 mls to
14. Ras Abu Soma, S. bay,
c. 7 mls to
15. Port Safâga, shore,
c. 15 mls to
16. Mersa Gawasis (anc. Sa'waw), inlets,
c. 18 mls to
17. Bir Queiʿ, boat-harbour,
c. 7 mls to
18a Hamrawein, boat-harbour,
c. 5 mls to
18bis Quseir Qadim (Myos Hormos)
c. 5 mls to
19. Quseir, shore.

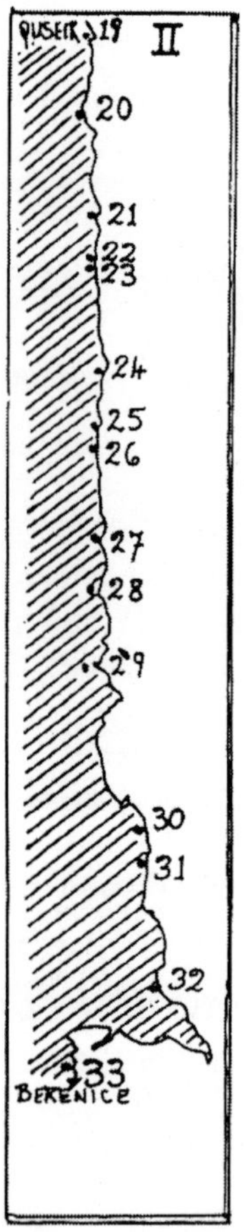

II. From Quseir to Berenice

(19 Quseir, shore)
c. 20 mls to
20. Sherm Medamer, inlet,
c. 10 mls to
21. Mersa Toronbi, small bay,
c. 12 mls to
22. Mersa Mubarak, inlet,
c. 1.5 mls to
23. Mersa Imbarik, deep inlet,
c. 11.5 mls to
24. Mersa (Abu) Dibbab, cove,
c. 7 mls to
25. Mersa Tarâfi, sheltered cove,
c. 3 mls to
26. Mersa Igli, narrow cove,
c. 16 mls to
27. Mersa Tundaba, anchorage,
c. 7 mls to
28. Wadi Ghadir, small harbour,
c. 18 mls to
29. Sherm Luli, deep inlet,
c. 30 mls to
30. Ras Qulʿan, cove in reefs,
c. 6 mls to
31. Mersa Wadi Lahami, good inlet,
c. 17 mls to
32. Mersa Sataiya, bay, c. 33 mls to
33. Berenice, small harbours.

Map 12:2 Red Sea: West Coast Gazetteer, Sections 1–11, Nos. 1–33

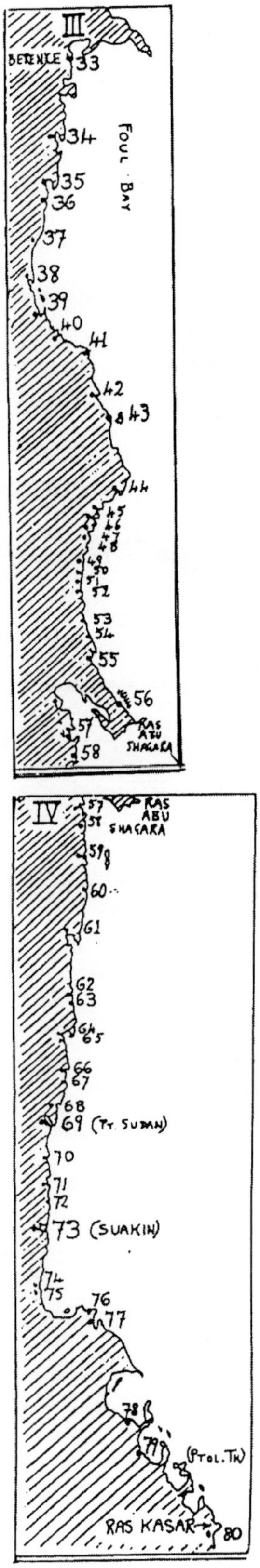

(*33.* Berenice, harbours)
c. 20 mls to
34. Mersa Abu Madd, inlet,
c. 10 mls to
35. Mersa Himeira, inlet,
c. 6 mls to
36. Scout Anchorage, shore
c. 16 mls to
37. Bir Shalatein, N. bay,
c. 18 mls to
38. Has(s)a (sandy) lagoon,
c. 9 mls to
39. Mersa Shaᶜab, large inlet,
c. 17 mls to
40. Mersa Abu Fissi, N. end,
c. 16 mls to
41. Ras Abu Dara, small bays,
c. 24 mls to
42. Mersa Girid, small inlet,
c. 18 mls to
43. Mersa Haleib, twin anchorage
c. 30 mls to
44. Mersa (Um)bella, small inlet,
c. 11 mls to
45. Khor el-Marᶜob, small inlet,
c. 3.5 mls to
46. Mersa Gwilaib,
c. 3 mls to
47. Khor Abu ᶜAsal, good inlet,
c. 3 mls to
48. Mersa Hamsayat, inlet,
c. 6.5 mls to
49. Mersa Wasiᶜ, inlet,
adjoining
50. Mersa/Khor Abu Fanadir,
inlet, c. 2.5 mls to
51. Mersa Gafatir, small inlet,
c. 5 mls to
52. Khor Delwein, small inlet,
c. 6 mls to
53. Mersa Abu Imama, inlet,
c. 6 mls to
54. Mersa Halaka, narow inlet,
c. 6 mls to
55. Khor Shinᶜab, good inlet,
c. 12 mls to
56. Shaᶜb Qumeira, coast
behind reef, c. 30 mls to
57/58. Dungunab Bay/
Muhammed Qol,
(c. 8 mls to next.)

III. From Berenice to Ras Abu Shagara (Rawai)

(*58.* Muhammed Qol, coral inlet)
c. 8 mls to
59. Khor Inkeifal, good inlet,
c. 9 mls to
60. Dabadib, anchorage,
c. 14 mls to
61. Mersa Salak, enclosed inlet,
c. 15 mls to
62. Mersa Arakiyai, small inlet,
c. 4 mls to
63. Mersa Aweitir, gap in reefs,
c. 7 mls to
64/65. Mersa Fijab/ᶜArus, inlets,
c. 10 mls to
66. Mersa Darur, small inlet,
c. 4 mls to
67. Mersa Halote, small inlet,
c. 8 mls to
68. Mersa (G)wi(y)ai, good inlet,
c. 4 mls to
69. Port Sudan, good inlet,
c. 14 mls to
70. Mersa Amid, small inlet,
c. 9 mls to
71. Mersa Ata, small nlet,
c. 6 mls to
72. Mersa Kuwai, good inlet,
c. 7 mls to
73. Suakin, good inlet,
c. 16 mls to
74. Mersa Sheikh Ibrahim, good
inlet, c. 4 mls to
75. Mersa Sheikh Saᶜad, coral
inlet, c. 22 mls to
76. Mersa Maqdam, anchorage
adjoining
77. Trinkitat, harbour,
c. 40 mls to
78. ᶜAqiq Gulf, S. shore,
adjoining
79. Khor Nawarat, inlet,
c. 24 mls
80. via Ras Kasar), to
81. Brassy bay, anchorage.

IV. From Ras Abu Shagara to Brassy bay

Map 12:3 Red Sea: West Coast Gazetteer, Sections 111–IV, Nos. 33–81

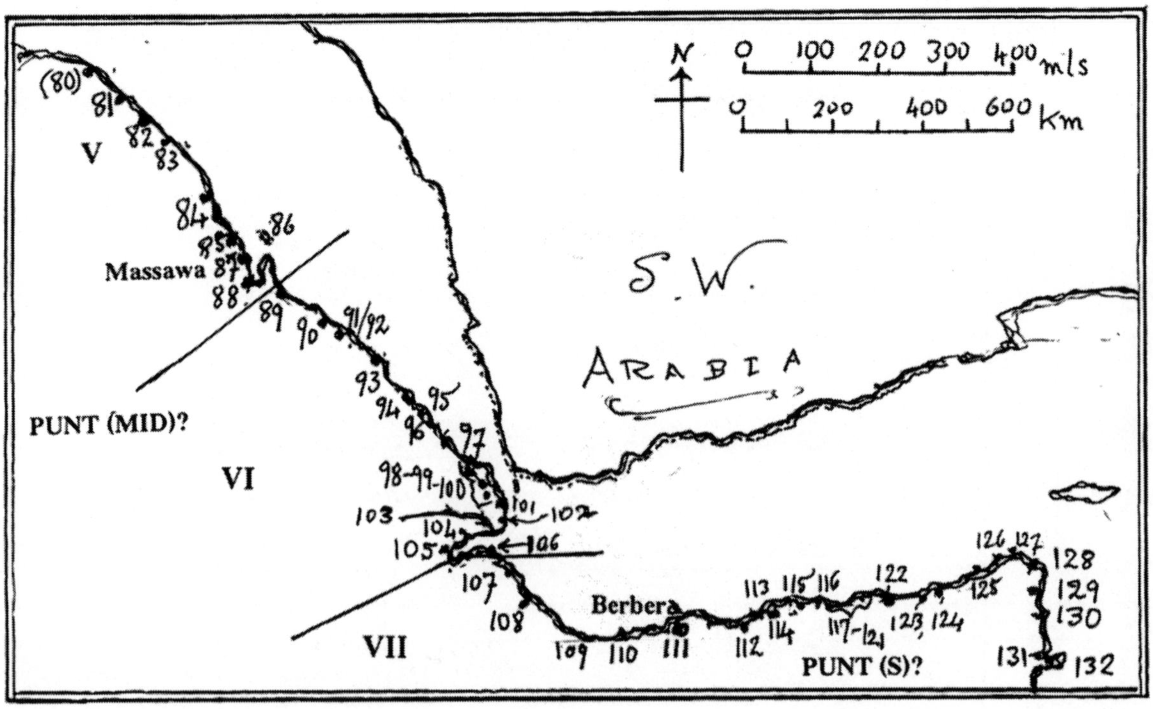

V. Brassy Bay to Zula (Adulis)

(80. Ras Kasar and then)
81. Brassy Bight,
c. 40 mls to
82. Mersa Teclai
c. 22 mls to
83. Mersa Dersa
c. 74 mls to
84. Mersa Kuba
c. 45 mls to
85. Khor Daklyat
(+Ghubbet Mus Nefit Isle)
c. 2 mls to
87. Massawa
c. 30 mls to
88. Zula ('Adulis')
c. 75 mls to (89. M. Fatma)

VI. Zula (Adulis) to Djibouti

89. Mersa Fatma, c. 32 mls S. of Corali pt. c. 20+ mls to
90. Midar, and
91. Amfile (Hanefa) bay
(+ 92. Anto Seghir & Is.)
c. 60 mls to
93. Edd & bay
c. 14 mls
94. Mersa Dudo
c. 22 mls
95. Barrassoli bay
96. Beilul bay
c. 16 mls to
97. Assab (Avalites)
c. 22 mls to
98. Ras Sintian, inlet
c. 8.5 mls
99. Ras Dumeira, N. side, shore
c. 21.5 mls to
100. Ras Siane, coves.
c. 6.25 mls to
101. Khor ('Crique') Angor'
c. 30 mls to
102. Anse Buret
c. 2.25 mls to
103. Obock (i)
c. 17 mls to
104. Ras Duan, S side, landing-beach; c. 26 mls to
105. Ghubbet Kharab
c. 26 mls to Djibouti
[103. Obock (ii), direct,
c. 25 mls to Djibouti]

VII. Djibouti to Ras Hafun

106. Djibouti
c. 11.5 mls to
107. Mersa Dolokhtiya
c. 18.5 mls to
108. Zeila
c. 40 mls to
109. Dagaritu area, beaches
c. 40 mls to
110. Bulhar
c. 37 mls to
111. Berbera (Malao)
c. 59 mls to
112. Karin/Ras Khanzir
c. 23 mls to
113. Ghubbet Ankhor
c. 18 mls to
114. Raguda
c. 6 mls to
115. Shulah
c. 14 mls to
116. Heis/Xiis (Mundu)
c. 16 mls to
117. Marso Senekhan
c. 6.5 mls to
118. Senacca
c. 42 mls to
119. Waghdaria
c. 28 mls to
120. Las Khireh/Khoreh
c. 30.5 mls to
121. Khor Durdureh
c. 16.5 mls to
122. Elayu (Mosyllon?)
c. 4.5 mls to
123. Bandar Ziada
c. 12.5 mls to
124. Bandar Kassim (Bosasso)
c. 44 mls to
125. Ras Fuluch (C. Elefante)
c. 9 mls to
126. Alula
c. 22 mls to
127. Damo [Bereda]
c. 23 mls to
128. Ras Asir - C. Guardafui
c. 40 mls to
129. Bargal
c. 8 mls to
130. W. Gondoli/Kh Binnah
c. 35 mls, to 131. Hordio bay &
132. Hafun (Opone), peninsula.

Map 12:4 Red Sea: West Coast Gazetteer, Sections 111–IV, Nos. 81–132

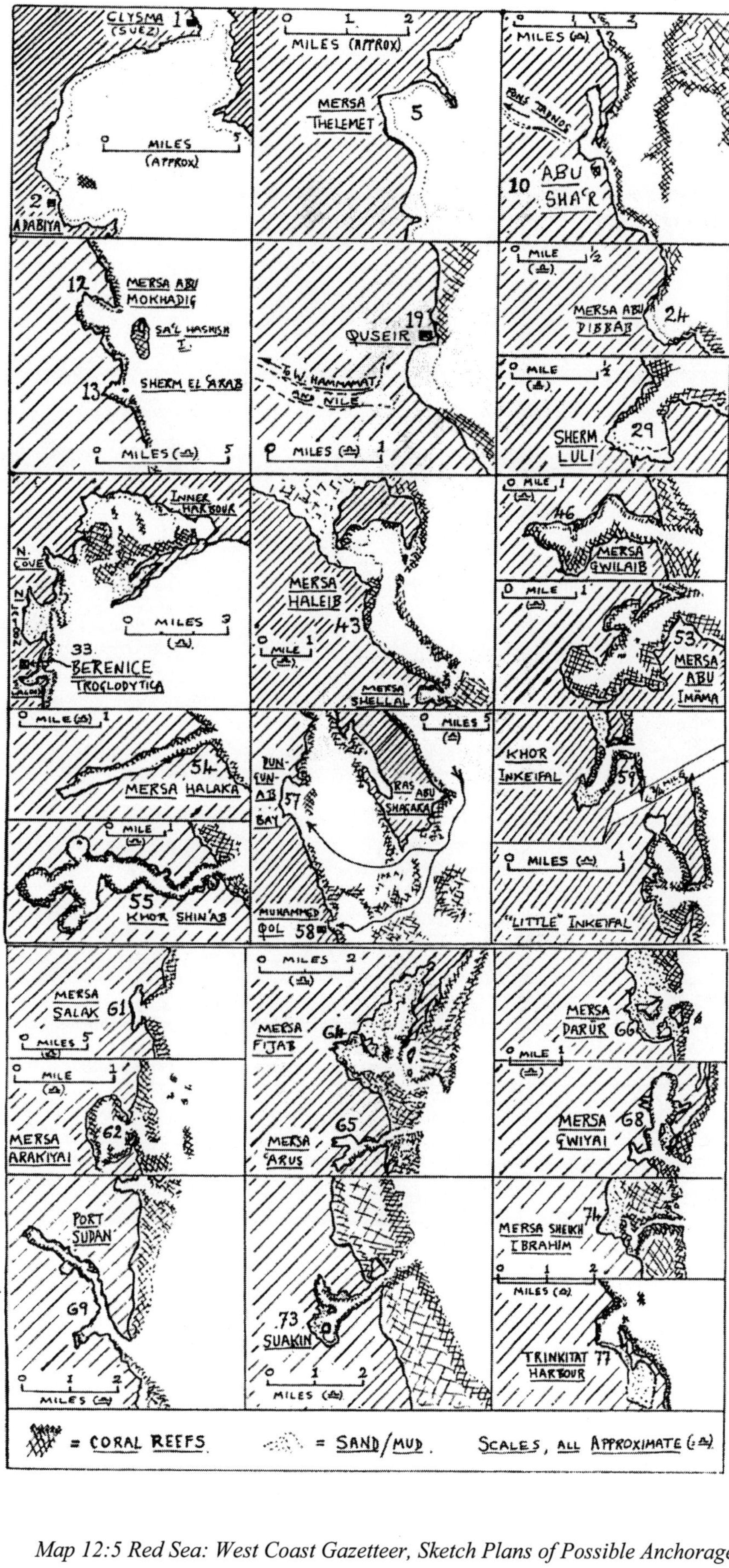

Map 12:5 Red Sea: West Coast Gazetteer, Sketch Plans of Possible Anchorages

I. Tiran Isle to Sharm Wadjh

1. Tiran Isle
 c. 30 mls to
2. Aynuna (Bay & valley)
 c. 27 mls to
3. Al-Muwailih
 c. 35 mls to
4. Sharm Naʿman, E. side of Naʿmn I,
 c. 4 mls to
5a. Sharm Yahar
 c. 3.5 mls to
5b. Sharm Jubba
 c. 14.5 mls to
6a. Sharm Zubeir [filled-in],
 c. 2 mls to
6b. Sharm Qafafa
 c. 1 ml.
6c. Sharm Jubba
 c. 20 mls to
7. Marsa Zubeida
 c. 22 mls to
8ab. Sharms Dumagha, ʿAntar,
 c. 25 mls to
9. Marsa Zaʿam
 c.3 mls to
10. Sharm Wadjh & Wadjh
 c. 14 mls to (11) Ras Kharaba.

II. Ras Kharaba to Yanbu

11. Ras Kharaba (coastline)
 c. 1.5 mls to
12. Marsa Wadi al-Miyah
 c.3.5 mls to
13. Sharm Habban
 c. 50? mls to
14. Umm Lajj
 c. 11 mls to
15. Sharm Mahar
 c. 60 mls to
16. Yanbu
 c. 38 mls to (17) Sh. Buraiqa.

III. Yanbu to Jiddah

17. Sharm Buraiqa
 c. 50 mls to
18. Sharm Rabigh
 c. 10 mls to
20. Sharm Bihar
 c. 12 mls to
21. Jidda.
 (6 mls to (22) Sumaima)

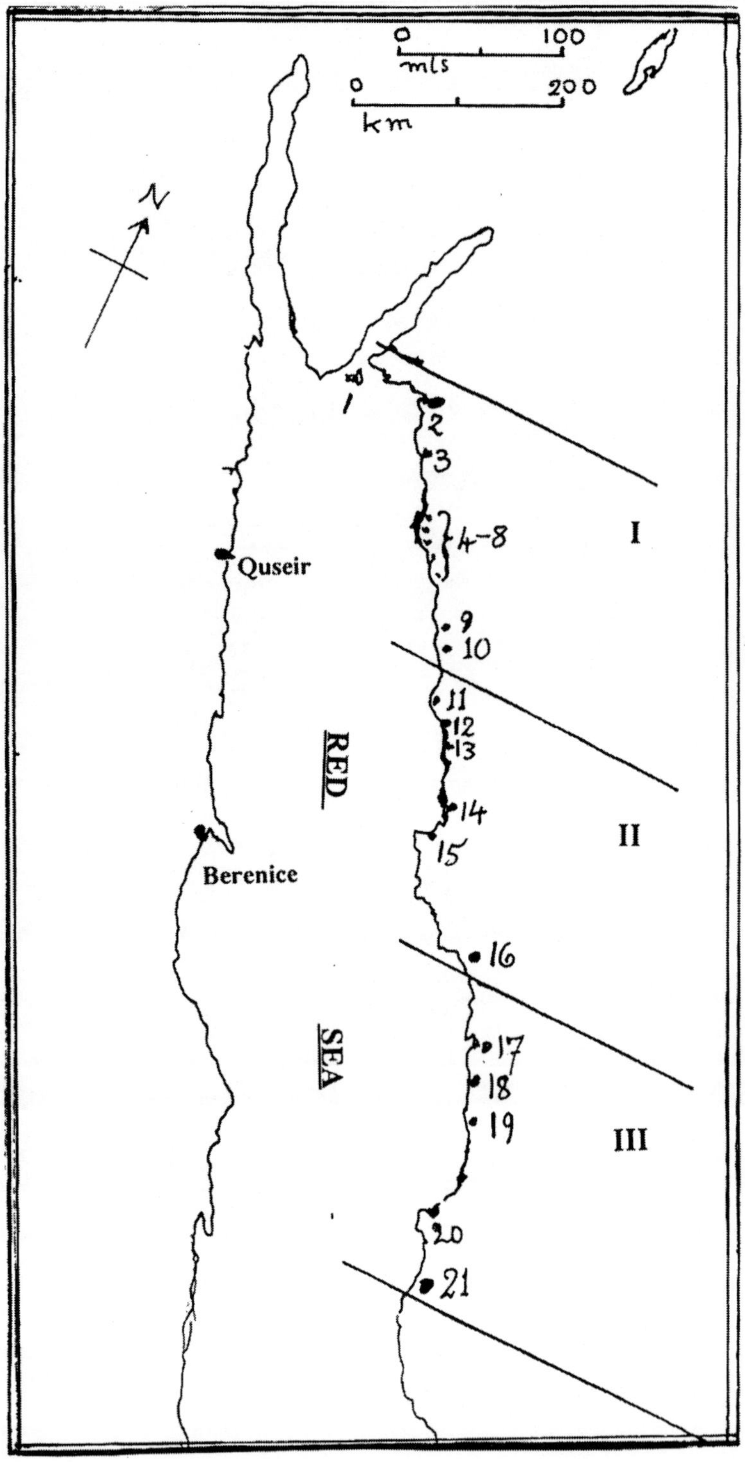

Map 12:6 Red Sea: East Coast Gazetteer, Sections 1–III, Nos. 1–21

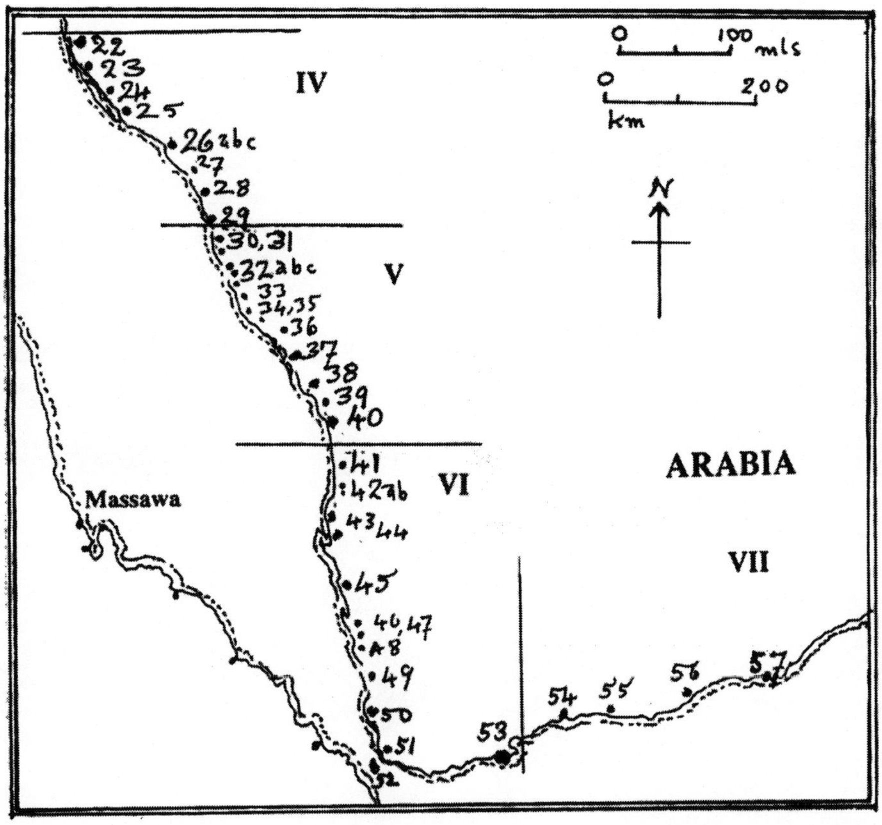

IV. Jiddah to Al-Qunfidha

22. Sumaima
 c. 7 mls to
23. Sarum
 c. 6 mls to
24. Kidan
 c. 3 mls to Abu Shauk
25. Abu Shauk
 c. 44 mls to
26ab. Al-Lith, Au Latt I., &
26c. Marsa Ibrahim
 c. 12 mls to
27. Marsa Raka
 c. 27 mls to
28. Jalajil
 c. 35 mls to
29. Al-Qunfidha
 c. 5 mls to (30) Ghubbat al-Qina (bay).

V. Al Qunfidha to Khor Wahlan.

30. Ghubbat al-Qina bay
 c. 6 mls to
31. Ras Makasir (small bay)
 c. 24 mls to
32a. Ras Hali, bay to E.,
 c. 7 mls to
32b. Jahfuf bay
 c. 3.5 mls to
32c. Khor Amiq/Amaq
 c. 14.5 mls to
33a. Khor Nahud,
 c. 2.5 mls to
33b. Khor Birk,
 c. 15 mls to
34. Khor Wasm N & S
 c. 14 mls to
35. Widan, inlet
 c. 8 mls to
36. Khor Makra,
 c. 23 mls to
37. Khor Itwad,
 c. 42 mls to
38. Khor Abu as Saba'a
 c. 14 mls to
39. Jizan
 c. 13.5 mls to
40. Khor Wahlan
 c. 33 mls to

VI. Marsa Baqila to Aden

41. Marsa Baqila
 c. 27 mls to
42a. Ras Khatit (& isl. anchorage)
 c. 8 mls to
42b. Luhiya
 c. 44 mls to
43. Kamaran bay/NE inlet, &
44. Kamaran bay, S head
 c. 40 mls to
45. Hodeida
 c. 10 mls to
46. Khor Ghulaifiqa, c. 14 mls to
47. Marsa Majalis
 c. 4.5 mls to
48. Marsa al-Fa'is
 c. 36 mls to
49. Marsa Fujaim
 c. 45 mls. to
50. Mokha
 c. 40 mls to
51. Khor Ghuraira, opposite:
52. Perim Isle, off B. al-Mandeb
 c. 85 mls E., to (53) Aden

VII. Aden to Kane

53. Aden
 c. 52 mls to
54. Shuqra
 c. 43 mls to
55. Maqatin bay
 c. 98 mls to
56. Balihaf
 c. 127 mls to
57. Bir Ali, anc. Kane.

Map 12:7 Red Sea: East Coast Gazetteer, Sections IV–VII, Nos. 22–57

Sea Port to Punt: New Evidence from Marsā Gawāsīs, Red Sea (Egypt)

Kathryn A. Bard, Rodolfo Fattovich and Cheryl Ward

Introduction

Fieldwork conducted at the coastal site of Marsā Gawāsīs, Red Sea (Egypt) in 2004–2005 and 2005–2006 confirmed that this was the sea port to Punt in the Middle Kingdom (*ca.* 2055–1650) and early New Kingdom (*ca.* 1550–1069).

Five parallel rock-cut rooms in the fossil coral terrace were used as a kind of ship arsenal. One of the rooms (Cave 5) is about 15 m long: the floor is covered with *ca.* 50 coils of ship rope, all neatly tied and knotted — just as the sailors left them almost 4,000 years ago. A geophysical survey and the identification of tiny sea shells in *wādī* deposits, as well as the discovery of a huge stone anchor and sherds of large Egyptian storage jars suggested that the edge of the ancient harbour was considerably inland from the present beach.

Large cedar timbers of ship planks and decking, some with the mortises and tenons and copper fastenings still in place, were found inside and outside the rock-cut caves. They included two blades from steering oars, dating on the associated ceramics to the early New Kingdom. Other wood / charcoal remains were identified as pine and two species of oak, all from south-west Asia, as well as species from the Nile Valley, and ebony from the southern Red Sea region. Over twenty-one wooden cargo boxes (there are more still in the sand) were found outside the caves. One of them (Box 2) had a painted hieroglyphic inscription with the cartouche of a king (probably Amenemhat III), year 8 of his reign, and '. . . the wonderful things of Punt.' This suggested that they originally contained products from Punt, maybe as part of a ship cargo. New stelae of Amenemhat III (*ca.* 1831–1786 BC) were also found near the entry to the caves. Exotic ceramics included fragments of vessels from the Yemeni Tihāmah and the region of Aden and possibly Eritrea, suggesting that in the early to mid-second millennium BC the Egyptians had maritime contacts with both Arabian and African regions of the southern Red Sea.

The site of Marsā Gawāsīs is located twenty-three km to the south of the modern port of Safāgah, on the top and along the slopes of a fossil coral terrace, which delimits the lower Wādī Gawāsīs to north. In 1976–1977 the site was partially excavated by Abdel Monem Sayed, University of Alexandria (Egypt).[1] On the basis of a few Middle Kingdom inscriptions recording expeditions to Punt at the time of Senusret I (*ca.* 1956–1911 BC), Amenemhat II (*ca.* 1911–1877 BC), Senusret II (*ca.* 1877–1870 BC) and Senusret III (*ca.* 1870–1831 BC),[2] a fragment of timber from a boat, and some limestone anchors Sayed identified this site with the port of *S3ww*, from where seafaring expeditions were sent to Punt. This identification, though accepted by most scholars, was rejected by A. Nibbi (1981) and C. Vandersleyen (1996), who denied the use of the site as a port and the Egyptian maritime trade to Punt.

In 2001 the University of Naples 'l'Orientale', Naples (Italy) and the Italian Institute for Africa and the Orient (IsIAO), Rome (Italy), in collaboration with Boston University, Boston (USA), resumed excavations at Marsā Gawāsīs, under the direction of Rodolfo Fattovich (UNO / IsIAO) and Kathryn A. Bard (BU) as part of a long-term project aimed at investigating the development of the Red Sea trade in late prehistoric to Classical times. In particular, the UNO / IsIAO and BU project at Marsā Gawāsīs was aimed at understanding the proper function of the site and collecting evidence about the ancient Egyptian navigation in the Red Sea, as well as validating or invalidating the hypothesis of a location of Punt in the northern Horn of Africa.[3]

Five field seasons were conducted in 2001–2002, 2002–2003, 2003–2004, 2004–2005, and 2005–2006. The results of the first three seasons confirmed that the site was certainly related to a maritime activity in the Middle Kingdom, possibly as far as the southern Red Sea and the Gulf of Aden, but no evidence of stable installations and a commercial function, supporting the identification of the site with a proper port, was found.[4] In 2004–2005 and 2005–2006 six rock-cut caves, large timbers of ship planks and decks, two blades of steering oars, and over twenty cargo boxes were discovered, supporting the identification of the site with a port.[5]

Fieldwork

In 2004–2005 and 2005–2006 excavations were conducted on the eastern terrace near the seashore and

1 See Sayed 1999.

2 The absolute chronology is based on Shaw 2000.

3 See Bard and Fattovich 2003–2004; Fattovich 2005; Fattovich and Bard 2006a.

4 Fattovich 2005.

5 See Bard and Fattovich 2005, 2006; Fattovich and Bard 2006a.

along the western and southern slopes of the coral terrace. A geophysical survey was also conducted on the top of the western coral terrace and at the base of the western and southern slope of the terrace along the *wādī*. Geo-archaeological investigations were conducted as well to collect more detailed palaeo-environmental information about the site.[6]

A) Eastern Terrace (Marsā Gawāsīs)

A stone platform (WG 29) was completely excavated on the top of the terrace near the seashore. This structure, *ca.* 1.2 m high from the original surface, was constructed with conglomerate slabs covered with coral and limestone blocks and consisted of an oval platform with a ramp to the west, *ca.* 9 m x 10 m in size. Originally, the top of the structure was covered with conglomerate slabs, which are now completely deteriorated, covering at the centre a frame of mangrove wood. Most likely this structure was an open-air altar facing the sea with a west-east orientation. On the top of this structure over 650 conch-shells from the Red Sea and Indian Ocean were collected in 2004–2005 and 2005–2006 seasons. The use of these shells is uncertain, as no evidence of possible use for manufacturing shell artefacts was found.

B) Western Terrace (Wādī Gawāsīs)

Six rock-cut caves were found along the western edge of the coral terrace.

Cave 1 was an isolated man-made cave (*ca.* 6 m x 4 m in area), with a rectangular entrance, *ca.* 1.6 m wide and 1.4 m high. A wooden threshold was at the base of the entrance. The timber was 1.35 m long, 0.15 m wide and 0.13 m thick. Mud-bricks had been placed against the threshold on the outside and inside. Fragments of storage pots, pieces of cedar boat parts, and five grinding stones were found inside the cave. A broken hieratic *ostracon* (inscription poorly preserved) and a possible tool made from a black-topped potsherd with a rim-band of incised triangles, similar to Early Kerma types, were also found in this cave. The pottery from this cave suggests that this structure was used in the late Old Kingdom (*ca.* 2345–2181 BC) and Middle Kingdom (*ca.* 2055 – 1650 BC).

Along the southwestern edge of the fossil coral terrace entrances to five man-made caves (Caves 2, 3, 4, 5, 6) were discovered after removing a deposit of *ca.* 2 m of wind-blown sand and associated artefacts. Caves 2, 3, 4 and 5 were mapped and surveyed, and the entrance of Cave 6 was investigated. Cave 2 was partially excavated. The five caves are located near each other with a northeast-southwest orientation. The caves were about 20–25 m long and 4 m wide, with collapsed coral rock and a large amount of sand deposited near the entrances (Figure 13:1)

Ship-breaking was apparently the main activity outside Caves 2, 3, and 4. Inside the caves, work areas were identified by extensive deposits of chipped and gribbled wood fragments, fastenings cut and broken with tools, and, in Cave 3, marine shell mixed with wood fragments, many of which are sponge-like with gribble, suggesting the trimming and reworking of planks. The occurrence of about fifty coils of rope inside Cave 5 suggests anyway that the caves were also used for storage of ship equipment. The ceramics from these caves date to the Middle Kingdom (*ca.* 2055–1650 BC). Only Cave 2 was surely reused in the eighteenth Dynasty (*ca.* 1550–1295 BC) as early New Kingdom potsherds were found inside the entrance corridor and were associated with two blades of steering oars on the top of the deposit. Twelve niches were cut in the wall of the fossil coral terrace to the east and above the entrance of Cave 2. The niches to the east of the cave were carved in two groups, each with five niches. Niches 1–5 formed the upper group and Niches 6–10 the lower one. Two more niches (11–12) were cut above the entrance of the cave, *ca.* 4 m to the west of the other ones. Four niches still contained limestone stelae. Other stelae had fallen out of the niches or may have been destroyed.

C) Western slope of the terrace

Evidence of some areas of activity was found along and at the base of the western slope of the coral terrace.

A man-made clay-plastered floor with a small undisturbed rectangular oven and the remains of one or perhaps two other, badly damaged ovens was found along the upper slope in front of Caves 2 and 3. The oven, 54 cm long, 45 cm wide and 27 cm high, was made with three vertical fragments of reddish-brown circular ceramic platters with a central groove on the sides, open to the west. Clay was used to plaster the oven bottom and to fill the corners and joints between the ceramic fragments. The oven was well cleaned, and then filled and covered with branches to be used again. The associated pottery dates to the Middle Kingdom.

A large functional area with at least five phases of occupation and use and evidence of living floors, post-holes, fire pits, and possible clay structures was identified at the base of the western slope. In this area some hundred broken bread moulds[7] were collected. The associated pottery dates to the Middle Kingdom.

---

[6] See Bard, *et al.* 2005; Fattovich and Bard 2006b.

[7] These artefacts were initially considered to be *tuyères*, but more detailed analysis demonstrated they are bread moulds.

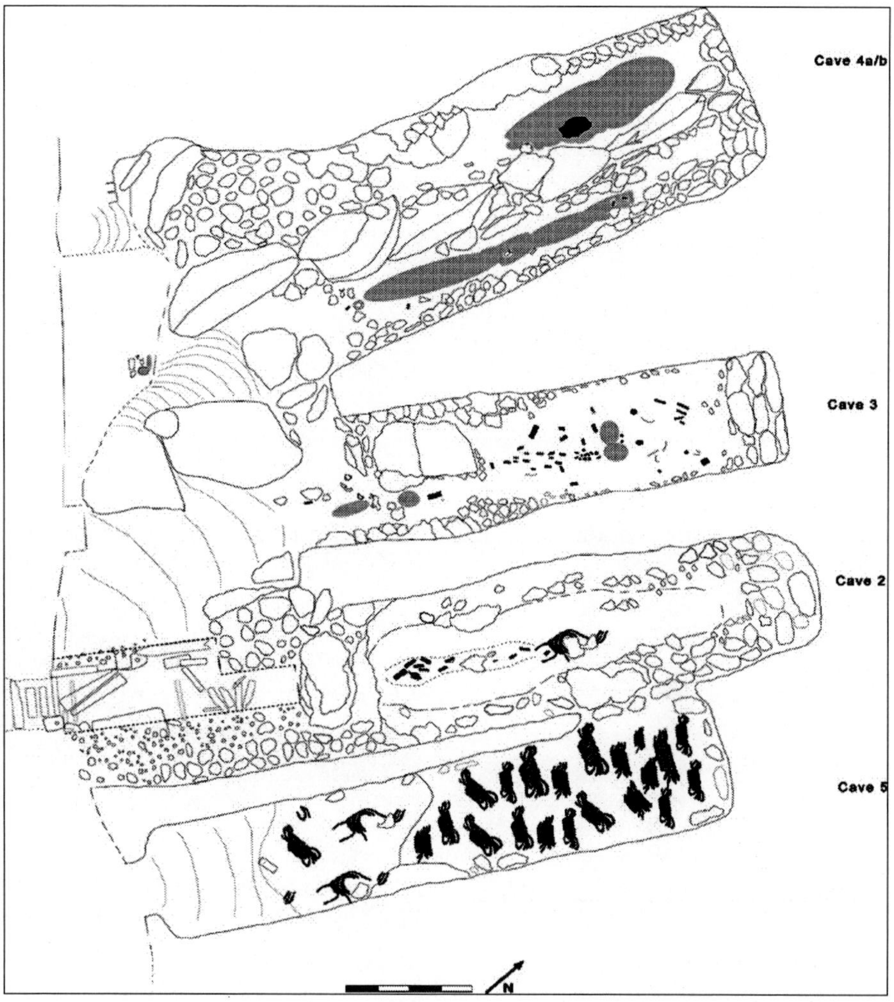

Figure 13:1 Plan of Caves 2–5

D) Southern slope

At the base of the southern slope along the *wādī* the geophysical survey identified an anomaly most likely corresponding to ancient river shore. An anchor of conglomerate stone and four large sherds of a storage jar were found over a layer of soft playa sand with many Middle Kingdom potsherds, a fragment of an imported pot, and many shells and fish bones. The lower stratum consisted of a soft playa sand with shells, but without any artefact.

Finds

Ship timbers and ropes, cargo boxes, sealings and a few inscriptions were the most relevant finds in 2004–2005 and 2005–2006 field seasons.

A) Ship timbers

Ship timbers provide the most ancient archaeological evidence for seafaring in complex watercraft. The technology and dimensions of hull components are consistent with what might be expected of seagoing ships in the Middle Kingdom, and marine incrustations and destruction by shipworms confirm they were actually used in the sea.

Hull planks up to 22 cm and 14–20 cm thick provide evidence of a characteristic Egyptian construction practice, that is, overbuilding, although in this case, because shipworm damage extends up to 5 cm into the plank edge, overbuilding does not seem to be an appropriate term. Some of the planks were virtually sponges with a thin layer of finished surface; no exterior coating survived to the present, but it is likely that the resinous nature of cedar, of which most planks share at least the general characteristics, functioned as a moderately effective repellent. Some planks probably from deck-level structures have small mortise-and-tenon joints, and do not have damage from shipworm.

Five major timber types were identified, so far. They include: a single, but complete deck beam. Rounded on its lower surface, the beam has ledges on either side of a raised central section. Its ends are adzed into precise curvatures that will reflect hull shape, and square holes, probably for lashing, are in an area originally covered by the planks on the side of the hull; hull planks, fastened to other timbers by deep mortise-and-tenon joints and secured by a band of copper composed of four strips threaded through a mortise in the plank's wide faces; possible deck planks, but some have gribble present, which mitigates against that identification. A few planks made with *Acacia nilotica*, about 2.5–3.5 cm thick, with mortise-and-tenon joints with a total length of about 7 cm or 14 cm for the maximum tenon size, and round holes that pass through the plank's wide faces and are associated with grooves about 4–5 cm long that extend to the plank edge. Two blades of steering oars, triangular in shape with rounded corners and a groove on the top, *ca.* 2.0 m long, 0.4 m to 0.15 m wide, 0.12 m thick, and *ca.* 0.2 m long, 0.09 m wide and 0.24 m thick, respectively (Figure 13:2).

Figure 13:2 Blades of steering oars from Cave 2, early New Kingdom

B) Ship ropes

At least 50 coils of rope were recorded on the surface inside Cave 5. Each coil bundle of line is about 1 m long and 60 cm wide, representing at least 20 and probably 30 m of line. Those easily visible from the viewpoint in Cave 2 have 'horizontal' wraps of 15 to 18 turns around 'vertical' loops of about 1 m, of which 15–20 may be counted in the visible portion of the coil (Figure 13:3). The cordage in Cave 5 could not be carefully examined because of its fragility and only preliminary observations have been made. Two kinds of ropes were tentatively distinguished: 1) with a fibre of 3–7 mm width, three yarns 7 mm in diameter, and a strand 3 mm in diameter, and 2) with a fibre of 3–7 mm width, three yarns 17–20 mm in diameter, and a strand 35 mm in diameter.

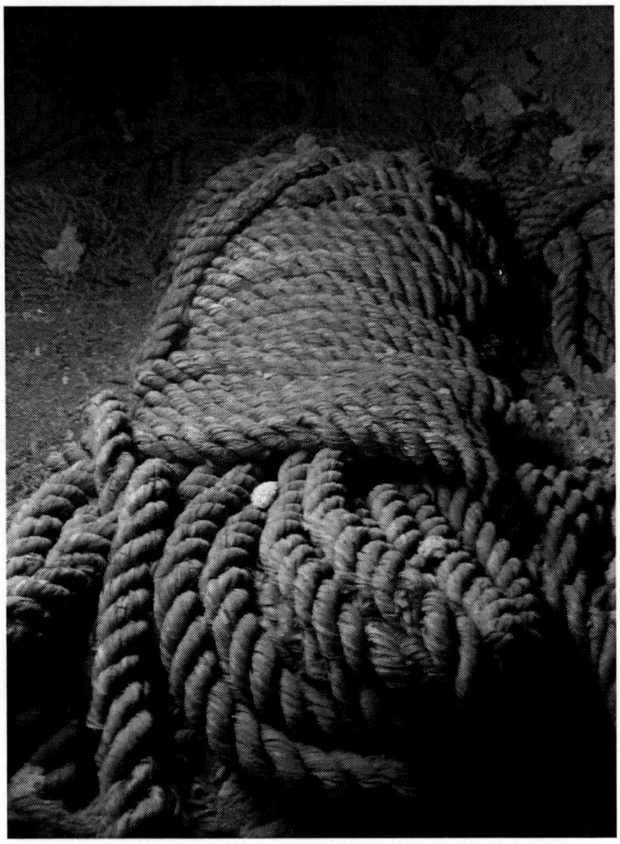

Figure 13:3 Cordage coil in Cave 5

C) Cargo boxes

The remains of twenty-one wooden boxes were found in a sand deposit outside the entrance to Cave 5 and were associated with Middle Kingdom potsherds. All boxes were rectangular, with two feet and, in some cases, the lid was also preserved. They were *ca.* 45–50 cm x 30–31 cm in size. The height could not be recorded as they were broken. An inscription was painted in black ink on the side of a box. The inscription consisted of four lines mentioning year 8 of Amenemhat IV (*ca.* 1786-1777 BC), the name of an official, Djedy, and '... the wonderful things of Punt.' This suggested that they originally contained products from Punt, maybe as part of a ship cargo.

D) Clay sealings

Fourteen clay sealings with sealing impressions were found close to the entrance to the caves, and were mainly associated with wood boxes. One sealing was in the filling of Box 13. Most of them are similar to late twelfth–thirteenth Dynasty types. Two sealings belonged to the same official, whose name is followed by the late Middle Kingdom epithet 'repeating life.'

E) Inscriptions

During the 2004–2005 and 2005–2006 seasons, some new epigraphic monuments and inscribed documents were found at Marsā Gawāsīs:

a) six inscribed stelae;
b) two wooden tags;
c) three 'ostraka'.[8]

The best preserved stela (Stela 5) was found in a sand deposit beneath the niches at the cave entrance. The stela records two expeditions led by officials named Nebsu and Amenhotep to Punt and Bia-Punt respectively during the reign of Amenemhat III. This stela provides new historical information about this king, who ordered a previously unknown expedition to these regions.

F) Exotic pottery

In addition to two potsherds similar in shape to Malayba types already recorded in the 2002–2003 season,[9] a few potsherds comparable with specimens from the Yemeni Tihāmah and Aden were found in the 2004–2005 and 2005–2006 seasons. These fragments were always associated with the remains of timber from ships. They include:

a) One fragment of the upper part (rim and shoulder) of a close bowl with a flat handle, decorated on the top with three lines of small impressed circles, brown ware with mineral inclusions, outside surface with a brown burnished slip and inside surface with a light wiping, from an assemblage dated to the first half of the Middle Kingdom (*ca.* 2000–1800 BC). This fragment is similar in decoration, shape and fabric to types from the region of Aden dated to the second millennium BC.[10]

b) One fragment of a shoulder from a jar, brown ware with burnished surface and mineral inclusion, decorated with two horizontal parallel moulded ledges and five vertical parallel ledges under them from an assemblage dated to the second half of the Middle Kingdom (*ca.* 1800–1650 BC). This fragment is comparable to specimens from Ma'layba (Aden), dated to phase 1 of the Sabir culture (*ca.* 2000–1500 BC).[11]

c) One fragment of a thickened rim from a bowl, dark grey ware with mineral inclusions, outside decorated with horizontal burnished lines under the rim and parallel burnished oblique lines on the body from an assemblage dating to the second half of the Middle Kingdom (*ca.* 1800–1650 BC). This fragment is comparable with types from the Aden region, tentatively dated to the second half of the second-early first millennia BC.[12]

d) Five fragments of closed bowls with thickened rim, brown ware with mineral inclusions, roughly smooth outside surface and burnished inside surface from assemblages dated to the early New Kingdom. These bowls are comparable with specimens from the northern Yemeni Tihāmah, dated to the late third–second millennia BC.[13] Middle Nubian ware was also collected in the 2004–2005 and 2005–2006 seasons. They occur in assemblages dated from late Old Kingdom to late Middle Kingdom, and can be ascribed to cooking vessels, suggesting they were related to domestic activities rather than trade.

G) Wood

The identification of charcoal and wood fragments demonstrated that woods originated from four different regions: 1) the eastern Mediterranean: cedar of Lebanon, pine, deciduous and evergreen oak; 2) the Nile Valley: Nile acacia, white acacia, and sycamore; 3) the Red Sea coastal region: grey mangrove, sea blite; and 4) the South: ebony (*Diospyros* sp.). Tamarisk occurs in the Nile Valley and also on the Red Sea.[14]

Wood remains included mainly cedar of Lebanon, Nile acacia and grey mangrove. For planks, mostly cedar wood was used, while tenons were made from wood of the Nile acacia. Planks of the cargo boxes are predominantly of sycamore, with a few of white acacia and Christ's thorn, while the sides were of tamarisk, Nile acacia and sycamore, and dowels of tamarisk and Nile acacia. Important finds include a few pieces of charred ebony, as this wood was often listed among the imports from Punt.

8 The inscribed documents were examined by El-Sayed Mahfouz (University of Assiut) and Rosanna Pirelli (UNO).

9 Fattovich 2005,

10 See Vogt and Buffa 2005: 440–1, Figure 6 / 6.

11 Ibid.: 439, Figure 2, 8.

12 Comparison with unpublished drawings of materials from Sabir investigated by B. Vogt.

13 Comparison with unpublished drawings of materials from Wādī 'Urq investigated by M. Cattani and M. Tosi.

14 Charcoal and wood were examined by Rainer Gerisch (Free University, Berlin, Germany).

Final remarks

The investigation at Marsā Gawāsīs in 2004–2005 and 2005–2006 demonstrated that the site was used as a seaport, possibly from late Old Kingdom / First Intermediate Period times, in the Middle Kingdom, and in the early New Kingdom. The site was not continuously occupied, but some large rock-cut storerooms were made in the fossil coral terrace. At Wādī Gawāsīs the excavated remains of ship planks, steering blades, anchors and riggings provide evidence of expedition ships, and inscriptions give information about the scale and destination of the seafaring expeditions. A few exotic ceramics from the eastern coast of the southern Red Sea region, and some remains of African ebony are evidence of the destination of these expeditions.

References

Bard, K.A., and Fattovich, R. 2003–2004. Mersa Gawasis: a Pharaonic coastal site on the Red Sea. *Bulletin of the American Research Center in Egypt* 184: 30–1.

———. 2005. Sea expeditions to the Land of Punt: Archaeology at a Pharaonic port in the Red Sea. *Context* (Boston University) 18 (2): 1–3.

———. 2006. Mersa / Wadi Gawāsīs, an Egyptian port on the Red Sea, *Newsletter of the Society for the Study of the Egyptian Antiquities*. Fall 2006: 1–3.

Bard, K.A., Fattovich, R., Arpin T., Childs S. T., Chen Sian Lim, Perlingieri C., Pirelli R. and Zazzaro C. 2005. *Recent Excavations at the Pharaonic Port of Mersa Gawāsīs on the Red Sea, 2004–2005 Field Season.* <http://www.archeogate.com>.

Fattovich, R. and Bard, K.A. 2006a. À la recherche de Pount. Mersa Gaouasis et la navigation ègyptienne dans la mer Rouge, *Égypte, Afrique et Orient* 41: 7–30.

———. 2006b. *Joint Archaeological Expedition at Mersa / Wadi Gawāsīs (Red Sea, Egypt) of the University of Naples 'l'Orientale' (Naples, Italy), Istituto Italiano per l'Africa e l'Oriente (Rome, Italy).*

Fattovich, R. 2005. Marsā Gawāsīs: A Pharaonic coastal settlement in the Red Sea, Egypt. 15–22 in J.C.M. Starkey (ed.), *People of the Red Sea.* Oxford: Archaeopress.

Nibbi, A. 1981. Some Remarks on the Two Monuments from Mersa Gawasis. *ASAE* 64: 69–74.

Sayed, A.M. 1999. Wadi Gasus. 866–8 in K.A. Bard (ed.), *Encyclopaedia of the Archaeology of Ancient Egypt.* London: Routledge.

Shaw, I. (ed.). 2000. *The Oxford History of Ancient Egypt.* Oxford: Oxford University Press.

Vogt, B. and Buffa, V. 2005. Cultural Interactions with the Horn of Africa – A View from Early Arabia. 437–456 in W. Rauning and S. Wenig (eds), *Afrikas Horn. Akten der Ersten Internationalen Littmann-Konferenz 2. bis 5. Mai 2002 in München.* Wiesbaden: Harrassowitz Verlag.

The *Arabægypti Ichthyophagi*: Cultural Connections with Egypt and the Maintenance of Identity

Ross Iain Thomas

The indigenous peoples of the Eastern Desert and Red Sea coast were known as the Trogodytes and the *Ichthyophagi* to the Greeks and Romans. These exonyms were used to describe culturally distinct groups who covered large geographical areas. For example, the term Trogodyte was most commonly used to describe the peoples who populated the area east of the Nile, Egypt and Nubia. The label *Ichthyophagi* was used to characterize the various peoples who populated the coast of what was known then as the Erythræan Sea (or our Red Sea and Indian Ocean).

Within these two groups there were distinctions made. Various labels were used for the nomadic peoples of the Eastern Desert including the Trogodytes and their various tribes such as the Blemmyes, Beja, Colobi, Megabaroi[1] and on occasion Arabs.[2] The Ptolemaic writer Agatharchides made clear distinctions between the *Ichthyophagi* from various parts of the Red Sea, Persian Gulf and South Arabia.[3] Ptolemy writing in the second century AD distinguished a group known as the *Arabægypti Ichthyophagi* in the northern Red Sea,[4] known as the Arabian Gulf, and it is on this group that this paper will focus. However, it is important to recognize that all these accounts are those of Greek or Roman authors whose characterization of these peoples shows a heavy bias.

This paper is based in part upon ongoing doctoral research entitled 'The Maritime Cultures of the Erythræan Sea Trade' and concentrates on the people who facilitated the trade, rather than the trade itself. The study encompasses the first–third centuries AD occupation deposits of the Red Sea ports of Berenike, Aila (modern 'Aqabah) and Myos Hormos[5] (al-Quṣayr al-Qadīm). Here some of the archaeological evidence for the *Icthyophagi* of the northern Red Sea area is presented, focusing on intra-site analysis of Myos Hormos, but also on occasion referring to relevant material from nearby sites such as Berenike or the Roman Eastern Desert forts and quarries (Map 14:1).

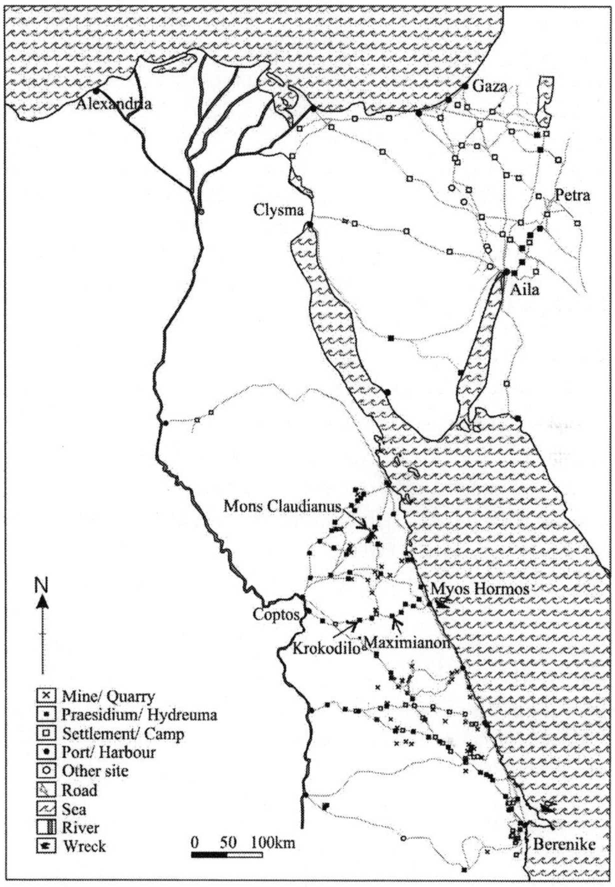

Map 14:1 Map of the northern part of the Red Sea

The Græco-Roman Characterization of the *Ichthyophagi*

It is clear that the Græco-Roman characterization of the *Ichthyophagi* present in the Classical literature of Geographies and Histories was based upon the Ptolemaic sources used by Agatharchides in his *On the Erythræan Sea*.[6] This account was subsequently reused by other authors such as Photius, Strabo, Diodorus and Pliny.[7] Agatharchides's sources were the people involved in the exploration and colonization of parts of the Erythræan Sea coast initiated by Ptolemy II. One such example is that of Simmias who encountered the *Ichthyophagi* when dispatched by Ptolemy III. Simmias described the *Ichthyophagi* as 'insensitive Æthiopians', then gave an

1 Barnard 2005: 23–5.
2 Pliny. *Natural History*: 6.167–9.
3 Agatharchides. *On the Erythraean Sea*: 3.15–22.
4 Ptolemy. *The Geography*: 4.5.
5 For the identification of *Myos Hormos* I follow the arguments cited in Peacock 1993: 226–32 and Bülow-Jacobsen, *et al* 1994: 27–42, subsequently confirmed by excavation discussed by Peacock and Blue 2006: 174.

6 Agatharchides. *On the Erythraean Sea.* tr. Burnstein 1989.
7 In Photius's *The Myriobiblion*, Strabo's *Geography*, Diodorus' *Library of History* and Pliny's *Natural History*.

account of how, despite brutal violence perpetrated against them, they showed no trace of language or indeed of emotions such as compassion or anger:

> They do not come into contact with other tribes nor does the strangeness of the appearance of those who visit them influence the natives, but, gazing at them intently, they remain impassive with their senses unmoved as though no one was present. For not even if someone draws a sword and strikes at them, do they flee; nor, if they suffer insult or blows, do they become angry. Further, the people as a whole do not share in the anger of the victims. Sometimes, even when their children or women are slaughtered before their eyes, they remain unmoved by what has happened, giving no indication of anger or, again, of compassion. In general, even if they experience the most fearful horrors, they remain calm, looking intently at what is happening and nodding their heads to each other. For this reason, people also say that they speak no language, but that they signify everything necessary by imitative gestures of their hands.[8]

Such categorization was clearly derogatory, but it is important to recognize that this is the product of Græco-Roman views on the distinction of other ethnic groups. The characterization of the other peoples of the world as deficient and uncivilized barbarians[9] was at the core of the Græco-Roman 'theory of ethnicity', how they defined ethnic groups and what features of society were perceived as culturally significant.[10] Indeed, from the common standing point of Greek anthropological thought at that time, the *Ichthyophagi*, with their supposed lack of language, would have been perceived as examples of the earliest stages of cultural evolution.[11]

Nevertheless, it is on such colonial accounts that the writers based their characterization of these peoples, which fit into a wider characterization of non-Greeks as somehow deficient barbarians. Agatharchides (and subsequent writers) go on to characterize these people by their way of life, their economy, diet, laws, language, political structure, burial practices, dress and descent.[12] The writer suggests that their environment determined their difference from the Greeks.[13] In this way Agatharchides and subsequent writers illustrated the superiority of Græco-Roman culture, through describing them as barbarians.[14] In doing so it constructed a picture, utilizing fantastic stories with mythical elements that subsequently became popular in medieval and post-medieval illuminated manuscripts (Figure 14:1).

Figure 14:1 Section of the ca. *1460 illuminated manuscript 'Le livre des merveilles de ce monde' depicting the lizard-eating Trogodytes and the headless Blemmyes*[15]

The characterization of and ascription to *Ichthyophagi* identity on the Red Sea

Ostraka recently discovered have revealed similarities between the characterization of the indigenous peoples of the Eastern Desert and Red Sea region in the writings of the Græco-Roman geographers and the actual inhabitants of the ports, quarries and forts. Twenty-two different references to *barbaroi* have been identified at the Roman quarry of Mons Claudianus and the Roman Fort Krokodilô in Wādī Ḥammāmāt.[16] These clearly refer to the elements within the local nomadic population as barbarians and as a threat to the Græco-Roman inhabitants of the Eastern Desert settlements. Other references to the nomadic population of the desert are present at Myos Hormos, where one *ostrakon* is labelled *Pet... Trogodyt.*,[17]

8 Agatharchides. *On the Erythraean Sea*: fragment 41b, after Burnstein tr. 1989: 79–80.

9 For example, see arguments in Hartog 1988 and Hall 1989.

10 A study of the Veso from Madagascar has identified significant differences between the Veso's perspectives on how ethnic identity is constructed, what features are culturally significant and modern anthropological models of the same. In her article Astuti describes different models of group identity construction that she labels 'ethno-theory'. Astuti 1995: 464–82.

11 Burnstein 1989: 79, notes similarities between Agatharchides's views on cultural evolution and those of Lucretius. *On the Nature of Things* 5: 1011–90, Vitruvius. *The Ten Books on Architecture* 2: 1 and Diodorus. *Library of History* 1: 8.

12 Agatharchides. *On the Erythraean Sea*: 31–50.

13 Ibid.: 34.

14 Diodorus. *Library of History*: 3.15.15.

15 'The monstrous races of Ethiopia', Ms 461. The Pierpont Morgan Library, New York, after Moser 1998: 89, plate 1.

16 Cuvigny 2003: 351–2.

17 Van Rengen personal communication: ostraka O543,

although as the exonym Trogodyte was used widely to denote various peoples from across east Africa this could equally represent someone from the region of Adulis or Aksum.[18] At Mons Claudianus, Arabs are referred to twice, although both times in conjunction with the purchase of fish.[19] However, as we do not know why these people have been labelled Arabs, we cannot be certain whether these represent members of one of the Arab nomadic tribes mentioned by Pliny[20] acting as middlemen for the *Ichthyophagi* of the coast, or whether they are the *Arabægypti Ichthyophagi* themselves.

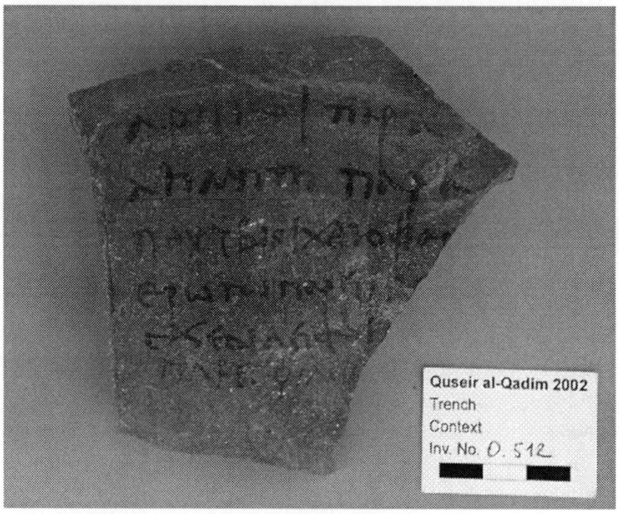

Figure 14:2 Ostraka *O.512 the* Pakubis Ichthyophagos ostraka[21]

In Myos Hormos another *ostrakon*[22] dated to the second century AD, contains the request for a permit for an individual named *Pakubis Ichthyophogos* (Figure 14:2) to move his *schedia*, a small fishing boat or raft, to Philoteras,[23] just north of Myos Hormos. The role of these fishing *schedia* in supplying the Eastern Deserts and quarries with fish are attested in an *ostrakon* from another Roman fort, called Maximianon, on the road between Myos Hormos and the Nile, dated to AD 11,[24] in which Ioulius Maximus was unable to send Gaius Apoliuanus his fish as the *schedia* had not returned to Myos Hormos in time for him to do so.

Archaeological evidence for maritime cultures on the Red Sea

In his paper on the evidence for the *Ichthyophagi* from the southern Red Sea region, Carl Phillips described a tradition of shellfish technology, including shellfish scrapers found in a number of shell middens dating up to the fifth century BC.[25] However this much earlier material culture is not found at Myos Hormos. Instead we have a range of shellfish artefacts, such as items of jewellery (pendants, rings, shell beads) and shell eating utensils, such as bowls, dishes and scoops (Figure 14:3). In itself the presence or absence of such material culture is not enough to identify specific maritime cultures in certain areas of a port. So in order to approach the archaeological evidence for various maritime cultures, it was decided to look at the concentration of different maritime activities taking place within different areas of Myos Hormos. Comparisons between maritime activities as represented by fishing or ship technology and the consumption of certain material culture and fauna can then suggest the presence of different group identities.

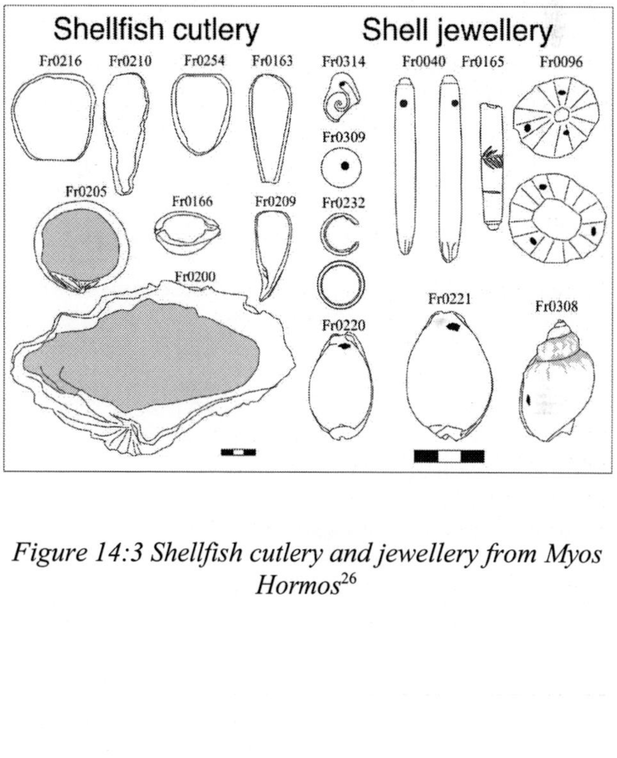

Figure 14:3 Shellfish cutlery and jewellery from Myos Hormos[26]

Tomber 2005: 41.

18 Ibid.

19 Leguilloux 2003: 345, *ostrakon* O. Claud 529 and 830.

20 Pliny. *Natural History*: 6.167–9.

21 Photograph taken by Van Rengen, courtesy of the Quṣayr al-Qadīm finds archive, Southampton University.

22 Van Rengen 2002: 54, ostraka O512.

23 The ancient harbour of *Philoteras* is not yet identified, though it is clearly represented as being the next coastal settlement north of *Myos Hormos* by Ptolemy 4.5.

24 Bülow-Jacobsen, *et al.* 1994: 30, ostraka O.Max 175.

25 Phillips 2004.

26 Drawing by author, after photograph taken by Hamilton-Dyer, courtesy of the Quṣayr al-Qadīm finds archive, Southampton University.

The concentration of different maritime activities such as fishing and ship maintenance can then be compared with the associated ceramic, faunal, epigraphic and other material culture that may represent identity. We are fortunate in possessing a wide range of artefacts preserved in the Eastern Desert, such as elements of fishing gear, including a creel net, floats, weights and hooks (Figure 14:6). If we needed any clues as to how these items were used, there are numerous mosaic depictions of such fishing activities (Figure 14:4). Ethnographic parallels with regard to the environment fished and the techniques used also corroborate the fish catch and species found in the archaeological record, and allow ancient techniques to be reconstructed.

Figure 14:4 Third-century AD depiction of fishermen from North Africa[27]

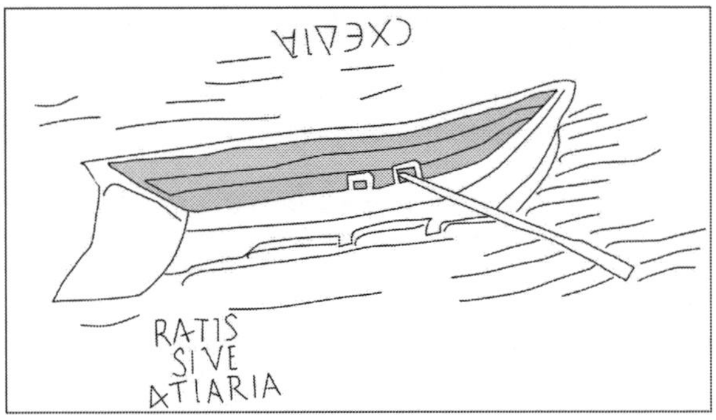

Figure 14:5 The third-century AD Althibarus mosaic, depicting the fishing boat schedia *(Σχεδια)*[28]

From the *ostrakon* discussed earlier, it would appear that fishing from boats was economically significant at Myos Hormos. The Althibarus Mosaic (Figure 14:5) depicts different vessels, and their names in Greek and Latin. The central boat is labelled *schedia*, which may resemble the *schedia* used by *Pakubis Ichthyophagos* and that kept Ioulius Maximus waiting.

From the finds it is possible to reconstruct the different fishing methods used. Passive fishing methods such as basket traps, tidal traps and creels would have been used to catch the large number of parrotfish that were consumed locally and traded with Mons Claudianus.[29] Various casting and dragnets of different sized mesh were used for catching different species of fish (Figure 14:6). A range of multiple and single-hooked lines are represented by the different form and size of hooks. It appears that multiple-hooked line technique was used to catch sea bream in antiquity[30] and some of this fish was then traded from Myos Hormos to the Eastern Desert settlements.[31] Also gorge lines were represented, with the use of baited sharpened sticks to catch large fish and shark species.

Not everyone was involved in fishing. Some people came to Myos Hormos to be involved in the long-distance trade with India, Arabia and East Africa. It is the wealth of this trade that caused the success of Myos Hormos in the first two centuries AD, when it would otherwise not have possessed the natural resources to support a large population. Evidence of the trade is substantial and the subject of ongoing publication by Southampton University.[32] Evidence of the ships used in the trade is also plentiful, a veritable gold mine for maritime archaeologists, looking at the construction of Mediterranean style ships on the Red Sea. A range of ships' artefacts have been discovered at Myos Hormos, including rigging, sail and hull elements (Figure 14:7).

As various artefacts represent different activities and skills involved in the maintenance of these ships, understanding the concentration of such activities across the site may well reflect a range of maritime specializations. For example, we have evidence of various sail-making, rigging, rope-work and carpentry skills involved in the production of the sails, running and standing rigging parts of a ship.[33]

---

27 Drawing by author, after Mosaic 46 from the Sousse Museum.

28 Drawing by author, after the Althibarus mosaic of the Bardo Museum, Tunis.

29 Hamilton-Dyer 2001: 285–7.

30 Bekker-Nielsen 2002: 216; 2004: 83–7, who quotes Oppian's *Halieutika*.

31 Hamilton-Dyer 2001: 285; Leguilloux 2003: 345–7.

32 Peacock and Blue 2006.

33 Running rigging represents the ropes that move, allowing for the sail to be operated and furled, whilst the standing rigging stay still whilst the ship is underway, holding up the mast and yard (which holds the sail).

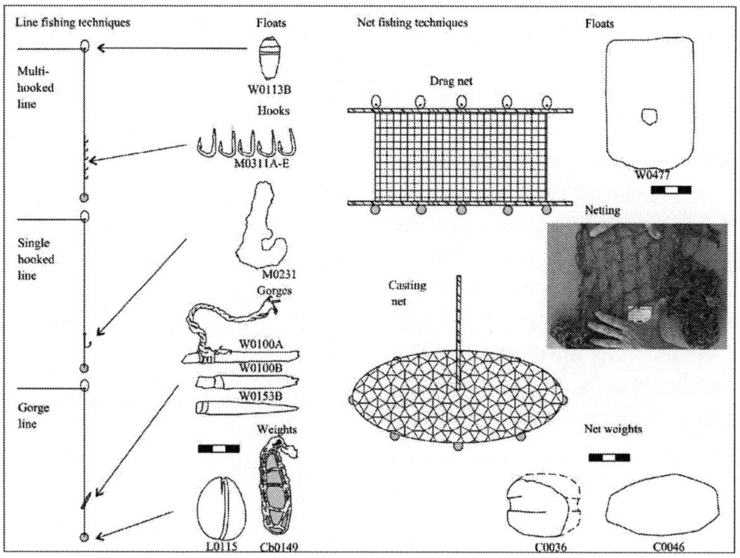

Figure 14:6 Fishing net and line techniques used at Myos Hormos[34]

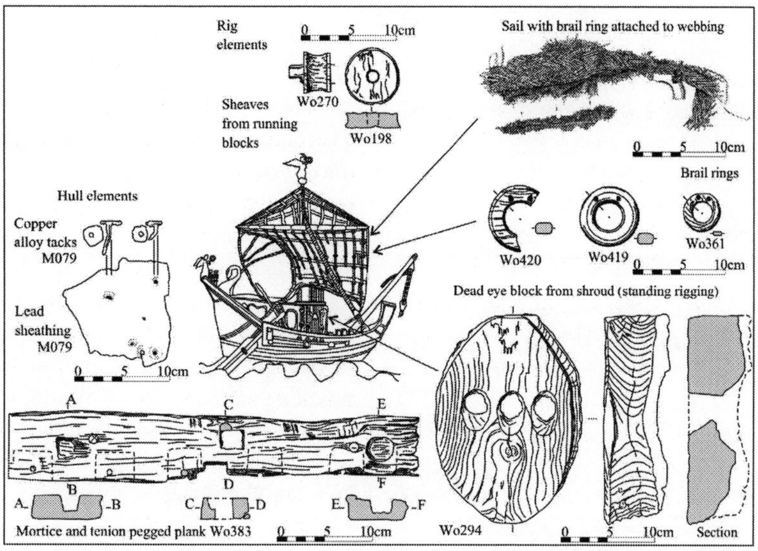

Figure 14:7 Diagram illustrating where artefacts of ship hull, sail and rig elements would have come from a Græco-Roman ship[35]

[34] Drawing by author, after photographs courtesy of the Quṣayr al-Qadīm finds archive, Southampton University.

[35] Copper tacks and lead sheathing by author, the *ca.* AD 200 Porto relief ship depiction redrawn by author after Torr 1895: plate 6.29. All other artefacts drawn by Whitewright, see this volume.

The hull construction of a Mediterranean vessel during the Imperial Roman period was very complicated.[36] This cabinet-like construction involved mortise, tenon and dowel connections that all have to be carefully cut and located (Figure 14:7). Whilst making the boat very sturdy, this method required much work whenever maintenance was needed. The hull was also sheathed with lead, attached by pine pitch (which offered additional waterproofing) and little copper tacks (Figure 14:7), of which there are many examples at Myos Hormos. The ship can then be interpreted as a particularly complicated artefact, made and maintained only by those with highly specialized skills, such as those possessed by shipwrights, riggers and sailmakers — specialized craftsmen for whom one would expect to pay a high premium.

Intra-site analysis of Myos Hormos

When the distribution of over 450 such maritime artefacts is plotted across the site, patterns appear as to what activities are concentrated in which areas (Map 14:2). It should be noted that the vast majority of finds were located in well-preserved dry *sebakh* (desiccated, well-preserved, refuse deposits), situated directly adjacent to domestic or industrial areas, making associations with the function of certain structures possible.

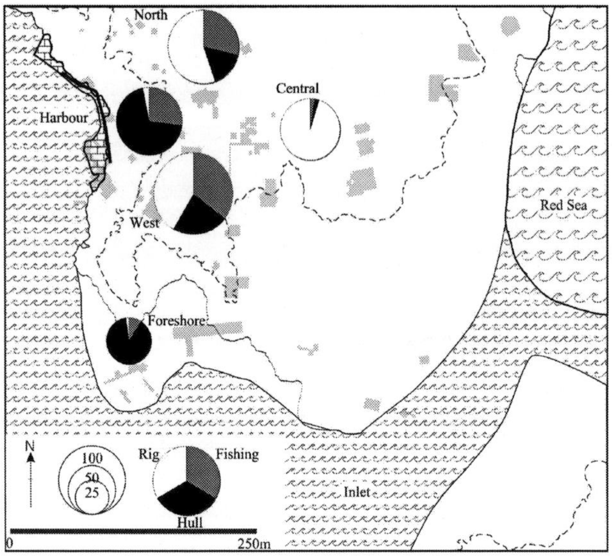

Map 14:2 Distribution of maritime artefacts across Myos Hormos[37]

From Figure 14:9 below it is possible to see how the distribution of maritime artefacts suggests that ship hull maintenance was, not surprisingly, clearly concentrated around the harbour area. Ships' rigging and sails appear to have been stored and maintained mostly in the central and eastern areas of the site. The greatest quantity and variety of fishing equipment were found in the western and northern areas of the site. These included a full range of basket traps, nets, gorge and hooked lines, illustrating a variety of specialized fishing techniques used by the people in that immediate vicinity. Intra-site analysis is only part of the picture: specific detail from certain archaeological contexts can provide a further insight into the relationship between maritime artefacts and the group identities associated with specific deposits or structures.

In the central area during the first and second centuries AD, ship's rigging accounts for the vast majority of the assemblage. These large two-story buildings (Figure 14:8) have been interpreted as possessing a warehouse ground floor and habitation levels on the first floor. The association of habitation areas with the first floor was based upon the presence of domestic occupation layers restricted to the areas around the stairs.[38] Evidence for storage amphoræ and their sealing is preserved, and the domestic artefacts appear to represent a few more of the Egyptian luxuries than are found elsewhere on the site. The people living here are likely to have been associated with the Red Sea trade and to have been wealthier than the other inhabitants of Myos Hormos.

The harbour was constructed from a large amphora and refuse deposit during the late Augustan period.[39] The subsequent use of the harbour rather unsurprisingly mainly consists of the hull maintenance of merchant ships and it is easy to imagine the ships being dragged ashore for maintenance work near the metalworking installations and hearths being used for heating pitch to make the hulls watertight.[40] In one location to the south, evidence of the gruelling annual job of cleaning the hull of its barnacles was preserved.[41] The actual barnacles knocked off the hull still had pitch attached and wood impressions from the hull on them. A number of fishing hooks and some weights were also found, although not the quantity or variety of artefacts found on the western ridge or in the northern limits of the site.

On the western ridge of the site, a complicated series of phases shows a number of different activities taking place (Figure 14:9), but the prevalence of fishing equipment across the site, along with a concentration of shellfish jewellery, shell bowls and scoops, suggests that these were quite different people to those inhabiting the central area. It was also in this area that the *Pakubis Ichthyophagos* and the *Pet...Trogodyt.. ostrakon* were found.

36 Parker 1992: 26–7.
37 Plan of inlet after Blue 2006: 59.
38 Masser 2006: 145.
39 Blue and Peacock 2006: 175.
40 Blue 2006: 84; Thomas 2006: 94.
41 Whittaker, *et al.* 2006: 80.

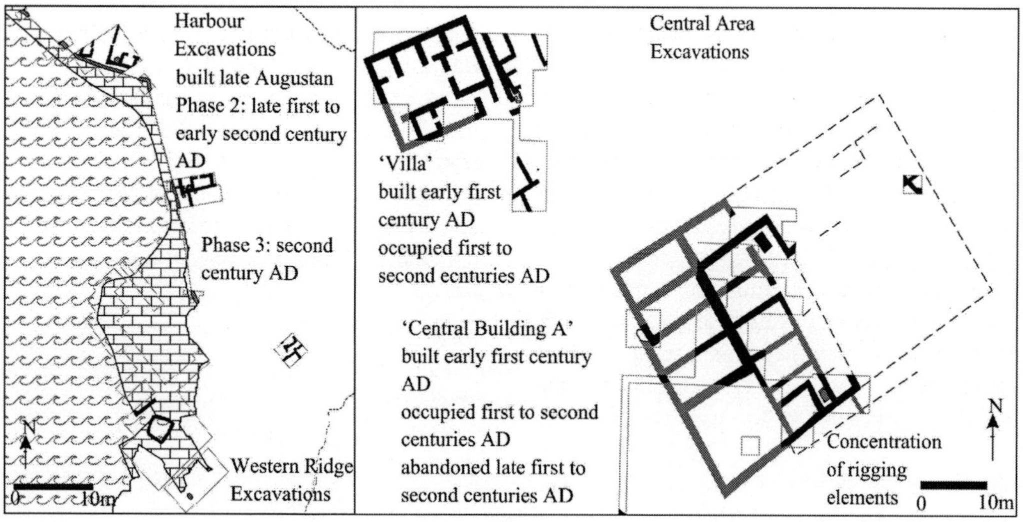

Figure 14:8 Myos Hormos harbour and central areas, with maritime artefacts distribution[42]

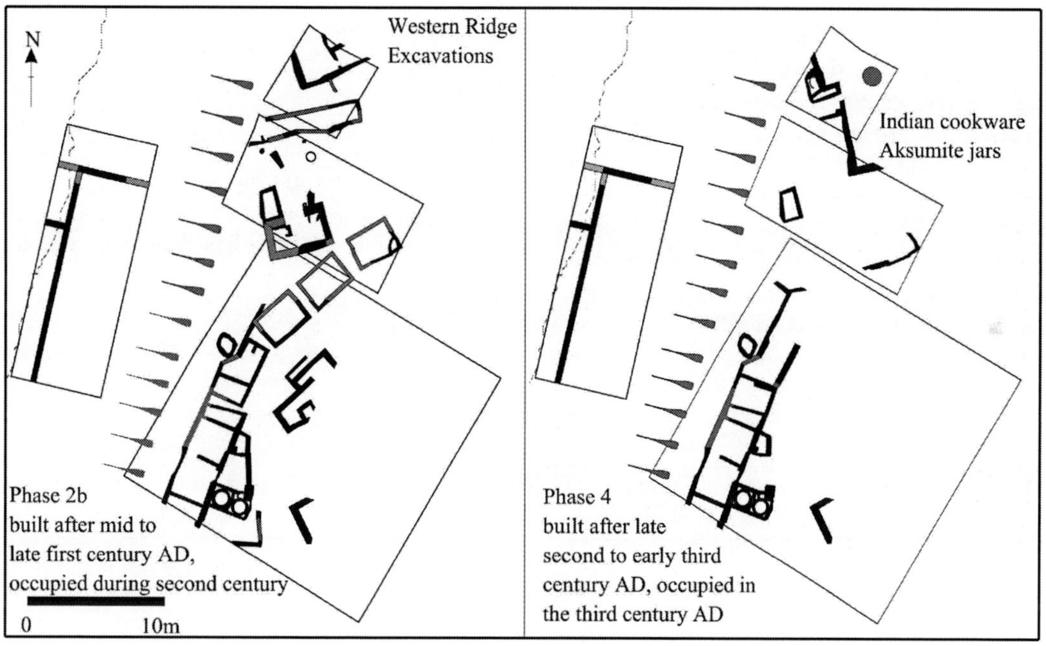

Figure 14:9 Trenches 6G and 8 in the second and third centuries AD[43]

42 Plan after Thomas 2006: 88, Masser 2006: 143, Whitcomb 1982: 33 and 38.

43 Plan after Thomas 2006: 131.

The final phase of occupation on the western ridge, dated to the third century and located only in a small area at the north of Trench 8 (Figure 14:9), shows a complete change from the earlier periods and other areas. Here a significant range of imported Aksumite and Indian pottery forms, such as cooking pots, lamps and jars, suggests close cultural contact with the southern Red Sea.[44] A variety of ship elements were also found in this location. Further evidence on the construction of identity across Myos Hormos is available from assessing the consumption patterns of the inhabitants of different areas of the site. This will reveal what and how they were eating and how this may have been culturally significant in the construction of group identities.

Consumption patterns at Myos Hormos

Interdisciplinary studies into the cultural significance of the consumption of fauna and of material culture[45] have highlighted the significant role that eating and drinking play in the construction of self identity, of which ethnic identity is an important part.[46] As a result of such 'culturalist' approaches to food consumption, recent integrated approaches to the archaeology of food, incorporating pottery, animal bones and plant remains, have been used to understand the cultural significance of how food was prepared and eaten in the Roman world.[47] At the Red Sea ports and Eastern Desert settlements, fauna were found to originate from four distinctively different environments or sources. The consumption of fauna from different environments may suggest culturally significant differences in the diets of different groups on site. These diets include:

- Domestic animals that had to be sourced from the Nile valley or were difficult to keep in the Eastern Desert, such as pigs, chicken, cattle and fish caught from the Nile itself,[48] including Nile catfish.
- Eastern Desert fauna, such as goats and hunted ibex or gazelle.
- Red Sea mammals, turtles and fish.
- Animals whose primary uses were for transport,[49] such as camels, horses and donkeys.

From the faunal remains, one can suggest culturally significant differences in the diets of certain groups at Myos Hormos and in the wider Eastern desert region. There were certainly similarities between the faunal refuse of the garrisons at the Roman Wādī Ḥammāmāt forts of Maximianon and Krokodilô, and the deposits at Berenike (Trench 7) and Myos Hormos[50] associated with the warehouses and ship maintenance required for the Erythræan Sea trade. These 'Græco-Roman' diets were heavily reliant on domesticated mammals, especially pig and chicken. Meanwhile the fish consumed, though large in quantity, were limited to certain species.

There were similarities in the heavy reliance upon diverse Red Sea fauna within some Ptolemaic and early Roman deposits at Berenike (Trenches 2, 11 and 13) and those of the fishermen at Myos Hormos present in the western and northern areas of the site (Trenches 8, 6B and 6D). The fish, turtle and sea mammals consumed suggest a much more varied used of Red Sea fauna as well as the presence of locally hunted wild animals and birds. How these people were eating was also different. This is clear from the fine wares used by all inhabitants of Myos Hormos in the act of preparing and serving food. It is also clear from the consumption of wine and oils from Egypt, represented archaeologically by *amphora* stoppers. Archaeologists have long attached cultural significance to Roman red-slipped terra *sigillata* wares, where 'the production and trade of Italian-style red pottery can ... be seen as a mechanism for both spreading and defining a "Roman" material culture and indeed a Roman identity.'[51] The cultural significance of how ceramic fine wares were used in the Roman period has been noticed before,[52] and approaches to how ceramics were used differently can highlight culturally significant differences in both form and ware.[53]

44 Thomas and Masser 2006: 137–8.

45 See examples in Falk 1994, Lupton 1996 and Appaduri 1986.

46 On archaeological approaches to ethnicity and group identities see Jones 1997 and Díaz-Andreu, *et al.* 2005.

47 Meadows 1995: 138, Hawkes 2002: 45.

48 Van Neer and Lentacker 1996: 346–50; Van Neer and Ervynck 1998: 365–8, 383–6; 1999: 333–40.

49 Hamilton-Dyer 2001: 296–9.

50 Such as the harbour Trench 7A and central areas labelled in Table 14:2 as Trenches 'C' and 2B.

51 Perkins 2000: 203.

52 For example, see Okun 1989, Swan 1992: 1–33 and Meadows 1995: 131–40.

53 For example, the consumer theory methodology used by Fincham 2002: 34–44, though any such methodology comparing the distribution of different ceramic forms requires a standard guideline for categorizing forms. In this study the standard guidelines for archiving Roman pottery are used, detailed in Webster 1969 and Darling 1994.

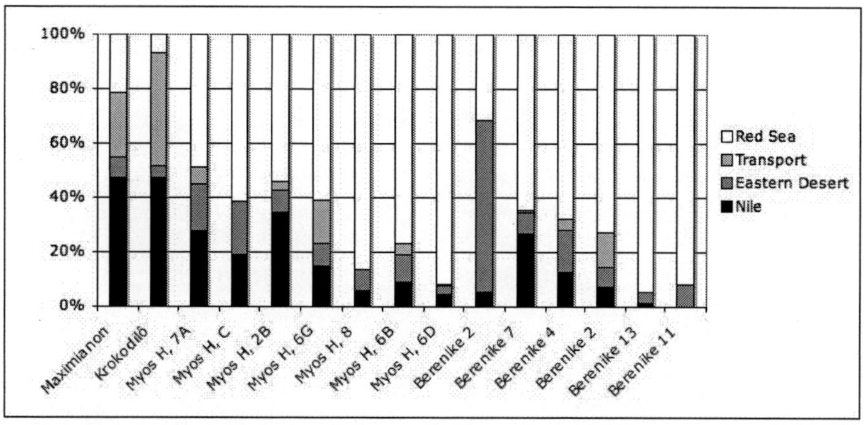

Table 14:1 The consumption of different fauna in the Eastern Desert ports of Myos Hormos and Berenike and the Eastern Desert forts of Maximianon and Krokodilô[54]

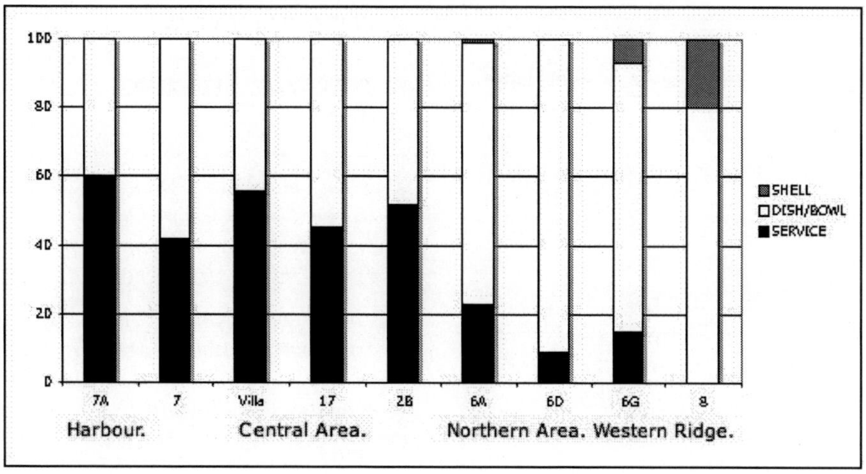

Table 14:2 The use of different fineware forms at Myos Hormos[55]

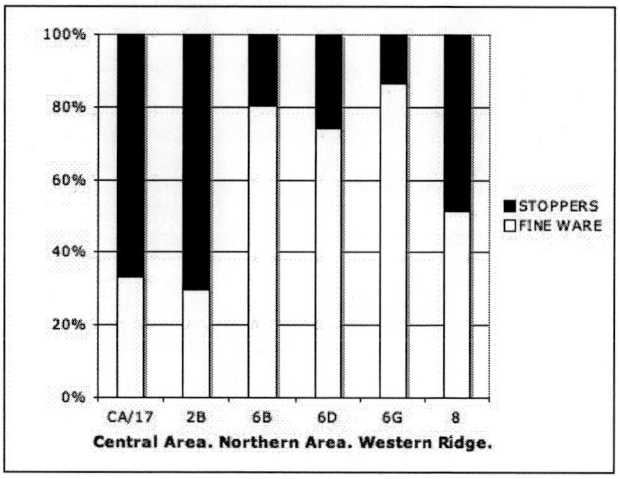

Table 14:3 The consumption of wine and oil represented by amphora stoppers, using fine-ware sherds as a proxy[56]

54 Based on bone and bone fragment counts. Data for *Maximianon* and *Krokodilô* after Leguilloux 2003, data for *Berenike* after Van Neer and Lentacker 1996; Van Neer and Ervynck 1998; 1999, data for *Myos Hormos* after Wattenmaker 1979 and unpublished data courtesy of Hamilton-Dyer, publication in progress.

55 The Villa data is after Whitcomb 1979; 1982. All other trenches are based on unpublished data courtesy of Tomber, publication in progress.

56 Fineware data from Whitcomb 1979; 1982 and Tomber, in progress. Stopper data from Thomas, in progress.

The typical fine wares found in Egypt during the first three centuries AD are well represented at Myos Hormos. The 'Roman' red-slipped *terra sigillata* wares, the Egyptian turquoise-blue faience wares and Upper Egyptian thin-walled wares[57] were found in all areas. It is, however, not the wares but the forms that appear to be culturally significant, which represent different ways of eating, since only specific forms were used in certain contexts. For example, the use of complementary service forms (represented in black in Table 14:2), including platters, cups, closed vessels, mugs and beakers, were only used by those who ate a 'Græco-Roman' diet, consumed large quantities of imported wine and oils (Table 14:3), and were involved in the Erythræan Sea trade.

Deposits limited to bowls or dish forms only (represented in white) represented a more Red Sea-fauna diet that also included numerous examples of fishing equipment. In these cases, shell bowls, dishes and scoops (Table 14:2, in grey) were relatively common. They also consumed a much smaller quantity of wine and oil (Table 14:3).

Conclusions

Despite the derogatory use of the characterization of the *Ichthyophagi* in the Græco-Roman literature, the *Ichthyophagi* were able to integrate into the poly-ethnic social system of the Erythræan Sea trade quite well. The example of *Pakubis* illustrates that they appear to have used the ethnonym given to them, at least in the context of applying for permits, to have written their own requests for permits in Greek, and they made themselves indispensable through supplying the Roman traders, forts and quarries with fish and fish products. It is also not unreasonable to assume that they were involved in the maintenance, crewing and piloting of trading vessels in local or more distant waters, as they would have possessed useful skills for this endeavour. What happened to them when Myos Hormos fell into disuse is unclear. Maybe they persisted at the site in a manner not yet archaeologically visible, or perhaps they moved towards other opportunities at Berenike or Aila.

References

Agatharchides. Burnstein, S.M. (tr.). 1989. *On the Erythraean Sea*. London: Hakluyt Society.

Appaduri, A. 1986. Introduction: commodities and the politics of value. 3-63 in A. Appaduri (ed.), *The Social Life of Things: commodities in cultural perspective.* Cambridge: Cambridge University Press.

Astuti, R. 1995. 'The vezo are not a kind of people': identity, difference, and 'Ethnicity' among a fishing people of Western Madagascar. *American Ethnologist* 3: 464–82.

Barnard, H. 2005. Sire, il n'y a pas de Blemmyes: a re-evaluation of historical and archaeological data. 23–40 in J.C.M. Starkey (ed.), *People of the Red Sea: Proceedings of Red Sea Project II Held in the British Museum October 2004*. BAR International Series 1395. Oxford: Archaeopress.

Bekker-Nielsen, T. 2002. Nets, boats and fishing in the Roman world. *Classica et Mediaevallia* 53: 215–33.

———. 2004. The Technology and productivity of ancient sea fishing. 83–95 in T. Bekker-Nielsen (ed.), *Ancient Fishing and Fish Processing in the Black Sea Region*. Aarhus: Aarhus University Press.

Blue, L. 2006. Trench 12. 81–4 in D.P.S. Peacock and L. Blue (eds), *Myos Hormos — Quseir al-Qadim: Roman and Islamic ports on the Red Sea.* Volume 1: *The Survey and Excavations 1999–2003*. Oxford: Oxbow Books.

———. 2006. The Sedimentary History of the Harbour Area. 68–74 in D.P.S. Peacock and L. Blue (eds), *Myos Hormos — Quseir al-Qadim: Roman and Islamic ports on the Red Sea.* Volume 1: *The Survey and Excavations 1999–2003*. Oxford: Oxbow Books.

Bülow-Jacobsen, A., Cuvigny, H. and Fournet, J. 1994. The Identification of *Myos Hormos*: new papyrological evidence. *Bulletin de L'Institut français d'archéologie orientale* 94: 27–42.

Cuvigny, H. 2003. Le fonctionnement du réseau. 295–360 in H. Cuvigny (ed.), *La Route de Myos Hormos: l'armée romaine dans le désert Oriental d'Égypte.* Cairo: IFAO.

Darling, M.J. 1994. *Guidelines for the Archiving of Roman Pottery*. London: Study Group for Roman Pottery.

Díaz-Andreu, M., Lucy, S., Babic, S. and Edwards, D.N. 2005. *The Archaeology of Identity*. Oxford and New York: Routledge.

Diodorus. Oldfather, C.H. (tr.). 1933. *Diodorus Siculus; Library of History*. Cambridge: Harvard University Press: Loeb Classical Library.

Falk, P. 1994. *The Consuming Body*. London: Sage.

Fincham, G. 2002. Consumer theory and Roman North Africa: a post-colonial approach to the ancient economy. 34–44 in M. Carruthers, C. van Driel-Murray, A. Gardner, J. Lucas, L. Revell and E. Swift (eds), *TRAC 2001*. Oxford: Oxbow Books.

Hall, E. 1989. *Inventing the Barbarian: Greek self-definition through tragedy*. Oxford: Clarendon Press.

Hamilton-Dyer, S. 2001. The Faunal Remains. 251–312 in V.A. Maxfield and D.P.S. Peacock (eds), *Survey and Excavation. Mons Claudianus*: Volume II *Excavations* part 1. Cairo: IFAO.

———. In progress. The Faunal Remains. In D.P.S. Peacock and L. Blue (eds), *Myos Hormos — Quseir al-*

57 For discussion of types found in the Eastern Desert, see Tomber 2006.

Qadim: Roman and Islamic ports on the Red Sea: fauna and flora. Oxford: Oxbow Books.

Hartog, F. 1988. *The Mirror of Herodotus: the representation of the other in the writing of history.* Berkeley, Los Angeles, London: University of California Press.

Hawkes, G. 2002. Wolves' nipples and otters' noses? Rural foodways in Roman Britain. 45–50 in M. Carruthers, C. van Driel-Murray, A. Gardner, J. Lucas, L. Revell and E. Swift (eds), *TRAC 2001.* Oxford: Oxbow Books.

Jones, S. 1997. *The Archaeology of Ethnicity: constructing identities in the past and present.* London: Routledge.

Leguilloux, M. 2003. Les animaux et l'alimentation d'après la faune: les restes de l'alimentation carnée des fortins de Krokodilo et Maximianon. 549–88 in H. Cuvigny (ed.), *La Route de Myos Hormos: L'armée romaine dans le désert Oriental d'Égypte.* Cairo: IFAO.

Lucretius. Esolen, A.M. (tr.). 1995. *On the Nature of Things.* Baltimore: Johns Hopkins University Press.

Lupton, D. 1996. *Food, the Body and the Self.* London: Sage.

Masser, P. 2006. Trench 17. 141–6 in D.P.S. Peacock and L. Blue (eds), *Myos Hormos — Quseir al-Qadim: Roman and Islamic ports on the Red Sea.* Volume 1: *Survey and Excavations 1999–2003.* Oxford: Oxbow Books.

Meadows, K. 1995. You are what you eat. 131–40 in S. Cottam, D. Dungworth, S. Scott and J. Taylor (eds), *TRAC 94: Proceedings of the Fourth Annual Theoretical Roman Archaeology Conference.* Oxford: Oxbow Books.

Moser, S. 1998. *Ancestral Images: the iconography of human origins.* Stroud: Sutton.

Okun, M.L. 1989. *The Early Roman Frontier in the Upper Rhine Area: assimilation and acculturation on a Roman frontier.* BAR International Series 547. Oxford: Archaeopress.

Oppian. Mair, A.W. (tr.). 1928. *Halieutika.* London: Heinemann.

Parker, A.J. 1992. *Ancient Shipwrecks of the Mediterranean and the Roman Provinces.* BAR International Series 580. Oxford: Archaeopress.

Peacock, D.P.S. 1993. The Site of *Myos Hormos*: a view from space. *Journal of Roman Archaeology* 6: 226–32.

Peacock, D.P.S. and Blue, L. (eds). 2006. *Myos Hormos — Quseir al-Qadim: Roman and Islamic ports on the Red Sea* Volume 1: *Survey and Excavations 1999–2003.* Oxford: Oxbow Books.

Perkins, P. 2000. Power, culture and identity in the Roman economy. 183-212 in J. Huskinson (ed.). *Experiencing Rome: culture, identity and power in the Roman Empire.* Milton Keynes and New York: The Open University and Routledge.

Phillips, C.S. 2004. The Ichthyophagi of the Southern Red Sea and Gulf of Aden. Unpublished paper presented at Red Sea Project II. *People of the Red Sea.* British Museum Study Day,

Photius. Freese, J.H. (tr.). 1920. *The Myriobiblion (The Library of Photius).* New York: Macmillan.

Pliny. Rackham, H. (tr.). 1993. *Natural History.* Cambridge: Harvard University Press.

Ptolemy. Stevenson, E.L. (tr.). 1932. *The Geography.* New York: Dover Publications.

Strabo. Jones, H. (tr.). 1917. *Geography.* Cambridge: Harvard University Press.

Swan, V. G. 1992. Legio VI and its Men: African legionaries in Britain. *Journal of Roman Pottery Studies* 5: 1–33.

Thomas, R. I. 2006. Trench 15. 87–94 in D.P.S. Peacock and L. Blue (eds), *Myos Hormos — Quseir al-Qadim: Roman and Islamic ports on the Red Sea.* Volume 1: *Survey and Excavations 1999–2003.* Oxford: Oxbow Books.

———. In progress. The vessel stoppers. In D.P.S. Peacock and L. Blue (eds), *Myos Hormos - Quseir al-Qadim: Roman and Islamic ports on the Red Sea: Ceramic and related objects.* Oxford: Oxbow Books.

Thomas, R.I. and Masser, P. 2006. Trench 8. 127–40 in D.P.S. Peacock and L. Blue (eds), *Myos Hormos — Quseir al-Qadim: Roman and Islamic ports on the Red Sea.* Volume 1: *Survey and Excavations 1999–2003.* Oxford: Oxbow Books.

Tomber, R.S. 2005. Trogodytes and Troglodytes: exploring interaction on the Red Sea during the Roman period. 41–50 in J.C.M. Starkey (ed.), *People of the Red Sea: Proceedings of Red Sea Project II Held in the British Museum October 2004.* BAR International Series 1395. Oxford: Archaeopress.

———. 2006. The Pottery. 3–328 in V.A. Maxfield and D.P.S. Peacock (eds), *Survey and Excavation Mons Claudianus.* Volume III: *Ceramic Vessels and Related Objects.* Cairo: IFAO.

———. In progress. The Pottery. In D.P.S. Peacock and L. Blue (eds), *Myos Hormos — Quseir al-Qadim: Roman and Islamic ports on the Red Sea: Ceramic and Related Objects.* Oxford: Oxbow.

Torr, C. 1895. *Ancient Ships.* Cambridge: Cambridge University Press.

Van Neer, W. and Ervynck, A.M.H. 1998. The Faunal Remains. 349-88 in S.E. Sidebotham and W.Z. Wendrich (eds), *Berenike 1996. Report of the 1996 Excavations at Berenike (Egyptian Red Sea Coast) and the survey of the Eastern Desert.* Leiden: CNWS.

———. 1999. The Faunal Remains. 325-48 in S.E. Sidebotham and W.Z. Wendrich (eds), *Berenike 1997. Report of the 1997 Excavations at Berenike (Egyptian Red Sea Coast) and the survey of the Eastern Desert.* Leiden: CNWS.

Van Neer, W. and Lentacker, A. 1996. The Faunal Remains. 337-54 in S.E. Sidebotham and W.Z. Wendrich (eds), *Berenike 1995. Report of the 1995*

Excavations at Berenike (Egyptian Red Sea Coast) and the survey of the Eastern Desert. Leiden: CNWS.

Van Rengen, W. 2002. Sebakh excavations and the written material. 53–4 in D.P.S. Peacock and L. Blue (eds), *Myos Hormos — Quseir al-Qadim: Roman and Islamic ports on the Red Sea.* Volume 1: *Survey and Excavations 1999–2003*. Oxford: Oxbow Books.

Vitruvius. Warren, H.L. (tr.). 1960. *The Ten Books on Architecture*. New York: Dover Publications.

Wattenmaker, P., Lacovara, P., Beck, C.W. and Moray, L. 1979. Flora and Fauna. 250-6 in D. Whitcomb and J.H. Johnson (eds), *Quseir al-Qadim 1978 Preliminary Report*. Cairo: ARCE.

Webster, G. 1969. *Romano-British Coarse Pottery*. CBA Research Reports 6. London: Council for British Archaeology.

Whitcomb, D.S. and Johnson, J.H. (eds). 1979. *Quseir al-Qadim 1978: Preliminary Report.* Malibu: ARCE, Undena Publications.

———. 1982. *Quseir al-Qadim 1980: Preliminary Report.* Malibu: ARCE, Undena Publications.

Whittaker, P., Walsh, M. and Blue, L. 2006. Trench 10A, 10B and 10C. 74–81 in D.P.S. Peacock and L. Blue (eds), *Myos Hormos — Quseir al-Qadim: Roman and Islamic ports on the Red Sea.* Volume 1: *Survey and Excavations 1999–2003*. Oxford: Oxbow Books.

Acknowledgements

Access to the data used in this study was only available because of an opportunity to participate at the Quṣayr al-Qadīm — *Myos Hormos* excavations, for which I owe David Peacock and Lucy Blue my gratitude. Access to unpublished data on the ceramics and fauna from *Myos Hormos* was very generously granted by Roberta Tomber and Sheila Hamilton-Dyer, whose important studies are in progress. Comments on aspects of and access to the Pakubis Ichthyophagos *ostraka* were granted by Wilfried van Rengen. I should also like to thank Louise Revell, Carl Phillips, John Cooper and Athena Trakadas, who have provided useful comments that have been incorporated within my study. Finally I would like to thank the Quṣayr al-Qadīm team for their input, specifically Julian Whitewright for the often long and detailed discussions on various aspects of my research topic (and some particularly fine illustrations).

Aila and Clysma: The Rise of Northern Ports in the Red Sea in Late Antiquity

Walter Ward

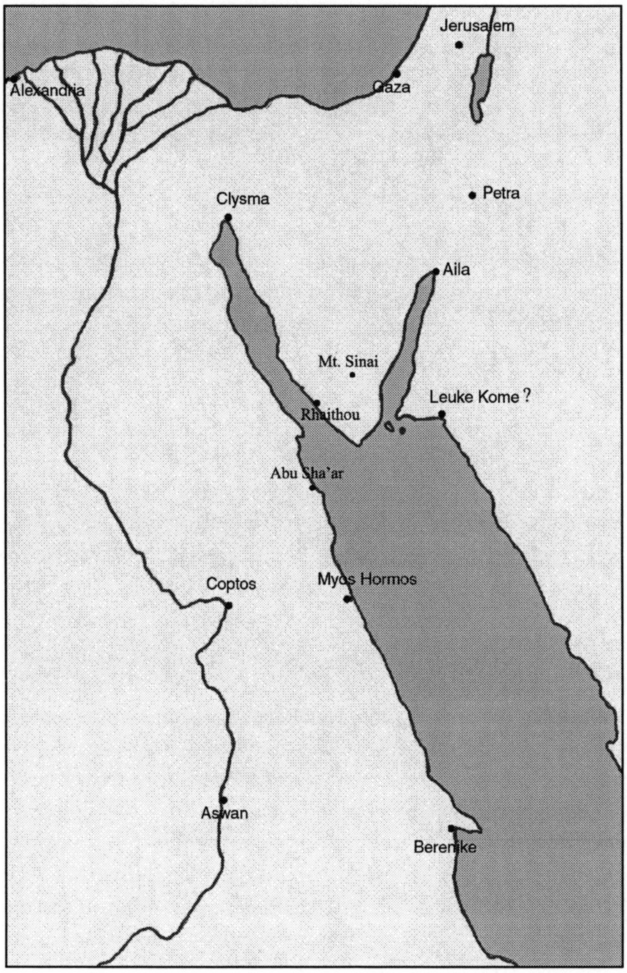

Map 15:1 Location of Red Sea Ports

During the Red Sea Project I in 2002, William Facey convincingly argued that merchants preferred southerly ports in the Red Sea because of the difficulty of sailing north against prevailing winds. He wrote,

> [i]t is this fact, that it is easy to sail south out of the Red Sea but hard to sail north, that provides some explanation why, in antiquity and Islamic times, ports on the Egyptian side show a tendency to be some way down the coast… Clysma / Suez at the northern end might have been in an obvious position geographically, but in navigational terms it was ill suited because of the difficulties of sailing into the wind.[1]

And yet, during the period of late antiquity, roughly dating from the fourth to the mid-seventh century CE, Clysma became one of the most important ports on the Red Sea. Another port, located at Aila, modern 'Aqabah, also rose to prominence during this period. These ports even outlasted the occupation of Berenike and for one hundred years were the principal ports in Roman territory on the Red Sea. This paper seeks to understand this conundrum. If Aila and Clysma were situated in such a bad location because of the prevailing winds, what led to their prominence?

Literary and archaeological evidence clearly demonstrate that the apex of trade in the Red Sea basin began with the Roman annexation of Egypt and lasted for about two centuries. Ports such as Berenike and Myos Hormos on the Egyptian side of the Red Sea, and Leuke Kome in the Nabataean kingdom flourished. However, the nature of Red Sea trade changed as a result of the decline of imperial authority, insecurity, and economic downturn during the third-century crisis. Myos Hormos and Leuke Kome were abandoned, and the Aksumite kingdom rose to prominence. Merchants from the Roman empire may have abandoned direct trade with India, although the causes and the results of this transformation are still largely mysterious.

Compared to the earlier Roman period, the study of the Red Sea in late antiquity has been relatively neglected. The reasons for this are understandable, since we lack the detailed written sources that exist for the earlier period. There is no *Periplus*, no Strabo, and no Pliny. The references to Red Sea trade are scattered through a wide variety of sources, such as pilgrimage accounts, minor histories, theological works, and hagiographic literature. However, the recent archaeological excavations at Berenike, Aila, Abū Sha'ar, Aksum, and other sites throughout the Red Sea basin help to remedy the lack of literary sources.

Overview of ports in the Red Sea in Late Antiquity

Four major Roman ports existed on the Red Sea during late antiquity: Berenike, Clysma, Aila and Iotabe. Of these four, Berenike and Aila have been extensively excavated.[2]

[1] Facey 2004: 11.

[2] On Berenike, see Sidebotham and Wendrich 1995, 1996, 1998, 2000, 2001–2002, and *forthcoming*; Wendrich 2003. For Aila, see Parker 1997, 1998, 2000b, 2002b, and 2003.

Clysma was the focus of an archaeological expedition before the Second World War, but the results of the excavation were not published until 1966.[3] The excavation report is of limited use. Iotabe has not been the subject of excavations, and its location remains to be discovered.

Berenike

Since Berenike has been the focus of numerous publication reports, articles, and papers, it needs no introduction. It is sufficient to state that Berenike suffered an economic decline in the late third century but rebounded in the mid-fourth century once imperial order was restored.

Archaeological evidence from Berenike clearly shows its prominent role as a port during late antiquity, in large part thanks to the extraordinary preservation at the site. Thousands of peppercorns, as well as other spices, including coconut, sesame and cumin, have been discovered in late antique contexts from Berenike.[4] Whether these were shipped directly from India or conveyed through Aksum or South Arabia is unknown.[5] Aksumite ceramics, as well as large quantities of *amphoræ* from Aila, show Berenike's contacts throughout the Red Sea.[6] Berenike's imports from within the Roman empire suggest that economic contact was primarily with the Eastern Mediterranean, paralleling contemporary developments at Alexandria.[7] This evidence suggests that Berenike, although maybe not as prosperous as it was in the first century, was still the principal Roman port in the mid-fourth and fifth centuries.

The exact date of Berenike's abandonment is unknown. The *Martyrium Sancti Arethæ*, in a passage dated to 524–525 CE, provides the last literary reference to maritime activities at the site.[8] Nevertheless, evidence from the port itself suggests that major activities had disappeared by the late fifth or early sixth century.[9]

Clysma

During the Ptolemaic period, a port was founded at the tip of the Gulf of Suez. Named Arsinoë, it seems to have been intended as a major port on the Red Sea, and there are a few indications that it functioned as a port, if a relatively minor one.[10] The name Clysma first appears in the second century CE in Ptolemy's *Geography*, where it is listed as a fort, not a port.[11] Ptolemy also mentions 'Trajan's River' which linked the Nile with the Red Sea at Clysma. It is unknown if this canal was navigable, but a comment in Lucian suggests that it was — unless this was intended to mock Trajan's attempt.[12] On the other hand, papyri mention conscripted labour in conjunction with the canal, but these occurrences might be related to irrigation expansion or maintenance rather than work on a navigable canal.[13]

Little is reported about Clysma between the second and the late fourth century, which led Mayerson to suggest that the site was relatively deserted.[14] There is little evidence that the site was inhabited until the visit of the pilgrim Egeria, who visited the site in 383 CE.[15] Her account served as Peter the Deacon's primary source in the eleventh-century *Liber de locis sanctis*.[16] According to Peter the Deacon, Clysma was an important port for trade with India (probably Aksum) and was the residence of a Roman *logothete* who travelled to India (once again, probably Aksum) each year as Roman ambassador. He also mentioned that this was the only port that Roman merchants used to trade with India, although this is clearly erroneous.[17] Later sources, such as the *Martyrium Sancti Arethæ* and the pilgrim Antoninus Placentinus suggest that Clysma remained a significant port throughout late

3 Bruyère 1966.

4 On the botanical remains discovered at Berenike, see Cappers 2006: 49–138 and 156–66.

5 Sidebotham 2002: 230–1.

6 Tomber 2004: 397–400.

7 Sidebotham 2002: 231–2. On Alexandria, see Majcherek 2004. Interestingly, although *amphoræ* from Gaza represent a large portion of the finds at Alexandria and Aila, they are little represented at Berenike. Tomber 2004: 400.

8 *Martyrium Sancti Arethæ* 44–5. Berenike supplied only seven out of sixty ships (transports or warships?) for an invasion of south Arabia; however, the historical accuracy of this source is questionable. As the ships were ordered to take part in an invasion of South Arabia by the Aksumite king Elesbas, these ships were more than likely Aksumite. This implies that this passage tells us more about Aksumite commercial interests than about the relative prominence of the Roman ports.

9 Sidebotham and Wendrich 2000: 417; Sidebotham and Wendrich 1998: 454.

10 The evidence comes from the fact that Agatharchides began his account of the Red Sea from this port, and Gallus departed from Arsinoë when he sailed to Leuke Kome; however, since the *Periplus* does not mention Clysma, its role in trade in the mid-first century CE was likely minimal. On Gallus and the expedition to Arabia, see Strabo 16.4.23 and Jameson 1968.

11 *Geographia* 4.5.54. The fort is also mentioned in a papyrus dated to 176 CE. See Fink 1971: 299, Section 76, column xviii, numbers 51 and 52, lines 4 and 16 = P. Hamb.39.

12 Lucian, *Alexander Pseudomantis* 44.16–18.

13 Sijpesteijn 1963: 72–9. See, for example, P.Oxy. 12.1426.

14 Mayerson 1996: 122.

15 Devos 1967: 188–94. Although this date has been accepted to a large extent (see Maraval 1997: 27–40), some scholars remain sceptical. See, for example, Mayerson 1991: 600.

16 See Wilkinson 1981: 179–80. Mayerson 1996: 124–5 downplays Egeria's importance as a source for Peter the Deacon.

17 Peter Diaconus Y.6. CCSL 175: 101.

antiquity.[18] Little is known about Clysma in the half century before the Muslim conquests, but it flourished later under Islamic rule.[19]

Aila

There is little evidence that Aila was a major port before the late third century CE. Sources from the early Roman period demonstrate that Aila was a major hub for overland commercial exchange, either directly with South Arabia or as an important transit site for maritime commerce shipped through Leuke Kome, but none of them describe Aila as a port.[20] Preliminary analysis based on pottery identification in the field also supports this conclusion; the early Byzantine period (fourth and fifth centuries) shows a tenfold increase in number of imported *amphoræ* sherds compared to both the Nabataean (late first century BCE and first century CE) and Roman periods (second and third centuries) of occupation. Perhaps more telling, the percentage of imported *amphoræ* sherds versus total pottery excavated shows a fourfold increase over the Nabataean period, and a nine-fold increase over the late Roman period.[21]

In the early fourth century, Eusebius describes Aila as a port; thereafter, numerous authors mention Aila's role in Red Sea trade throughout late antiquity.[22] Many types of imported *amphoræ* have been discovered at Aila, and Aila produced its own *amphoræ* from the late fourth century through the seventh century. These *amphoræ* have been found throughout the Red Sea region, including Berenike and Adulis, the port of Aksum.[23] However, it is unknown exactly what these *amphoræ* transported. One possibility is wine made from dates, which ancient sources connect to the Nabataeans and other Arab tribes.[24] Another possibility is *garum*. Fish bones from the Red Sea were discovered at Nessana in the Negev, which must have been transported from Aila.[25] A final possibility is that goods were repackaged in Aila *amphoræ* for shipment.[26] This theory is supported by the lack of finds of Aila *amphoræ* inside Aila's hinterland and the Levant.[27]

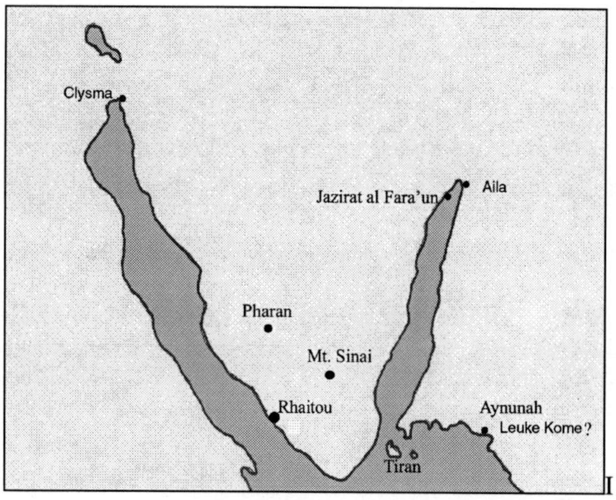

Map 15:2 Location of Ports around Sinai and the possible locations of Iotabe

In 630, John, the Christian governor of Aila, probably the bishop, surrendered the city to the Prophet Muḥammad and obtained protection of Aila's ships and caravans through the agreement. Aila seems to have been completely abandoned by the imperial authorities as a result of the Persian conquest in the early seventh century. The city apparently lacked the means to defend itself and chose to submit to Muḥammad rather than be the focus of a campaign.[28] Archaeological evidence shows that Aila continued to prosper after the Islamic conquests.[29]

Iotabe

Little is known about the fourth major port, the island of Iotabe, but it appears to have been a customs station for Aila. Although Procopius describes the location of the

18 *Martyrium Sancti Arethæ* 44–5; Antoninus Placentinus 41. In addition, a *commercius* was stationed at Clysma in the reign of Anastasius. See Sartre 1982: 112–9.

19 See Mayerson 1996: 125–6.

20 Strabo 16.2.30, 16.4.4; Pliny 5.12.65, 12.32.64–5. The *Periplus* does not mention Aila and makes clear that Leuke Kome was the most important port in the Nabataean kingdom (see *Periplus* 19).

21 Ward 2002: 124–42 and 2003. S. Thomas Parker, director of the excavations at ‘Aqabah, is currently subjecting the pottery to a more rigorous analysis. Although the exact numbers of pottery will surely change, I doubt that the overall impression created by the revised pottery counts will substantially alter my thesis. It is important to point out that a larger section of Byzantine Aila was excavated than of Nabataean / Roman Aila. This may have skewed the quantitative results in favour of Byzantine Aila; however, I think the increase in the percentage of *amphoræ* sherds vs. excavated sherds mitigates this *caveat* somewhat.

22 Eusebius, *Onomasticon* 6; See Parker 1997: 21 for a summary of the sources.

23 Tomber 2004: 397–8; Melkawi, *et al.* 1994.

24 See, for example, Diodorus Siculus 19.94.9–10. Dolinka 2003: 95 strongly argues that the Aila *amphora* contained date wine; however, his main point, that an Aila *amphora* at Berenike contained the painted inscription ‘oinos’ has been questioned by Tomber 2004: 398, who believes that the lack of pitch on the inside of the containers could rule out wine as a primary content and that the inscription indicates ‘reuse’.

25 See Dolinka 2003: 95–6 for a detailed discussion of Red Sea fish bones present throughout the southern Levant region. These bones presumably originated at Aila and may represent *garum* production at the site.

26 See Melkawi, *et al.* 1994: 463.

27 Parker 2005: 228 concludes that although a small number of Aila *amphoræ* have been discovered at Humayma, trade was clearly oriented to the Red Sea.

28 Mayerson 1964: 169–77.

29 Whitcomb 1994.

port with concrete details, and it must have controlled an important passage on the route to Aila, it has not been located.[30] It has been suggested that Iotabe was located at *Jazīrat al-Fara'ūn* (Pharoah's island), just south of Aila, and a few 'Byzantine' sherds were discovered on the island.[31] However, the only architectural material on the island dates to the Crusader period.[32] The island of Tiran, located where the Gulf of 'Aqabah flows into the Red Sea, has also been suggested, but archaeologists have not found any remains.[33] Based on these two problems, Mayerson suggested that a possible location for Iotabe could be on the islands to the east of the Gulf of 'Aqabah along what is now the Saudi border.[34] He suggests that instead of controlling the trade route, Iotabe served as a transit station, where large ships unloaded their cargos. These cargos were then shipped to Aila on smaller vessels.[35] However, since Aila supplied fifteen ships for the invasion of South Arabia, Mayerson's suggestion seems unlikely. These fifteen ships must represent larger vessels and not small boats.[36] Nevertheless, Mayerson's suggestion that the port may lie outside of the Gulf of 'Aqabah could still be correct. There was a port at Onnē in late antiquity, which some scholars have connected with Aynunah in Saudi Arabia.[37]

Iotabe appears in literary sources for less then a century, from 451 until 536 CE.[38] During the reign of Leo in 473 CE, an Arab leader named Amorkesos ended his association with Persia, travelled across the Arabian Peninsula, and captured Iotabe. His first action was to remove the Roman tax collectors and to keep the taxes for himself.[39] Twenty-five years later, in 498 CE, the *dux* of Palestine, Romanus, fought a campaign against Arab tribes, probably the Ghassānids and the Kindites. In the same operation, he retook Iotabe. While merchants were allowed to control the port, they sent a portion of the taxes to the emperor.[40] Under Justinian about 534 CE, another expedition was mounted to retake Iotabe. A transfer of power away from the imperial authorities before this expedition is implied. The motivation for the invasion seems to be related to taxes, but religious motives are also mentioned, possibly as justification.[41] No other source mentions Iotabe, and it is unknown how long the Roman authorities controlled the island or when the port was abandoned.

Security Threats?

Just as the third-century crisis altered the nature of Red Sea trade and brought changes to the occupation of Roman ports it also marks the turning point in the security of the Red Sea region. Although the Roman controlled ports of the Red Sea were not usually within striking distance of Persia, literary sources suggest that nomadic groups living on the edge of Roman control threatened these ports and their trade routes. In Third Palestine, the province containing the Sinai Peninsula and southern Jordan, literary sources report that nomadic Arab tribes, which are almost universally described in the Roman sources as Saracens, threatened the settled population.[42] These nomadic tribes lived both inside the territory of the Roman empire in the Sinai, in the Negev desert, and throughout Transjordan, and outside of directly Roman controlled territories in the northern Arabian Peninsula. These are the very regions where Aila, Clysma and Iotabe were located and through which merchants were required to travel to reach the Mediterranean. In southern Egypt, numerous sources mention the existence of nomadic indigenous tribes collectively known as Blemmyes. These sources describe attacks that the Blemmyes launched on

30 Procopius, *Persian War* 1.19.4.

31 Rothenberg and Aharoni 1961: 86–92.

32 Mayerson 1992: 3. Rothenberg and Aharoni 1961: 92 report finding a Byzantine capital on the island.

33 Abel 1938: 510–38; Rothenberg and Aharoni 1961: 161–2.

34 Mayerson 1995: 34; Mayerson 1992: 1, notes that 'the island ... was beyond the bounds of Palaestina Tertia.' The entire Sinai was within the province, but the Arabian shore was not. However, whether the Roman authorities could project their power into the Sinai Peninsula is unknown.

35 Mayerson 1992: 3.

36 *Martyrium Sancti Arethæ* 44–5.

37 Marcianus, frag. 18, Muller (ed.) 1861: 527; Bosworth 1984: 53–4. Aynunah is the commonly accepted location of Leuke Kome. See Kirwan 1984: 57–9. If Onnē is also located at Aynunah, then Leuke Kome may not have been abandoned. An inscription from Adulis, which was recorded by Cosmas Indicopleutes, suggests that Leuke Kome was still active in the middle of the third century. See Munro-Hay 1989: 8; Kirwan 1979: 95–6. However, a survey of Aynunah published a large corpus of Nabataean and early Roman pottery, but nothing which conclusively proves occupation of the site after the fourth century. See Ingraham, *et al.* 1981.

38 Mayerson 1992: 3, no.1. These are the dates of ecclesiastical councils where bishops of Iotabe are attested.

39 Malchus frag. 1. Blockly 1983: 404–6. On Amorkesos, see Shahīd 1989: 59–113 and Letsios 1989.

40 Theophanes AM 5990 (de Boor 1883) 141; Mango and Scott 1997: 217. Shahīd 1989: 120–31.

41 I follow Mayerson 1992: 2 who links the expedition of Aratius with Justinian's action. The island was inhabited by a substantial Jewish population. Procopius, *Persian War* 1.19.4; Choricius (Foerster and Richtsteig 1929: 3.2.67–76.

42 Where the term 'Saracen' originated is still hotly debated. See Shahīd 1984: 123–41. Ptolemy provides the first usage of the term for a tribe in the Sinai and the Ḥijāz. Although Graf and O'Connor 1977: 57 attack Ptolemy for giving two locations for the tribe, I do not think this mitigates Ptolemy's usefulness because nomadic groups could easily inhabit both the Sinai and the Ḥijāz. Graf maintains that the term 'Saracen' derives from the Arabic *širkat* 'federation'. See Graf and O'Connor 1977; Graf 1978; Graf 1997: xii–xiii. An alternative designation for Saracens is the 'tent dwellers' (*scenitae*). See Ammianus 23.6.13. *Scenitas Arabas quos Saracenos posteritas appellavit.*

merchants of the Red Sea and the ports of Berenike and Clysma.[43]

The Saracens first become a problem for the Roman authorities during the third-century crisis.[44] Diocletian fought a campaign against Saracens, although this may have been in Syria and not in the southern Levant.[45] The Xth Fretensis legion was moved from Jerusalem to Aila to help defend the frontier, and the Arabian frontier reached its highest state of defence. Afterwards, the security of this frontier slowly declined. Justinian removed many of the units for his wars in Africa and Italy, and Arab tribes increasingly took on the main security role along the Syrian / Arabian border. The final collapse of security must have taken place around the time of the Persian conquests in the early seventh century, and there was little opposition when the Muslim Arabs entered Roman territory.[46]

While the Saracens could not permanently occupy Roman territories, their raids could injure weakly defended targets, such as monastic communities, villages, and caravans laden with goods. The large numbers of anecdotes do not need to be reiterated in this paper, since the discussion of Romans and Saracens has produced an enormous bibliography.[47] Most current theories do not see the *limes* as a fortified border against a Saracen menace and argue that the fortified positions in southern Levant were intended to deal with internal threats, such as banditry.[48] However, these theories do not adequately explain why the majority of units in late antiquity were situated along the frontier, rather than in major population centres.[49] Regardless, whether the Roman military was intended to face internal or external threats, it is clear that nomadic tribes could pose both kinds of threats. And although the various Saracen tribes were but one security threat, they appear most frequently in the Roman sources. While there were a few 'high profile' wars between the Romans and these tribes, such as the revolt of Mavia and the campaigns fought with the Persian-allied Lakhmids, this paper will focus on the smaller scale, everyday interactions which could directly threaten merchants and their caravans.[50]

Three examples from the Sinai illustrate that Saracen tribes were located inside Roman territory and could raid the Christian communities in the peninsula. The Christian sources stress the cruel, barbaric nature of the Saracens. There is no way to prove the historicity of these events; however, they must have created a perception that the Saracens were anti-Christian and dangerous.

In the late fourth century, the monk Ammonius visited the Sinai. While there, he reported that when a Saracen chief had died, his followers attacked the monks around Mount Sinai. Ammonius goes into great detail how the Saracens hacked off the heads, hands and feet of monks, and sliced open the bellies of others.[51] During approximately the same period, Pharan, a town in the Sinai, contracted a treaty with a Saracen leader. When a group of Saracens attacked the monks at Mount Sinai, the Pharanites appealed to this leader and received his assurances that justice would be served. The emissaries from Pharan found the chief in the northern Sinai desert.[52] In the late sixth century, the pilgrim Antoninus Placentinus reported a disturbance among the nomadic Saracens. He was able to cross the Negev and Sinai deserts only because of a religious festival. While at Mount Sinai, Antoninus described the rituals of a pagan Saracen priest on the slopes of Mount Sinai.[53]

That the Roman authorities believed that the Saracens were a danger to Mount Sinai and Palestine in general is illustrated by the erection of Saint Catherine's monastery. Procopius describes how Justinian ordered the monastery to be built at Mount Sinai to protect the monks against Saracen raids.[54] Although Mayerson has questioned Procopius's logic in the passage, it shows that the Romans (or at least Procopius) believed that the Saracens threatened the Sinai and could travel from north Arabia, through the Sinai, and into Palestine.[55] Aila lies between

43 The Blemmyes are also sometimes called Beja.

44 The Nabataeans had fought against some of the tribes on their borders. The Daif, Masikat, and Muharib tribes participated in a rebellion against the Nabataean state. See Graf 1989: 363. A number of military installations were constructed along the eastern frontier in the Severan period, which were most likely directed against nomadic tribes. Unfortunately, there is no literary or epigraphic evidence to confirm this. See Parker 2000: 370.

45 *Panegyrici Latini* 11.5.4; 7.1. Parker 2000: 372; Graf 1989: 346–7. The federate tribes of both Rome and Persia were mostly concentrated along the Syrian frontier rather than the Arabian. On the federate tribes, and Arabs in general along the eastern frontier, see Shahīd 1984, 1984b, 1989, 1995.

46 See Parker 2000: 381–3. A recent article argues that the frontier was largely abandoned in the late fourth century, but this idea has been meet with scepticism. See Fisher 2004.

47 See Parker 1986, 1987 and 2000, Graf 1989, Shahīd 1984b, 1989, Mayerson 1989, Banning 1986, 1987, and 1992, Rosen 1987, Haiman 1995.

48 Isaac 1984 and 1990, Graf 1989.

49 Parker 2000: 373–9.

50 The most famous 'Saracen' attack is the revolt of Mavia. Although I do not agree with all of his conclusions, Shahīd 1984b: 138–202 provides the most in-depth discussion of the revolt. See also Bowersock 1980 and Mayerson 1980b.

51 Ammonius [Greek] 6. See Mayerson 1980 for a summary and analysis of the historical nature of the text.

52 [Nilus], *Narrationes* 6.9, 6.11, 6.17; Mayerson 1975 provides an interesting analysis and summary of this complex text.

53 Antoninus Placentinus 38, 39.4.

54 Procopius, *De aedificiis* 5.8.

55 Mayerson 1978. This passage is also discussed by Gatier

the Sinai and the northern Arabia peninsula, suggesting that Saracens could easily threaten both the city itself and its trade routes through the Negev or up the *via nova Traiana* to Syria.

There is substantial evidence from Aila that the city possessed a strong garrison and increasingly strong fortifications. In the late third century, the Xth Fretensis legion, probably numbering between one and two thousand soldiers, was transferred from Jerusalem to Aila. It was clearly meant to anchor the southernmost point of the *via nova Traiana*. In the late fourth or early fifth century, a city wall with projecting towers was constructed surrounding the city. About 120 m of the wall was excavated, in some places extant up to four m in height, and four towers have been discovered. This wall was constructed about a century after the transfer of the legion and may be a response to an increasing Saracen threat.[56] In the late sixth century, small mudbrick installations were constructed along the inside of the wall, which were probably intended to buttress a section of the wall that had collapsed.[57] These fortifications show that the authorities of the city took the threat of raids seriously, and that the wall was still in use during the late sixth century.

I have already described how the Saracens were able to seize Iotabe and divert tax revenues from the imperial government. The fact that Iotabe was captured four times, twice by the Romans, in less than a century suggests that its trade routes were also insecure. That it took twenty-five years for the Romans to recapture the island implies that the Roman authorities did not have the strength in Third Palestine to retake the island easily.[58]

In southern Egypt, the Roman sources describe another nomadic, 'outsider' threat, the Blemmyes. Although Roman accounts of the Blemmyes begin in the first century CE, they first appear as hostile invaders during the reign of Decius (249–251) in the third-century crisis.[59] They continued to raid southern Egypt, including Coptos, until Diocletian pulled Roman forces behind the First Cataract and gave those lands to the Nobatai to act as a buffer against the Blemmyes.[60]

In many ways, the scholarly debate about the Saracens parallels that of the Blemmyes. First, it appears that there were many different populations living in the region between Egypt and Aksum whom the Romans grouped together under the name Blemmyes.[61] Secondly, they seem to have presented the same type of threat to the settled Roman populations. Thirdly, it is clear that some of the groups lived within Roman territory.

The monk Ammonius also described an incursion of Blemmyes into the Sinai, and once again, the historical realties of the text are less important than the perception of the Blemmyes that it created. In the fourth century, a number of Blemmyes captured a vessel from Aila and demanded to be taken to Clysma.[62] They intended to sack the city. They anchored off the coast at Rhaithou, intending to raid the community before continuing on to Clysma. When they could not find enough plunder, they killed forty monks. Ammonius describes the atrocities committed by the Blemmyes in the same terms as those committed by the Saracens.[63] These raiders were then defeated by the inhabitants of Pharan, who had recently converted to Christianity. That this episode is not just a hagiographic *topos* is suggested by Procopius's claim that Diocletian's settlement with the Nobatai was not working, and that the Blemmyes continued to plunder Egypt. He also mentions that they practiced human sacrifice.[64] Also, *papyri* report that around 525 CE Anastasius, *dux* of the Thebaid, fought against a revolt of the Blemmyes. This might be related to a report in the *Martyrium Sancti Arethæ* which notes that the Blemmyes and Nobatai raided both Coptos and Berenike; however, this text reports that these forces were driven out by the Aksumites, and not the Romans.[65]

Archaeological evidence suggests that a new, desert oriented population was infiltrating the Eastern Desert in the fifth and sixth centuries.[66] At Berenike, the traditional Mediterranean diet slowly gave way to one based more on desert flora and fauna.[67] Handmade pottery (termed Eastern Desert Ware) is the most extensive evidence of this desert-oriented population.[68] Although the scholars studying the Eastern Desert Ware are hesitant to attribute it to the Blemmyes, this connection seems plausible.[69]

1989: 507–10.

56 Parker 2002: 80.

57 Parker 2003: 326.

58 Fisher 2004: 52; Letsios 1989: 533. Shahīd 1989: 70–1 suggests that the Roman garrisons were temporarily withdrawn from the area for Leo's invasion of Africa when the island was originally taken.

59 Pliny, 5.46; Updegraff 1988: 69. See Barnard 2005: 25–33 for a list of literary references to the Blemmyes.

60 Procopius, *Persian War* 1.19.

61 Barnard 2005: 34.

62 Ammonius [Greek version] 8–9, 18–38.

63 Compare Ammonius [Greek] 6 and 28.

64 Procopius, *Persian War* 1.19.

65 *Martyrium Sancti Arethae* 42–3.

66 Cited as a possible occupation at five sites in the Eastern Desert. Sidebotham, Bernard, and Pyke 2002: 222–3.

67 Sidebotham 2002: 234–5.

68 Barnard 2002.

69 Barnard 2006. Barnard 2005: 38 argues that '[t]he association with the Blemmyes, however, is doubtful and not just because this name may not refer to a stable ethnic entity … the period in which Eastern Desert Ware (third to eighth centuries CE) was produced is much shorter than the period in which Blemmyes are present in the written sources (seventh century BCE, probably to the present). And although the written sources are far from

Literary sources suggest that the Blemmyes controlled large areas of the Eastern Desert in the fifth century and specifically mention the emerald mines between Berenike and the Nile.[70] Many examples of Eastern Desert Ware have been discovered in Wādī Sikait, identified as Mons Smaragdus. Since the literary sources demonstrate the presence of the Blemmyes in roughly the same topographic and chronological parameters as the Eastern Desert Ware, it seems likely that this pottery represents the people to whom the Romans were referring, no matter how misinformed they may have been.

Strangely, little evidence of a garrison from the fourth century onwards has been published from Berenike, despite the numerous examples from the earlier centuries. The early Roman port was surrounded by at least ten forts, all of which seem to have been abandoned by the fourth century.[71] One would expect a garrison to be stationed at a port of this significance. The *Notitia dignitatum* mentions that in the early fifth century the *Legio prima Valentiniana*, along with an auxiliary unit of cavalry, was based at Coptos, and detachments of these units probably patrolled the desert and guarded Berenike.[72] It is unknown how long these units were based at Coptos.

It is possible that the presence of Blemmyes made merchants hesitant to use Berenike, either because of disturbances to the water supply or the harassment of merchant caravans. This, coupled with the problems of supplying Berenike and the maintenance of the harbour, may have caused the Roman abandonment of the port. These merchants may have sought the relative safety of Clysma and Aila. The fort at Abū Sha'ar may have been constructed to defend the Eastern Desert routes from threats such as the Blemmyes, and Abū Sha'ar may have also served as a defended anchorage for merchants.[73] There was a fort at Clysma, and Egeria reports that soldiers escorted pilgrims in the later fourth century along the pilgrim routes of Egypt and the Sinai.[74] Although there is little evidence of a garrison at Clysma and Aila in the later fifth and sixth centuries, these ports may have seemed more secure based on their locations closer to the centre of imperial power.

Although this paper has focused on the security threats posed by these two groups, archaeological, anthropological and historical evidence shows that there was a range of potential relationships between the nomadic and sedentary populations, ranging from symbiosis to antagonism. The relationship between the nomadic groups and the sedentary population was probably almost always neutral, if not amiable. Mutually beneficial agreements were often reached between the sedentary and nomadic peoples; however, our sources rarely focus on these relationships.[75] The Roman, increasingly Christian, sources dwell on the hostile incidents in a successful smear campaign that becomes increasingly potent as the Christian sources describe attacks on monks and the 'demonic' religious practices of the nomadic groups.

Conclusion

It is clear that Red Sea trade recovered quickly after the restoration of imperial order in the late third century. The major ports, Berenike, Aila, Clysma and Iotabe, all demonstrate evidence of maritime trade throughout this period. It is also clear that no major power threatened these ports, although groups of Saracens allied to Persia or operating independently could cause major problems for the imperial authorities. The threats presented by the Blemmyes and Saracens could normally be held in check by strong governmental supervision; however, if that supervision disappeared, the Saracens and Blemmyes could raid merchant caravans, disrupt the transportation of supplies, or actually attack the ports. I suggest that the two ports located the farthest from major Roman settlements and control, Berenike and Iotabe, disappeared because they were the hardest to defend, while Aila and Clysma continued to serve as major ports.

A century and a half after the abandonment of Berenike, Aila's city wall had gone out of use, and imperial power was impotent after the Persian conquest of the east. The

comprehensive, the region controlled by the Blemmyes seems smaller that [sic] the area in which Eastern Desert Ware is found.' These arguments do not seem compelling to me. First, it is easy to assume that cultural change could account for the smaller chronological period for Eastern Desert Ware as opposed to the Blemmyes. Second, it seems likely that the term 'Blemmyes' is an outsider amalgamation for various ethnic groups. Only one (or a few) of these groups may have been responsible for Eastern Desert Ware. These vessels could have been exchanged throughout the deserts of northeastern Africa. While this would imply that the literary sources lack essential details about the ethnic composition of these peoples, this does not mean that one of the groups under the umbrella of 'Blemmyes' was not responsible for the pottery.

70 Olympiodorus. Blockley 1983 frag. 35.2

71 See Sidebotham 1999 for a discussion of the military remains at the site. The reign of Vespasian witnessed the highest construction of military sites in the eastern desert. See Bagnall, Bülow-Jacobsen, and Cuvigny 2001. Sidebotham 2000: 365 mentions that these forts defended Berenike 'to a lesser extent' in late antiquity.

72 *notitia dignitatum, oriens* 31.

73 See Sidebotham 1989 on the Abū Sha'ar excavations. He notes that the fort was not built to outlast a prolonged siege, but rather 'to defend against occasional raids by local Bedouin marauders or bandits' (138). In a footnote he mentions the Blemmyes and Nobatae as possible threats.

74 Egeria 7.

75 A pact is mentioned in Nilus' *Narrationes*, but the text focuses on comparing the horrible atrocities and customs of the Saracens and the noble lives of the monks.

danger to Aila's land and sea shipping reached the point where the city surrendered to the Prophet Muḥammad to secure the safe passage of its traders. We know little about Clysma at that time, but it is probably reasonable to assume that it too was relatively undefended in the seventh century. Its chief advantage lay in its distance from any potential threats. Therefore, it appears that throughout late antiquity, the southern ports, Berenike and Iotabe, suffered harassment from outside tribes that eventually led to the abandonment of these ports, whereas Aila and Clysma, being closer to the Mediterranean and imperial control, continued as ports. This suggests that the trade routes which previously flowed through Berenike and Iotabe had moved north to the ports of Aila and Clysma, where merchants felt more secure. Merchants deemed the security of their cargos more important than the difficulties in sailing north in the Red Sea as a result of the 'wind regime'.

References

Abel, F. 1938. L'Île de Jotabé. *Revue Biblique* 47: 510–38.

Ammianus Marcellinus in C. Clark (ed.). 1910–1915. Berlin: Weidmann; 1935–1939. J. Rolfe (tr.). Cambridge: Harvard University Press.

Ammonius Monachus. [Aramaic version]. *Relatio*. C. Müller-Kessler and M. Sokoloff (eds and tr.). 1996. 3: 9–69 in *The Forty Martyrs of the Sinai Desert, Eulogios, The Stone-Cutter, and Anastasia*. Styx: Publications Groningen, Corpus of Christian Palestinian Aramaic; D.G. Tsames and K.G. Katsanes (eds). 1989. [Greek version] 194–234 in *To Martyrologion tou Sina*. Sinaitika keimena 2. Thessalonike: Ekdoseis P. Pournara.

Antoninus Placentinus. *Itinerarium*. P. Geyer (ed.). 1965. 175: 129–53 in *Itineraria et alia geographica. CCL* Turnholt: Brepols.

Bagnall, R., Bülow-Jacobsen, A. and Cuvigny, H. 2001. Security and water on the Eastern Desert roads: the prefect Julius Ursus and the construction of *praesidia* under Vespasian. *JRA* 14: 325–33.

Banning, E.B. 1986. Peasants, Pastoralists and 'Pax Romana': mutualism in the Southern Highlands of Jordan. *BASOR* 1986: 26–50.

——. 1987. De Bello Paceque: a reply to Parker. *BASOR* 265: 52–4.

——. 1992. Saracen Encounters: a reply to Mayerson. *BASOR* 286: 87–8.

Barnard, H. 2002. Eastern Desert Ware: a short introduction. *Sudan & Nubia* 6: 53–7.

——. 2005. Sire, il n'y a pas de Blemmyes: a re-evaluation of historical and archaeological data. 23–40 in J.C.M Starkey (ed.), *People of the Red Sea: Proceedings of Red Sea Project II held in the British Museum, October 2004*. BAR International Series 1395. Oxford: Archaeopress.

——. 2006. Eastern Desert Ware: fine pottery from an arid wasteland. *Egyptian Archaeology* 28: 29–30.

Boissonade, J. (ed.). 1962. *Martyrium Sancti Arethæ*. 5: 1–62 in *Anecdota Græca*. Hildesheim: Olms.

Bowersock, G. 1980. Mavia, Queen of the Saracens. *Studien zur antiken Sozialgeschichte* 28: 477–95.

Bosworth, C. 1984. Madyan Shu'ayb in pre-Islamic and early Islamic lore and history *JSS* 29.1: 53–64.

Bruyère, B. 1966. *Fouilles de Clysma-Qolzoum (Suez): 1930–1932*. Cairo: IFAO.

Cappers, R. 2006. *Roman Food Prints at Berenike*. Los Angeles: Cotsen Institute of Archaeology.

Casson, L. (tr.). *Periplus maris erythræi*. 1989. *The Periplus Maris Erythræi. Text with introduction, translation, and commentary*. Princeton: Princeton University Press.

Choricius Gazae. *Opera*. R. Foerster and E. Richtsteig (eds). 1929. Leipzig: Teubner.

Devos, P. 1967. La Date du voyage d'Égérie. *AnBoll* 85: 165–94.

Diodorus Siculus. *Bibliotheca historica*. Vogel (ed.) after I. Bekker and L. Dindorf. 1964. Leipzig: Teubner.

Dolinka, B. 2003. *Nabataean Aila (Aqaba, Jordan) from a Ceramic Perspective*. BAR International Series 1116. Oxford: Archaeopress.

Egeria. *Itinerarium*. Maraval (ed.). 1997. *Journal de voyage* SC 296. Paris: Éditions du Cerf.

Eiring, J. and J. Lund (eds). 2004. *Transport, Amphorae and Trade in the Eastern Mediterranean. Acts of the International Colloquium at the Danish Institute at Athens, September 26–29, 2002*. Athens: Danish Institute at Athens.

Eusebius. *Onomasticon*. E. Klostermann (ed.). 1904, repr. 1966. *Das Onomastikon der biblischen Ortsnamen*. Leipzig: J.C. Hinrichs.

Facey, W. 2004. The Red Sea: the wind regime and location of ports. 7–18 in P. Lunde and A. Porter (eds), *Trade and Travel in the Red Sea Region. Proceedings of Red Sea Project I held in the British Museum October 2002*. BAR International Series 1269. Oxford: Archaeopress.

Fahd, T. (ed.). 1989. *L'Arabie préislamique et son environnement historique et culturel: Actes du Colloque de Strasbourg, 24–27 juin 1987*. Leiden: Brill.

Fink, R. 1971. *Roman Military Records on Papyrus*. Philological Monographs of the American Philological Association 26. Cleveland: American Philological Association.

Fisher, G. 2004. A New Perspective on Rome's Desert Frontier. *BASOR* 336: 49–60.

Freeman, P., *et al.* (eds). 2002. *Limes XVII: Proceedings of the XVIIIth International Congress of Roman Frontier Studies held in Amman, Jordan (September 2000).* BAR International Series 1084. Oxford: Archaeopress.

Gatier, P.-L. Les traditions et l'histoire du Sinaï du IVe au VIIe siècle. 499–523 in T. Fahd. 1989. *L'Arabie préislamique et son environnement historique et culturel: Actes du Colloque de Strasbourg, 24–27 juin 1987.* Leiden: Brill.

Graf, D. and M. O'Conner. 1977. The Origin of the Term Saracen and the Rawwāfa Inscriptions. *Byzantine Studies* 4: 52–66.

Graf, D. 1978. The Saracens and the Defense of the Arabian Frontier. *BASOR* 229: 1–27.

——. 1989. Rome and the Saracens: reassessing the nomadic menace. 342–400 in T. Fahd. 1989. *L'Arabie préislamique et son environnement historique et culturel: Actes du Colloque de Strasbourg, 24–27 juin 1987.* Leiden: Brill.

——. 1997. *Rome and the Arabian Frontier: from the Nabataeans to the Saracens.* Brookfield, VT: Ashgate.

Haiman, M. 1995. Agriculture and Nomad-State Relations in the Negev Desert in the Byzantine and Early Islamic Periods. *BASOR* 297: 29–53.

Jameson, S. 1968. Chronology of the Campaigns of Aelius Gallus and C. Petronius. *JRS* 58: 71–84.

Ingraham, M., *et al.* 1981. Saudi Arabian Comprehensive Survey Program: C. Preliminary report on a Reconnaissance survey of the northwestern province (with a note on a brief survey of the northern province). *Atlal* 5.Ic: 59–84.

Isaac, B. 1984. Bandits in Judaea and Palestine. *Harvard Studies in Classical Philology* 88: 171–203.

——. 1990. *The Limits of Empire: the Roman army in the East.* Oxford: Oxford University Press.

Kirwan, L. 1979. The Arabian background to one of the 'Cosmas' inscriptions from Adulis (Ethiopia). *SHA-I:* 93–9.

——. 1984. Where to search for the ancient port of Leuke Kome. *SHA-II*: 55–61.

Leadbetter, B. 2002. Galerius and the eastern frontier. 85–9 in P. Freeman, *et al.* (eds). 2002. *Limes XVII: Proceedings of the XVIIIth International Congress of Roman Frontier Studies held in Amman, Jordan (September 2000).* BAR International Series 1084. Oxford: Archaeopress.

Letsios, D. G. 1989. Amorkesos and the Roman Foederati in Arabia. 525–38 in T. Fahd. 1989. *L'Arabie préislamique et son environnement historique et culturel: Actes du Colloque de Strasbourg, 24–27 juin 1987.* Leiden: Brill.

Lucian. *Alexander Pseudomantis.* A.M. Harmon (ed.). 1925, repr. 1961. 4: 174–252 in *Lucian.* Cambridge: Harvard University Press.

Lunde, P. and A. Porter (eds). 2004. *Trade and Travel in the Red Sea Region. Proceedings of Red Sea Project I held in the British Museum October 2002.* BAR International Series 1269. Oxford: Archaeopress.

Majcherek, G. 2004. Alexandria's long-distance trade in Late Antiquity — the amphora evidence. 229–37 in J. Eiring and J. Lund (eds). 2004. *Transport, Amphorae and Trade in the Eastern Mediterranean. Acts of the International Colloquium at the Danish Institute at Athens, September 26–29, 2002.* Athens: Danish Institute at Athens.

Malchus. In R. Blockley (tr.). 1983. *The Fragmentary Classicizing Historians of the Later Roman Empire.* Liverpool: Cairns.

Marcianus. *Periplus maris exteri.* K. Müller (ed.). 1855, repr. 1965. 1: 515–62 in *Geographi Graeci Minores.* Hildesheim: Olms.

Mayerson, P. 1964. The first Muslim attacks on southern Palestine (AD 633–634). *TAPA* 95: 155–99.

——. 1975. Observations on the 'Nilus' Narrationes: evidence for an unknown Christian sect? *JARCE* 12: 51–74.

——. 1978. Procopius or Eutychius on the construction of the monastery at Mount Sinai: which is the more reliable source? *BASOR* 230: 33–8.

——. 1980. The Ammonius narrative: Bedouin and Blemmye attacks in Sinai. 133–48 in G. Rendsburg, *et al.* (eds). *The Bible World, Essays in Honor of Cyrus H. Gordon.* New York: Ktav Pub Inc.

——. 1980b. Mavia, Queen of the Saracens: a cautionary note. *IEJ* 30: 123–31.

——. 1989. Saracens and Romans: micro-macro relationships. *BASOR* 274: 71–9.

——. 1991. Review of T. Fahd (ed.).*L'Arabie préislamique et son environnement historique et culturel: Actes du Colloque de Strasbourg, 24–27 juin 1987. Journal of the American Oriental Society* 111.3: 598–600.

——. 1992. The Island of Iotabe in the Byzantine sources: a reprise. *BASOR* 287: 1–4.

——. 1995. Aelius Gallus at Cleopatris (Suez) and on the Red Sea. *GRBS* 36: 17–24.

——. 1996. The Port of Clysma (Suez) in transition from Roman to Arab rule. *BASOR* 55.2: 119–26.

Melkawi, A., 'Amr, K. and Whitcomb, D.S. 1994. The excavation of two seventh-entury pottery kilns at Aqaba. *Annual of the Department of Antiquities of Jordan* 38: 447–68.

Munro-Hay, S.C. 1989. *Excavations at Aksum: an account of research at the ancient Ethiopian capital directed in 1972–1974 by the late Dr Neville Chittick.*

Memoirs of the British Institute in Eastern Africa 10. London: British Institute in Eastern Africa.

Mynors, R.A.B., Nixon, C.E.V. and Rodgers, B.S. (tr.). 1994. *In Praise of later Roman emperors*: the Panegyrici Latini. Berkeley: University of California Press.

[Nilus]. *Narrationes.* Conca (ed.). 1983. Leipzig: Teubner; also, *PG* 79 cols. 589–694.

Seeck, O. (ed.). 1876. *Notitia Dignitatum*. Berlin: Weidmann.

Olympiodorus. In R. Blockley (tr.). 1983. *The Fragmentary Classicizing Historians of the Later Roman Empire.* Liverpool: Cairns.

Parker, S.T. 1986. *Romans and Saracens: a history of the Arabian Frontier.* ASOR Dissertation Series 6. Winona Lake: Eisenbrauns.

——. 1987. Peasants, Pastoralists, and 'Pax Romana': a different view. *BASOR* 265: 35–51.

——. 1997. The 1994 Season of the Roman 'Aqaba Project. *BASOR* 305: 19–44.

——. 1998. The Roman 'Aqaba Project: the 1996 campaign. *ADAJ* 42: 375–94.

——. 2000. The Defense of Palestine and Transjordan from Diocletian to Heraclius. 367–88 in L.E. Stager, *et al.* (eds), *The Archaeology of Jordan and Beyond: essays in honor of James A. Sauer.* Winona Lake: Eisenbrauns.

——. 2000b. The Roman 'Aqaba Project: the 1997 and 1998 campaigns. *ADAJ* 44: 373–94.

——. 2002. The Roman Frontier in Jordan: an overview. 77–82 in P. Freeman, *et. al.* (eds). 2002. *Limes XVII: Proceedings of the XVIIIth International Congress of Roman Frontier Studies held in Amman, Jordan (September 2000).* BAR International Series 1084. Oxford: Archaeopress.

——. 2002b. The Roman 'Aqaba Project: the 2000 campaign. *ADAJ* 46: 409–28.

——. 2003. The Roman 'Aqaba Project: the 2002 campaign. *ADAJ* 47: 321–33.

——. 2006 Roman Aila and the Wadi Arabah: an economic relationship. 223–30 in P. Bienkowski and K. Galor (eds), *Crossing the Rift: Resources, settlement patterns and interaction in the Wadi Arabah.* Oxford: Council for British Research in the Levant and Oxbow.

Peter the Deacon. *Liber de locis sanctis. Appendix ad Itinerarium Egeriae*, II. P. Geyer (ed.). 1965. 175: 93–103 in *Itineraria et Alia Geographica. CCL.* Leipzig: Teubner.

Procopius. J. Haury (ed.). 1913. *Opera*. Leipzig: Teubner; H. Dewing (tr.). 1962–1978. Cambridge: Harvard University Press.

Ptolemy. K. Müller (ed.). 1883. *Geographia.* Paris: Didot.

Rosen, S. 1987. Byzantine nomadism in the Negev: results from the emergency survey. *Journal of Field Archaeology*, 14(1): 29–42.

Rothenberg, B. and Aharoni, Y. 1961. *God's Wilderness: discoveries in the Sinai.* Toronto: Nelson.

Sartre, M. (ed.) 1982. *Inscriptions grècques et latines de la Syrie*, 13. Paris: Institut Français d'Archéologie du Proche-Orient.

Shahīd, I. 1984. *Rome and the Arabs. A Prolegomenon to the Study of Byzantinum and the Arabs*. Washington: Dumbarton Oaks.

——. 1984b. *Byzantium and the Arabs in the Fourth Century*. Washington: Dumbarton Oaks.

——. 1989. *Byzantium and the Arabs in the Fifth Century*. Washington: Dumbarton Oaks.

——. 1995. *Byzantium and the Arabs in the Sixth Century*. Washington: Dumbarton Oaks.

Sidebotham, S., Barnard, H., and Pyke, G. 2002. Five enigmatic Late Roman settlements in the Eastern Desert. *Journal of Egyptian Archaeology* 88: 187–225.

Sidebotham, S. and Wendrich, W. (eds). 1995. *Berenike 1994.* Leiden: CNWS.

——. 1996. *Berenike 1995.* Leiden: CNWS.

——. 1998. *Berenike 1997.* Leiden: CNWS.

——. 2000. *Berenike 1998.* Leiden: CNWS.

——. forthcoming. *Berenike 1999–2000.* Los Angeles: Costen Press.

Sidebotham, S. and Wendrich, W. 2001–2002. Berenike. Archaeological fieldwork at a Ptolemaic-Roman port on the Red Sea coast of Egypt 1999–2001. *Sahara* 13:23–50.

Sidebotham, S. 1989. Fieldwork on the Red Sea Coast: the 1987 season. *JARCE* 26: 127–66.

——. 1999. Berenike, trade and the military: investigations at a Red Sea port in Egypt. 251–7 in N.. Gudea (ed.). 1999. *Roman Frontier Studies: Proceedings of the XVIIth International Congress of Roman Frontier Studies.* Zalău: The County Council of Sălaj, The County Museum of History and Art Zalău: 'Porolissum'.

——. 2002. Late Roman Berenike. *JARCE* 39: 217–40.

——. 2002b. The Roman Empire's southeastern-most frontier; recent discoveries at Berenike and environs (Eastern Desert of Egypt) 1998–2001. 361–72 in P. Freeman, *et al.* (eds). 2002. *Limes XVII: Proceedings of the XVIIIth International Congress of Roman Frontier Studies held in Amman, Jordan (September 2000).* BAR International Series 1084. Oxford: Archaeopress.

Sijpesteijn, P. 1963. Der ΠΟΤΑΜΟΣ ΤΡΑΙΑΝΟΣ. *Aegyptus* 43: 70–83.

Starkey, J.C.M. (ed.). 2005. *People of the Red Sea: Proceedings of Red Sea Project II held in the British*

Museum, October 2004. BAR International Series 1395. Oxford: Archaeopress.

Strabo. Meineke (ed.). 1877, repr. 1969. *Geographia.* Leipzig: Teubner.

Theophanes. *Chronographia.* C. de Boor (ed.). 1883. Leipzig: Teubner; C. Mango and R. Scott (tr.). 1997. *The Chronicle of Theophanes Confessor.* Oxford: Oxford University Press.

Tomber, R. 2004. Amphorae from the Red Sea and their contribution to the interpretation of Late Roman trade beyond the Empire. 393–402 in J. Eiring and J. Lund (eds). 2004. *Transport Amphorae and Trade in the Eastern Mediterranean. Acts of the International Colloquium at the Danish Institute at Athens, September 26–29, 2002.* Athens: Danish Institute at Athens.

Updegraff, R. 1988. The Blemmyes I: the rise of the Blemmyes and the Roman withdrawal from Nubia under Diocletian (with additional remarks by L. Török, Budapest). *ANRW* II.10.1: 44–106.

Ward, W. 2002. Roman Red Sea Ports: Berenike, Myos Hormos, Clysma, Leuke Kome, and Aila from Augustus to Diocletian. Unpublished MA thesis, North Carolina State University, Raleigh, North Carolina.

——. 2003. Camels or Ships? An Economic Comparison of Nabataean, Roman, and Byzantine Aila. Unpublished paper presented at the American Schools of Oriental Research Annual Meeting. 20 November 2003. Atlanta, Georgia.

Wendrich, W., *et al.* 2003. Berenike Crossroads: the integration of information. *JESHO* 46(1):46–87.

Whitcomb, D. 1994. *Ayla: art and industry in the Islamic port of Aqaba.* Chicago: Oriental Institute Museum.

Wilkinson, J. 1981. *Egeria's Travels to the Holy Land.* Jerusalem: Ariel.

Acknowledgments

Generous financial support was supplied by the UCLA History Department and the British Academy. I would like to thank everyone at the conference who offered suggestions and comments, whether I heeded these or not. I would especially like to thank S. Thomas Parker for providing access to the unpublished archaeological material from Aila, Hans Barnard for supplying unpublished articles on Eastern Desert Ware, Roberta Tomber for answering questions about *amphoræ* in the Red Sea, John Cooper for help with the Red Sea canal, and Willeke Wendrich for answering questions regarding Berenike. Above all, I would like to thank my dissertation chairs, Claudia Rapp and Ronald Mellor, for their continued encouragement and advice.

Shipwrecks, Coffee and Canals: the Landscapes of Suez

Janet Starkey

Ship me somewheres east of Suez
Where the best is like the worst
Where there aren't no Ten Commandments
And a man can raise a thirst.
For the temple bells are ringing
And it's there that I would be,
By the old Moulmein pagoda
Lookin' lazy at the sea ...

('Mandalay'. 1890)[1]

Travel writing is a delicate blend of autobiography, geography, philosophy, ethnography, fiction and above all, history. In this volume we have begun to map geographies, archaeologies, histories, and ideologies that shape the way we think of the Red Sea. This paper dissects travel writings linked to the landscapes and seascapes of the northern Red Sea and specifically on those surrounding the harbour-town of Suez (al-Suways), a provincial capital at the western shore of the bay of Suez, north-west of the mouth of the Suez Canal. In 1783 the French savant, comte Constantin François Chassboeuf Volney (1757–1820) identified the vicinity with 'Kolzoum, the Clysma of the Greeks'.[2] As the southernmost city of the Suez Canal, it has an international importance far beyond its dark and depressing site — this location being in marked contrast to any unreal image conveyed by billboards of films and novels such as *Suez, Passport to Suez, Wings over Suez,* and W. Somerset Maugham's novel *East of Suez* (1922, filmed in 1925), or Twentieth-Century Fox's *Suez* (1938) in which Tyrone Power played Ferdinand de Lesseps, the architect of the Suez Canal. The pivotal position of the harbour-town with all its multicultural and commercial connections is more complicated than any simplistic East-West dialogue.

Whilst travel writing has become a fashionable topic for academic research, what do accounts of Suez offer apart from nostalgic memories or antiquarianism, a reflection of an exotic Oriental harbour-town? The miserable conditions and poor water supplies described by visitors to Suez, such as the explorer John-Louis Burckhardt (1784–1817) who visited in 1816,[3] hardly reflect their aesthetic enjoyment of Oriental travel. As the 1929 *Baedeker* noted: 'before the construction of the canal it was a miserable Arab village'. It refers to 'the Arab quarter, with its seven mosques and unimportant bazaar'[4] and lists its chief attractions as a visit to the harbour and to the nearby 'Ayn Mūsa, 'an oasis of luxuriant vegetation'. Whilst we may well agree with Said and Nash[5] that the *topoi* of travellers to the Middle East in an overworked topic, our stereotypes of the town can be reassessed by reconsidering different descriptions by travellers, many of whom may have been neglected or almost forgotten, Whilst in travelogues the narrator defines a presence in the literary locations that is ideological, nevertheless, some accounts also provide valuable detail that may shed light on the harbour-town's archaeological material culture; on its fishermen and boats (Niebuhr 1792), its commerce (comte Volney 1787; Richard F. Burton 1885) and the state of the town and its inhabitants. R.F. Burton, W.T. Thackeray, and Anthony Trollope described the harbour-town's incorporation into a cosmopolitan imperialist world after the Suez Canal was opened in 1869. These travel accounts enable us to reflect on memory as memoir, in the form of autobiographical travel writing and fictional narratives for, collectively, these literary descriptions and cultural connections may well enhance our understanding of its physical landscape.

Figure 16:1 Constantin-François Chasseboeuf, comte de Volney

1 'Mandalay'. 1890. In Kipling 1982.
2 Volney 1787: I, 213, 216.
3 Burckhardt 1822. On-line at http://etext.library.adelaide.-edu.au/b/burckhardt/john_lewis/syria/chapter7.html
4 Baedeker 1902: 174.
5 Nash 2005: 1–9.

Landscape as a literary object

In travel writing, land has physical and symbolic functions. Yet the material reality of location in travel literature is more than a *trope* with its function within the travelogue. The travel writer as observer engages with and revises physical and perceptual accounts of a landscape. Apart from providing a backdrop for any metaphoric journeys, any observant commentator also provides useful contemporary detail about a specific location that can be used to substantiate archaeological evidence and historical records.

In 1762 Carsten Niebuhr (1733–1815), a German geographer and traveller and sole survivor of one of the earliest 'scientific expeditions' to Arabia, was despatched by Frederick V, king of Denmark, in 1761 to undertake a rigorous survey of its people, flora and fauna. He later published *Travels through Arabia and Other Countries in the East*.[6] In August 1762 the Danish expedition left Cairo by caravan for Suez to sail to Jiddah. The expedition took with them a tent, a number of camp beds, copper cooking utensils and provisions, Pehr Forsskål's Ellis microscope and Niebuhr's Hadley astrolabe. Niebuhr, the expedition's surveyor, recounts in his meticulous journals that their journey took 32 hours and 40 minutes and that they arrived in Suez on 31 August 1762 at 10 am:

> The city of Suez stands upon the western side, but not just upon the western extremity of the Arabian Gulf. It is not surrounded with a wall; but the houses are built so closely together, that there are only two passages into the sea, of which that nearest the sea is open, the other shut by a very insufficient gate. The houses are very sorry structures; the khans being the only solid buildings in the city ... The ground lying around it is all one bed of rock, slightly covered with sand. Scarce a plant is to be seen anywhere in the neighbourhood. Trees, gardens, meadows and fields are entirely unknown in Suez.[7]

In 1816 when Burckhardt visited Suez the eastern part of the town of Suez was 'completely in ruins, but near the shore are some well built Khans, and in the inhabited part of the town are several good private houses.'[8] Furthermore,

> The air is bad, occasioned by the saline nature of the earth, and the extensive low grounds on the north and north-east sides, which are filled with stagnant waters by the tides. ... The inhabitants endeavour to counteract the influence of this bad atmosphere by drinking brandy freely; the mortality is not diminished by such a remedy, and fevers of a malignant kind prevail during the spring and summer.[9]

Sir John Garner Wilkinson (1797–1875) gave Suez scant attention in his guidebook of 1847: 'The environs are monotonous and barren. The town is small and insignificant ... the part of the sea most likely to be effected ... "by a strong east wind".'[10] Suez was still a depressing and squalid town when Richard F. Burton (1821–1890) visited it in 1853.[11]

Niebuhr found the town 'very thinly inhabited' in 1762. Before 1810, the town had eleven quarters, about 112 houses, two mosques, a mill, several ovens, some eighteen larger shops and khans, six markets with 120 shops and workshops and a *zāwiya*. In 1816 Burckhardt also found the town in a ruinous state and 'neither merchants nor artisans live in it. Its population consists only of about a dozen agents, who receive goods from the ports of the Red Sea, and forward them to their correspondents at Cairo, together with some shop-keepers who deal chiefly in provisions.'[12] He noted: 'The aspect of Suez is that of an Arabian, and not an Egyptian town, and even in the barren waste, which surrounds it, it resembles Yembo and Djidda; the same motley crowds are met with in the streets, and the greater part of the shop-keepers are from Arabia or Syria.'[13] In 1853 Burton described the people of Suez as a 'finer and fairer race than the Cairenes' and more like Arabs, their dress was 'more picturesque', their 'eyes carefully darkened with kohl' and they 'wear sandals not slippers' — but they were also 'a turbulent and fanatic set, fond of quarrels, and slightly addicted to "pronunciamentos".'[14] In 1837 the population of Suez was under 3,000, by 1840 around 3,000. In 1841, violent March storms caused several buildings to collapse. By 1850, as many as 1,500 had died in Suez as a result of a cholera epidemic but by 1853 Burton found the population between 4,800 and 6,000.

Sweet Water

There were difficulties supplying inhabitants of Suez with fresh water: supplies from Bir Suez and the 'pretended' wells of Moses were poor. Boats could be attacked by Bedouin if they stopped at al-Ṭūr to take on sweet water: for example, in 1783 'after plundering it of 15,000 bags of coffee, they abandoned the vessel to the wind, which threw it upon the coast.'[15]

6 Niebuhr 1792.
7 Ibid.: 175–6.
8 Burckhardt 1822: 467.
9 Ibid.
10 Wilkinson 1847: 209–210.
11 Burton 1855–1856: Chapter 9.
12 Burckhardt 1822: 465.
13 Ibid.: 467.
14 Burton 1856: 118.
15 Volney 1787: I, 217–8.

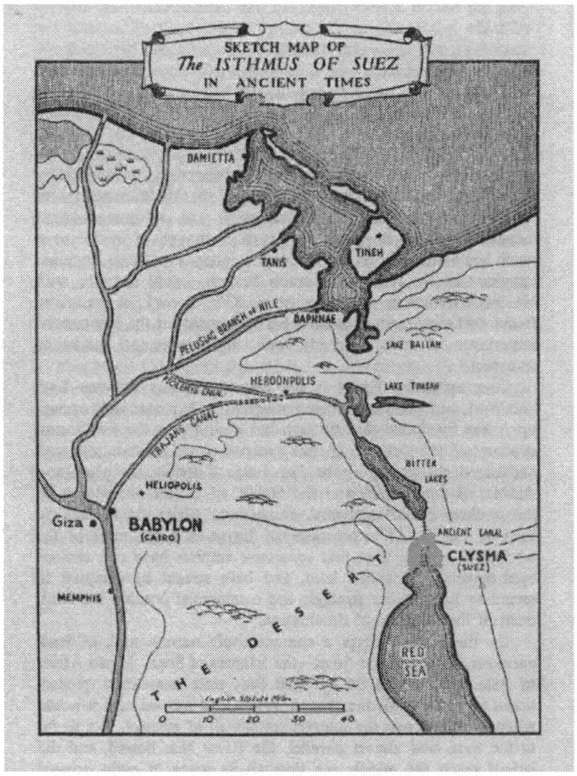

Map 16:1 Sketch map of canals on the Isthmus of Suez (Schofield 1969: 2)

A canal from the Nile to the Red Sea at Suez was built in Pharaonic times. According to Strabo this was first executed under Senusret I (1965–1920 BC) using the Pelusiac branch of the Nile just north of Bubastic, along Wādī Tumaylāt (the land of Goshen, east, then south, reaching the Red Sea through the Bitter Lakes at the port of Clysma, A canal from the Nile to the Red Sea at Suez was built in Pharaonic times. It was then partly restored by Pharoah Necho (612 BC) and completed by the Persian ruler Darius Hystaspes (521 BC) and his successor, Xerxes; the Ptolemies, Philadelphus (286 BC) and Euergetes (246 BC) reconditioned the canal with a terminus at Arsinoë, near the modern Suez, and it was again restored by the Roman Emperor Trajan (AD 98). A journey along the canal took four days according to Herodotus.[16] A canal terminated at Qulzum, dug about AD 641–642, at the time of Caliph 'Umar ibn al-Khaṭṭāb, so that corn and barley could be transported from the Nile Valley to Makkah and al-Madīnah,[17] but closed in AD by al-Manṣūr, the second 'Abbāsid caliph, to blockade these holy cities.

When Jean de Thévenot visited the Sinai peninsula in 1658 he had to take drinking water with him, and as he could not buy wine in Suez, he had to stock up on brandy.[18] The Arabs charged high prices for water or threatened to ruin the city by cutting off water supplies. Burckhardt described Bir Suez in 1816, as 'a copious spring enclosed by a massive building'.[19] The only good drinking water came from the wells of al-Naba, 'three hours journey on the Arabian shore' according to Volney: 'though reputed the best, it is still very bad' according to Niebuhr, and a spring with sweet water but a 'very indifferent taste' that 'becomes putrid in a few days if kept in skins' according to Burckhardt.[20] In 1744, Volney commented that 'without a mixture of rum', it [the water of al-Naba] is insupportable to Europeans'.[21] Although Volney found traces of the ancient canal, commerce between Suez and Cairo was by caravan as the canal was choked up and destroyed by Bedouin. In the 1790s, a group of Napoleon's technicians traced the former Nile-Red Sea canal and explored possibilities of restoring it; Niebuhr had plotted the Rosetta branch of the Nile so accurately in the 1760s that his drawings were used in the reconstruction of the old sweet-water canal in the early nineteenth century.

Seascapes — of boats and commerce

Vessels had to navigate despite sudden winds, infamous reefs and shoals. Johann Wild (b. *ca.* 1585), a German slave to a Persian merchant, recorded that on their safe arrival in Suez from Jiddah in 1606 each passenger sacrificed two or three sheep to be distributed to the poor.[22]

In 1547 Pierre Belon du Mans counted about thirty to forty Turkish boats drawn up on the shore, to avoid the effects of winter wind.[23] They had been brought from Constantinople via Cairo, taken apart and the pieces carried across the desert to Suez where they were reassembled.

Vessels that were overloaded could not navigate in the winds and through the reefs; if too light they could overturn. In the seventeenth century, larger vessels had two or three holds above each other, to avoid water damage:[24] between 1995 and 1998, Cheryl Ward, Peter Hitchcock and their team discovered such a wreck of a vessel dated to about 1765, on coral reefs off Sadana Island at about 30 m below sea level.[25] The wreck provides archaeological evidence to support descriptions of shipping by contemporaries such as Volney and Niebuhr. In 1783, Volney described Suez harbour: 'a wretched quay, where the smallest boats are unable to reach the

16 Rennell 1830: 57.
17 Volney 1787: I, 213.
18 Thévenot 1681. 312.
19 Burckhardt 1822: 464–5.
20 Ibid.: 468.
21 Volney 1787: I, 216.
22 Wolff 2003: 241–2.
23 Ibid.: 243.
24 Ibid.: 242.
25 Ward 2004: 165–71. The boat is estimated to be about 50 m long and 18 m wide and around 900 tons.

shore, except at the highest tides.' He saw twenty-eight boats in the road at a time and he found that 'their number diminishes every year, since, by continually coasting along a shore full of shoals, one out of nine, at least, is shipwrecked.'[26] Yet in 1853, Burton found ninety-two ships (*baghlah*) in Suez between 25 and 250 tons, and recorded thirty-eight departures in 1852–1853, noting that, according to Henry Levick,[27] a strict rotation system (*farzah*) operated from 1818.

The artist Baurenfeind was taken ill when the Danish Expedition arrived in Suez in 1762. Botanist Pehr Forsskål, the surveyor Niebuhr and the doctor Kramer were hardly on speaking terms with the philologist, Friedrich von Haven, especially as he had threatened to poison Baurenfeind. Yet Von Haven insisted on exploring Mount Sinai in search of inscriptions, for which he set out on 6 September, accompanied by a reluctant Niebuhr and a group of Bedouin, including Sawalha, Leghat and Said to act as protector-guides (*ghafir*). The botanist, Pehr Forsskål,[28] remained to look after Baurenfeind and to explore the deserts around Suez. Forsskål also talked to its fishermen,[29] merchants and shipbuilders who told him that dhows were expensive to build being constructed from pine from Antioch or the Greek islands and that the keel was teak from India.

The Sadana Island wreck had an oak frame, with pine planking, which again indicated a Mediterranean source for its timbers. Cheryl Ward suggested that raw materials were probably brought from Alexandria, up the Nile to Cairo, and carried 150 km (90 miles) by camel to the shipyards at Suez. In 1853, Henry Levick, Esq. later Vice-Consul, and afterwards Postmaster at Suez noted: 'Teak comes from India via Jeddah, and Venetian boards, owing to the expense of camel-transport, are a hundred per cent dearer here than at Alexandria. Trieste and Turkey supply spars, and Jeddah canvas: the sail-makers are Suez men, and the crews a mongrel mixture of Arabs and Egyptians; the Rais, or captain, being almost invariably, if the vessel be a large one, a Yambu' man.'[30]

Smaller boats were made from local timber: cypress, acacia and mimosa. In 1855 Burton identified two kinds of craft, distinguished from each other by tonnage, rather than build: 'The Baghlah (buggalow), is a vessel above fifty tons burden, the Sambuk (a classical term) from fifteen to fifty.'[31] Niebuhr also recorded an awkward rudder, made of a large beam, 'the use of which is dangerous and inconvenient.'[32]

In 1783 Volney recorded that they scarcely built a *cayasse*[33] in three years, the dock at Suez being ill adapted to repair boats, but Burckhardt recorded that Suez was one of the few harbours in the Red Sea where ships could be repaired, and that vessels are constantly seen at the wharf.

As in Roman and Ottoman times,[34] boat-builders were often Greek even into the early nineteenth century. Burckhardt noted that repairs were carried out 'by Greek shipwrights and smiths, in the service of the Pasha, who are let out to the ship-owners by the commanding officer'.[35] By 1816 Burckhardt found no Europeans living in Suez though Niebuhr visiting in 1762 noted that 'Among its inhabitants are some Greeks, and a few families of Copts'.[36] In 1816 Burckhardt noted that Greeks of Suez visited St Catherine's monastery in Sinai every summer, camping with their families in its garden, and that they were the only persons who ventured to undertake the journey through the desert to reach it. He recorded the arrival of a group of Greeks from Suez: 'being friends of the monks, they were invited in the evening to the private apartments of the latter, where they were plied so bountyfully with brandy that they all retired tipsy to bed.' Succeeding generations of Greeks continued as ship-builders, depite difficulties in obtaining materials. Two new quarters were built in the 1810s when Greeks were brought to Suez by Muḥammad 'Alī Pasha to build ships to transport troops for his Ḥijāzī wars (1811–1818).

---

26 Volney 1787: I, 218.

27 Levick wrote a long description of Suez between 1838 and 1853 and gave a copy to Richard F. Burton, who quoted (1855–1856) extensively from it. Henry Levick was vice-consul and later post-master in Suez and had a brother who was also a trader in the area. I think they lived in the house in which Napoleon Bonaparte stayed when he visited in 1798. This original document is lodged in the Swindon and Wiltshire Record Office with the Papers of Sir Richard Burton (1821–1890), 2667 26/2/v 1870–1881 'Letters to Richard and Isabel Burton on a range of subjects'. Package (v) 11 includes a bundle of letters entitled 'Khedive mines' and 'Levick' (I have requested access to these archives.).

28 For more detail about the botanical collections of Pehr Forsskål see Hepper 2007, this volume.

29 Volney 1787: I, 216 found that 'Arabs seldom attempt fishing, at which they are far from expert', whilst Burckhardt found shellfish called *Zorombat* (زرنبات) being sold by the fishermen at al-Ṭūr and Suez and gives details of fish preservation (1822: 504).

30 Levick, quoted by Burton 1855–1856, repr. 2004: 337.

31 Burton 1855–1856: 178.

32 Niebuhr 1792, quoted by Nance 1920: 39.

33 Possibly 'cavasse' or from 'caisson', i.e. a dry dock?

34 See papers by Arenson and P. Starkey, this volume.

35 Burckhardt 1822: 590.

36 Niebuhr, in Pinkerton 1811: 5.

Long-Distance Trade

Cairo was the centre for circulation of trade from Arabia and India via the Red Sea and through Suez as well as by the Nile with Abyssinia and Africa, and by the Mediterranean from Marseilles, Leghorn and Venice to Alexandria via Rosetta to Cairo. There were several different routes from Cairo to Suez, including that taken by the Towara 'called Derb el Ankabye (درب العنقبية)', 'which lies mid-way between the great Hadj route, and the more southern one close along the mountains: the latter is pursued only by the Arabs Terabein, and other Syrian Bedouins.'[37] Burckhardt noted that Suez was supplied 'with provisions from Cairo (cost 25% more than in Cairo and of the worst quality); and that 'vegetables are found only at the time of the arrival of the caravan'. Caravans run by Terabein Arabs also travelled between Suez,[38] Gaza and Hebron carrying 'manufactures of Damascus, soap, glass-ware, tobacco, and dried fruits, which are shipped at Suez for the Hedjaz and Yemen'.[39]

Thus a greater part of merchandise from India and Yemen passing through Suez, especially coffee, spices, textiles and porcelain, was in transit to other countries and was paid in goods from Europe and Turkey. The Sadana Island wreck was heavily laden with coffee as well as small earthenware jars (*qulal*), frankincense, 'pearl oyster shells, spices, packing materials, foodstuffs, and about a hundred coconuts, originally stuffed into every possible nook and cranny of the ship'.[40] It also carried a cargo of Chinese porcelain, as well as Imari ware, probably for the Ottoman court. In al-Mukhā', European traders exchanged Chinese porcelain for coffee and often brought porcelain north to Jiddah and Suez with their coffee cargoes. Egypt consumed imported finished articles of luxury in return principally for raw materials so that, Volney noted, this commerce did not 'contribute greatly to the real riches of Egypt, or the benefit of the people'.[41]

In 1783 Volney identified the merchandise from Cairo to be sent to Jiddah, Makkah and al-Mukhā' to be bartered for coffee from Arabia as well as Indian goods including arms, fur, passengers, wrought silk from Constantinople; cloths from Languedoc, Lyons stuffs and laces, grocery, paper, mercery[42] and 'wood, sails, and cordage for the ships at Suez; in some anchors carried each of them by four camels, iron bars, carded wool, and lead; it likewise carried bales of cloth, and barrels of cochineal, corn, barley and beans, Turkish piastres, Venetian sequins,[43] and Imperial dahlers,'[44] By 1852 Levick noted that:

> imports were contained in 36,840 packages, the exports in 13,498: of the staple articles — coffee and gum-arabic — they were respectively 15,499 and 14,129 bales, each bale being valued at about L5. Next in importance was wax from al-Yaman and the Hijaz, mother-of-pearl from the Red Sea, sent to England in rough (sic), pepper from Malabar, cloves brought by Moslem pilgrims from Java, Borneo, and Singapore, cherry pipe-sticks from Persia and Bussora,[45] and Persian or Surat 'Timbak' (tobacco). Minor articles of exportation were 'general spiceries (ginger, cardamons, &c.); Eastern perfumes, such as aloes-wood, attar of rose,[46] attar of pink and others; tamarinds from India and Al-Yaman, Banca tin, hides supplied by the nomade Badawin, senna leaves from Al-Yaman and the Hijaz, and blue chequered cotton Malayahs (women's mantillas), manufactured in southern Arabia. The total value of these smaller imports may be L20,000 per annum.[47]

In 1853 Levick recorded imports into Suez as 41,395 packages:

> Specie makes up in some manner for this preponderance of imports. ... Imports were about L350,000[48] ...

37 Many travellers described these routes, including Wilkinson 1847: 207.

38 Burckhardt 1822 : 571.

39 Volney 1787: I, 209.

40 Ward on http://www.anthro.fsu.edu/people/faculty/ward/-7seas.pdf

41 Volney 1787: I, 209.

42 'Mercery' refers to silk, linen and fustian textiles and goods made from these fabrics.

43 Venetian *sequins* were still a major trading coin (indeed the principle gold coin) in the Mediterranean and Asian worlds in the eighteenth century. Sequin is probably an Anglicization of the Venetian term *zecchino*, the name of the main Venetian gold coin from the early sixteenth century, when the term *ducat* shifted to become a silver coin and accounting term (Cook, personal communication).

44 Volney 1787: I, 209, 215. According to Harris the British pound sterling was equal to 23.17 *livres tournois* during the 1790s. 1 *livre* = 24 *Kreuzer rhein.* £5 in 1780 was worth about £330 in modern terms according to Bank of England exchange rates. The Rhenish *florin* or *gulden* (as a unit of account) = 60 *kreuzer*. In 1766 the *florin* was equal to 3s. 1¼d., the *thaler* or 'Rix dollar' was worth 4s.8d. sterling (Cook, personal communication).

45 Miss Julia Pardoe describes 'the street of the pipe-stick makers [in Constantinople], a race of men who are sure of success in their calling, and who are comparatively independent on their manner of doing business; and many a bargain is struck between the itinerant dealer and these worthy perforators of cherry-sticks and jasmin-wood' (1838: 38). Cherry sticks were also an overland import from Iran into the Ottoman empire (Simpson, personal communication).

46 Rose attar is also partly smoking related as it was a preferred additive to water-pipe tobacco (Simpson, personal communication).

47 In 1850, £20,000 was worth about £1,220,000 in modern terms.

48 In 1850, £350,000 was worth about £21,350,000 in modern terms, according to the Bank of England which provides advice on values of the pound across time in terms of 2006 values. As Cook reflects, however, giving modern

> principally of coffee and gum-arabic; of these there were respectively 17,460 and 15,132 bales, the aggregate value of each article being from L75,000 to L80,000, and the total amount L160,000[49] ... There were also (A.D. 1853) of cloves 708 packages, and of Malabar pepper 948: the cost of these two might be L7,000.[50] Minor articles of exportation are, — general spiceries (ginger, cardamons, &c.); Eastern perfumes, such as aloes-wood, attar of rose, attar of pink and others; tamarinds from India and Al-Yaman, Banca tin, hides supplied by the nomade Badawin, senna leaves from Al-Yaman and the Hijaz, and blue chequered cotton Malayahs (women's mantillas), manufactured in southern Arabia. The total value of these smaller imports may be L20,000 per annum.

Exports in 1853 were 15,988 packages, with export trade to Jiddah at L300,000 per annum. L30,000 to L40,000, in crown, or Maria Theresa, dollars annually left Egypt for Arabia, Abyssinia, and other parts of Africa. The exports in 1852–1853 listed by Levick chiefly consisted

> of English and native 'grey domestics,' bleached Madipilams, Paisley lappets, and muslins for turbands; the remainder being Manchester prints, antimony, Syrian soap, iron in bars, and common ironmongery, Venetian or Trieste beads, used as ornaments in Arabia and Abyssinia, writing paper, Tarbushes, Papushes (slippers), and other minor articles of dress and ornament.

Coffee

In order to understand a little more about commerce in Suez, details of the coffee trade are discussed in more detail. Throughout the seventeenth century, Egypt dominated the coffee market; and coffee made up two-thirds of the value of Egypt's imports from the Red Sea even in the latter part of the eighteenth century. In 1718 the coffee price in Yemen reached a record level due to fierce competition between Turkish, English, French, Belgian, and Dutch buying agents, so that the supply ran short.

In May 1783, a year when there was great demand for coffee, the Jiddah fleet of twenty-eight boats brought 30,000 *sardes* of coffee to Suez.[51] In 1783 the duties[52] on coffee were enormous and the value of coffee increased as it was transported West; According to Volney's account, the *sarde* or bale of coffee weighed 370–375 lb and cost 54 *pataques* in al-Mukhā',[53] 'the name given there to the *dahler* of the empire,[54] which was worth 5 *livres* 5 *sols* (four and four pence half-penny), or 236 *livres Tournois* (£9/16/8)'.[55] In addition sea duties (*baḥr*) of 147 *livres* (£6/2/6)[56] were charged plus an addition of 69 *livres* (£2/17/6), plus another 6 per cent added at Jiddah, which meant that the duties were nearly the same as the initial cost of the coffee! Additional costs included freight, losses and waste so that it was not astonishing that Mocha coffee sold at 45 and 50 *sols* per lb (1s 10d to 2s 1d) and in Marseilles at 3 *livres* per lb (half a crown).[57] By 1816 according to Burckhardt the Pasha owned most of the imports of coffee and had fixed its transport across the desert at a low price, so that none of the agents dare offer more to the camel drivers. Thus few were encouraged to come to Suez except those engaged in transporting the Pasha's merchandise. In 1852 Levick recorded 17,460 bales of coffee (c. L75,000) and in 1853 he noted 15,499 bales of coffee, each being L5.

The Dutch East India Company records note that in Mukhā', European traders exchanged Chinese porcelain for coffee and often brought porcelain north to Jiddah and Suez with their coffee cargoes.[58] As Cheryl Ward concluded, trade in Chinese porcelain and coffee was so profitable that boat owners were able to recoup their shipbuilding costs after only three voyages between Suez and Jiddah. Curiously, there were several important types

equivalences can be unreliable (personal communication).

49 In 1850, £160,000 was worth about £9,760,000 in modern terms

50 In 1850, £7,000 was worth about £427,000 in modern terms.

51 At the rate of 370 lb for each *sarde* this meant that the total trade was about 11,100,000 lb or 101,000 quintals. More normally on average the coffee trade was from 60,000–70,000 quintals annually.

52 According to Volney 1787: I, 220, duty on the *sarde* was 216 *livres* (£9) at Suez; thus the 30,000 *sardes* of 1783 produced to the Customs House in Suez the sum of 6,480,000 *livres Tournois* (£270,000) in duty.

53 Volney's text (1787: I, 220) suggests the *pataque* is the local term for *thalers* (it may be derived from the Netherlands *patagon*), and worth 4s. 4½d. 54 *pataques* were worth in modern terms £792 (Cook, personal communication).

54 For exchange rates in this period Snelling's *Current Coins of Europe* (1766) has been used. For example, the *livre* was roughly 24 *kreuzers* or just under a shilling (about 11 pence): the exact level varied from year to year and place to place (Cook, personal communication).

55 In France, the *livre tournois* and the currency system based on it became a standard monetary unit of accounting and continued to be used even when the 'livre tournois' ceased to exist as an actual coin. Livres would normally be the *livre tournois*, the main French unit of account. One livre was equal to 10½d (though Snelling says people often reckoned it at 11d.). In 1766 Snelling's list gives 22 6/7 *livres* to the pound sterling. On these rates, 26mn *livres* is equivalent to about £1,130,000. The modern equivalent of this would be £74,580,000 (Cook, personal communication).

56 To arrive at a rough modern equivalent of currencies for the 1760s–1790s, multiply the figure by 65–70 (Cook, personal communication). In mid-eighteenth-century urban England a family of four could live modestly on £40 sterling a year, and a gentleman could support his standard of living on £300 sterling a year.

57 Volney 1787: I, 220–1.

58 Brouwer 1998.

of local non-porcelain coffee cups manufactured and in circulation in the eighteenth and nineteenth centuries in the region: E.J. Keall, for example, described Hays ware, tiny coffee cups made for the coffee-drinking elite, manufactured in the peripheral settlement of Hays near Zabīd in Yemen.[59]

Pilgrimage

Pilgrim caravans from Makkah brought back 'Indian stuffs, shawls, gums, pearls, perfumes, and especially the coffee of Yemen'.[60] These commodities were also shipped from Jiddah to Suez, then transported to Cairo where considerable profits were made from duties charged and from sums spent by the pilgrims there. Yet Suez was a modest harbour for pilgrims travelling to Makkah and al-Madīnah. Caravans with 3,000 to 4,000 camels came from as far away as the river of Senegal, as well as the Mediterranean coasts, from Algiers, Tripoli and Tunis, via the deserts of Alexandria. They travelled to Cairo where they joined the Egyptian caravan via the old pilgrim road through Wādī al-Ṭīh to Suez, returning a hundred days later, those from Morocco returning home after a year. Buckhardt described the Great Ḥajj route that ran from Dār al-Hamra to the Birkat al-Ḥajj, four hours from Cairo, where pilgrims encamped before setting out for Makkah. On 29 September 1762 Niebuhr recorded the arrival in Suez of a great caravan of over 6,000 camels with pilgrims en route for Makkah. On 5 October 1762 the Danish expedition, surrounded by chests, baggage and equipment, took a rowing boat in order to board the ship that would take them to Jiddah before the pilgrims came on board. Once the pilgrims came aboard, there were over 500 on their ship alone, with about 72 crew members, including their wives and children. Volney noted that the caravans waited for the arrival of vessels into the port of Suez around the end of April or the beginning of May, as well as in July and August, before setting off from Cairo. He accompanied a caravan in 1783 with about 3,000 camels and 5,000 to 6,000 men which took at least forty days to assemble and took twenty-nine hours 'by the route of the Haouatat Arabs'.[61] He also recorded that the Ayaidi Bedouin also controlled part of the route. Volney noted: 'Pilgrims, who preferred the voyage by sea to a land journey' also carried 'rice, meat, wood and even water; for no place in the world is more destitute of every necessity than Suez.'[62]

Burckhardt saw Syrian, Turkish and Maghribi pilgrims in Suez, waiting for the departure of ships. He found three pilgrim boats in the harbour, and calculated that one sailed to the Ḥijāz every fortnight. By 1838 Henry Levick[63] noted the affluent merchants of Suez and between 10,000 to 12,000 pilgrims, but Burton recorded that there were only 4,893 pilgrims in 1851–1852 with 3,136 recorded in 1852–1853. On 6 July 1853 Burton sailed for twelve days, south to Yanbū', on the 'Silk al–Zahab' ('Golden Thread'), a two-masted 50-ton steamer, which sailed without a compass, log, chart or spare ropes, carrying ninety-seven Syrian and Maghribi pilgrims in a boat designed to hold no more than sixty passengers; he returned to Suez from Jiddah on the 'Dwarka' after his pilgrimage to Makkah and al-Madīnah in September. In 1855 passengers from Suez to Jiddah were charged 'as much as 6 or even 8 dollars for standing room — personal baggage forming another pretext for extortion — and the higher orders of pilgrims, occupying a small portion of the cabin, paid about 12 dollars.'[64]

Changing landscapes and seascapes

Post and passengers to and from India

Although there was intermittent contact between European communities in India and Europe via Suez and the overland route to Alexandria, with various *ad hoc* postal arrangements, it was not until the nineteenth century that arrangements through Suez were more regulated. In 1830 the 'Hugh Lindsay', a steamboat, built in Bombay at the expense of the Bombay Government, arrived in Suez from Bombay.[65] In 1829–1830 and again in 1835, Lieutenant Thomas Waghorn (1800–1850) explored the possibilities of the Suez route to send mail to India, thus saving over sixty days compared to the Cape route. As a direct result the British Government made an agreement for the Peninsular and Orient Company (P&O, founded in 1837, with 'Orient' added after 1840) to regularly convey mails to Alexandria, then via the Nile and overland to Suez, from where ships of the East India Company took them to Bombay. Waghorn was responsible for the Egyptian sector and from 1838 inward mails bore the cachet: 'Care of Mr. Waghorn, Suez.' From

[59] Keall 1992: XXII, 29–46. There were also local handmade version(s) on the Karak plateau; Tophane (and probably Asyut) red clay versions from the 1840s; as well as Kutahya-ware cups throughout the southern Levant (Simpson, personal communication). None of these wares appear to have been mentioned as being imported into Suez in the travellers' sources quoted in this text, though this does not mean that this was not the case.

[60] Volney 1787: I, 208.

[61] Ibid. 215.

[62] Ibid. 218.

[63] According to maritime pension records 1833/34, OIOC at the British Library, found as a loose leaf, is a note of Salaries of Agents in Egypt, including Capt Johnson, Principle Agent in Egypt, Mr Alfred Warne, Packet Agent, Cairo and Henry Levick, Packet Agent, Suez, who were all paid £750 *per annum*, more than the agent in Alexandria was paid at the time.

[64] Burton 1857: 167.

[65] Searight, introduction to Thackeray 1846: 19.

1838, Suez was the terminus of a lucrative new post road via Alexandria and Cairo and became the embarkation point for passengers on the new steamships to Bombay.

Waghorn's company provided hotels in Alexandria, Cairo and Suez and made all the travel arrangements across Egypt, building a series of rest-houses and supplying guides, and including alternatives of carriage, donkey chairs, camels, or horses from Cairo to Suez.[66] Thackeray, travelling at the invitation of the P & O in 1844, described the arrival of passengers at Waghorn's Hotel d'Orient in Cairo from Bombay and Suez: 'As a hundred Christian people, or more, come from England and from India every fortnight, this inn has been built to accommodate a large proportion of them; and twice a month, at least its sixty rooms are full'[67] ... 'the road between Cairo and Suez is *jouché* with soda-water corks.'[68]

In 1858 Anthony Trollope (1815–1882) was commissioned by the Post Office to visit Egypt for two months to discover if bags or metal boxes were more suitable for sending mail across Egypt after the railway line between Alexandria and Suez was completed that year, replacing the 80-90 camel postal caravan. The railway was also used to import fresh water into Suez, which gradually turned into a town. Trollope also negotiated a postal treaty (signed in London on 16 July 1858) with Nuba Bey (1825–1899), to use the railway to convey post between Alexandria and Suez.[69]

Figure 16:2 French postcard of the Railway Station, Suez, 1915

Trollope went to Suez for five days as part of his mission and subsequently described Suez in *The Bertrams* as a 'triste, unhappy, wretched place ... a small Oriental town, now much be-Europeanised ... it has neither water, air, nor verture. No trees grow there, no rivers flow there. Men drink brine and eat goats; and the thermometer stands at 80 in the shade in winter. The oranges are the only luxury.' Through the *motif* of the 'traveller abroad' in Suez, Trollope mercilessly lampoons English cultural connections with the Orient. In his short story 'George Walker at Suez', published in 1861, [70] Suez 'is by far the vilest, the most unpleasant and the least interesting. No women there, no water and no vegetation.'[71] It had changed little in essence from the town described by Niebuhr a hundred years previously.

Indo-European connections and the impact of the Suez Canal

European interests in Suez were entwined with the expansion of commerce and were based upon the increasing use of sea lanes from the Mediterranean Sea via Suez even before the Suez Canal was opened in 1869. From the early seventeenth century, European powers were preoccupied with the idea of building a canal to link the Mediterranean and the Red Sea. The seventeenth-century trader, Jacques Savary, in his work *The Complete Merchant*, believed that whilst Holland and England could use the Cape routes, for France trade on competitive terms was impossible as long as goods from India had to use caravan routes from Suez to Cairo[72] and canal to Alexandria.[73]

By Volney's time the port of Suez was barred to the shipping of Christian powers, yet English vessels sometimes made illicit use of the port. The British collector, George Annesley, Viscount Valentia (1770–1844) accompanied by his draughtsman and later British Consul-General in Egypt, Henry Salt (1780–1827), sailed up the African coast on their way back from India, and after a stormy voyage arrived in Suez on 26 January 1806 on board the 'Panther'. The joined the Ḥajj caravan with its 1,500 camels, 300 armed Arabs, and thirty Turkish soldiers with two officers to guard the *maḥmal* as it returned across the desert to Cairo.[74]

66 Schonfield 1969: 15.

67 Thackeray 1846: 129–30.

68 Ibid.: 145.

69 Anthony Trollope had written eleven chapters of *Doctor Thorne* when he left Dublin on 20 January 1858.

70 Trollope 1861.

71 George Walker at Suez, *Public Opinion* (12–15 April 1861) and then published in 1863. *Tales of All Countries*. London: Chapman and Hall.

72 There were several different routes across the desert from Cairo to Suez, including the great Ḥajj route, and most controlled by Bedouin Terabein.

73 Schonfield 1969: 7.

74 Manley and Rée 2001: 33–4.

Figure 16:3 Suez in 1798 from the Déscription de l'Égypte, *plate 575*

lan du port de Soueys et du fond du golfe arabique. Profil du canal projeté entre les deux mers.

Map 16:2 Suez harbour in 1798, from the Déscription de l'Égypte, *plate 574*

In May 1817, a small fleet of ships (some English and others belonging to Muḥammad ʻAlī Pasha) arrived at Suez direct from Bombay: 'among the articles imported were two elephants destined by the Pasha as presents to the Porte. This has been the first attempt within the last forty years to open a direct trade between India and Egypt, and', as Burckhardt commented, it 'will be as profitable to the Pasha as it must be ruinous to his subjects'.[75]

Creating the Canal

In 1798 Napoléon Bonaparte's forces invaded Egypt, partly to disrupt and destroy British links with India, so he revived the idea of a Suez route. Napoléon himself stayed in Suez in the house that was later to become the British agent's residence.[76] Between 1798 and 1802, Napoléon's savants surveyed the isthmus of Suez and published plans and drawings in the greatest monument to Napoleon, the wonderful *Déscription de l'Égypte*, published between 1809 and 1828.[77] In 1821, under the direction of Father Enfantin, Linant's Saint-Simonian study group, interested in opening up the world to the free movement of commodities,[78] proposed cutting through the low-lying Isthmus of Suez at its narrowest point, establishing a large internal port in the basin of Lake Timsah, and making the harbours of Suez and Pelusium accessible to the largest vessels. Linant de Bellefonds Bey, an able director of the canal works of Egypt, made the Suez Canal the study of his life.

It took Ferdinand de Lesseps (1805–1894), French vice-consul in Egypt, a man of soaring accomplishments, great notoriety and scandal, to implement Napoleon Bonaparte's dream of building a canal across the Isthmus of Suez as a short-cut to the riches of the East. De Lesseps' reports provide impressive statistics[79] and included the positive impact on the Ḥajj pilgrimage: 'the pilgrimage to Mecca henceforth rendered not only possible but easy to all Mussulmans, an immense impulse given to steam navigation and travelling generally, for countries on the Red Sea and Persian Gulf.'[80] He describes Suez as 'an isolated point ... its population a very miserable one, having only brackish water to drink. Our canal will bring it water and activity, which it lacks.' In his journal he recorded meteors and ancient Egyptian texts as evidence that he alone was destined to build the Canal. As he wrote of 15 November 1854 when he obtained a royal concession from Saʻīd Pasha, viceroy of Egypt, to set up a company to construct a maritime canal, 'the moment for the fulfilment of Napoleon's prophecy has arrived'.

75 Burckhardt 1822: 466.

76 See fn 27, above.

77 France, Commission des sciences et arts d'Égypte: 1809–1828: plates 574–577.

78 Mitchell 1991: 16–17.

79 For example, the distance was 1,800 leagues to Constantinople via the Canal as against 610 leagues via the Atlantic route (London 3,834 leagues via the Canal versus 5,950 leagues via the Cape).

80 Lesseps 1876: 46.

In 1835 when Alexander Kinglake (1809–1891) visited Suez from Cairo en route to Palestine and Syria, there was a British agent for the East India Company who welcomed him kindly.[81] In 1855, in an official report to the East India Company, Burton suggested that a consul should be established in Suez to extend the British sphere of influence.[82]Richard F. Burton, visiting a transformed Suez in 1869 to view preparations for the opening of de Lesseps' canal,[83] wrote: 'In a few years ancient Suez will be no more. The bazaars are not so full of filth and flies, now that the pilgrims pass straight through and hardly even encamp. The sweet water canal ... renders a Hammam possible; coffee is no longer hot saltish water, and presently irrigation will cover with fields and gardens the desert plain...the railway station, close to the hotel, the new British hospital, the noisy Greek casino, the Frankish shops, the puffing steamers, the ringing of morning bells, gave me a novel impression.'[84]

Figure 16:4 From Land of Pharaohs – Illustrated by Pen and Pencil *by Revd Samuel Manning, 1875*

In 1873 Burton noted that 'The noble works of the Canal Maritime, which should, in justice, be called "Lesseps Canal", shall soon transfer Clysma into a modern and civilised city.'[85] Burton visited Suez again in 1877 on his way to search for gold in Midian; his earlier forecast had not been fulfilled; another Suez was developing around the 'New Docks' [two new permanent artificial harbours 3 km south of Suez at the entry into the Canal] 'while the old town is falling to pieces[86] ... the port now temporarily ruined by its own folly and the ill-will of M. de Lesseps;

81 Kinglake 1844: 190–5.

82 McLynn 1990: 113.

83 Burton 1873: note to 3rd edn.

84 Ibid.

85 Ibid.

86 Burton 1879: note to 4th edn.

... I would have bought the (Suez) Canal... put a fortress at each end... I would annex Egypt and protect Syria, occupy the Dardenelles, and, after that, let the world wrangle as much as it pleased...!'[87]

Traders, soldiers, politicians, Indian Service administrators, engineers and tourists, as well as their families, like the small Rudyard Kipling (and my own father and grandparents), travelled from the British Empire in India through the Suez Canal after 1869. For Rudyard Kipling (1865–1936) the voyage from India in the East through Suez to Europe in the West reflected the loss of 'emotional and sensual security of a childhood Orient',[88] when, as a six-year-old Anglo-Indian child, he was sent back to a gloomy, unfamiliar England. In the symbolic geography of the voyage, the East was for Kipling an Edenic space: a 'sphere of communication and poetic fulfilment' that 'belongs to that time and space which is "East of Suez"':[89] a reflection of the European imperial interests beyond the Red Sea theatre.

Figure 16:5 Poster for the film 'Suez' *(1938)*

Conclusion

Travel writing was once thought to be an artless genre but more recently given advances in the analysis of narrative discourse, it is seen as an imaginative art, as much filled with fiction as with fact, with clouds of memories and the artful manipulation of details and events that acquire the status of facts. Travel accounts, whilst aiming to recreate the past through the processes of memory, can provide only a trace of an earlier experience. Nevertheless, fine travel narrative is based on extensive historical research and appreciation of local knowledge. The literary landscape of the travelogue, driven by its own fictive conventions — arrival, records based on careful observation leading to fascinating detail on the physical and cultural landscape, and departure — may, however provide useful data and about the physical landscape, resources and cultural connections of a location.

87 Burton's *Essay* that Isobel appended to her *Life*, see Burton 1893: 497.

88 http://social.chass.ncsu.edu/jouvert/v6i1-2/baneth.htm

89 Ibid.

References

Baedeker, K. 1902. *Egypt: handbook for travellers.* Leipzig: K. Baedeker; New York: C. Scribner's Sons.

———1929, 8th revised edn. *Egypt and the Sudan: handbook for travellers.* Leipzig: Karl Baedeker.

Brouwer, C.G. 1998. *Dutch-Yemeni Encounters: activities of the United East India Company (VOC) in South Arabian waters since 1614.* Amsterdam: D'luyte Rarob.

Burckhardt, J.-L. 1822. *Travels in Syria and the Holy Land; published by the association for promoting the discovery of the interior parts of Africa.* London: Association for Promoting the Discovery of the Interior Parts of Africa; John Murray.

Burton, I. 1893. *The Life of Captain Sir Richard F. Burton by his wife, Isabel Burton, with numerous portraits, illustrations and maps.* London: Chapman & Hall.

Burton, Sir R.F. 1855. Chapter 9 in *Personal Narrative of a Pilgrimage to El Madinah and Meccah.* London: Longman, Brown, Green and Longmans, repr. 1857; also London: G. P. Putnam & Co, 1856. Also Burton, Note in 3rd ed. 1873; Burton, Note to 4th ed. 1879.

——. 1885. *Supplemental Nights, to The book of the thousand and one nights.* London: Benares: VI.

——. 2004. *A Secret Pilgrimage to Mecca and Medina.* Introduced by Tim Mackintosh-Smith. London: Folio Society; prev. *Personal Narrative of a Pilgrimage to El Medinah and Meccah.*

France, Commission des sciences et arts d'Égypte. 1809–1828. *Description de l'Égypte où, Recueil des observations et des recherches qui ont été faites en Égypte pendant l'expédition de l'armée française.* 21 volumes. Paris: Imprimerie impériale.

Gindy, N. 2001. 'While I was in Egypt, I finished Dr Thorne', 139-51 in P. Starkey and J. Starkey (eds), *Unfolding the Orient.* Reading: Ithaca.

Harris, R.D. 1976. French finances and the American War, 1777-1783. *Journal of Modern History* 48 (June), 233-58

http://social.chass.ncsu.edu/jouvert/v6i1-2/baneth.htm

Keall, E.J. 1992. Smokers' pipes and the fine pottery tradition of Hays. *Proceedings of the Seminar for Arabian Studies* 22: 29–46.

Kinglake, A. 1844. *Eothen*. London: J. Olivier; repr. J.M. Dent, 1908.

Kipling, R. 1982. *The Portable Kipling*. Harmondsworth: Penguin.

Lesseps, F de. 1876. *The History of the Suez Canal: a personal narrative*. Tr. Sir H.D. Wolff. Edinburgh: W. Blackwood.

——. 1887. *Recollections of Forty Years*. Tr. C.B. Pitman. London: Chapman and Hall.

Manley, D. and Peta Rée, P. 2001. *Henry Salt: artist, travellers, diplomat, Egyptologist.* London: Libri Publications.

McLynn, F. 1990. *Burton: snow upon the desert*. London: John Murray.

Mitchell, T. 1991. *Colonising Egypt*. Berkeley and Oxford: University of California Press.

Nance, R.M. 1920. Fresh light on Terradas and Gelves [Indian Ocean]. *Mariner's Mirror* 6: 34–9.

Niebuhr, C. 1792. *Travels through Arabia and Other Countries in the East.* R. Heron (tr.). Edinburgh: printed for R. Morison and Son booksellers, Perth, G. Mudie, Edinburgh; and T. Vernor, Birchin Lane, London.

Pardoe, J. 1838. *The Beauties of the Bosphorus*. London: George Virtue,

Pinkerton, J. 1811. *A General Collection of the Best and Most Interesting Voyages and Travels in All Parts of the World.* London: Longman, Hurst, Rees, and Orme.

Rees, T. 2003. *Merchant Adventurers in the Levant*. Stawell: Talbot.

Rennell, J. 1830. *The Geographical System of Herodotus Examined and Explained.* London: C. J. G. & F. Rivington.

Schonfield, H.J. 1969. *The Suez Canal in Peace and War, 1869–1969*. London: Vallentine, Mitchell.

Thackeray, W.T. 1846. *Notes of a Journey from Cornhill to grand Cairo, by way of Lisbon, Athens, Constantinople, and Jerusalem: performed in the steamers of the Peninsular and Oriental Company*. London: Chapman and Hall. 1991, new edn with introduction by Sarah Searight. Heathfield: Cockbird Press, 1991.

Thévenot, Jean de. 1681. *Recueil de voyages de Mr Thevenot.* Paris: Chez Estienne Michallet

Trollope, A. 1861. George Walker at Suez. *Public Opinion* (28 December). On-line at http://www.info-motions.com/etexts/gutenberg/dirs/etext03/grgwk10.htm

Volney, comte C.-F.C. 1787. *Travels through Syria and Egypt in the years 1783, 1784, and 1785: containing the present natural and political state ... of the Turks and Arabs.* London: printed for C.G.J. and J. Robinson.

Ward, C. Chinese porcelain for the Ottoman Court: Sadana Island, Egypt. 186–90 in *Eighteenth-Century Wrecks.* http://www.anthro.fsu.edu/people/faculty/ward/7seas.pdf (See also http://www.adventure-corps.com/sadana/index.html and http://ina.tamu.edu/sadana.htm.)

——. Luxury wares in the Red Sea: the Sadana Island shipwreck. 165–171 in P. Lunde and A. Porter (eds), *Trade and Travel in the Red Sea Region. Proceedings of Red Sea Project I.* BAR International Series 1269. Oxford: Archaeopress.

Wild, J. 1973. V*oyages en Égypte de Johann Wild, 1606–1610*. Cairo: IFAO.

Wilkinson, Sir J.G. 1847. *Handbook for Travellers in Egypt: including descriptions of the course of the Nile to the second cataract, Alexandria, Cairo, the Pyramids, and Thebes, the overland transit to India, the peninsula of Mount Sinai, the Oases, &c*. London: John Murray.

Wolff, A. 2003. *How many Miles to Babylon?* Liverpool: Liverpool University Press.

Acknowledgements

An earlier version of this paper was presented at an ASTENE conference in Nuwaiba, Sinai in March 2006. Many thanks for information about currencies from Dr B.J. Cook, Curator of Medieval and Early Modern Coinage Department of Coins and Medals, British Museum, London; for information about coffee cups, rose of attar and cherry-sticks to St John Simpson, and to St John, Professor Dionisius Agius and William Facey for discussions on the meaning of *cayasse*.

Part IV: The Cultural Connections of the Red Sea

What is the Archaeological Evidence for External Trading Contacts on the East African Coast in the First Millennium BC?

Paul J.J. Sinclair

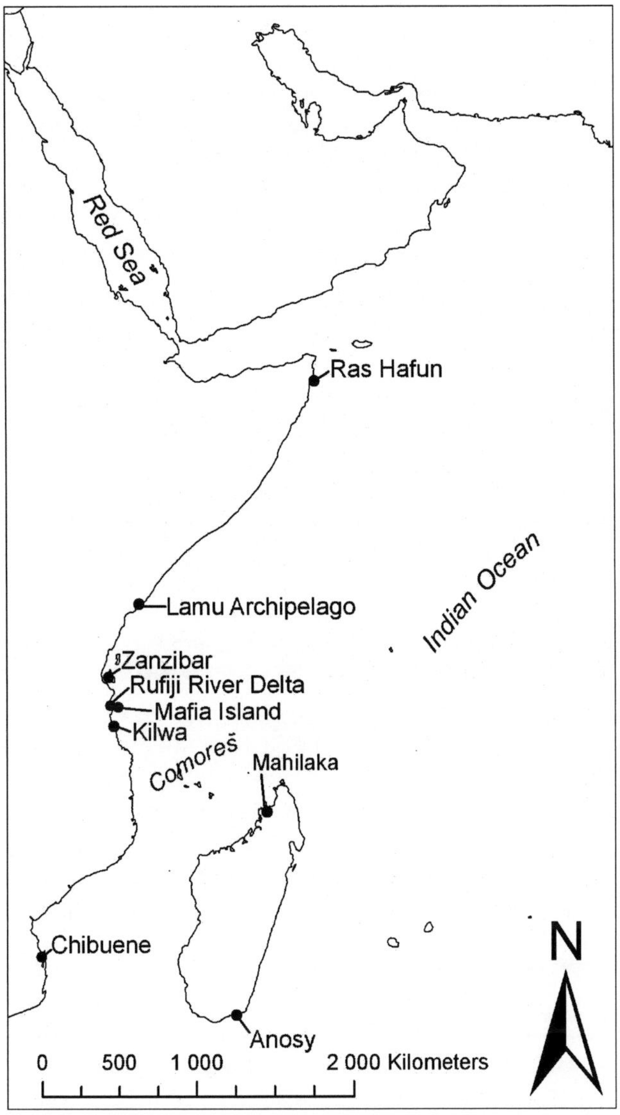

Map 17:1 Sites on the East African Coast

The aim of this paper is to identify potential sources of evidence for first-millennium BC trade along the East African coast. Examples from Zanzibar and Mafia Islands off the coast of Tanzania will be compared to material from southern Mozambique. I argue that recently reported scattered finds of early imports are best interpreted in relation to the regional cultural succession. Evidence for first-millennium BC trade is limited and in need of confirmation. A number of material culture indicators support the idea of Red Sea contacts in the first millennium AD as is well known from documentary sources, but South Asian contacts have also to be considered.

Archaeological investigations along the coast of East Africa and more specifically the islands of the Lamu and Zanzibar archipelagos have concentrated mainly on the extensive open sites containing architectural remains of the Swahili civilization and documentary evidence for trade, from the early first millennium AD onwards. The early focus on ceramic assemblages in East Africa by team members from the British Institute's programme on origins of the Bantu-speaking languages documented the widespread distribution of ceramic complexes throughout eastern and southern Africa and these have been attributed to iron-using early-farming communities probably speaking variants of Bantu languages.[1] Research, especially in the Rift, concentrated on early cattle keepers thought to speak variants of Cushitic languages.[2] Other work focused on establishing the basic chronologies of coastal urban settlements and the extent of late-first-millennium AD trade links.[3] Notable also for the present topic is the important contribution identifying ceramic assemblages from Ras Hafun, the late-first-millennium BC / early-first-millennium AD maritime station just south of the Horn.[4] Further challenges to established paradigms include evidence for very early trade contacts with Iraq and South Asia and the remarkably early presence of South-East Asian food crops in West and Central Africa as well as the early presence of African food crops in South Asia and South Asian cattle in Africa.[5] Archaeologists in East Africa are now facing the need to grapple with new interpretive paradigms in order to integrate the archaeological evidence from these disparate research contributions.[6]

As with any pioneer undertaking in archaeology, significant gaps were left in the sampling process particularly along the Tanzania coast and on the offshore islands. A number of these gaps have been filled with the work of F. Chami and his co-workers from the University of Dar es

1 Soper 1971; Phillipson 1985.
2 Phillipson 1985 and see Lane, *et al.* 2007.
3 For example, Chittick 1974, 1984; Horton 1996, Abungu 1989; Kusimba 1999; Wright 1992; La Violette and Fleisher 1995; Breen and Lane 2004.
4 Smith and Wright 1988.
5 Meyer, *et al.* 2001; Mbida, *et al.* 2000; Shinde 2002; Blench 2003; Fuller 2003; Neumann 2003; Misra and Kajale 2003; Gupta 2004; Magnavita 2006, Lejju, *et al.* 2006.
6 See Lane, *et al.* 2007 for a recent reconsideration of the conceptual framework of the pastoralist debate; Chami 2006a: 49–59.

Salaam who have demonstrated the presence of iron-working farming communities along the coast of Tanzania and on the near off-shore island complexes of Mafia and Kilwa.[7] Trade goods in the form of beads in association with early iron-using farming-community fluted pottery are documented from the coastal hinterland south of Dar es Salaam and in the Rufiji delta.[8] The segmented examples said to be Roman seem more securely dated to the first millennium AD than to the first millennium BC[9] and some similar examples exist in ninth- and tenth-century AD collections in Scandinavia.[10] The early occupation at Unguja Ukuu on Zanzibar, a site excavated by A. Juma, dates to the second half of the first millennium AD.[11] A wide range of glass beads and fragments seem mostly Islamic in origin[12] but some fragments of Roman / Egyptian earthenwares dating to the sixth century AD have been recovered from period I(a), broadly dated from the sixth to the tenth centuries AD. In addition, blue-green glazed Sasanian Islamic wares and white glazed far eastern wares are well attested at the site. Local earthenwares include characteristic linearly incised triangular motifs rather than the fluted ones of the earlier first-millennium AD iron-working, farming-community assemblages elsewhere on the coast. Blue-green glazed Sasanian Islamic wares have very wide distribution around the Indian Ocean rim and Glover[13] considers finds in East Africa to be Islamic in date but others[14] are more open to a pre-Islamic date.[15]

The emphasis of initial pioneer contributions upon visible architectural remains of the Swahili urban settlements[16] and ceramic assemblages of the early iron-working farming communities, and even the later responses focused on urbanism in the 1980s, resulted in relatively little effort being made to investigate other archives with potential for evidence of hunter-gatherer and pastoralist activities. Consideration of the role of pastoralists in urban formation on the Lamu archipelago by Horton was followed by a series of exchanges focusing on the presence or otherwise of pastoralist ceramics on the coast.[17] Currently the balance of evidence particularly on the Tanzanian coast and the Kilwa area[18] seems to favour the presence of pre-iron-using farming-community ceramics, some of which are similar to 'pastoral neolithic' wares known from the Rift Valley, but others such as pottery from Kitere seem comparable to first-millennium AD coastal wares of the Nampula and Monapo traditions from Mozambique.[19] In addition, sherds from Kilwa illustrated by Chami[20] seem similar to pottery from the north Mozambique coast Lumbo Bridge and Ibo Island, the former dated to the fourteenth century AD and the latter just as in Chami's illustration[21] by an associated spindle whorl similar to those from Chittick's excavation of stratified deposits on Kilwa and dated by him to period IIa, about the twelfth and thirteenth century AD[22]. A detailed comparison of all of these wares including thin sections still remains to be done but there is no doubt that the ramifications of the new work at Kilwa and on the southern coast of Tanzania by Chami and his team are potentially significant.

In a series of path-breaking investigations on the off-shore islands of Juani, near Mafia and Unguja (Zanzibar), Chami[23] has directed his attention at a number of cave deposits. All are small-scale, pioneer excavations aiming at establishing a preliminary sequence and will be followed by more detailed analysis. At Unkunju a single test pit was located in the spoil heap of a previous disturbance leading to the need, at least in my opinion, of considering all finds as a single stratigraphic unit. Beads found at the site are difficult to use as temporal markers[24] but the excavator argues on the basis of an eye bead and a scalloped bead for a pre-Islamic 300 BC–AD 400 date.

Considerable interest has been taken in the possible presence of South Asian earthenware ceramics.[25] Early preliminary identifications of two Harrapan potsherds have been withdrawn by Gupta. All of the sherds initially identified as Early Historic and Historic of Indian origin (with the exception of a single sherd of probable Arikamedu basket-impressed ware) cannot, according to Indian specialists present at the Indo-Pacific Prehistory Association meeting in Manila in March 2006, be taken as confirmed early historic or historic or even South Asian, given the absence of characteristic time markers in the collection of small sherds. Additional associated finds include mixed limestone and quartz stone assemblages studied by Knutsson. Further finds of possible South Asian pottery dated 200 BC–AD 400 were obtained from

7 Chami 1994, 1999a, 1999b, 1999c, 2001a, 2001b, 2005, 2006a, 2006b; Chami and Msemwa 1997; Chami and Kwekeson 2003.

8 Chami 1999a, 1999b.

9 Chami 2006a: 145.

10 Callmer 1977; Ljungkvist personal communication. In addition, both K. Andersson and F. Herschend in Uppsala have clarified earlier comments on the segmented bead from Rhodos 400 BC–AD 100 to be within the range of first-millennium AD collections in the Baltic.

11 Juma 2004.

12 Eighth to tenth century AD, according to St J. Simpson's personal communication.

13 Glover 2002.

14 Horton 1996, Juma 2004 and Chami 2006: 133.

15 See Tampoe, 1989, Juma 2004 for further discussion.

16 For example, Kirkman 1963, Chittick 1974, 1984.

17 Chami 2001; Chami and Kwekeson 2003; Sutton 2002; Phillipson 2005.

18 Chami 2006b.

19 Sinclair, *et al.* 1993: 424–5.

20 Chami 2006a: 143 Plate 12.

21 Ibid.: 143 Plate 13.

22 Sinclair 1985; Chittick 1974: 430 fig 166 a and h.

23 Chami 1999a, 1999c, 2001a, 2004, 2006a; Chami and Kwekeson 2003.

24 Chami 2004: 81.

25 Chami 2004, 2006a.

Kinunda Cave, also on Juani.[26] Gupta now places both ceramic collections in the first half of the first millennium AD.[27] In order for these highly significant possibilities of South Asian contact / presence to be confirmed there is broad agreement that more excavation and larger collections are required.

At Machaga Cave on Unguja, the main island of the Zanzibar archipelago, Chami has reported a sequence of occupation with stone tools and pottery ascribed by him to the Neolithic dating back to *ca.* 2800 BC and with a range of wild and domestic fauna, stone and bone tools and pottery.[28] Osteological samples of chicken bones are difficult to positively identify and have been questioned by some academics and defended by the excavator.[29] The bones from Machaga and from Kuumbi (see below) are currently the focus of further comparative analysis both in regard to the identifications and also the presence or otherwise of worked tools

The identification by Boussac of a single monochrome glass bead from Machaga similar to those produced at Arikamedu[30] and a single carnelian stone bead are both interesting indicators but in view of the long duration of production of both well into the first millennium AD it might be argued that finds from Machaga should not be taken as confirmation of first-millennium BC trade. On the other hand three associated carbon dates indicate a first to third-millennium BC occupation.[31] The interest aroused by the finds and carbon dates obtained from Machaga is considerable and further, it is worthwhile to note the cave deposit benefits from two intact white calcium-rich horizons in the stratigraphy indicating relatively undisturbed strata and underlining the value of further specialist geomorphological study and continued excavation at the site.

At Kuumbi Cave on Unguja, Zanzibar test pit excavations have recovered a 2.5 m sequence of more than 20,000 years of occupation.[32] Three stone-tool assemblages, coral stone at the base, quartz fragments in the mid section and crystalline limestone higher up are represented.[33] The well preserved osteological assemblage is dominated throughout to more than 50 per cent of the total identified fragments by a range of small antelopes. Early occurrence of zebra and rare giraffe gives way to a range of smaller animals higher up the sequence. Above the basal deposit is a 'sterile?' level *ca.* 40 cm thick (dated Ua 24922 to 21695 +-300 BP) lacking evidence of human activities and with an osteological collection largely restricted to remains of bats and small rodents and apparently not derived from human activities. These deposits might well represent an occupational hiatus during the last glacial maximum. In the lowermost deposits there are abundant remains of giant land snail *Achatina sp.*, but no marine shell occurs.

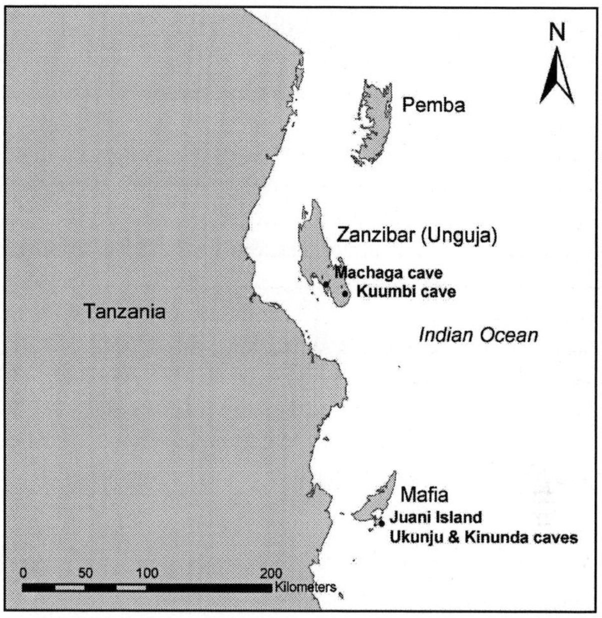

Map 17:2 Location of cave on Unguja and Juani island.

After an extended period of abandonment the cave was re-occupied by people using micro-lithic quartz stone tools and in addition decorating bone, as shown by a single example. Previous preliminary identifications of cattle bones[34] in the deposit cannot be confirmed yet. The deposit comprises mixed ash midden with remains of food processing and is dated by three samples from the lower, mid and upper sections. This unit is dated by Ua24919 4005+–40 BP 85cm, Ua 24920 1815+–40 BP 139 cm, and Ua 24921 5350+–45 BP 170 cm. It contains a quartz flake assemblage as well as some crystalline limestone flakes.[35] The reversal of the dates points to a need for caution in chronological interpretation. Terrestrial shell continues and marine shell appears. Some shells show signs of working to facilitate meat extraction and at least one marine shell operculum has been retouched into a scraper. Earlier reported remains of cattle and chicken and bone points at least from Trench 6 extension (finds from which have been analysed in detail) are not yet confirmed. The upper layers contain an apparently contemporary limestone flake assemblage. A range of fragmented ceramic sherds was recovered from the upper levels of the sequence and incised decoration motifs indicate the likelihood of a second-millennium AD date. The three

26 Chami 2004: 93.
27 Gupta 2006 unpublished, Gupta personal communication.
28 Chami 2006a: 142 Plate 9.
29 Chami 2001b, 2006a; Sutton 2002.
30 See discussion in Chami 2006a: 133.
31 Chami 2001b, 2006a: 100.
32 Sinclair, *et al.* 2006.
33 Preliminary analysis by Kjel Knutsson, see Sinclair, *et al.* 2006.
34 Sinclair, *et al.* 2006.
35 Ibid.

glass beads recovered from trench 6 have not been identified.

From these preliminary findings we know that hunter gatherers using a heavy duty stone tool assemblage lived in Kuumbi Cave prior to 21,000 years ago, hunting fauna in part no longer found on Zanzibar. Given the present depth of the channel (75 m) Zanzibar was probably joined to the mainland during different periods throughout the last Glaciation.

Results from Kuumbi show that Unguja was occupied much earlier than previously appreciated and given that Unguja has very probably been an island for the last 15,000 years[36] it seems not unlikely that at least from the mid Holocene the inhabitants of Unguja had a seagoing capacity which perhaps even included the possibility of reaching the Comores and Madagascar. Continued research is planned which will include a detailed reassessment of stratigraphy and dating and osteology in the caves of the Zanzibar and Mafia archipelagos. Further analysis of stone technology and resource use will also be undertaken.

Madagascar

On Madagascar, beginning with the seminal pioneer contributions of Pierre Vérin, a whole series of surveys and investigations have been undertaken by *inter alia* Wright, Dewar, Rakotoarisoa and Radimilahy and co-workers from Antananarivo University Museum.[37] These important contributions have resulted in a series of culture historical sequences from different parts of the island from the eighth and nineth centuries AD. Ethnographic evidence for contact between Oceania and East Africa is provided by Blench.[38] Colonization of Madagascar from the eastern Indian Ocean seaboard seems to be confirmed on archaeological, linguistic and genetic grounds.[39] The contribution of African populations is not as clearly stated but by no means denied and seems to have been most clearly expressed archaeologically by a possible fusion shown in the early ceramics of African incised motifs and Indian Ocean red slipped wares. Finds from secondary contexts which potentially document early occupation include dwarf hippo bones showing cut marks dated to the early centuries AD and giant lemur bones showing butchery marks apparently induced by humans dated to late centuries BC from Taolambiby and Tsirave southern Madgascar. These finds provide further indication of occupation of Madagascar from c. 300 BC. already documented palynologically. [40] Particular attention is focused now on the as yet undated finds of ceramics and fauna at the Andakatomena Cave in St Augustine Bay in south west Madagascar and the excavator suggests the use of now extinct *Aepyornis* shell as water containers by the occupants of the cave.[41] Notwithstanding a series of well planned and implemented archaeological sites surveys elsewhere in different coastal areas of the island by the Anatanarivo team, no occupation of Madagascar earlier than the eighth-century cave-shelter deposits at Andovakoera[42] has so far been archaeologically documented. The extensive and detailed investigation of Mahilaka on the north-west coast of Madagascar dating from the ninth century AD provides the best evidence for the establishment and development of a settlement from a small-scale limited occupation to a fully urban centre measuring 2 km by 1 km. Evidence for trading activities in this period including remains of imported glazed ceramics, glass and glass beads, as well as gold probably produced locally has been documented by Radimilahy.[43] In the Anosy region of the far south east of the island Rakotoarisoa[44] has provided a detailed geographical interpretation of the settlement system development from the late first millennium AD. Similar dates are obtained from the early occupation of the highlands in the vicinity of Antananarivo.[45]

Comores

Until very recently there were no indications of the occupation of the Comores archipelago by early-mid-first-millennium AD iron-using farming communities with a ceramic repertoire similar to that of the Tanzanian coast. A recent surface find of a fluted earthenware sherd from a cave in Anjouan might prove to be the first such indication but this is still not confirmed or stratigraphically controlled.[46] The Dembeni phase materials presented by Allibert and Wright[47] and dated from the ninth century AD still provide the earliest reliably attested evidence for occupation of the Comores. The early trading site of Mro Dewa on Mwali,[48] which is still not well dated radio-metrically, does however provide extensive remains of blue-green Sasanian Islamic tin-glazed wares similar to those found at Unguja Ukuu on Unguja island Zanzibar and elsewhere on the East African coast.

36 Shackleton 1987, Mörner 1992 and see also Breen and Lane 2004.
37 For example, Vérin 1986; Wright and Rakotoarisoa 1990; Wright 1993; Dewar 1996; Rakotoarisoa 1998; Radimilahy 1998, 2006.
38 Blench 1996, 2006 unpublished.
39 Soodyall, *et al.* 1996 and see Radimilahy 2006 and forthcoming, for a summary.
40 MacPhee and Burney 1991; Burney *et al.* 2004, Perez *et al* 2005, Radimilahy 2006.
41 Radimilahy 2006.
42 Dewar 1996; Radimilahy 2006.
43 Radimilahy 1998.
44 Rakotoarisoa 1998.
45 Wright and Rakotoarisoa 1990.
46 Sherd shown at African Archaeology Network meeting Kampala 2006.
47 Wright 1984; Allibert, *et al.* 1990, Allibert and Vérin 1996.
48 Chanudet and Vérin 1983.

Mozambique

Archaeological developments along the coast of Mozambique over the last two decades are summarized in different publications from Eduardo Mondlane and Uppsala Universities.[49] Extensive work by Adamowicz in Nampula province documenting the widespread presence of iron-using farming communities from the early first millennium AD onwards is still not fully published. Fluted pottery of the iron-using farming communities dated to the early centuries AD is found as far south as Maputo and arguably similar wares into Natal. So far, however, despite careful observation no obviously imported trade items have been recorded from any of these sites.

Trading activities are well attested at Chibuene in southern Mozambique from the mid first millennium AD onwards.[50] Some earthenware pottery decoration motifs including flutes are very reminiscent of Kenyan and Tanzanian coastal wares;[51] others are similar to wares from Siraf and the Persian Gulf. Also present are hundreds of glass fragments and glass beads of the so-called Zhizo series similar to those recorded from the southern Zimbabwe plateau Phase II iron-using community sites and the Schroda and Bambandyanalo complex of the Limpopo Valley. The recovery of two eye beads has caused some discussion. Marilee Wood considers the possibility that these are Egypto-Phoenician from *ca.* 600–400 BC as admixtures in an otherwise standard Zhizo series dating to the later half of the first millennium AD. St John Simpson of the British Museum, London,[52] does not believe these eye beads are Egypto-Phoenician but dates them to the later phase of eye-bead production in the first millennium AD. Similar eye beads are well known in late first-millennium AD assemblages from Scandinavia.[53] Glass beads from the early-second-millennium AD Zimbabwe-tradition site of Manyikeni represent the Indo-Pacific trade beads series.[54] Contacts with the near off-shore islands in southern Mozambique are confirmed with pottery similar to Phase I Gokomere Ziwa wares on Bazaruto dated elsewhere to mid-first-millennium AD, found together with surface finds of blue-green glazed Sasanian Islamic imports[55] similar to those reported from Mro Dewa and Unguja Ukuu and other sites of the Lamu archipelago.

49 Sinclair 1987, Morais 1988, Sinclair, Morais, Adamowicz and Duarte 1993; Ekblom 2004 and recently by Macamo 2006.
50 Sinclair 1982, 1987; Ekblom 2004.
51 Soper 1971, Chami, 1994.
52 St J. Simpson personal communication.
53 Calmer 1977; J. Ljungkvist personal communication.
54 M. Wood personal communication.
55 Sinclair 1987.

Discussion

Perspectives on the peopling of the East African coast and near off-shore islands are changing rapidly. Two alternative hypotheses seem to be emerging to account for the new finds. The first and less controversial is that stone tools on coastal sites as well as Mafia and Zanzibar indicate the presence of hunters and gatherers.[56] The question of the presence of pastoralist communities, if this entails the co-occurrence of domesticated plants and animals and characteristic pottery and food processing technology,[57] seems much less obvious in the evidence so far presented on the islands. Although the evidence for the participation of these early inhabitants of the islands in external trade exchanges is sparse, it is repeated at a number of sites and in different contexts and should be taken seriously. A pattern is emerging which, given confirmation, promises new insights into cultural dynamics of the East African coast which increasingly can be seen to have been continuously occupied throughout the Holocene. Evidence for contact between Africa and South Asia from the second millennium BC in regard to food crops such as cow peas and sorghum seems firmer in India than in Africa.[58] However, the lack of African data can quite likely be accounted for as a sampling problem in the Sudan / southern Ethiopian regions.[59] The transmission of food crops from Africa and possibly cattle from South Asia[60] as well as the tree resin from Zanzibar / Mozambique found in third-millennium BC context at Tell Asmar in Iraq[61] seems more likely to have taken place as a component of coastal traffic to and from the Horn rather than direct trans-Oceanic contact to East Africa. Recent discussions on the peopling of Madagascar from the eastern Indian Ocean rim and the still debated early presence of South-East Asian food crops in West Africa do,[62] however, point to the need to keep an open mind on the subject. Recent assertions of Libyco / Berber trading activities down the West coast of Africa from 600–100 BC, including the colonization of Madagascar,[63] seem far-fetched and are based on a highly selective and questionable reading of historical, linguistic and rock art sources which in my view adds little to a balanced reassessment of the important archaeological research results achieved by the Dar es Salaam team on the coast and islands.

As discussed above, the broader regional picture along the coast of East Africa shows a number of possibilities of first-millennium BC trade. Imports of glass beads into East Africa have been discussed in a Mediterranean and Red

56 Breen and Lane 2004.
57 Sinclair, Shaw and Andah 1993.
58 Fuller 2003.
59 Blench, personal communication.
60 Magnavita 2006.
61 Meyer, *et al.* 1991.
62 Mbida, *et al.* 2000.
63 Chami 2006a: 187–203.

Sea perspective[64] but also increasingly including South Asia, for example, in documenting links between Madagascar and the eastern Indian Ocean.[65] As the South Asian connections come into focus with the direct participation of South Asian scholars, the possibility that copies of Mediterranean beads were made in South Asia and then traded (and *vice versa*) has also to be borne in mind.[66] In my view, the ascription of single examples as evidence for trade in a given period, for example, the first millennium BC, seems fraught with uncertainty. On the other hand, some African archaeologists feel strongly and not without reason that their European colleagues have consistently underestimated both the antiquity and complexity of the African cultural historical record. We do seem to be in a position of the glass half full or the glass half empty with the pivot point at the BC / AD divide. For me, the evidence of trade in the first half of the first millennium AD is stronger than that for the first millennium BC. It is not a matter of rejecting these possibilities out of hand but rather the expression of a need to continue with basic archaeological research in order to better place East Africa in relation to the continental interior and the extended Indian Ocean trade and cultural networks.

Acknowledgements

Thanks are due to Roger Blench who read and commented on an early version of the paper and to F. Chami, A. Juma, D. Phillipson, S. Gupta, V. Shinde, K. Knutsson, J. Ekman, K. Lindholm and A. Berger and those mentioned in the footnotes for comments at different stages in the production of the paper. Excavations at Kuumbi Cave are part of the African Archaeology Network Programme coordinated by Professor Felix Chami of the University of Dar es Salaam. The Kuumbi Field team included Felix Chami, Abdurahman Juma, Gido Laseway, Fadhili Ngacho, Jonh Amini, Sassi Emmael, Nguye Anton, Juma Khator, Hamza, Abdallah Mohammed, Markku Pyykönen and the present author. Funding was provided by Sida SAREC and additional support by Uppsala University, Dar es Salaam University and the Zanzibar Department of Museums and Archives.

References

Abungu, G. 1989. Communities on the river Tana Kenya: an archaeological study of relations between the delta and river basin AD 700–1800. Unpublished PhD thesis University of Cambridge.

Allibert, C., Argant, A. and Argant, J. 1990. Le site de Démbeni (Mayotte, Archpel des Comores). *Études Océan Indien* 11: 63–172.

Allibert, C. and Vérin, P. 1996. The early pre-Islamic history of the Comores Islands: links with Madagascar and Africa. 461–70 in J. Reade (ed.), *The Indian Ocean in Antiquity*. London, Kegan Paul.

Blench, R. 1996. The ethnographic evidence for long distance contacts between Oceania and East Africa. 417–38 in J. Reade (ed.), *The Indian Ocean in Antiquity*. London, Kegan Paul.

——. 2003. The movement of cultivated plants between Africa and India in prehistory. 15: 273–92 in K. Neumann, A, Butler and S. Kahlheber (eds), *Food, Fuel and Fields, progress in African Archaeobotany. Praehistorica*, Cologne, Heinrich-Barth-Institut.

Blench, R. 2006. The origins of domestic and translocated animals in Madagascar: surveying the linguistic evidence. Paper for the International Conference on Austronesian Languages X, held at Puerto Princesa, Palawan, 17–20 January 2006. On-line at http://www.rogerblench.info/Linguistics%20papers%20opening%20page.htm#_top and subsequently revised as The Austronesians in Madagascar and on the East African coast: surveying the linguistic evidence for domestic and translocated animals. Cambridge, February 2006, on-line at http://www.sil.org/asia/-philippines/ical/papers/Blench-Malagasy%20animal%-20names.pdf

Breen, C. and Lane P. 2004. Archaeological approaches to East Africa's changing seascapes. *World Archaeology* 35(3): 469–89.

Burney, D.A., Burney, L.P., Godfrey, L.R., Jungers,W.L., Goodman, S.M., Wright,H.T. and Jull, A.J.T. 2004. A chronology for late prehistoric Madagascar. *Journal of Human Evolution* 47 (1-2):25-63.

Callmer, J. 1977. Trade beads and bead trade in Scandinavia *ca.* 800–1000 AD. Lund: LiberLäromedel / Gleerup.

Chami, F. 1994. *The Tanzanian coast in the first millennium AD: an archaeology of the iron-working, farming communities.* Studies in African Archaeology 7. Uppsala: Societas Archaeological Upsaliensis.

——. 1998. A review of Swahili archaeology. *African Archaeological Review* 15: 199–221.

——. 1999a. Roman beads from the Rufiji Delta, Tanzania: first incontrovertible archaeological link with Periplus. *Current Anthropology* 40(2): 237–41.

——.1999b. Graeco-Roman trade link and the Bantu migration theory. *Anthropos* 94: 205–15.

——.1999c. The Early Iron Age on Mafia Island and its relationship with the hinterland. *Azania* 34: 1–10.

——. 2001a. The archaeology of the Rufiji region 1987 to 2000: coast and interior dynamics from AD 0–500. 7–20 in F. Chami, G. Pwiti and C. Radimilahy (eds), *People, Contacts and the Environment in the African Past.* Dar es Salaam: Dar es Salaam University Press.

——. 2001b. Chicken bones from a Neolithic limestone cave in Zanzibar. 81–97 in F. Chami, G. Pwiti and C.

64 Chami 1999, Chami 2006a: 134.

65 Robertshaw, *et al.* 2006, Radimilahy, forthcoming.

66 Glover, personal communication.

Radimilahy (eds), *People, Contacts and the Environment in the African Past*. Dar es Salaam: Dar es Salaam University Press.

——. 2004. The Archaeology of the Mafia archipelago, Tanzania. 4: 73–101 in F. Chami, G. Pwiti and C. Radimilahy (eds), *African Archaeology Network: Reports and a Review*. Dar es Salaam: Dar es Salaam University Press.

——. 2005. The Ancient Western Indian Ocean world market. *Indian Ocean Archaeology* 2: 1–7.

——. 2006a. The Unity of Ancient African History 3000 BC to AD 500. Mauritius: E&D Ltd.

——. 2006b. The archaeology of pre-Islamic Kilwa kisiwani (island). 5: 119–50 in F. Chami, G. Pwiti and C. Radimilahy (eds), *African Archaeology Network: Reports and a Review*. Dar es Salaam: Dar es Salaam University Press.

Chami F. and Kwekesan, A. 2003. Neolithic pottery traditions from the islands, the coast and the interior of East Africa. *African Archaeology Review* 20 (2): 65–80.

Chami, F.A. and Msemwa, P.J. 1997. A New Look at Culture and Trade on the Azanian Coast. *Current Anthropology* 38(4): 673–7.

Chanudet, C. and Vérin, P. 1983. Une reconnaissance archéologique de Mohéli. *Études Océan Indien* 2: 41–58.

Chittick, N. 1974. *Kilwa: an Islamic trading city on the East African coast*. 2 vols. Nairobi: British Institute in Eastern Africa.

——. 1984. *Manda: excavations at an island port on the Kenyan coast*. Nairobi: British Institute in Eastern Africa.

Dewar, R. 1996. The archaeology of the early settlement of Madagascar. 417–38 in J. Reade (ed.), *The Indian Ocean in Antiquity*. London, Kegan Paul.

Ekblom, A. 2004. *Changing Landscapes. Global Studies in Archaeology 5*. Uppsala: Department of Archaeology and Ancient History, Uppsala University.

Fuller, D. 2003. African crops in prehistoric South Asia: a critical review. 15: 239–71 in K. Neumann, A. Butler and S. Kahlheber (eds), *Food, Fuel and Fields, progress in African Archaeobotany. Praehistorica*, Cologne: Heinrich-Barth-Institut.

Glover, I. 2002. West Asian Sasanian Islamic ceramics in the Indian Ocean, South and South East Asia. *Man and the Environment* 27 (1): 165–77.

Gupta, S. 2004. An overview of Indian Ocean Archaeology. *Journal of Indian Ocean Archaeology* 1: 1–9.

——. Early Historic East Africa in the Indian Ocean World with special reference to contacts with India. Paper presented at the 18th IPPA Conference Manila March 2006.

Horton, M. 1996. *Shanga: the archaeology of a Muslim trading community on the coast of East Africa*. London: The British Institute in Eastern Africa.

Juma, A. 2004. *Unguja Ukuu on Zanzibar. An Archaeological Study of Early Urbanism* PhD thesis. Studies in Global Archaeology 3. Uppsala: Department of Archaeology and Ancient History.

——. 2006. Identity of Aboriginal people in Zanzibar: an overview. 5: 107–18 in John and Jill Kinahan (eds), *The African Archaeology Network: Research in Progress. Studies in the African Past.* Dar es Salaam: Dar es Salaam University Press.

Kirkman, J. 1963. *Gedi, the Palace*. The Hague: Mouton & Co.

Kusimba, C. 1999. *The Rise and Fall of Swahili States.* London: AltaMira Press.

Lane, P., Ashley, C., Seitsonen, O., Harvey, P, Mire, S. and Odede, F. 2007. The transition to farming in eastern Africa: new faunal and dating evidence from Wadh Lang'o and Usenge, Kenya. *Antiquity* 81 (311): 62–81.

LaViolette, A, and Fleisher J. 1995. Reconnaissance of sites bearing triangular-incised ware on Pemba Island, Tanzania. *Nyame Akuma* 44: 59–65.

Lejju, B.J., Robertshaw, P. and Taylor, D. 2006. Africa's earliest bananas? *Journal of Archaeological Science* 33: 102–13.

Macamo, S. 2006. *Privileged Places in South Central Mozambique.* Studies in Global Archaeology 4. Uppsala: Department of Archaeology and Ancient History.

Magnavita, C. 2006. Ancient humped cattle in Africa: a view from the Chad basin. *African Archaeological Review* 23 (3–4): 55–84.

Mbida, M.C., Van Neer, W., Doutrelepont, H., and Vrydaghs, L. 2000. Evidence for Banana Cultivation and Animal Husbandry during the First Millennium BC in the Forest of Southern Cameroon, *Journal of Archaeological Science* 27: 151–62.

McPhee, R.D. and Burney, D. 1991. Dating of modified femora of extinct dwarf Hippopotamus from southern Madagascar: implications for constraining human colonization and vertebrate extinction events. *Journal of Archaeological Science* 18: 695–706.

Meyer, C., Todd, J. and Beck, C. 1991. From Zanzibar to Zagros: a copal pendant from Eshnunna. *Journal of Near Eastern Studies* 50 (4) (October 1991): 289–98.

Misra, V.N. and Kajale, M.D. (eds). 2003. *Introduction of African Crops into South Asia.* Pune: Society for Prehistoric and Quaternary Studies.

Mörner, N. 1992. Ocean circulation, sea level changes and East African coastal settlements. 256–66 in *Urban Origins in Eastern Africa: Proceedings of the 1991 workshop in Zanzibar.* Stockholm: Swedish Central Board of National Antiquities.

Neumann, K. 2003. The late emergence of agriculture in sub-Saharan Africa: archaeobotanical evidence and ecological considerations. 15: 50–71 in K. Neumann, A, Butler and S. Kahlheber (eds), *Food, Fuel and Fields, progress in African Archaeobotany. Praehistorica*, Cologne, Heinrich-Barth-Institut.

Perez, V.R., Godfrey, L.R., Nowak-Kemp, M., Burney, D.A., Ratsimbazafy, J. and talia Vasey, N. 2005. Evidence of early butchery of giant lemurs in Madagascar . *Journal of Human Evolution* 49 (6): 722-742.

Phillipson, D. 1983. *African Archaeology*. Cambridge: Cambridge University Press.

Radimilahy, C. 1998. Mahilaka: an archaeological investigation of an early town in northwestern Madagascar. *Studies in African Archaeology* 15. Uppsala: Department of Archaeology and Ancient History.

Radimilahy, C. 2006. Contacts between Madagascar, South-East Asia and Africa. New light from recent archaeological works. Paper presented at the 18th IPPA Conference Manila, March 2006.

Rakotoarisoa, J.-A. 1998. *Mille ans d'occupation humaine dans le sud-est de Madagascar: Anosy, une île au milieu terres*. Paris : L'Harmattan.

Robertshaw, P., Rasoarifetra, B., Wood, M., Melchiorre, E., Popelka-Filcoff, R.S. and Glascock, M.D. 2006. Chemical analyses of glass beads from Madagascar. *Journal of African Archaeology* 4 (1): 91–109.

Shackleton, N.J. 1987. Oxygen isotopes, ice volume and sea level. *Quaternary Science Review* 6: 183–90.

Shinde, V. 2002. The Emergence, Development and Spread of Agricultural Communities in South Asia. 89–118 in Y. Yasuda (ed.), *The Origins of Pottery and Agriculture*. New Delhi: Roli Books.

Sinclair, P. 1982. Chibuene, an early trading site in southern Mozambique. *Paideuma* 28: 149–64.

——. 1987. *Space, Time and Social Formation: a territorial approach to the archaeology and anthropology of Zimbabwe and Mozambique, c. 0–1700 AD*. AUN 9. Uppsala: Societas Archaeologica Upsaliensis.

Sinclair, P., Shaw, T., and Andah, B. 1993. Introduction. 1–31 in T. Shaw, P. Sinclair, B. Andah and A. Okpoko (eds). *The Archaeology of Africa: food, metals and towns*. London: Routledge.

Sinclair, P. Morais, J. Adamowicz, L. and Duarte, R. 1993. 409–31 in T. Shaw, P. Sinclair, B. Andah and A. Okpoko (eds). *The Archaeology of Africa: food, metals and towns*. London: Routledge.

Sinclair, P. Juma, A. and Chami, F. 2006. Excavations at Kuumbi Cave on Zanzibar in 2005. *Studies in the African Past* 5: 95–106.

Smith, M. and Wright, H. 1988. The ceramics from Ras Hafun in Somalia: notes on a classical maritime site. *Azania* 2: 1–7.

Soodyall, H., Jenkins, T., Hewitt, R., Krause, A., and Stoneking, M. 1996. The peopling of Madagascar. 156–70 in A.J. Boyce and C.G.N. Mascie-Taylor (eds), *Molecular Biology and Human Diversity*. Cambridge: Cambridge University Press.

Soper, R. 1971. A general review of the early iron age in the southern half of Africa. *Azania* 5: 39–52.

Sutton, J. 2002. A review of people contacts and the environment in the African past. *Journal of African History* 43: 503–5.

Tampoe, M. 1989. *Maritime Trade between China and the West: an archaeological study of the ceramics from Siraf (Persian Gulf), 8th to 15th centuries AD*. Based on D.Phil thesis. Oxford: BAR International Series 555.

Vérin, P. 1986. *The History of Civilisation in North Madagascar*. Rotterdam: A.A. Balkena.

Wright, H.T. 1984. Early seafarers of the Comoro Islands: the Dembeni phase of the IXth–Xth centuries AD. *Azania* 19: 13–60.

——. 1993. Trade and politics on the eastern littoral, AD 800–1300. 683–93 in T. Shaw, P. Sinclair, B. Andah & A. Okpoko (eds), *The Archaeology of Africa: food, metals and towns*. London: Routledge.

Wright, H.T. and Rakotoarisoa, J.A. 1990. The archaeology of complex societies in Africa, case studies in cultural diversification. 21-30 in P. Sinclair and J.A. Rakotoarisoa (eds), *Urban Origins in Eastern Africa, Proceedings of the 1989 Madagascar Workshop*. Stockholm: Central Board of National Antiquities.

The 'Arabians' of pre-Islamic Egypt

Tim Power

In the first quarter of the twentieth century, the desert explorer and antiquarian George Murray pitched camp by the well of Bi'r Nakhīl in the Eastern Desert of Egypt. He gives a description of the site in his field-journal:

> We moved camp here two days ago. The well is a pool in the *wady* bed, about five feet by seven and eight inches deep. Just across the *wadi* are the ruins of some seventy huts of rubble stone, each with a well-built central room with a *mastabah* for the *harim*, and another *mastabah* in the court-yard for the master of the house, while subsidiary stone circles denoted pens for poultry, goats, etc. Many broken fragments of ribbed amphorae showed that the inhabitants could not have been Bedouin, who hardly use pottery, while the presence of *harim* and animals forbids one to suppose a mining settlement or garrison. A small cemetery of about twenty graves, circular stone heaps, across the *wady* showed that the occupation had been of short duration.[1]

Clearly, Murray was at a loss as to what exactly to make of the remains at Bi'r Nakhīl. Words such as *mastabah* and *harim* belong better to an Orientalist repertoire than to that of the Classics, yet he quickly moves to preclude a Bedouin hypothesis, and turns instead to an altogether more convoluted resolution: namely, that the remains represent 'a temporary refuge for some of the inhabitants of al-Quṣayr in Roman times, perhaps during time of pestilence or foreign invasion.'[2]

Then, at the start of the twenty-first century, Bi'r Nakhīl was 'shot-in' with an EDM, rendered on CAD and published on the NET as part of an altogether less romantic approach to the site (Map 18:1).[3] This hinterland survey associated with the University of Southampton's Quṣayr al-Qadīm project, and undertaken by G. Earl and D. Glazier, suggested an entirely new interpretation — that Bi'r Nakhīl may have been 'a community of Desert Fathers'.[4] Already, D. Peacock, during the course of his work at Mons Claudianus, having struck across a similarly ambiguous site at Umm Diqal, had developed the anchorite hypothesis, which he interpreted as 'an early monastic settlement of the Desert Fathers'.[5] Both sites could be dated to the fifth and sixth centuries AD on the basis of ceramic surface finds, yet neither advertized any obvious function. At the same time, the architecture of largely single-roomed rectilinear structures, built of low walls without obvious provision for roofing, and only intermittently furnished with low benches, was felt to be evocative of the hermit's cell. Moreover, given the relative proximity of the great desert monasteries of St Anthony's and St Paul's, and of the myriad Coptic hagiographies written at this time, there seemed to be a weight of circumstantial evidence towards an anchorite hypothesis. This evidence was further informed by the Palestinian monastic communities studied by Y. Hirschfeld, that presented Peacock with a model for the Egyptian material.[6]

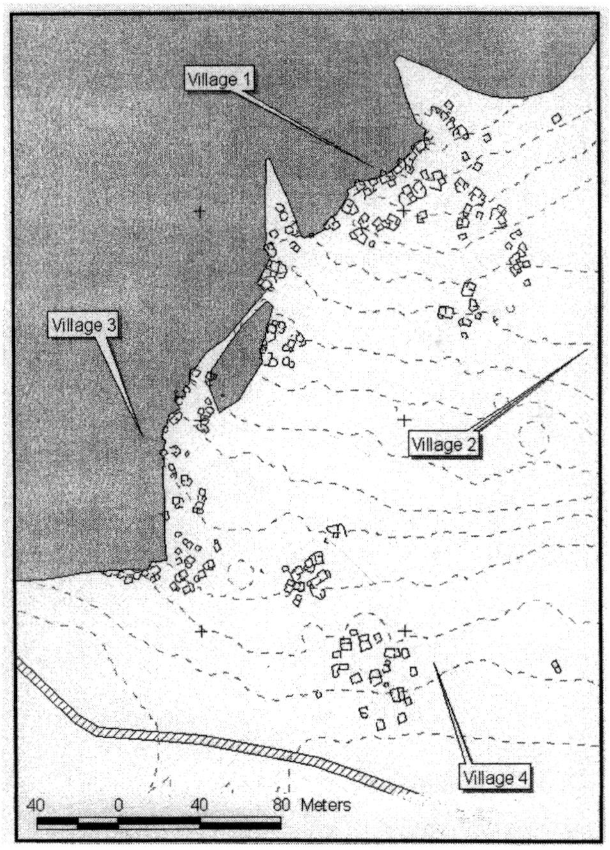

Map 18:1 Bi'r Nakhīl (Earl and Glazier 2006)

1 Murray 1925: 149.
2 Ibid.
3 Earl and Glazier 2006. Publication on the internet preceded full publication by some time.
4 Ibid.: 32.
5 Peacock 1997: 153.
6 Hirschfeld 1992.

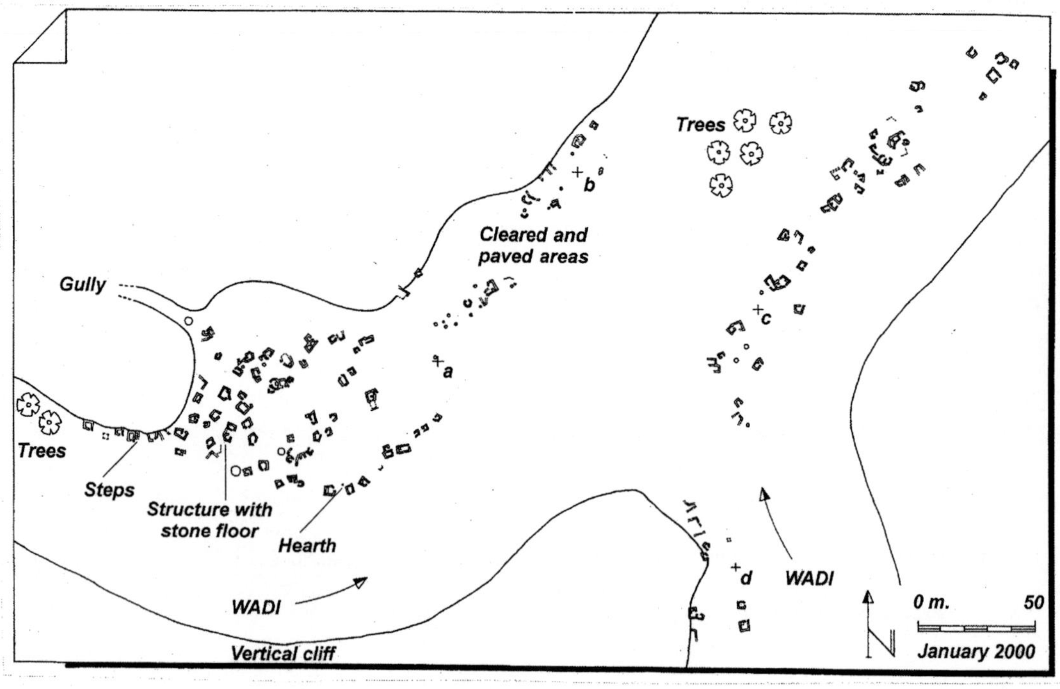

Map 18:2 Qaryat Mustafa (Sidebotham, et al. *2002)*

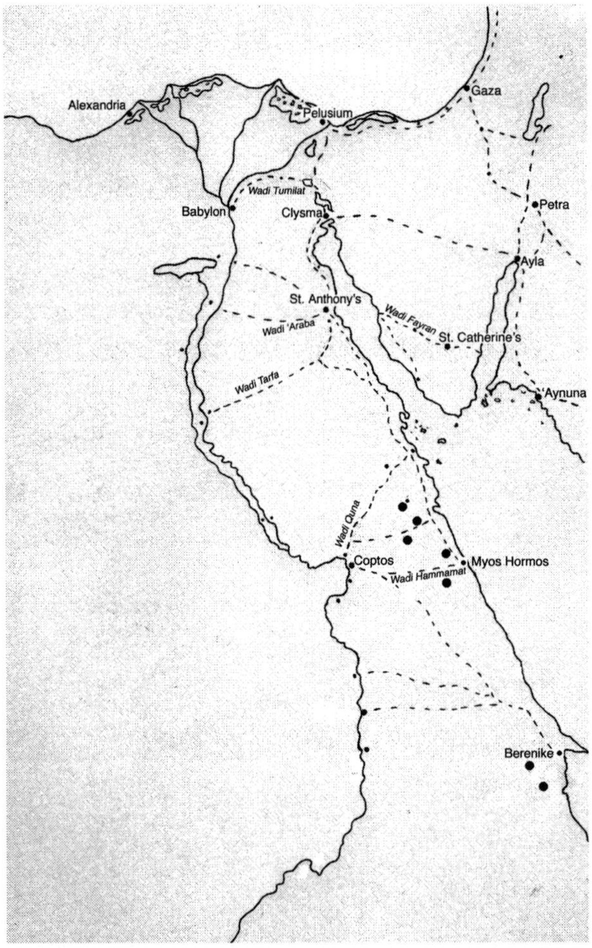

Map 18:3 Distribution Map of the 'Enigmatic Settlements'

The matter was then considered by S. Sidebotham, H. Barnard and G. Pyke in a paper discussing what they dubbed 'the enigmatic Late Roman settlements of the Eastern Desert' (Maps 18:2 and 18:3).[7]

They presented five analogous sites and returned to Murray's discarded interpretations, thereafter presenting five possible solutions to the problem of the 'enigmatic settlements'. The authors made clear from the start that not any one of these solutions was without fault. There was no evidence for the waste products of industrial processing that might be expected of mining or quarrying sites. The settlements were simply too dense for charcoal burners or herb gatherers, or else they were too haphazard and poorly defended to be military installations.

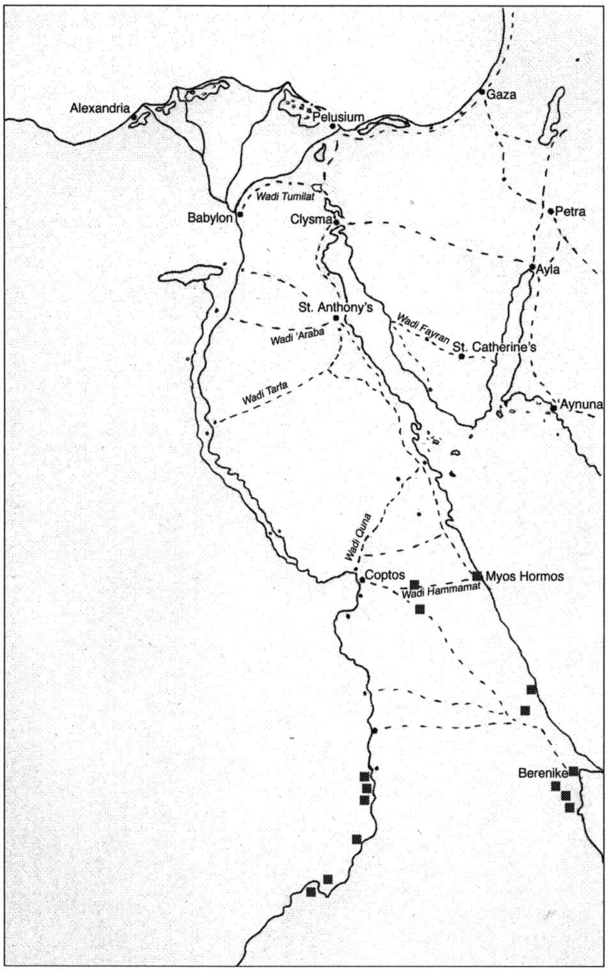

Map 18:4 Distribution Map of EDW (after Barnard 2002)

As for the Bedouin hypothesis, whilst the egalitarian nature of the architecture found in favour, the absence of occupation debris or burials spoke against this idea. In particular, the lack of Eastern Desert Ware was considered particularly problematic.

Barnard has made a special study of this decorated hand-made ceramic tradition, which seems most densely distributed in Lower Nubia and the Eastern Desert south of the Wādī Ḥammāmāt, and presents a working hypothesis for its association with the Blemmyes (Map 18:4).[8] For Sidebotham and Barnard, the historical sources of late antiquity indicate that the Blemmyes comprised the nomadic population of the Eastern Desert. No Eastern Desert Ware means no Blemmyes, and no Blemmyes means no nomads, so that the 'enigmatic settlements' could not be considered semi-permanent nomadic encampments.

We will return shortly to the Bedouin hypothesis, but must first consider the conclusions reached by Sidebotham and Barnard. In short, they concurred with Peacock's team, that the balance of probability lay with the anchorite hypothesis. Yet they express some unease as to this conclusion, for much that one might expect from ascetic Christian communities is lacking. Where are the churches, Christian graffiti or the hermit-caves attested at the monastic sites of the Nile Valley and Judean Desert (Maps 18:5a and 18:5b)?[9] Clearly, there were problems with the anchorite hypothesis even at its inception.

In fact, the anchorite hypothesis does not accord at all well with the current understanding of Late Antique Egyptian monasticism, as gleaned from the findings of papyrologists. An important paper by J. Goehring has been accepted as demonstrating the deployment of the desert as a literary *topos* in Late Antique hagiography. He traces this as far back as the late first century, where it appears in a moralizing poem by Babrius:

> A man journeying into the desert found Truth standing alone and said to her, 'Why revered lady, have you left the city and now dwell in the desert?' To which with profound wisdom she straightaway replied, 'Falsehood found a place with a few amongst those of old, but now it has spread to all humankind'.[10]

---

7 Sidebotham, *et al.* 2002.

8 Barnard 2002. He builds on the work of John Hayes (1995) and Pamela Rose (1995) who made the link between the Berenike EDW and the Nubian material published by Strouhal (1982). Rose first linked EDW with the Blemmyes.

9 See further the discussion in Earl and Glazier 2006: 28–32, which reproduces similar misgivings.

10 Goehring 1993: 281.

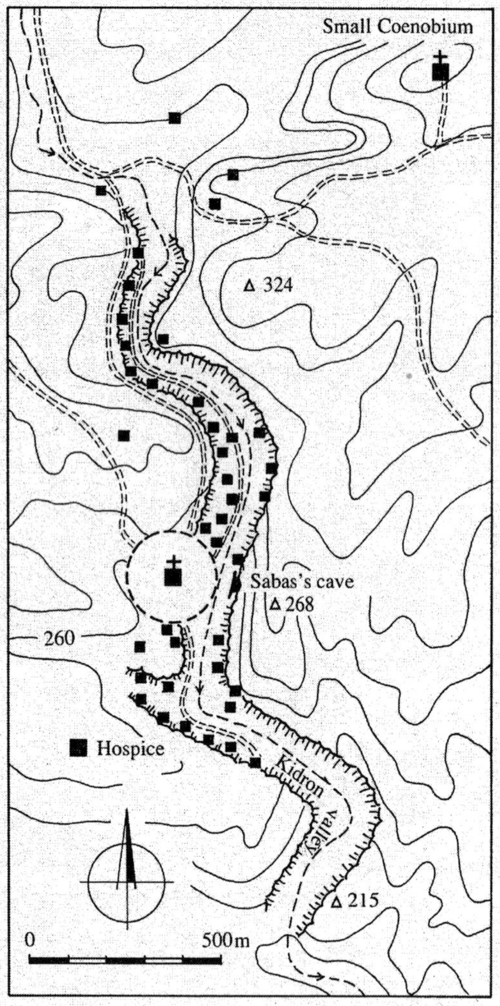

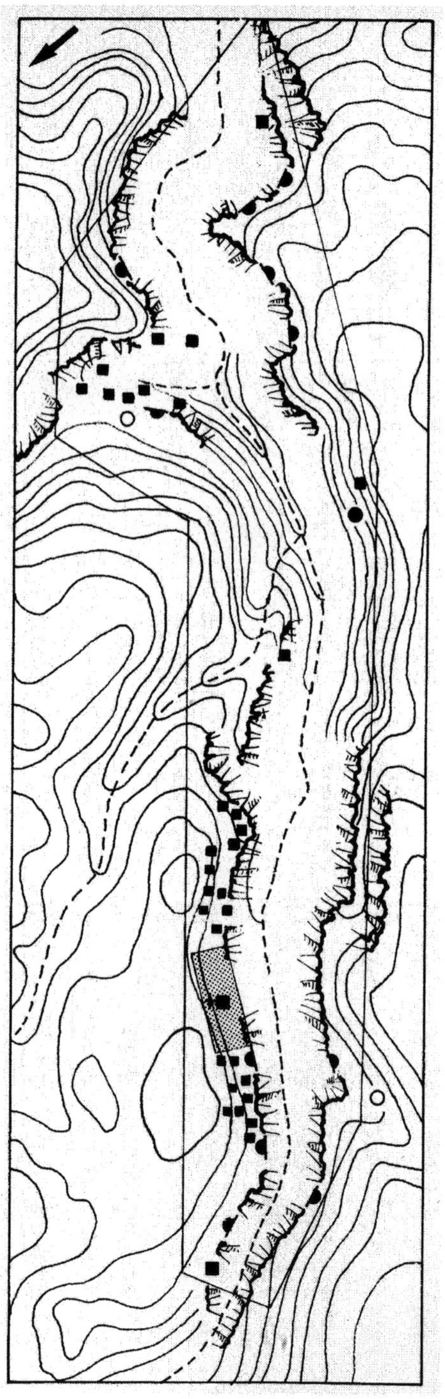

Maps 18:5a and 18:5b Monastic Settlements of the Judaean Desert (Hirschfeld 1992)

Goehring goes on to elucidate the employment of this literary device with reference to an episode from the *Life of Pachomius*.[11] Pachomius was apprenticed to the anchorite Palamon who, we are told, lived outside the village of Sheneset. Yet at the same time he is described as living an ascetic ideal 'in those deserts, in the acacia forest that surrounded them, and in the far desert'.[12] The apparent contradiction dissolves before the topography, whereby an outcropping of rock sits hard by the village and surrounded by arable lands, so that the further desert lies at the edge of the alluvium. The Coptic hagiographies

11 Ibid.: 289.

12 Bohairic, *Vita Pachomii* 10.

of the Desert Fathers which supply the circumstantial evidence underlying the anchorite hypothesis cannot, therefore, be taken at face value, and demand a much greater historiographic awareness than has been marshalled in its cause.

Indeed, the anchorite movement was largely spent by the time of the enigmatic settlements in the fifth and sixth centuries. P. Crone and M. Cook, noted authorities on Late Antique and early Islamic historiography, write:

> With Pachomius the caves gave way to large monastic settlements, the hermits to thousands of inmates, solitary autonomy to the rules and regulations of increasingly powerful abbots, and by the fifth century Egypt all but unanimously subscribed to the coenobitic ideal. If the anchorites still held formal pride of place, their eremetical ideal was now suspected of ascetic virtuosity and discouraged in favour of communal life, obedience and, above all, work.[13]

Accordingly, R. Bagnall observes that in practice almost all pious settlements were to be found within the cultivated areas of the Valley and Delta, at the edge of the alluvium, and at the 'inner desert'.[14] These last were rarely more than a day's journey from the Nile. The determining rationale for the location of monastic communities was dictated by the visitations of bishops, according to M. Krausse's study of the papyri, by whose peregrinations orthodoxy might be enforced.[15] Doctrinal disputes and heresies amongst the burgeoning and often truculent Christian communities ever threatened to rend the Church asunder. It is unlikely that anchorite settlements beyond the reach of the Church authorities would have been tolerated, so that the balance of probability shifts away from the anchorite hypothesis for the enigmatic settlements.

At the same time, there is a deal of historical evidence that might be used circumstantially to support an 'Arabian' association with the enigmatic settlements. Before considering this material, a historiographic note on ethnicity is in order. The correspondence between the ethnic labels used by ancient writers and the ethnicities (that is, self-appointed personal and communal identities) which they purport to describe is hardly exact. As such, I have used the broad term 'Arabian' in the title of this paper, rather as historians of the Western Roman empire write of 'Germanic' peoples. Yet throughout the paper I refer to Arabs rather indiscriminately, for the fact is that given both the impossibility of resolving the issue and its familiarity to anyone working with the subject, further qualifications would be cumbersome and essentially gratuitous.[16] The proviso delivered, the argument may be resumed.

It has long been recognized that Egypt's Eastern Desert approaches lie within the orbit of Arabia, and that this state of affairs has maintained since the Iron Age when first we hear of the Arabs. The ethnonym 'Arab' is first attested in 853 BC, when 'Gindibu the Arab' flees Shalmaneser III with a thousand camels.[17] Somewhat later, 'Idibi'ilu the Arab' is given 'wardenship of the entrance to Egypt' by Sargon II, whilst a government decree allows Badi'ilu 'pasture in the midst of the land'.[18] Their descendents play a leading role in Herodotus's account of Cambyses's conquest of Egypt in 525 BC, affording no less than 'passage into Egypt, which the Persians could not enter without the consent of the Arabs'.[19] Excavations at the Saite-Achæmenid fortress of Tall al-Maskhūtah in the Wādī al-Ṭūmaylāt unearthed a silver bowl dated to *ca.* 400 BC. It bears an Aramaic inscription referring to known Arab tribal groups and Arab deities: 'that which Qaynu son of Gesham, king of Qedar, brought in offering to the [goddess] Allat.'[20] Later still Strabo wrote of Coptos that it is a 'town inhabited by Egyptians and Arabs together.'[21] This brief sketch of the evidence from the first millennium BC is sufficient to posit an autochthonic 'Arabian' association with the Eastern Desert approaches of the Nile Valley.

When in AD 270 Zenobia of Palmyra usurped the purple and seized eastern Anatolia and Egypt, she provoked a crisis for Rome in the east met only by Aurelian three years later with the annihilation of Palmyra. In the account of al-Ṭabarī, the ninth/tenth-century author of a universal history widely regarded as definitive, the Arab tribal confederation of Tanūkh was in the thick of the action. Jadhīmah al-Abrash ibn Malik slew 'Amr ibn Zarīb, the father of Zenobia.[22] Jadhīmah's nephew joined Aurelian in the sack of Palmyra, and the son of this nephew was the Imru' al-Qays buried at Nemara in 328.[23] The funerary inscription describes him as 'king of all the Arabs', and in so doing speaks volumes as to the emergence of an aspirant Arab leadership drawing on a self-declaiming Arab identity, and expressed — for the first time — in the Arabic language.[24] With the reduction of the Nabatæans

13 Crone and Cook 1977: 52.

14 Bagnall 1993: 295.

15 Krausse 1985.

16 Excellent discussions on ancient 'Arabian' ethnicity and ethnic labels are to be found in Macdonald 1998; 2003; Hoyland 2001.

17 AR 1.611. See Hoyland 2001: 58–63.

18 Eph'al 1982: 93–100.

19 Herodotus III, 88.

20 Brooklyn Museum of Art 545034. Dumbrell 1971: 36.

21 Strabo 8.119–21; also 8.71, 85 on Arabia beginning east of the Delta.

22 Ṭabarī (4.138–50). The Umm al-Jimāl inscription (PAES 4A.41) is bilingual Greek-Nabataean. See Hoyland 2001: 235.

23 Beeston 1979.

24 Albeit in the Nabatean script. See the discussion in

and destruction of Palmyra the Romans unwittingly undid their buffer states, preparing the ground for the Arabs to make something of a 'comeback' in late antiquity. This they were to do with astonishing success, eventually establishing an empire which stretched from Spain to China. From the fourth century, the Late Antique resurgence of the Arabs becomes noticeable in the Eastern Desert approaches to the Nile Valley. Athanasius tells us that St Anthony joined the Saracen caravan bound for the desert interior in AD 313, whilst according to tradition his monastery was founded in the reign of Julian the Apostate, between AD 361 and 363.[25] Sozomen dates the conversion of some Palestinian Arabs to the same sort of time — 'not long before Valens',[26] who succeeded Julian in the east and ruled from AD 364 to 378. Cyril of Scythopolis quipped that 'these people who had previously been the wolves of Arabia joined the flock of Christ.'[27] As for the reign of Valens, Sozomen relates that upon the death of an Arab *fœderatus*, his wife Mawia acceded and rose in revolt. In the course of the revolt she raided Palestine and the coastal plain 'as far as the regions of Egypt lying to the left of those sailing up the Nile which are generally denominated by Arabia.'[28] The *casus belli* was ostensibly the Arian heresy of Valens, and the matter was concluded only when Byzantium allowed Mawia her choice of bishop, 'a certain man named Moses, who practiced asceticism in a neighbouring desert and who was noted for performing divine and miraculous signs.'[29] The exact location of Mawia's people is not given by Sozoman, but Irfan Shahid makes a careful study of the topography and suggests Sinai as a likely candidate.[30] Such sources attest an 'Arabian' presence stretching from the Wādī ʿArabah in Egypt, through the Sinai and coastal plain towards the southern Levant.

Broadly speaking, the Græco-Roman sources of the fifth to seventh centuries continue to support this picture. At the end of the fourth century, the western pilgrim Egeria describes the necessity of a military escort through the Arab tribes settled around the Wādī Ṭūmaylāt.[31] In the first half of the fifth century, Jerome mentions that the towns of northern Sinai had a strong Arab element[32] and Sozomen notes Saracens and Ismaelites throughout the coastal plain.[33] Some twelve and a half thousand Saracens are claimed by Antoninus Placentinus to have attended a religious festival in honour of a stone idol of the Sinai.[34] The *Notitia Dignitatum* lists Saracen and Thamudæan military units stationed along the coastal plain,[35] though it might be objected that the names of Late Roman units no longer correspond to the ethnic composition of the troops. At any rate, it gives camel corps in Akhmīm and Qinā, which does rather suggest Arab auxiliaries.[36] Further indications of an Arab presence south of the Wādī ʿArabah are to be found in the sixth-century Antaioupolis papyri. Accordingly, military units from Wādī Fīrān in the Sinai are attested in AD 524 and 529, and fought with the *dux* of the Thebaid against the Blemmyes around AD 568–570.[37] Indeed the poet Dioscorus mentions that these same units fought with the *dux* against Saracens.[38] The ethnic identity of the Fīrānīs is unclear, though the purportedly fourth-century *Ammonii Monachi Relatio* attests to Arab *fœderati* settled in the *wādī*, and Shahid makes much of it in his *Byzantium and the Arabs*.[39] However, there are issues as to the authenticity of this source, and some have claimed it as an outright forgery.[40]

The sources of the seventh century are particularly fascinating. According to an epitome of the *Life of John*, Patriarch of Alexandria at the time of the AD 616 Persian conquest, numerous Saracens fled before the invaders and sought refuge in Alexandria.[41] In his discussion of this episode, W. Kaegi wonders whether these were Sinaitic Arabs or those of Palestine;[42] it might equally well be wondered if they were the Arabs of the Eastern Desert. He goes on to suggest that these Arab refugees may have subsequently been a source of information for the invading Muslims. According to al-Maqrīzī, after the fall of Pelusium the armies of ʿAmr ibn al-ʿĀṣ were swelled by the local Bedouin,[43] and he must have had local knowledge to thereafter strike south towards the Wādī Ṭūmaylāt and emerge in the Delta at Bilbais. But then he may not have needed the help of the local Arab population in this, for the Islamic historical tradition has it that ʿAmr was accustomed to trade with Egypt long before he ever threw his lot in with the Muslims.

Hoyland 2001: 79 and 229–47.

25 Athanasius 49.1–50.4

26 Sozomen 6.38. Quoted in Hoyland 2001: 238.

27 Cyril of Scythopolis 18.24–5.

28 Sozomen 6.38. From Hoyland 2001: 149.

29 Ibid.

30 Shahid 1984: 152–8.

31 Wilkinson 1981.

32 Jerome, Com Isa V, Is 19:18. Cf. Figueras, 2000: 64–87.

33 Sozomen 6:38.

34 Antoninus Placentinus 148.

35 Respectively at Scennae Veteranorum 28:17, 26 and Birsama 72, 10–73, 22.

36 According to Meredith and Littmann 1954: 241.

37 According to Shahid 1984: 295–7.

38 MacCoull 1986.

39 Shahid 1984: Chp. 8.4, 287–308 '*Ammonii Manachi Relatio*', and Chp. 8.5, 308–19 'The Authenticity of the *Ammonii Monachi Relatio*'.

40 Devreesse 1940: 218–20, considers it a sixth-century forgery serving the cult of martyrdom. See further Mayerson 1980.

41 Lappa-Zizicas 1970: 272.

42 Kaegi 1998: 56.

43 Butler 1978: 213.

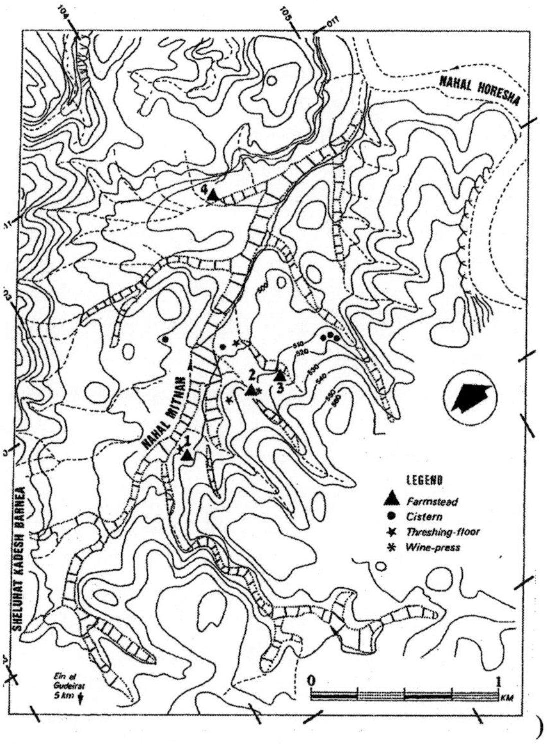

Map 18:6a The Nahal Mitnan Farms (Haiman 1995: 1, Plan 1)

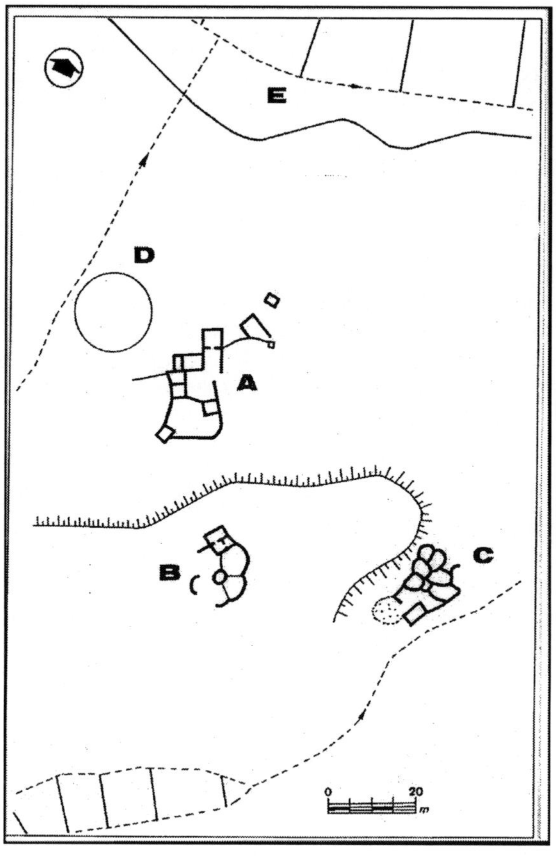

Map 18:6b Farm Cluster no. 1 (Hairman 1995: 1, Plan 2)

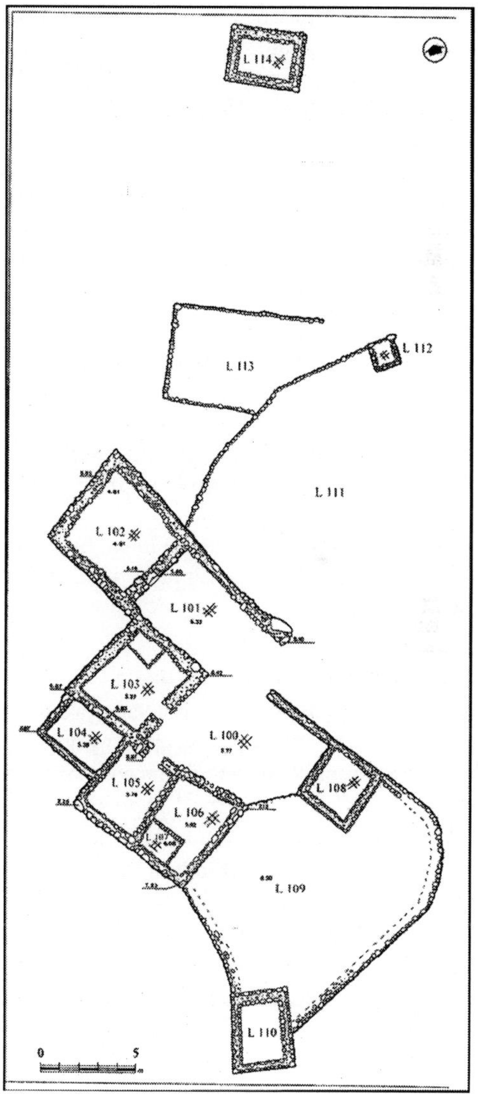

Map 18:6c The Excavated Farmhouse (Haiman 1995: 3, Plan 3)

Though these sources demonstrate an Arab presence from the Wādī 'Arabah in Egypt reaching up towards the Syrian steppe between the fourth and seventh centuries, it should be noted that they cannot compare with the Levantine material in either the frequency or depth of treatment. In particular, it might be expected that the Coptic sources possibly tell us more of their posited Arab neighbours. This, I would suggest, means that the Arab population of the Eastern Desert at no time approached that of Syria-Palestine, no matter how many Saracens Antoninus Placentinus claims to have seen. Yet absence of evidence does not necessarily mean evidence of absence, and the historiography of Coptic literature needs to be taken into account. As Crone and Cook note, 'the social keynote of the Coptic Church in late antiquity is village rusticity... (and its) emotional keynote is ethnic and linguistic chauvinism: solidarity of Monophysite Monks against Heraclius' persecution of the Copts, and the glory of Egypt in the panegyrics of Egyptian saints.'[44] It is as such a rather introverted and parochial tradition, absorbed with the business of salvation and the wages of sin, and consequently little concerned with the barbarians of the fringe.

Approaching the enigmatic settlements of the Late Antique Eastern Desert from the 'Arabian' paradigm serves to replace one set of circumstantial evidence for another. Having removed the Eastern Desert from the literary conceit of the Desert Fathers, it may now alternatively be located in the 'Arabian' *Völkerwanderung*. At this point we can return to the Bedouin hypothesis and finally move beyond circumstantial evidence to the evidence of analogy.

Just as Peacock looked to Palestine to find anchorite *comparenda* for the enigmatic settlements, we turn first to the Negev to seek analogies supporting the Bedouin hypothesis. Hundreds of ancient farmsteads were recorded by Mordechai Haiman along the Egyptian border during the Negev Emergency Survey throughout the 1980s.[45] Four farms were surveyed in detail and one excavated along the Nahal Mitnan tributary of the Nahal Horsha (Maps 18:6a, 18:6b and 18:6c), where a ceramic assemblage stretching from late antiquity into the early Islamic period was recorded (specifically, the sixth–eighth centuries). Haiman concludes that 'these farms should be regarded as evidence of an Umayyad state-sponsored enterprise to sedentarise a semi-nomadic population which had inhabited the margins of permanent settlement since Byzantine times.'[46] The Nahal Mitnan farms, then, are to be associated with an Arab population before, and more particularly, after the Arab conquest of Palestine.

Numerous typological parallels immediately become apparent with the architecture of the enigmatic settlements in the Eastern Desert, with which they overlap chronologically. Both are characterized by a cellular arrangement of small rectilinear structures, grouped together by less substantial communicating walls so as to form outer courtyards. These communicating walls are shown on the Bi'r Nakhīl survey plans, and whilst Sidebotham's team did not mark them on their plans, they note that 'many structures have a semi-circular or rectilinear cleared area beside them or in between them, sometimes outlined by a one- or two-course high wall'.[47] There is, therefore, a shared architectural rationale in the creation of domestic space, which is further borne out by the construction techniques.

In the Eastern Desert, Sidebotham, *et al.* recorded walls to a height of between 0.7 and 1.2 m, whilst Peacock gives a maximum height of 1.5 m, and both note that the lack of tumble indicates the walls were not intended to have been taller.[48] At Nahal Mitnan, Haiman states that the walls are preserved to a height of 1.5 m.[49] Sidebotham, *et al.* give the width as between 0.5 and 0.6 m, with which Earl and Glazier's plans agree, whilst Haiman gives 0.7 m — though his plans clearly show the walls of abutting structures as rather narrower.[50] Importantly, all concerned record that the walls were dry-stone and double-skin with a rubble fill.[51] Similarly, a wooden roof was conjectured by the archaeologists in the Eastern Desert, and traces of such a structure were indeed found in the Negev.[52] *Mastabahs* comprise the only evidence of furnishing in both regions, and are similarly bordered by a single course / row of stones. Peacock gives the average dimensions as 1.4 m x 0.7 m x 0.3 m, and records a gravel fill; Haiman's plans concur with these dimensions, though he notes a beaten earth fill.[53] Construction techniques were therefore virtually identical.

Whilst the parallels between the Negev sites and those of the Eastern Desert are striking, there are noticeable differences in typology and construction. The clustering of rooms at Nahal Mitnan and arrangement of courtyard space displays a greater degree of cohesion than any of the

44 Crone and Cook 1977: 54.
45 Haiman 1995.
46 Ibid.: 11.

47 Sidebotham, *et al.* 2002: 189.
48 Ibid.
49 Haiman 1995: 1 and 3.
50 Sidebotham, *et al.* 2002: 192; Earl and Glazier 2006: Figure 2.42, 29; Haiman 1995: 1.
51 Sidebotham, *et al.* 2002: 189; Earl and Glazier 2006: 27; Haiman 1995: 1.
52 Sidebotham, *et al.* suggest a wooden frame covered by hides or mats, analogous with traditional 'Ababdah *bayt bursh* 2002: 189 and note 6. Earl and Glazier suggest a frond roof 2006: 30. Haiman found a charred beam 1.5 m long, 1995: 4.
53 Earl and Glazier 2006: 27; Haiman 1995: 4.

Eastern Desert sites. Moreover, the walls of the excavated farmhouse were provided with a solid foundation of large, roughly hewn blocks of stone, and included architectural features such as door-jambs, thresholds and sockets. That such features do not appear in the Eastern Desert is hardly surprising, for the Nahal Mitnan farms fell within a steppe ecological zone where crops were cultivated on terraced *wādī* slopes fed by cisterns, and appear to have been associated with permanent agrarian communities. Their architecture consequently represents a much more substantial investment of resources than the semi-permanent pastoralist encampments of the Eastern Desert.

What seems clear, however, is that the architectural typology and construction techniques repeat themselves in both regions. This, I would argue, implies that the Nahal Mitnan farms and enigmatic settlements of the Eastern Desert of Egypt belong to the same cultural tradition. Given the clear association of the Nahal Mitnan farms with the assemblage of post-conquest Arab Palestine, it is further possible to claim the Eastern Desert settlements as belonging to the architectural traditions of Arabia.

Earlier we saw how Sidebotham and Barnard used the lack of Eastern Desert Ware at the enigmatic settlements as an argument against the Bedouin hypothesis. Having demonstrated that the Blemmyes are not the only historically attested nomadic population in the region, the very absence of Eastern Desert Ware may be put to the service of a particularly Arab version of the Bedouin hypothesis. Of the seven enigmatic settlements discussed by Peacock and Sidebotham, five are to be found in the region stretching north from the Wādī Ḥammāmāt. At the same time the distribution of Eastern Desert Ware, as plotted by Barnard, falls south of the Wādī Ḥammāmāt. If the association of the enigmatic settlements with an Arab presence in the northern section of the Eastern Desert is at all valid, and the general association between Eastern Desert Ware and the Blemmyes is accepted, then the mutually exclusive distribution of the two respective data sets assumes a new significance. This is all the more intriguing when it is remembered that the Wādī Ḥammāmāt provides the contemporary tribal boundary between the Arab Ma'aza to the north and the Beja 'Ababdah to the south, and that this arrangement has maintained for as long as can be remembered.

This still leaves two enigmatic settlements to the south west of Berenike, to which might be added another site in the same vicinity, though of a very different nature. Early visitors to Hitan Shenshef had variously thought it a satellite settlement of people from Berenike or else a medieval Arab slave-dealer's stronghold, and Murray decided it was an 'autumn station for the officials and merchants of Berenike' (Map 18:7).[54] He notes the lack of mines and quarries, or millstones and slag-heaps associated with processing minerals and considers that there was no ground to be cultivated in the immediate surrounds. Survey and excavations undertaken by Sidebotham and Wendrich's Berenike team in 1996 and 1997 found limited evidence for limited agricultural processing.[55] However, both the function of the site and the origin of its inhabitants remained undetermined, so that the excavators confessed that 'it is still not clear whether the population consisted of Romans, a Romanised local population — perhaps Blemmyes? — or a combination.'[56]

Yet the large courtyard houses of Shenshef (Map 18:8) display an architectural typology without parallel in either the Græco-Roman Mediterranean or the Hamito-Semitic Nilotic traditions (Maps 18:9 and 18:10). R. Alston's study of the domestic architecture of Roman Egypt is largely based upon the University of Michigan's 1928–1935 excavations at Karanis.[57] According to his analysis, ground plans have an average of about 70 m^2 — much smaller than Shenshef. Typically, the houses possessed a small external yard for domestic work, whilst the flat roofs of these frequently multi-storeyed buildings were similarly employed as working space. Two types of larger house were attested. The first, known as *aithrion,* seems essentially Greek, with rooms arranged around an internal courtyard integral to the house. Such a house is uniquely illustrated on a ground plan from the Oxyrhynchus papyri (Map 18:10). The second larger house type is a peculiarly Egyptian style characterized by two towers flanking the main gate. This seemingly goes back to Pharaonic times, when the gate was the cultic centre of a house, and recalls the pylons of temple architecture. Romano-Egyptian architecture, as briefly outlined here, seems to find no expression at Shenshef, which speaks against a Roman population.

As for the Blemmyes, the Late Antique sources agree that they were a nomadic people without architecture, though the accounts are fragmentary and apparently rather cursory. Luckily the early Arabic sources give more detailed descriptions of the Beja. For instance, al-Ṭabarī states that 'the Beja are nomads, owners of camel and sheep. Their country is a sandy desert, devoid of all vegetation and water, without villages or fortresses.'[58]

54 Murray 1926: 166.

55 Aldsworth and Barnard 1996; Aldsworth 1999; Gould 1999.

56 Gould 1999: 379.

57 Alston 1997; 2002; Cf. Husselman 1979.

58 Ṭabarī, *Ta'rīkh* iii, 1430.

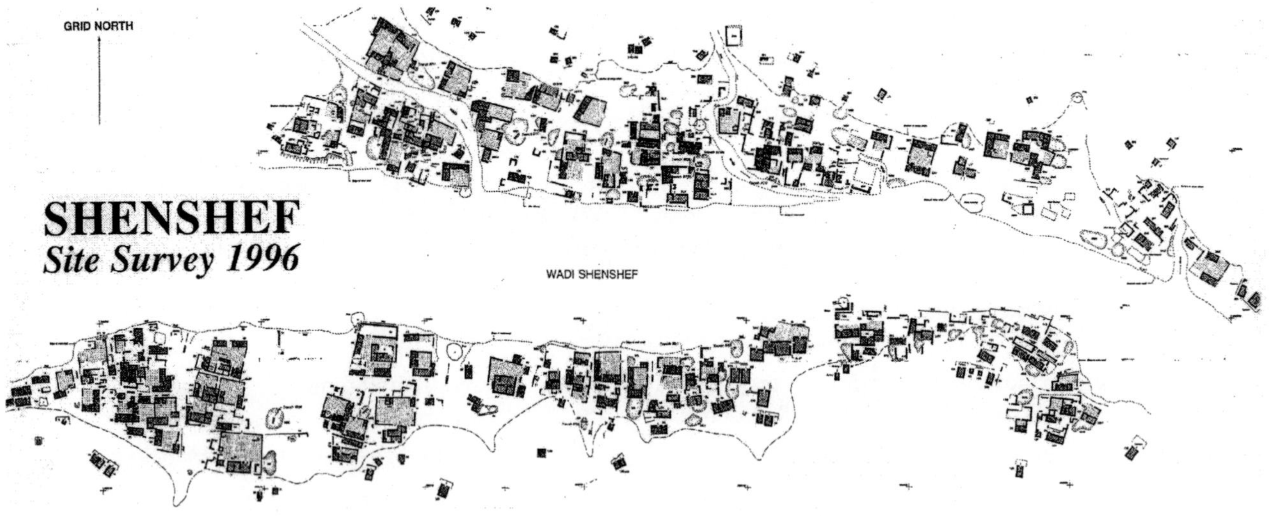

Map 18:7 Shenshef (Aldsworth and Barnard 1996)

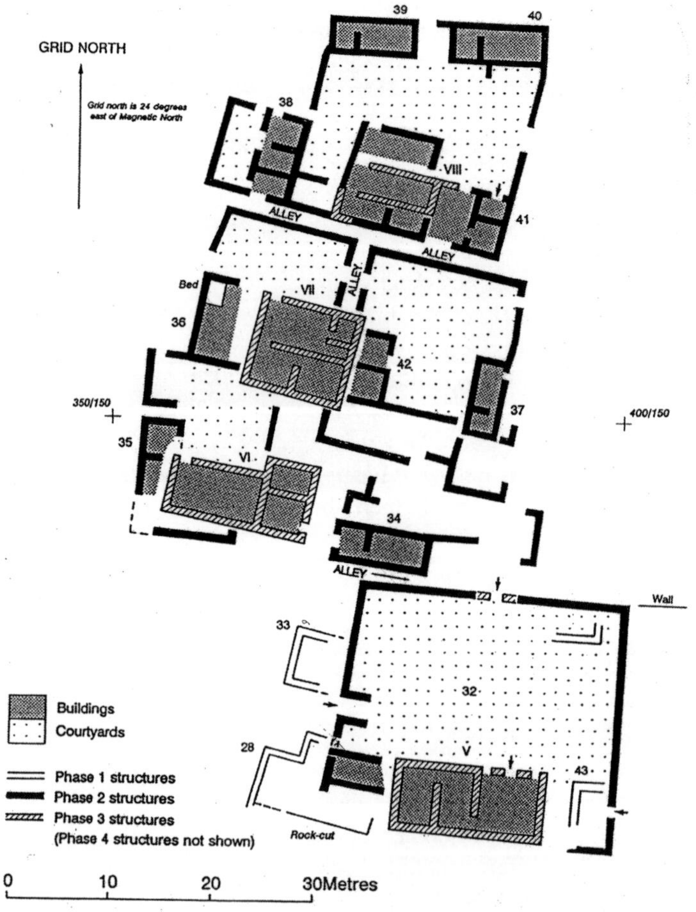

Map 18:8 Houses at Shenshef (Aldsworth and Barnard 1996)

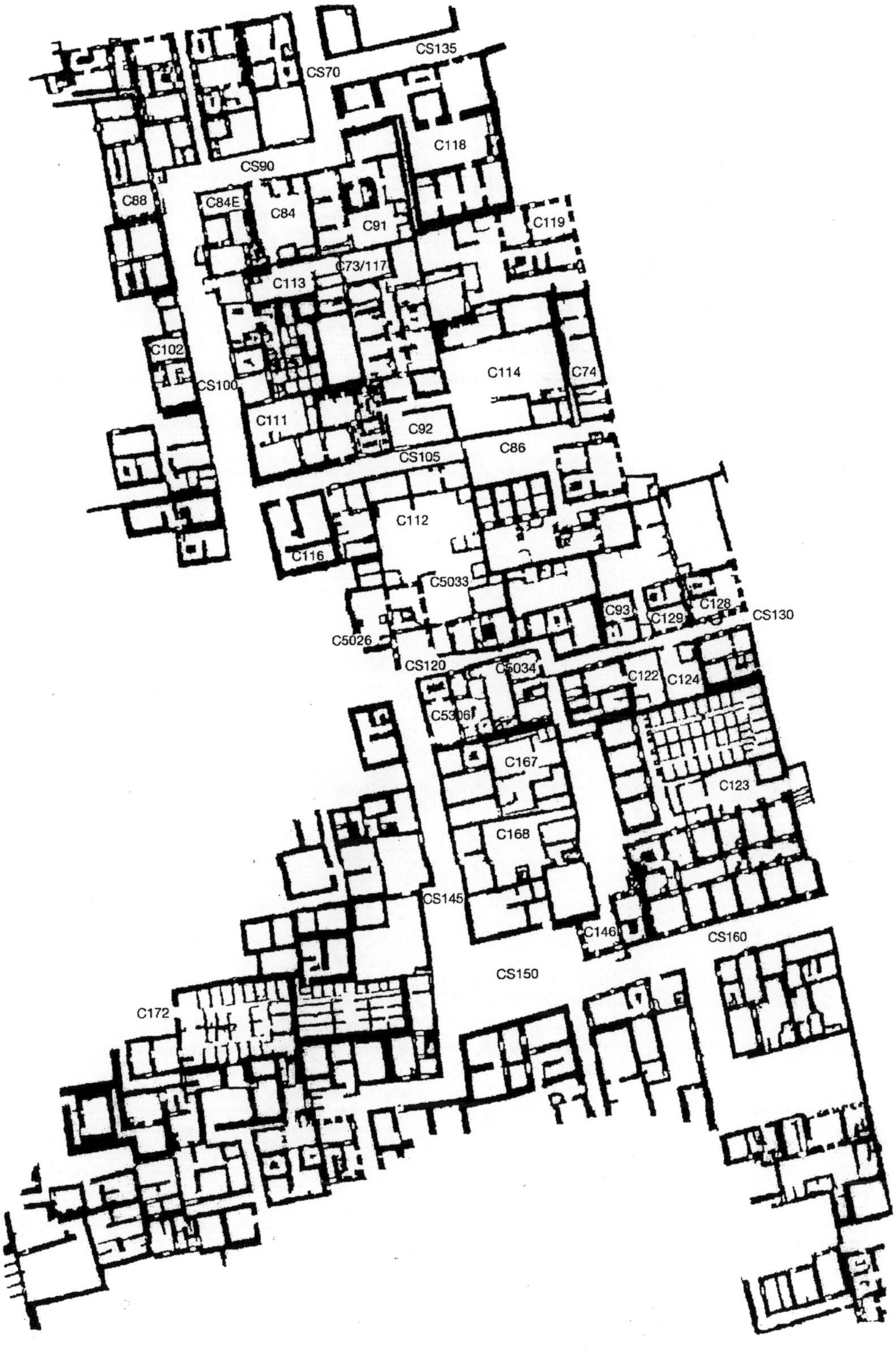

Map 18:9 Karanis and Oxyrhynchus (Alston, 2002)

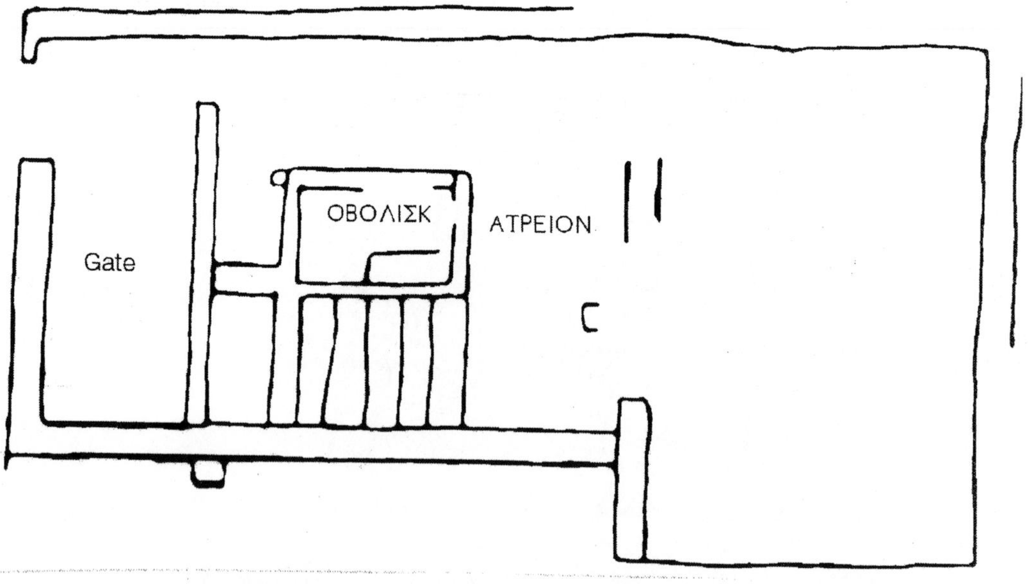

Map 18:10 An Aithron house from the Oxyrhynchus Papyri (Alston 1997)

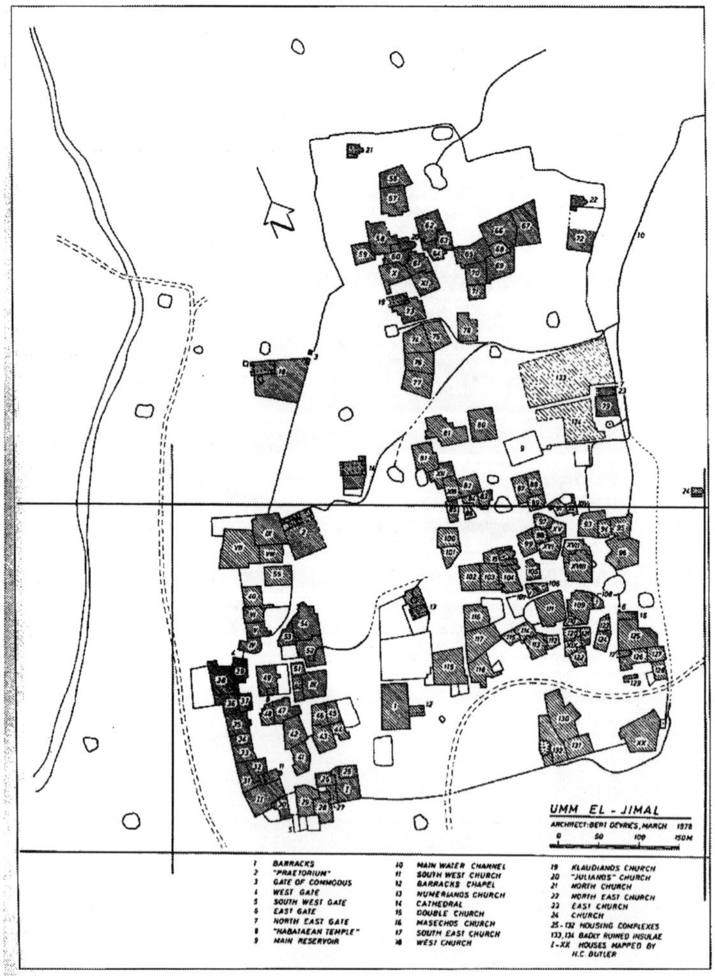

Map 18:11 Umm al-Jimāl (DeVries 1995)

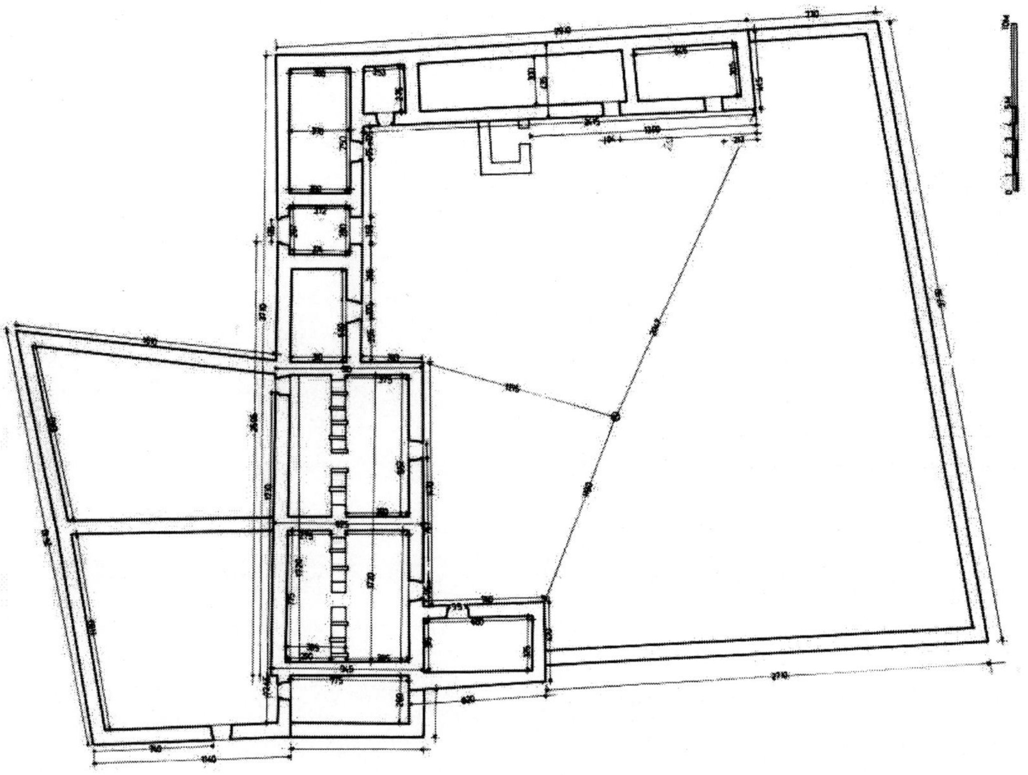

Map 18:12 House 119 at Umm al-Jimāl (DeVries 1995)

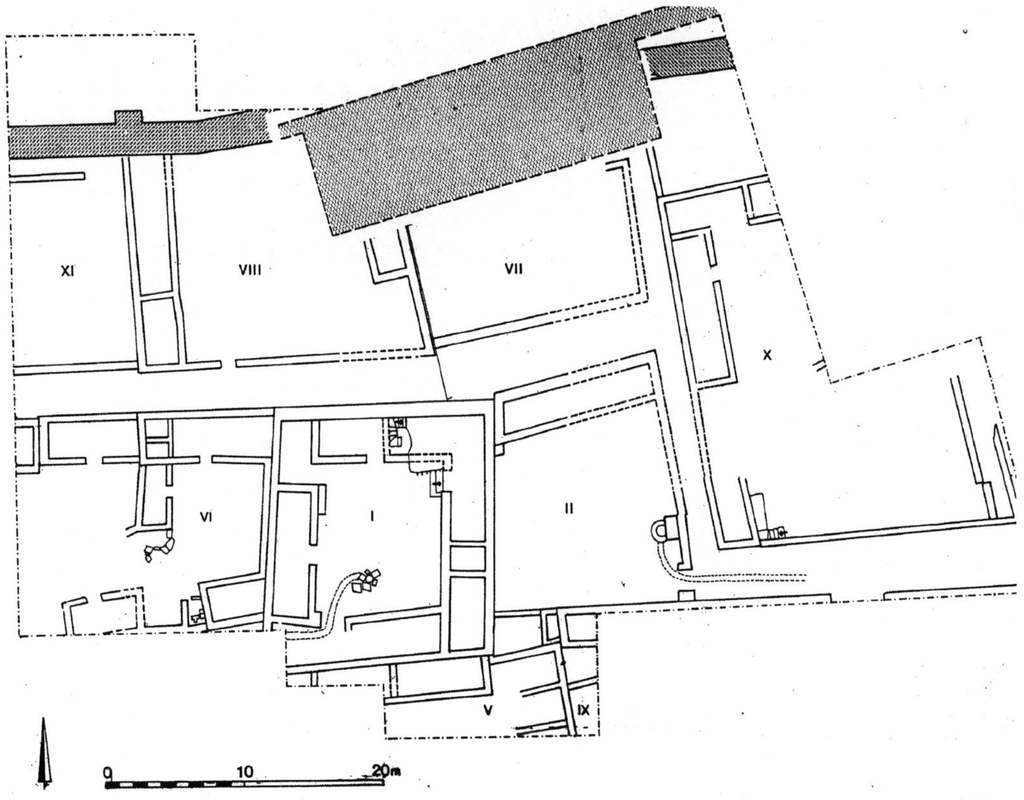

Map 18:13 Residential Area at Sétif (Fentress, et al. *1991)*

Similarly Ibn Ḥawqal tells us 'they dwell under hair tents and possess neither villages nor towns, nor cultivated fields.'[59] In the early twentieth century, Murray described the *bayt bursh* of the Beja as being 'in colour and shape like a hay-cock, built of matting from the dom-palm. The mats are stretched over long curved sticks, and fastened there with wooden skewers, whilst the door, only 2 or 3 feet high is curtained generally with a piece of sacking. The interior is only about 10 feet square in all.'[60] Such accounts would tend to preclude the nomadic Blemmyes as the builders of so sophisticated a settlement as Shenshef.

It falls, then, to consider other parallels for the courtyard houses of Shenshef, and such are readily found in the early Islamic architecture of the Umayyad Levant and North Africa. The point of noting such parallels is not to claim Shenshef for the early Islamic period, which the ceramic sequence would seem to preclude, but rather to place it in the architectural traditions of Arabia and so suggest its association with the 'Arabians' of pre-Islamic Egypt. It might be wondered why, then, analogies are not made with the Late Antique architecture of Arabia, which would after all be contemporary with the date of Shenshef as evinced by its pottery. Yet the current state of research does not allow for this, with archaeological interest in Late Antique Arabia still nascent, and one is forced to cast somewhat farther and turns as such to the archaeology of post-conquest Bilād al-Shām and al-Maghrib for *comparenda*.

Umm al-Jimāl in Jordan (Map 18:11) provides a particularly useful parallel for Shenshef, for it has strong Arab associations in the Late Antique and Umayyad periods. As has been noted, the third-century Jadhīmah al-Abrash ibn Malik is attested as 'king of the Tanūkh' in an inscription from the site. B. DeVries' excavations have revealed continuous settlement through the Late Antique and early Islamic periods, which demonstrate extensive remodelling following the Arab conquest (Map 18:12).[61] The beaten floor of House 119, for instance, was found embedded with Late Roman and Umayyad ceramics of the seventh century, and this and other evidence led DeVries to conclude that it was Umayyad construction on a cleared Byzantine domestic site.[62] The plan shows clear similarities with the houses of Shenshef, most obviously the massive open courtyard with narrow rectilinear rooms arranged around the perimeters. This is to provide clear parallels with an architectural tradition unattested prior to the Arab conquests, and so almost certainly belonging to the tradition of pre-Islamic Arabia.

59 Ibn Ḥawqal 48.
60 Murray 1935: 81.
61 DeVries 1995.
62 Ibid.

Another early Islamic site with continuous occupation through late antiquity is Sétif, in eastern Algeria (Map 18:13). A residential area was excavated by E. Fentress and though the buildings here date from the second half of the tenth century to the mid-eleventh century, they are of the same basic type as those from seventh-century Umm al-Jimāl, and provide further analogies for the houses of Shenshef.[63] The same rooms flank the courtyards, and as at Shenshef, are furnished with *mastabahs*. What is significant about the Sétif houses is the clear break with the Late Antique housing typology, so that they may be clearly identified as belonging to the material culture of the Arab settlers. Sétif therefore provides clear Arab *comparenda* for Shenshef, implying an 'Arabian' as opposed to a Romano-Blemmyes population.

In brief, I would suggest that most 'enigmatic settlements' represent semi-permanent encampments associated with 'Arabian' nomadic pastoralists. At Shenshef, however, there is clearly something different going on. Its location close by the Late Roman emporium of Berenike might well imply some sort of economic relationship, so that it might be understood as a mercantile satellite settlement of 'Arabian' merchants.

So it is that the 'enigmatic settlements' discovered by Peacock and Sidebotham – hitherto attributed to the Desert Fathers — may now be identified as material evidence for the historically attested 'Arabian' population of Late Antique Egypt. And yet there is no 'smoking gun', and an argument from circumstance and analogy can only go so far. Particularly problematic are the lack of Arabic inscriptions and rock-art, which are found in abundance at the desert fringes of pre-Islamic Syria and Palestine. This document, then, should be considered a desk-based assessment informing future survey work in the Eastern Desert, raising intriguing questions that cannot as yet be answered.

References

Aldsworth, F.G. 1999. The Buildings at Shenshef. 385–418 in S.E. Sidebotham and W.Z. Wendrich (eds), *Berenike 1997. Preliminary report of the 1997 excavations at Berenike (Egyptian Red Sea coast) and the survey of the Eastern Desert.* Leiden: Research School CNWS.

Aldsworth, F.G. and Barnard, H. 1996. Survey of Shenshef. 427–44 in S.E Sidebotham and W.Z. Wendrich (eds), *Berenike 1995. Preliminary report of the 1995 excavations at Berenike (Egyptian Red Sea coast) and the survey of the Eastern Desert.* Leiden: Research School CNWS.

63 Fentress 1991: 114–51.

Alston, R. 1997. Houses and Households in Roman Egypt. In R. Laurence and A. Wallace-Hadrill (eds), *Domestic Space in the Roman World: Pompeii and beyond. Journal of Roman Archaeology: Supplementary Series* 22. Portsmouth.

———. 2002. *The City in Roman and Byzantine Egypt.* London and New York: Routledge.

Ammonii Monachi Relatio. R. Devreesse. 1940. Le christianisme dans la péninsule sinaïtique, des origines à l'arrivée des musulmans. *Revue Biblique* 49: 205–23. Partial publication of the Greek recension.

Antoninus Placentinus. *Itinerarium.* P. Geyer (ed.). 1965. Turnholt. J. Wilkinson (tr.) 1977. *Jerusalem Pilgrims before the Crusades.* Warminster: Aris & Phillips.

Athanasius. T. Vivian, A.N. Athanassakis, and R.A. Greer (tr.) 2003. *Life of Anthony.* Kalamazoo: Cistercian Publications.

Bagnall, R.S. 1993. *Egypt in Late Antiquity.* Princeton: Princeton University Press.

Barnard, H. 2002. Eastern Desert Ware, a Short Introduction. *Sudan & Nubia* 6: 53–7.

Beeston, A.F.L.1979. Nemara and Faw. *Bulletin of School of Oriental and African Studies* 42: 1–6.

Butler, A.J. 1978. *The Arab Conquest of Egypt.* P.M. Fraser (rev. ed.). Oxford: Clarendon Press.

Crone, P. and Cook, M. 1977. *Hagarism: the making of the Islamic World.* Cambridge: Cambridge University Press.

Cyril of Scythopolis. E. Schwartz (ed.) 1939. Leipzig. R.M. Price (tr.) 1991. *Lives of the Monks of Palestine.* Kalamazoo: Cistercian Publications.

DeVries, B. 1993. The Umm el-Jimal Project, 1981–1992. *Annual of the Department of Antiquities of Jordan* 37: 433–60.

———. 1995. The Umm el-Jimal Project, 1993 and 1994 Field Seasons. *Annual of the Department of Antiquities of Jordan* 39: 421–35.

Dumbrell, W.J. 1971. The Tell el-Maskhuta bowls and the 'Kingdom' of Qedar in the Persian period. *Bulletin of the American Schools of Oriental Research* 203: 33–44.

Earl. G. and Glazier, D. 2006. Survey at Bi'r an-Nakhil. 26–32 in Peacock, D.P.S. and L. Blue (eds). 2006. *Myos Hormos — Quseir al-Qadim: Roman and Islamic ports on the Red Sea.* Volume 1: *Survey and Excavations* 1999–2003. Oxford: Oxbow Books.

Egeria. *Itinerarium.* J. Wilkinson (ed. and tr.). 1981. *Egeria's Travels to the Holy Land.* Warminster: Aris & Phillips.

Eph'al, I. 1982. *The Ancient Arabs: nomads on the borders of the Fertile Crescent 9th–5th centuries BC.* Jerusalem: Magnes Press.

Fentress, E., Mohamedi, A., Benmansour, A., Amamra, A.A. 1991. *Fouilles de Sétif (1977–1984).* Algiers: Agence d'Archéologie.

Figueras, P. 2000. *From Gaza to Pelusium: materials for the historical geography of North Sinai and South-West Palestine, 332 BCE–640 CE.* Tel Aviv: Ben-Gurion University of the Negev Press.

Gould, D.A. 1999. The Excavations at Shenshef. 371–84 in S.E. Sidebotham and W.Z. Wendrich (eds), *Berenike 1997. Preliminary report of the 1997 excavations at Berenike (Egyptian Red Sea coast) and the survey of the Eastern Desert.* Leiden: Research School CNWS.

Goehring, J.E. 1993. The encroaching desert: literary production and ascetic space in Early Christian Egypt. *Journal of Early Christian Studies* 1: 281–96.

Haiman, M. 1995. An early Islamic period farm at Nahal Mitnan in the Negev Highlands. *'Atiqot* 26: 1–19.

Hayes, J.W. 1995. Summary of pottery and glass finds. 33–41 in S.E. Sidebotham and W.Z. Wendrich (eds), *Berenike 1994. Preliminary report of the 1994 excavations at Berenike (Egyptian Red Sea coast) and the survey of the Eastern Desert.* Leiden: Research School CNWS.

———. 1996. The Pottery. 147–78 in S.E. Sidebotham and W.Z. Wendrich (eds), *Berenike 1995. Preliminary report of the 1995 excavations at Berenike (Egyptian Red Sea coast) and the survey of the Eastern Desert.* Leiden: Research School CNWS.

Hirschfeld, Y. 1992. *The Judean Desert Monasteries in the Byzantine Period.* New Haven and London: Yale University Press.

Hoyland, R.G. 1997. *Seeing Islam as Others Saw It: a survey and evaluation of Christian, Jewish and Zoroastrian Writings on Early Islam.* Princeton: Darwin Press.

———. 2001. *Arabia and the Arabs: from the Bronze Age to the coming of Islam.* London and New York: Routledge.

Husselman, E.M. 1979. *Karanis: excavations of the University of Michigan in Egypt 1928–1935: topography and architecture.* Ann Arbor: University of Michigan Press.

Ibn Ḥawqal. *Kitāb ṣūrat al-arḍ.* J.H. Kramers (ed.). 1938–1939. Leiden: E.J. Brill.

Jean l'Aumônier, *Life of John.* E. Lappa-Zizicas. 1970. Un épitomé inédict de la vie de S. Jean l'Aumônier. *Analecta Bollandiana* 88: 272.

Kaegi, W.E. 1998. Egypt on the eve of the Muslim conquest. 34–61 in C.F. Petry (ed.), *The Cambridge History of Egypt.* Volume 1: *Islamic Egypt, 640–1517.* Cambridge: Cambridge University Press.

Krausse, M. 1985. Die Beziehungen zwischen den beiden Phoibammon-Klostern auf dem thebanischen Westufer. *BSAC* 27: 31–44.

Lappa-Zizicas, E. 1970. Un épitomé indécit de la vie de S.Jean l'Aumônier. *Analecta Bollandiana* 88: 272.

Littmann, E. and Meredith, D. 1953. Nabataean inscriptions from Egypt — I. *Bulletin of the School of Oriental and African Studies* 15(1): 1–28.

———. 1954. Nabataean inscriptions from Egypt — II. *Bulletin of the School of Oriental and African Studies* 16(2): 211–46.

MacCoull, L. 1986. Dioscorus and the Dukes. *Byzantine Studies / Études Byzantines* 13: 29–39.

Macdonald, M.C.A. 1998. Some reflections on epigraphy and ethnicity in the Roman Near East. *Mediterranean Archaeology* 11: 177–90.

———. 2003. 'Les Arabes en Syrie' or 'la pénétration des Arabes en Syrie': a question of perceptions? *Topoi*, Suppl. 4: 303–18.

Mayerson, P. 1980. The Ammonius Narrative: Bedouin and Blemmyes attacks in Sinai. 148–64 in G. Rendsburg, *et al.* (eds), *The Bible World, Essays in Honor of Cyrus H. Gordon.* New York: Ktav Publishing House.

Murray, G.W. 1925. The Roman roads and stations in the Eastern Desert. *Journal of Egyptian Archaeology* 11: 138–50.

———. 1926. Note on the ruins of Hitan Shenshef near Berenice. *Journal of Egyptian Archaeology* 12: 166–7.

———. 1935. *Sons of Ishmael: a study of the Egyptian Bedouin.* London: G. Routledge; repr. 1967.

Peacock, D.P.S. 1997. *Survey and Excavation at Mons Claudianus, 1987–993.* I: *Topography and Quarries.* Cairo: IFAO.

Peacock, D.P.S. and Blue, L. 2006. *Myos Hormos — Quseir al-Qadim: Roman and Islamic ports on the Red Sea.* Volume 1: *Survey and Excavations* 1999–2003. Oxford: Oxbow Books.

Peter the Deacon. *Liber de Locis Sanctis. Corpus Christianorum* 175. Turnhout and Leuven : Brepols.

Retsö, J. 2003. *The Arabs in Antiquity: their history from the Assyrians to the Umayyads.* London: Routledge.

Seeck, O. (ed.). *Notitia Dignitatum.* 1876. Berlin: Weidmann.

Shahid, I. 1984. *Byzantium and the Arabs in the Fourth Century.* Washington: Dumbarton Press.

———. 1995. *Byzantium and the Arabs in the Sixth Century.* Washington: Dumbarton Press.

Sidebotham, S.E. 1986. *Roman Economic Policy in the Erythra Thalassa, 30 BC– AD 217.* Leiden: E.J. Brill.

Sidebotham, S.E., Barnard, H., and Pyke, G. 2002. Five enigmatic Late Roman settlements in the Eastern Desert. *Journal of Egyptian Archaeology* 88: 187–225.

Sozomen. *Ecclesiastical History.* 2: 239–47 in R. Hussey (tr.) 1860. Oxford. C.D. Hartranft (tr.) 1891. *Nicene and post-Nicene Fathers of the Christian Church.* Oxford: Clarendon Press.

Strabo. Jones, H. (ed. and tr.) 1917. *Geography.* Cambridge: Harvard University Press.

Strouhal, E. 1982. Hand-made pottery of the IVth to VIth centuries AD in the Dodecaschoinos. Pages 215–22 in J.M Plumley (ed.), *Proceedings of the Symposium for Nubian Studies. Selwyn College, Cambridge.* 1978. Warminster: Aris & Phillips.

———. 1984. *Wādī Qitna and Kalābsha-South.* Vol. 1. *Archaeology.* Prague: Charles University: 157–77, 195–200, Tabs. 31–4, Pls. 66–70.

———. 1991. Further analysis of the fine handmade pottery of Egyptian Nubia in 3rd–5th centuries AD. 3–9 in W. Godlewski (ed.), *Coptic and Nubian Pottery.* Part II. *International Workshop, Nieborów. August 29–31, 1988.* Warsaw: National Museum in Warsaw Occasional Paper.

al-Ṭabarī. *Annales.* M.J. de Goeje (ed.) 1879–1901. Leiden: E.J. Brill.

Red Sea and Indian Ocean: Ports and their Hinterland

Eivind Heldaas Seland

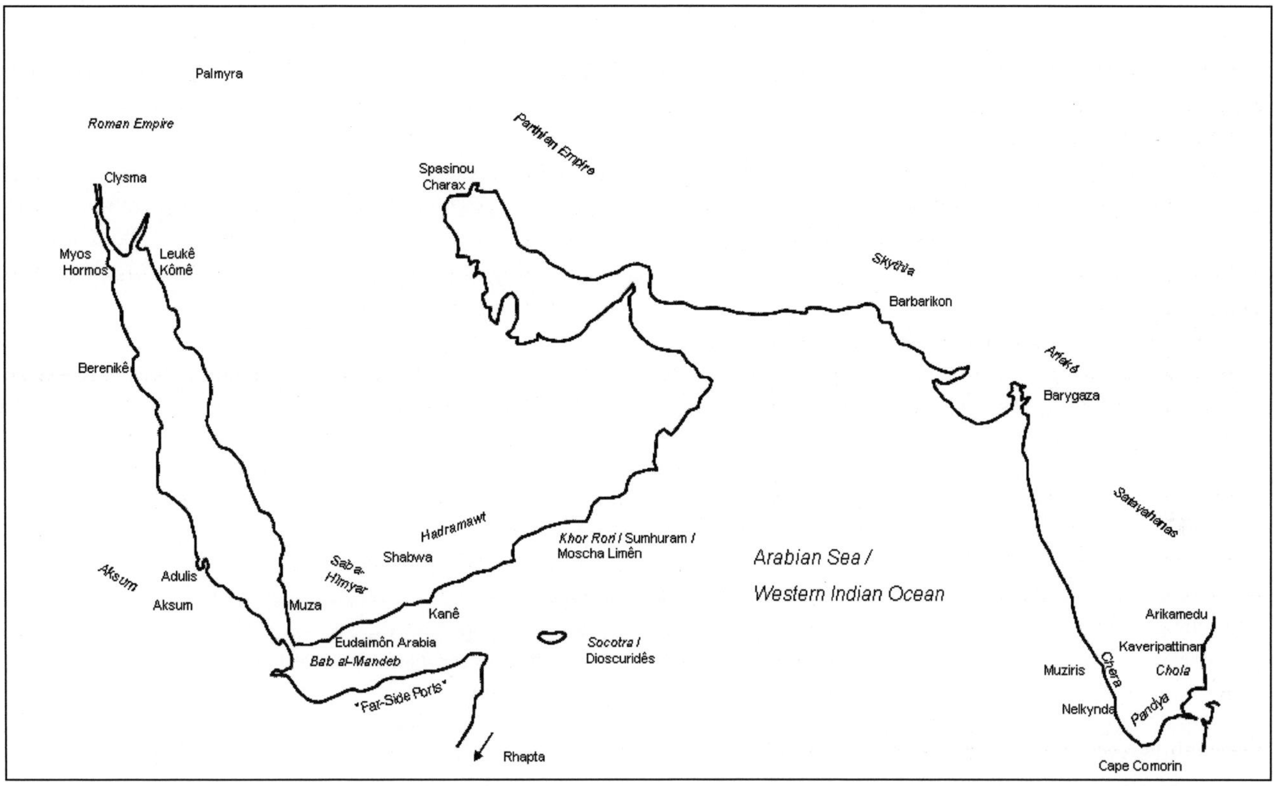

Map 19:1 The Indian Ocean and the Red Sea in the first century CE

While states on the Red Sea and Indian Ocean rim in the ancient period were primarily located inland, maritime long-distance exchange facilitated by the monsoon winds brought these societies, which were often separated by huge stretches of water, into close commercial contact over many centuries. Our main literary source for this trade, the *Periplus of the Erythræan Sea*, reveals a picture of inland states actively engaged in maritime trade. These states interacted in a system where political centres on high ground inland mobilized key resources from extensive hinterlands in order to coordinate and facilitate long-distance maritime exchange, from coastal settlements established and maintained specifically for that purpose. In this paper I argue that maritime trade as an agent of change in Red Sea and Indian Ocean societies is reflected in the consistent use of terminology describing hierarchies of settlements in the *Periplus*. This, in turn, broadens our understanding of the relationship between ocean, coast, inland and inland-periphery in the regions participating in the monsoon exchange.

The early states on the Red Sea and Indian Ocean rim were deeply interconnected by networks carrying goods, people and ideas from Tamil south India in the south-east to Egypt in the north-west. Through Indian ports the system linked overland and maritime networks connecting to central and south-east Asia, and indirectly also to China. On the African side the Indian Ocean exchange connected with African and Mediterranean hinterlands and networks. Societies in the Red Sea and Indian Ocean region were separated by huge stretches of water, and when explaining similar developments across such distances, maritime exchange stands out as the most likely common agent of change.

While the states on the Red Sea and Indian Ocean were connected by maritime trade, they were not primarily coastal states. Political centres were situated in good agricultural areas inland. On the African Red Sea coast precipitation was too scarce for dry farming,[1] while extensive areas suitable for cultivation were available in the highlands of modern Ethiopia and Eritrea. The situation resembles that of Arabia, where dry-farming in some areas and irrigation in others enabled high population densities in parts of central Yemen and Wādī Ḥaḍramawt.[2]

1 Foreign Office 1920: 6–7; Fattovich 2003: 16–7.

2 Naval Intelligence Division 1946: 476–7; Wilkinson 2002: 102–7; Sedov 1996: 69, 86 (on Ḥaḍramawt).

Most Indian coasts receive plenty of rainfall in normal years, but wastelands and marshes dominate large parts of the border area between modern India and Pakistan, and the western coast of India is dominated by a narrow coastal plain giving way to the steep Ghat mountains. While cultivation is possible on pockets of good soils and in estuaries,[3] the Deccan and modern Gujarat have offered better possibilities for the centralization of agricultural surplus necessary to establish political dominance over larger regions. Red Sea and western Indian Ocean littorals have thus generally been subject to hinterland rulers, but the evidence from an ancient period suggests that coastal settlement nevertheless played important roles as interfaces between agricultural hinterlands and maritime commercial networks.

The *Periplus of the Erythræan Sea* is an anonymous merchant's guide from the first century CE.[4] It is written in the Greek *koinê* variant, probably by an Egyptian captain or merchant involved in Red Sea and Indian Ocean commerce.[5] With respect to its contents the small work is unique in the preserved ancient corpus. The *Periplus* gives detailed sailing directions for the African coast southwards to Rhapta,[6] probably in modern Tanzania,[7] and along the coast of Arabia and India eastwards to Cape Comorin,[8] the southernmost point of India. The description of the Indian coasts further east[9] is sketchy and unreliable.[10] The work lists ports, markets and commodities and frequently also details about local populations and rulers and their attitude to foreign traders. Moreover, the work indirectly sheds light on the relationship between coast and hinterland, between state and non-state areas, and between maritime and overland networks, through a consistent use of terminology describing rulers and particularly settlements.

While the Indian Ocean and Red Sea trade was, of course, maritime, the products traded were generally inland or transit products. The state of Aksum in modern Ethiopia and Eritrea exported mainly ivory from the African hinterland through the 'regulated port of trade', *emporion nomimon,*[11] of Adulis on the Red Sea.[12] Muza, the port of Saba-Ḥimyar was also an *emporion nomimon* and exported mainly myrrh[13] from the highlands of modern Yemen.[14] Kanê, the port of Ḥaḍramawt, exported frankincense. Now, frankincense is not an inland commodity, and the most important source in antiquity as today seems to have been the Dhofar region in modern Oman;[15] but the source is situated hundreds of kilometres away from the main population centres of Ḥaḍramawt and from their most important port at Kanê. This seems to have led to a conscious policy of expansion on behalf of the kingdom of Ḥaḍramawt,[16] with the establishment of outposts and settlements in the core frankincense-producing regions, like Syagros, Moscha Limên and on Soqotra,[17] in order to centralize the trade in this important commodity, which was mainly traded with Mediterranean merchants at the port of Kanê.[18]

Across the Indian Ocean, the situation is the same. At the port of Barbarikon at the mouth of the Indus, traders could find products from the inland part of the Skythian or Indo-Parthian kingdom in control there, but also silk from China and precious stones from modern Afghanistan.[19] This reveals the connections of Barbarikon to overland networks, which went northwards and eastwards and connected to the route later called the Silk Road. At the port of Barygaza at the mouth of the Narmada in western India, Mediterranean merchants were able to buy the same products from the Indian interior, and the same transit goods from China and Central Asia.[20] From the Tamil kingdoms in southern India, merchants acquired pepper, grown in the southern Ghats, precious stones from the Coimbatore district,[21] textiles from the Kaveri Valley, aromatics in transit and silk from the Bay of Bengal, as well as pearls, which were of course a coastal commodity but sold not from the areas where they were harvested, the Gulf of Mannar and the Palk Strait,[22] but from certain ports on the west coast.[23]

In sum, this reflects a conscious strategy on the part of rulers situated in inland cities in good agricultural areas.

---

3 Ray 1986: 12–20.

4 Consensus now seems to have been reached on a mid first-century date, see Robin 1991 and Fussman 1991.

5 Huntingford 1980: 6–8; Casson 1989: 8; Schoff 1995: 15–6.

6 *Periplus* 1–18.

7 Chami 1999; Horton 1990; Casson 1989: 141–2.

8 *Periplus* 19–58.

9 Ibid.: 59–66.

10 Fabricius 1883: 28; Schoff 1995: 16, 234, but see Casson 1989: 8, n.14 and 17 for a more optimistic view.

11 In L. Casson's edition of the *Periplus* (1989), which is not only the best but also the most widely cited, *emporion nomimon* is translated as 'legally limited port of trade' (1989: 51, 63, 71). I prefer 'regulated port of trade', because I find no evidence of the royal monopoly that Casson claims characterized these ports (1989: 274–6); but the important term is *nomimon,* meaning something like 'legitimate', 'customary' or 'lawful' (LSJ 1179b), which implies some sort of official status and regulation of trade in the place.

12 *Periplus* 4, 6.

13 Ibid.: 24.

14 See Van Beek 1958: 143–4, 152; Groom 1981: 96–7, 116–20.

15 Van Beek 1958: 142, 152; Groom 1981: 98–115.

16 Seland 2005: 272–6.

17 *Periplus* 30–2.

18 Ibid.: 27–8.

19 Ibid.: 39.

20 Ibid.: 41, 48–9, 50.

21 Warmington 1995: 250–1.

22 Sarma 1978: 423–5.

23 *Periplus* 56, 59.

They collected and mobilized resources from diverse hinterlands, and these resources were offered to merchants from other parts of the Red Sea and Indian Ocean from ports especially established for commercial purposes, and in most cases unable to support a sizeable population by themselves. This pattern repeats itself in all states on the Indian Ocean rim in the first century. The way that Red Sea and Indian Ocean states organized themselves in order to take advantage of maritime trade, combined with the fact that only states with access to maritime trade survived in internal power struggles over time,[24] shows that maritime trade was a significant factor in the emergence and development of these states.

The description of the Red Sea in the *Periplus* provides two examples of how these states organized themselves with respect to maritime trade. These are the relevant parts of the description of first-century Aksum:

> About 3000 stades beyond Ptolemais Thêrôn is a legally limited port of trade, Adulis...From Adulis it is a journey of three days to Koloê, an island city that is the first trading post for ivory, and from there another five days to the metropolis itself, which is called Axômitês; into it is brought all the ivory from beyond the Nile through what is called Kyêneion, and from there down to Adulis. The mass of elephants and rhinoceroses that are slaughtered all inhabit the upland regions, although on rare occasions they are also seen along the shore around Adulis itself.[25]

Here we learn that Adulis was called an *emporion nomion,* 'regulated port of trade',[26] and the use of the word *emporion* identifies Adulis as a commercial settlement. It is elsewhere described as a 'moderately sized village', a '*kômê symmetros*'[27] in Greek, indicating its moderate scale and thus limited importance outside the commercial sector.

We also learn that three days inland from Adulis was the yet unidentified city,[28] *polis,* of Koloê, and that from there you could reach the capital, *mêtropolis*, of Aksum in another five days. Koloê was the first market, or *emporion*, for ivory and into Aksum was brought 'all the ivory from beyond the Nile through what is called Kyêneion, and from there down to Adulis'. So Aksum centralized and controlled the trade in ivory for a large part of the African hinterland through the commercial settlement of Adulis on the Red Sea coast.

This small passage allows us to reconstruct the geographical and economic layout of the first-century kingdom of Aksum in the following way: The capital of Aksum, in the highlands, coordinated the trade in the most important commodity, ivory, through a port established for that purpose, Adulis. Other centres existed: the old Ptolemaic elephant-hunting station of Ptolemais Thêrôn, which is labelled a small market, *mikron emporion*,[29] and the secondary centre and city, *polis*, of Koloê. (Figure 19:1).

If we turn to the kingdom of Saba–Ḥimyar on the other side of the Red Sea, the picture turns out to be roughly similar. The *Periplus* gives the following account in excerpt:

> Beyond these regions, on the very last bay on the left-hand shore of this sea, is Muza, a legally limited port of trade on the coast, about 12,000 stades from Berenicê if you follow a course due south...A three-day journey inland from Muza lies Sauê, the city of the province, called Mapharitis, that surrounds it. The governor, Cholaibos, has his residence there. Nine days further inland is Saphar, the metropolis, residence of Charibaêl, legitimate king of the two nations, the Homerite and the one, lying next to it, called the Sabaean; he is a friend of the emperors, thanks to continuous embassies and gifts...Its [Muza's] exports consist of local products — myrrh...[30]

Here we learn of another regulated port of trade,[31] Muza; a capital, *mêtropolis*, called Saphar, which was the royal residence; and a city, *polis,* called Sauê, where a royal vassal, a *tyrannos*, resided. Saphar and Sauê were situated in good agricultural areas inland. Muza, on the coast, would not be able to sustain an agricultural population on its own. The main production areas for myrrh, the most important export of Saba–Ḥimyar, were also inland.

24 In Southern Arabia, the inland powers of Saba' and Qataban were among the dominant polities in the first century BCE (De Maigret 2002: 213). At this time trade in aromatics with the Mediterranean seems to have been carried out along caravan routes (Pliny 12.64). By the mid first century CE, trade had moved to the maritime routes on the Red Sea as described by Strabo (2.5.12, 17.1.3) and in the *Periplus*. Qataban is not mentioned in the *Periplus*. Its probable maritime outlet at Aden had been taken over by Saba-Ḥimyar by the mid-first century (*Periplus* 26). Over time Qataban was destroyed by Ḥaḍramawt and Saba Ḥimyar (De Maigret 2002: 229, 238–9). And Ḥimyar eventually conquered both Ḥaḍramawt and their former liege of Saba (De Maigret 240–4). See Champakalakshmi 1999: 94 on the situation in Tamil South India.

25 *Periplus* 4, excerpt, L. Casson (tr.)

26 See note 11 above.

27 *Periplus* 4:2.6.

28 Wenig 2003: 93–5.

29 *Periplus* 3.

30 Ibid.: 21–4, excerpts, L. Casson (tr.).

31 See note 11 above.

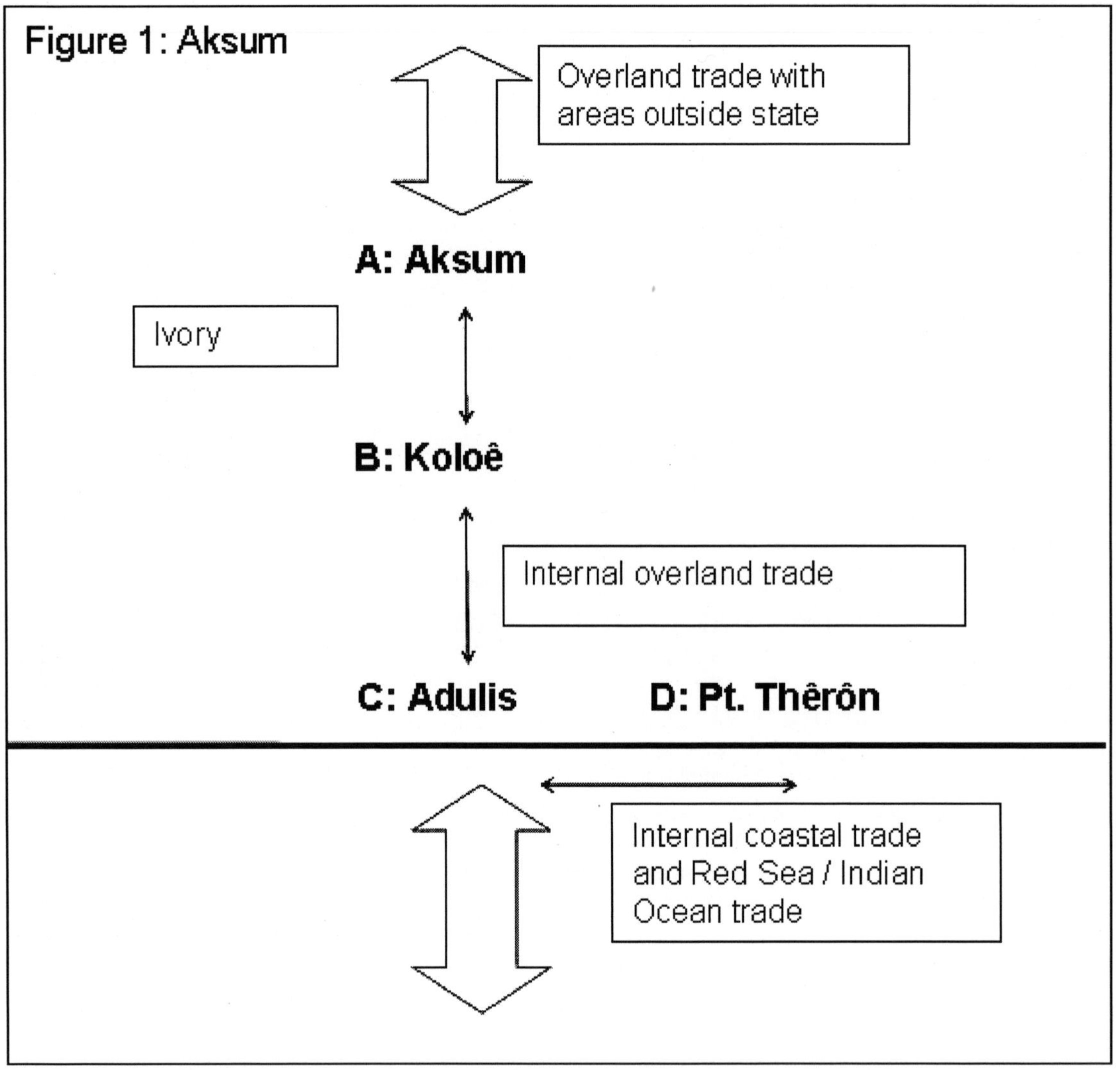

Figure 19:1 Aksum

These are not the only centres in the kingdom of Saba-Ḥimyar mentioned in the *Periplus*. Along the coast, we also find Okêlis, on the Straits of Bāb al-Mandab, described as 'not so much a port of trade' (*emporion*) 'as a harbour and a watering station' (*hormos kai hydreuma*);[32] and Eudaimôn Arabia, modern Aden, which is described not as an *emporion,* but as a 'seashore village' (*kômê parathalassios*), that however had a prosperous past as a market in Arabian trade with India and the Mediterranean.[33]

The picture is the same as at Aksum. A range of secondary settlements are controlled from an inland capital, but although the main export, myrrh, is available throughout large parts of the kingdom of Saba–Ḥimyar, and there are a number of suitable harbours, all export takes place from one appointed port of trade, the *emporion*, while other coastal settlements are referred to as harbours, villages or watering stations, not markets. (Figure 19:2)

The other five established kingdoms described in the *Periplus*: Ḥaḍramawt, Skythia, Ariakê, Chera, and Pandya, all seem to follow the same pattern The only notable exceptions are that commodities of coastal origin, frankincense and pearls, take prominence among exports from the Ḥaḍrami and Pandya kingdoms respectively, while inland exports dominate from other regions. The presence of such important commercial goods on the coast forced inland centres to invest in infrastructure and administrative presence in coastal areas in order to ensure control.[34]

32 *Periplus* 25.

33 Ibid.: 26.

34 See page 212 above on frankincense. The situation seems to be the same in the Pandya kingdom, where we learn that pearl fisheries were conducted by convicts and that pearls were gathered in an inland centre (*Periplus* 59), only to be sold from a second port (*Periplus* 56).

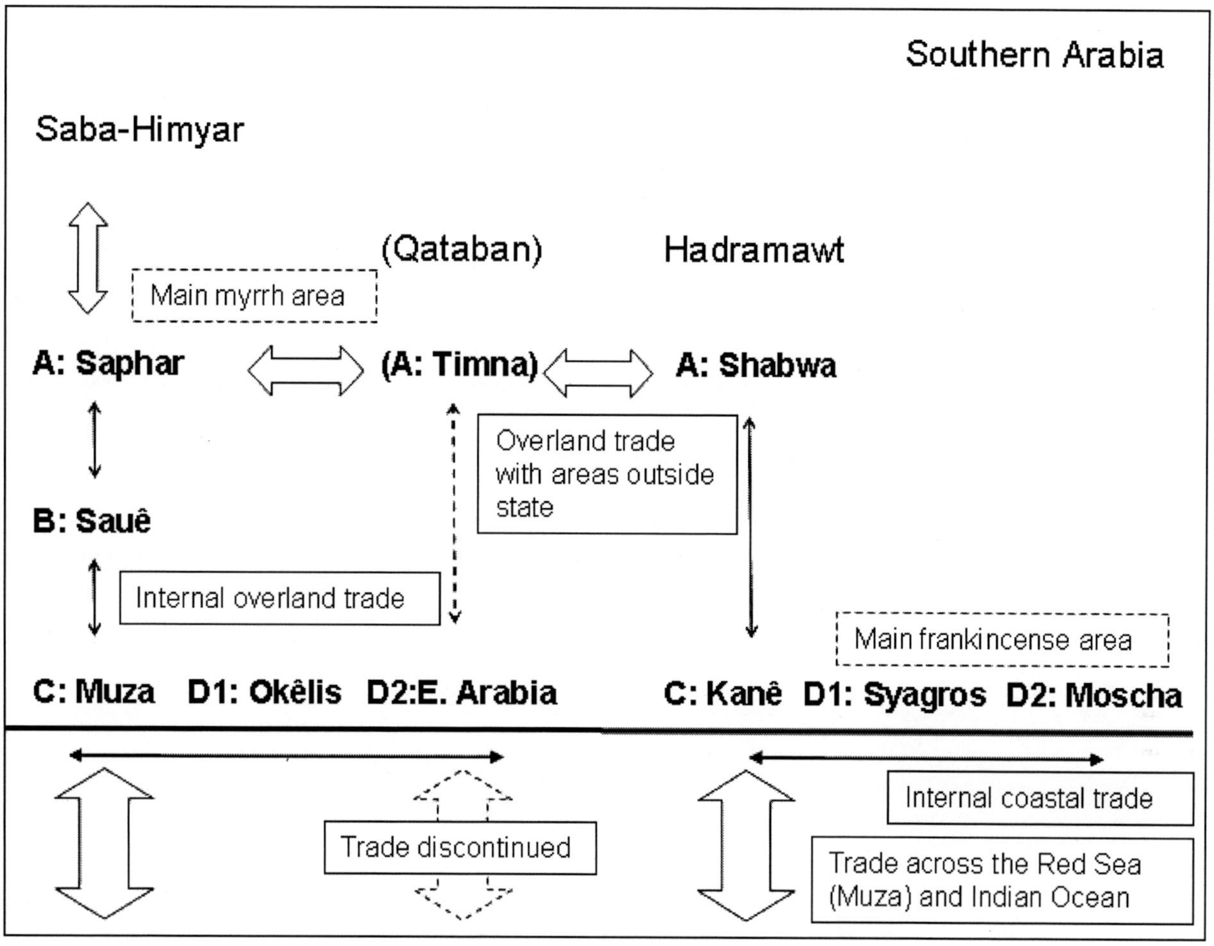

Figure 19:2 Southern Arabia

The similarity, however, does not end with the superficial geographical and economic layout of these kingdoms as I describe them here. On closer investigation, it proves also to be reflected in the terminology of the *Periplus* itself. Figure 19:3 lists all centres mentioned within Indian Ocean and Red Sea kingdoms in the *Periplus*, together with the terminology used to denote them: The list is remarkably consistent. Places of royal residence are generally called *mêtropoleis* in the *Periplus,* literally 'mother-cities' or rather 'capitals' in our context. Other important inland centres are called *poleis*, 'cities'. Coastal settlements serving as centres of trade are invariably called *emporia*, 'markets' in some cases with an additional epithet like 'regulated', *nomimos,* or 'lawful', *enthesmos*. Other ports where trade took place also carry the label *emporion*, but when they occur within areas under state control they always carry labels like 'local', *topikon* or 'small', *mikron.* Coastal settlements from which little or no long-distance exchange took place are simply called villages, *kômai,* and harbours, *hormoi* or *limenes*.

This hierarchy is compatible with the geographical and economic layout of states exemplified with the structure of Saba–Ḥimyar and Aksum described above. The *Periplus* here draws a picture of an Indian Ocean model state with a four-level hierarchy. The king ruled from a capital / *mêtropolis* (A). Most states had large centres of secondary political importance called cities / *poleis* (B). All maritime trade took place from one appointed port of trade (C). There were other coastal settlements (D), but these were not involved in long-distance maritime trade. The *Periplus* is a practical and descriptive handbook, not a treatise on the ancient model state and cannot be expected to be complete or consistent. As long as that is kept in mind, the model provides a useful tool which allows us to compare the states around the Indian Ocean and to some extent fill in the blank spaces from other sources. For instance, both Tamil and classical sources mention Karur and Madurai as the cities of royal residence in the Chera and Pandya realm, and they can fill in the blank *mêtropolis* spaces in those states. In Aksum, the two archaeologically attested large inland settlements of Matara and Qohaito could both represent the Koloê of the *Periplus* and could both possibly fit into the *polis* slot under Aksum in Figure 19:3, above.

Rank	Term	Aksum	Ḥimyar	Ḥaḍramawt	Skythia	Ariakê	Chera	Pandya
A	*mêtropolis*	Aksum	Saphar	Saubatha	Minnagar	Minnagara	(Karur)	(Madurai)
B	*polis*	Koloê (Qohaito) (Metara)	Sauê			Ozênê Kalliena		Kolchoi
C	*emporion*	Adulis	Muza	Kanê	Barbarikon	Barygaza	Muziris	Nelkynda
D	*komê, hormos, limên, mikron emporion, topikon emporion*	Pt Thêrôn	Okêlis Eudaimôn Arabia	Syagros, Moscha		Kammoni Akabaru Suppara Kalliena	Tyndis	Bakarê Balita

Figure 19:3 Terms denoting centres in the Periplus Maris Erythræi[35]

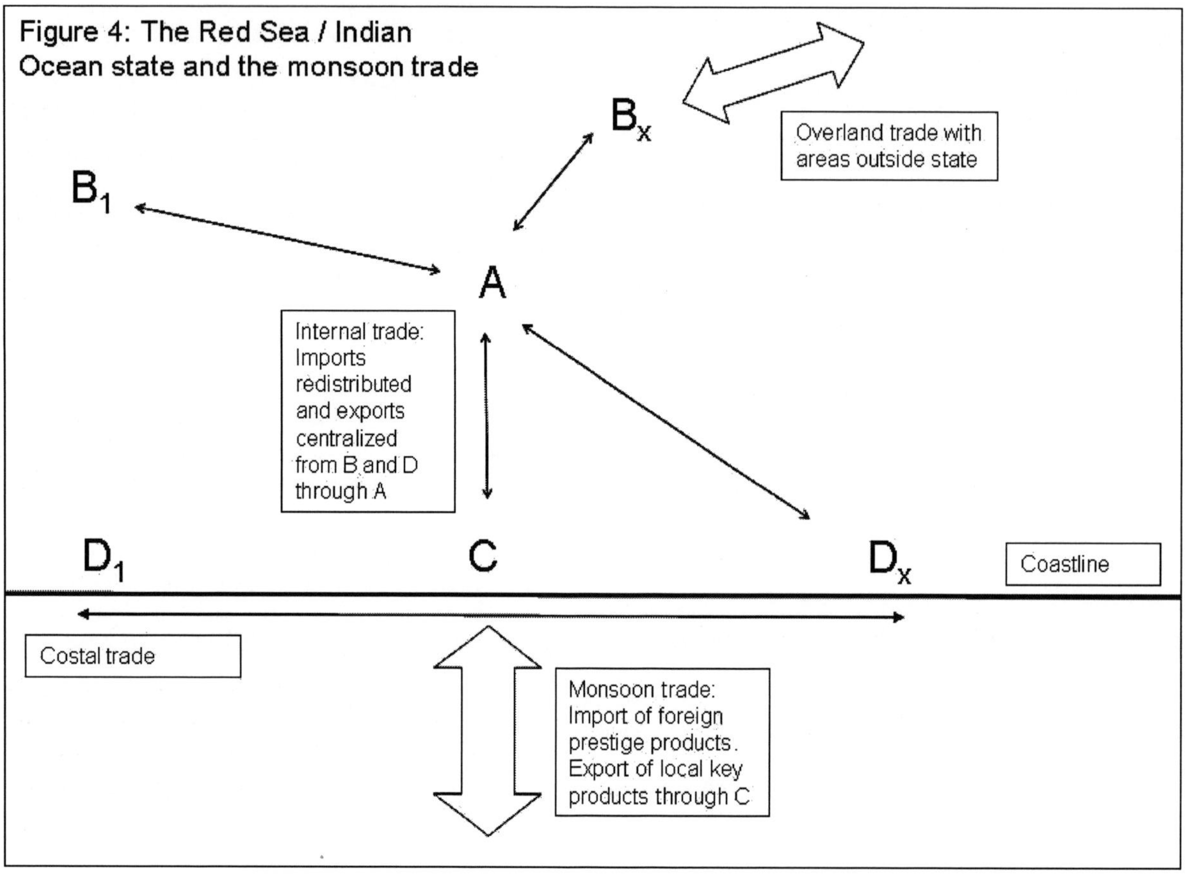

Figure 19:4 The Red Sea / Indian State and the Monsoon Trade

[35] Names in parenthesis refer to contemporary centres not mentioned in the *Periplus.*

This hierarchy of centres described in the *Periplus* lays the foundation for a descriptive model of commercial aspects of the first-century Indian Ocean state. A model greatly facilitates the comparison with other regions — for example, Bennett Bronson's models of trade, ecology and state development in early south-east Asia,[36] and other periods. It gives a framework for the interpretation of a fragmentary source material and it provides a picture of how polities reacted to the common agent of change represented by the monsoon trade.

By the mid-first century a common structure had evolved in all the Indian Ocean states (Figure 19:4). From an inland centre (A), the political elite controlled the flow of export commodities from peripheral regions with secondary centre(s) (B_x) and (D_x). Typically, these export commodities were inland products, either from mountainous or forested regions within the centre's area of political dominance, or acquired through overland trade with areas outside the state. In some cases, most prominently frankincense in Ḥaḍramawt and pearls in the Pandian kingdom, coastal or marine products constituted important exports. This would prompt a heavier administrative presence on the coast and a more direct involvement in the harvesting of the commodity than with inland commodities, which would have to pass through the political centre on their way to the coast anyway. In this way the political centre was also able to control the redistribution of imported goods from the appointed port of trade (C) to other centres.

Virtually all maritime, long-distance exchange would take place from one and only one *emporion* / port of trade (C) in each state. C also took part in coastal exchange, but had little economic importance apart from its role in the monsoon trade. Except for the presence of drinking water and the existence of a good harbour, C's special position was founded on its supply of trade goods from the interior, an administrative presence from A and the port's offer of security and services to visiting traders. In other words, while D was cut off from direct involvement in the monsoon trade, C's role in the exchange was dependent on the policy of A. The model provides a graphical expression of ruler effort to benefit from trade as well as trade influence on state structure.

The hierarchy reflects the variables of rank and function, rather than of size. While it is likely that a capital would be larger than a city and a city larger than a village, the important difference was the former being the seat of the king. The port of trade was of greater commercial importance than the harbour or even the local or small market, but the *Periplus* gives us no information as to size. The *polis* was probably larger than the port of trade, but in most cases we know little of the political relation between the two and between each of them and the capital. Rather than an A–B–C–D hierarchy with the former controlling the latter, we have a model with *one* political centre, A, which relates to a number of centres, B, C and D with different functions. The model is flexible as to the number of centres B, D and even A, but cannot accommodate several ports of trade (C) if it is not attestable that they played different roles in the system.

What does this tell us about the importance of maritime trade for the states on the Red Sea and Indian Ocean rim? The relative role of trade compared to other variables such as religion, agriculture, irrigation and conquest can hardly be established. The main clue to the importance of trade compared to other variables lies in the similar influence trade had on the spatial organization of these states, which allows the construction of a model valid for all of them. While the role of trade compared to other factors can never be established beyond doubt in the absence of statistical records, the similar manner in which all the states in the survey organized their productive, commercial and administrative activities in order to participate in the monsoon exchange, points toward trade taking precedence over other factors influencing the political-economical organization of the states.

[36] Bronson 1978.

References

Bronson, B. 1978. Exchange at the upstream and downstream ends: Notes toward a functional model of the coastal state in Southeast Asia. 39–52 in K.L. Hutterer (ed.), *Economic Exchange and Social Interaction in Southeast Asia: perspectives from prehistory, history and ethnography*. Ann Arbor: University of Michigan, Center for South and Southeast Asian Studies.

Chami, F.A. 1999. Roman Beads from the Rufiji Delta, Tanzania: first incontrovertible archaeological link with the *Periplus*. *Current Anthropology* 40: 237–41

Champakalakshmi, R. 1999. *Trade, Ideology and Urbanization South India 300 BC to AD 1300*. New Delhi: Oxford University Press.

De Maigret, A. 2002. *Arabia Felix: an exploration of the archaeological history of Yemen*. London: Stacey International.

Fabricius, B. 1883. *Der Periplus Des Erythräischen Meeres — Von Einem Unbekannten — Griechisch und Deutsch mit Kritischen und Erklärenden Anmerkungen Nebst Vollständigem Wörterverzeichnisse*. Leipzig: Von Veit & Comp.

Fattovich, R. 2003. *The Development of Urbanism in the Northern Horn of Africa in Ancient and Medieval Times*. University of Uppsala. E-text available from http://www.arkeologi.uu.se/afr/projects/BOOK/fattovich.htm.Uppsala. Accessed 10 October 2006.

Foreign Office, Historical Section. 1920. Spanish and Italian Possessions: Independent States, 126: Eritrea. *Peace Handbooks* XX. London: HMSO.

Fussman, G. 1991. 'Le Périple et l'histoire politique de l'Inde.' *Journal Asiatique* 279: 31–8.

Groom, N. 1981. *Frankincense and Myrrh: a study of the Arabian incense trade.* London: Longman.

Horton, M. 1990. The Periplus and East Africa. Review of L. Casson, *The Periplus of the Erythraean Sea. Azania* 25: 95–9.

Huntingford, G.W.B. 1980. The Periplus of the Erythraean Sea — *by an Unknown Author; with some extracts from Agatharkhides 'on the Erythraean Sea'.* Hakluyt Society Second Series 151. London: Hakluyt Society.

Hutterer, K.L. (ed.). 1978. *Economic Exchange and Social Interaction in Southeast Asia: perspectives from prehistory, history and ethnography.* Ann Arbor: University of Michigan, Center for South and Southeast Asian Studies.

L.S.J. [Liddell, H.G., Scott, R., and Jones, H.S.]. 1996. *A Greek-English Lexicon.* Oxford: Clarendon Press.

Naval Intelligence Division. 1946. Western Arabia and the Red Sea. *Geographical Handbook Series* BR 527. London: Naval Intelligence Division.

Periplus maris erythrœi. L. Casson (tr.). 1989. *The Periplus Maris Erythrœi. Text with introduction, translation, and commentary.* Princeton: Princeton University Press.

Ray, H.P. 1986. *Monastery and Guild: Commerce under the Satavahanas.* Delhi: Oxford University Press.

Robin, C. 1991. L'Arabie du sud et la date du Périple de la mer érythrée. *Journal Asiatique* 279: 1–30.

——. (ed.) 1996. *Arabia Antiqua: early origins of South Arabian states.* Roma: Istituto Italiano per il Medio ed Estremo Oriente.

Sarma, A. 1978. The Paleoecology of Coastal Tamilnadu, South India: chronology of raised beaches. *Proceedings of the American Philosophical Society* 122: 411–26.

Schoff, W.H. 1995 (1911) *The Periplus of the Erythraean Sea — Travel and Trade in the Indian Ocean by a Merchant of the First Century.* Delhi: Munshiram Manoharlal.

Sedov, A.V. 1996. *On the origin of agricultural settlements in Hadramawt.* 67–86 in C. Robin (ed.), *Arabia Antiqua: early origins of South Arabian states.* Roma: Istituto Italiano per il Medio ed Estremo Oriente.

Seland, E.H. 2005. Ancient South Arabia: trade and strategies of state control as seen in the *Periplus Maris Erythraei. Proceedings of the Seminar for Arabian Studies* 35: 271–80.

——. 2006. Indian Ocean in Antiquity: trade and the emerging state. Unpublished PhD thesis, University of Bergen.

Simpson, St J. (ed.). 2002. *Queen of Sheba.* London: British Museum Press.

Van Beek, G.W. 1958. Frankincense and myrrh in ancient South Arabia. *Journal of the American Oriental Society* 78: 141–52.

Warmington, E.H. 1928, repr. 1995. *The Commerce between the Roman Empire and India.* New Dehli: Munshiram Manoharlal.

Wenig, S. 2003. Enno Littmanns Deutsche Aksum Expedition 1906 und die German Archaeological Mission to Eritrea (G.A.M.E.) 90 Jahre Später. *Nürnberger Blätter zur Archaeologie* 18: 79–98.

Wilkinson, A.J. 2002. Agriculture and the countryside. 102–9 in St J. Simpson (ed.), *Queen of Sheba.* London: British Museum Press.

Acknowledgements

This article is based on my dissertation in ancient history (Seland 2006) submitted to the University of Bergen. The dissertation was supervised by Professor Jørgen Christian Meyer. Opponents were Professor Vincent Gabrielsen (Copenhagen) and Dr Sunil Gupta (National Museum, Allahabad). I am much obliged to them and to Professor emeritus Richard Holton Pierce (Bergen) for advice, comments and criticism on different parts of the material presented here.

Bishops and Traders: The Role of Christianity in the Indian Ocean during the Roman Period

Roberta Tomber

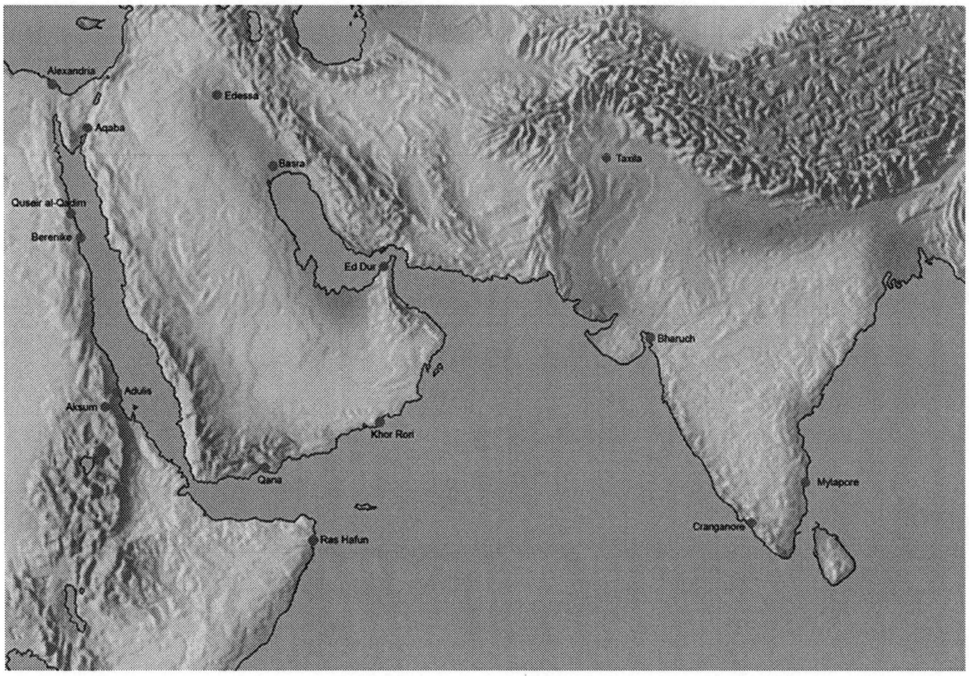

Map 20:1 Main sites mentioned in the text (Antony Simpson)

Introduction

This paper developed from work that I undertook some years ago, comparing artefact assemblages on the Red Sea, from Aila in the north to Aksum in the south.[1] It was clear that materially these Red Sea sites were much more united during the late Roman period, from the fourth century onwards, than in the early centuries. This uniformity is visible particularly through the distribution of Roman amphora types, including the vessel made at 'Aqabah. Frequently adorned with Christian symbols, including the *chi-rho*, it is found at all the Red Sea sites discussed here. During the fourth century there also seems to be population increase on the Egyptian Red Sea and, more generally, resurgence in Indo-Roman trade.

I attributed this growing uniformity in part to the annexation of the Nabataean kingdom as the province of *Arabia* in AD 106. A more significant factor in this process was, from the third and fourth century, the ascendancy of the Aksumite kingdom. From this period onwards cultural links were fostered between the Roman and non-Roman Red Sea, aided by the spread of Christianity.[2] This paper investigates the role that Christians and Christianity may have played in the Indian Ocean trade by bringing together evidence from the Roman world and India (Map 20:1).

The Red Sea: Early Roman period evidence

Indian Ocean trade through the Red Sea was well-established, and generally considered at its apex, during the first century AD. The most informative document for Red Sea trade, the *Periplus Maris Erythrœi*, dates to the mid-first century AD.[3] The Red Sea ports at 'Aqabah, Myos Hormos, Berenike and Adulis (Map 20:2) were all functional by at least the late first century BC / early first century AD. This is the period that Christianity first arrived in Egypt from Judea, and was particularly centred in Alexandria, but there are few manifestations of it even there.[4] The earliest Christians were converted from the Jewish communities, of which Alexandria had a large population, for Christianity was originally considered a sect within Judaism. As expected, there is no evidence for Christianity on the Red Sea at this period, but there may

1 Tomber 2004.

2 Ibid.

3 Casson 1989.

4 Finneran 2002: 72.

be some for Judaism. At al-Quṣayr al-Qadīm or ancient Myos Hormos, where Roman period occupation is limited to the Early Roman period, from the late first century BC into the third century,[5] a Hebrew name is recorded on an *ostracon*.[6] Excavations by D.P. Peacock and L. Blue have uncovered one monumental building, of a civic or religious nature. Copeland[7] has argued for a religious function, suggesting that it may be a synagogue. The material evidence for this is primarily negative, including the absence of votive objects that would be expected from other denominations; furthermore, the enormous variety in synagogue architecture excludes a firm identification from the plan of a rectangular building with courtyard. The lack of primary deposits associated with the building make interpretation difficult and any identification must be regarded as speculative. However, the Hebrew *ostracon* reminds us that Jews, like Greeks, Romans and Egyptians, were involved in trade[8] and are likely to have been resident at al-Quṣayr.

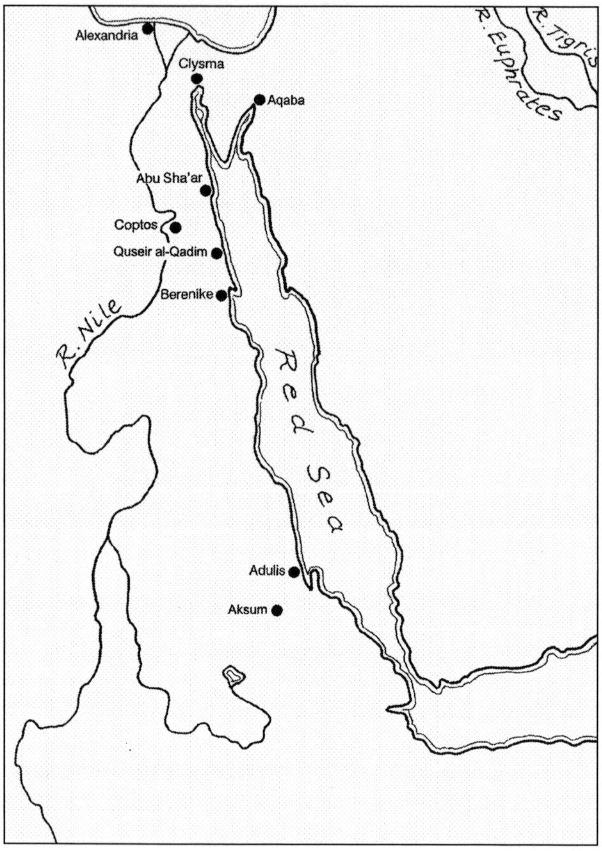

Map 20:2 Red Sea sites in context

The Red Sea: Late Roman period evidence

By the fourth century the Christian population of Egypt had grown enormously, possibly accounting for as much as 40 per cent of the population of Alexandria,[9] a substantive change reflected at the Red Sea sites. This section outlines the evidence for Christianity from these sites from the fourth through early seventh century (Map 20:2); Myos Hormos, discussed above, is no longer active. Clysma may also be relevant to the discussion, as a Justinianic monastery and fortified church has been reported from there[10] and more recently a double chapel used as a mausoleum,[11] but little other information is available.

'Aqabah / Aila

Excavations by S.T. Parker at 'Aqabah or ancient Aila have revealed an occupation sequence spanning from the Nabatean in late first century BC through the Byzantine and Islamic periods.[12] Here a mudbrick structure with eastern orientation has been tentatively interpreted as a church.[13] Its construction is dated to the turn of the fourth century, which if a church would make it the earliest church in Jordan and one of the earliest purpose built churches in the Roman world.[14] Parker has emphasized the significance of its construction before the Edict of Toleration (AD 313)[15] and suggested that it may have been privately funded and built 'shortly before the church building programme launched by Constantine in Palestine after 325'.[16]

Its identification as a church has been controversial, but in support are its plan with eastern orientation and associated artefacts.[17] Certainly by AD 325 Christianity was well-established, for a bishop from Aila attended the Council of Nicaea.[18] Artefacts include glass lamps and fragments from a cage cup, and possibly an offering table.[19] A wooden box containing 100 coins dating to around AD 360 has been tentatively interpreted as a collection box.[20] Parallels have been drawn with Egyptian mudbrick structures and Parker has suggested that the high percentage of Egyptian pottery might imply the presence of an Egyptian Christian community at Aila.[21] An adjacent cemetery,

5 Peacock and Blue 2006: 175 citing R. Tomber personal communication.
6 Copeland 2006: 126, citing W. van Rengen personal communication.
7 Ibid.: 125–7.
8 Haas 1997: 95–6.

9 Finneran 2002: 65.
10 Gatier 1989: 502.
11 Grossmann, *et al.* 2005.
12 Parker 2003: 321.
13 Parker 1999.
14 Ibid.: 326.
15 Parker 2000: 392.
16 Parker 2003: 332.
17 Ibid.: 326.
18 Parker 2000: 392.
19 Parker 2003: 325–6.
20 Parker 2000: 383.
21 Parker 1998: 383.

slightly later in the fourth century but similarly oriented, includes a burial with a cross.[22]

Abū Sha'ar

Unlike the other coastal sites included here, Abū Sha'ar is not a port, but a military site. Excavated by S.E. Sidebotham, it was established in the early fourth century and occupied into the early seventh century.[23] A fort, it seems to have also functioned to monitor international trade and police nomads in the vicinity, as indicated by a gate inscription reading]um mercator[, possibly reconstructed as '*ad usum mercatorum*'.[24] During the late fourth or early fifth century the *principia* was converted into an apsidal church built primarily of gypsum blocks with some upper courses of mudbrick.[25]

Sidebotham describes a range of finds with Christian associations, including an embroidered cloth cross.[26] Within the structure was a cloth wrapped burial, possibly indicative of a martyr or saint — a tradition in the Coptic Church.[27] Epigraphic evidence includes Christian *graffiti* incised on a gypsum block within the apse carved with crosses and the Greek letters Π and K;[28] and a Greek inscription on stone reading 'Lord Jesus Christ, save and have mercy on your servant Salamanis' — a particularly Syrian name.[29] Furthermore, Sidebotham[30] draws parallels between this church and others in Egypt, Syria, Palestine and Jordan, and suggests that the fort assisted Christian pilgrims travelling between holy places, via Aila, and that later it may have been a pilgrimage site.

Berenike

Excavations by S.E. Sidebotham and W.Z. Wendrich have uncovered a sequence from the third century BC through the early sixth century AD.[31] The site provides evidence of diverse religious activities, including a large fifth-century basilica plan church. It is the largest religious building on site, holding up to about eighty people.[32] In addition to the main church the complex includes an outer area for food preparation. Christian artefacts from the building include a bronze cross and lamps with Christian motifs, such as one with a Coptic inscription reading 'Jesus forgive me'.[33] Two Hebrew *ostraca* from a late fourth- to early fifth-century deposit have been published by Schmitz,[34] one of which is linked to Jewish merchants who lived at or visited Berenike.[35] Additionally there are two Greek jar labels referring to 'Jewish' and 'Jewish delicacies'.[36]

Aksum and Adulis

Ethiopia was officially converted to Christianity in *ca.* AD 340 during the reign of Ezana by Frumentius, a legend recounted by Rufinus (*ca.* AD 345–410).[37] Prior to this several different religious traditions were followed including one with possible ties to Judaism.[38]

Basilica churches are present both at Adulis and Aksum, as well as numerous structures in the adjacent regions.[39] The cathedral at Aksum is traditionally thought to have been built during the reign of Ezana or possibly Kaleb in the sixth century as a five-aisled basilica that survived until the sixteenth century.[40] An apsidal basilica was excavated in the 1970s by the Italians at Beta Giyorgis, north Aksum; finds included a variety of crosses in ceramic, stone and metal, as well as ceramic vessels decorated with crosses.[41] Aksumite material culture in general exhibits Christian motifs: crosses, for example, are commonly found on ordinary objects such as coins and pottery.[42]

Three basilica churches have been excavated from Adulis. One, reported on by Munro-Hay,[43] was uncovered by Napier in 1869, the two others by Paribeni.[44] Finds from Adulis with Christian associations include imported white marble decorated with Greek crosses interpreted as liturgical furniture[45] and a marble slab decorated with a cross.[46] More portable objects are two gold crosses,[47] a lamp decorated with crosses,[48] numerous 'Aqabah amphorae and other ceramics with Christian monograms,[49] an amphora stopper decorated with a cross[50] and an Abū Minā flask.[51]

22 Ibid.
23 Sidebotham 1994.
24 Bagnall and Sheridan 1994: 162–3; Sidebotham 1994: 141, 158.
25 Sidebotham 1994: 136–46.
26 Ibid.: 141.
27 Ibid.: 138.
28 Sidebotham, *et al.* 1989: 143.
29 Bagnall and Sheridan 1994: 163–4.
30 Ibid.: n. 19, 138, 158.
31 Sidebotham and Wendrich 2001–2: 23.
32 Ibid.: 32–4
33 Ibid.: 33.
34 2000: 183–6.
35 Ibid.: 186; Steiner 2004 for an alternative interpretation.
36 Bagnall, *et al.* 2000: nos 99 and 109; Schmitz 2000: 186.
37 Munro-Hay 1991: 202–4.
38 Finneran 2002: 122–5
39 Ibid.: 137; Munro-Hay 1991: 211.
40 Phillipson 2000: 476.
41 Ricci and Fattovich 1987.
42 Finneran 2002: 133.
43 Munro-Hay 1989.
44 Paribeni 1907.
45 Munro-Hay 1989 50; Paribeni 1907: 477, fig. 15.
46 Munro-Hay 1989: 48–9.
47 Paribeni 1907: 484–5, figs 20–1.
48 Ibid.: 499, fig. 28.
49 Ibid.: 549–53, figs 59–60; Munro-Hay 1989: 50.
50 Paribeni 1907: 455, fig. 4.
51 Ibid.: 537–8, fig. 54.

These flasks, produced during the sixth and first half of the seventh century AD, commemorate the late third-century Egyptian martyr St Menas whose shrine is at Mariot, south-west of Alexandria. They are widely distributed from Asia Minor to Britain, including Ethiopia.[52] Interestingly, occasional sources identify Abū Minā as a patron of merchants,[53] but this would not seem to be a significant attribute as most established scholars do not mention this aspect of him.[54] Kiss notes that Ethiopian texts describe the miracles and cures that took place at the tomb.[55]

Bishops on the Red Sea

Of these sites, Aila, Berenike, Aksum and Adulis were all bishoprics and those in Egypt and Ethiopia were appointed by the Patriarch of Alexandria. Certainly, given the size and status of Aila, Aksum and possibly Adulis, this is unsurprising. As a barometer of the stronghold of Christian institutions, by AD 303 most of the Egyptian nome capitals had a bishop[56] and by AD 320 there were twenty-nine bishoprics in the Nile Valley (middle and upper Egypt) and forty-four in the Delta.[57] It is surprising to me that Berenike had a bishop, but the Synaxarion or list of the Coptic Saints records that this was the case.[58] Apparently his seat or residence was in Coptos since he was sub-ordinate to the Bishop of Coptos. A bishop was needed at Berenike so that merchants and mariners who travelled the Red Sea would be able to receive the sacraments. Interestingly, this information dates to the early seventh century, after the Roman abandonment of Berenike. However, Coptos had a bishop from AD 325 and it seems this arrangement was in place 'from the beginning'.[59] From this we know that at least some of the Christians at Berenike were merchants and sailors.

Christianity in India

From India the evidence for Christianity is a mixture of myth and oral tradition with more tangible evidence from a much later period. There are two main traditions relating to the origins of Christianity, both of which revolve around St Thomas. The first is a Western or non-Indian one based on the Acts of St Thomas, which are generally agreed to date to the early third century and to have been written in Syriac, possibly at Edessa.[60] From the Acts comes the oldest description of St Thomas' mission to India:

> … and we portioned out the regions of the world, in order that each one of us might go into the region that fell to him by lot, and to the nation to which the Lord had sent him. By lot India fell to Judas Thomas, also called Didymos. And he did not wish to go, saying that he was not able to travel on account of the weakness of his body. He said 'How can I, being a Hebrew, go among the Indians to proclaim the truth?' And while he was considering this and speaking, the Saviour appeared to him during the night and said to him 'Fear not, Thomas, go away to India and preach the word there, for my grace is with you.' But he would not obey saying, 'Wherever you wish to send me, send me, but elsewhere. For I am not going to the Indians.'[61]

After this refusal, the Acts go on to describe the sale of Thomas by Jesus to an Indian merchant by the name of Abban visiting Jerusalem.[62]

One of the difficulties in interpreting this and other texts is determining what was meant by India, for it may have referred to modern India, Ethiopia or South Arabia. Mayerson[63] has summarized many ancient texts that refer to India and has concluded that the Hellenistic and early Roman sources had a much more accurate perception of India than the Byzantine writers, with the mid-sixth-century writer Cosmas Indicoplestues an exception in this respect. Other scholars consider that it is only the East Syrian or Nestorian writers, with their greater contact with India, who refer to modern India.[64] These difficulties are further complicated by the variety of names for 'India'; for example depending on the writer Aksum might fall within areas referred to as Inner India, Innermost India and Further India.[65] If modern India is meant, the question remains whether north-west or south India is intended. The *Christian Topography* of Cosmas is considered the first historical document to conclusively refer to the Church in south India[66] and more specifically the Malabar Coast, although even Cosmas may have known of Malabar only second hand.[67]

To return to the Acts, St Thomas reached north-west India, at that time under Parthian influence, from Edessa. The Acts describe Thomas' apostolate in India as beginning in the kingdom of Gūdnaphar, who had a brother Gad. Both equate reasonably with historical figures of the Partho-Indian king Gondophares and his brother, named and dated through coinage and a Gandhara inscription that place their rule between AD 19 and AD 45.[68] Thus although the Acts are thought to have been written in the third

52 Kiss 1989: 11; Bangert 2006.
53 Cross and Livingstone 1974: 902.
54 For example, Meinardus 2004: 151–4; Kamil 2002: 278.
55 Kiss 1989: 9.
56 Bagnall 1993: 278.
57 Ibid.: 285.
58 Fournet 2000: 208.
59 Ibid.
60 Most 2005: 89.
61 Ibid.: 107.
62 Ibid.: 107–8.
63 1993: esp. 171.
64 Brown 1982: 46–7.
65 Mayerson 1993: 171.
66 Brown 1982: 68.
67 Wolska-Conus 1968: 17.
68 Atiya 1968: 363; Neill 1984: 28.

century, the origins of the legend seem to be historically traced to the first century. In the Acts, Thomas travelled to another kingdom, where he was martyred. Some attempt has been made to equate its king Mazdai (Misdeus in Greek) with a first-century AD Indian king of Kerala, Coromandel or Karnataka.[69] Eventually St Thomas's tomb was lifted and found to be empty, the corpse apparently having been taken to Mesopotamia.

A second legend is derived from south Indian oral tradition[70] with some input from the East Syrian church, and has St Thomas landing at Cranganore in *ca.* AD 52. From where he sailed is not explicitly stated, but it can be inferred as the West rather than Persia since south Indian trade routes were linked to the Red Sea. Some versions of the fable, not traceable to a particular source, even suggest Alexandria. Others merge the two interpretations together: that Thomas was forced out of the Indo-Parthian empire by Kushan invaders in AD 50, making his way to Soqotra and from there returning to south India.[71] Doe[72] refers to a tradition that has St Thomas introducing Christianity to the island when he was shipwrecked there in the fourth, and building a church out of the ships' timbers. Archaeologically and historically Soqotra can be shown to be a strategic meeting place for different ethnic groups from throughout the Indian Ocean.[73]

If AD 52 is taken as an historic date, it matches well with the period of the *Periplus*. Thomas' landing at Cranganore, or locally Kodungallur, is interesting since it has long been equated with the important *Periplus* port of Muziris. Although Dr Shajan, Dr Selvakumar and I have suggested a different location for Muziris, at the village of Pattanam *ca.* 10 km south of Kodungallur town,[74] the association between the landing place of St Thomas and Cranganore / Muziris is striking. To resume the legend, in Malabar Thomas converted many, travelled to Coromandel and eventually to China. On his return to Malabar he established a number of churches after which he again went to the Coromandel and was eventually martyred on or near the Little Mount and buried at Mylapore, now the site of the St Thom cathedral.

A Malayalam song, the Rabban Puttu[75] or Thomas Ramban[76] was allegedly the work of a disciple of St Thomas. Although it was not written down until the seventeenth and eighteenth centuries, it shows influences from the Acts of St Thomas and the East Syrian tradition, with possible additions up to Portuguese times.[77]

The Rabban Song has Thomas sailing from Arabia to Maliankara (just south of Cranganore) and arriving in December / January *ca.* AD 50. Travelling to Coromandel and China he then returned to Malabar and established seven churches; after additional trips to Coromandel and Malabar he was eventually martyred, again at Little Mount, in AD 72. His arrival at Maliankara in December / January conflicts with the conditions described by Casson,[78] who concludes that it would be difficult to land on the south-west coast during those months.

The seven churches supposedly established by St Thomas are also of interest in the context of trade. At one of these sites, Kokkamamgalam, a hexagonal-based monument (Figure 20:1) commemorates the locations of the other six churches, one on each face, as follows: Kodungallur (Cranganore, Figure 20:2), Cayal (Chayal / Nilakkal), Kollam (Quilon), Kottakavu (Paravur), Niranam and Palayur.[79]

Figure 20:1 The monument at Kokkamamgalam commemorating the seven churches established by St Thomas

69 Mundadan 1984: 25–6.
70 Ibid.: 29.
71 Atiya 1968: 363.
72 1992: 31–2.
73 De Geest 2006: 19.
74 Shajan, *et al.* 2004.
75 Mundadan 1984: 29–32, including n. 33.
76 Gillman and Klimkeit 1999: 163.
77 For example, Brown 1982: 57.
78 1989: 289.
79 For other variants see also Neill 1984: 33.

Map 20:3 shows all seven locations and demonstrates the observations made by many scholars, that apart from Cayal they are located near the coast or on the Periyar and its channels.[80] As potential ports they are likely to have had cosmopolitan populations that were fertile grounds for the spread of Christianity. Humphries[81] has demonstrated for the Roman Empire that port towns frequently play a role as regional centres as well.

In later times all seven Kerala locations have Christian associations — apart, again, from Cayal. It is furthermore stated that there were Jewish enclaves near most of these sites and indeed a synagogue still exists at Paravur.[82] As for Alexandria, an existing Jewish population would have provided a group suitable for conversion. Jewish tradition holds that Jews settled in Muziris in AD 68 / 69 and scholars have suggested that they fled to Kerala from persecution in the West or Arabia and became established as traders.[83] The presence of Jewish enclaves during the first century is, however, not universally accepted. One of the arguments against this is that the earliest copper-plate charter post-dates this time. Dates for the charter vary between the sixth and eleventh centuries: for example, Gillman and Klimkeit[84] place it *ca.* AD 700 with another school of thought supporting AD 1000.[85]

Figure 20:2 A detail from the Kokkamamgalam monument illustrating the church at Cranganore

The association between these locations and trade sites is explicit in two cases: Cranganore with Muziris and, less well known, Niranam with Nelcynda.[86] If one disputes the equation between Cranganore and Muziris and instead places ancient Muziris at Pattanam, it is, as the crow flies, only *ca.* 1.5 kilometre north-west of St Thomas's church at Paravur.[87] Archaeological evidence for either trade sites or churches is sparse, coming only from Pattanam,[88] although the entire coastline (including the Pattanam area) is rich in megalithic urn burials.[89]

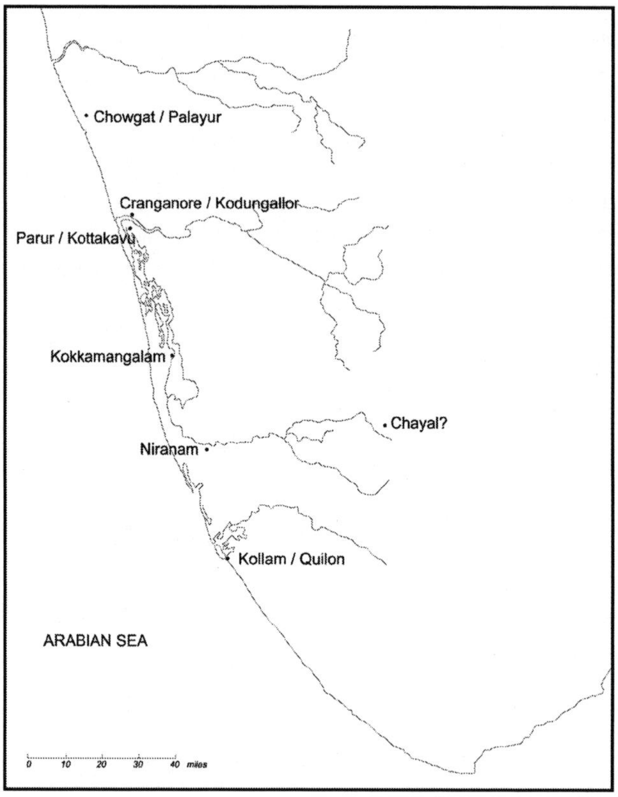

Map 20:3 Location of the seven churches established by St Thomas (Antony Simpson, after Brown 1982)

In common, Western and Indian legends both place the spread of Christianity within the first century AD. They differ substantially as to whether St Thomas (or more generally early Christianity) emanated from Persia or the region of the Red Sea, and whether his apostolate took place in north or south India. The more tangible evidence comes from south India, through the presence of Christian communities reported on when the Portuguese arrived[90] and the supposed burial place of St Thomas at Mylapore.

80 Brown 1982: 52.
81 1998: 221.
82 Brown 1982: 52, 62.
83 Ibid.
84 1999: 164.
85 Gurukkal and Whittaker 2001: 345, n. 41 citing Brown 1982: 90.

86 Casson 1989: 296–8.
87 See Shajan, *et al.* 2004: fig. 1.
88 Selvakumar, *et al.* 2005.
89 Shajan and Seralathan 1999.
90 Mundadan 1984: 108–114; Brown 1982: 11–42.

It is more difficult to distinguish the origins of these early Christians. The modern Christian community in Kerala is divided into West and East Syriac groups, and owes more to the East Syriac or Persian influence. When this balance was achieved is not certain: it is generally assumed to be in the fourth century, but the earliest references in Chaldean documents to Christians in south India date to the early or mid-fifth century.[91] Yet another oral tradition places an influx of Persians with the merchant Thomas of Cana in AD 345, but a more accurate date is likely to be the mid-eighth century.[92] An early seventh-century Pahlavi cross exists at Mylapore; other crosses are known from Kerala, but are thought to be sixteenth-century copies of the Mylapore one.[93]

In general Christianity is thought to have spread via trade routes.[94] An exemplary case study where rich archaeological evidence is available is that by Humphrey[95] for northern Italy, where he established a strong connection between Christian and trading communities at Aquileia. In our case, even those who accept the apostolate of St Thomas in India as literal acknowledge the importance of trade routes in facilitating his journey, including land routes to the north, sea routes to the south[96] and sea routes via the Gulf.[97] We have already established that there were Christian sites along the Red Sea; equally there were over twenty bishoprics in the Tigris-Euphrates Valley and the borders of Persia,[98] including those at Basra and in the province of Fars.[99] A bishopric existed at Beth Katraye, opposite Bahrain, in either AD 225[100] or the fourth century.[101] A number of Christian sites have been identified archaeologically in East Arabia, but are broadly dated.[102] Cosmas[103] refers to a Persian church and Persian bishops in India and Sri Lanka.[104]

Roman historical evidence

It is likely that both regions were influential in the spread of Christianity to India but here we will concentrate on the Red Sea and tales of travellers from Egypt to India; this is not intended as a comprehensive survey of the literature but to provide a few key examples. Writing in the fourth century Eusebius describes the second-century journey of Pantaenus, who as head of the Catechetical School of Alexandria travelled from Alexandria to India to preach. He found that Christianity was already known in India (possibly brought by Bartholomew rather than Thomas, but this is another story), and was being practiced in Hebrew, that is, by Jewish Christians. In this context, as elsewhere, opinion is mixed as to what is meant by India,[105] and some consider that Pantaenus travelled only to South Arabia. Neill[106] argues strongly against this, noting that given the established trade between Alexandria and Egypt it is unlikely that such confusion would have arisen. Interestingly, Pantaenus's student Clement of Alexandria makes the first unambiguous reference to Buddhism, its spread like that of Christianity linked with traders.[107] While this reference to Buddhism suggests contact with Indians it need not have happened in India: for example in the early fifth century Palladius's interest in Brahmans is recorded as having taken him, with Moses bishop of Adulis, to India.[108] An alternative viewpoint is that Palladius never ventured beyond an Indian community in Somalia, where a Theban informant who had spent many years in north-west India provided the information needed for his *Account of the Life of the Brahmans*.[109] The textual evidence for Christianity or Christians in India is confusing, and the more thoroughly one delves into it the shakier it becomes. With the Early Roman trade document, the *Periplus*, we are on firmer ground, clearly dealing with foreigners travelling to India proper.

From the mid-fourth century onwards the Christian Church gradually acquired landholdings, although it was not until the mid-fifth century that these were of a significant and documented quantity.[110] However, rare earlier evidence does include two fourth-century texts that describe Nile boats owned by the Church, in one case for transporting grain.[111] Despite this early silence, the overall trend is of an increasingly wealthy Church.

By the nature of the goods exchanged in Indian Ocean trade, including pepper, gems and other costly items, it was above all a monumentally expensive business. The Muziris papyrus, a mid-second-century legal agreement between two merchants, highlights the vast sums required to participate in Oriental trade.[112] Despite the great profits to be accrued from trade there is little to suggest that the Church had any systematic involvement in long-distance trade, and their official attitude seems to be to denigrate it,

91 Gillman and Klimkeit 1999: 167; Atiya 1968: 364.
92 Gillman and Klimkeit 1999: 164–9.
93 Gropp 1991: 86.
94 Latourette 1954: 75, 78.
95 Humphrey 1998.
96 Mundadan 1984: 25.
97 Brown 1982: 2.
98 Latourette 1954: 78–9.
99 Brown 1982: 66.
100 Atiya 1968: 258.
101 Brown 1982: 66.
102 Bin Seray 1996: 325–7; see also Ball 2000: 130.
103 Book XI, 14.
104 Wolska-Conus 1973: 343–4.

105 Stevenson and Frend 1987: 179; Gillman and Klimkeit 1999: 158; Fox 1988: 278; Mayerson 1993: 171–2; Neill 1984: 40.
106 Ibid.
107 Whittaker 1998: 19.
108 Munro-Hay 1991: 82.
109 Muckenstrum-Poulle 1995: 157–8.
110 Bagnall 1993: 291.
111 Wipszycka 1972: 63; Bagnall 1993: 291.
112 Rathbone 2001: 49.

particularly in contrast to agriculture;[113] however, an analogous situation might be drawn with Republican senators who were legally prohibited from long-distance seaborne activities but nevertheless participated indirectly.[114]

Despite this general antipathy on the part of the Church, Mango[115] has compiled some rare evidence in support of their involvement: the early seventh-century *Life of John the Almsgiver* recounts that the Church of Alexandria owned a fleet of over thirteen ships of 10,000 and 20,000 *modii* used for both subsistence (grain) and luxury goods. This is reinforced by two horoscopes dating to the third quarter of the fifth century that attest to the role of the Church of Alexandria in long-distance trade. One of the cargoes mentioned is *xerophorta* or dry goods, which Mango suggests may refer to spices and aromatics imported from the East.

Another tantalizing hint pertaining to the fourth century comes from the *Liber Pontificalis* (Book of the Popes) that lists private estates given to the Church at Rome. Although most estates paid the Church in money, some from Egypt (and elsewhere in the Orient) instead paid with large quantities of cinnamon, pepper, cloves and nard oil.[116] It has been suggested that estates had to buy these goods on the open market and send them on to Rome where they were sold by the Church;[117] in this way the Church became a middleman for the spice trade.[118] That a mechanism could have existed to involve the Church, either practically or through influence, at an earlier process in the spice trade is an interesting alternative.

This might be sensible given that aromatics played a role in Christian ritual. *Exodus* 30 mentions frankincense, myrrh and cinnamon.[119] Frankincense and myrrh originate from South Arabia and East Africa and cinnamon or cassia from India, Sri Lanka or even South-east Asia.[120] Whether these products reached the Roman world directly or indirectly, they are nevertheless part of the overall intersecting system of Oriental trade. Exotic spices or aromatics were not only exchanged through commerce, but as gifts between important persons as recorded by St Gregory the First (d. AD 604).[121]

Summary

The different strands of evidence compiled here, from archaeology, texts and oral tradition, are frustratingly vague and inconclusive. In India there is no archaeological evidence for Christianity during the Roman timeframe, but it is strongly held on the basis of the Acts of St Thomas and oral tradition that Christianity was established in the first century. On the Red Sea, there is extensive, concrete evidence for Christianity, but not until the fourth century. The relative contribution of the Red Sea region and Mesopotamia in the spread of Christianity to India remains unresolved, but this paper focuses on the Red Sea with its undeniable trading links to India.

In both India and on the Red Sea, Christian centres are located on well-established external trade routes. That trade facilitated not only the exchange of objects, but also of ideas is commonplace but nonetheless important. Port towns comprised diverse populations, including Christians and Christian merchants, and provided the perfect milieu for the spread of Christianity. In this case, not only was Christianity spread from West to East, but Eastern ideals influenced the West. As you remember, whether or not they travelled to India, Palladius was interested in Brahman philosophy; and Clement of Alexandria in Buddhism; their interests reflect inter-connections between the two regions in matters other than commerce. To progress further in our understanding of Christians in the Indian Ocean, the degree and nature of their involvement, archaeological evidence is needed from India and if possible future fieldwork should target sites in order to address these questions.

113 For example, Meijer and van Nijf 1992: 18–21.
114 D'Arms 1981: 45–6.
115 1999: 96–8.
116 Hopkins 1983: 87.
117 Ibid.: 38–9, 116.
118 Duchesne 1886: cl.
119 Dalby 2002: 136–7.
120 Ibid.: 38–9, 116.
121 Duchesne 1886: cl.

References

Atiya, A.S. 1968. *A History of Eastern Christianity*. London: Methuen.

Bagnall, R.S. 1993. *Egypt in Late Antiquity*. Princeton, NJ: Princeton University Press.

Bagnall, R.S., Helms, C. and Verhoogt, A.M.F.W. 2000. *Documents from Berenike*, I. *Greek Ostraka from the 1996–1998 Seasons*. Papyrologica Bruxellensia 31.

Bagnall, R.S. and Sheridan, J.A. 1994. Greek and Latin documents from Abu Sha'ar, 1990–1991. *Journal of the American Research Center in Egypt* 31: 159–68.

Ball, W. 2000. *Rome in the East. The Transformation of an Empire*. London: Routledge.

Bangert, S. 2006. Menas ampullae and Saxon Britain: Coptic objects in a pagan kingdom. *Minerva* 17(4): 20–1.

Bin Seray, H.M. 1996. Christianity in east Arabia. *Aram* 8, 315–32.

Brown, L. 1982, 2nd rev. edn. *The Indian Christians of St Thomas. An Account of the Ancient Syrian Church of Malabar*. Cambridge: Cambridge University Press.

Casson, L. 1989. *The Periplus Maris Erythræi. Text with Introduction, Translation and Commentary*. Princeton, NJ: Princeton University Press.

Copeland, P. 2006. The Roman town: Trench 2B. 116–27 in D. Peacock and L. Blue (eds), *Myos Hormos – Quseir al-Qadim. Roman and Islamic Ports on the Red Sea. Survey and Excavations 1999–2003*. Oxford: Oxbow.

Cross, F.L. and Livingstone, E.A. (eds). 1974, 2nd edition. *The Oxford Dictionary of the Christian Church*. Oxford: Oxford University Press.

Dalby, A. 2000. *Dangerous Tastes. The Story of Spices*. London: British Museum Press.

D'Arms, J.H. 1981. *Commerce and Social Standing in Ancient Rome*. Cambridge, MA: Harvard University Press.

De Geest, P. 2006. Caves and Archaeology, Socotra. 19 in C. Cheung and L. DeVantier (eds), *A Natural History of the Islands and their People*. Hong Kong: Odyssey Publications.

Doe, B. 1992. *Socotra. Island of Tranquillity*. London: IMMEC Publishing Ltd.

Duchesne, L. 1886. *Liber Pontificalis Texte, introduction et commentaire*. Bibliothèque des Écoles Françaises d'Athènes et de Rome series 2.

Fox, R. Lane 1988. *Pagans and Christians*. London: Penguin.

Finneran, N. 2002. *The Archaeology of Christianity in Africa*. Stroud, Glos.: Tempus Publishing Ltd.

Fournet, J.-L. 2000. Copts dans l'Antiquité tardive (fin IIIe–VIIe siècle). 196–215 in *Coptos. L'Egypte antique aux portes du désert. Lyon, musée des Beaux-Arts 3 février–7 mai 2000*. Paris: Réunion des musées nationaux.

Gatier, P.-L.1989. Les traditions et l'histoire du Sinaï du IVe and VIIe siècle. 499–523 in T Fahd (ed.), *L'Arabie pre-islamique et son environment historique et culturel*. Leiden: E.J. Brill.

Gillman, I. and Klimkeit, H.-J. 1999. *Christians in Asia before 1500*. Richmond, Surrey: Curzon.

Gropp, G. 1991. Christian maritime trade of Sasanian age in the Persian Gulf. 83–8 in K. Schippmann, A. Herling, and J.-F. Salles (eds), *Golf-Archäeologie*, Internationale Archäologie 6.

Grossmann, P., Salib, M.S. and al-Hangury, M.S. 2005. Survey of an early Christian burial chapel at Tall al-Yuhudiyya-Suez. *Bulletin de la Société d'Archéologie Copte*, 44: 45–53.

Gurukkal, R. and Whittaker, C.R. 2001. In search of Muziris. *Journal of Roman Archaeology* 14: 335–50.

Haas, C. 1997. *Alexandria in Late Antiquity. Topography and Social Conflict*. Baltimore: The Johns Hopkins University Press.

Hopkins, K. 1983. Models, ships and staples. 84–109 in P. Garnsey and C.R. Whittaker (eds), *Trade and Famine in Classical Antiquity*. Cambridge Philological Society Suppl. 8.

Humphries, M. 1998. Trading gods in northern Italy. 203–24 in H. Parkins and C. Smith (eds), *Trade, Traders and the Ancient City*. London: Routledge.

Kamil, J. 2002. *Christianity in the Land of the Pharaohs. The Coptic Orthodox Church*. London: Routledge.

Kiss, Z. 1989. *Alexandrie V. Les ampoules de Saint Ménas découvertes à Kôm el-Dikka (1961–1981)*. Warsaw: Éditions Scientifiques de Pologne.

Latourette, K.S. 1954, 2nd edition. *A History of Christianity*. London: Eyre and Spottiswoode.

Mango, M. Mundell. 1999. Beyond the amphora: non-ceramic evidence for late antique industry and trade. 87–106 in S. Kingsley and M. Decker (eds), *Economy and Exchange in the East Mediterranean during Late Antiquity: Proceedings of a Conference at Somerville College, Oxford, 29th May, 1999*. Oxford: Oxbow.

Mayerson, P. 1993. A confusion of Indias: Asian India and African India in the Byzantine sources. *Journal of the American Oriental Society* 113(2): 169–74.

Meijer, F. and Nijf, O. van. 1992. *Trade, Transport and Society in the Ancient World. A Sourcebook*. London: Routledge.

Meinardus, O.F.A. 2004, 2nd edition. *Two Thousand Years of Coptic Christianity*. Cairo: American University in Cairo Press.

Most, G.W. 2005. *Doubting Thomas*. Cambridge MA: Harvard University Press.

Muckensturm-Poulle, C. 1995. Palladius' Brahmans. 157–66 in M.-F. Boussac and J.-F. Salles (eds), *Athens, Aden, Arikamedu. Essays on the Interrelations Between India, Arabia and the Eastern Mediterranean*. New Delhi: Manohar.

Mundadan, A.M. 1984. *History of Christianity in India*, I. *From the Beginning up to the Middle of the Sixteenth Century (up to 1542)*. Bangalore: Theological Publications in India.

Munro-Hay, S. 1989. The British Museum excavations at Adulis, 1968. *Antiquaries Journal* 69: 43–52.

——. 1991. *Aksum. An African Civilisation of Late Antiquity*. Edinburgh: Edinburgh University Press.

Neill, S. 1984. *A History of Christianity in India. The Beginnings to AD 1707*. Cambridge: Cambridge University Press.

Paribeni, R. 1907. Richerche nel luogo dell'antica Adulis. *Monumenti Antichi*. Rome: Reale Accademia dei Lincei 18: 438–572.

Parker, S.T. 1998. The Roman 'Aqaba project: the 1996 campaign. *Annual of the Department of Antiquities of Jordan* 42: 375–94.

——. 1999. Brief notice on a possible early 4th-c. church at 'Aqaba, Jordan. *Journal of Roman Archaeology* 12: 372–6.

——. 2000. The Roman 'Aqaba project: the 1997 and 1998 campaigns. *Annual of the Department of Antiquities of Jordan* 44: 373–94.

——. 2003. The Roman 'Aqaba project: the 2002 campaign. *Annual of the Department of Antiquities of Jordan* 47: 321–33.

Peacock, D. and Blue, L. (eds). 2006. *Myos Hormos – Quseir al-Qadim. Roman and Islamic Ports on the Red Sea. Survey and Excavations 1999–2003*. Oxford: Oxbow.

Phillipson, D.W. 2000. *Archaeology at Aksum, Ethiopia, 1993–7*. Memoirs of the British Institute in East Africa 17. London.

Rathbone, D. 2001. The 'Muziris' papyrus (SB XVIII 13167): financing Roman trade with India, in *Alexandrian Studies II in Honour of Mostafa el Abbadi. Bulletin de la Société d'Archéologie d'Alexandrine* 46: 39–50.

Ricci, C. and Fattovich, R. 1987. Scavi archeologici nella Zona di Aksum. B. Bieta Giyorgis. *Rassegna di Studi Etiopici* 31: 123–95.

Schmitz, P.C. 2000. Semitic graffiti. 183–9 in S.E. Sidebotham and W.Z. Wendrich (eds), *Berenike 1998. Report of the 1998 Excavations at Berenike and the Survey of the Egyptian Eastern Desert, including Excavations in Wadi Kalalat*. Leiden: Centre for Non-Western Studies.

Selvakumar, V. Gopi, P.K. and Shajan, K.P. 2005. Trial excavations at Pattnam – a preliminary report. *The Journal of the Centre for Heritage Studies* 2: 57–66

Shajan, K.P. and Seralathan, P. 1999. Holocene sea level changes inferred from geo-archaeological studies in the Kodungallur area, south-west coast of India. 315–7 in Y. Saito, K. Ikehara and H. Katayama (eds), *Land-Sea Links in Asia. Proceedings of an International Workshop* Organized *by the Geological Survey of Japan, March 15–19, Tsukuba, Japan*. Tsukuba: Geological Survey of Japan

Shajan, K.P., Tomber, R., Selvakumar, V. and Cherian, P.J. 2004. Locating the ancient port of Muziris: fresh findings from Pattanam. *Journal of Roman Archaeology* 17: 351–9.

Sidebotham, S.E. 1994. Preliminary report on the 1990–1991 seasons of fieldwork at Abu Sha'ar (Red Sea coast). *Journal of the American Research Center in Egypt* 31: 133–58.

Sidebotham, S.E., Riley, J.A., Hamroush, H.A. and Barakat, H. 1989. Fieldwork on the Red Sea Coast: the 1987 season. *Journal of the American Research Center in Egypt* 26: 127–66.

Sidebotham, S.E. and Wendrich, W.Z. 2001–2002. Berenike. Archaeological fieldwork at a Ptolemaic-Roman port on the Red Sea coast of Egypt 1999–2001. *Sahara* 13: 23–50.

Steiner, R.C. 2004. A Jewish Aramaic (or Hebrew) laissez-passer from the Egyptian port of Berenike. *Journal of Near Eastern Studies* 63(4): 277–81.

Stevenson, J. with Frend, W.H.C. (eds). 1987, 2nd edition. *A New Eusebius. Documents Illustrating the History of the Church to AD 337*. London: SPCK.

Tomber, R.S. 2004. Amphorae from the Red Sea and their contribution to the interpretation of late Roman trade beyond the empire. 393–402 in J. Eiring, and J. Lund (eds), *Transport Amphorae and Trade in the Eastern Mediterranean. Acts of the International Colloquium at the Danish Institute at Athens, September 26–29, 2002*. Monographs of the Danish Institute at Athens 5.

Whittaker, C.R. 1998. 'To reach out to India and pursue the dawn': the Roman view of India. *Studies in History* 14: 1–20.

Wipszycka, E. 1972. *Les resources et les activités économiques des églises en Ègypte du IVe au VIIIe siècle*. Papyrologica Bruxellensia 10.

Wolska-Conus, W. 1968. *Cosmas Indicopleustès, topographie chrétienne* 1. *Sources Chrétiennes* 141. Paris: Les Éditions du Cerf.

——. 1973. *Cosmas Indicopleustès, topographie chrétienne* 3. *Sources Chrétiennes* 159. Paris: Les Éditions du Cerf.

Acknowledgements

Warms thanks are due to Drs K.P. Shajan and V. Selvakumar, who enabled me to visit many of the South Indian Christian sites mentioned here, and discussed them with me, adding a dimension to this subject that would otherwise be absent. I am particularly grateful to Dr Niall Finneran for many stimulating comments and bibliographic suggestions on a draft of this paper. I am also thank Dr A. Haeckl and J. Cooper, as well as participants of the conference, for additional useful discussion.

Arabic Sources for the Ming Voyages

Paul Lunde

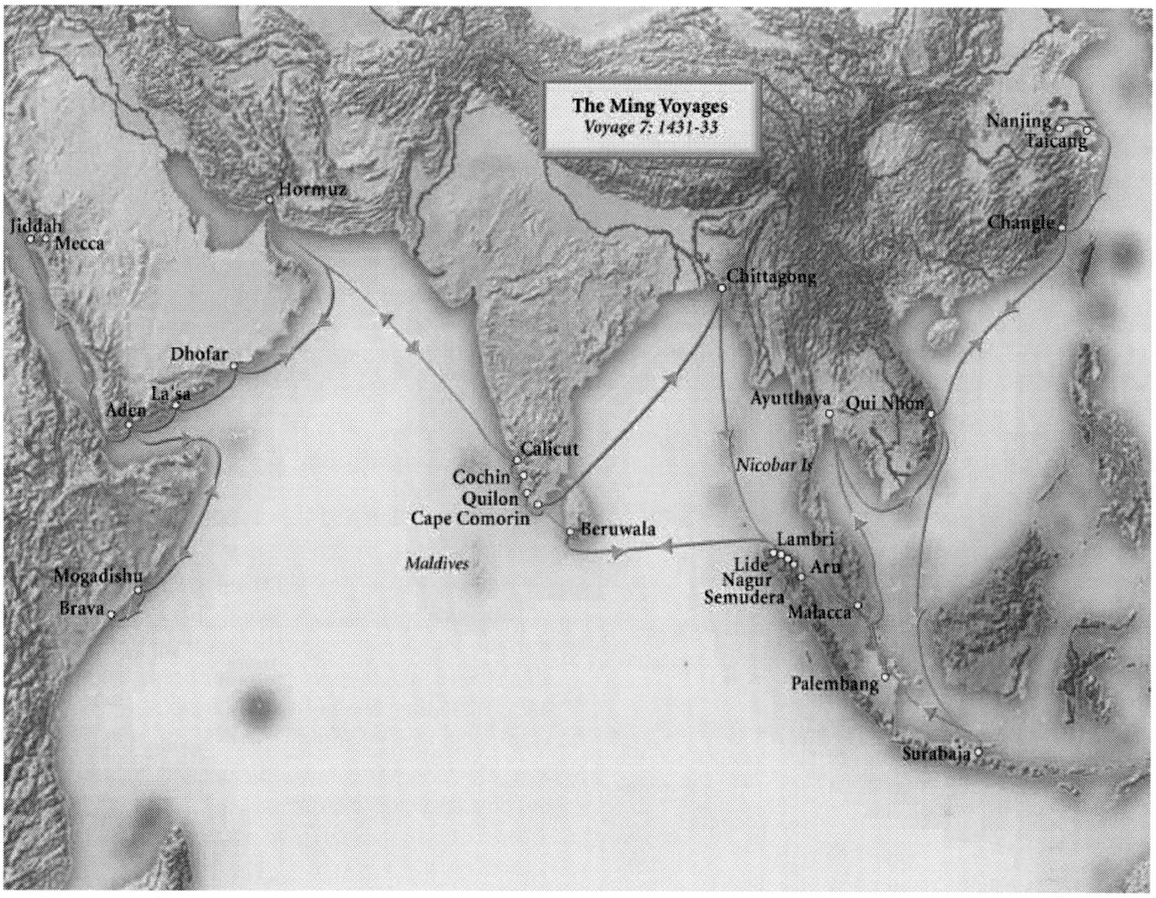

Map 21:1 'The Ming Voyages' by Mukhtar Sanders, courtesy the Golden Web Project

The Ming maritime expeditions

Between 1405 and 1433, the Ming dynasty sent seven major naval expeditions to the Western Ocean under the overall command of the Muslim eunuch Zheng He (Cheng Ho). They were initiated by the usurping Yongle (Yung-lo) Emperor (1402–1424), who also dispatched a concurrent series of overland diplomatic missions to Central Asia, first to Tīmūr-i Lang in Samarkand and then, after the conqueror's death in 1405, to his successor Shāhrūkh (1405–1447) in Herat.

His motives for sending these missions were varied, ranging from a desire to legitimize his rule by bringing as many countries as possible into the Chinese tributary system,[1] to ensuring a supply of horses for the army and securing pepper, spices and pharmaceuticals from India and the Indonesian archipelago. The collection of precious stones, exotic birds, animals and plants from far-off lands, aromatic wood for the construction of the palace in his new capital of Beijing (Peking), the gathering of military and geographical intelligence and perhaps above all, displaying Chinese military and naval power, all played a part. Most important was the establishment of diplomatic relations with foreign rulers, sixty-seven of whom, including the rulers of Yemen, Dhofar, and the *sharīf* of Makkah, sent envoys to China with the returning fleets to pay homage to the Chinese emperor.[2] Trade too played a considerable role: the 'treasure ships' of the armadas were loaded with silks, porcelain, lacquer, copper cash and other trade goods, as well as valuable gifts for foreign potentates. These were exchanged for local products and exotics. So much pepper was brought back from the seventh voyage in 1433 that the Imperial troops were paid in pepper, rather than the customary silk, for years afterwards.

1 Church 2007: forthcoming, suggests that this was the primary motive of the voyages.

2 Mills 1970: 2.

These costly expeditions came to an abrupt end with the death of the Yongle Emperor on 12 August 1424, after the return of the sixth voyage. On 7 September 1424, the day he ascended the throne, his successor, the Hongxi (Hung-his) Emperor, issued an edict abolishing all further maritime expeditions:

> The ships (for fetching) precious stones which go to the barbarian countries of the western ocean are all stopped. If there are any that are already anchored in Fu-chien or in T'ai-tsang, they should all return to Nanjing (Nanking). The building of seaships for going to the barbarian (countries) should everywhere be stopped.[3]

Court officials, resentful at the growing power and wealth of the eunuchs to whom command of the expeditions had been given, and appalled at their vast expense, using funds vitally needed for public works, had long lobbied for their cessation. Now the voyages were stopped and Zheng He and a number of eunuchs associated with him in the expeditions were assigned to shore duty, principally in renovation of the palace buildings in Nanjing.[4]

The Chinese sources

Yet for reasons that are not clearly understood, a seventh — and last — expedition was unexpectedly dispatched by the Xuande (Hsüan-te) Emperor (1425–1435) in 1431. Once again Zheng He was put in command, and many of his former associates took part, including Ma Huan, Fei Xin (Fei Hsin) and Gong Zhen (Kung Chen), all of whom later wrote accounts of the places they visited on this and earlier expeditions. These accounts, together with a number of references in the *Ming shilu* (*Ming shih-lu*) and the *Ming shi* (*Ming shih*) and several inscriptions — two memorial inscriptions erected by Zheng He in Chinese ports and one erected in Galle in Sri Lanka — constitute the principal primary sources for the Ming voyages.

We also possess a series of forty 'cartograms', which was incorporated into a scroll map probably from the collection of Mao Kun (Mao K'un) (1511–1601), and may be based on information derived from the voyages of Zheng He.[5] They depict the coastlines of countries from China to Hormoz and Arabia, routes of the ships and the stellar altitudes of major ports and landmarks.[6] They are not in scale, and occasionally a number of countries are compressed, higgledy-piggledy, onto the same cartogram.

Archival documents in the Imperial Library dealing with the voyages were hidden and probably destroyed by the zealous conservative Confucian official Liu Daxia (Liu Ta-hsia) during the Chenghua (Ch'eng-hua) period (1465–1487); he is reported to have said:

> The expeditions of the Sanbao [San-pao, that is, Zheng He] to the Western Ocean wasted tens of myriads of money and grain, and moreover the people who met their deaths [on these expeditions] may be counted by the myriads. Although he returned with wonderful precious things, what benefit was it to the state? This was merely an action of bad government of which ministers should severely disapprove. Even if the old archives were still preserved they should be destroyed in order to suppress [a repetition of these things] at the root.[7]

The seven expeditions

The first expedition (1405–1407) is said to have consisted of 317 ships of different sizes, sixty-two of which were designated 'treasure ships', and loaded with silks, porcelains and other precious things as gifts for rulers and to trade for the exotic products of the Indian Ocean.[8] The ships were manned by an approximate total of 27,800 men, including not only sailors and soldiers, but helmsmen, anchor-men, interpreters, business factors, accountants, doctors, iron-anchor mechanics, caulkers, scaffold-builders and other craftsmen.[9]

This first fleet, which set sail from Nanjing, called at Champa, Java, Samudra (Sumatra), Lambri (Atjeh), Malacca, Ceylon, and Calicut, 'the great country of the Western Ocean', as Ma Huan calls it, where it lay at anchor four months. The Chinese brought so much merchandise to Calicut that it took three months to price it all. It is noteworthy that all seven expeditions docked at Calicut, then the principal emporium of the Indian Ocean trading network, and used it as a base from which detached expeditions were sent to Arabian and East African ports.

---

3 Duyvendak 1938: 388–9.

4 Ibid.: 389–90.

5 Mills suggests that the Mao Kun map was based on information gathered during the first six voyages, and that it was probably derived from one prepared 'about 1422' (Mills 1970: 241). It occurs in the military compendium *Wubei zhi* (*Wu-pei chih*) by Mao Kun's grandson, Mao Yuanyi (Mao Yuan-i), printed in 1621 and presented to the throne in 1628.

6 For a detailed account of the Mao Kun scroll map, see Mills 1970: 236–302.

7 Duyvendak 1938: 395–9; Church 2007: forthcoming.

8 The figures for the numbers of ships is somewhat speculative; the sixty-two treasure ships are documented in the sources, but Pao Tsen-p'eng, although probably not far wrong, engages in a complicated set of calculations to arrive at his estimate of 317. See his *On the Ships of Cheng Ho* (National Historical Museum Collected Papers on the History and Art of China, 1st series, 6; Taibei and Hong Kong: Zhonghua congshu, 1961), 26–30.

9 Mills 1970: 15.

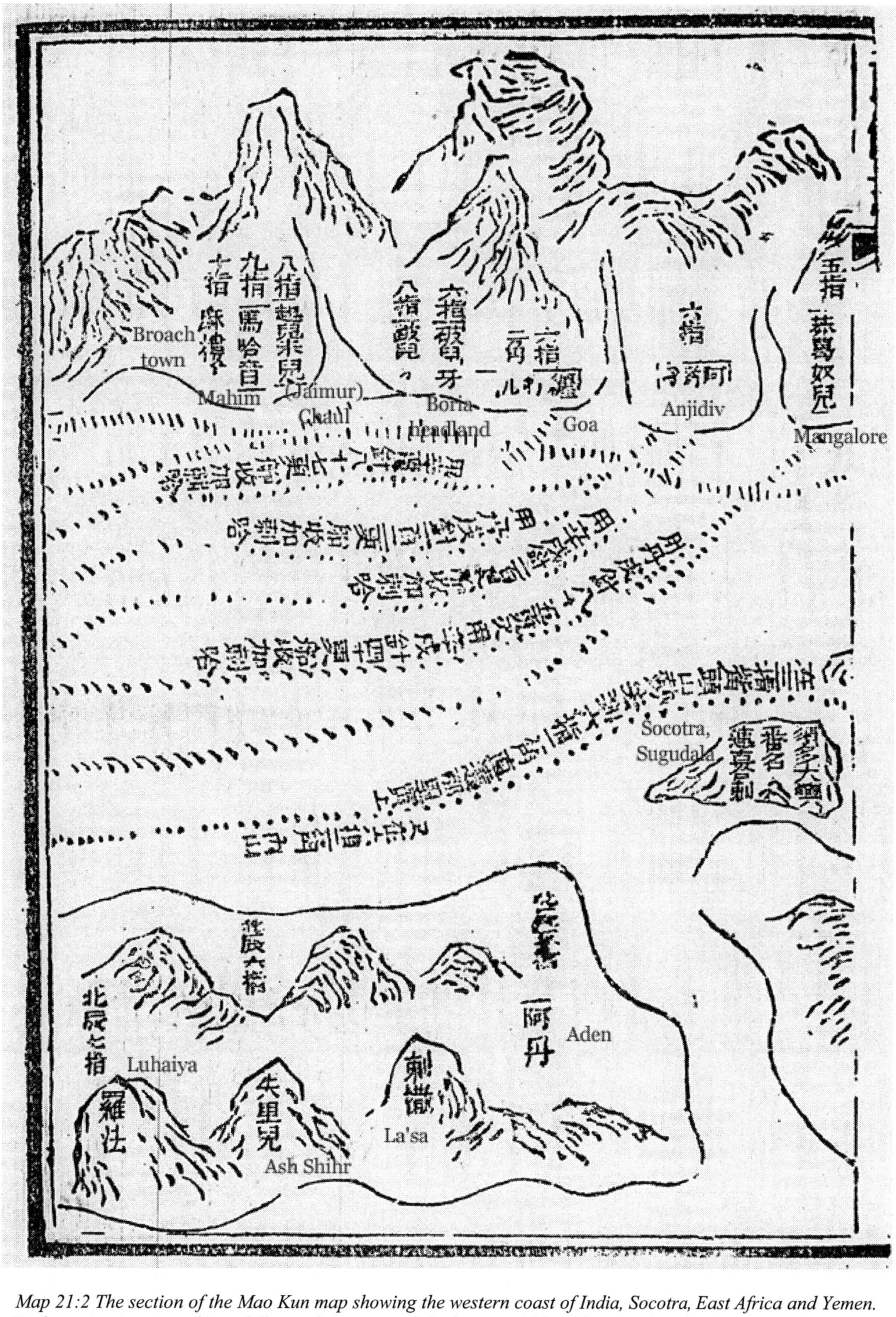

Map 21:2 The section of the Mao Kun map showing the western coast of India, Socotra, East Africa and Yemen. Each portion is oriented in a different direction, and the map would have been useless for navigational purposes. The identification of the Yemeni place names courtesy Dr Sally Church

The second expedition (1407–1409) consisted of approximately 249 ships and visited Thailand, Java, Aru and Lambri, Coimbatore, Kayal, Cochin and Calicut, where the fleet spent some four months, between the end of December 1408 and April 1409. This is the only expedition Zheng He did not accompany.

The third expedition (1409–1411) consisted of forty-eight 'treasure ships' and an unknown quantity of other vessels, shipping 30,000 men. It visited Champa, Java, Malacca, Semudera, Ceylon, Quilon, Cochin and Calicut.

The fourth expedition (1413–1415) was accompanied by Ma Huan, attached to the armada, as he himself informs us, as a 'translator of documents'.[10] Born into a Muslim family near Hangzhou (Hangchow), he is said to have learned Persian and Arabic as a young man, probably from Muslim merchants. This fourth expedition was allegedly composed of sixty-three ships and 28,560 men and was the first to sail west of India. The objective was Hormoz in the Gulf. Ma Huan took notes on the ports visited, and began to write them up on 19 November 1416, fourteen months after the return of the fleet, under the title *Yingya shenglan* (*Ying-yai Sheng-lan*), 'The Overall Survey of the Ocean's Shores'. He later took part in the sixth and seventh expeditions and added descriptions of Bengal, Dhofar, Aden and Makkah. Mills thinks the work received its final form in 1434–1435; Pelliot says it was first published in 1451.[11] Surviving printed versions, of which there are three, are late; the earliest dates from 1617.[12] Ma Huan's account is by far the most detailed and comprehensive of the three books produced by men who took part in the voyages. Those by his travelling companions, Fei Xin and Gong Zhen, add little or nothing to his accounts of Aden, Jiddah and Makkah, which are what concern us here.

The fourth expedition was, Ma Huan says in his preface, 'a wonderful opportunity [such as occurs only once] in a thousand years.'

> I followed the [mission] wherever it went, over vast expanses of huge waves for I do not know how many millions of *li*; I passed through the various countries, with their [different] seasons, climates, topography, and peoples; and I saw [these countries] with my own eyes and I walked [through them] in person... So I collected [notes about] the appearance of the people in each country, [and about] the variations of the local customs, also [about] the differences in the natural products, and [about] the boundary limits.[13]

10 Ibid.: 69.

11 Ibid.: 36.

12 For an account of these printed editions and the editorial problems associated with them, see ibid.: 37-41.

13 Mills 1970: 69–70.

For unknown reasons, Ma Huan did not accompany the fifth expedition (1417–1419), which visited Champa, Pahang, Java, Palembang, Malacca, Samudra, Lambri, Hormoz, 'La'sa' (tentatively identified by Mills and later Serjeant as al-Hasā' / Lahsā, near Mukallā), Aden, Mogadishu, Brava and Malindi. The Chinese sources give no information about the number of ships or men who took part. This expedition was the first to touch at Arabian and East African ports.

The sixth expedition (1421–1422) visited Thailand, Malacca, Aru, Samudra, Lambri, Coimbatore, Kayal, Ceylon (Sri Lanka), the Maldives, Cochin, Calicut, Hormoz, Dhofar, La'sa, Aden, Mogadishu and Brava. It was composed of forty-one ships; the number of men is unknown. This time Ma Huan was on board one of three ships sent on a branch expedition to Dhofar and Aden while others were sent to the East African coast, putting in at Brava and Mogadishu.

Then, after the hiatus of seven years that followed the 1424 prohibition, Zheng He was despatched once again to the Western Ocean. Ships from this seventh and final expedition called at Champa, Thailand, Java, Palembang, Malacca, Samudra, Ceylon (Sri Lanka), Calicut, Hormoz, Aru, Nagur, Lide, Lambri, the Nicobars, Bengal, Quilon, Cochin, Coimbatore, the Maldives, Dhofar, La'sa, Aden, Makkah, Mogadishu and Brava. It was composed of more than 100 ships and around 27,550 men. The fleet left Nanjing on 19 January 1431 and reached Calicut on 10 December 1432. The main fleet spent only four days at anchor, then sailed for Hormoz, which it reached on 17 January 1433 after a voyage of thirty-five days. It was on this expedition that Ma Huan visited Makkah, not sailing with the main fleet, but with an advance branch expedition to Calicut, and then in a local craft to Jiddah. Zheng He's main fleet was back in China by July 1433.

Even this brief resume shows the colossal scale of the Ming voyages. Fleets of comparable size were not seen again in the Indian Ocean until the Second World War, and they dominated the waters of the Indian Ocean for almost a quarter of a century. A Chinese governor was installed in Palembang, pirates were driven from the Malacca Strait and Chinese support had much to do with the rise of Malacca itself. Those who refused to bring tribute, like the king of Ceylon and two Sumatran rulers, were taken to the Chinese capital in chains.

Not only were the fleets enormous, but the largest of the 'treasure ships' are said to have been 450 feet long with a 183 foot beam. The dimensions are clearly impossible, but these were still huge ships, surely the largest then sailing the waters of the Indian Ocean.[14] Yet the long Chinese presence in the waters of the Indian Ocean, their huge fleets and gigantic ships, left little trace in the records of

14 On this and related questions, see Church 2005.

the peoples they visited. Faint memories of the visits to Calicut persisted into early Portuguese times; a temple was dedicated to Zheng He in Malacca; Niccolò de' Conti caught a glimpse of a junk in the Red Sea, and told Fra Mauro, who drew a junk on his world map, labelling it *zonchi da India.* The historical tradition in pre-Moghul India was weak, and only just beginning in Malaysia and Indonesia. Persian chronicles are silent on the visits to Hormoz, for reasons explained by Jean Aubin.[15] The only non-Chinese sources for the Ming expeditions to the Indian Ocean are, as one might expect, in Arabic. Although disappointingly meagre, they are still of considerable interest, both confirming the Chinese sources and at the same time raising some new questions.[16]

The Arabic sources

The most important Arabic source is the *Anonymous Rasūlid Chronicle* (*ARC*) published by Yajima from BN Arabe 4609.[17] It was composed in 1441 and covers the years AH 439 / AD 1048 to AH 840 / AD 1436 in annalistic form. It contains information found nowhere else, particularly on the period from the reign of the Rasūlid Sultan al-Malik al-Nāṣir (AH 803–827 / AD 1401–1424) to almost the end of the reign of al-Malik al-Ẓāhir (AH 831–842 / AD 1428–1438), under both of whom the author clearly lived and about whose reigns he is minutely informed. This chronicle seems to have been unknown to later Yemeni historians. The *ARC* mentions the arrival of junks in Aden harbour from the fifth, sixth and seventh expeditions.

The Egyptian historian al-Maqrīzī (1364–1441) needs no introduction: a friend of Ibn Khaldūn and an original and innovative writer himself, his *Kitāb al-Sulūk li-ma'rifat duwal al-mulūk* (henceforth *Sulūk*) shows a deep interest in Yemen, the Ḥijāz and the Red Sea area, about which he was well informed. He was in Makkah in 1431, the year before the arrival in Jiddah of two junks from the seventh Ming expedition, and was an acquaintance of Sa'd al-Din Ibrāhīm ibn al-Murrah, the comptroller of the port of Jiddah at the time of the arrival of the Chinese junks the following year. Sa'd al-Dīn was probably the source for the account of the junks in his *Sulūk*.

Ibn Ḥajar al-'Asqalānī (1372–1449), famous as a *ḥadīth* scholar, biographer and historian, came from a wealthy family of merchants; his mother's brother was a *kārimī* merchant and his sister married a member of one of the wealthiest *kārimī* families, the Kharrūbī. Although he contributes but a single sentence to the record of Chinese junks in Jiddah, it significantly mentions that their merchandise found a ready market in Makkah.

Ibn al-Dayba' (1461–1537) lived and wrote under the successors of the Rasūlids, the Ṭāhirids (1454–1517). His historical works were commissioned by the last of the Ṭāhirid sultans, 'Āmir II (AH 488 / AD 1517). Unlike the author of the *ARC,* al-Maqrīzī and Ibn Ḥajar al-'Asqalānī, Ibn al-Dayba' was not a contemporary of the events he described, and relied on written sources and perhaps oral tradition for his account of the arrival in Aden of junks from the sixth expedition in 1422, long before he was born.[18]

The fifth expedition in the *Anonymous Rasūlid Chronicle*

The *ARC* records the arrival in Aden of junks from the fifth Ming voyage in Dhū al-Ḥijjah 821 / 30 December 1418–27 January 1419:

> Arrival of ships of the junk [*marākib al-zank*] [19] at the Protected Port accompanied by a messenger [*rasūl*] from the lord of China with precious gifts for our master, the Sultan al-Malik al-Nāṣir in the month of Dhū al-Ḥijjah the Sacred in the year 821.[20]

15 Aubin 1988: 87.

16 The Arabic sources that mention the Ming voyages that touched Aden were first studied by the editor of the *ARC*, Hikoichi Yajima. In his introduction, he refers to his article 1964. On the Descriptions of the Chen-Ho (sic) Expeditions descrived (sic) in an Arabic Source. *Shigaku* [*Historical Review of Keio University*], 38(4): 95–101 and Some Aspects of the Indian Ocean Trade in the Beginning of the 15th Century — On the Arrival of Chinese Ships at Aden. *Journal of Asian and African Studies* (Tokyo) 8, forthcoming. I have not been able to consult these papers. Serjeant 1988 reviews the mentions in the *ARC* and Ibn al-Dayba' and partially translates some passages, pointing out the chronological difficulties. I have borrowed the felicitous phrase 'How nice of you to come!' from Serjeant's translation of the passage from the *Qurrat* (Serjeant 1988: 75). Chaudhuri 1989 merely reprints an entry from Popper's translation of Ibn Taghrībirdī's *Nujūm,* which is in fact lifted from al-Maqrīzī's *Sulūk*, my text 7b.

17 Yajima 1976.

18 There are also two seventeenth-century sources, both Zaydī. Most Zaydī chronicles rely principally on Ibn al-Dayba' for their information on Rasūlid and earlier times. One of these is the author of the *Ghāyat al-Amānī fī akhbār al-Yamānī*, attributed by its editor, mistakenly, to Yaḥyā ibn al-Ḥusayn; see note 32. The other is al-Ḥasan ibn al-Ḥusayn, whose *Tuḥfat al-Zaman fī ta'rīkh mulūk al-Yaman* is contained in BL Ms. Or. 3330. He mentions Chinese junks in Aden (from the seventh expedition?) on ff. 82a-82b (Yajima 1976: 21, n. 28; Darrag 1961: 200, n. 5). I have not yet been able to examine this ms.

19 The earliest forms of this word in European sources are similar: *zuncum* in Odoric da Pordenone (1331), *zonchi* on the Fra Mauro map (1459). See Yule and Burnell 1985: 472–3.

20 Appendix, Text 5a.

A further entry describes the arrival at al-Janad, near the Rasūlid capital of Ta'izz, of the gifts sent to the sultan by the Yongle emperor:

> Our master the Sultan al-Malik al-Nāṣir entered al-Janad the Protected from the victorious encampment and the gifts of the lord of China were carried to him in procession. They were striking gifts, among them different sorts of rarities and silk cloth woven with gold [*al-thiyāb al-kamkhāt al-mudhahhaba*], best quality musk, storax and many sorts of China-ware vessels. The value of the present was estimated at 20,000 *mithqāls*. It was escorted by the Qāḍī Wajīh al-Dīn 'Abd al-Raḥmān ibn Jumay'; this occurred on Tuesday, 26 Muḥarram 822 / 22 February 1419.[21]

After an unrelated entry, dated 22 Ṣafar 822 / 20 March 1419, the *ARC* resumes with an account of the return gifts sent by al-Malik al-Nāṣir to the Chinese envoys in Aden:

> Our master the Sultan al-Malik al-Nāṣir ordered the messengers of the lord of China to be presented with gifts in return for his gifts. Among them were different kinds of rarities and a branch of coral polished in the Frankish manner, and different kinds of wild animals, like the wild cow and wild ass and striped lions and cheetahs and trained cheetahs and they arrived in Aden escorted by the Qāḍī Wajīh al-Dīn 'Abd al-Raḥmān ibn Jumay' in the month of Ṣafar 822 / 27 February–27 March 1419.[22]

Wajīh al-Dīn 'Abd al-Raḥmān ibn Jumay' is frequently referred to in the *ARC*, and here seems to have been responsible for the *matjar al-sulṭānī* in Aden. He is first mentioned in an entry for 7 Jumādā II / 7 October 1410, taking an inventory of the sultan's treasury in Aden.[23] He later appears elevated to the position of *sayyid al-wuzarā'*.[24]

Wajīh al-Dīn was almost certainly related somehow to a slightly earlier 'Ibn Jumay'', 'Alī ibn Yaḥyā al-Ṭā'ī al-Sa'dī , 'called Ibn Jumay'', a wealthy *kārimī* merchant and a friend of Ibn Ḥajar al-'Asqalānī's maternal uncle, to whom the Rasūlid Sultan al-Ashraf first entrusted the task of overseeing the royal *matjar* in Aden, then the governorship of the whole city; both the *amīr* and the *nāẓir* were subordinate to him. Ibn Ḥajar knew him personally and adds that he was a secret Zaydī, welcomed foreign merchants and treated ordinary people with love and consideration.[25]

This first Ibn Jumay' died at the age of sixty in AH 803 / AD 1400. He did much to attract merchants to Aden and greatly increased its customs revenues; in 1396 the customs duties on imports totalled one million *dīnārs*.[26]

The sixth expedition (1421–1422)

This was the last voyage dispatched during the reign of the Yongle Emperor, and the least known. Chinese sources mention the number of ships — forty-one — but not the number of men. All the other voyages lasted two years, while this is said to have lasted only one. It was the second expedition accompanied by Ma Huan, whose description of Aden clearly dates from this voyage. The Emperor's order authorizing the voyage was issued on 3 March 1421, but Zheng He was apparently still in China on 10 November 1421. Since he returned to the Chinese

---

21 Appendix, Text 5b.

22 Appendix, Text 5c.

23 Yajima 1976: 85.

24 Six years later, in Rabī' I 816 / 29 April–28 May 1416, a delegation of Makkan merchants led by the Qāḍī Amīn al-Dīn Mufliḥ al-Turkī arrived at the court of the Sultan al-Malik al-Nāṣir with a considerable sum of money which had been confiscated for unexplained reasons from Wajīh al-Dīn by the *sharīf* of Makkah, Ḥasan ibn 'Ajlān. The Makkan delegation was ceremoniously welcomed by the Sultan, and the merchants that accompanied it were granted exemption from the *'āshūr* for that year. The Sultan also ordered the moneychangers (*al-mutaṣarrifīn*) in the ports and coastal towns to treat merchants honestly. It is clear from this episode that al-Malik al-Nāṣir was eager to attract merchants to Aden by offering them good terms (Yajima 1976: 91).
The next year, on 17 Jumādā II 817 / 1 August 1417, Wajīh al-Dīn presented the sultan with rich gifts, including textiles, scents and other rarities and these were gratefully received by the sultan and the merchants in attendance upon him. These gifts may well have been recompense for the Sultan's intervention with the *sharīf* of Makkah to obtain the restoration of his confiscated wealth (Yajima 1976: 93–4). Whatever the case, the Sultan's pleasure in his gifts did not last. Wajīh al-Dīn was arrested and his wealth confiscated the following month, on 10 Sha'bān 820 / 22 September 1417 (Yajima 1976: 102). He was not released until 22 Muḥarram 821 / 1 March 1418 (Yajima 1976: 105). A year later he was back in favour; he reappears, escorting the gifts of the Chinese Emperor to the Sultan in al-Janad (Yajima 1976: 105; Appendix, Text 5b). He next appears in the *ARC* during the reign of al-Malik al-Ẓāhir (1428–1439), in an entry dated 8 Muḥarram 834 / 26 September 1430, escorting the royal treasure from Aden to Zabid (Yajima 1976: 134). The following year, on 28 Ramaḍān 834 / 9 June 1431, he escorted valuable gifts and port revenues worth 5 *lakk* from Aden to the Sultan in Zabīd; in this passage, for the first time, he is given a title: *sayyid al-wuzarā'* (Yajima 1976: 142). In September of the same year he was arrested once again and his wealth confiscated 'because of certain matters that angered the Sultan' (Yajima 1976: 143). When the seventh Ming voyage arrived in Aden on 28 February 1432, Wajīh al-Dīn had been replaced as *sayyid al-wuzarā'* by Shihāb al-Dīn Aḥmad ibn Ibrāhīm al-Muhālibī. Wajīh al-Dīn died the same year, on 27 June 1432, still in disgrace (Yajima 1976: 147).

25 Ibn Ḥajar 1971: 175–6.

26 Khazrajī 1918: 288; Darrag 1961: 199.

capital on 3 September 1422, only ten months later, he could not possibly have personally accompanied the fleet to all the ports it visited. For unknown reasons, he must have gone only as far as Samudra, then returned almost immediately to China. According to Ma Huan, the fleet was divided at Samudra and some vessels, under the command of a eunuch named Zhou Man (Chou Man), continued on to Aden, probably via Calicut.[27]

The arrival of this expedition in Aden is mentioned by the *ARC*, by Ibn al-Dayba‘ in both the *Bughyat al-Mustafīd* and the *Qurrat al-‘Uyūn*, and by the author of the *Ghāyat al-Amānī,* whose account is clearly lifted from Ibn al-Dayba‘. Only the *ARC* gives a precise date for the arrival of the ships: 18 Ṣafar 826 / 31 January 1423.[28] Ibn al-Dayba‘ in both the *Bughyat* and the *Qurrat*, merely gives the year, AH 823 / AD 1421. The *Ghāyat al-Amānī* also gives 1421, but the late date of this work (seventeenth century) and the fact that the author is copying Ibn al-Dayba‘ mean this is devoid of significance. The date given by the *Anonymous Rasūlid Chronicle*, 31 January 1423, is the more credible. Ma Huan's shipmate, Gong Zhen, says three ships visited Aden in 1422.[29] If they left from Calicut in December of that year, they would have arrived in Aden in January 1423 as stated in the *ARC*.

> The Sultan our master al-Malik al-Nāṣir received the news of the arrival of the junk [*al-zank*] and in them [sic!] the messenger [*rasūl*] of the ruler of China, escorting rich gifts from the Emperor [*al-malik khāqān*] to our master the Sultan al-Malik al-Nāṣir. Our master the Sultan al-Malik al-Nāṣir issued a decree [*marsūm*] to the Qāḍī Jamāl al-Dīn ibn Isḥāq and to the eunuch, the messenger of the ruler of China, that they should proceed to the Noble Gate of the Protected Port. So they arrived and the gifts accompanied them. Among them were rarities and musk deer and young civet cats and colourful parrots and Chinese *ūd*[30] and splendid China ware and textiles and carpets and extremely fine mosquito nets [*al-bashākhīn al-‘ajība*][31] and top quality aloe-wood and other sorts of wares. An order was issued to the Victorious Army and all the amirs to receive them. This occurred on Sunday, the 18th of the month of Ṣafar, 826.[32]

In Rabī‘ I 826 / 12 February–13 March 1423 al-Malik al-Nāṣir received the Chinese envoy in Ta‘izz:

> The Qāḍī Jamāl al-Dīn Muḥammad ibn Abī Bakr ibn Isḥāq and the eunuch Jalāl al-Dīn, the messenger [*rasūl*] of the ruler of China, arrived in Ta‘izz the Protected in the month of Rabī‘ I 826.[33]

When the *ARC* speaks in Text 6a of 'the arrival of the junk', he is clearly using *zank* in the sense of *marākib al-zank*, as in Text 5a, shown by the immediately following plural pronoun in *fī-him*.

This is the only text to attempt a translation of 'emperor', here rendered *al-malik khāqān,* a title used in Arabic and Persian sources going back to Yuan times. In all the other texts, the Chinese emperor is referred to either as *ṣāḥib al-ṣīn*, 'ruler of China', or in one case simply *malik*, 'king'. It is quite possible that the phrase *al-malik khāqān* occurred in the Arabic (or Persian?) translation of the Imperial Edict presented to al-Malik al-Nāṣir, and that the *ARC* reflects this usage.

Most interesting is the reference to the name of the Emperor's messenger, the eunuch Jalāl al-Dīn. This man must be identical to the eunuch Zhou Man of the Chinese sources.[34] The admiral Zheng He and Ma Huan were both Muslims, and presumably adopted Muslim names as well as Chinese, so it would not be surprising if Chou Man too were Muslim and should be referred to as Jalāl al-Dīn in an Arabic source.

Ibn al-Dayba‘ refers to the same expedition in both the *Bughyat al-Mustafīd* and the *Qurrat al-‘Uyūn*, although as we have seen he places the arrival of the Chinese envoy in 1421, not 1423. Although the versions in the *Bughyat* and the *Qurrat* are almost identical, the account in the *Qurrat* contains a significant difference that throws much light on the reception of the Chinese envoy. The text of the *Bughyat* reads:

> And in the year [8]23 the envoy [*qāṣid*] of the ruler of China arrived with three huge [*‘aẓīma*] ships in which were precious gifts to the value of 20 *lakk* of gold. He was received by al-Malik al-Nāṣir but did not kiss the ground before him. Instead he said: 'Your master, the ruler of China, greets you and advises you to treat your subjects with justice.' [Al-Malik al-Nāṣir] said to him: 'How nice of you to come!' and entertained him and lodged him in the guest house. Then al-Nāṣir wrote a letter to the ruler of China, saying: 'It is yours to command; my country is your country.' He sent him wild beasts and a generous quantity of splendid royal robes and ordered him to be escorted to the city of Aden.[35]

The *Qurrat* repeats this entry, with a few small changes: the value of the Chinese gift is computed in both gold and silver rather than just gold and the sentence detailing the

27 Mills 1970: 155.

28 Yajima 1976: 114.

29 Mills 1970: 58.

30 I can offer no explanation for this term.

31 Mosquito nets were among the gifts given by the Yongle emperor to the king of Borneo in 1412. See Groeneveldt 1887: 234.

32 Appendix, Text 6a.

33 Appendix, Text 6b.

34 Mills 1970: 155, note 3.

35 Appendix, Text 6c.

gifts sent to the Chinese envoy is omitted. Ibn al-Dayba‘ then adds a revealing passage:

> And this advice from the ruler of China to al-Malik al-Nāṣir was given in deadly seriousness.[36]. The phrase that was making the rounds on everyone's tongue was: 'The king of China thinks everyone is his slave!', and that this showed they were stupid and ignorant of the affairs of foreign countries and their kings. Furthermore, anyone who looks carefully into the matter knows that courtesy demands that nothing be said (on such occasions) but pleasant and acceptable things.[37]

Ibn al-Dayba‘ is of course describing an event that happened before he was born, under the previous dynasty. Whatever his sources, they did not include the *Anonymous Rasūlid Chronicle.* His reference to 'the phrase making the rounds on everyone's tongue' argues an oral source, or written account of one. The outrage at the presumption of the Chinese envoy in referring to the Emperor as 'your master' (*sayyidu-ka*), the refusal to bow to the ground before the sultan, and the Imperial Edict urging the sultan to treat his subjects with justice is still palpable in Ibn al-Dayba‘s account and had apparently persisted long after the name of the Chinese envoy and the specific nature of the Chinese gifts, as recorded by the *ARC,* had been forgotten. It is also clear that the Anonymous Chronicler, writing while the Rasūlid dynasty was still in power, has diplomatically drawn a veil over the episode of the Chinese envoy's refusal to prostrate himself before the sultan and the arrogant tone of the Imperial Edict.

The author of the *Ghāyat al-Amānī*, copies the account of Ibn al-Dayba‘ almost verbatim.[38] He refers to the Chinese envoy as a *rasūl*, as does the Anonymous Chronicler, rather than a *qāṣid*, as in Ibn al-Dayba ‘. The three ships are 'stuffed with cargo' (*mashḥūna*) rather than 'huge' (*‘aẓīma*), an adjective that he rather inelegantly transfers to the Emperor's gifts in place of Ibn al-Dayba's *nafīsa*. His most important change is to soften the arrogance of the Chinese envoy's address by simply replacing *sayyidu-ka ṣāḥib al-ṣīn* 'your master, the ruler of China' with the more diplomatic '*sayyidī ṣāḥib al-ṣīn*, 'my master, the ruler of China'.

The Imperial Edict itself, with its protest against al-Malik al-Nāṣir's treatment of his subjects, was of course regarded as an unwarranted intrusion into Yemeni affairs, as is made clear by the account in Ibn al-Dayba's *Qurrat al-‘Uyūn*. The protest was almost certainly motivated by pressure upon the Ming court from Calicut merchants trading in Aden, especially the *kārimī* merchants and their agents, who handled the bulk of the spice trade between Aden and Egypt, in particular the pepper shipped out of Calicut.[39] Complaints about the high taxes levied on imports to Aden had almost certainly been carried back to China by envoys from Calicut and other ports touched by Zheng He's fleets. These merchants must have hoped that the huge Chinese fleets would overawe rulers like al-Malik al-Nāṣir, and dissuade them from imposing arbitrary import duties.

A hint of the displeasure evoked in Aden by the tone of the Imperial Edict and the behaviour of the Chinese envoy is perhaps discernible in a phrase at the beginning of Ma Huan's account of Aden. After mentioning that the country is rich and well-populated, that the people are Muslim and speak Arabic (*a-la-pi*), he adds: 'The people are of an overbearing disposition';[40] this is an uncharacteristic comment from this remarkably non-condemnatory observer.

Ma Huan goes on to describe how the 'king' received the Imperial Edict from the eunuch Zhou: 'When the king heard of his arrival, he led his major and minor chiefs to the sea-shore, and welcomed the imperial edict and the bestowal of gifts. At the king's palace they rendered a ceremonial salutation with great reverence and humility.'[41] It seems clear from the *ARC* that al-Malik al-Nāṣir gave the Chinese permission to disembark in Aden port, and that they were ceremonially met by the *amīr* of Aden and his troops at the main gate of the city, but that the reception of the eunuch Zhou Man / Jalāl al-Dīn by al-Malik al-Nāṣir occurred not in Aden, but later in Ta‘izz, as one might expect. Ma Huan discreetly omits any mention of the envoy's refusal to prostrate himself before the sultan, just as does the author of the *ARC*.

Once the Imperial Edict had been read out to al-Malik al-Nāṣir, Ma Huan says the sultan gave permission for merchants to sell and barter with the Chinese. The Chinese traded for gems, pearls, branches of coral, amber, rose water, giraffes, lions, zebras, 'golden-spotted leopards' (cheetahs?), ostriches and white pigeons.

Ma Huan ends his account of Aden with a list of the 'tribute' items sent to the Yongle Emperor by al-Malik al-Nāṣir:

> The king of the country was filled with gratitude for the imperial kindness, and specially made two gold belts inlaid with jewels, a gold hat studded with pearls and

36 In Arabic, this phrase has an almost proverbial ring: *al-‘ārī ‘an al-laṭāfa al-mutasarbil fi l-kathāfa,* literally, 'denuded of lightness, clothed in density'.

37 Appendix, Text 6d.

38 Whoever he was, he was not 'Yaḥya ibn al-Ḥusayn', as given on the title page of ‘Ashūr's edition. For this author and the deplorable edition of the text, see the comments of Rex Smith 1984: 149.

39 For the activities of the *kārimī* merchants, see Fischel 1958 and Lapidus 1967: 116–30.

40 Mills 1970: 154.

41 Ibid.: 155.

> precious stones, besides *ya-ku* [*yaqūt,* rubies] and all other such kinds of precious stones, two local horns,[42] and a memorial to the throne written on gold leaf; [and] he presented these things as tribute to the Central Country.[43]

Ma Huan says that the Imperial Edict was accompanied by gifts of robes and hats, gifts that al-Malik al-Nāṣir's return gift seems nicely calculated to reciprocate. Strangely, Ma Huan does not mention the gifts listed by the *ARC* and which Ibn al-Dayba' says were valued at 20 *lakk* of gold, equivalent to two million *mithqāl* (*dīnārs*). This colossal sum should be compared with the gifts worth 20,000 *mithqāl* brought by the fifth Chinese expedition in 1419. The figure 20 *lakk* is probably exaggerated.

Ma Huan's account of Aden (*a-tan*) carefully avoids comment on the political situation. He confines himself, as in his descriptions of other ports, to describing local costume, male and female, including the formal dress of the sultan and his officials, local crafts, coinage, climate, calendar, food and drink, domestic and exotic animals (including elephants, giraffes, zebras, ostriches and lions), local architecture, and plants. Aside from mentioning that the country has 'seven or eight thousand well-drilled horsemen and foot-soldiers', he says nothing of Aden's impressive fortifications or its dramatic setting. Indeed, at the beginning of his account he makes the puzzling statement that 'The country lies beside the sea, and is far removed from the mountains.'[44]

His remarks on women's costume, on the other hand, are accurate and of great value, especially since we have no representations of Yemeni costume before the time of Carsten Niehbuhr:

> As to the dress of the women: over the body they put on a long garment; round the shoulders and neck they set a fringe of gem-stones and pearls — just as Kuan yin [the Chinese goddess of mercy] is dressed; in the ears they wear four pairs of gold rings inlaid with gems; on the arms they bind armlets and bracelets of gold and jewels; [and] on the toes they also wear toe-rings; moreover, they cover the top of the head with an embroidered kerchief of silk, which discloses only the face.[45]

42 Dr Church informs me that the characters read here as 'local horns' can be read 'snake horns' in the parallel passage in Gong Zhen 1961: 37. The reading in Mills is the more likely, but should be understood as '(animal) horns of the country', and probably refers to oryx or gazelle horns.

43 Mills 1970: 159.

44 Fei Xin, who never visited Aden, does mention the walls, Fei Xin 1996: 98.

45 Mills 1970: 156. Fei Xin's *Overall Survey of the Star Raft* was originally illustrated, but the illustrations have not survived.

The decline of Aden

Al-Malik al-Nāṣir, faced throughout his reign with Zaydī revolts and the incursions of Arab tribes, was in constant need of cash to pay his army. He raised it by levying a wide variety of non-canonical taxes on the merchant community, at times resorting to outright confiscation. The Cretan merchant Emmanuel Piloti, reporting from Alexandria, says that in the early 1420s, about the time the junks of Zheng He's fleet reached Aden on their sixth voyage, the combined taxes and duties levied on imports amounted to 50 per cent of the value of the merchandise, 'and this occasions great damage and harm both to pagans and Christians'.[46] Ships coming into Aden were detained there, and merchants awaiting their spices in Damascus and Alexandria had to wait for them to be brought overland by what was called the 'Aden caravan', accompanied by Yemeni merchants and the agents of al-Malik al-Nāṣir.[47] What Piloti says of the exorbitant taxes levied in Aden is confirmed by the Arabic sources.[48]

These exactions eventually caused an exodus of the *kārimī* and other merchants; some transferred their operations to Jiddah, others to the Indian ports of Calicut, Cambay and Surat. The Chinese protest at al-Malik al-Nāṣir's policies, however undiplomatic, was a reaction to policies that were adversely affecting China's export trade and the Indian Ocean trading network as a whole.

Al-Malik al-Nāṣir died, unlamented, in 1424 and was succeeded by his son, al-Manṣūr 'Abd Allāh (AH 827–830 / AD 1424–1427), who continued his father's disastrous policies.[49] In fact, the Rasūlid state was rapidly un-

46 Dopp 1950: 42.

47 Ibid. This important passage reads: 'Et est vray que en celle mer si a ung seigneur d'une ysole, lequel seigneur s'apelle le seigneur d'Adem; et si seigneurise aulcunes ysoles que en ceste ysole crest espices. Et pource que cestuy seigneur estoit puissant, et que toutes lez espices dez aultres ysoles ne povoyent passer sans que premièrement se aprésentassent à luy, lequel estoit mal dispost et empecchoit tousjours lez navilz des espices, lesquelx navilx faisoit demorer per force jusques à tant qu'ilz magnoyent la mjoytié de leurs espices, et estoit occasion d'ung très grant dommage et mal, tant de poyens comme de crestiens, par quoy lez nostrez crestiens attendoyent à Damasque et aussi en Alexandrie en tant que cestuy seigneur destenoit tant et si longuement qu'il mandoit ses espices à caravannes en gran quantité avecques ses citoyens et par ses facteurs, en si grant quantité qu'ilz s'appelloyent la caravanne d'Adem.'

48 Darrag 1961: 200, note 2.

49 al-Maqrīzī says in his necrology: 'He was one of the worst kings in the world, vicious, tyrannical and greedy' (al-Maqrīzī 1972: 675). He and Ibn Ḥajar al-'Asqalānī attribute his death to a thunder-clap, probably an allusion to Q. 13: 13. The *ARC* makes no mention of a thunder-clap, and places his death not at the castle of Qawārīr, near Zabīd, but al-Fass (Yajima 1976: 118).

ravelling, and the Mamlūk Sultan, Barsbay (AH 825–841 / AD 1422–1438), was quick to take advantage of Rasūlid weakness to extend his power over the southern Red Sea.

Barsbay and the Red Sea

During the hiatus between the return of the sixth Ming expedition and the departure of the seventh and last, the political and commercial situation in the southern Red Sea was radically transformed.

On 26 February 1425, the year following the deaths of both the Yongle emperor and al-Malik al-Nāṣir, Barsbay sent an *amīr* of Ten named Urunbughā with a corps of one hundred *mamlūks* to Jiddah by sea. Barsbay thus placed the port of Jiddah under direct Mamlūk control, installing a garrison and appointing a secretary named Sa'd al-Dīn Ibrāhīm ibn al-Murrah specifically to collect the taxes on merchandise brought by ship from India.[50] This official was dismissed from office the following year and replaced by a *kārimī* merchant, but was subsequently reinstated; he was in office as *nāẓir* when Ma Huan docked in Jiddah in 1432.[51]

Although forced for political reasons to share the revenues of the port with the *sharīf* of Makkah, Barsbay reserved the taxes and customs duties levied on the India ships entirely to himself. In order to ensure that ships docked at Jiddah, and not the old *kārimī* ports of 'Aydhāb and al-Quṣayr on the African coast, both by now eclipsed by al-Ṭūr but still sporadically functioning, Barsbay destroyed 'Aydhāb in 1426.[52] He made sure ships heading up the Red Sea from Jiddah off-loaded at al-Ṭūr, where their merchandise was once more subjected to customs-duties, rather than at al-Quṣayr. Under Mamlūk control, Jiddah rapidly began attracting the India ships that had formerly docked in Aden: fourteen vessels in 1425, another fourteen in 1426, soon thereafter fifty and then a hundred.[53] Substantial public works were undertaken, the port was restored, government offices built and a new mosque constructed.

One immediate consequence of these measures was the increase in the numbers of *mujawwarūn*, the 'interlopers', as Serjeant termed them.[54] These were merchant ships that tried to evade the high taxes levied in Aden by running through the Bāb al-Mandab directly for Jiddah. Al-Malik al-Nāṣir almost certainly founded the port of al-Fāzzah on the Red Sea coast opposite the off-shore island of Jabal Zuqar to police the strait and intercept these interloping ships.[55] Armed galleys and soldiers patrolled the Bāb al-Mandab, even using Greek fire to good effect.[56] Interloping ships were sometimes forced into Yemeni ports by contrary winds, usually because they tried to sail up the Red Sea during the summer. The merchants aboard were often treated with clemency, probably in order to lure them back to trading in Aden.

Barsbay's strategy in the Red Sea was simple and for a time effective. He succeeded in making Jiddah the leading Red Sea port, to the detriment of Aden. In 1429 he issued a decree establishing a state monopoly of the pepper and spice trade. The *kārimī* merchants who wished to stay in business were reduced to becoming state functionaries; those who refused to do so emigrated.

Al-Maqrīzī refers to Jiddah's eclipse of Aden a number of times, both in the *Mawā'iẓ* and the *Sulūk*, telling the story of how the *nākhūdhā* Ibrāhīm, one of the 'interlopers'

50 Darrag 1961: 206.

51 This official is frequently mentioned in al-Maqrīzī's *Sulūk* in entries between 1424 and 1433. al-Maqrīzī travelled with him to Makkah in a caravan that departed from Cairo 7 January 1431; between al-Wajh and Akrah they found the remains of the pilgrims who had died there from thirst the previous year and buried a thousand of them. The caravan was attacked by the *sharīf* of Madinah and his Bedouin allies and only escaped after a fierce battle and the payment of 1100 *dīnārs* plus 400 *dīnārs* worth of broadcloth and woollen robes (al-Maqrīzī 1972: 854). It is clear from al-Maqrīzī that Sa'd al-Dīn ibn al-Murrah was not permanently stationed in Jiddah, but went there to levy the *mukūs* and return with it to Cairo. In 1432 he left Cairo for Jiddah on 15 February, travelling light and probably arriving early in March (al-Maqrīzī 1972: 867).

52 Refugees from the destroyed city were then massacred by the ruler of Sawākin. This event still resonated a century later, when Leo Africanus wrote his *Della Decrittione dell' Africa;* he says the Beja ('Bugiha') used to control 'una città grossa sopra il mar Rosso chiamata Zibid (sic! 'Aydhāb), dove è un porto, che dirittamente risponde al porto del Zidem (Jiddah) il quale è vicino alla Mecca quaranta miglia, ma da cento anni in qua per cagione, che costoro rubbarono una caravana, che portava robba & vettovaglia alla Mecca, il Soldano si sdegnò & mando un'armata del mar rosso, laquale assediò & disfece la detta città, & il porto de Zibid, che dava loro d'entrata dugento mila saraffi (*ashrafī*?) alhora quelli, che fuggirono, incominciarono a girsene à Dangala & Suachin qualche piccolo cosa guadagnano, ma di poi il Signor di Suachin col favor di certi turchi armati di schioppi & d'archi, gli dette una rota, percioche in una giornata ammazzarono di questa canaglia che andava nuda piu che quattro mila persone, et mille ne menarono vivi a Suachin qual furono uccisi dale femine & da fanciulli.' (Ramusio 1970: 80v). Garcin 1972 regarded this passage as a garbled account of the 1507 Mamlūk attack on Yanbū'; it does contain evident anachronisms,and confuses 'Aydhāb with Zabīd, but the destruction of the port rings true and is consonant with Barsbay's Red Sea policies.

53 Darrag 1961: 203.

54 Serjeant 1994: *passim.*

55 According to the *ARC*, the order for founding the port was issued on 18 Jumādā I, 822 / 12 June 1419 (Yajima 1976: 106).

56 Yajma 1976: 164–5; Serjeant 1994: 87.

studied by Serjeant, disgusted at his treatment in Aden, Sawakin and Dahlak, investigated the possibilities of Jiddah in 1424, and the following year arrived with fourteen ships: 'News of him reached the sultan (Barsbay), and as he wanted to appropriate (Jiddah's) customs-duties to himself, he despatched Ibn al-Murrah for that (purpose). From that time henceforth Jiddah became a great Bandar, while Aden Bandar fell into disuse, all but a little.'[57] Aden's decline can be graphically illustrated by the steady diminution of the *khizānah*.

The Aden *khizāna*

Once a year the accumulated customs duties (*'ashūr*) and other tax receipts (*'ashūr al-shawānī, dilāla*)[58] levied in the port of Aden, together with gifts received from merchants and foreign potentates, were carried with great ceremony to the Rasūlid capital at Zabīd if the sultan were in residence or to wherever he might be camped if he were not. Although the transfer of the *khizāna* is frequently mentioned in the *ARC*, in only eight cases is the amount recorded. For some reason, no estimate of the amount occurs in the chronicle between AH 817 / AD 1414 and AH 834 / AD 1431. The extraordinary value of the gifts brought by the sixth Ming expedition — 20 *lakk* according to Ibn al-Dayba' — is not mentioned in the *ARC*, and the figure must be treated with caution, for it is well in excess of even the largest amount recorded in the *ARC*, the 17 *lakk* in revenues in 1399, when the first Ibn Jumay' was so efficiently administering Aden city and port. The gifts brought to the sultan by the fifth expedition in 1419, according to the *ARC*, amounted to only 20,000 *mithqāl* (*dīnārs*), a reasonable sum, and it is hard to believe that they should have been increased to 20 *lakk* on the sixth.

796 / 1394	5 *lakk*
802 / 1399	17 *lakk*
813 / 1410	10 *lakk*
817 / 1414	10 *lakk*
834 / 1431	5 *lakk*
835 / 1432	3 *lakk*
836 / 1433	4 *lak*k + 1 *lakk* in gifts
840 / 1436	1 *lakk*

It is unfortunate that this series of figures is not more complete and that it does not include the years of the fifth and sixth Ming voyages. The seventh voyage did not trade at Aden, according to our sources, but made for Jiddah, where the customs charges would have been collected by the agents of Barsbay. It is hard to believe, however, that the junks would have been allowed to proceed from Aden to Jiddah without paying a substantial indemnity. This may be reflected in the entry in the *ARC* for 10 Ramaḍān 835 AH / AD 11 May 1432, which reads: 'The Qāḍī Shihāb al-Dīn Aḥmad ibn 'Abd al-Raḥmān al-Sayyāhī arrived in Zabīd from Aden with a fine *khizāna* which included coin, gold, silver, silk and cloth worth more than 3 *lakk*'.[59] The relatively large figure for 1433, particularly the 1 *lakk* of gifts (which included fifty bales of cloth, scent, rarities, slaves and other gifts), was partly due to a mission from Calicut led by a ship-owner (*nākhudhā*) named Kirwah, beseeching the sultan to levy only the *'ashūr*, on Calicut merchants. This confirms Arabic sources that speak of the crippling effect of additional taxes on trade. Kirwah was given a slight rebate on the *'ashūr* and the merchants' minds, says the *ARC*, were set at rest by the Sultan, who promised reforms.[60] But these measures, assuming they were implemented, were too little and too late. As the table above clearly shows, the customs' revenues of Aden steadily dwindled during the first third of the fifteenth century. After 1425, they correspondingly rose in Jiddah, the new Red Sea entrepôt of the India trade.

The seventh expedition (1431–1433)

This was the background against which the seventh Ming voyage took place. It was accompanied by Ma Huan, Fei Xin and Gong Zhen, the authors of the three principal sources for the Ming voyages.[61] Thanks to a certain Zhu Yunming (Chu Yün-ming), who preserved an itinerary of the voyage, probably from a log book, we have the exact dates when the main fleet put in at its various ports of call, both for the outward and for most of the homeward journey.[62] Unfortunately, it does not include the dates or routes of branch expeditions, one of which is our concern here. The main fleet sailed out of Dragon Bay in Nanjing on 19 January 1431 and made its slow progress west, stopping in many ports along the way. It arrived in Calicut on 10 December 1432. Four days later the main body of the fleet sailed for Hormoz, reached on 17 January 1433. The fleet returned to Calicut on 9 March, docking on 31 March after a voyage of twenty-three days. They set out on the return voyage to China on 9 April; by 22 July Zheng He, accompanied by envoys from many of the places the fleet had visited, was in Beijing.

Ma Huan did not accompany the main fleet. Instead, he shipped out of Nanjing with the eunuch Hong Bao (Hung Pao) on a detached expedition sent directly to Calicut sometime early in 1431. In Calicut, Hong Bao chose seven emissaries, among them Ma Huan, and sent them in a 'ship of the country' to Jiddah.[63]

At the beginning of his entry on 'The Country of the Heavenly Square' (Tianfang [T'ien fang], Makkah / Arabia) in the *Overall-Survey of the Ocean's Shores,* Ma Huan says that Jiddah (Zhida [Chih-ta]) is three months

57 al-Maqrīzī, *Sulūk* 4: 680; Serjeant 1994: 84.
58 The galley and brokerage taxes; see Smith 1996: 210–4.

59 Yajima 1976: 146.
60 Ibid.: 160–1.
61 Mills 1970: 18.
62 From his work entitled *Qianwen ji* (*Ch'ien-wen chi*), 'A Record of Things Once Heard', printed *ca.* 1526 but preserved in a later compilation (Mills 1970: 14).
63 Mills 1970: 35–6.

sail south-west of Calicut,[64] and at the end of his description of Makkah explains how he and his companions came to be sent there from Calicut:

> When a division of the fleet reached the country of Ku-li [Calicut], the grand eunuch Hung saw that this country was sending men to travel there; whereupon he selected an interpreter and others, seven men in all, and sent them with a load of musk, porcelain articles and other such things [and] they joined a ship of that country and went there. It took them one year to go and return.
>
> They bought all kinds of unusual commodities, and rare valuables, ch'i-lin [giraffes], lions, 'camel-fowls' [ostriches], and other such things, in addition they painted an accurate representation of the 'Heavenly Hall' [*Ka'bah*]; [and] they returned to the capital.
>
> The king of the country of Mo-ch'ieh [Makkah] also sent envoys who brought some local articles, accompanied the seven men — the interpreter [and others] — who had originally gone there, and presented the articles to the court.[65]

He makes no mention of having docked at Aden on this voyage, and his statement that Jiddah was three months sail from Calicut implies that he went directly there. Mills, basing himself on suggestions by Pelliot, dated Ma Huan's departure from Calicut to 'about July 1432', and his arrival in Jiddah three months later to October. He thought Ma Huan and his companions spent some three months in Makkah, left in January 1433 and arrived back in Calicut in time to join Zheng He's fleet, which sailed for home on 9 April.[66] This chronology seems unlikely. It would have been difficult, if not impossible, to sail from Calicut to Aden in July, against the south-west monsoon. It is much more likely that Ma Huan and his companions left for Jiddah earlier in the year.

The *Anonymous Rasūlid Chronicle*, records the arrival of a Chinese junk in Aden on 19 Jumādā II 835 / 28 February 1432. Since the main Ming fleet was still at sea somewhere between Champa and Surabaja, this could only be one of the junks in Hong Bao's detached expedition, perhaps even a ship commanded by Hong Bao himself. Here is the brief entry from the *ARC*:

> The *nākhudhā* of the junk, the eunuch [*khādim*] of the ruler of China, arrived at Lahj on Wednesday, 25 Jumādā II 835 / 28 February 1432, with gifts for our lord the Sultan,[67] may God All-powerful make him victorious. He was escorted by our lord the *sayyid al-wuzarā'*, Shihāb al-Dīn Aḥmad ibn Ibrāhīm al-Muhālibī and the shaykh Jamāl al-Dīn Muḥammad Abū Jayyān.[68]

An entry in al-Maqrīzī's *Sulūk*, dated 22 Shawwāl 835 / 22 June 1432, apparently referring to the same junk(s), both confirms the arrival of the Chinese in Aden in that year and shows how the changed political situation in the Red Sea was affecting the port of Aden:

> News arrived from Makkah that a number of junks [*zunūk*] had arrived on the coast of India from China. Two of them anchored in Aden, but did not sell their porcelain, silk, musk and other merchandise because of the disorders in the Yemen. The captain [*kabīr*] of these two junks wrote to the Sharīf Barakāt ibn Ḥasan ibn 'Ajlān, the *amīr* of Makkah and to Sa'd al-Dīn Ibrāhīm ibn al-Murrah, the comptroller [*nāẓir*] of Jiddah, requesting permission to come to Jiddah. They in turn requested permission from the Sultan [Barsbay] and incited his cupidity by [telling him] of the great wealth he would gain by their coming. The Sultan replied to allow them to come to Jiddah and to treat them well.[69]

Al-Maqrīzī was well informed about events in the Red Sea and Yemen. He had accompanied Sa'd al-Dīn ibn al-Murrah to Makkah the previous year, on his way to collect the taxes from the port of Jiddah, and Sa'd al-Dīn was almost certainly the source for the entry in his *Sulūk*.[70] His reference here to the arrival of 'a number of junks' off the coast of India, must refer to the ships of the detached expedition commanded by Hong Bao, for the main body of the Ming fleet did not reach Calicut until 10 December 1432, six months later.

A single sentence in Ibn Ḥajar al-'Asqalānī completes the story: 'And in [835 / 1432] a number of Chinese junks [*zunūk*] arrived with rarities beyond description which were sold at Makkah'.[71] Despite its brevity, this important passage proves that the junks actually did make it to Jiddah and there sold their cargoes.

---

64 Ibid.: 173.

65 Ibid.: 178.

66 Ibid.: 35–6; Pelliot 1933: 322–4.

67 The Rasūlid Sultan, al-Malik al-Ẓāhir (1428–1439) now reigned in Yemen. On 19 Jumādā II 835 / 22 February 1432 he arrived in Aden from Ta'izz, and after a short stay left for Lahj, 25 miles north-west of Aden, arriving on 24 Jumādā II / 27 February (Yajima 1976: 145). He received the Chinese envoy the following day.

68 Yajima 1976: 145; Text 7a. Shihāb al-Dīn was Wajīh al-Dīn's replacement as *sayyid al-wuzarā'*; he is frequently mentioned in the *ARC*. This is the only occurrence of the name Jamāl al-Dīn Muḥammad Abū Jayyān in the *ARC*.

69 al-Maqrīzī 1972: 872–3; Appendix, Text 7b. The message to Barsbay requesting permission for the junks to land must incidentally have been sent by carrier pigeon (Darrag 1961: 208).

70 al-Maqrīzī 1972: 854.

71 Appendix, Text 7c.

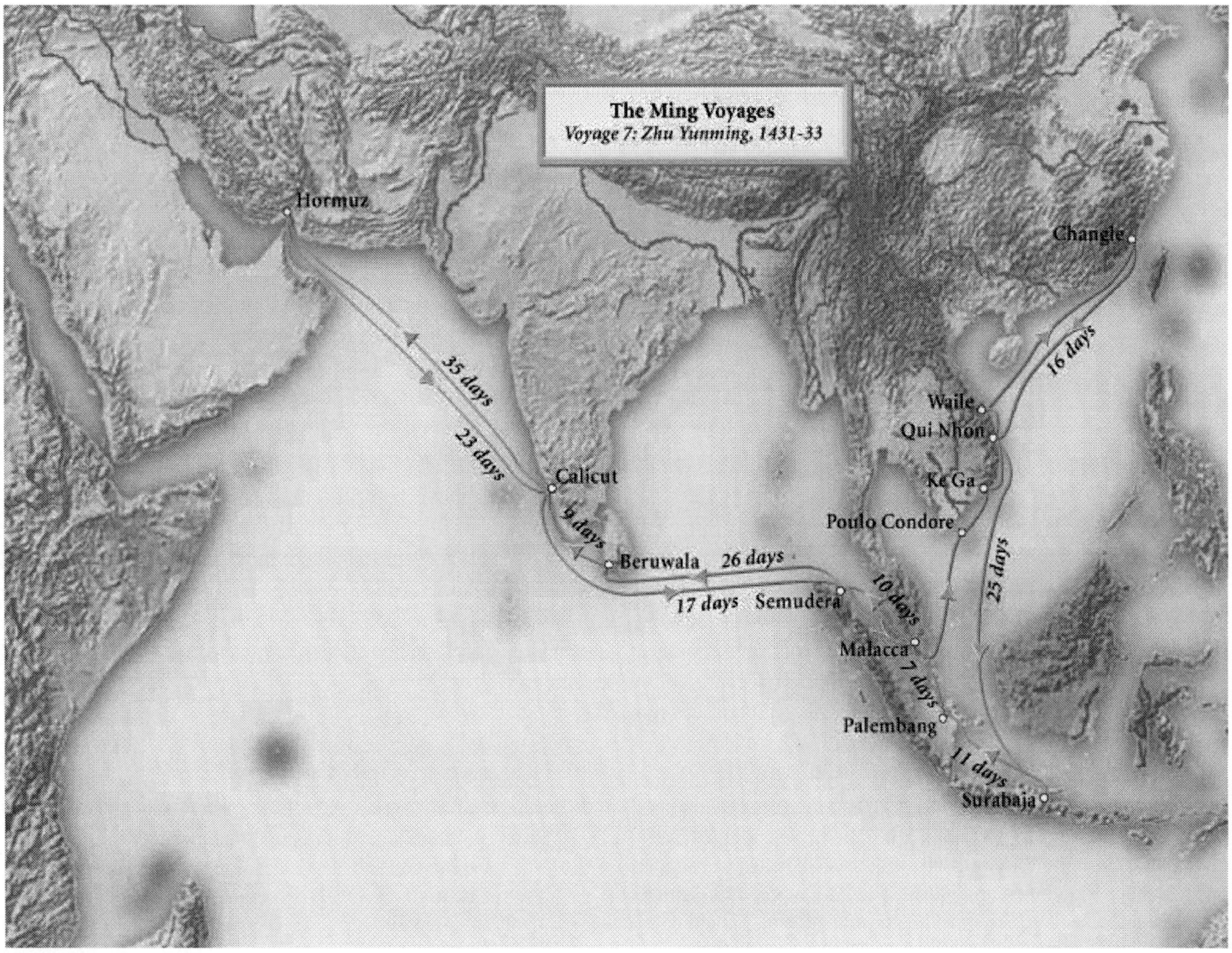

Map 21:3 The seventh expedition

The return to China

The ceremonies of the pilgrimage in 1432 took place between 9 and 19 August. They were accompanied by the customary trade fair, to coincide with which the Chinese probably timed their arrival.

It is a little hard to believe, given the circumstances, that the junks could have comfortably remained at anchor off Aden for four months. Sailing against the wind up the Red Sea in summer is a difficult, and often impossible, undertaking.[72] Some ships of the 'interlopers' were blown back by the *shamāl* into the hands of the Rasūlids in July of 1434.[73] Perhaps they awaited their answer at some intermediate port? Junks from this expedition also put into Dhofar and 'La'sa' (al-Aḥsā'). Hong Bao brought an envoy from the 'king' of Dhofar named 'Hazhihuxian' (Ḥajjī Ḥusayn?) to Beijing on his return. Junks under Hong Bao's command also visited Mogadishu and Brava on this expedition.[74] No matter where they put in, they would still have to make for Jiddah before the onset of the summer monsoon. Or did they simply sail for Jiddah soon after arriving in Aden, and wait off Jiddah for permission to land?

The two junks that docked in Jiddah in 1432 must have been sent, not only to trade, but to pick up Ma Huan and his companions and the menagerie of exotic animals he and his companions had acquired — a giraffe, lions and ostriches — to say nothing of all the other 'unusual commodities' they accumulated. According to the *Ming*

72 Facey 2004: 10, Fig. 2.

73 Serjeant 1994: 88.

74 An entry in the *Shilu* under the year 1448 records the return to China of three men who had been in Hong Bao's fleet on the 1431–1433 voyage. They were the survivors of a ship with a complement of 300 men that ran into difficulty off the African coast and drifted to Brava (*Buguo*). Other survivors of this expedition are said to have ended up in Pate, Kenya. *Ming Yingzong shilu*, Zhengtong 13 (1448), 8th month, *renxu*, *j.* 169, pp. 2b–3a, pp. 3260–61. I would like to thank Dr Church for this reference. See also Levathes 1994:195-203.

Xuanzong Shilu ('Veritable Records of the Ming: Xuanzong Period'), Hong Bao's ships returned to China with an envoy from the 'chief' (*toumu*) of Makkah named Shaxian (Shāhīn?) and a number of other Makkans, probably merchants. Hong Bao's ships also brought envoys from the kings of Hormoz, Dhofar, and Aden and other countries. These envoys were received in Beijing on 14 September 1433, two months after the reception of Zheng He, which argues that they sailed separately.[75] It is probable that the junks stayed in Jiddah for the pilgrimage, which in 1432 fell between 9 and 19 August, and the trade fair that followed, leaving in September. This would allow a year for the voyage back to China.

Epilogue

The envoys that accompanied Hong Bao on the voyage back to China remained there until 11 August 1436, when they received orders to return to their native countries. They were sent in the company of a Javanese envoy who had brought tribute and was returning to his country on a Javanese ship.[76] Several junks were allotted to take them from Java to their respective countries. Whether the envoys from Hormoz, Dhofar, Aden and Makkah sailed home on these junks or some other vessels is unrecorded.

The Venetian traveller Niccolò de' Conti told Pero Tafur, whom he met in Sinai in 1437, that he had seen Chinese junks sailing the Red Sea:

> He described their ships as like great houses, and not fashioned at all like ours. They have ten or twelve sails, and great cisterns of water within, for there the winds are not very strong, and when at sea they have no dread of islands or rocks. These ships carry all the cargoes which the caravans receive from them at Makkah [that is, Jiddah], which is the port where they unload.[77]

These could have been the junks that docked in Aden and Jiddah in 1432. Niccolò clearly thought their presence in the Red Sea a common occurance. Curiously, Khalīl ibn Shāhīn al-Zāhirī (1410–1468), who was in Makkah in 1436 and Sinai in 1437, also refers to 'a ship with seven sails' in Jiddah harbour; the context implies that it was a regular visitor.[78]

---

75 The entry from the *Ming Xuanzogn shilu* for 14 September 1433 reads, in Dr Church's translation: 'The king of Samudra, Zainuli Abiding [Zayn al-'Ābidīn], sent his younger brother Halizhihan and others. The king of Calicut, Bilima, sent the envoy Gebumanduluya and others. The king of Cochin, Keyili, sent the envoy Jiabubilima and others. The king of Ceylon, Bulagemabahulapi [Parakramabāhu VI, 1412–1467], sent his envoy Mennidenai and others. The king of Dhofar, Ali ['Alī ibn 'Umar, see Mills 1976: 153, n. 15] sent the envoy Hazhihuxian [Ḥajjī Ḥusayn] and others. The king of Aden, Molikenasi'er [Malik al-Nāṣir, long deceased] sent the envoy Puba and others. The king of Ganbali [Coimbatore], Douwalada, sent the envoy Duansilijian and others. The king of Hormuz, Saifuding [Sayf al-Dīn)] sent the foreigner [*fanren*] Malazu and others. The king of Cail [Jiayile] sent the envoy Adulu Haman and others. The chief [*toumu*] of Makkah, Shaxian [Shāhīn?)], and others came to present a *qilin* (the word for an auspicious mythical beast, used by the Chinese envoys for the giraffe in order to flatter the emperor; Fei Xin used the word *zulafa*], [as well as] elephants, horses, and various products. The emperor went to Fengtianmen to receive them. The minister of the Beijing branch of the Board of Rites, Hu Ying, regarded the *qilin* as an auspicious gift and led the various officials in praise and congratulations. The emperor replied: "It is not necessary to express congratulations. I do not covet things that come from distant regions, but consider that because they come from such distant places and are given in earnest, I should accept them"' (tr S.K. Church). This entry is for the first day (*xinhai*) of the intercalary eighth month in the eighth year of Xuanzong (14 September 1433); see *Ming Xuanzong shilu* (Veritable Records of the Ming:xuwanzong Period), Zhongyang yanjiu yuan series (Taibei, 1962–1967, juan 105, 1a,p.2341).

76 Vandermeersch 1973: 273.

77 Tafur 1926: 93.

78 Niccolò de' Conti (ca.1420-44) had visited many of the ports in India and south-east Asia visited by the Ming voyages; he saw and described junks in the account of his travels he dictated to the famous humanist and papal secretary, Poggio Bracciolini, who included it in a chapter of his *HIstoriae de varietate fortunae* (1447). The version of his travels recounted to Pero Tafur is quite different and more highly coloured. The chronology of Niccolò's travels is very uncertain. When Pero Tafur met him in 1437, he was apparently returning to Egypt with the pilgrimage caravan, accompanied by his wife and three children.. He told Tafur he had been forced to convert to Islam in Jiddah. It is not known how long he resided in Jiddah / Makkah but if he saw Hong Bao's junks he must have been in Jiddah in 1432. Either that, or his description of junks sailing the Red Sea was based on hearsay or residence in some other Red Sea port, possibly Aden. Niccolò was a wealthy Venetian merchant, and it is not impossible that he should have been trading in Aden or Jiddah.The main body of the *hajj* of 841/1437 arrived back in Cairo on 17 July (al-Maqrīzī 1972:1018) which means the encounter between Niccolò and Pero Tafur in Sinai must have taken place at the beginning of July. For more detail on Niccolò de' Conti, consult Jiménez de la Espada 1982: 57–74. The passage from Khalīl ibn Shāhīn's *Zubdat kashf al-mamālik* reads: 'As for Jiddah, it is the port of Makkah and one of the greatest of ports. More than a hundred ships bring their cargoes there every year, among them a ship with seven sails [*markab bi-sab'at qulū'*]. He goes on to say that the port revenues averaged an annual 200,000 *dīnārs*, shared between the Sharīf and Barsbay (Ibn Shāhīn 1894:13-14). Khalīl ibn Shāhīn was *amīr al-hajj* in 1436 and *hākim* of al-Karak in 1437 (appointed 7 September). These dates coincide closely with those of Niccolò de' Conti. Is it possible that both men saw the junk that brought back the Sharīf's 'envoy', 'Shaxian'?

The laconic entries in the Mamlūk and Rasūlid chronicles evince little surprise or wonder at the arrival of Chinese junks in Aden and Jiddah. The Arabic chronicles do not mention the envoys sent to China by the rulers of Dhofar, Makkah and Yemen, whose arrivals at and departures from the imperial court were so meticulously recorded by the Chinese annalists. It is probable that these were in fact merchants, assuming the guise of envoys to facilitate their passage, with the tacit knowledge of the Chinese. This practise was common, and may explain why their names are not recorded in the Arabic chronicles. Aside from the single adjective 'huge' (*'aẓīma*) used once by Ibn al-Dayba', the junks themselves excited no comment, and are never described; nor are the physical appearance and costume of the Chinese envoys and their retainers.

Nevertheless, these Arabic sources, taken together with the Chinese, add to our understanding of the Indian Ocean trading network and its complexities on the eve of the coming of the Portuguese. It is to be hoped that more Yemeni sources on the Ming voyages and their reception in South Arabian and Red Sea ports will someday come to light.

References

Chaudhuri, K.N. 1989. A Note on Ibn Taghrībirdī's Description of Chinese Ships in Aden and Jedda. *Journal of the Royal Asiatic Society* 1989: 112.

Church, S.K. 2005. An investigation into the plausibility of 450-ft. Treasure Ships. *Monumenta Serica* 53: 1–43.

——. 2007. The Ming Voyages and the Silk Road of the Sea. (article, forthcoming).

Darrag, A. 1961. *L'Égypte sous le regne de Barsbay 825–841 / 1422–1438*. Damascus: Institute Français de Damas.

Dopp, P.H. 1950. *L'Égypte au commencement du quinzième siècle d'après le traité d'Emmanuel Piloti de Crète (Incipit 1420)*. Cairo: Imprimerie Université Fouad 1er.

Duyvendak, J.J.L. 1938. The True Dates of the Chinese Maritime Expeditions in the Early Fifteenth Century. *T'oung Pao* 34: 341–412.

Facey, W. 2004. The Red Sea: The Wind Regime and Location of Ports. 7–17 in P. Lunde and A. Porter (eds), *Trade and Travel in the Red Sea Region. Proceedings of Red Sea Project I, Held in the British Museum October 2002*. Society for Arabian Studies Monographs 2. BAR International Series 1269. Oxford: Archaeopress, 2004.

Fischel, W. 1958. The Spice Trade in Mamluk Egypt. A Contribution to the Economic History of Medieval Islam. *Journal of the Economic and Social History of the Orient* 1: 157–74.

Fletcher, J.F. 1968. China and Central Asia, 1368–1884. 206–24 in John K. Fairbank (ed.), *The Chinese World Order*. Cambridge, Mass.: Harvard University Press.

Garcin, J.-C. 1972. Jean Léon l'Africain et 'Aydhāb. Annales Islamologiques XI: 189-209. Repr. No. II in J.-C. Garcin. 1987. *Espaces, pouvoirs et ideologies de l'Egypte médiévale*. Aldershot : Variorum.

Gong Zhen [Kung Chen]. 1961. *His-yang Fan-kuo chih*. Beijing: Chung-hua shu-chü.

Groeneveldt, W.P. 1887. Notes on the Malay Archipelago and Malacca. Volume 1: 126–262 in R. Rost (ed.), *Miscellaneous Papers relating to Indo-China and the Indian Archipelago*. Second Series. London: Trübner.

Ibn al-Dayba'. 1979. *Bughyat al-mustafīd fī ta'rīkh mad-īnat zabīd.* A. al-Ḥibshī (ed.). Sana'a: Markaz al-Dirāsāt wa l-Buḥūth al-Yamanī.

——. *Qurrat al-'uyūn fī akhbār al-yaman al-maymūn.* Cambridge University Library Ms. Or. (10) 226.

Ibn Ḥajar al-'Asqalānī. 1971. *Inbā' al-ghumr bi-anbā' al-'umr.* Volume 2, R. Ḥibshī (ed.). Cairo: al-Majlis al-A'lā lil-Shu'ūn al-Islāmīyah.

——. 1972. *Inbā' al-ghumr bi-anbā' al-'umr.* Ed. R. Ḥibshī. (Cairo: al-Majlis al-A'lā lil-Shu'ūn al-Islāmīyah, 1972). Vol. 3.

Ibn Shāhīn, Khalīl. 1894. Zoubdat kachf el-mamâlik. Tableau politique et administratif de l'Égypte, de la Syrie et du Hidjâz sous la domination des sultans Mamloûks du XIIIe au XVe siècle par Khalîl ed-Dâhiry. P. Ravaisse (ed.). (Paris : Imprimerie Nationale).

al-Khazrajī. 1918. *Kitāb al-'uqūd al-lu'lu'īyah fī dawlat al-rasūliyah.* M. 'Asal (ed.). Gibb Memorial Series. Cairo: Maṭba'at al-Hilāl, 1914; Leiden: Brill, 1918.

Levathes, L. 1994. *When China Ruled the Seas: the treasure fleet of the Dragon Throne, 1405-1433*. New York: Simon and Shuster.

al-Maqrīzī, Aḥmad ibn 'Alī. 1972. *Kitāb al-sulūk li-ma'rifat duwal al-mulūk.* Volume 4, Part 2 (A.H. 824–841). S. 'Ashūr (ed.). Cairo: Maṭba'at Dār al-Kutub, 1972.

Mills, J.V.G. 1970. *Ma Huan. Ying-Yai Sheng-Lan, 'The Overall Survey of the Ocean's Shore.* Tr. from the Chinese text, edited by Feng Ch'eng-Chün, with introduction, notes and appendices by J.V.G. Mills. Cambridge: Cambridge University Press for the Hakluyt Society.

Pao, Tsen-p'eng. 1961. *Zheng He xia xi yang shi bao chuan kao. On the Ships of Cheng-Ho* [Text in Chinese and English]. Collected Papers on History and Art of China (First Collection) 6. Taipei: National Historical Museum.

Pelliot, P. 1933. Les grands voyages maritimes chinois au début du XVe siècle. *T'oung Pao* 30: 237–452.

Ptak, R. 1989. China and Calicut in the Early Ming Period: envoys and tribute embassies. *Journal of the Royal Asiatic Society* 1989: 81–111.

Ramusio, G. B. 1563; repr. 1970. *Navigationi et Viaggi. Venice 1563–1606*. Volume 1. Amsterdam: Theatrum Orbis Terrerum.

Serjeant, R. 1988. Yemeni Merchants and Trade in Yemen: 13th – 16th centuries. Pp. 61-82 in D. Lombard and J. Aubin, J. (eds), *Marchands et hommes d'affaires asiatiques dans l'Océan Indien et la Mer de Chine 13e-20e siècles*. Paris: Éditions de l'École des Hautes Études en Sciences Sociales. Repr. No.I in R.B. Serjeant. 1996. *Society and Trade in South Arabia*, G.R. Smith (ed.). Aldershot: Variorum.

——. 1991. Tihama Notes. 45–60 in A. Jones (ed.), *Arabicus Felix: Luminosus Britannicus. Essays in Honour of A.F.L. Beeston on his Eightieth Birthday*. Reading: Ithaca Press. Repr. No. XVI in R.B. Serjeant, 1996. *Society and Trade in South Arabia*, G.R.Smith (ed.). Aldershot: Variorum.

——. 1994. Fifteenth century 'interlopers' on the coast of Rasūlid Yemen. 83–91 in *Itinéraires d'Orient: Hommage à Claude Cahen*. Res Orientales 6. Bures-sur-Yvette: Groupe pour l'étude de la civilisation du moyen-orient. Repr. No. IV in R.B. Serjeant. 1996. *Society and Trade in South Arabia*. G.R. Smith (ed.). Aldershot: Variorum.

Smith, G.R. 1984. The Tahirid sultans of the Yemen (858–923 / 1454–1517) and their historian Ibn al-Dayba'. *Journal of Semitic Studies* 29: 141–54. Repr. No. XV in G.R. Smith. 1997. *Studies in the Medieval History of the Yemen and South Arabia*. Aldershot: Variorum.

——. 1995. Have you anything to declare? Maritime trade and commerce in Ayyubid Aden: practices and taxes. *Preceedings of the Seminar for Arabian Studies* 25: 127–40. Repr. No.X in G.R. Smith. 1997. *Studies in the Medieval History of the Yemen and South Arabia*. Aldershot: Variorum.

——. 1996. More on the port practices and taxes of medieval Aden. 208–18 in G.R. Smith, J.R. Smart and B.R. Pridham (eds), *New Arabian Studies* 3. Repr. No.XI in G.R. Smith. 1997. *Studies in the Medieval History of the Yemen and South Arabia*. Aldershot: Variorum.

Tafur, P. 1926. *Travels and Adventures, 1435–1439*. M. Letts (tr. and ed.). London : George Routledge & Sons.

——. 1982. *Andanças e Viajes de un Hidalgo Español. Pero Tafur (1436–1439)*. M. Jiménez de la Espada (ed.). Barcelona: Ediciones El Albir.

Vandermeersch, L. 1973. Les relations sino-arabes au XVe et au XVIe siècle: un chapitre de l'histoire des Ming. *Cahiers de linguistique d'orientalisme et de slavistique* 1–2: 271–8.

Yaḥyā ibn al-Ḥusayn. 1968. *Ghāyat al-Amānī fī akhbār al-quṭr al-yamānī*. S. 'Ashūr (ed.). Cairo: Dar al-Kātib al-'Arabī li-l-Ṭibā'ah wa l-nashr. Turāthunā. 2 vols.

Yajima, H. (ed.). 1976. *A Chronicle of the Rasūlid Dynasty of Yemen from the unique MS Paris No. Arabe 4609*. Study of Languages & Cultures of Asia and Africa Monograph Series No. 7. Tokyo: Gaikokugo Daigaku.

Yule, H. and Burnell, A.C. 1985, 2nd ed. *Hobson-Jobson*. W. Crooke (ed.). London: Routledge & Kegan Paul.

Appendix

Fifth expedition (1417–1419)

Text 5a: *Anonymous Rasūlid Chronicle*, Dhū al-Ḥijja 821 / 30 December 1418–27 January 1419[79]

وصول مراكب الزنك إلى الثغر المحروس و معهم رسول من صاحب الصين بهدية سنية لمولانا السلطان الملك الناصر في شهر ذي الحجة الحرام سنة ٨٢١

Text 5b: *Anonymous Rasūlid Chronicle*, 26 Muḥarram 822 / 22 February 1419[80]

دخل مولانا السلطان الملك الناصر دار الجند المحروس من المحطة المنصور و زقّت هدية صاحب الصين إليه و كانت هدية فاخرة فيها من أنواع التحف و ثياب الكمخات المذهّبة المفتخرة و المسك العال و العود الرطب و الأنية الصيني أ نواع كثيرة قوّمت الهدية بعشرين ألف مثقال و صحبتها القاضي وجيه الدين عبد الرحمان بن جميع و ذلك في يوم الثلاثاء ٢٦ من شهر المحرّم سنة ٨٢٢

79 Yajima 1976: 105.

80 Ibid.: 105.

Text 5c: *Anonymous Rasūlid Chronicle*, 17 February–27 March 1419[81]

أمر مولانا السلطان الملك الناصر بتجهيز رسل صاحب الصين بهدية عوض هديته فيها من أنواع التحف و شجر المرجان يجلي بالمينة الإفرنجي و أنواع الوحوش كالمهاة و حمر الوحش و الأسود المؤلفة و الفهود و الفهود المودّية و سافروا إلى الثغر المحروس عدن صحبة القاضي وجيه الدين عبد الرحمان بن جميع في شهر صفر سنة ٨٢٢

Sixth expedition (1421–1422)

Text 6a: *Anonymous Rasūlid Chronicle*, 18 Ṣafar 826 / 31 January 1423[82]

وصل العلم إلى مولانا السلطان الملك الناصر بوصول الزنك و فيهم رسول صاحب الصين و صحبته هدية سنية من الملك خاقان إلى مولانا السلطان الملك الناصر فورد مرسوم مولانا السلطان الملك الناصر إلى القاضي جمال الدين بن إسحاق هو و الطواشي رسول صاحب الصين بان يصلوا إلى الباب الشريف من الثغر المحروس فوصلوا و صحبتهم الهدية و فيها من التحف و ظباء المسك و فطير الزباد و الدرر الملوّنة و الأود الصيني و الأواني الصيني المفتخرة و الثياب و الفرش و البشاخين العجيبة و العود العال و غير ذلك من الأواني و ورد المرسوم على العسكر المنصور ان يلقوا هم و الأمراء كافة و كان ذلك نهار الأحد ١٨ من شهر صفر سنة ٨٢٦

Text 6b: *Anonymous Rasūlid Chronicle*, Rabīʿ I 826 / 12 February–13 March 1423[83]

تقدم القاضي جمال الدين محمد بن أبي بكر بن إسحاق هو و الطواشي جلال الدين رسول صاحب الصين إلى تعز المحروس في شهر ربيع الأول سنة ٨٢٦

Text 6c: Ibn al-Daybaʿ, *Bughyat al-Mustafīd*, 823/1421[84]

و في سنة ثلاث و عشرين قدم عليه قاصد صاحب الصين بثلاثة مراكب عظيمة فيها من هدايا النفيسة ما قيمته عشرون لكا من الذهب واجتمع بالملك الناصر فلم يقبل الأرض بين يديه بل قال سيدك صاحب الصين يسلم عليك و يوصيك بالعدل في رعيتك فقال له مرحباً و نعم المجيئ جئت وأكرمه وأسكنه بدار الضيافة ثم كتب الناصر إلى صاحب الصين كتاباً الأمر أمرك والبلد بلدك و جهز له من الوحوش البرية و الثياب الفاخرة السلطانية جملة مستكثرة

Text 6d: Ibn al-Daybaʿ, *Qurrat al-ʿUyūn* 823 / 1421[85]

و في سنة ثلاث و عشرين قدم عليه قاصد صاحب الصين بثلاثة مراكب عظيمة فيها من الهدايا النفيسة ما قيمته عشرون لكاً من الذهب و الفضة و اجتمع قاصده بالملك الناصر فلم يقبل الأرض بين يديه بل قال له سيِّدك صاحب الصين يسلم عليك و يوصيك بالعدل في رعيتك فقال له مرحباً بك و نعم المجئ جيت و اكرمه و اسكنه دار الضيافة ثم كتب الناصر إلى صاحب الصين كتاباً يقول فيه الامر امرك والبلدبلدك و هذا الخطاب من ملك الصين للملك الناصر العاري عن اللطافة المتسربل في الكثافة يصدّق الكلام الداير على الالسنة من قولهم ملك الصين يظنّ ان كل الناس عبيده و الظاهر انّ فيهم حمقاً و جهلاً باحوال البلاد و ملوكهم والا فالأدب موجب لمن يحقق من نفسه الكمال ان لا يخاطب غيره الا باللطف و الاجمال

Text 6e Yaḥyā ibn al-Ḥusayn, *Ghāyat al-Amānī,* beginning of 823 / 1421[86]

81 Ibid.: 106.

82 Ibid.: 114.

83 Ibid.

84 al-Hibshī 1979: 104.

85 Cambridge University Libarary Or. (10) 226, f. 167v.

86 Yaḥyā ibn al-Ḥusayn 2: 565.

فيها قدم إلى اليمن رسول من عند ملك الصين
بثلاثة مراكب مشحونة فيها من الهدايا العظيمة
ما قيمته عشرون لكا من الذهب فاتصل
بالسلطان الناصر أحمد بن إسماعيل و لما دخل
عليه لم يفعل كغيره من تقبيل الارض و نحو
ذلك بل قال له سيدي صاحب الصين يسلم
عليك و يوصيك بالعدل في رعيتك فقال له
مرحباً بك و نعم المجيء جئت ثم أنزل الرسول
دار الضيافة و بالغ في إكرامه و كتب إلي ملك
الصين كتاباً يقول فيه و الأمر أمرك و البلد
بلدك و اهدى إليه من الثياب السلطانية و مىن
الوحوش البرية جملة مستكثرة

Seventh expedition (1431–1433)

Text 7a: *Anonymous Rasūlid Chronicle*, 25 Jumādā II 835 / 28 February 1432[87]

وصل ناخوذة الزنك و هو خادم صاحب
الصين بالهدية لمولانا السلطان نصره الله تعالى
إلى لحج و وصل صحبته مولانا سيد الوزراء
شهاب الدين أحمد بن إبراهيم المحالبي و الشيخ
جمال الدين محمد أبو جيّان نهار الأربعاء ٢٥
من شهر جمادى الأخرى سنة ٨٣٥

Text 7b: al-Maqrīzī, *Sulūk*, 22 Shawwāl 835 / 22 June 1432[88]

و قدم الخبر من مكة المشرفة بان عدة زنوك
قدمت من الصين إلى سواحل الهند و أرسى
منها إثنان بساحل عدن فلم تنفق بها بضائعها من
الصيني و الحرير و المسك و غير ذلك لإختلال
حال اليمن فكتب كبير هذين الزنكين إلى
الشريف بركات بن حسن إبن عجلان أمير مكة
و إلى سعد الدين إبراهيم بن المرة ناظر جدة
يستأذن في قدومهم إلى جدة فاستأذنا السلطان
في ذلك و رغباه في كثرة ما يتحصّل في
قدومهم من المال فكتب بقدومهم إلى جدة و
إكرامهم

Text 7c: Ibn Ḥajar, *Inbā'*, 835 / 1431–1432[89]

و فيها وصل من جنوك الصين عدة و معهم من
التحف ما لا يوصف فبيع بمكة

Acknowledgements

I would like to thank Dr S.K. Church of Wolfson College, Cambridge, for her valuable suggestions and help with the Chinese sources, and in particular for allowing me to refer to the typescript of her forthcoming paper, 'The Ming Voyages and the Silk Road of the Sea'.

87 Yajima 1976: 145.
88 al-Maqrīzī 1972: 872–3.
89 Ibn Ḥajar al-'Asqalānī 3: 472.

From the White Sea to the Red Sea: Piri Reis and the Ottoman Conquest of Egypt

Paul Starkey

Introduction

It is often instructive to look at a period involving major cultural shifts and changes through the life or career of a particular individual. In this respect, the career of the Turkish traveller and cartographer Piri Reis b. Ḥājjī Meḥmed (*ca.* 1470–1553/1554), is a fascinating one from several points of view, spanning as it did a period when the Ottomans were extending their empire over much of the central Arab world, including Egypt and into the Red Sea. Piri Reis is today almost certainly most widely known for his 'world map', dated 1513 and preserved in the Istanbul Topkapı Saray Library,[1] and this work, which continues to be surrounded by controversy, is certainly his most distinctive contribution to the intellectual history of the time. Less controversially, however, Piri Reis was also the author of a major navigational work, the *Kitab-ı Baḥriye*,[2] designed as a complete manual for Turkish navigators in the Aegean and Mediterranean seas. Later, with the Ottoman advance into Syria and Egypt in 1516–17, the focus of his career switched from the Mediterranean to the Red Sea and he again saw active service in the Ottoman Red Sea fleet based in Suez, but his career seems to have come to an untimely end when he was apparently executed in Cairo around 1554 for dereliction of duty, following a less than successful encounter with the Portuguese in the straits of Hormoz in 1552.

How did a sailor who had apparently spent most of his early career in the Mediterranean come to end it in such an apparently ignominious fashion so far from home, and what can his career tell us about the cultural connections of the Red Sea area during this period?

Piri Reis's Early Career

Piri Reis's early life, if somewhat sketchy, seems routine enough. He was born Muhiddin Piri into a seafaring family around 1470 or shortly before, almost certainly in Galibolu (English Gallipoli), and initially learned the art of navigation from his uncle, Kemal Reis, who between *ca.* 1481 and 1495 appears to have earned a living as a corsair in the Mediterranean. These exploits, which took him as far as the Western Mediterranean and the coasts of France and Spain as well as those of North Africa, gave him an intimate knowledge both of seafaring in general and of the Mediterranean in particular — a knowledge which he was later to put to good use in his major navigational work, the *Kitab-i Baḥriye* (of which, more later). In 1495, his career changed direction when his uncle was summoned to serve in the Ottoman fleet, and from then until Kemal Reis's death in 1510 or 1511, Piri Reis participated in various naval assignments in the Mediterranean alongside his uncle, including not only the 1499–1502 war with Venice, but also, very likely, the evacuation to North Africa of the Muslim and Jewish population of Spain during the *reconquista* of Ferdinand and Isabella. Following the death of his uncle, Piri Reis returned to Gallipoli and devoted himself to cartography and the art of navigation.[3]

The 1513 'World Map'

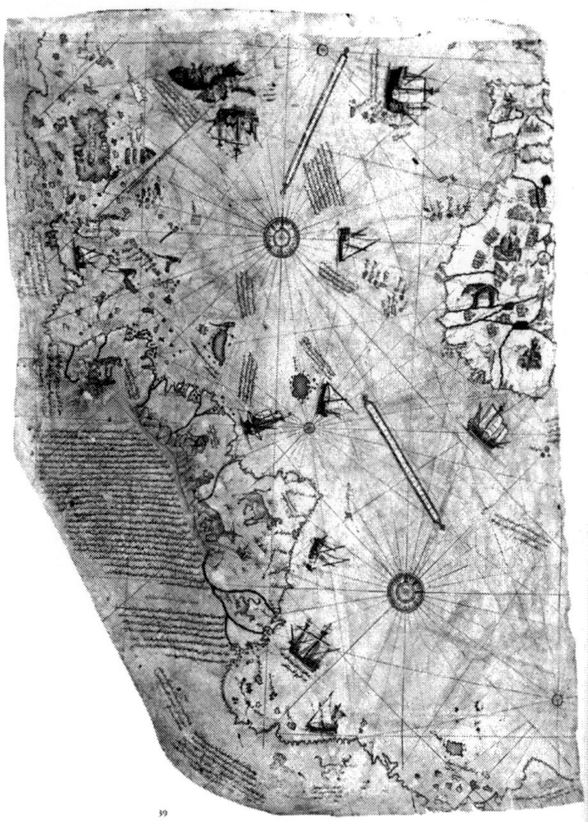

Map 22:1 Piri Reis's 'World Map'

[1] For a general discussion of which, see McIntosh 2000; Afetinan 1975.

[2] See Piri Reis 1988 (facsimile edition with Ottoman Turkish transcription, and translations into modern Turkish and English.)

[3] Afetinan 1975; Soucek 1995 ; Soucek in EI^2 s.v. 'Piri Reis', 'Kemal Reis'.

Despite his authorship of the *Kitab-ı Baḥriye*, and his distinguished career as an active seaman, Piri Reis would probably have remained a respected if rather obscure historical figure, had it not been for the rediscovery in 1929, in the Topkapı Saray Library in Istanbul (where it is still kept), of an imperfectly preserved 'world map', showing the Atlantic Ocean with part of the coasts of Europe and Africa and a portion of the New World consisting mainly of South America. The remainder of the map (probably between a half and two thirds in total), which included the majority of Europe and Africa and all of Asia (including the Middle East itself, of course), had been lost in unknown circumstances.

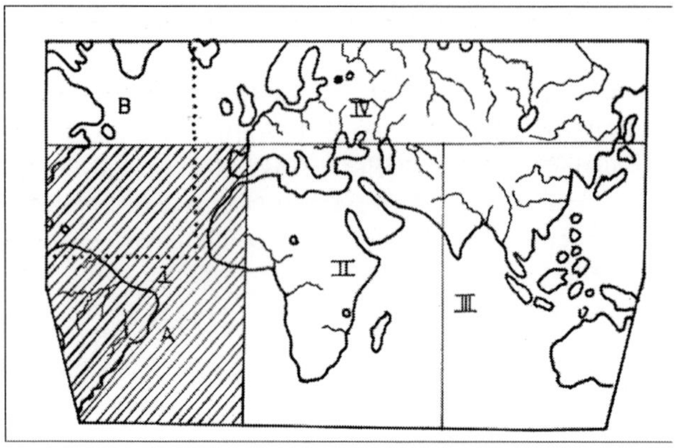

Map 22:2 Extant portion of 'World Map' (after Afetinan)

Map 22:3a Detail from 'World Map'

The map, which is drawn on gazelle hide and dated 1513, had been presented to the Ottoman Sultan Selim I in Egypt in 1517 — the date of the Ottoman conquest of Egypt — and has sometimes misleadingly been described, among other claims made for it, as 'the oldest map of America'. In addition to the cartography itself, the map is interesting for the notes appended to it (in Ottoman Turkish), which make clear that it had been based on some twenty earlier charts, among which the author numbers 'the map of Western lands drawn by Columbus', and he boasts that 'No one up to this day and age has made a similar kind of map'. Among the other sources mentioned by Piri Reis are the 'Mappa Mundi' and 'charts drawn in the days of Alexander, Lord of the Two Horns' — though it seems more likely that these were actually the maps of Claudius Ptolemeus, the astronomer and geographer who lived in the second century AD, whom Muslim authors habitually confused with Ptolemy I, friend of Alexander and ruler of Egypt, who died in the third century BC.

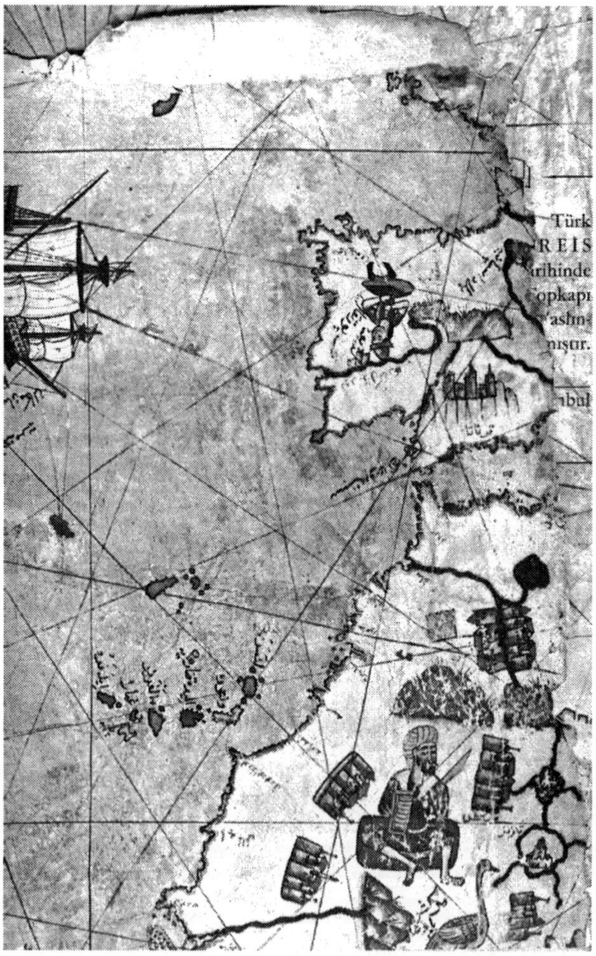

Map 22:3b Detail from 'World Map'

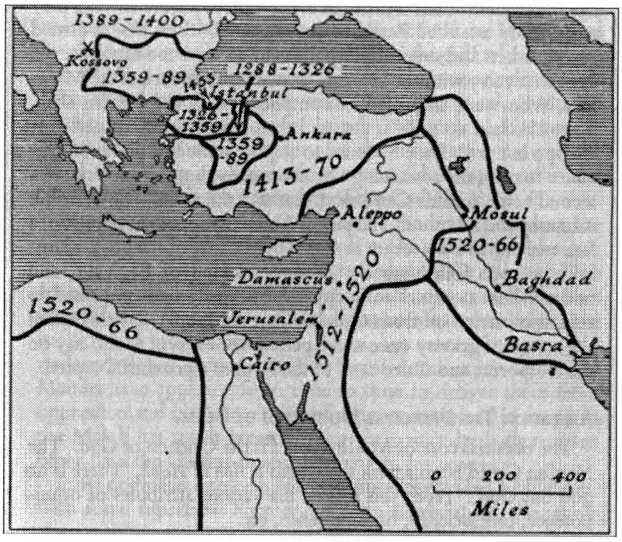

Map 22:4 The Ottoman Expansion into Africa and the Red Sea

The discovery, or rediscovery, of this map obviously raised a number of immediate questions: most obviously, was it authentic? What was a map of such a nature doing in Istanbul? How had the source materials for such a map — whether or not they included a map drawn by Columbus himself, as alleged — come to be in the hands of an Ottoman seafarer such as Piri Reis? Despite extensive research and debate, definitive answers to these and other related questions have continued to prove elusive, discussion having not infrequently become blurred by the sometimes bizarre claims that have been made for the map: they include (to quote a convenient recent summary by Gregory McIntosh) the claim 'that it shows evidence of the ability of the mapmaker to measure and perform spherical trigonometry calculations centuries ahead of its time, that it provides evidence of a worldwide seafaring civilisation existing thousands of years ago, and that it proves Earth was visited by aliens from other planets.'[4]

Perhaps the most controversial section of the map, and certainly the one that has been responsible for the most bizarre theories, is that supposedly relating to Antarctica and the so-called 'Eastward-Tending Coast'. 'Officially', if we may use the word, Antarctica was not 'discovered' until 1818, even though from the early fifteenth century, mapmakers had often indicated a huge southern landmass that linked Africa to Asia and made a landlocked sea of the Indian Ocean — a geographical notion ultimately derived from Ptolemy's references to a 'southern land'. Perhaps the most mundane explanation for the feature, however — and a not implausible one, in my view — is that Piri Reis simply ran out of gazelle skin when he came to drawing the southernmost portion of South America, so rather than consign the rest of the continent to oblivion, he simply turned the coastline to the east and continued along the edge of the page.

The Ottoman Advance into Egypt

Let us, however, return to Piri Reis's career and his progress towards the Red Sea. The historical context is a somewhat complex one, for in addition to a period of fluctuating relations between Europe and the Islamic world, the fifteenth century and first years of the sixteenth century were witnessing major shifts in the balance of power within the Middle East itself. The fall of Constantinople in 1453 had announced to the world that the Ottomans were becoming a dominant power in the region, and the event quickly acquired symbolic importance. In Eastern Anatolia and elsewhere, Ottoman and Mamlūk rivalries had been apparent for some time, reaching a head in a series of battles between 1485 and 1491. The competition between the two empires was also apparent in an argument over responsibilities for the *ḥajj* route. Meanwhile, further east, the Safavids were consolidating their power in a Shī'ite state that posed a potential, and indeed soon an actual, danger both to the Mamlūks and the Ottomans. In another parallel, and perhaps even more significant, development, the economic stability of the Mamlūk state had been threatened by the discovery by the Portuguese in 1497 of the passage around the Cape of Good Hope, which quickly led to the loss of the Indian spice trade route through the Red Sea and Egypt. This had always been a cumbersome route, for reasons that are discussed in other papers in this volume – not least, because of the dependency of the route on the vagaries of the winds. The effect of the Portuguese discovery was catastrophic for many Arabs: indeed, one scholar has written that 'the real cause of the recession of the culture and prosperity of the Arabs is to be found in the activities of the Portuguese and not in the conquest by the Turks of the Mamelūk Empire over ten years later.'[5]

Although the precise interplay of some of these factors remains a matter for speculation, the fate of Syria was effectively sealed in a single battle at Marj Dābiq on 24 August 1516, when the Mamlūk army was decisively defeated by an Ottoman one that not only enjoyed a numerical advantage but also, and most crucially, a decisive superiority in the use of modern firearms, which the Mamlūks, for one reason or another, had failed to adopt. The battle of Marj Dābiq was followed by a rapid Ottoman advance southwards, through Aleppo to Damascus, which they reached at the end of August 1516, and to Gaza, where, following some abortive negotiations between the two sides, a major battle took place on 22 December 1516. The struggle for Egypt was in turn to all intents and purposes lost in a single battle at al-Raydāniyya, outside Cairo, on 13 January 1517, which the

4 McIntosh 2000.

5 Stripling 1942; see also Lunde 2004; Smith 2004.

Mamlūks effectively lost in some twenty minutes. Rearguard actions continued for some time, but in April 1517 the newly appointed sultan Tūmānbay, who had been in hiding in the west of the country, was handed over to the Ottomans and hanged at Bāb Zuwaylah in Cairo like a common criminal. The Ottoman conquest of Egypt was now effectively complete.

These events explain how in 1517 Piri Reis found himself in command of several ships that first accompanied the Grand Vizier Ibrahim Pasha to Alexandria in Egypt. From there, he sailed with a portion of the Ottoman fleet up the Nile to Cairo, where he presented his world map to Sultan Selim the Conqueror, or Selim the Grim as he was also known (*r.* 1512–1520). Piri Reis's 'world map' of 1513 was followed, in 1528/9, by a second 'world map', of which only a fragment again survives. This second map, which covers the north-western part of the Atlantic and the eastern coastal regions of the northern America,; is also preserved in the Istanbul Topkapı Saray Library, though for a number of reasons (most obviously, its later date) it does not appear to have aroused the interest of the first map.

The *Kitab-ı Baḥriye*

In the meantime, however, Piri Reis had embarked on a work that was more closely related to his own personal experience, the *Kitab-ı Baḥriye* (the title of which has been variously translated as 'The Book of Maritime Matters' or 'The Book of Seafaring'). Two versions exist of the *Kitab-ı Baḥriye*, the first completed in 1521, the second reworked in 1526, complete with a long introduction in verse, apparently worked up by the poet Murādī, for presentation to the Turkish Sultan Süleyman, through the Grand Vizier Ibrahim Pasha; the later version also includes a description of the Portuguese voyages around the Cape of Good Hope.

The object of this work was primarily to provide a complete manual for Turkish navigators in the Aegean and Mediterranean seas, and on this level, the work is clearly based in the European tradition of 'portolans'[6] — though the verse additions to the 'presentation copy' obviously add an additional diplomatic and political dimension.

The verse preface includes a section describing the 'seven seas', starting with the 'Chinese Sea'; and although it contains no explicit references to the Red Sea, it does include an extended reference to the island of Hormoz, which makes clear the extent of contemporary Portuguese domination and which, in view of Piri Reis's subsequent fate, could perhaps be regarded as almost prophetic:

Know then that Hormuz is an island and many merchants call there:
It is calculated that the entire circumference of the island is thirty-five miles:
There is a marvel here, a mountain made of salt. Be not surprised at the commands of God:
Because of this salt nothing ever grows there spring or summer:
Every part of the island is arid: nor is there any water to drink.
Ships bring their own water from elsewhere and some sell it in this city:
Good friend, because of the heat of the day, all their commerce takes place at night:
The island is twelve miles by ship from the harbour of Bandar on the Iranian coast:
For two peninsulas face one another and if one looks carefully, one may even see a man on the opposite shore:
But now the Portuguese have reached this place and they have built a fort on that cape:
There they wait and collect tolls from ships that pass. You have now learned the circumstances of that place:
The Portuguese have overcome them all and the khans of the islands are filled with their merchants:
In fall or summer, no trading takes place unless the Portuguese are present.[7]

Following this wide ranging preface, the bulk of the work (the first version of which is subdivided into 130 chapters and the second into 210) consists largely of a series of detailed descriptions of sections of the Mediterranean clearly derived from the author's own voyages; each chapter of the work being accompanied by a related chart, showing features such as shallows and sandbanks, safe harbours, sources of water, fortresses and inhabited villages. Starting from the Dardenelles' fortresses, the work moves north-west showing islands and fortresses in the Aegean and Mediterranean, then works its way around the northern coasts of the Mediterranean before turning back along the African coast to Algiers, Tunis and Alexandria and returning to its starting point via Palestine, Syria, and the southern Turkish coast.

[6] On which, see Soucek 1995; the derivation of the term 'portolan' itself is disputed.

[7] Piri Reis 1988: 165.

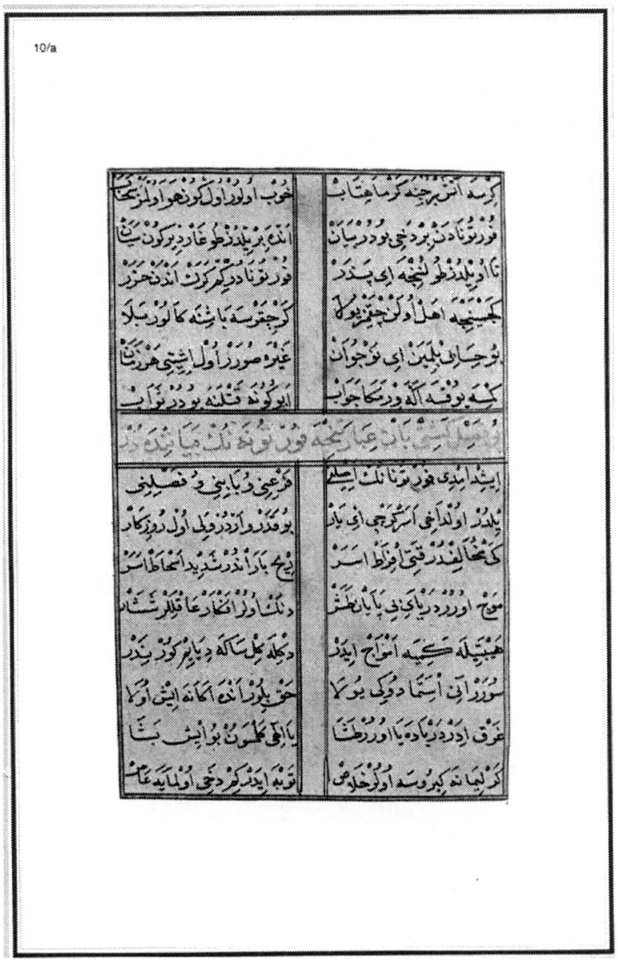

Figure 22:1 Verse introduction to Kitab-ı Baḥriye

The author also includes an interesting detour in a chapter purporting to describe the 'Banks of the Nile River from the Mouth at Reşid as far as Mişr [i.e. Cairo]'; he adds, however, that 'it is not our intention to treat them for practical navigation as we have done in the Akdeniz [Mediterranean].' In practice, his description of the Nile is less than minimal, and though he does include a brief explanation of the annual Nile flood, the main results of his observations are rather recorded in a series of maps, of which the most fascinating are undoubtedly those of contemporary Cairo.

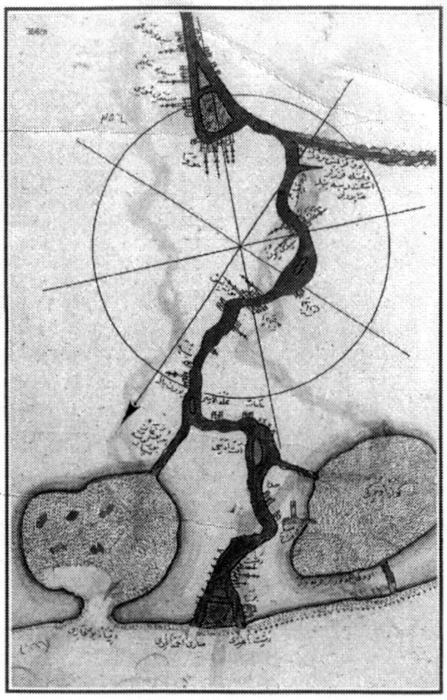

Map 22:5 The Nile Delta

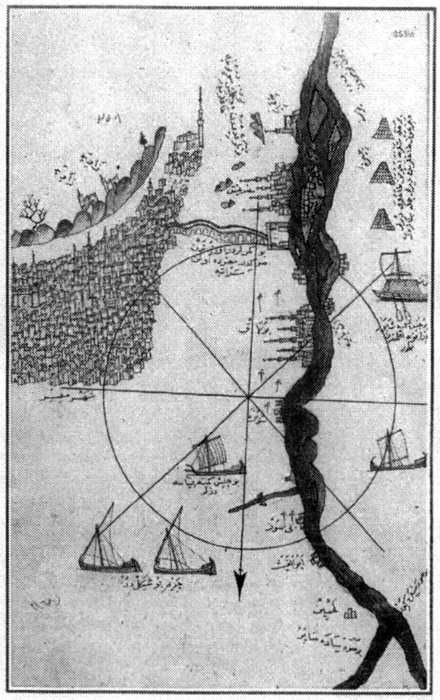

Map 22:6 Mısır Şehri, Cairo

Map 22:7 Mısır Şehri, Cairo (detail)

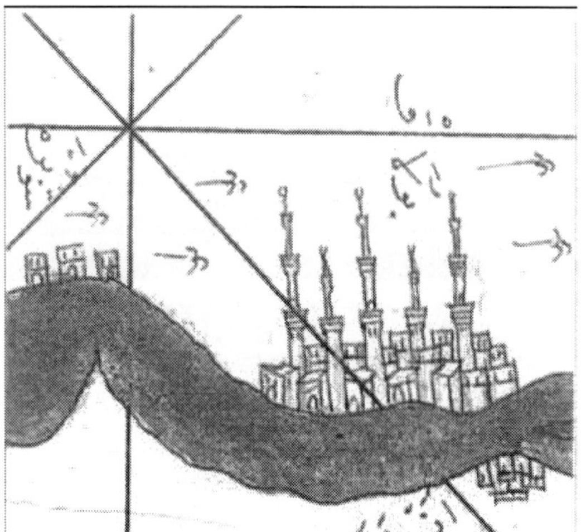

Map 22:8 Bulaq port of Cairo on the Nile

Piri Reis's Later Career

At this point, until around 1547, information on Piri Reis's life itself becomes somewhat sketchy. In the meantime, however, the Portuguese had built up their eastern empire with an astonishing speed, using their naval power to gain control over the Indian Ocean and diverting the stream of merchandise, principally spices, from Asia to Portugal via the Cape of Good Hope. The Red Sea route, whose importance as a trade route had already begun to deteriorate under the later Mamlūks, sank further into insignificance as the Portuguese blockaded the entrance to the waterway. The port of Suez, inherited from the Mamlūks by the Ottomans, quickly assumed an importance as the main base for Ottoman naval activities against the Portuguese. What followed is a little difficult to disentangle in detail in terms of the precise sequence of events, but essentially attempts by the Ottomans to encroach on the power of the Portuguese through forays into the Indian Ocean were countered by Portuguese attempts to sail up the Red Sea to capture Suez. An Ottoman expedition into the Indian Ocean in 1538, however, secured control over Aden and Zabīd in Yemen for the Ottomans. A counteroffensive by the Portuguese with the intention of retaking Suez failed, and shortly afterwards Ottoman influence in the region was further extended with their occupation of Basra in 1546.[8]

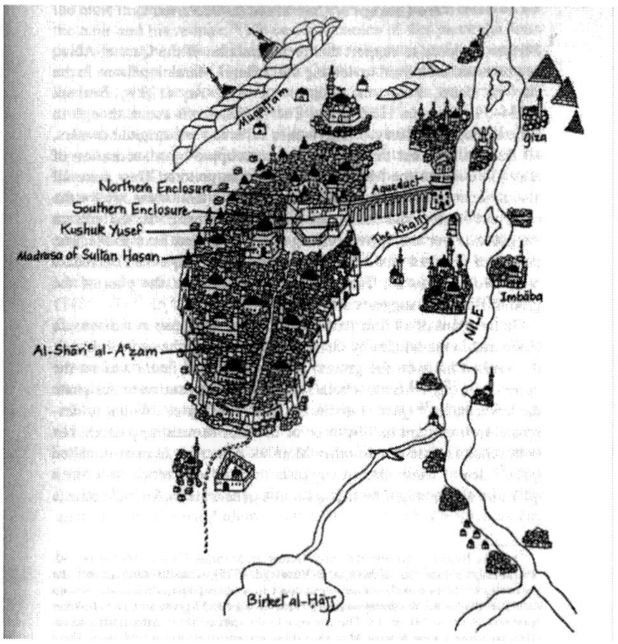

Map 22:9 Piri Reis's Plan of Cairo (after Rabbat)

The difficulties encountered by the Ottomans in administering the Suez-based Red Sea fleet around this period were noted by the French traveller Pierre Belon du Mans, who visited Suez around 1547 and, having recorded the customary rude remarks about this 'most disagreeable town',[9] noted that the Turkish ships had had to be brought from Constantinople and up the Nile to Cairo, where they had had to be dismantled, carried by camel and cart to Suez and then reassembled.

The miserable fate of Piri Reis was sealed in 1552, when he received orders that he should bring under Ottoman control the strategically important island of Hormoz and also that of Bahrain.

8 See Lunde 2004; Smith 2004.
9 Wolff 2003: 243.

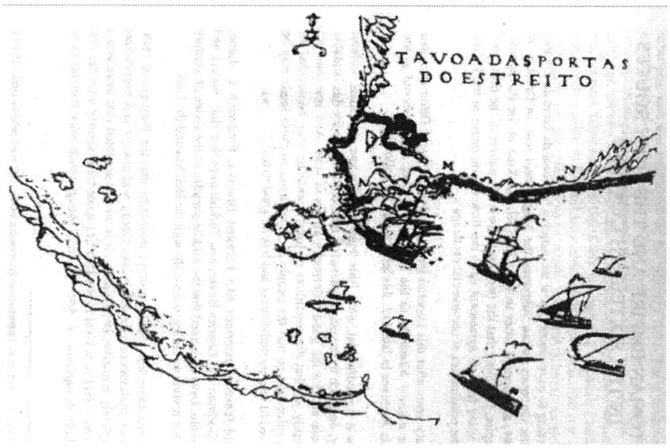

Map 22:10 Entrance to the Red Sea

Although what precisely happened is slightly uncertain, it clearly spelled the end of Piri Reis's career. The account of the well-known Turkish historian Kâtib Çelebi[10] reads as follows:

> Piri Pasha, the capudan of Egypt, left Suez AH 959 with a fleet of thirty sail, consisting of galleys, bashderdés, golettas, and galleons; and proceeding to Aden by Jedda and Babelmandel, sailed thence towards Ras-al-had, passing Zaffar and Shedjar. On his route he was overtaken near Shedjar by a storm, in which several of his barges were destroyed. With the remains of his fleet he attacked Muscat, a fortress in the Persian Gulf, in the country of Oman, which he took, and made the inhabitants prisoners. He then laid waste the islands of Ormuz and Barkhet. On his arrival at Bassora he heard that the fleet of the vile infidels was advancing towards him; a report which was confirmed by the infidel capudan whom he took at Muscat, and who now advised him to remain no longer in his present situation, on account of the impossibility of escaping by the strait of Ormuz. The pasha, being unable to clear the whole of his fleet, departed before the arrival of the infidels, with three galleys, his private property. One of these he lost near Bahrein, and with the remaining two returned to Egypt. Of the vessels left at Bassora, Kobad Pasha, the governor of that city, offered the command to Ali Beg, a beg of Egypt, and a commander in the army; who, however, refused it, and returned by land to Egypt: and the vessels, thus abandoned, were soon destroyed. The Pasha of Egypt, apprised of these events seized and imprisoned Piri Reis on his arrival at Cairo, and sent information of the circumstance to the Sublime Porte, whence he immediately received an order to put to death, the admiral, who was beheaded accordingly in the divan of Cairo. He left immense riches, which were confiscated to the treasury. The inhabitants of Ormuz, from whom he had extorted large sums of money, came to complain of his exactions and crave an indemnity; but no attention was paid to their demands, and the gold was put into gilt vases and sent to Constantinople.[11]

Figure 22:2 Aden

Figure 22:3a and 22:3b Portuguese views of battles against the Ottoman fleet in the Red Sea

[10] Also known as Ḥājji Khalīfeh.

[11] Çelebi 1831: 71–2.

Conclusion

Given Piri Reis's fate in Cairo, we might conclude that contemporary Ottoman standards of justice were, by modern yardsticks, sometimes rather crude. This sort of execution is of course a particularly harsh fate for someone who would apparently have been an octogenarian by this time and it has caused some modern historians to wonder whether two different people have here been confused, and that the 'Red Sea' Piri Reis was a different man from his 'White Sea' namesake — though the doubts that have been raised by modern scholars do not appear to have been shared by the Ottoman historians. The simple fact is that, compared with the Portuguese fleet, the Ottoman Suez fleet (most of which, as previously noted, had to be transported from the Mediterranean via Cairo by caravan) was extremely weak; and in view of the problems being encountered by the Ottoman Red Sea fleet, it seems not unnatural that the authorities should have brought out of retirement one of their most distinguished sailors. There seems there no good reason to doubt that this is one and the same man, It is hard to imagine what Piri Reis would have made of some of the more bizarre theories about his world map; but in his progress from the Mediterranean to the Red Sea, Piri Reis seems in some way to symbolise the shifting horizons of the Ottoman state, forced through the conquest of Egypt to refocus so much of its attention to the south-east rather than the west. It is a fascinating life from a period of shifting horizons and cultural boundaries in which the Red Sea plays a prominent role and it has led us back to some of the themes that have held a dominant position through all three stages of the Red Sea Project.

References

Afetinan, A. 1975. *Life and Works of Pirî Reis: the oldest map of America.* Publications of Turkish Historical Association S.VIII, 69a. Ankara: Turkish Historical Association.

Ibn Iyās. 1982–1984. *Badā'i' al-zuhūr wa-waqā'i' al-duhūr.* Cairo.

Kahle, P. 1926. *Piri Re'īs. Bahriyah-i Piri Ra'is = Piri Re'is bahrije: das türkishce Segelhandbuch für das Mittelländische Meer vom Jahr 1521.* 2 vols. Berlin: de Gruyter.

Kâtib Çelebi. 1831. *Tuḥfat al-kibār fī asfār al-biḥār.* James Mitchell (tr.). *The History of the Maritime Wars of the Turks.* London: Volpy; Oriental Translation Fund.

Lunde, P. 2002. 'What the devil are you doing here?' Arabic sources for the arrival of the Portuguese in the Red Sea and Indian Ocean. 131–6 in P. Lunde and A. Porter (eds), *Trade and Travel in the Red Sea Region: Proceedings of Red Sea Project I held in the British Museum October 2002.* BAR International Series 1269. Oxford: Archaeopress.

McIntosh, G.C. 2000. *The Piri Reis Map of 1513.* Athens and London: University of Georgia Press.

Piri Reis. 1988. *Kitab-i Bahriye.* 4 vols. Istanbul: Istanbul Research Center.

Smith, C. 2002. Mamluk and Ottoman activity in Yemen in the sixteenth century: coastal security and commercial significance. 137–144 in P. Lunde and A. Porter (eds), *Trade and Travel in the Red Sea Region: Proceedings of Red Sea Project I held in the British Museum October 2002.* BAR International Series 1269. Oxford: Archaeopress.

Soucek, S. 1960–2004a. 'Kemal Reis' in *Encyclopaedia of Islam.* Leiden: Brill.

——. 1960–2004b. 'Piri Reis' in *Encyclopaedia of Islam.* Leiden: Brill.

——. 1995. *Piri Reis and Turkish Map-Making after Columbus: the Khalili Portolan Atlas.* Volume 2 of *Studies in the Khalili Collection.* London: Nour Foundation, in association with Azimuth Editions and Oxford University Press.

Stripling, G.W.F. 1942. *The Ottoman Turks and the Arabs, 1511–1574.* Urbana: The University of Illinois Press.

Wolff, A. 2003. *How many Miles to Babylon?* Liverpool: Liverpool University Press.

Index

European interests 180 ; maritime expansion 4
European-Ottoman relations in the Red Sea 6
Eusebius 225
Exana 221

F

Facey, Capt R. 122, 124, 126
Facey, W. 14, 78, 121
Farasān Islands 27, 122
Fars 225
Farzah (rotation system) 176
fashīn 104
Fāṭimid period 91
fauna 54, 57–62, 151, 156–7, 166
al-Fāzzah 238
Fei Xin (Fei Hsin) 230, 239
Fīrānīs 200
First Intermediate Period 148
fish 2, 4, 51, 54, 60, 63–74
fisheries 53, 63–4, 67, 152
fishing 4, 27, 59, 65, 152–3
Fisker, Commander 57
Flint Island 123
flora 2, 57–62, 166
fog 124
Forsskål, P. 2, 57–62, 174, 176
France 124
frankincense *see* aromatics
Frederick V, king of Denmark 57, 174
French Dépôt de la Marine 124
Friis, Professor Ib 59, 61
Frumentius 221
Fujairah 106

G

Gad 222
Galle 230
Gallipoli 247
Gallus 92
Gandhara 222
Genebtyw 135
Geniza 92
Genoa 91; galleys 91
geomorphological mapping 14–6
Gh al-Ghulayfīqah 13
ghanjah 97–8, 105
Ghat mountains 212
ghurab 91
Gibraltar 57
glass: beads 5, 189, 191; ware 177
Gokomere Ziwa wares 191
gold 132–5, 235
Golden Web Project 229
Gondophares, Partho-Indian king 222
Gong Zhen (Kung Chen) 230, 239
Gordon Reef 122
Greece 48
Greek 150, 221
Greek *koinê* 212
Greeks 4, 92, 176
'Groenland' 57, 58
Grouper (Serranidae) 71
Gūdnaphar 222
Gujarat 212

H

Hadie 60
Haḍramawt 40, 214, 217
Haines, Capt 121
al-Ḥajjāj ibn Yūsuf 89–92
al-Hamid 26, 28
Hangzhou (Hangchow) 232
Hanish al-Kubra 124
harbours 1–4, 131–42; natural 3, 131–5
harbour-towns 3
al-Ḥarīrī, Abū al-Qāsim bin 90, 98, 102, 106, 117
al-Hasā' / Lahsā 232
Hatshepsut, Queen 90
Havilah 133
Hawlan 133
Haycock islands 122
Hays 26, 179; Hays ware 179
Hazhihuxian' (Ḥajjī Ḥusayn?) 241
Hebrew 135, 220–1
Hellenistic Mediterranean 45, 48
Herat 229
herbarium specimens 58
hero stone 98, 100
Herodotus 175, 199
Hilcoat, D. 61
Himyarites 6
Hina 89
Hiram, king of Tyre 90
Hodaida *see* al-Ḥudaydah
Holocene period 2, 13–4
Hong Bao 239–41
Horden P. 1, 86
Hormoz 5, 6, 92, 230, 232, 239, 242, 252
Horus, eye of 104
Horvat Karkur 53
hospital ships 123
Hospitallers 53
Hourani, G.F. 92
al-Ḥudaydah (Hodeida) 16, 26, 60, 133
'Hugh Lindsay' 122, 179
Hunter, F.M. 113, 117
hūrī 104–5, 107, 113
Huzayyin 13
Hyksos 134
Ḥaḍramawt 133–4, 212
Ḥajj 182; caravan 180
Ḥijāz 4, 233
Ḥijāzī wars (1811-1818) 176
Ḥimyar 35, 134

I

Iberian Peninsula 112
Ibn al-Dayba', Rasūlid sultan 233, 235–6, 239, 243; *Bughyat al-Mustafīd* 235; *Qurrat al-'Uyūn* 235
Ibn Baṭṭūṭah 113
Ibn Ḥajar al-'Asqālānī 233–4, 240
Ibn Ḥawqal 208
Ibn Jubayr 90, 112–3
Ibn Jumay' 239
Ibn Khaldūn 233
Ibn Mājīd 117–8
Ibn Rustah 89
Ibo island 188
Ibrahim Pasha 250
Ichthyophagi' (fish-eaters') 4, 6, 149–60
identity 101–11, 149–60
Imari ware 177
India 3–5, 35, 60, 77, 78, 105, 116, 110, 121–4, 161–2, 180, 182, 188, 211–8, 229, 232, 239, 249
Indian Ocean 3–6, 35, 64, 67, 77–8, 83, 86, 89, 91–3, 95–100, 112, 116, 126, 143, 190–1, 211–28, 252
indigenous knowledge 3, 6
Indo-European Telegraph 3, 121
Indonesian archipelago 229
Indo-Pacific trade beads 191
Indo-Parthian empire 212, 223
Indo-Roman trade 219–28
Indo-West Pacific 64
Indus 92, 212
Iotobe 161–7
Iran 90
Iranians 116
Iraq 5, 89–91, 187
Iren 134
Irjet 134
iron 190
Iron Age 26–7
Islam 4, 5, 26, 48, 53, 107, 109, 208; pottery 48
Ismaelites 200
Israel 64–5
Istanbul 249; Topkapı Saray Library 6, 247–8
Italians 124
Italy 225
Iraq 191
ivory 12, 132–3, 211–3

J

Jabal al-Madhbah 50–1
Jabal Isbil 40
Jabal Jusassiyyah 106
Jabal Lisa 40
Jackson Reef 122
Jaffa 53
Jafura Desert 22
Jahran 24
jalabūt 117
jalbah 3, 104, 107, 111–120
jālbūt 105
al-Janad 234
Java 230, 232, 242; ships 242
Jazīrat al-Fara'ūn (Pharoah's island) 164
Jazīrat Fir'awn 91
al-Jerahi 16
Jerim 60
Jerome 200
Jerusalem 53, 90–1, 165, 222; kingdom of 91; Armenian monastery 53
Jewell, J.J.H. 116
Jewish communities 219
Jiblah 60
Jiddah (Jeddah ; Zhida [Chih-ta]) 5, 59, 86, 112–3, 123–4, 133, 174, 175, 177–9, 232–3, 238–42
jilāb 113
Jizan 133
John, governor of Aila 163
jolly boat 112

Q

R

S